contents

Eyak Alaska Classic

Jay Miller, PhD, ed

THE EYAK INDIANS
OF THE COPPER RIVER DELTA, ALASKA

KAJ BIRKET-SMITH AND FREDERICA DE LAGUNA

KØBENHAVN
LEVIN & MUNKSGAARD
EJNAR MUNKSGAAHD
1938 Det Kgl. Danske Videnskabernes Selskab

PART I: DESCRIPTION OF EYAK ETHNOLOGY

© 2020

contents

PART II: EYAK FOLKLORE

PART III: CRITICAL ANALYSIS OF PREVIOUS WRITERS ON THE EYAK

PART IV: ANALYSIS OF EYAK ETHNOLOGY

BIBLIOGRAPHY

ILLUSTRATIONS

TEXT FIGURES

contents

PLATES

NB: *Edits herein {add within curved brackets}
preferred tribal names,
call out obsolete & now offensive usages,
underline the italics in Analysis section,
& simplify punctuations.

INTRODUCTION

Most of the material for this report was gathered during an archaeological and ethnological expedition to Prince William Sound during the summer of 1933. The expedition was sponsored by the Danish National Museum (represented by Dr. KAJ BIRKET-SMITH, the Danish author of this report) and by the University of Pennsylvania Museum (represented by Dr. FREDERICA DE LAGUNA, the American author). The participation of the first-mentioned member of the expedition was made possible by a grant of the Rask-Ørsted Foundation of the Danish Government, and a smaller contribution from the Julius Skrike Institution. Our two assistants were NORMAN REYNOLDS, a student of Anthropology at the University of Washington, and Dr. WALLACE DE LAGUNA, then a student at Harvard University. The latter devoted himself exclusively to the archaeological work, but NORMAN REYNOLDS took an active part in the collection of the ethnological material, especially in the recording of the Tales and the Vocabulary.

In 1930, while making an archaeological survey of Prince William Sound for the University of Pennsylvania Museum, the American author met two of the Eyak, Galushia Nelson and old Chief Joe, and also met Mr. CHARLES ROSENBERG, the first white trader among the Eyak. With Galushia Nelson as guide, a rapid survey was made of the [8] original Eyak village sites, all of which arc now abandoned. As a result of this preliminary trip, enough was .learned about these Indians to show that they were a tribe distinct in language and culture from the neighboring Prince William Sound Eskimo, that they were distinct, too, from the Tlingit to the east, and from the Atna, or Athapaskan speaking tribes of the Copper River valley. On the basis of that information the hypothesis was suggested that the Eyak were a group of Athapaskans who had come from the Interior down the Copper River to its mouth.[1] This hypothesis, together with other theories about the cultural position of the Eyak, will be discussed in the following pages. After the information obtained from the natives had been compiled, the American author had the unique opportunity of a week's visit in the fall of 1935 with Colonel ABERCROMBIE, the first American explorer to visit the Eyak. His written report on that expedition contains perhaps the most important information to be found in any published source, but it is very little in comparison to what he was able to tell in conversation. In spite of the fact that his visit to the Eyak was 51 years ago, the Colonel retains a vivid and detailed memory of what he saw, and this valuable information has been included in this report.

A few remarks about our native informants would be of interest. The chief of these was Galushia Nelson, a man about 54 years old in 1933. He was born and brought up at Alaganik. His parents were Eyak, but on his mother's side, at least, there seems to have been some admixture of Tlingit blood. At the age of ten he was taken to the United States by an American couple who were interested in him. [9]

He was educated there and had special training as a mechanic. His family, however, succeeded in inducing him to return to Alaska, offering him false hopes of earning a living at his trade. He had left his people living a more or less unspoiled and happy life at Alaganik. He returned to find them reduced in numbers by poverty and disease, leading a miserable existence on the outskirts of Cordova. The shock of disillusion was so great that the night he landed Galushia attempted to commit suicide. The wound in his breast was not fatal, hut it may have

---

[1] DE LAGUNA 1934, 156.

been one reason why he later contracted tuberculosis of the lungs. In 1933 he was sick and unable to work. All during the early months of 1935 he was thought to be at the point of death, and again attempted to kill himself. This attempt was fortunately unsuccessful, and he made such a miraculous recovery from his sickness that he was able to resume fishing that summer.

Shortly after his return to Alaska, Galushia married an Eyak woman, Annie, by whom he had two sons; Johnny, about (6 or 7 years old, and a baby born about the beginning of 1935. His wife has also had a sad history. As an orphan she was brought up by an Eyak family who neglected her shamefully. A disfiguring scar on her neck is said to be the result of some skin disease which went untended. The little girl had to sleep with the dogs beside the fire and it is their tongues which are supposed to have cured her. After she was married she was kidnapped by the oriental crew of a cannery and was kept imprisoned for some weeks before she was rescued. During her husband's illness she supported her little family by working in a cannery.

(Galushia was a very intelligent informant and was genuinely anxious to help us. He speaks good English and [10] was always careful to explain exactly what he knew and what he did not know. Annie, moreover, was often able to supplement her husband's information. Most of the tales which we have recorded she had learned from Old Chief Joe, now dead. She would tell them to her husband in Eyak, and he would translate them for us, usually verbally, sometimes in writing. Annie was also our chief source for kinship terms.

We attempted to use Mary Nelson, the wife of Galushia's older brother, Gus, but she proved unreliable and could not speak English very well. There was bad feeling between Gus and Galushia, because the latter refused to work for his older brother as the old customs required.

Most of our information about shamanism was obtained from Johnny Stevens. a younger man than Galushia, but who was supposed by most of the Eyak and Eskimo to have shamanistic powers. Johnny, himself, did not claim them openly to us, but there is no doubt that many of his statements about shamanism in general are autobiographical in character. He married a Copper River woman and had been associated with a famous Copper River shaman, Chitina Joe, from whom he was supposed to have acquired his powers, Johnny also worked at one time for the Copper River Railway and is very proud of this distinction.

A little information was obtained from Old Man Dude, a shaman much feared by both the Eskimo and Eyak. An account of some of his doings is given in *Stories about Shamans*. He speaks very poor English, which is rendered even more unintelligible because of a stutter. He could say neither the sonant or surd *th* sounds of English, but rendered them as glottalized surd *l*. Curiously enough, his stutter is absent when speaking either Eyak or Eskimo. [11]

Of the written sources of information about the Eyak the most important arc the narratives of JACOBSEN and ABERCROMBIE. The former visited the Eyak in 1883, while making ethnological collections for the Berlin Museum. His observations, however, are not very critical. Colonel ABERCROMBIE visited the Eyak the following year on his expedition up the Copper River. He explained in conversation that his report on this expedition was published during his absence in the field. He did not know that it had appeared in print until a friend mentioned the matter, and he found then that the manuscript had been greatly cut. Some of the discrepancies between the written report and the account which he gave verbally are undoubtedly due to errors in the printed version; a few, however, seem to be due to forgetfulness. At the time of his visit to Alaganik he had with him as interpreter a white man. Pete Johnson, who had married an Eyak woman. ABERCROMBIE not only learned a good deal about the natives from this man, but also made close observations at first hand, all the more remarkable considering that his purpose at Alaganik was not ethnological but to secure guides for his explorations up the river. It is only proper to remark that what he seems chiefly to have forgotten is the extent to which the Eyak in 1884 had been influenced by contact with the whites. In his written report he mentions their guns and poor skill in shooting, but he now reports that the Eyak had no imported tools or weapons in 1884. The point is purely academic, for his detailed verbal descriptions of stone adzes and axes, bows and arrows, and methods of hunting and fishing leave no doubt that the Eyak in 1884 were still living a very primitive life. Whatever they may have acquired from the whites was at that time only an addition [12] to the native culture, and had not yet transformed the old modes of living.

Colonel ABERCROMBIE is distrustful of PETROFF'S observations on the Eyak and believes that the latter did not visit these people himself, and that it is only second-hand information about them which is published in the Tenth and Eleventh Census reports on Alaska. On the whole, it is surprising how little has been written about the Eyak, and of lhal little what a large proportion is valueless. A discussion of the written sources is reserved for Part III.

Colonel ABERCROMBIE'S published report of his expedition of 1884 appears in the *Compilation of Narratives of Explorations in Alaska*, 1900. Reference is made in the text to two figures: one illustrates the small Eyak canoe, the other is a diagram of the potlatch house at Alaganik during a ceremony. Neither of these two figures appears in the volume. This omission at once suggests that the report has been reprinted from an earlier edition which contained the illustrations, and this supposition is strengthened by the fact that most of the other articles in the volume have actually appeared before, generally as separate books. For example, ALLEN'S account of his expedition up the Copper River in 1885 was first published in 1887 as a separate book with illustrations, and it is from this edition that the references in the following pages are drawn. The report was afterwards republished, but without the illustrations, in the volume of *Compilation of Narratives*. MR. HENRY B. COLLINS, JR, of the United States National Museum very kindly undertook to discover if possible the original edition of ABERCROMBIE'S report. He found that unfortunately this hypothetical "original" edition does not exist, and the Library of Congress has no record that it ever did exist. [13]

Since Colonel ABERCROMBIE says that the published version of this report is very much cut, the American author tried to find the original manuscript. After lengthy inquiries at the Army War College in Washington, D.C., where such documents are kept, it was learned that ABERCROMBIE'S manuscript had been destroyed many years ago, by permission of an Act of Congress. There remains, however, a *Photographic Album*, consisting of a number of original photographs taken by ABERCROMBIE in 1884, accompanied by short explanatory captions. Details of Plates 3 and 6, which are the most important for our study of the Eyak, have been reproduced by permission of the Army War College, and appear in our Plate 10. Some of the line drawings published in the original edition of ALLEN'S report of his expedition of 1885 have been copied from these photographs taken by ABERCROMBIE. The pictures which appear as text figures in the present monograph were drawn by the American author, according to Colonel ABERCROMBIE'S verbal descriptions and were made with his help. None of them are the text figures to which he referred in his published report. They must be considered, therefore, only as approximations and not as accurate representations.

The authors wish to express their thanks for the help given them in the field. Among the many persons in Cordova who gave welcome assistance, Mrs. MYRA MACDONALD, formerly teacher at the native school at Cordova, and her successors, Mrs. HAROLD E. SMITH, and Mrs. TILLIE BURNELL, have given the most help for this particular phase of our work. We also wish to thank Colonel W.R. ABERCROMBIE for his invaluable assistance. A grant from the [14] Carlsberg Foundation made it possible for the Danish author to study JACOBSEN'S collections in the *Museum für Völkerkunde* in Berlin in 1935. Our best thanks are due to Professor W. KRICKEBERG, Director of the American department of this museum, for allowing the publication of descriptions and photographs of several interesting specimens. We are also deeply indebted to Dr. MELVILLE JACOBS, Department of Anthropology of the University of Washington, for his never failing assistance in preparing the linguistic material for publication. The photographs of specimens in the University of Pennsylvania Museum have been prepared by Mr. W.H. WITTE. The authors also wish to express their appreciation to the Rask-Ørsted Foundation, Copenhagen, and the American Philosophical Society, of Philadelphia, for the grants which have made possible the publication of the present volume.

PART I
DESCRIPTION OF EYAK ETHNOLOGY

Material Culture

Territory and Villages

The [17] few surviving Eyak live at Old Town, Cordova, on the shores of Eyak Lake. The shaman, Old Man Dude, and his younger son, Billy, have a cabin in Simpson Bay, Prince William Sound.

In former times, according to Galushia, the Eyak territory extended from Cordova Bay, just inside the eastern edge of Prince William Sound, to Martin River, and included the Copper River valley as far up as Childs and Miles Glaciers, above which the Eyak did not venture. They sometimes went to Kayak Island, though this was Tlingit territory. (Galushia knew nothing about the Eskimo claims to Kayak Island. According to Makari, our Eskimo informant, Kayak Island and the mainland from Cape Martin to Bering River belonged originally to the ṭɫqaɣmiut, a branch of the Shallow Water People, the Eskimo tribe whose chief village was Palugvik on Hawkins Island, the site which we excavated in 1931. The eastern branch of the Shallow Water People were named for their village, *ṭɫqat*, Chilkat, on Bering River. The Eskimo claim to Kayak Island is supported by the reports of early voyagers — see Part III. It is, however, quite clear that the Tlingit later drove the Eskimo out of this territory.) The Eyak used to hunt sea-otter off the Egg Islands and off Strawberry Point, [18] Hinchinbrook Island, in spite of opposition from the Shallow Water Eskimo, to whom this region belonged. They also dug clams at the present site of Point Whitshed Radio Station, although this was also trespassing on Eskimo territory. They "went up Orca Inlet after bear, but never in single canoes because of the Eskimo. The nearest foreign villages "were those belonging to the Eskimo on Mummy, Hinchinbrook, and Hawkins Islands, and the Tlingit villages of Katalla and Chilkat, after the latter had driven out the Eskimo.

Johnny Stevens claimed that the Eyak territory extended as far into Prince William Sound as Knowles Head beyond Port Gravina, and that the Eyak used to go as far north as Ellamar to hunt. He admitted, however, that they never went to Port Gravina before they had guns. It seems clear that this expansion could not have taken place until the Russians had enforced peace between the Eyak and the Eskimo. The Eyak at one time had a settlement somewhere in Port Gravina, for "we were given the name of a potlatch house there (see *Houses*). Johnny Stevens' statement that the Eyak used to hunt at Canoe Pass and Makaka Point on Hawkins Island is probably untrue for the early days.

The Eyak villages were (1) Eyak, *i•γíyáq*, near Mile Six of the Copper River Railway, on Eyak River about a mile below the outlet of Eyak Lake; (2) Alaganik, ənáx̱ànaq, near Mile Twenty-one of the railroad, on the westernmost distributory of the Copper River; (3) glacatł, "Fort." below Eyak on Eyak River, where a Russian post is said to have been established; (4) t'cí•cqέiGətɫέ, translated by Chief Joe as "beach", but evidently derived from *t'cí•*, "whelk," on the narrow isthmus between Eyak Lake and Cordova Bay. The site roughly corresponds to the present native village [19] at Cordova, called Old Town. There was also a summer camp on Mountain Slouch, called *tsà•láxà•tɫəu*, from *tsà•láxà•tɫ*, "gravel," and another camp at Point Whitshed, called tɫíx̱àtɫ, "lots of clams."

(1) Captain JACOBSEN, who visited Eyak in 1883 when collecting ethnological specimens for the Museum für Völkerkunde in Berlin, reported that Eyak ("Iggiak") consisted of 10 houses.[1] ABERCROMBIE, who visited the village the following year, writes:

"The village is situated on a small stream flowing from a lake into the tide water about 8 miles to the westward of the extreme western mouth of Copper River. It consists of a dozen houses built of logs slabs, and roughly hewn planks. At high tide it can be reached from the cast by boats, and from an arm of the sea extending inland from Cape Whitshed. In going down from Eyak to Nuchek [Eskimo village and trading post at Port Etches, Hinchinbrook Island] the latter route, although involving a short portage across a marsh, is preferred on account of its saving something in distance, but more particularly as avoiding the rough sea common off Cape Whitshed."[2]

Colonel ABERCROMBIE now remembers seeing only 1 house and 4 ruined houses at Eyak. In 1885, Lieutenant ALLEN found only 5 houses at the same place, in which lived 8 men and their families.[3] The U.S. Census of 1890 reports 27 houses and 28 families.[4] The village was raised about the end of the century to make a site for a cannery that was never built, and the natives moved to Cordova. The differences between the number of houses [20] at Eyak as reported by these various writers may in part be due to the fact that *glacatł* was so close that some visitors (as ABEHCROMBIE admitted in conversation) may have included the houses of both villages in their reports on Eyak, while ALLEN may have been reporting for Eyak alone.

(2) Though JACOBSEN also visited Alaganik, he gives no description of the village. ABERCROMBIE writes:

"Besides Eyak the chief village is a small fishing station, Ataganik, on one of the innumerable branches of Copper River, 9 miles from the western mouth. Here upon a small island are two houses of the general type already described [see Eyak], and upon the mainland near by are five more. Boats drawing over 18 inches of water can not, except during the season of high water, and even then only at flood tide, approach nearer than 2 miles. The population of this village is constantly changing, few people living there in winter."[5]

ABERCROMBIE now remembers only three houses at Alaganik, in which about 120 people were living in 1884. These houses were the two large buildings, probably potlatch houses (see *Houses*), and the small hut in which the shaman lived with his two companions. The two large buildings seemed to be new at the time, and showed white influence in the manner of their construction. Colonel ABERCROMBIE is mistaken, however, in believing that Alaganik was founded in 1868, the year of the measles epidemic. From what the natives told us, Alaganik must have been one of their oldest villages. ABERCROMBIE has probably forgotten the other

---

[1] JACOBSEN 1884, 386.

[2] ABERCROMBIE 1900, 397

[3] ALLEN 1887, 37.

[4] PETROFF 1893, 158.

[5] ABERCROMBIE 1900, 397.

houses which he mentioned in his report, probably because he did not enter them. CHARLES ROSENBERG, with whom the American author of [21] the present monograph had a conversation before his death in 1930, established the first trading post at Alaganik. The store building is still standing (Plate 5, 2). Though we do not know the exact date of its establishment, ABERCROMBIE thinks it was about 1890. At the time of the first gold rush, many prospectors took the Copper River route into the interior. ROSENBERG kept a .record of their names, the date of their entry, and a brief note of their subsequent fortune. This record is now preserved by the U.S. Marshal at Cordova. ROSENBERG was familiar with ABERCROMBIE'S report and said that the latter was incorrect in speaking of Alaganik as a slimmer village, since it was inhabited the year round. This assertion is also supported by the natives, and in conversation, Colonel ABEHCHOMBIE also corrected his written statement. Alaganik was abandoned in 1892 or 1893, following a severe epidemic, and the natives moved to Old Town, Cordova. In 1890 the U.S. Census reported 12 houses and 12 families at Alaganik.[1]

(3) We have not been able to find any reference to the village or to the Russian trading post at gIacatL In 1884, however, ABERCROMBIE noticed some houses at this place, but supposed them to be part of the larger village of Eyak on the other side of the river.

(4) In 1883 JACOBSEN encountered a few Indians from Eyak encamped at the present site of Old Town. Apparently the original village had been abandoned at that lime. Colonel ABERCROMBIE says that he noticed the remains of an old village on the flats between Eyak Lake and Cordova Bay when he was there in 1884. The large houses had fallen in. but there were a number of small huts, about 6 by 8 feet. These were made of rough planks, set vertically, [22] with bits of cloth tacked around the walls inside. He thinks these were temporary shacks occupied by the natives while they were drying herring. Between 1884 and 1890, two canneries were built here. The Eleventh U.S. Census reports the "Odiak Canneries" as supporting a population of 273 persons, of whom only 12 could have been Eyak. PETROFF writes: "Quite a settlement of Ugalentz Thlingit [Eyak] has sprung up about these canneries, but their houses are generally deserted during the winter for their own homes."[2] In 1899 there were 59 Eyak living at the canneries.[3] The buildings have since been torn down and the site is now occupied by the buildings and yards of the Copper River and Northwestern Railway.

(5) We have no record of the number of families that used to occupy the fishing camps on Mountain Slough and at Point Whitshed. In 1885 ALLEN found an old native and his wife stringing clams in a small cove west of Point Whitshed.[4]

ALLEN reports that in 1788 a single redoubt (Russian) was built at the mouth of the Copper River, a few miles south of Alaganik ("Anahánuk"), "but at present [1885] no traces of it remain. It is probable that a village of two miserable *barábarras*, called by the natives 'Skátalis,' is on the site of the old odinátishka of the Russians."[5] "Sákhalis" (as he also spells it) at that time

---

[1] PETROFF 1893, 158.

[2] PETROFF 1893, 158, 66.

[3] ELLIOT 1900, 739.

[4] ALLEN 1887, 36.

[5] ALLEN 1887, 19.

consisted of 2 houses, each about 12 by 13 feet, one of which sheltered 29 natives and 10 dogs.[1] This village or camp is not mentioned by the natives.

JACOBSEN visited a village of three families at Cape [23] Martin. He writes: "The inhabitants of the above-mentioned places on the Copper River delta [Eyak, Alaganik, and Cape Martin], including the village of Tschilkat [Chilkat], east of Cape Martin, form one group, who, according to the seasons, have their dwellings preponderantly now in one, now in another of these places."[2] At that time, 1883, Captain ANDERSON used to trade with the natives at Cape Martin. JACOBSEN has probably confused the Eyak with their nearest Tlingit neighbors, for the Tenth U.S. Census lists Cape Martin as a Tlingit village, containing 6 permanent residents,[3] and PETROFF writes in 1890: "One of the favorite hunting and fishing grounds of the Ugalentz tribe [Eyak], and also a point of rendezvous with their Yaktag neighbors [Tlingit], is the vicinity of Cape Martin, near the easternmost mouth of Copper river. A small trading post has been located here for many years."[4] In 1884 Colonel ABERCROMBIE met a number of Cape Martin Indians at Alaganik. He believes them to be Eyak, because they looked like the Alaganik people and seemed to speak the same language, as far as he could tell. In any case, he thinks that the Cape Martin people could not have been in close communication with the Yakutat Tlingit, because he gave these visitors at Alaganik a letter to deliver to Yakutat. Some years later they brought the letter to Nuchek and confessed that they had been afraid to attempt the rather dangerous voyage down the coast to the eastward. In view of this conflicting testimony we cannot be quite sure what tribe lived at Cape Martin. The population may have been mixed, especially in later days. It should be mentioned, however, that JACOBSEN'S [24] collections from Cape Martin, now in the Berlin Museum, are decidedly Tlingit in character.

From time to time various estimates of the number of Eyak have been made. These are summarized below:

1818 – 117 (51 males, 66 females). Census made by Inspector KOSTLIVTSEV.[5]
1834 – 150. VENIAMINOV.[6]
1839 – Not more than 38 families. WRANGELL.[7]
1863 – 148 baptized Christians (73 males, 75 females). TIKHMENEV.[8]
1870 – Some 200 families. DALL speaking of the "Eskimo Ugalakmutes."[9]
1880 – 117 persons at "Ighiak" and "Alaganu." PETROFF.[10]
1884 – 33 able-bodied men. ABERCROMBIE.[11] 120 persons at Alaganik.
1890 – 154 (78 males, 76 females). PETROFF.[1]

---

[1] ALLEN 1887, 38.

[2] JACOBSEN 1884, 389.

[3] PETROFF 1884, 29.

[4] PETROFF 1893, 65.

[5] PETROFF 1884, 33.

[6] PETROFF 1884, 36; ELLIOT 1875, 227.

[7] WRANGELL 1839, 96.

[8] ELLIOT 1875, 227.

[9] DALL 1870, 410; 1877, I, 21. DALL is probably referring, however, to the Eskimo inhabitants of Kayak Island.

[10] PETROFF 1884, 29.

[11] ABERCROMBIE 1900, 397.

We append a list of Eyak Indians which we compiled in 1933. It may nut be complete, and it may include Indians who had already died. Chief Joe and his Eskimo wife died during the winter of 1930 - 1931. Lucy, Annie, and Emma (the last three on the list) can hardly be counted as members of the tribe, since one is living in Kodiak, while the other two are somewhere in the States. Of the 38 persons on the list, 19 are pure Eyak as far as our genealogical information would show, though Galushia and Gus Nelson, [25] Annie Nelson, and Minnie Stevens claim some Tlingit blood. Four are half white, one is a quarter white, six are half Eskimo, one is three-quarters Eskimo, five are half Copper River Athapaskan, two are half Japanese. Not included is the second son (name unknown) born to Galushia and Annie Nelson in 1935.

1. Gus Nelson.
2. Mary Nelson, his wife.
3. Nikita, their son.
4. Annie, their daughter.
5. Mary, their daughter, wife of Willy Dude.
6. Willy Dude, step-son of Old Man Dude, by a white father.
7. Evaline, daughter of Willy and Mary Dude, one quarter white.
8. Galushia Nelson, brother of Gus Nelson.
9. Annie Nelson, his wife.
10. Johnny, their son.
11. Eleaua Saski, wife of Pete Saski, and niece of Gus and Galushia Nelson.
12. Rosie, daughter of Eleana and Pete Saski, half Eskimo.
13. John, son of Eleana and Pete Saski, half Eskimo.
14. Alfred, son of Eleana and Pete Saski, half Eskimo.
15. Old Man Dude.
16. Billy Dude, his son.
17. Johnny Stevens.
18. Daughter of Johnny Stevens and his first wife, half Eskimo.
19. William, son of Johnny Stevens and his second wife,
        one half Copper River Athapaskan.
20. Donny, son of Johnny Stevens and his second wife.
21. Jack, son of Johnny Stevens and his second wife. [26]
22. Earl, son of Johnny Stevens and his second wife.
23. Richard, son of Johnny Stevens and his second wife.
24. Scar Stevens.
25. Minnie Stevens, his wife.
26. Pete, their son.
27. Malia or Mary, their daughter.
28. Sophie, their daughter, wife of William Saitu (Japanese),
29. Billy, son of Sophie and William Saitu. half Japanese.
30. Mabel, daughter of Sophie and William Saitu, half Japanese.
31. Mike Duval, son of Minnie Stevens and Scar Stevens' older brother.
32. Molly, daughter of Chief Joe and his Eskimo wife. Half Eskimo.

---

[1] PETROFF 1893, 158.

33. Pauline, daughter of Chief Charlie and his Eskimo wife,
      three-quarters Eskimo, and half-sister to Molly.
34. Johnny MacIntyre.
35. Son of Johnny MacIntyre and an Eskimo wife, half Eskimo.
36. Lucy, daughter of Johnny MacIntyre's sister and a white man, half white.
37. Annie, daughter of Johnny MacIntyre's sister and a white man.
38. Emma, daughter of Johnny MacIntyre's sister and a white man.

For the relationships of these individuals see the genealogical table. Appendix I.

Village Sites.

With Galushia Nelson as guide, the American author made a short excursion in 1930 to the sites of the principal Eyak villages. [27]

The site of Alaganik is about 75 yards (70 m.) west of Mile Twenty-one on the Copper River Railway, on the north side of the tracks. The old houses stood on both sides of a small stream which flows into Alaganik Slough just south of the tracks. The site is now overgrown with bushes except for a small grassy patch on the right (west) bank of the stream, where ROSENBERG used to cut hay for his mules. Here is the grave of J.W. SNEIDAKER, a white man, whom ROSENBERG buried in 1899. The site is surrounded by woods. The old houses have entirely fallen down, but it was possible to trace the outlines of one house near the grave, three walls of a second house higher up on the same side of the stream, and a single wall on the opposite (east) bank. We attempted an excavation in front of the best preserved ruin and found only a pile of chips, a few glass beads, scraps of iron, broken china, three wooden wedges (Plate 11, 4, 5, 6), the prow handle of a dugout (Plate 11, 7), two spits for roasting fish (Plate 11, 1, 2), and part of a dead-fall for mink (Plate 11, 3). The objects of native manufacture are described below in the appropriate sections. We also uncovered the wooden foundations of what may have been a front porch, or other addition to the house, and the foundations of an earlier structure.
The house was 29 feet 6 inches by 24 feet 6 inches (9 by 7.5 m.). The doorway, indicated by two upright posts, was 2 feet wide, and was in the middle of one of the longer walls, facing the stream. About 6 feet (1.82 m.) inside the house walls, partitions ran along the two sides and across the back, which marked off either the edge of the sleeping bench, or less probably the rows of box-like sleeping rooms, since no cross-partitions separating individual cubicles were seen. All of these walls were indicated [28] by horizontal logs. Unfortunately we did not uncover them, and so we do not know if they were grooved to receive the lower ends of the vertically placed wall planks, as described by Galushia, or whether they were dovetailed at the ends, as described by ABERCROMBIE (see *Houses*). Remains of upright posts were seen in the two front corners, and a similar rotted post was in the line of the rear partition, 10 feet (3.05 in.) from the right wall. Our excavations were not extensive enough to indicate whether the front porch, if it was a porch, ran all the way across the front of the house. It was 8 feet (2.44 m.) wide. This house seems to have been rather unusual, since Galushia was not familiar with porches on the old-style houses, and had never seen a house with the door in one of the longer walls. It was usually located in one of the shorter end walls.
In front and to the right of this house we uncovered the rotted foundations of what may have been an earlier structure. The left rear corner of this ruin just touched the right front corner

of the first house. The second building was 22 feet 4 inches by 22 feet 10 inches (6.80 by 6.96 m.), with the longer side parallel to the stream. It was not possible to determine where the door had been, but it may have been between the two overlapping sections of the front wall, which formed a short passage 2 feet wide.

The native graveyard of Alaganik is on a high spur of rock, about 150 yards (140 m.) east of the village. When the railway was built, the rock was cut in two to make a place for the tracks, and the graves in the middle of the cemetery were thus destroyed. There are several modern graves there, each marked with a Russian cross and enclosed in a picket fence. There is also one of the old-style grave houses or boxes for ashes. This is a little house built out [29] of hand-adzed planks, but it lacks the four supporting posts seen on a similar grave box at Eyak. This house has a plank floor about 4 feet by 5 feet 10 inches (1.22 by 1.77 m.), with a gable plank roof, 3 feet 6 inches (1.06 m.) high, the eaves of which touch the floor. That is, there were no side walls. The ridge pole of the roof is supported at each end by a wide plank, notched at the top to hold the pole, and fitted at the bottom into a grooved plank set on edge across the end of the floor. The ends of the house are enclosed by smaller planks, set into the same grove. The boards are held by iron nails. Beside the grave box was lying a much weathered post, which Galushia identified as the grave post of a chief of the Wolf People (see *Moieties and Chiefs*). The post was hollowed out behind, like a Tlingit totem pole, making a V-shaped cross-section. The top, in front, is carved to represent an animal's head with pointed ears, eyes, and a rather indefinite mouth. The bottom of the post had rotted so that it was impossible to tell how high it had stood (Plate 8, 1).

Mr. ROSENBERG'S trading post was not at the village, but was built at the present site of Alaganik Station, at Mile Twenty-two on the railway, on the same side of the slough as the village. The original log cabin is still standing (Plate 5, 2) and is occupied by Mr. MCALLISTER.

About a quarter of a mile (400 m.) above the station, on the north side of the tracks, is a dry cave. Galushia told us that in his boyhood a shaman used to store his paraphernalia here. Galushia removed the drum, but was whipped by his parents and made to return it. We visited the cave but found nothing but some adzed planks, which Galushia thought might indicate that there had once been a burial here. (The Prince William Sound Eskimo used to [30] bury their dead in coffins made by lining a hole with adzed planks. We found such graves both in caves and in a shell heap on Hawkins Island. The Eskimo also placed their dead in rough stone or plank coffins in caves, without covering the coffin with earth.)

We also stopped at the site of glacatł, "Fort," on the west (right) bank of Eyak River, about half a mile (800 m.) below the site of Eyak. The village is supposed to have been just below the large rock, which, because of its resemblance to a fort, has given the name to the village (Plate 4, 2). We dug in a few indefinite pits but found nothing except a few fire-cracked rocks and traces of charcoal to a depth of 2 feet.

The site of Eyak is on the left (east) bank of Eyak River, about half a mile (800 m.) below the railroad bridge at Mile Six. It is at present occupied by a white man, Mr. NELSON, and his Eskimo wife. The old houses are supposed to have stood on land now used for a garden (Plate 5, 1), just north of a small tributary stream. Several objects, including a stone mortar and pestle, and an old gun, are said to have been found in the garden. The graveyard is on the same side of the river, about a quarter of a mile (400 m.) above the village. It is now almost entirely overgrown with trees and bushes. Most of the graves are marked with Russian crosses and picket fences (Plate 6, 1). We found the remains of one old grave box. It stood on four posts, 4 feet 8 inches (1.42m.) high. Two of these posts were braced by slanting beams, nailed to them, with their lower ends set into the ground. The floor of the box, or house, was of planks, and measured 4 feet 3 inches by 4 feet (1.30 by 1.22 m.). The roof was missing, though one of the supports for the gable, 3 feet (0.91 m.) high, and a pair of slanting rafters at one end were left. [31]

The site of t'cí•cqɛiGətłɛ is now entirely obliterated. Chief Joe said that it is now occupied by buildings belonging to the Copper River Railway. There are no surface indications to show whether the old houses were on the flat beside the lake where the freight office and the railway yards are located, or whether they were on top of the bank, on the northwest side of the flat where the homes of the railway employees have been built.

The American author also visited the small site at Point Whitshed Radio Station. It is called txałam qidl•ua by the Eskimo, meaning "behind Mummy Island." According to Gus Nelson this was Eskimo territory. Both the Eskimo, Makari, and Galushia Nelson said that the Eyak used to come here to dig clams, so that we cannot be sure which people made the few objects found here. There is a small midden, containing razor clam shells, horse clam shells, and cockle shells. It is 75 feet (22.86 m.) long and 6 inches (0.15 m.) thick, and extends from the cannery building on the right to the nearest cabin on the left. In the midden is a stump, the roots and lower part of which are covered by the shells. This stump was burned during the period of occupation, for the charred part is covered by midden deposit containing fire-cracked rocks. The site, therefore, cannot be very old. In this midden was found: a greenstone axe (roughly grooved after the fashion of the large "splitting adzes," but with the blade at right angles to the plane of these adzes), a planing adze blade, a slate "awl-like" weapon point, and two pieces of cut bone. On the beach we found a stone man's knife like an ulo(?). These specimens are to be described in our monograph on *The Archaeology of Prince William Sound.* [32]

Houses

The Eyak house has been described by several writers. WRANGELL writes: "They live in huts built of beams (*Balken*), on the sides of which separate places are divided off for each family, but in the middle a fire is made for all together. Thus from two to six families are accustomed to occupy in common a single shed."[1] PETROFF states in the Tenth Census: "Their houses are built of planks, and in the Tlinget style of architecture, with circular openings in front."[2] In the Eleventh Census, he also writes: "The houses in these 2 settlements [Eyak and Alaganik] are constructed altogether after the Thlingit model, large square structures, built of huge logs and covered with bark, and set in a single row along the shore, each with a platform in front, upon which the inhabitants pass much of their leisure time in summer."[3] Briefer descriptions of Eyak houses have been mentioned above, under Territory and Villages.

The Eyak house, as described by Galushia Nelson, was an unpainted rectangular structure, built of hemlock planks. The ruins seen at Alaganik, roughly 25 by 30 feet (7.02 by 9.14 m.), and 22 by 23 feet (6.71 by 7.01 m.), he judged to be of average size, though he said he had never seen one with a doorway in the longer side. The door was square and so low that one had to stoop to enter. The roof was of gable construction. The central ridge pole running the length of the house passed through the middle of the smoke-hole. The framework of the roof was of poles, on which were laid planks, not overlapping, but extending from the ridge to the

---

[1] WRANGELL 1839, 97.
[2] PETROFF 1884, 146.
[3] PETROFF 1893, 65f.

eaves. The whole was covered with bark. The [33] walls were of planks set vertically into a grooved frame of logs at the bottom and a corresponding frame at the top. Galushia thinks there were posts in the four corners (supporting the upper log frame?) and a post on each side of the door. Some of these posts could be seen in the ruin at Alaganik. He denies the existence of the front porch, however, or of an entrance room or entrance passage. Sometimes dirt was piled about the outside of the walls to keep the planks from rattling. Inside, there was a central room, with dirt floor, in the middle of which a single(?) fire was built, directly under the smokehole. There was no fire pit, and no stones were set about the hearth. Along the two sides and across the back were the sleeping rooms, like boxes. They reached as high as the eaves, and were not quite high enough to allow a man to stand upright. They were ceiled, and floored(?) with planks. On top of these sleeping rooms were kept the stores of dried meat and fish, etc. Each sleeping room had a sliding door in the middle of the front wall, as high as the roof of the room. The door slid between the front wall of the room and stakes driven into the ground at the bottom and a horizontal beam at the top. The front door of the house was barred at night and the doors of the sleeping rooms were also closed. Each family occupied a single room in these communal houses. The archaeological evidence would suggest that these rooms were about 6 by 10 feet (1.8 by 3m.). The last community house was that of Chief Joe and his two brothers. Each of the three families had its own room, but these were box-like additions built on the outside, like the bathrooms also used as sleeping rooms by the Prince William Sound Eskimo and the Tnaina Athapaskans of Cook Inlet. Joe's house was not partitioned on the inside, [34] as "was the old Eyak style, Galushia thinks that in former times a greater number of families may have shared a single house. The place of honor, occupied by the head of the house, was at the rear, opposite the front door. A chief and his family occupied the central rear room, and the space in front of it was where the chief sat, where guests were entertained, and where a dead body was kept during the wake. It was not considered impolite to walk between a person and the lire, since all were accustomed to sit around the sides of the house, leaning back against their own sleeping rooms. Little children, slaves, and dogs slept in the open space around the fire. Unmarried girls probably slept with their parents, but Galushia is not sure. Annie Nelson, his wife, was an orphan child adopted by an Eyak family, and she slept among the dogs beside the fire. (It is possible that only orphans had to sleep there.) Strangers were accommodated with sleeping places along one side of a special house in each village. In *Tale* 17, the two daughters of Chief Calm Weather not only had separate rooms, but lived in a house of their own.

There were also small houses for single families, and a man could live either in a community house or in a private house of his own, according to his choice.

The entire floor space in the sleeping room was covered by the skin bedding, so that the clamshell lamp was set on a shelf. A sloping board, long enough to accommodate all the occupants of the room, was used as a pillow. (See *Tale* 28.) Undecorated grass mats were hung on the walls and laid on the floor under the bedding. The lamp was never used in the main room, where the open fire was supposed to provide sufficient illumination.

Clothing was dried on poles which ran across the house [35] between the eaves. In war time, or when snow drifts blocked the door, it was possible to climb out of the house through the smokehole, by means of a rope attached to the central roof beam or a ladder (cf. ABERCROMBIE'S description p. 40). Dead bodies were taken out through a gap made in the wall, not through the smokehole.

Besides the single and communal dwelling houses there were special houses for smoking fish. These were built like ordinary houses, hut lacked the separate sleeping rooms. There was a fire in the middle of the floor, with smokehole above. A lattice of poles was laid the entire length and breadth of the house roughly at the height of the eaves. There were actually two levels of racks, the upper a foot higher than the lower. Fish to be smoked were placed first on the lower rack, and when partly cured were moved to the upper. Unfortunately we neglected to find out if there were planks above the fire to spread the smoke. There were smokehouses in the three main villages, Eyak, Alaganik, and Old Town, for fish could be obtained near by. When curing fish in these villages, the families probably continued to occupy their regular houses. There were also special fishing camps at Point Whitshed and on Mountain Slough. The smokehouses there were built like a lean-to, with a shed roof, and a door in the higher end (side ?). These sheds were made of poles covered by hemlock bark, and served as dwelling houses for single families during the fishing season, as well as smokehouses. There were a number of houses at Point Whitshed that were occupied in October after the salmon runs were over, when the people were drying clams, and some families might even stay there the whole year. (It is not clear from Galushia's description whether these bark sheds were located only at the [36] two camps, or whether some of the smokehouses in the main villages were of this type. Nor do we know if there were any wooden smokehouses or ordinary dwelling houses at Point Whitshed. Galushia saw these camps when he was a boy.)

In the main villages there were quite a few houses. The central structure was the fort (see below), and near it were the two moiety potlatch houses (see below). Dwelling houses were located wherever anyone wanted to build. There was no moiety segregation and no streets or other regular arrangement. Each family had a residence at Eyak and at Alaganik and moved back and forth at pleasure.[1] In *Tale* 24 distinct mention is made of a winter house and a summer camp. We do not know how common it was for the family to live in the regular house throughout the year or how large a proportion of the people moved into the summer camps.

In each village were two potlatch houses, one for each moiety. The potlatch house was built like the dwelling house, except that above the lower set of wall planks there was a second tier, set into the upper frame of logs and capped by a third frame. Only the potlatch house was built with these walls of double height. Inside was a single fireplace under the smokehole. In his description of the potlatch given by the Tlingit on Kayak Island, Galushia mentioned windows, but we do not know if the Eyak potlatch house ever had windows, nor do we know if there were any sleeping rooms, unless the sleeping quarters for guests, mentioned above, were in one of the pollatch houses. Outside at the front of the house was a post, the top of which was carved to represent the moiety bird, Raven or Eagle. [37]

The head of the bird was above the door; sometimes the post was higher than the house, sometimes not so high. Galushia does not know if the bottom of the post was set into the ground, but has a vague remembrance that entrance to the house was through a hole in the post. As a child he saw an Eagle post at Katalla. It was probably in front of the potlatch house which his maternal (?) Tlingit uncle built to accommodate the Eyak Eagles when they came to potlatches. This house could accommodate 26 families. Galushia later changed the figure to 16. At ordinary times it is doubtful if any one slept in the potlatch house. There were no totem poles in front of the dwelling houses.

All the Eyak potlatch houses had names. Thus the Raven house at Alaganik was called

---

[1] PETROFF 1893, 65: "Their situation affords these villages unimpeded communication through sheltered inland channels, and taking advantage of this circumstance their people intermingle freely."

the "Goose House." and the Eagle house was the "Bed House." At Eyak, the Raven house was the "Raven House," and the Eagle house the "Skeleton House," or more literally "Old Dead Body's House." At Gravina Bay there was a Raven house called "The One We Burned Down on the Beach." The Tlingit group that were adopted by the Eyak Eagles were supposed to have been in such a hurry to build their potlatch house that they made it of bark, thus acquiring the name "Bark House People." This tradition might indicate that the two subgroups. Bark House People and Wolf People, in the Eagle and Raven moieties respectively, may have had their own potlatch houses, but that would be at variance with Galushia's express statement that there were only two in each village, serving the two moieties as a whole. (For the Eyak names of these houses, see the Vocabulary, Appendix II.)

These names for potlatch houses can all be duplicated by the house names recorded by SWANTON among the [38] Tlingit,[1] with the exception of the "Goose House." Thus the "Raven house" is used as the name of a house or house group among the following Tlingit Raven clans: GānAXA'dî of Tongas and Taku, Tē'nedî ("bark house people") of Henya, Dē'citān of Hutsnuwu, and Łuqā'xadî of Chilkat. The Ka'gwAntān, a widespread Raven clan, is called "people of the burnt-down house," and they have a house of this name at Sitka. The Eyak "Skeleton House" suggests the "eagle's-bones house" of the Chilkat Ka'gwAntān. This is "said by the Wrangell people to have been claimed only in very recent times, the eagle not properly belonging to them." Eagle crest and names seem to have been taken over by the Tlingit Wolf moiety from the NēxA'dî of Sanya, a clan with Eagle names and crest, which stands outside both the Wolf and Raven moieties. The Raven clan, T!A'q!dentān, at Huna has a "raven's-bones house." The "Bed House" of the Eyak Eagles suggests the "sleeping house" of the L!ūk!naxA'dî at Sitka, but this was a Raven clan. Among the Tlingit two Raven clans, the Tē'nēdî of Henya and the Tī hît tān of Stikine, are both called "bark house people" and each have a house or house group of the name "bark house." The Wolf clan, Ka'gwAntān, of Chilkat had a "wolf house."

A house-warming potlatch was given when the potlatch house was finished. We must note that there is no reference to the potlatch house in any of the tales.

As already mentioned, Colonel ABERCROMBIE remembers only two houses at Alaganik, besides the small house occupied by the shaman and his two attendants. These two houses he describes in some detail. Although 60 persons were actually living in each of these two houses at the time of [39] his visit in 1884, the buildings differed in construction from the communal dwelling house as described by our native informants. Moreover, the dances that he witnessed were held in one of these houses. In his report he referred to it as "a native hotel used for visiting and passing friendly tribes. All entertainments are given in the casina."[2] These two houses, therefore, must have been the two potlatch houses, even though, contrary to what Galushia led us to understand, they were also serving as dwellings. It will be remembered that both buildings were new when ABERCROMBIE saw them in 1884, and the style of architecture showed Russian influence, as he suggests. It is possible that the potlatch house was then undergoing a transformation into a communal dwelling house, while the old style of dwelling house was being abandoned. Or the chief and some of the people may always have lived in the potlatch house. On the other hand, this may have been a temporary arrangement at Alaganik. In his report, ABERCROMBIE mentioned 7 houses at Alaganik. It is a pity that he did not enter any of them, for his memory of their character might help us to determine more accurately that of the two houses

---

[1] SWANTON 1908, 398ff.
[2] ABERCROMBIE 1900, 384.

that he did visit.

These two houses were rectangular, one-room buildings, about 60 feet (18.3m.) long and 20 feet (6.1 m.) wide, with the door at one end. The walls were of horizontally laid logs, dovetailed together, about six being used on the sides to reach the eaves. Colonel ABERCROMBIE suggests that the crude dovetailing may have been in imitation of the Russian buildings at Nuchek. The central ridge pole of the gable roof passed through the middle of the smoke-hole, and two of the parallel beams (purlins) that helped [40] to support the roof formed the lower edges of the smoke-hole. The roof was of logs, sloping from the roof to the eaves. Over these were laid strips of spruce bark, held down by a layer of clay. The walls were about 6 feet (1.8 m.) high, and the slope of the roof was only about 15°. The center of the gable would have been, therefore, about 10 feet (3 m.) high. The walls were chinked with moss and the women used to keep a round stone among their tools to pound the moss back in when it came loose. To protect the smokeholc from the wind, there was a moveable screen which could be set up on either side. This screen was made of several planks, pegged to two logs that hung down over the roof of the house and by their weight prevented the screen from being blown over. Two alder pegs, about 20 inches (0.5 m.) long, projected from the inner side of the screen at the bottom, and were hooked inside the lower edge of the smokehole (Figure 1). There were no extra boards to protect the ends of the smokehole. When the wind shifted, some one would climb to the roof on a ladder, made of a notched log, and move the screen to the opposite side. [41]

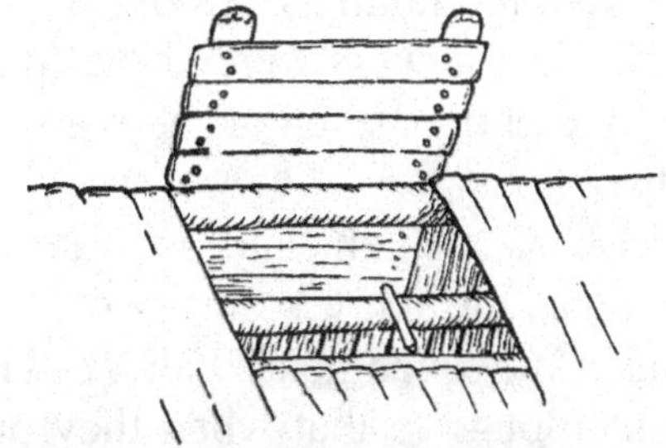

Fig. 1. Smokehole and windscreen, as described by ABERCROMBIE.

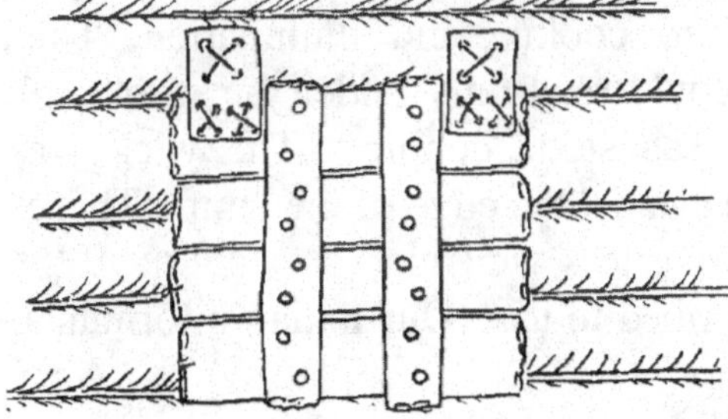

Fig. 2. Door of Eyak house, as described by ABERCROMBIE.

The doorway of the house was almost square, and "was considerably wider than our doors. One had to step over a log to enter, but did not need to stoop unless one stepped on the log sill. The logs of the wall had been roughly hacked off at the sides of the doorway with stone axes. The door itself was of hewn planks, set horizontally, and fastened together by two vertical planks on the outside (Figure 2). Each plank was nailed to these cross-planks by two wooden pins on each side. A hole had been drilled through the two planks, and after the wooden peg was inserted, both ends of the peg were spread by means of small wedges so that it could not work loose (Figure 3). The door was hinged at the top by two strips of white whale(?) hide, which were laced by rawhide thongs to holes in the door and holes in the log above the doorway.

ABERCROMBIE remembers no fastening for the door. There were no decorations outside the house and no carved post, but a large eye, in red and black, was painted on the door. [42]

In the center of the house was the fireplace. This was a depression in the dirt floor, about 4 or 5 feet (1.2 or 1.5 m.) by 3 or 4 feet (0.9 or 1.2 m.), filled with gravel to within 4 or 5 inches (10 or 12 cm.) of the floor level. The edges of the pit were faced with a log frame.

Fig. 3. Wooden nail used for pegging together door, etc., as described by ABERCROMBIE.

Along the two sides of the house and across the back was a continuous plank bench, about as high as the counter of a store, and wide enough so that a man could lie extended across it. The bench sloped down slightly towards the outer edge, along which was fastened a pole against which the sleepers braced their feet. Under the bench was a series of lockers with sliding doors, each compartment belonging to the family who sat and slept on the bench above. The lockers were about 6 feet (1.8 m.) long and as deep as the bench was wide (7 feet?). The dour of the locker was about 25 inches (0.7 m.) wide, just big enough to admit a man, and was as high as the bench. The door was always located at the end of the locker nearest the front of the house and slid between grooved logs at top and bottom. Each locker had partitions separating it from those on either side. The locker doors were carved and painted with what ABERCROMBIE understood to be the family totems of the owners. These designs were like those of the Tlingit, but were much more crudely made, and he was not able to identify the figures represented. In addition to these designs, each door had a black and red eye painted on it. In the lockers were kept the family's belongings — bedding, food, tools, clothing, toys, and ceremonial paraphernalia. The lockers were not used as sleeping places. The chief or headman and his family occupied the entire bench at the rear of [43] the house. His locker was more elaborately decorated than the others.

The benches were used as beds at night and as seats during the day. On them were spread mats made of reeds. At night the natives slept on a mountain goat skin and covered themselves with a homemade blanket of woven goat's hair(?). The blanket was only about a yard (0.9 m.) wide and five feet (1.5 m.) long, so that when they pulled it up over their heads and shoulders, their feet were uncovered. The chief had a bear skin or two in addition. The fire in the middle of the room served for cooking and illumination. The house had no windows, and it was so dark inside that one could read only under the smokehole. A few people had seal-oil lamps, made of a hollowed sandstone cobble. The wick was of twisted cotton from the cottonwood tree, and was laid against the edge of the lamp. These stone lamps were like those of the Eskimo at Nuchek, but were less well made. ABERCROMBIE saw no lamps made of clam shells such as the natives described to us. (Our Indian informants, on the other hand, denied the use of stone lamps.)

In the center of the village, according to Galushia, stood the fort or stockade, used as a refuge in time of war. It was built of upright posts instead of planks, and because of its construction was given the same name as the fish trap. There was a single door. A space inside was excavated for a depth of a few feet. Galushia does not know whether this structure was roofed, or whether a house was built inside the stockade. Food was stored in the fort. Once, when people were besieged in a fort, their supply of water was exhausted. A man ran to get some, but was shot down by arrows. In *Tale* 16, the Sun's children build a fort when they come down to earth to attack the Alders. [44]

When men were on hunting trips, they usually camped in the open. However, if they were to be out for a long time, they might build a brush shelter or lean-to against a cliff. Johnny Stevens said that hunters also made a dome-shaped hut of branches, like that used by adolescent girls. Hunters also camped sometimes under an overturned canoe. No skin tent was used.

Gus Nelson's wife denied that a special hut was built for menstruating girls. She said that they were secluded in a sleeping room. Galushia, however, was sure that girls at puberty were sent to a special hut, built of planks like an ordinary house. Later, both he and Johnny Stevens described a conical hut, built like a tipi and covered with bark. Johnny Stevens also mentioned a dome-shaped puberty hut, made of arched branches, their ends stuck into the ground to form a structure like an inverted basket. Galushia thought this type was a late introduction.

We were told that the sweat bath was not originally an Eyak institution but was borrowed from the Eskimo, before the Russians came, according to Galushia. The bath is taken in a small log hut, like those built by the Prince William Sound Eskimo, Friends sometimes would take a bath together to see who weakened first, but even now it has not become very popular among the Eyak. Colonel ABERCROMBIE saw no sweat-bath houses at Alaganik in 1884, and curiously enough, does not remember any at Nuchek, though they were common in the Copper River Valley.

Caches were sometimes built for meat. These were platforms set up on four poles, the edges of the platform projecting beyond the supports so that animals could not climb up. There was no roof to the cache. A cache is mentioned in *Tale* 2. Galushia knew of no pit caches to store meat in [45] the ground. Caches were not used much, for the people were in a hurry to get their meat home. The caches which ABERCROMBIE remembers at Alaganik were more like those used in the interior, and it is possible that he has confused those of the two regions. He described them as little log houses, about 6 feet square, set on top of 10-foot (3 m.) posts. The house had a gable roof and was built of horizontal logs. There was no projecting platform in front. The doorway was square, just large enough to crawl through, and lacked a door. The house rested on four blocks of wood that capped the four posts. These blocks were about 15 inches (38 cm.) square, and were kept well oiled, which made them so hard that no animal could climb them.

Though the Eyak built no permanent dwellings of bark or brush, they tell about the Tree People, a tribe of cannibal giants who live in the interior and who make houses of boughs (*Tale* 20).

Boats

The Eyak formerly built wooden canoes. At present these dugouts have been almost entirely abandoned in favor of skiffs and gas boats, but in 1933 we found two which we measured and photographed. One, partially completed at that time, is the work of Gus Nelson, the other, an old cracked boat, belongs to Old Man Dude. Gus Nelson's boat (Plate 9, 1) more closely follows the traditional pattern than does Dude's. It measures 16 feet 4 inches (4.98 m.) in length at the gunwale, and 15 feet 6 inches (4.72 m.) at the keel, the extra 10 inches (26 cm.) representing the overhang of the stern. The beam is 2 feet 10 inches (86 cm.), and the stern and bow both stand 2 feet 4 inches (71 cm.) high. The stern is simply curved under, but the prow is undercut in a V for a depth of 9 inches (22 cm.), leaving both the [46] gunwale and keel projecting. Galushia explained that this was to make the boat easier to steer. The boat was round-bottomed in the middle, only at bow and stern was it narrowed to produce a false keel. Since it was unfinished, we were unable to see what arrangements Gus may have been planning for thwarts. The canoe was being shaped with an adze, and was kept covered with a piece of canvas to prevent it from cracking in the sun.

Old Man Dude's canoe (Plate 5, 4) measures roughly 17 feet (5.02 m.) in length, the inside length being lo feet 7 inches (4.85m.). The beam is 2 feet 11 inches (89cm), the height of the stern is 1 foot (30 cm.), that of the prow 1 foot 6 inches (46 cm.), hut this was not the original height. since the gunwales arc broken. As the canoe stands now, the profile of the bow and stern is like that of the Eskimo dugouts found in Palutat Cave in Prince William Sound. The projecting keel at the prow has recently been hacked off, but even in its original condition this canoe must have lacked the graceful shape of Gus Nelson's boat. Now the wood has sprung apart and the cracks have been mended with tin. The whole surface is painted. In the angle of the prow is a wooden handle like that found at Alaganik in 1930. The sides of the canoe have been forced apart to permit the insertion of the sharpened ends of the handle into slots. When the canoe was allowed to spring back into shape, the tension of the wood held the handle firmly in place. The specimen from Alaganik (P-UM 30-25-99d, Plate 11, 7) is a naturally curved section of alder(?), flat on one side, and sharpened to a wedge at both ends. It is 21 cm. long and 3 cm. wide. In the middle of Dude's canoe, just under the gunwales, are cleats to hold a seat or thwart, 7 inches (18cm.) wide. There was perhaps another thwart about 3 feet (92 cm.) from the stern. [47]

There were no taboos connected with canoe-building, Galushia explained, and any man could make one. Fire may have been used in felling the tree. To hollow it out, two or three fires were built along the middle, and were kept pushed back from the edges with a stick. Afterwards the charred wood was adzed out. The sides were forced out after boiling water in the canoe by means of hot rocks. The sides of the larger canoe (of the small canoes also?) were kept in position by three thwarts. In the forward thwart of the large canoe was a hole to step the mast. The sail was square; one side was fastened to the mast, and the outer peak was held up by a diagonal boom. When not in use canoes had to be kept out of the sun to prevent their cracking. They were painted black with charcoal mixed with oil. When traveling on lakes they were loaded to leave a 6-inch (15 cm.) freeboard, but lighter loads were carried on salt water.

The largest canoes carried 10 persons (Mrs. Gus Nelson) or 16 (Galushia). Old Man Dude mentioned a canoe with 50 occupants in *Tale* 14B, but this is certainly an exaggeration. In the large canoes the occupants sat on thwarts. In the small canoes they sat on wooden stools, which they straddled in a half kneeling position. The stool was shaped like an overturned box, open at both ends, and was cut from a single block of wood. Some of the small canoes carried 4 persons (Mrs. Gus Nelson). If a man was paddling alone, he sat in the middle of the canoe. He might paddle only on one side, steering the canoe by a transverse motion at the end of the stroke. The canoe was always paddled by men unless the party was small and the man sick (Galushia). Thus in *Tale* 14A one old man takes three women in a canoe to pick berries. Slaves helped to paddle. [48]

Mrs. Gus Nelson, however, said that both men and women paddled. She showed me a photograph of her mother and a man in a canoe at Alaganik. They were both paddling on the same side. It was customary, she explained, for all to paddle three strokes on one side, then shift simultaneously to the other. This is the Eskimo method of paddling the three-man baidarka. According to Galushia, when a large party traveled there was a special pilot who sat next the steersman in the stern but did not himself paddle or steer. Johnny Stevens said that the shaman never paddled when he was with a party.

In conversation Colonel ABERCROMBIE adds the following information: The small canoes usually carried two occupants, but might hold four; the large canoes carried six or eight persons. He is full of admiration for the small canoe, but says that the larger boat was not nearly so well designed. Not only was it without the graceful lines of the smaller craft, but lacked the projecting keel in the bow. On the smaller canoe this keel acted like a drift rudder and made the boat easy to handle in swift water, and prevented it from broaching in rough seas. The boats at

Alaganik were made of yellow cedar, which ABERCROMBIE suggests may have been obtained in trade from the Eskimo near Valdez, where he observed a stand of yellow cedar. Canoes were shaped with a large stone adze. The inside was filled with water, which was heated with hot stones, so that the sides could be forced out. The thwarts were then inserted, two for the small canoe, three for the large. These thwarts were small poles, about $2^{1/2}$ inches (6 cm.) in diameter, and were lashed on just below the gunwale by a thong which passed through a horizontal hole in the thwart and, two, holes in the side of the canoe. The sides of the canoe bulged from [49] the bow and stern to these thwarts and then ran straight between them. The model made at Alaganik in 1884, and generously given by Colonel ABERCROMBIE to the University Museum, was made to scale and reflects accurately the shape of the smaller canoes (Plate 11, 8). The two paddlers in the small canoe sat on two stools. Just behind the thwarts. These stools were made of a hollow section of log, about 2 feet (61 cm.) long, 9 inches (23 cm.) high, and 6 inches (15 cm.) wide. On a hunting trip the arrows were laid under the stool. Any load was always placed in the center of the boat. In the large canoe the paddlers did not sit on thwarts or stools, but squatted, side by side, a pair behind each thwart. Colonel ABERCROMBIE saw no mast or sail. The steersman sat on a small triangular wooden seat, lashed into the angle of the stern. ABERCROMBIE noticed no prow handles, but remembers that the natives used to take hold of the thwarts when drawing the canoe up on the beach. None of the canoes were carved or decorated, but some (Long Jim's, for example) were painted black outside. When not in use, the canoes were drawn up on the bank and were covered with grass, skins, or brush to prevent them from cracking.[1]

According to Galushia, the paddle had a crutch handle and a longer and more pointed blade then the Eskimo paddle. A broken paddle was found at Old Man Dude's house (P-UM 33-29-2, Plate 12, 1). The blade had been broken [50] off and the handle was reshaped for an axe. The total length of the paddle must have been about 175cm. The blade is about 80 cm. long and 11 cm. wide, pointed at the tip, with the greatest width in the middle. The blade widens more evenly into the handle than on Eskimo specimens from Prince William Sound. The handle is oval in section, 3.5 by 3 cm., with the greater diameter in the plane of the blade. The end is carved to a crutch-shaped grip, 6 cm. wide. The paddle is unpainted. The Eyak never used a double-bladed paddle. The canoe was steered with the paddle, and for large canoes special steering paddles with long handles were used.

According to Colonel ABERCROMBIE, the paddle had a pointed blade, the widest part being near the handle. The handle was carved with a crutch-shaped grip. The blade was thicker in the middle than at the edges, but lacked a prominent ridge. When in use, the paddle was slid along the gunwale, and the handle was eventually worn through by the friction. The blade was painted, hut the only feature of the decoration which ABERCROMBIE can remember was the large eye which appeared on all the paddles. Like the eye on the doors of the house and lockers, it had a black pupil and a red and black outline. Other symbols were painted above and below it.

In his written report, ABERCROMBIE makes the following observations about the Eyak and

---

[1] In this connection it may be of interest to cite GRINNELL'S description of the small Yakutat canoes: "They are light, and until one has become accustomed to them, seem very cranky and likely to tip over. The shape of the cutwater is peculiar, for under the prow the wood is cut away backward, and beneath this again projects forward just above the water's level, with the result that this projecting point of wood first strikes and pushes away the ice cakes which so thickly float upon the water's surface, and prevents them from chafing the bows of the canoe." (GRINNELL 1902, 162f).

their small canoes. "They are not hunters, and use their canoes as a means of transportation entirely. These are made out of trees hollowed out, and are beautiful models. The boats are about 18 feet long, have a 3-foot beam, and are handled with great dexterity in the sloughs and even in quite rough water. The Indians never ascend the river [Copper River] more than 8 or 10
[51] miles as their boats are easily cracked', and in the terrific swash of rapids they would stand a poor show."[1] "Situated as they are without trails, the water is their highway and the canoe the universal means of transportation. They own no large canoes. Those in common use are 15 feet in length, 18 inches beam when spread, round bottomed, sharp at stem and stern, and weigh from 80 to 125 pounds. They will carry two natives or, upon an emergency, three, with their supplies for a week. In experienced hands they will ride out in safety a considerable sea, provided it is not breaking, and in open water, where rocks, brush, floating logs, or ice do not endanger them, are exceedingly serviceable. For river work they are not so satisfactory, as in addition to readily capsizing they are easily split by a blow. Much care has to be taken, also, that when not actually in use they are kept constantly moist in the shade. They are valued at from $4 to $6, and every native owns one or more. Even the children are expert in their management."[2] In Plate 10 we reproduce enlargements of photographs of Eyak canoes, taken by ABERCROMBIE in 1884.

ALLEN also published pictures of Eyak canoes, some of them drawings made from ABERCROMBIE'S photographs. ALLEN and another man and four Eyaks traveled in one "small canoe." He speaks of meeting "a canoe with a small piece of cotton cloth for sail." The Eyak canoes "draw only a few inches of water, and along the flats when the tide is low are propelled by using the paddle as a pole."[3] WRANGELL says only that they are similar to those of the Tlingit.[4] [52]

PETHOFF more specifically states: "The Thlingit wooden canoe forms their principal means of transportation. Of these craft two kinds are in use among the Ugalentx [Eyak], the large traveling canoe with prominent uprising prow, resembling in shape those of the Yakutat tribe, from which they are frequently purchased, and the smaller hunting or fishing canoe, also of wood, easily propelled by one man and of exceedingly graceful shape, with a ram-like protuberance at the bow, which they claim facilitates the ascent of rapid streams."[5]

The natives made no statement to us about the use of the kayak. ABERCROMBIE writes, however: "The bidarka in such general use to the westward is not used to any extent by the Eyaks."[6] In 1890 PETROFF wrote: "To a limited extent the Ugalentz Thlingit [Eyak] also make use of the kayak, or Eskimo canoe, but this is done only for the purpose of sea-otter hunting, and the canoes are purchased from their Eskimo neighbors. A few of these canoes can also be found among the Yaktags or Chilkahts living along the shores of Controller bay, and even among their fellow tribesmen beyond Cape Suckling. Here also, however, the use of the kayak is confined to the pursuit of the sea otter."[7] In 1880 he wrote: "Even the manufacture of {this} kaiak has been abandoned and is now forgotten by the hybrid tribe."[8] PETROFF'S statements are colored by his

---

[1] ABERCROMBIE 1900, 384f.

[2] ABERCROMBIE 1900, 398.

[3] ALLEN 1887, 36f.

[4] WRANGELL 1839, 97.

[5] PETROFF 1983, 66.

[6] ABERCROMBIE 1900, 398.

[7] PETROFF 1893, 66.

[8] PETROFF 1894, 146.

assumption that the Eyak were originally an Eskimo group who became absorbed by the Tlingit. There seems no warrant, however, to suppose that the Eyak ever made kayaks. Their limited [53] use of the kayak in historic times we must ascribe to Russian influence, since whatever its disadvantage as a means of travel for long distances or in dangerous waters,[1] there is no doubt that the kayak or baidarka was better adapted than the dugout for sea-otter hunting in the open sea.[2] It is significant that Galushia did not mention the kayak at all, even when describing sea-otter hunting. According to our native informants, the small canoe was used for sea-otter hunting, for fishing, and for hunting seals on the river.

In 1884 ABERCROMBIE saw about 15 or 20 baidarkas at Alaganik. He suggests that they may have been made by a renegade Eskimo living among the Eyak. These boats had two or three manholes. At that lime there were no one-hole kayaks in use, even at Nuchek. He does not think that the Eyak used baidarkas for anything except sea-otter hunting, and that they did not dare to hunt sea-otter unless invited by their Eskimo neighbors. The baidarkas at Alaganik were exactly like those at Nuchek, with sinew cords across the deck under which were thrust the spears and club. When not in use the baidarkas, with hunting gear in place on the decks, were kept on top of racks. The paddles were put inside the manholes to protect them from the sun. At frequent intervals the owner would oil his boat to keep the seal skin in good condition. Oil for (his purpose was carried in a small skin bag-The dugout was used as a vessel in boiling out eulachon oil (Johnny Stevens).

For canoe races the Eyak formerly built special canoes, longer, lighter, and more slender than ordinary canoes.

Special canoes were built for war. These had a carved prow, representing either the Raven's or the Eagle's head. [54] The people worked together when making a war canoe and it was owned by the whole tribe. (Does Galushia mean by the moiety?) They carried 16(?) persons. In *Tale* 25, mention is made of a man whose sole duty was to bail out the war canoe. We do not know if every war canoe carried such a man. The bailer was a spruce-root basket. No wooden bailers or wooden tubes for sucking up water were used.

Galushia also says that for war the Eyak sometimes used a sealskin or goatskin boat, built like an Eskimo umiak. The frame was of wood, with gunwales, keel, and frames. There were only a few ribs, and these were made in two pieces, one for each side, fastened at the bottom to the keel. The keel was curved, making both the bow and stern turn up. The gunwales were heavier than the other frames, and were tied together at the bow, so that there were no projecting horns as on Eskimo umiaks. The bottom was rounded. All the parts of the framework were lashed together, and no pegs were used. As a boy, Galushia saw such a sealskin boat at Alaganik. The owner would not let anyone touch it. ABERCROMBIE also saw a sealskin umiak, and it may even be the same boat. When his native crew deserted him on the Copper River, Long Jim went back to Alaganik to get them. They returned in an umiak, similar to those at Nuchek. This boat is illustrated in Plate 10, 2.

The Wolf People, a fabulous cannibal tribe, are supposed to make bark canoes (*Tale* 19), but the Eyak never made them. The canoe of the Land-Otters is a live skate and their paddles are live mink (*Tale* 12). Mention is made of a people who own a self-paddling canoe of seal skin (Raven, incident 22), and in another story (*Tale* 17) a self-paddling canoe is mentioned. The canoes of the Blackfish can dive (*Tale* 9). Travel by canoe is frequently mentioned in the stories. [55]

---

[1] PETROFF 1882, 569, 571.
[2] BANCROFT 1888, 347.

Sleds

Johnny Stevens asserted that the Eyak used a sled with upturned ends (Kutchin type). These stood a foot high, and were made of pieces lashed together. The runners were of wood, without bone shoeing. Dogs were hitched tandem to the sleds, and this form of transportation was used both for travel and for bringing home game.

It can be accepted without question, however, that the Eyak did not use dogs for dragging their sleds. Dog traction and the tandem style of hitching were introduced by the Americans, and since the terrain is ill adapted for sledding, it is doubtful if the Eyak ever made much use of this method of transportation.

Whether or not the original Eyak sled was of Kutchin type is less easy to determine. Galushia does not mention this kind, but describes two other types of sled. The first was a very crude contrivance, made only for dragging home across the ice loads of fish that were too heavy to carry. The sled was pointed, since it was made of a forked branch, across which were set cross-bars, morticed into the branches without lashings. The number of cross-bars depended on the length of the sled. Boughs were laid on top. For bringing home game a Yukon type sled was used, but Galushia was not sure if it was indigenous. This sled had runners made of two naturally curved branches. Galushia thought that it was of necessity only a temporary contrivance, because he believed that the friction on the snow would soon wear out the unprotected wooden runners. He also explained that a sled was never taken from the village with the hunting party, but was only fetched after they had killed game. To make or take along a sled in advance would spoil the hunters' luck.

No mention is made of sleds in the tales. [56]

Snowshoes

Snowshoe frames were made from small spruce trees. The frame was of two pieces, lashed together, with pointed heel, and rounded, spliced, upturned toe. The bent-up toe was held in position by a Y-shaped lashing, the two ends of the Y being fastened to the toe, and the bottom of the Y running back to the first cross-bar. There were three cross-bars, the last two being close to the heel. The forward and rear spaces were left open, but a webbing of seal thong was laced between the two first cross-bars, where the foot rested. The webbing was run through horizontal holes drilled in the frame, and ran back and forth in a simple rectangular weave, leaving an open space for the toe of the foot. Men made both the frame and the webbing. No netting needle was used. The Copper River Indians used sinew for webbing, but the Eyak never did.

A pair of snowshoes owned by Gus Nelson (Plate 7, 2) departs somewhat from the traditional pattern described by his brother. The length is 125.7 cm., the distance from the toe to the first cross-bar is 34 cm., and the distance between the first and second cross-bars is 36 cm. The maximum width of 23 cm. is at the first bar; the width at the second is 18.7 cm. The toe is turned up for a height of 10 cm. The arrangement of webbing and strings can be seen in the photograph.

When setting snares wooden snowshoes were worn to prevent the hunter from leaving his scent. These wooden shoes were used only for this purpose. While Galushia was unable to give us any detailed description of them, we can assume that they were roughly shaped like the netted

snow-shoes since Galushia called them "wooden snowshoes." and denied that they were skis.
Snowshoes are mentioned only in *Tale* 2. [57]

Dogs

The Eyak dogs were about the same size as the Eskimo "husky." They had pointed prick ears, bushy tails, and looked something like police dogs. According to Galushia, they were used only for hunting. They were never harnessed to a sled and were never used to carry packs. He tells how shocked he was at first seeing dogs used as pack animals. Some Copper River Indians had come down to trade at Orca Cannery, near Cordova. They loaded their dogs each with two one-hundred pound sacks of flour, so that the poor animals could hardly walk. Eyak dogs were trained to hunt and were never kept as pets. It would spoil a dog's luck to play with him (see *Tale* 24). The natives always took a dog when hunting. He was kept on a leash until the hunter was ready to let him go. Galushia does not know what kind of a dog collar was used. Dogs were also trained to slay behind the hunters. Dogs chased mountain goats and held them until the hunter came. They also smelled out bears' dens (*Tale* 6B).

Each dog had a name. The owner gave him whatever name he fancied, but it was always a dog's name and it was usually the name of a dead dog, just as a child was always named after a dead relative. Some dog names had a meaning, such as "Would always bring game to the man." Dogs were kept in the house and slept beside the fire. It was stated that they never had rabies before the introduction of white men's dogs. Animal bones were usually given to dogs, since there was no taboo against it. A dog was never killed, either when the owner died or at any other time, because it was had luck to do so. There was no objection to touching a dead dog, however.

Johnny Stevens, in describing what we have identified [58] as the American innovation of dog driving, said that the animals were hitched tandem and wore ordinary collars. The dog whip was made of one long tapering thong, or of several thongs fastened together, attached to a wooden handle. The whip was about five feet long and had a knot at the end of the lash. Galushia is not certain whether the dog whip was used formerly.

We were not able to learn anything definite about the inheritance of dogs. When Galushia's mother died, her dogs went to her daughter. This would indicate that a woman might own dogs, which seems curious since they were used only for hunting. Probably it was the husband of the nominal owner, in such a case, who actually used the dogs.

The use of the dog skin by the witch will be discussed later (p. 207).

Colonel ABERCROMBIE was surprised to see only a few dogs at Alaganik. He thought that perhaps the people had eaten them in a time of famine.

Personal Adornment

Men wore their hair parted in the middle and tied into a bunch on each side. It fell to their necks (Johnny Stevens). Most men wore their hair long and greased it with seal oil. They put eagle down on it at potlatches(?). They did not wear a headband except at a potlatch, and at the mourning feast for slain warriors feathers were stuck in the band (Galushia). Shamans wore their hair combed back and fastened behind with a double-pronged pin. Their hair fell to their shoulders (Johnny Stevens). Men wore a mustache but no beard.

Colonel ABERCROMBIE describes the haircut of the men as a "Dutch bob," reaching to the nape of the neck behind, [59] with bangs across the forehead. Kai, the shaman, wore his hair parted in the middle, falling loose lo his shoulders, except for a front lock on each side which was threaded through a copper ring. This drew the hair forward to expose the ears (Figure 4).

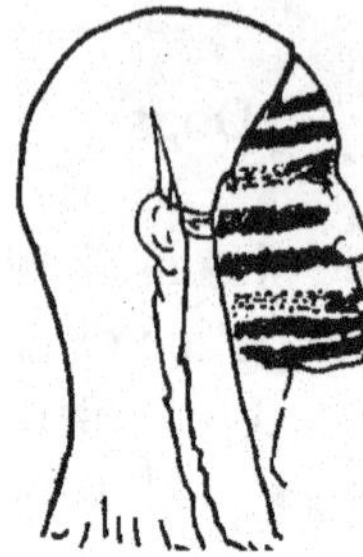

Fig. 4. Kai, the shaman, as described by ABERCROMBIE.
The dotted areas on the face represent red paint.

At the dances which ABERCROMBIE saw, all the male performers wore headbands, or rather crowns of wood, about 3 inches (7.6 cm.) wide, covered with skin. They were decorated with glass and obsidian beads, stitched to the skin. The latter were obtained from the interior, he thinks, because he saw similar obsidian beads among the Copper River Indians. There were no shell beads at Alaganik. The beads were sewn to the crown to form a row of diamond-shaped figures. Most of the men had beads only in front, but Kai, the shaman, had beads all the way around. There were holes in the upper edge of the crown into which feathers were set (Figure 5). The feathers seemed to be replaceable, for at the end of the dance they would be badly mussed, and yet the men would appear for the next dance with fresh feathers. These crowns were like the headbands worn by the Copper River Indians at Taral, though the latter lacked feathers.

According to Galushia, women and girls wore their hair in one braid down the back. tied at the end with a thong, and were very proud of its length. They wore a headband (material?). In *Tale* 5, the tail of the animal becomes her headband when she assumes human shape. In *Tale* 28, [60] the girl asks her mother to fix her hair so that she will not be mistaken for a slave, thus implying that slave women wore their hair in a different style from other women, though we have no information about that style. Colonel ABERCROMBIE says that the Eyak women wore their hail-in two braids, generally hanging down over the breast, less often down the back. At the dances, some of the wealthier women threaded dentalium shells on their hair to decorate their braids, but Galushia knew nothing about women's hair ornaments.

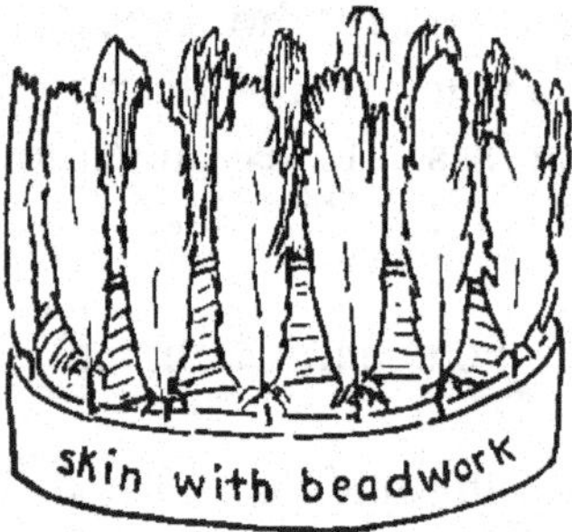

Fig. 5. Wooden crown with leathers, worn at dances, as described by ABERCROMBIE.
The wooden frame is covered with skin and beadwork.

It is not certain if the comb was formerly used by the Eyak. Galushia denied that they knew either the comb or the porcupine-tail hairbrush in old days. In *Tale* 5, however, the old woman chides the hunter: "You eat, too, while your women are combing their hair." In incident 23 of the Raven cycle, Raven had a magic comb that would bring hack the color to white hair and restore youth.

Both sexes painted the face, though we do not know if this was done daily or only for special occasions. The moieties had their own patterns (?). The designs were straight lines(?). Later, Galushia said that at potlatches a diamond-shaped figure was painted on the cheek, though he did not known who wore this pattern. Diamond-shaped figures used in basketry are called "face painting." Before going to fight, the warriors painted their faces black and red.

From what Colonel ABERCROMBIE relates, it would seem that face paint was used only for dance. Thus, the women [61] of the chorus had their faces painted black and red,[1] and some of Ihe wealthier people in the audience were painted. All of the performers were masked, except Kai, the shaman, whose face was painted.[2] Kai was not painted all the time, but appeared in paint to greet ABERCROMBIE when he landed at Alaganik, and was painted for the dances which were held every afternoon during the week of ABERCROMBIE'S slay. Kai had two black stripes across his forehead, a red stripe across his eyes, two black stripes across his cheeks (the last three interrupted at the nose), a red stripe across his mouth, and two black stripes across his chin. These lines were all horizontal (Figure 4). The red paint was a much brighter color that the stain used for wood. "Kai looked like a devil."

Both sexes (or only women?) tattooed the wrist. The tattooing was in one or more (?) lines around the wrist, like a bracelet. A hole was made under the skin with an awl, and a thread stained with blueberry juice or with charcoal mixed with grease was drawn through. Galushia thought that tattooing was also done by pricking. No food taboos were associated with tattooing. It is still practiced, but Galushia knows of no reason for this type of decoration. Women also burned their wrists with a glowing stick. This was to accustom themselves to pain, so that if they were speared in time of war they would not cry out. ABERCROMBIE does not remember such scars or tattooing.

Both men and women wore ear ornaments. Galushia's [62] ears were pierced when he was such a small child that he does not remember the occasion. He does not think that any ceremonies were connected with making holes in the ears or in the septum of the nose. Captain JACOBSEN, who visited the Eyak in 1883, makes the following statement:

"As soon as a child is born, the septum of the nose and both ears are pierced, and rings are put through the holes without further ceremony."[3]

While beads, animal teeth, especially seal teeth, and seal whiskers were used as ornaments, we are not sure just what was worn in the ears. The natives say that only the chief and his family wore earrings and headdresses of dentalium shells, and these only on special occasions. The chief wore strings of dentalium shells hanging from his ears. Galushia knows of no type of men's ornaments that were forbidden to women. He says that women alone wore nose ornaments. He has seen many women with nose rings made of roots or bone, but never a man or a little girl. Neither sex wore labrets. The chief's family wore necklaces of beaver teeth or seal teeth. In *Tale* 4B, the Salmon Boy is wearing his sister's necklace.

Colonel ABERCROMBIE remembers no ornaments except copper finger rings. These, like

---

[1] Compare with the statement in his report (p. 385) that the seven women who sang had their "faces painted red and black and hair and persons ornamented with swan's-down [eagle down?]".

[2] At the same performance the "dancer" (actually the shaman who did not dance, but told the story) was a "grotesquely arrayed native with painted face". (ABERCROMBIE 1900, 398).

[3] JACOBSEN 1884, 394.

Kai's hair rings, were made of a thin band, bent around to overlap. These rings were worn by both men and women, chiefly on the fourth finger of the right hand. The rings were probably obtained from the interior, for the Copper River Indians wore similar rings. Long Jim, an exiled Indian from Taral, had a number of rings, which he was always trading off. He wore them on the ring finger of his right hand, and they flashed in the sun when he was spearing salmon. [63]

There was no pulling out or filing off of teeth, though there were rules for the disposal of teeth, nail parings, etc. Baby teeth were put outside a mouse hole so that the mouse would bring new teeth in exchange. Nail pairings had to be buried outside, all in one place, "so that they might be found again if necessary." Hair combings were burned. Mention will be made below of the fear that hair, nail parings, or scraps of clothing might fall into the possession of witches, There was no rigid rule for the disposal of spittle. Galushia, who was tubercular, was careful to spit into a piece of paper which he carefully burned, but he had evidently been advised by a doctor to do this for the protection of his family.

JACOBSEN mentions that the natives wore amulets of bone and stone hanging from their necks. These objects were evidently highly prized, for he was unable to buy a single specimen.[1] ABERCROMBIE does not remember any amulets, except those which Kai wore in a small skin bag hung around his neck. These were sharks' teeth, claws, animal bones, and similar objects.

ABERCROMBIE says that the Eyak were very dirty and were covered with lice. They ate so much fish that when they sweated they had a fishy smell. They smeared their bodies with seal oil to prevent their skins from chapping in the wind. When scratched by bushes, their skin would be scratched white, but would not be cut. They were able to sit in the cold rain without apparent signs of discomfort. They were much tougher than the Nuchek Eskimo.

Galushia thinks that before the sweat bath was adopted the only method of taking a bath was to jump in the river, and he doubts if the women did this very often. [64]

Clothing

The dress of both men and women consisted of shirt, trousers, and boots (*Tales* 3, 6B, 17, 18).

The shirt was a pull-over frock, slit far enough down the front to admit the head. The woman's shirt reached the knees, but there is some uncertainty about the length of the man's. Mrs. Gus Nelson said that it reached only to the waist. Galushia says that some men's shirts reached the knees (the winter shirt?), while some merely covered the hips. They were cut evenly around the bottom. RICHARDSON writes: "The shirts of the Ugalents reach to the knee or lower, and are cut evenly round without peaks."[2] The shirt was made in two pieces, back and front, seamed at the sides. The sleeves were separate pieces, sewed up on the outside of the arm. The shirts of the chiefs and their families were decorated along this seam with a fringe, which may have been part of the material of the sleeve, or a separate piece sewn on (Galushia is not certain). There were also fringes along the other seams, but these were not made of separate pieces. Animal teeth and undyed porcupine quills were sometimes sewn to the seams. In summer, and in winter when in the house, only an inner shirt was worn. This had the hair turned next the body, and lacked a hood. This shirt seems to have been made of seal skin; at least we have

---

[1] JACOBSEN 1884, 387.
[2] RICHARDSON 1851, I 404. Since this writer confused the Eyak with the Prince William Sound Eskimo, it is hazardous to place much reliance on his statements.

explicit information to that effect regarding the man's shirt. The outer shirt worn in winter had a hood attached, and was of eagle or swan skins from which the large feathers had been plucked to leave the down. Makari, our Eskimo informant, said that the Eyak were so poor [65] that they dressed only in eagle skins. There were no moiety or social restrictions limiting the use of eagle skins. It was stated that when the shirt was made of bird skins or the skins of small animals, the separate pelts were first sewn together to make a large piece, which was afterwards cut down to fit the pattern. It does not seem improbable, however, that the skins were sewn together in long strips which were joined horizontally to make the shirt; this would he in accordance, at least, with the Eskimo pattern. Only the chiefs and their families wore shirts of weasel (ermine) skins. In *Tale* 6 A, the woman is wearing a shirt made of groundhog skins, with the tails hanging down for decoration. Sea-otter skins were worn only by the chief and his family. Mountain goat skins were worn principally by women, seal skins by the men. The daughter of Chief Calm Weather (*Tale* 17) had dentalium shells at the hem of her skirt.

While the hood of the winter frock was sewn to it, a separate hood was worn with the inner or summer shirt. This was made of two pieces of skin, sewn together up the middle of the head. These separate hoods were of two kinds. One was really a cap, reaching only to the neck. It is not certain if it was tied under the chin. The other was a true hood, fitting around the face, and seamed under the chin. It was without a peak and had no fringe around the face. The hood attached to the winter shirt was of this type, except that it fitted more closely about the face. Hoods worn by the chiefs were decorated across the front. In winter a piece of fur was worn across the nose. It might be detachable or be sewn to the hood.

Colonel ABERCROMBIE visited Alaganik in June and again in October. He noticed no difference in the clothing worn by the natives at these two seasons. The women were [66] dressed only in a shirt that reached to the knees. The garment was pulled on over the head and lacked a hood. The sleeves reached only to the elbows. They wore no other clothes. The shirts of the ordinary women were of depilated seal skin; the wealthier women dressed in mink. When traveling or working around the village, the men wore jackets reaching to the middle of the thighs. For lounging, they put on instead a similar shirt which reached just below the knees, so that when they squatted the hem touched the ground and kept their feet warm. The sleeves were long and loose, and they used to warm their hands by folding their arms and tucking their hands into the opposite sleeve. All of the men's shirts lacked hoods. The longer shirts were made of duck skins with the feathers turned outside, or of fur seal with the fur outside. There were also some of ground squirrel skins like those worn by the Copper River Indians at Taral. These were traded from the interior, ABERCROMBIE believes, because he doubts if there were any ground squirrels on the coast. The skins had been taken off whole, so that the coat had the fur both on the outside and on the inside. The little tails hung down outside. The jackets were all cut straight around the bottom and lacked the points of the Copper River jackets.

It is uncertain if the Eyak wore hats. Neither the wooden helmet nor basketry hat was recognized, Galushia's statements are somewhat confused since he says that dentalium shells were attached to the hats of the chiefs and their families. He spoke of a cap, however, (the short, separate hood, mentioned above?), which had a small peak to shed the rain. He does not think that the Eyak wore wooden eyeshades or snow goggles of any kind. ABERCROMBIE saw no hats or headcovering at Alaganik, except the head dresses [67] worn on special occasions which we have already described.

In rainy weather shirts of bear intestines were worn (over the inner shirt?). The strips of gut were sewn in horizontal bands. This shirt lacked a hood(?). ABERCROMBIE said that the men wore waterproof shirts of seal intestines, with a hood which could be fastened tightly about the face with a drawstring.

Both sexes wore trousers of seal skin. Those of the women had the same cut as the men's except that they were looser. They were seamed down the inside and outside of the legs, (and were made in two pieces?). Mrs. Gus Nelson says that they were drawn up about the waist by a cord running in a hem at the top. They were not embroidered. It is not clear whether two pairs were worn in winter, and often none were worn in summer. Since the women's summer boots were short, there was a strip of bare skin between the top of the boot and the hem of the shirt (Mrs. Gus Nelson). Galushia believes that the men wore an ordinary apron, somewhat similar to that worn in war (see below), but he was unable to give any definite information about it. Curiously enough, no mention was made of a woman's apron or genital covering.

ABERCROMBIE says that the men wore trousers of depilated seal skin which came to the knee. Their sealskin boots, which they wore only for traveling and hunting, came to just below the knee, so that there was a gap between the trousers and boots. Around the village neither men nor women wore boots, and the children were even running barefooted in the snow. The children wore the same type of clothing as the adults.

Our native informants state that boots were worn by both [68] sexes in winter. Though special summer boots for women were mentioned, we have no information about men's summer footgear. Hoods were made of seal skin, with the hair turned inside on the sole and on the upper. Though the Eyak removed the hair from skins, we were not told whether depilated skins were ever used for boots. Boots were made in two pieces, the sole and the upper. The sole covered only the bottom of the foot. The upper was gathered at the toe with three stitches before it was sewed to the sole, and it was seamed up the back. While this type of boot resembles those of the Eskimo, Mrs. Gus Nelson said that the Eyak boots were different from those of their Eskimo neighbors. The Eyak sewed the boot seams clear through the skin; they were not blind-stitched to make them waterproof. The boots of chiefs were decorated about the top with porcupine quills and beads. Soles were replaced as they wore out. Thongs to fasten on the boots were sewn on at the ankle and at the top. Both short and long boots were of the same pattern. Men's hunting hoots reached to the thigh; their ordinary hoots to the calf (to just below the knee, Mrs. Gus Nelson). Women's boots were short in summer (below the knee), and long in winter, though the exact length for the latter was not specified. No sandals and no shoes of fish skin were made. Bear skin was sometimes used for boots. In incident 21, Raven teaches the people to make "moccasins" of bear skin.

Both mittens and gloves, called by different names, were worn. Muskrat skins and sometimes the skins of young beavers were used for mittens. No mittens with rattling puffin beaks were used in dances. ABERCROMBIE saw no mittens or gloves.

Women had a robe or blanket, made of small skins [69] sewed together, which fell from the shoulders to the heels. The skins of mink (Mrs. Gus Nelson), marmot, goat, eagle or swan (Galushia) were used. The robe was not worn when the woman was active. It did not seem to have any fastenings, but the edges were grasped with the arms crossed and the blanket wrapped about the body. The robe was chiefly used as a covering at night. Men also had robes. We do not know if they were much worn during the day. That they may have been worn commonly, probably as an overcoat in cold weather, is suggested by PETROFF'S observation in 1880: "The fur garments or parkas of the Eskimo have been supplanted by the blanket worn by the

Thlinket."[1]   The value of the statement is, however, considerably weakened by PETROFF'S erroneous assumption that the Eyak were originally Eskimo who had adopted TIingit culture. From ABERCROMBIE'S descriptions we know that even in 1884 the Eyak were commonly wearing clothing of an Eskimo pattern. Galushia also described a blanket worn by the chief's daughter, which had a design of buttons sewn on it. We do not know if the blanket was of white man's manufacture (though the buttons themselves seem to have been made by the natives), nor whether the button blanket was a copy of the recent button blankets farther .south. It is possible that it represents an aboriginal garment. The buttons were made from a rare kind of clam shell with a pearly interior, which was called by the same name as the dentalium. Pieces of the shell were cut and ground into shape, generally round. No description was given of the patterns. [70]

At the death potlatch, the next of kin(?) would wear the dead man's robe and his other clothes. Raven (incident 21) teaches the people to make blankets of bear skin. ABERCROMBIE mentioned (see Houses) bedding of goat and bear skins, and woven goat wool, but the natives denied that they made blankets of wool or woven fur strips. In *incident* 5, Raven acquired a grass blanket. While it is possible that this was the grass mat used as floor and wall covering in the house, it is more likely that the blanket of the story refers to the cedar bark robes worn by the more southerly Northwest Coast Indians, and does not represent an Eyak article of dress. Grass and bark mats were worn by the Prince William Sound Eskimo, at least as grave wrappings.

ABERCROMBIE says that when fishing the men wore only a breech clout. This was a strip of skin pulled between the legs and tucked into a belt in front and in back. Galushia also mentioned an "apron," though he was unable to give any definite description of it.

Special clothing was worn for war, for potlatches, and for shamanistic performances. In war time, the men wore a rectangular apron, fastened by a cord around the waist, the lower end hanging free in front. No band of skin passed between the legs. There was no decoration reserved for great warriors. As already stated, at the mourning ceremony for slain warriors the men wore feathers in their headbands.

Every one had a best suit of clothes to be worn when visiting or on important occasions. Johnny Stevens said that these were decorated with dentalium shells and porcupine quills, but according to Galushia these decorations were reserved for the chiefs and their families. At some of [71] the dances connected with the potlatch, fancy costumes were worn, either comic or representing animals and birds. Men wore headbands. The chief of each moiety wore a skin headdress embroidered with shell beads in the shape of the clan bird (this was probably the dentalium shell headdress, already mentioned). A man from each moiety wore a wooden mask representing the Eagle or the Raven. These masks were painted and were decorated around the edges with teeth and beads. There were holes for the eyes, nose, and mouth. The mask was attached by a string around the head(?). In the dance witnessed by ABERCROMBIE at Alaganik, one of the dancers was a "young man representing the 'totem' of his family."[2] He may have worn a mask, though ABERCROMBIE did not so describe him.

In conversation, Colonel ABERCROMBIE was able to describe in some detail the costumes worn at the dances. All of the male performers, with the exception of Kai, the medicine man,

---

[1] PETROFF 1884, 146. In his report (p. 397), ABERCROMBIE also observed that in 1884 the Eyak dressed in the same manner as the Tlingit. His oral account confirms, however, the natives' own descriptions of their more Eskimo-like costume.

[2] ABERCROMBIE 1900, 385.

wore masks depicting the characters they represented, both human and animal. The masks were painted black and red, and were tied on by a sinew cord around the head. There could have been no mouthpiece for additional support because all the actors took part in the dialogue. Around the edges of the masks were feathers, but none had arms, legs, or wings. In each case, the feathers in a man's mask were like those in his crown. Thus, Kai's assistant had raven tail feathers, and the dancers had either eagle wing or tail feathers. ABERCROMBIE thinks there was some significance in the choice, though he does not know what it was.

On ordinary occasions, according to Galushia, the shaman dressed like other men, but "when practicing he wore [72] some sort of special costume. He did not wear an animal disguise, but had a mask of some kind, a bone necklace, and a belt. Johnny Stevens denied any special costume for shamans, though he mentioned the doctor's belt. He said that except for the method of wearing the hair, there was nothing about the shaman's appearance to indicate his profession. Colonel ABERCROMBIE can remember only that Kai's clothing was distinguished in some way. JACOBSEN, however, describes a shaman's costume, and also mentions purchasing one at Cape Martin. Unfortunately we cannot be sure if this was Eyak or Tlingit. When about to hold a seance: "The shaman clothes himself first of all in his festival dress, which consists of a kind of apron, hung with bird beaks or the hoofs of wild mountain goats. He paints his face, covers his head with a kind of hat, or, according to the medicine that he wants to make, with a mask, and takes his rattle in his hand. ... As soon as one song is ended and a new one is to be begun, the medicine man puts on another costume, or mask, or headdress, and sprinkles eagle down on his head, etc."[1]

Several taboos relating to clothing should be mentioned. There was no special season prescribed for making clothing, but a woman was not allowed to do so while her husband was out hunting. Women were not allowed to wear fresh seal skins, hut we do not know how long the skins had to age before they could be worn. There was no such restriction on men. There was a taboo against sewing together in one garment the skins of land and sea animals. Thus sea-otter fur and seal skin might be combined, but seal skin could not be mixed with goat skin or with the fur of any land animal, Galushia thought that the taboo would [73] not apply to skins that were six months old, but Johnny Stevens believed that the taboo was absolute. The prohibition applied most strongly to seal and goat skins. Galushia was not sure about goat and sea-otter when the question was specifically asked, nor was he sure how land-otter and beaver were classified. While he could tell us nothing about hair embroidery, he was of the opinion that the taboo against mixing the two types of fur would have prevented its use (or largely restricted it). Apparently the rule did not apply to sinew thread, for mountain goat sinew was used for all sewing (Mrs. Gus Nelson). In incident 21, Raven teaches the women how to sew with bear sinew.

Tools and Techniques

Methods of working stone have been forgotten by the Eyak and little information could be obtained on this subject. Thus Galushia knew only that stone was pecked and polished, and could not say whether a flaking tool was used for chipping. It is probable that flaking was little employed, since neither the Prince William Sound Eskimo nor the Tlingit seem to have flaked stone to any appreciable extent.

---

[1] JACOBSEN 1884, 390f.

Both a stone adze and a stone axe were used (*Tales* 12A, 14A, 17). The blades were of greenstone, obtained somewhere in Boswell Bay, Hinchinbrook Island, and were grooved for attachment to the handle. They were difficult lo make and easily broken. In *Tale* 17, the slave who has broken the edge of his axe fears a beating. We have already mentioned the grooved, greenstone axe blade, found at Point Whitshed Radio Station, a site which may have been cither Eyak or Eskimo. Grooved stone axes. though rare, were certainly used by the prehistoric Chugach Eskimo of Prince William Sound. [74]

Colonel ABERCROMBIE says that in 1884 the Eyak were still using tools of stone and native copper, and had no Russian or American implements. His memory is probably at fault; it is more likely that they possessed a few imported tools. The only adze used was the large grooved blade, which we have elsewhere described as a "splitting adze."[1]

As far as the Eyak are concerned this term is a misnomer, since ABERCROMBIE reports that the adze was used for shaping wooden objects, such as the dugout, while a stone axe was used for splitting wood. The blade of this axe was about as big as a man's two hands laid with the palms together. It was ungrooved. The wooden handle was lashed to one side of the head. The blade would be used and resharpened until it was worn down to the butt. He did not see any of the small "planing adze" blades set into a bone haft, like those used by the Chugach Eskimo. There were apparently three types of knives. The woman's knife of stone (*Tales* 20 and 24) is said to have been like the Eskimo ulo. There was also a man's knife about which the natives were able to give us no information, but since both the Chugach[2] and the Tlingit[3] had daggers of copper, we should imagine the Eyak knife to have been of this type. Men also used a crooked knife for carving. Beaver teeth and walrus ivory arc said to have been used for carving (as blades for the crooked knife?), but no thumb protector was worn.

ABERCROMBIE does not remember seeing any stone [75] knives at Alaganik. Both men and women used long, double-edged copper daggers, which they obtained in trade from the Copper River Indians. These had a blade with three beveled surfaces on one side, the other side being flat; the handle was wound with skin and ornamented with two ear-like spiral projections. A specimen, obtained at Taral in 1884, was generously given to the University Museum by Colonel ABERCROMBIE as a typical example (Plate 13, 3). It is 34cm. long; the blade proper is 21 by 2.8cm.; the handle, without the skin wrapping, is 1.4cm. wide and 0.4cm. thick. The edges of the blade were sharpened by grinding on the beveled side only. Every native carried a fine-grained sandstone for this purpose. Even the women used these daggers for cutting up fish and game, or else used a sharpened clam shell. ABERCROMBIE noticed no ulo except this clam shell, and no crooked knife.

We have no information about weapon blades, except that they were of stone. Galushia hazarded that they were of chipped slate, but it is far more likely that any slate blades were ground. It is curious that he had no information about copper blades, since copper seems to have been commonly acquired in trade by the Eskimo and Tlingit from the Copper River Indians. The agate spear head in the story about the dwarfs (*Tale* 18) was only a miniature weapon. No agates were found big enough for real use.

---

[1] DE LAGUNA 1934, 56 & passim.

[2] COOK 1785, 400; SAUER 1802, 196. Copper was traded from the Copper River Indians.

[3] LA PÉROUSE 1797, II. 172 (Yakutat of Lituya Bay). SWANTON (1908, 437) reports that all the copper for copper plates is said to have come from the Copper River.

ABERCROMBIE does not remember seeing any stone weapon blades. Arrows were tipped with bone points; the spears or harpoons for fish had detachable barbed heads of bone or copper. Only Long Jim had a spear with an iron head. This specimen will be described in the section on *Fishing* (Plate 12, 2).

According to our native informants no stone pots or stone [76] lamps were used. The only lamp was described as a clam shell filled with seal oil or pitch, with a lump of fat for a wick. It was used only to illuminate the sleeping room and was never used for cooking. Curiously enough, ABERCROMBIE saw stone but not shell lamps. These were roughly hollowed sandstone cobbles, with a wick of cottonwood fluff leaned against the rim. He also saw dried eulachon used as candles. Galushia had never heard of stone mortars and pestles, though specimens are said to have been found at the site of Eyak. One of the pestles was shaped like a telephone receiver. In Russian days a wooden mortar was used for snuff, but the Eyak did not use a snuff tube.

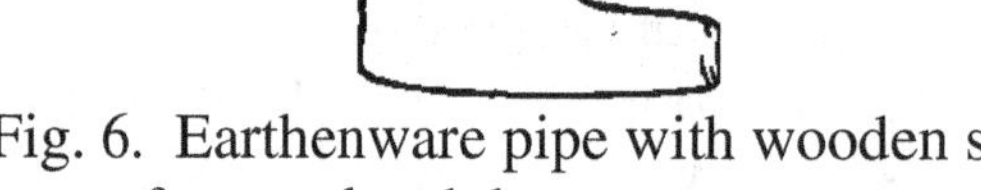

Fig. 6. Earthenware pipe with wooden stem,
from a sketch by ABEBCROMBIE.

ABERCROMBIE reports that tobacco was little used either by the Eskimo or the Eyak. In 1884, HOLT, the trader at Nuchek, was the only white man in the region who smoked. ABERCROMBIE does not remember seeing any native using snuff, either at Nuchek or Alaganik., Only a few Eyak men and women smoked, and when white men's goods were offered, they preferred tea to tobacco or flour. The tobacco that they obtained was chewing plug, from which they whittled off chips to smoke. Their pipes, of which ABERCROMBIE saw only four or live at Alaganik, were small, affording only a few whiffs. The bowls were of native pottery: clay mixed with sand, crudely shaped and imperfectly fired. The color ranged from dark blue to yellow, and was different on the two sides, showing that the pipes had been dried beside an open fire. These were the only objects of native pottery that ABERCROMBIE saw at Alaganik. The [77] stems of the pipes were of arrowwood, from which the pith had been extracted, and were 4 or 5 inches (10 or 12 cm.) long (Figure 6).

Fire was made by means of a fire board and a drill (*Tale* 12A). Old Man Dude described both a hand and a cord drill. He said that it was customary for two persons to collaborate in making fire, one to operate the drill, the other to press down on the brace in which the drill revolved. Galushia described a pump drill, but we may assume that this was of recent introduction. Punk was used for tinder. Care was taken to keep the drill always dry. There seems to have been no knowledge of pyrites. Fire was used for felling trees(?), and in hollowing out the dugout. ABERCROMBIE did not see fire made. When traveling by canoe, lie says that the natives used to carry a glowing coal between two pieces of punk. They did not take fire when hunting mountain goats.

The drill seen by ABERCROMBIE for making holes was a pump drill, about 18 inches long. The shaft was of arrow-wood, about as thick as a man's little finger, he judged; a stone point was lashed to it with sinew. He did not see any bow drills. Similar pump drills, sometimes larger in size, were used at Nuchek.

All wood working was done by the men. Wooden wedges were used for splitting wood. Three specimens were found in front of the house ruin at Alaganik. The first of these (P-UM 30-

ii5-99a, Plate 11, 4) is very roughly made, 29 cm. long and 6 or 7 cm, in diameter. The second (Plate 11, 5) is carefully made, and measures 33 cm. in length and 3 cm. in diameter. The smallest specimen (Plate 11, 6) is only 13.5 cm. long and 3cm. in diameter. ABERCROMBIE says that in splitting a log, the stone axe was used to make the first cuts. Then wooden wedges were inserted along the cut. [78] These were hit in succession, not very hard, with a large unworked stone. The man stood astride the log and held the stone in both hands. As the wedges were driven in, longer ones were inserted until they were finally driven through the log. In this way the Eyak were able to split out planks only 2 or 3 inches (5 or 7 cm.) thick.

Before bending, wood was warmed, but was not steamed or put in water. However, for bending out the sides of the canoe, boiling (Galushia) or hot (ABERCROMBIE) water was used. ABERCROMBIE says that when adzing out the inside of the canoe, the Eyak chopped away the wood in long parallel grooves. When the ridges between were removed, the wood was finished with long lines of adze marks. He also says that wooden pins were used for nailing together the planks of the house door, the planks of the grave house and of the picket fence around the grave (see *Death and Burial*). A hole was drilled first, and after the pin was inserted, both ends of the pin were forced apart by small wooden wedges, which fastened the pin securely in the same manner that we fasten an axe handle into the head (Figure 3).

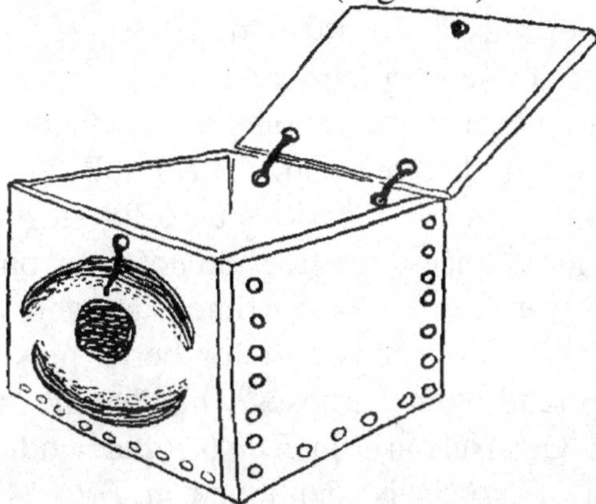

Fig. 7. Painted wooden box, as described by ABERCROMBIE.
The dotted areas indicate red paint. He has forgotten other details of decoration.

Spruce-wood boxes with lids were used for storage. The box was square, with vertical sides and a flat bottom. As described by Galushia, it was made in five pieces, the sides and bottom grooved and fitted together. The lid had a flange around the edge, so that the thicker central part fitted into the top of the box. It was tied on and lacked hinges. According to ABERCROMBIE, these boxes were about 12 inches square, and were made of four sides and a bottom that fitted between the sides. These pieces were all nailed together. Holes were drilled, and then round pegs with small wedges in the ends were driven into the holes. When the peg hit the bottom of the hole, the wedge was forced [79] into the peg, widening it so that it stuck fast. The outer end of the peg was also fastened by a small wedge. The lids were hinged on two sinew rings, twisted so that the ends of the sinew were hidden. There was also a braided sinew cord, attached to the front of the box, which could be passed through a hole in the lid to tie it shut. The ends of the cord were braided to form a knob. This fastening and the sinew hinges were kept pliable with oil. The boxes were decorated with paintings on the covers and on the sides. ABERCROMBIE does not remember what these patterns were, except that on the front of the box was the same eye that was painted on doors and canoe paddles (Figure 7). According to Galushia, boxes were usually plain, but some were painted, and some (?) carved. He believes there was red paint, and blue paint made from blueberry juice. ABERCROMBIE thinks the reddish-brown stain was made by boiling skunk cabbage leaves (more probably hemlock bark?). Neither the red nor the black paint was affected by water. [80]

According to the tales, seal oil was kept in the boxes (*Tales* 4A, 17; *Raven*, incident 2 "bucket;" incident 11). In *Tale* 6B, berries are put up in a "barrel," probably a box of this type. ABERCROMBIE says that small belongings were kept in these boxes. In the play which he witnessed the sun was kept in a small wooden box, and in incident 3 of the *Raven* cycle, the sun, moon, and stars were kept in a wooden box hanging from the ceiling. In *Tale* 8, the woman keeps a porpoise head in a box in her sleeping room.

JACOBSEN reports that he saw at Alaganik "many utensils carved out of wood which looked exactly like objects seen in British Columbia."[1]

Storage vessels were also made of hemlock bark which was gathered in spring by the women. The bark was cut across at the bottom of the desired strip, and was pried off the tree with a sharp flat stick (bark-stripping wedge). Sometimes if a great deal of bark were required the men would cut a tree down. Later, Galushia said that a piece of bark might be used for a temporary dish but that there were no regular bark dishes. When telling incident 21 of the Raven cycle, Johnny Stevens explained how bark pails were made. The bark was taken in the spring. One piece was used for the side, and one for the bottom. Holes were drilled (punched ?) for the peeled young spruce roots used for sewing the pail together. (The side of a birchbark vessel of this type was found in an Eskimo cave burial on one of the islands of the Mummy Island group). In this talc, goat fat was tried out in the bark pail. In *Tale* 6B, a bark basket was used for berry picking. ABERCROMBIE saw open birchbark baskets used for storing dried berries. He does not know where the bark was obtained, since birch trees do not grow on the coast. [81]

Baskets of spruce roots were made by the women and were used for cooking, for fetching water (compare *Tale* 17), for drinking cups and for berry picking (compare *Tale* 6A), The baskets used for berry picking (and other purposes?) had handles across the top like a pail, but none had shoulder straps (Mrs. Gus Nelson). In *Tale* 6A, the handle of the woman's berry basket broke. A "pack basket" (full of crows) is mentioned in *Tale* 14B. (The use of this term in describing it suggests that it may have had shoulder straps.) Water was kept in large baskets, and small baskets were used as cups. Each family in the house had their own cup. Not much water had to be kept in the house because it was always close to the stream. ABERCROMBIE saw no baskets used as cups or for storing water, but said that the natives at Alaganik fetched water from the slough as it was required. He saw no elaborately decorated baskets, like those described below. The spruce root cooking baskets which he remembers had only a ring of red around the top. This was actually woven into the basket, and was not put on as false embroidery, because he could see the line on both sides.

Mrs. Gus Nelson showed us a basket she was making to sell. The weave was common twining, with bands of open diagonal pattern. In the old days, she explained, all baskets were woven closely to make them water-tight. While working on the basket the root fibers were kept moist. She worked with the basket held upright, twining on the nearer edge in a counter-clockwise direction (against the sun), and held one of the two spiral strands in her mouth. Unfortunately we neglected to record the direction of the twist. Formerly baskets were decorated with false embroidery of grass. Blue was obtained by boiling the grass in blueberry juice, and red by boiling with hemlock bark. [82]

---

[1] JACOBSEN 1884, 389.

Emmons reports, probably on the basis of statements made by his Tlingit informants, that the Eeak tella (whom he supposed to be Tlingitized Eskimo on the eastern shore of Prince William Sound) learned from the Tlingit how to weave with roots. "They work on a very limited scale, producing but a few small, coarse baskets, ornamented in color, but seldom embroidered with grass-stems." He also mentions a tribe, called the Guth-le-uk-qwan, living on Controller Bay and Kayak Island, who may or may not be the Eyak, but who have been classed with the Eyak by the *Handbook of American Indians* (see Part III). Of them he writes: "Their basket-work differs only in the coarser strands of root employed in the woof," as compared to that used by the Yakutat Tlingit.[1] Certainly the latter statement fits the original Eyak basketry better than the first, and we suggest that it does actually apply to older Eyak work, while his reference to the Eyak tella applies to the recently degenerated Eyak basketry. In other words, both people are probably the Eyak.

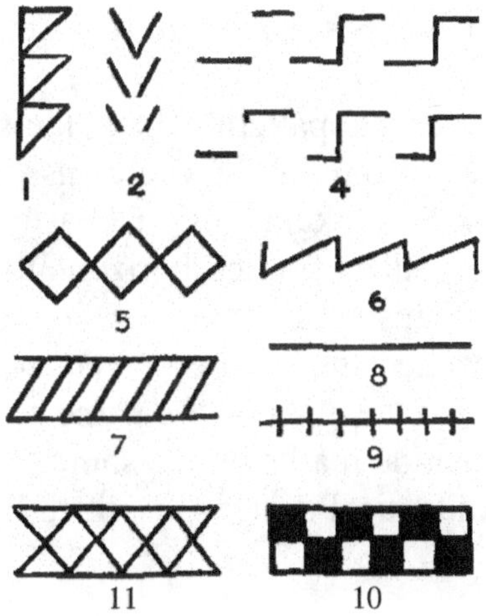

Figure 8. Basketry designs, from a sketch by Annie Nelson.

Annie Nelson sketched and named the following basketry patterns (Figure 8). (For the native names sec Appendix II):
1. "One above each other — pointed"
2. "Amphineura (chiton) shells"
3. "Cockle meat" [83]
4. "Yakutat basket straws (or design)"
5. "Face painting"
6. "One after another" like waves
7. "Heat waves"
8. not translated
9. "Brown bear's ulna"
10. "Together — each other"
11. "Raven bone."

The first two patterns were used by young girls in making their first baskets.
These designs can be duplicated by similar or analogous Tlingit patterns described by

---

[1] EMMONS 1903, 232, 231.

EMMONS.

(1) This is similar to EMMONS 25. Any triangle is called "the head of the salmonberry." Triangles may be variously combined. Triangles on a diagonal line are called "the spear barb;" in a vertical or horizontal line, EMMONS 15, they are "the teeth of the killer-whale."[1]

(2) This is like EMMONS 13, a horizontal row of chevrons. This and similar angular designs are called by the Yakutat "the outside of the tent-shell (limpit)". Specific names are: EMMONS 8, "the tail of the tern;" 9, "the feather wings of the arrow;" and 13, "the peculiar flake-like appearance of the flesh of a fish cut along the line of the greater axis."[2]

(3) This is identical with EMMONS 36, "the work or embroidery around the head" on the helmet or basket hat of the shaman, and is supposed to represent the terraces on a mountain side.[3]
3

(4) This is EMMONS 35, a vertical pattern called "the squirrel's tail," apparently equated with a similar isolated [84] figure. Both of these are also called "old-person-hand-back-of-tattooed."[4] Curiously enough Eyak 4, "Yakutat design," has a strong resemblance to one variety of EMMONS 37, which is the same pattern applied horizontally, but with the addition of a short horizontal line in each open space. This is called by the Tlingit "Guth-luh-ku — a word from the tongue of an older race that descended the Copper River and peopled those shores before the coming of the Tlingit." According to the Yakutat the name refers to the tide, either as reflecting a floating and bobbing object, or as tide marks on the shore.[5] The "older race" are probably the Eyak, and so we have two almost identical designs, ascribed by the Yakutat to the Eyak, and by the Eyak to the Yakutat.

(5) This is a combination of diamonds. An isolated diamond, EMMONS 29, is called "the eye" by the Yakutat, or a "drop of liquid" by the Tlingit farther south. A series of diamond-shaped outlines strung on a horizontal median line is called "the beaver-skin stretching frame."[6]

(6) This is EMMONS 3, which appears in oblique bands, and is called "the lightning."[7]

(7) This may be EMMONS 10, a horizontal band of rhomboid figures, alternating in color, called "the leaves of the fire-weed", or EMMONS 11, the same design spaced in pairs, called the rainbow, literally "the wings of different colors." Or it may be EMMONS 22, horizontal bands of diagonal lines, but without bordering lines, woven with colored woof strands and not embroidered. This is called "the strawberry basket."[8] [85]

---

[1] EMMONS 1903, 270, 268.
[2] EMMONS 1903, 267.
[3] EMMONS 1903, 274.
[4] EMMONS 1903, 273.
[5] EMMONS 1903, 274.
[6] EMMONS 1903, 271.
[7] EMMONS 1903, 265.
[8] EMMONS 1903, 266f and 269.

(8) This is EMMONS 20, "one straight." or "the cross-piece of the fish drying-frame on which rest the small rods which carry the split fish."[1]

(9) This resembles EMMONS 30, which is, however, an isolated single or double cross. The latter is called "towards each other."[2]

(10) This is EMMONS 47, "checkers-under-board." or "checkcrs-foot-board."[3]

(11) This may be a combination of EMMONS 42. The single X is called "crossing." Or, if the diamonds and triangles are to be considered as solid units, it might be variation of the triangle pattern, like EMMONS 15 "teeth of the killer-whale," or EMMONS 25 "small sand-hills," both of which are composed of horizontal hands of triangles.[4]

While there is thus a close similarity between the designs used by the Eyak and the Yakutat, the names do not exhibit a one-to-one correspondence. On the whole, however, the system of naming was essentially the same for both people. In addition to the names quoted above, the Tlingit also have "the foot print of the brown bear," "the back-bone or ribs of the hair seal," "the hood of the raven," "the tail of the raven," "the outside of the smaller scallop shell," "joining together," and "one within another."[5] Were basket-making still as live an art now among the Eyak as it was when EMMONS visited the Tlingit, we should probably have been able to obtain a list of names and patterns from them quite comparable to those recorded by EMMONS. [86]

EMMONS illustrated a "Guth leuk" basket obtained on Kodiak Island,[6] which is probably of Eyak manufacture. It is decorated by a row of diamonds connected by a medial line, probably our design 5, "face painting," and the checkerboard pattern, our design 10. Another basket, collected at Nuchek, EMMONS believes was made either at Kayak Island or at Yakutat.[7] His guess as to its provenience is equivalent to saying that it was either Eyak or Yakutat work. The designs are our numbers 3 and 10, and a figure formed by a square in the middle, from which four triangles (half-squares) project at the corners. The latter EMMONS groups with the triangle combinations (his design 25).

A few baskets are included in the JACOBSEN collection (B-MV, IV A 6359-612). The two former specimens are both cylindrical twined baskets made of spruce roots with a reinforced rim. Two pairs of similar reinforcements also occur on IV A 6360 near the bottom, which is more bowl-shaped than on the other specimen. The decoration will appear from the illustrations (Plate 14, 1-2). IVA 6359 has a diameter and height of about 28 cm. The colors of the decoration are yellow, brown, and gray. IV A 6360 has a diameter of 14.5 and a height of 18.5cm. Colors: yellow, brown, and black. There is a short, twisted loop attached to the rim.

The other two baskets are of less interest, since both are imitations of ordinary tea-kettles

---

[1] EMMONS 1903, 269.

[2] EMMONS 1903, 272.

[3] EMMONS 1903, 277.

[4] EMMONS 1903, 276, 268, 270.

[5] EMMONS 1903, designs 6 (p. 265), 12 (p. 267), 16 (p. 268), 31 (p. 272), 23 (p. 270), 21 (p. 269), and 45 (p. 276).

[6] EMMONS 1903, pl. V, 3.

[7] EMMONS 1903, pl. X, 4.

produced in the same twined technique as the preceding ones. IV A 6362 is decorated with bands of chevrons and obliquely arranged stripes, and on the lid there is a whirl ornament. Colors: yellow, brown, and gray. IV A 6361 is somewhat smaller, and the bottom is provided with an off-set like that which [87] on real kettles is intended for placing in the hole of the stove. The decoration consists of bands of diamonds, chevrons, and triangles, and on the lid concentric circles. The colors are the same as on IV A 6362.

A mother would put her daughter's nail parings into a basket that she was making, so that the girl would grow up to be skillful in this work (Galushia). Basket-making is mentioned in *Tale*s 6, 16, and 18.

Grass mats used in the sleeping room and Raven's grass blanket have already been mentioned. We have no information from the natives about the manufacture of the grass mat, and might assume that they were twined like those of the adjacent Eskimo. Colonel ABERCROMBIE, however, reports that the reed mats spread on the benches of the large houses were woven. The strands ran diagonally, not parallel to the edges of the mat, and were woven over-one under-one. The goats hair blanket used for bedding has already been mentioned, and though ABERCROMBIE cannot describe it further, we can assume that it was twined.

Besides baskets, skunk cabbage leaves were used as cups. A drinking tube made of a swan's wing bone was also used, and Galushia did not think it was restricted to adolescent girls. Galushia says that clam shells were used as dishes, and ABERCROMBIE remembers them as cups.

Food was served in wooden bowls, either round or square, and long wooden dishes. Meat was also served on round or square wooden plates. Mrs. Gus Nelson specified that the wooden dish or bowl was about 18 inches long, 3 inches high, and oval in shape. The men, of course, made these vessels. Each family had its own dish, from which all ate at the same time. From what Colonel ABERCROMBIE says, food was not served in wooden platters except at feasts. [88]

Ordinarily each member of the family went to the cooking basket with his own spoon, and ate the food from his spoon with his fingers. After the two dances that ABERCROMBIE attended, food was passed about in wooden plates and platters. The plates were round, about 12 inches in diameter, and 2½ or 3 inches deep. The platters were like large boat-shaped ladles, about t8 inches long. They were pointed at one end, and cut squarely across the other, from which projected a shorthandle. They were carved from cotton-wood (Figure 9).

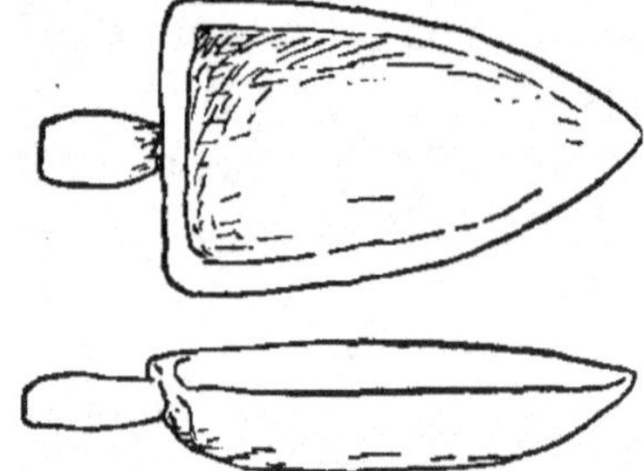

Fig. 9. Boat-shaped wooden serving platter with handle,
as described by ABERCROMBIE

Galushia told us that spoons were made of wood or goat horn. Water in which meat had been boiled was drunk from wooden spoons. There was a large spoon or ladle for serving meat and this was kept in the cooking basket. Sometimes a sharp stick (meat fork) was used in serving meat. Each person had his own individual spoon. Spoons were also made of eagle beaks tied to sticks.

ABERCROMBIE saw spoons of goat horn but none of sheep horn. He does not know how the natives were able to remove the horn from the skull without breaking it, but suggests that the skull with the horns may have been boiled. The horn was cut across diagonally as far up as the ?? natural hollow extends (Figure 10, a). The handle of the spoon was made from the top of the horn and retained its natural curve. The bowl was cut from the butt end, which had to be bent up. Before being worked the horn was softened and made pliable in hot water. The horn was shaped by [89] rubbing with a long thin piece of sandstone, about 2½ inches wide and 7 inches long. The total length of the finished spoon was about 7 or 8 inches (17 or 20 cm., Figure 10, b). The wooden spoons that ABERCROMBIE saw were of the same general shape, though the handles were straight (Figure 10, c). The ladles used in cooking were all of wood and were bigger. The total length might be as much as 15 inches, but the bowl was never more than 3 inches (7cm.) long. None of the spoons were decorated. As already mentioned he saw spoons used both as cups and as plates.

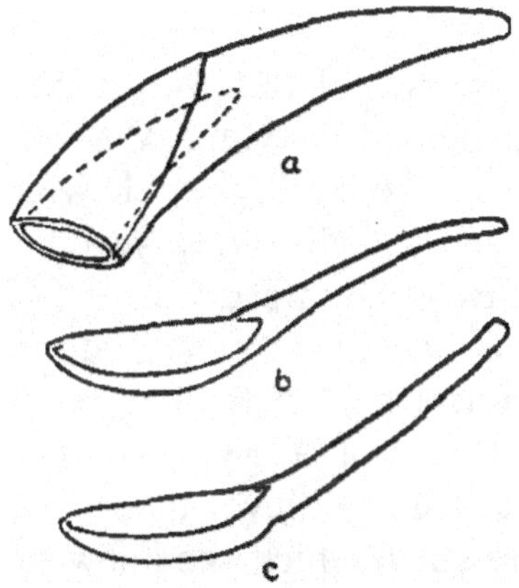

Fig. 10 a, Method of cutting mountain goat horn to make a spoon;
b, horn spoon; c, wooden spoon. As described by ABERCROMBIE.

When stranded whales were found, the baleen was used for dishes, spoons, and in later times, for snuff boxes with separate wooden bottoms, ABERCROMBIE remembers a few spoons of baleen.

For carrying packs or bundles a special strap was worn that went across the chest, not the head, and had loops for the arms. A pack bag is mentioned in *Tale* 19, hut we do not know if this was supposed to be peculiar to the Wolf People (not the Eyak clan, but a mythical cannibal tribe).

ABEBCROMBIE saw the women at Alaganik carrying their babies on their hacks by means of a pack strap across the mother's chest. This was fastened to the top of the sack or wrappings in which the baby was swaddled, and lacked arm loops(?). The baby faced backwards and there was nothing to protect its face from the sun or rain. The baby [90] was always kept swaddled. When in the house, the child was laid on the bench beside the mother; when traveling, in the bottom of the canoe. As soon as a child could toddle, it was no longer carried.

In old days fat and flesh were scraped from skins with a stone knife or scraper (compare Raven, incident 21). Now, Mrs. Gus Nelson puts the skin over a thick pole, held horizontally, and scrapes the skin with a butcher knife. Galushia explained that this use of the knife was recent. Raw goat skins (all skins?) were first washed in running water, then stretched, scraped and pounded with a stone until soft. On hunting trips, skins were dried and stretched on stakes driven into the ground. A drying frame of some kind was used in the village. After the fat had been removed from bird skins, they were washed and rubbed between the hands. Intestines used for waterproof shirts were first squeezed to remove the contents. Then they were washed, and for drying were inflated with air, after the ends had been tied. When dry, they were split open. Hair was removed from skins by soaking them in warm water for several weeks. We believe that this statement of the time is exaggerated. A skin soaked so long would rot. The Central Eskimo, who employ the same method, only soak the skin a few days. Urine or brains were not used for this (Galushia). Mrs. Gus Nelson insisted that only the Copper River Indians at Chitina used to remove hair from skins. ABERCROMBIE says that the hair was scraped from seal skins with a clam shell. He does not mention the use of hot water, but says only that the skin was rolled up with the hair inside and kept this way for some time until the hair had rotted loose.

Thongs were made by the men from fresh or dried seal skins. If the skin was dry, it ,was soaked before the thongs [91] were cut. Since the skin was always cut up the belly of the animal before being removed, thongs were cut from a flat piece. The thong was cut in a spiral, beginning at the outer edge of the skin. Then the line was stretched and dried, but no thong smoother was used.

Formerly the Eyak had no needles. Holes for the thread were punched with a bone awl, and the edges of the skin were softened by chewing. ABERCROMBIE saw the women sewing with bone awls in 1884. Before they made the holes, they chewed the skin and allowed it to dry. He reports that the stitching was from left to right and was well done. He did not notice any fringes on clothing. According to the natives, the thread was of sinew, dried, split, and twisted into a three-strand thread. The end of the thread was moistened in the mouth, and pushed through the hole made by the awl. Mrs. Gus Nelson said that only goat sinews were used, but in incident 21, Raven teaches the people to make thread of bear sinews. The Eyak used to buy thread from the Chitina Indians, she claims, but Galushia believes that this trade was modern (after game was scarce along the coast?). The only stitch which she knew was overcasting, from back to front, and from left to right. Apparently blind stitching to make waterproof seams was not known. Since this stitch pierces only half the thickness of one piece of skin, it would have been very difficult to make without needles.

Women's sewing bags were of skin and had three pockets. There were no bags of birds' feet or animal leg skins. (Makari, our Eskimo informant, said that though his people did not make bags of birds' feet, they were made by the Eyak and Yakutat). The sewing hags seen by ABERCROMBIE were made of two pieces of seal oesophagus, overcast together. The bottom was rounded. About the top was [92] a drawstring, which passed through holes which had been buttonhole-stitched with sinew (Figure 11). He also saw sewing bags of young dehaired seal skin, and understood that the skin was obtained from Nuchek in exchange for goat skin. In these bags the women carried hunks of sinew from which they pulled off strips to use for thread as they were needed. The natives said that clothes were washed in urine. Colonel ABERCROMBIE does not believe that the Eyak ever washed their clothes in urine or cleaned them with clay as did the Copper River Indians, because their garments were always filthy. Galushia did not think that the Eyak washed themselves in urine, though washing the hands in urine is specifically mentioned in *Tale* 12A. Galushia remembers seeing only one urine tub. This was owned by the man at Alaganik who had the sealskin war canoe. The tub was square, and was hollowed out

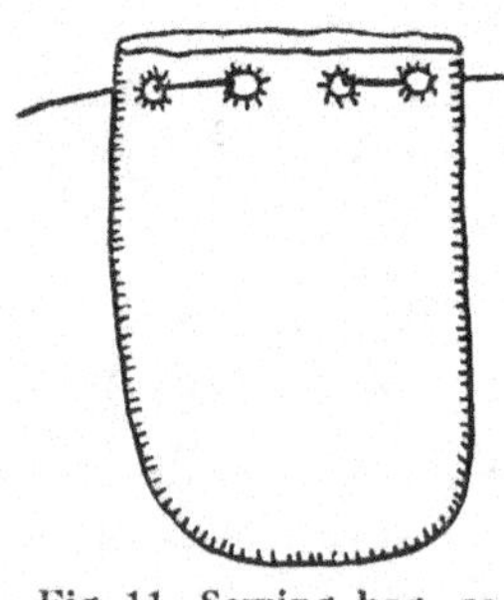

Fig. 11. Sewing bag, as described by ABERCROMBIE.

of a log. Apparently urine was not much used, in any case, for ABERCROMBIE did not notice that the Eyak saved it, as did the Indians whom he visited on the Copper River.

Both the natives and ABERCROMBIE mention lines and lashings of braided or twisted sinew. ABERCROMBIE says that these had to be kept pliable with oil. Galushia believes that no rope was made of bast or fiber, though in *Tale* 16 a rope of roots is mentioned, and he admitted that halibut fishing lines were made of dried kelp. ABERCROMBIE also reports that the fish line was a 6(?)-strand braid of dried fibers of some sort (grass or roots – perhaps kelp). It was about as thick as the sinew line on Long Jim's spear head [93] (Plate 8, 1), and was dyed brown. It had to be dried out after use. JACOBSEN says that the rope used by the shaman in one of his exhibitions was made of bast or leather.[1]

The snow shovel was made of a single flat board. There was no separate edging on the blade, and no handle on the blade for the left hand.

Measurements were estimated by the span of a man's outstretched arms, by half that distance, by the length of a hand, by the span between the tip of the thumb and the tip of the middle finger, and by the length of the last joint of the thumb.

Preparation of Food

Both meat and fish were eaten fresh. The former was taboo to menstruating or pregnant women. Fresh herring and whitefish were specifically forbidden to pregnant women. Meat and fish were boiled in spruce-root baskets with hot stones (see *Raven*, incident 21).

No salt was used when boiling meat. It was usually cooked in fresh water, but sometimes salt water was used, (individual preference, or only when fresh water was unobtainable?). ABERCROMBIE says that at Alaganik fresh salmon were cooked in salt water by choice. Blood of all game animals was saved and was added to the soup in which the meal had been boiled. The soup was eaten with the regular meal. Meat of sea mammals might be eaten at the same meal with the meat of land animals, and they might even be cooked together in the same pot, though the latter was seldom done since it would spoil the flavor of both. There was no taboo against it, however (Galushia and Johnny Stevens). Vegetable products were never cooked in [94] the same basket with meat, (see, however, the green stuff cooked with the first salmon).

ABERCROMBIE says that though there was only one fire in the middle of the house, each woman when cooking would pull out a few coals and burning sticks for her own use, so that there would be as many little subsidiary fires as there were cooks. The stones used for boiling water were special round hard rocks which must have been brought to Alaganik from some distance, he thinks. Some of these had been chipped to the desired shape. Only one stone was needed to boil and cook a basketful of fish. The stone was heated under a little fire, made by setting up three sticks, tipi-fashion, against which other sticks were leaned. When red hot, the stone was forked out on two long sticks. The sticks were grasped together at one end by the right hand and were slightly spread by the left. One stick was placed between the left thumb and forefinger, the other between the middle and ring finger (Figure 12). The fingers of old women were stiffened in this position. The stone was not grasped between the sticks, but was scooped up on them.

---

[1] JACOBSEN 1884, 391.

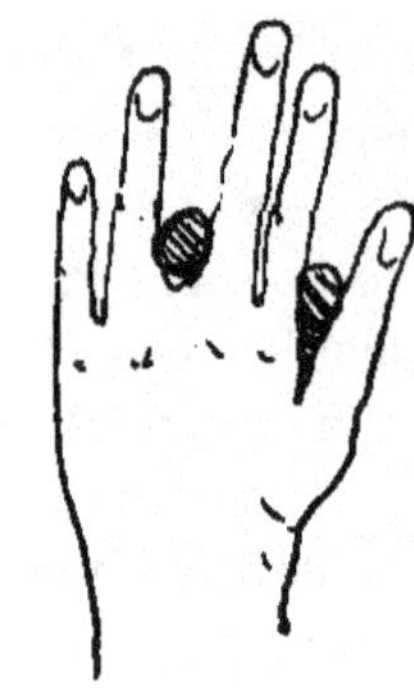

Fig. 12. Method of holding wooden tongs,
as described by ABERCROMBIE

Meat and fish were also roasted on spits (*Tale* 4B and *Raven*, incident 21), and meat was roasted on a plank. Two flat wooden stakes, 30.5 and 35 cm. long respectively, were found at Alaganik and were identified by Galushia as spits for fish (Plate 11, 1, 2). The spits were set into the ground beside the fire and were inclined towards it. Johnny Stevens specified that the spit (for fish or for meat only?) was made of three sticks. In *Tale* 9, seals were roasted around the [95] camp fire. Before Raven taught the people how to roast meat on spits, they cooked it on hot stones (incident 21), ABERCROMBIE, however, did not notice any roasting on spits at Alaganik, though it was common in the interior. All the cooking that he saw was by boiling. The Copper River Indians often baked birds in a clay jacket, but he did not see the Eyak practice this method. Galushia told us that salmon were sometimes baked in a hole dug in the beach, over which a fire was built (Raven, incident 9).

Most of the supplies for winter were obtained in the summer. Meat to be dried was cut in strips and smoked over a slow fire of green hemlock (green alder?) because it burns slowly with little heat. In incident 11, Raven's partner smokes both fish and meat with drift wood. It takes about a week to smoke meat. Sometimes meat was boiled before smoking. Dried meat was put up in wooden boxes with seal oil and these were kept on top of the sleeping rooms. No pemmican was made. In incident 21, Raven teaches the people to put up goat fat in bark pails. The liver of animals was never dried, but was always eaten fresh. Seal brains were eaten.

In June, when ABERCROMBIE was at Alaganik, he saw salmon drying on racks in the sun but did not see any being smoked. It was the work of the women to unload the canoes, split the fish and hang them up to dry. Eulachon and herring were also dried. The Eyak whom he saw camped at Old Town. Cordova, were drying herring on the rocks. The herring had not been split, and as they were drying the women would roll them frequently to expose them to fresh surfaces of warm rock.

Quantities of fish were put up in the summer. Galushia described two ways of cutting up salmon for smoking. The [96] first method was to split the fish up the back and belly, and hang it up with the boneless meat on one side and the piece with the backbone and tail on the other. The second method was to split it up the back and hang it lengthwise over the rack. Meat and fish were smoked in the smokehouse. The present method of smoking fish is to cut it in strips free of bones. It takes about 8 days to smoke fish cut in this style, and probably took much longer for the old methods. Fish smoked in the old way had a strong taste. As soon as the salmon was cured, the bones were removed and the fish were stacked head to tail, and tied in bundles. The drying of fish (*Tale* 21), the fish rack (*Tale* 4, and *Raven*, incident 2 A), and bundles of dried fish (*Tale* 17) are mentioned in the folklore.

Seal oil and fish oil were tried out and put up in boxes (*Tale* 4A and 17). The box of seal oil, in incident 11 of the Raven cycle, is supposed to have been a square box with a lid that was tied on. Eulachon (candlefish) oil was tried out by boiling the fish in a canoe.

Sockeye and silver salmon were sometimes buried in the ground on a layer of skunk cabbage leaves. The fish were allowed to rot and were eaten in the winter. Meat was never buried.

Clams were strung on spruce roots for drying. Hemlock roots were not used because they have a bitter taste. The needle for stringing clams was made of wood, about 5(?) inches long, and had an eye. After the clams were dry they were put up in a bark or wooden box with seal oil. When eaten fresh, they were roasted with eggs in a pit. There seems to have been no method for preserving eggs.

The Eyak ate the root of the Kamchatka lily, locally known as "wild rice." The root was dried, and then rubbed [97] into small particles like grains of rice. These were boiled.

Another plant, said to resemble an artichoke, was dug in early spring on the mud flats. It has branching roots. Only the main part of the root was eaten. It is now dug with an axe. The root was eaten raw or roasted and is said to have a sweet taste-In the spring the sap from the inner bark of the hemlock was scraped off in mussel shells. It was dried and served as a sweet dessert.

Blueberries, salmonberries, high-bush cranberries (with a bitter taste) and low-bush cranberries (like huckleberries but with a more "oily" taste) were gathered. The women picked them into baskets with handles (*Tale* 6A). All of these berries were preserved for winter. Some were put fresh into oil, others were dried in the sun on racks made of sticks, then pounded and put up in boxes (*Tale* 6B, "in a barrel"). Before dried berries were served, they were cooked in oil. Berries (dried or fresh?) were boiled with salmon eggs to make a jelly. Colonel ABERCROMBIE saw dried berries kept in open birchbark baskets. One dish that he remembers was a pudding made of boiled dried berries, the stalks of the wild celery, and the inner bark of the cottonwood. It was the latter ingredient which thickened the mixture to the consistency of a pudding. He did not notice that any special dishes were served exclusively for certain meals.

Three kinds of seaweed were gathered in July and August, but only two kinds were eaten from choice (*Tale* 20). The first of these is black and grows on the rocks, especially around Mummy Island. The second kind is thick and brown at the base, with long tapering ribbons. In times of famine (late winter or early spring?) they ate the stems of [98] seaweed described as having balls at the end which pop when crushed (*Fucus sp.*?). Probably all these seaweeds were boiled. They were also dried for winter use.

When starving, the Eyak would cook and eat their skin clothing, but they never ate clay or bark, and Galushia had never heard of cannibalism from hunger. He admitted, however, that the only severe famine of which he had heard was that of *Tale* 28.

Before the Russians came, the Eyak had no tea, no fermented beverages, and no tobacco. The Russians introduced snuff, which the Eyak mixed with fungus and prepared in a wooden mortar. No snuff tube was used. We have already mentioned snuff boxes of baleen. It will be remembered that ABERCROMBIE did not see any natives taking snuff, hut that he saw clay tobacco pipes of native manufacture. At present the natives make a strong and sour beer, and obtain liquor from the local bootleggers. In 1884, ABERCROMBIE found that tea was in universal demand- It was brewed in a spruce-root cooking basket, and was drunk from spoons. The Eyak did not care for flour and bacon; ABERCROMBIE thinks that the latter was too salty. At the present time their diet differs but little from that of the poorer whites in the region.

The Eyak used to eat in the morning when they got up and at night before they went to bed. There were no regular meal times during the day, though people ate whenever they were hungry. There were no special styles of cooking and no special types of food peculiar to breakfast or dinner. The women prepared the food, unless there was a slave to cook and serve. On hunting trips the men cooked for themselves. They seldom bothered to take along a cooking basket unless they were going by canoe. [99]

Seal fat was stuck on a stick and given infants to suck (compare *Tale* 24). Marrow was never given to young people because it was supposed to make their bones ache. Young people were also forbidden to eat bear liver (and that of other animals?), bear paws, and bear(?) kidneys, because it would make them slow. (In Raven, incident 14 slowness seems to have been associated with the stomach, and in the Eskimo version of the same story with other entrails). There was no taboo against young people eating eggs. Seal flippers, considered the best part of the seal, were never given to children, though Galushia could not give the reason. Menstruating or pregnant women were forbidden to touch or eat fresh meat, the first salmon, fresh whitefish and herring, and fresh fish roe (perhaps all fresh fish?). Nursing mothers used to drink a great deal of fish soup, that is, seal meat cooked in the same water in which fish had been boiled, and a great deal of porcupine soup, because these were supposed to produce milk.

Though the Eyak did not kill whales, there was no taboo against eating a stranded one (compare Raven, incident 13).

Our Eskimo informant, Makari, told us that the Eyak were so poor that they had very little to eat, and used to buy food from the Eskimo in exchange for blankets, snow-shoes, axes, and wedges. The only possible truth in this statement, which clearly illustrates the contempt of the Eskimo for the Eyak, may be that the Eyak sometimes bought such marine products as seal oil or whale oil from the Eskimo, who were certainly more adept in sea-mammal hunting. There is, however, no indication of such trade in the statements made by the Eyak themselves. ABEKCHOMBIE thinks that the Eyak must have had hard winters, with a great deal of snow and not much game. [100]

Land Animal Hunting

Goats and bears were the most important land animals hunted by the Eyak. The former were sought in the mountains above Mountain Slough. They were commonly driven towards hunters in ambush, but fences were not built for these drives, nor could fire be used because it was generally too wet. Dogs were trained to chase and hold a goat until the hunters could kill it. Goats were killed with arrows or with spears if the hunter could get close enough. Pits were never dug for goats because of the rocky nature of the country in which they lived. *Tale* 3 illustrates the dangers of falling from a cliff when goat hunting. It was considered the most dangerous type of hunting, and (his is reflected in the taboos (see *Magic*). ABERCROMBIE says that the natives had to climb above the goat in order to get close enough to shoot, because the goat always looked down the mountainside for its enemies. They would shoot the goat between the ribs and the arrow would almost protrude from the farther side.

Both brown (Kodiak grizzly) and black bear were hunted. The Eyak sometimes went up Orca Inlet after bear, though this was trespassing on Eskimo territory. Bears were hunted in winter. Dogs would locate the dens and the hunters would tease the, bear until it came out. A man stood above the hole and speared the bear as it emerged. Another method was to erect a number of spears in the ground, if a soft place could be found. The spears were set with their points inclined forward. A man would tease the bear, and when pursued would dodge behind the spears, allowing the bear to become impaled. A deadfall was built for bears. It was made of an upper and a lower log, both furnished with [101] wooden spikes, those of one log dovetailing into the spaces between the spikes on the other. The upper log was propped up against a notch cut in a tree, and a trigger string was set across the bear trail. When the animal passed and pulled the string, the upper log fell, and the bear was either killed outright or was held by the spikes. Pits for bears were dug in the ground, hut were not furnished with stakes. No snow pits were made. Bears were also killed with an automatic bow, so arranged that the animal in passing would release the arrow. This bow was different from the ordinary bow, stronger(?), and lacked the sinew backing. The hunter was not accustomed to talk to the bear except to tease him. In incident 21, Raven kills a bear with a spear.

The beaver was not hunted under the ice in winter, but was killed in spring and fall with a deadfall set in the beaver trail.

The fox and lynx were killed with snares fastened to bushes. Other animals may have been killed in snares, but Galushia is not sure. The snare is mentioned in *Tale* 20. The fox was also caught in a pit.

Mink and martins were taken in deadfalls. A piece of wood with a slot in it, found at Alaganik (P-UM 30-25-99f, Plate 11, 3), was identified by Galushia as part of a deadfall for mink, but he did not describe the trap. *Tale* 5 tells of catching groundhogs in deadfalls.

The muskrat was shot with bow and arrow.

The weasel or ermine was caught in a box trap, buried in the ground. A little plank was so arranged that the animal would walk out on it and be tipped into the box.

Only the Eskimo used the torsion trap or "klipski."

The land-otter was not purposely hunted but was [102] occasionally caught in a deadfall. The unwillingness to kill the land-otter is undoubtedly due to the belief that these animals are transformed human beings. It is true that in both versions of *Tale* 12, the man clubbed to death the land-otters that had kidnapped or were trying to kidnap him, but this is rather an act of revenge than a regular hunt. In version A he used the skins.

Wolves were not hunted because they were also supposed to have been men. The Eyak believed that if attacked by a wolf they could speak to it and induce it not to hurt them.

The spear used for hunting was of wood, with a diamond-shaped blade of hone, sharp on the edges and furnished with a tang for hafting. The blade was secured by a lashing. After stabbing an animal, the hunter would twist the blade in the wound.

Besides the automatic bow already mentioned, there were two kinds of bows. A short bow was used for hunting in the woods, a longer bow on the open flats. Except for size there was no difference between them(?). The bow was of hemlock, with a sinew backing to make it stronger. The backing was tied at each end and on each side of the arrow notch in the middle, but was not twisted after it was put on (Galushia). Johnny Stevens says that the bow was of spruce with a string of braided sinew. He denies that sinew hacking was used. The bow was notched at one edge in the middle where the arrow rested which, however, seems to be an inadequate way of describing the ordinary Northwest coast type with a narrow grip and flat wings (cf. the bow in the JACOBSEN collection described below). There was no projecting wooden string guard. The bow was held horizontally, the arrow was pulled between the [103] thumb and forefinger, i.e. the so-called primary release. The bow was notched as a tally of game killed. Not all game, only certain (what?) kinds were recorded. The tally was kept only for personal gratification.

Colonel ABERCROMBIE describes the Eyak bow as short, about 3 feet (90 cm.) long, with a sinew cord and sinew backing. It was so stiff that an inexperienced white man could not bend it. The Eyak bent their bows with a quick jerk. The hunter wore a wrist guard of skin which protected the side of his wrist and his thumb from the recoil of the string. The guard was cut at the upper edge to make room for the arrow, which rested between the forefinger and middle finger of the bow hand. The Eyak were excellent shots. ABERCROMBIE saw a man shoot an arrow, and when it fell. 25 or 30 yards away, he hit it with a second arrow. (Compare, however, his written statement quoted in the next section.) When not in use the bowstring was loosened. To restring it, the natives would bend the bow around one knee and slide the loop at the end of the bowstring until it engaged in the notches at the end of the bow.

The bow in the JACOBSEN collection (B-MV, IVA 6350, native name "kot'l-krat'l", Plate 12, 3) has a stave supposed to be made of spruce. It is the ordinary Northwest Coast type with a narrow, almost cylindrical grip and two flat wings. While the back of the wings is somewhat rounded, the belly has two facettes sloping from a median ridge to meet the hack at sharp edges at the sides. The nocks are short and cylindrical. The string is a four-ply braid of sinew thread, ending in a loop at one end. There is no sinew backing. Length 140cm., maximum width of wings 4.2cm.

The arrows had a head of bone (compare Raven, incident 21), or stone, attached directly to the wooden [104] shaft. The butt was enlarged to make a grip for the fingers and was notched for the string. The feathers were eagle feathers, split in two and fastened on straight, not in a spiral, by a lashing at both ends. The Eyak knew nothing about gluing on feathers.

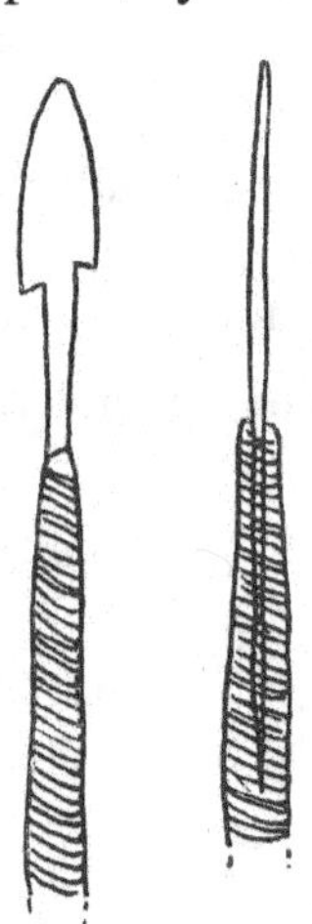

Fig. 13. Wooden arrow with iron blade, owned by Gus Nelson. From a sketch by NORMAN REYNOLDS.

A bow and arrow belonging to Gus Nelson were shown us but we were unable to measure or photograph them. The bow was like that made by the Eskimo of Port Graham, Cook Inlet (close relatives of the Chugach), but lacked string and backing. The arrow had a barbed iron blade with a long tang. The notch at the butt was at right angles to the plane of the blade (Figure 13).

ABERCROMBIE adds the following information: The arrows were made of arrow-wood and were about 2½ feet long. The halves of three feathers were used. The heads were of bone, with a single barb, slanting Fig. 13. Wooden back more closely than those on the spear head. The end of the arrow shaft fitted into the hollow bone head and was firmly fixed with glue of some kind. The barb served to keep the arrows in the wound. If a wounded goat bled externally he would run until he bled to death, but if he bled internally he would soon fall. ABERCROMBIE saw no blunt-pointed bird arrows.

There are five arrows in the JACOBSEN collection (B-MV, IV A 6351-55, native name "tak'l", Plate 12, 4-7), all belonging to the bow described before. They are all very much alike and said to be used for hunting land animals and for war. IVA 6351 has a slender iron head with a barb on either [105] side and a pointed tang sunk into a wooden shaft and secured by a whipping of sinew thread. There are three split feathers lashed at the ends with sinew thread and cut like the arrow feathers of the Pacific Eskimo, i.e. so that the outer edge of the vane forms a regular curve. The nock forms a knob with a notch for the bow string. Total length 98.2cm., of which the head is 9.5 by 1.2cm. IV A 6352 has a total length of 97.8cm.; the head is 9.4 by 1.2 cm. IV A 6353 has a broken shaft and could not be measured accurately. IV A 6354 differs from the rest in having a spruce-root(?) lashing at the fore end of the shaft instead of sinew thread. Total length

102.5 cm., head 6.4 by 1.1cm. IVA 6355 has a total length of 93cm., the head 10.6 by 1.1 cm.

Besides there are two loose arrow heads of bone for land animal or bird hunting (IV A 6337-38, native name "krich", Plate 13,8). The stem is four-sided, ending in a short, pointed blade with a barb on both sides. The tang of IV A H338 is wedge-shaped. Total length 17.8 and 14.1 cm., breadth 1.6 and 1.3cm. respectively.

Arrows were kept in a wooden quiver without a lid. It was circular in section, widening at the top to accomodate the feathers, and had a slight bulge in the middle. It was made of two pieces, hollowed out and lashed together. It was carried on a strap across the shoulders. ABEHCHOMBIE does not remember seeing either wooden or skin quivers at Alaganik. When goat hunting the men used to carry their arrows wrapped in their bedding; when hunting in the small canoes they put their arrows under the hollow stool.

The Eyak generally hunted in groups, led by a chief(?) whose orders the others had to obey. Only the best hunters went out alone. When a goat was killed (with spears?), all [106] the hunters participating got a share of the meat, but the actual killer obtained the larger share and the horns and skin. When the animal was killed with arrows, the first to strike the game received all (the major share?), provided the arrow remained in the wound, even though he did not actually kill it. The successful hunter would give a share of his game to all the women in camp. He would keep what he needed for his own family, and give away the rest, first to the old people in his own house, then lo people in the other houses, as far as the meat went. If a hunter failed to share his game, he would be ostracised. These statements are not very consistent, because Galushia did not remember clearly.

The Eyak used smoke for signalling when hunting, to indicate that the party had a great deal of meat and needed help (to carry it back?). Galushia docs not know the signals.

There were no special hunting grounds reserved for families or moieties or village groups. There was not much of a yearly cycle in hunting.

By 1884 the Eyak were armed with guns. ABERCROMBIE writes: "The natives of this village [Alaganik] were armed with the old three-band, brass-bound Springfield musket, and shoot home-manufactured bullets. The natives are indifferent shots at more than 60 yards, depending mainly on the spear for their fish supply ... The natives never shoot at a greater distance than 75 yards."[1] "Like the rest of the Coast Indians, the Eyak are armed with the double rifle and shotgun combined."[2] Apparently they did not possess revolvers, these "being held in greater fear and more [107] incomprehensible to the natives than a rifle, as they fire so often without reloading,"[3] and we doubt if they own any now. This record is difficult to reconcile with Colonel ABERCROMBIE'S oral statements that the Eyak in 1884 had no white men's weapons or tools. It is possible that he has forgotten their guns, or that they had only a few. It is less likely that the written statement should apply to some other tribe.

Sea Mammal Hunting

The only sea mammals hunted by the Eyak were the seal and sea-otter. They did not hunt fur seals because they were afraid of them, but killed the small harbor or hair seal. They did not hunt porpoises like their Eskimo neighbors, and they were afraid of the walrus because these

---

[1] ABERCROMBIE 1900, 384f.

[2] ABERCROMBIE 1900, 397.

[3] ABERCROMBIE 1900, 385.

animals were supposed to be transformed human beings. Walrus, moreover, always seem to have been scarce in this region. They did not hunt whales, but when a dead one was found they ate the flesh(?), and the fat, and utilized the baleen.

Seals were hunted in the water, on rocks and sandbars, and on the ice. Most of the seals were killed on the river bars in summer, when a large number could be found in one place. They were killed with a club. The club is described by Johnny Stevens as having a tapering handle ending in a knob. Seals were also clubbed in the shallow water around the Egg Islands, and on the rocks off Gravina Point (Johnny Stevens).

Seals on the sandbars were sometimes harpooned. Johnny Stevens said that one hunter would act and cry like a seal to decoy the animal, while another hunter would lie [108] hidden in a pit dug in the sand, with just his head showing. He denied that one hunter alone could use this method. Galushia, however, said that while it was customary for several hunters to help each other, one man could hold decoy and kill the seal. The harpoon was thrown from the hand.

Seals in open water were killed by harpoons (*Tale* 10) thrown by hand (Galushia) or with a throwing-board (Johnny Stevens). A bow and arrow were also used (JS). This must have been a harpoon arrow, like that used for the sea-otter. Seals were usually killed in the river, rarely in the open sea.

Seals were not often hunted on the ice, because of the danger of drifting away. The hunter always had to have a canoe at hand. However, in the spring, when seals were basking on the ice, they were sometimes hunted. The hunter was dressed in seal skins (as indeed he would be for any hunting), and while stalking would imitate the noise and movements of a seal. No special sealing scratcher was used. For hunting on the ice, a harpoon was used. We were told that a bladder was attached to the shaft, but this must probably be due to confounding it with the harpoon employed from the canoe, for on an ice-hunting harpoon a bladder will not only be useless, but also an inconvenience. Johnny Stevens seemed to think that the Eyak never hunted seals on the ice before they had guns. That is why, he said, they never went to Gravina Bay in the old days, whereas in Russian times they began to hunt seals on the ice in Simpson Bay, Sheep Bay, and Port Gravina. We feel certain that the reason the Eyak did not go to these places in former days was because they were afraid of the Eskimo. He also told us that in summer seals enter Eyak Lake and ascend the Copper River as far as "Tea Kettle" (Tiekel at Mile [109] Ninety-six on the Copper River Railway). In winter they apparently stay in the open sea, and that is why he did not know that seals have to keep open their breathing holes when they are imprisoned under solid ice. There was, therefore, no hunting of seals at their breathing holes.

Galushia maintained that the throwing-board for the scaling harpoon was used only by the Eskimo. Johnny Stevens claimed it for the Eyak also, though the type he described was almost identical with the Chugach Eskimo form. It was made of wood, with a pitted projection at the end into which the butt of the dart fitted. There was a hand grip at the other end with a hole to accommodate the forefinger. The Chugach throwing-board differed only in possessing a pointed projection which fitted into the hollowed butt of the dart.

The harpoon, according to Galushia, had a detachable barbed head with tang. The toggle harpoon head with socket was unknown. The harpoon shaft was a little longer than the span of a man's outstretched arms. There was no socket-piece, and the head was hafted directly into a hole in the wooden shaft, bound about with lashings to prevent splitting. The head was fastened by a short line to the fore end of the shaft, where the line was attached at two places, one above the other, and was further secured by sinew lashings. At the butt of the shaft another line, or the continuation of the harpoon line, was also fastened on at two places, and then led to the float, an inflated seal stomach, just in front of the float, another line was fastened to the main line and this was tied about the hunter's waist. In case the seal dragged him too close to the edge of the ice, the hunter would cut this line. The same harpoon was used when sealing from the canoe. When not in use, the harpoon was kept outside the house, under the overturned canoe. [110]

In the JACOBSEN collection there are five hone and two iron harpoon heads, the native name of which is given as "katt", (Plate 13, 5,6,7). For one of the iron specimens (B-MV, IV A 6335) it is expressly stated that it is used both for seals and salmon; as, however, the name and the type are the same for all, there is hardly any doubt that this information may apply also to the rest of them.

IV A 6337 is a bone head with four strongly projecting, unilateral barbs. The tang is pointed and provided with a line hole near the barbed edge. Length 18-7 cm. IV A 6339 and 6340 are also made of bone, but provided with five barbs and wedge-shaped tangs. Lengths 14.7 and 11.1 cm, respectively. IV A 6341 and 6342 are similar to the two proceeding pieces, though having only three and four barbs respectively. Lengths 11.7 and 11 cm. The iron heads, IV A 6335 and 6363, have four barbs, but are otherwise of the same type as the bone specimens. Lengths 19 and 12.2cm. To IV A 6363 there is fastened a double line, 22 cm. long and made of seal thong whipped with sinew thread.

ABERCROMBIE does not think that the Eyak did much seal hunting, though Long Jim (from Taral on the Copper River) and Shorty (an exiled Tlingit) used to kill them. The Eyak used the kayak to some extent in sealing, but speared most of their seals from the shore. ABEBCROMBIE says that they used the same spear or harpoon for both fish and seals, see, therefore, Plate 12, 2, and Plate 13, 1, 2, which will be described in the section on Fishing. ABERCROMBIE did not see any harpoons with throwing-board nor any harpoons with float.

In describing sea-mammal hunting, ABERCROMBIE wrote:

"The old musket is used for sea otter, and occasionally for [111] seal, but they also use the how and arrow. The how is not very powerful, although sufficiently so for the short ranges at which it is employed. While it throws an arrow fairly well, the bowmen show no great degree of skill. The arrow has a detachable barb fastened to the shaft by a thong of twisted sinew. This arrangement leaves the point implanted in the body of the sea], or otter, and not only tends to interfere with the animal when it dives, but also impedes the animal's attempts to escape."[1]

Sea-otter were hunted off the Egg Islands and Strawberry Point, Hinchinbrook Island. The use of the kayak in sea-otter hunting has already been discussed. ABERCROMBIE adds in conversation, however, that he doubts if the Eyak ever went after sea-otter unless invited by the Eskimo when the latter needed extra men to fill out the circle of baidarkas. We suspect that he exaggerates the Eyaks' timidity. The Eskimo at Nuchek, he says, had an old man who acted as a weather prophet for the sea-otter hunt. During the day he used to climb the hills north of Nuehek to keep watch for Eyak poachers, because the Eskimo regarded the sea-otter grounds as their own territory.

Five harpoon arrowheads for sea-otter in the JACOBSEN collection are made of copper (B-MV, IV A 6343-47, native name "katt-klistilkrat'l"). They all belong to the same barbed type as the big harpoon heads previously described, having three unilateral barbs, a wedge-shaped tang,

---

[1] ABERCROMBIE 1900, 397.

and a line hole close to the barbed edge. IV A 6343 has a length of 4.3 cm. Attached to the head there is a fragment of a line made of finely braided sinew thread forming two parallel strands. At regular intervals red thread and while hair have been wound around the strands, thus producing a sort of [112] chequered pattern. IV A 6344 has a length of 4 cm.; fragment of a simple line of braided sinew thread. The lengths of IV A 6345, 6346, and 6347 are 3.8, 3.5, and 3.2 cm, respectively. The last mentioned specimen has also a fragment of a simple sinew line like IV A 6344.

Bird Hunting

The birds hunted by the Eyak include the various species of duck, geese, swan, ptarmigan, and grouse. The last two could be hunted during the winter, since they remained all the year round. The other birds, however, were killed chiefly in August when they were moulting. The Eyak used sharp-pointed arrows or clubs. It was customary for all the inhabitants of the village to join in driving the moulting birds along the sloughs to a narrow place where they could be forced ashore. In that case, they could be killed by simply wringing their necks. The best time for these drives was in the early morning or evening. All the people shouted when driving the birds. In incident 21 of the Raven cycle, a duck is shot with bow and arrow.

ABERCROMBIE saw the natives chasing moulting geese on the mud flats near Alaganik. The whole village — men, women, and children — would run after them. The geese could outrun a man, so that to catch them, the natives formed a big circle, gradually closing in. The birds would try to hide behind drift wood, and some would succeed in breaking through the circle. Those caught were killed with clubs. The clubs were about 2 feet (60 cm.) long, round in section, and narrowed for a grip with a knob at the end of the handle, as on a baseball bat. They were tough, and ABERCROMBIE thinks that they were made of green wood which had been purposely seasoned. He saw no special [113] multipronged darts or arrows for birds, and no blunt-headed arrows for stunning birds and small game. The natives denied the use of slings and bolas. The loon was not hunted, because a boy had once turned into one (*Tale* 11).

Fishing

Both our native informants and Colonel ABERCROMBIE recognized the salmon as the most important source of food in Eyak economy. Five species were known: the king, the sockeye or red, called by a special name when it turns red in fresh water just before spawning, the humpbacked, the dog, and the silver. The first of these to run is the king, and its appearance is announced by the arrival of the tern. Information about the runs of these different species has very kindly been furnished by the U.S. Bureau of Fisheries. We quote from a letter by SETON H. THOMPSON, Division of Alaska Fisheries:

"Considering the entire Copper River delta from Martin River to Point Whitshed and including Martin and Eyak Rivers with Copper River as the Copper River region, it may be said that only three species of salmon enter these waters. These are the king [or chinook, *Oncorhynchus tschawytscha*], the red [or sockeye, O. *nerka*], and coho salmon [or silver, O. *kisutch*]. The run of kings begins from about the first of May and ends about June 1. The red salmon run extends from about May 5 to July 15. There are some red stragglers in the delta waters as late as August 10 but they are comparatively few and cannot be regarded as constituting a run. The principal part of the red salmon run in this region has ascended the spawning streams before June 25. Red salmon are abundant on the spawning grounds of Eyak [114] Lake and Martin River during July and early August. Spawning on most of the tributaries of Copper River takes place in late July or August.

"The coho salmon runs in the Copper River region begin about August 1 and continue until the end of September. These fish have been observed on the spawning grounds as late as November."

In Prince William Sound, however, there are only a few kings, reds, and silvers. The most important salmon are the pink or humpbacked (*Oncorhynchus gorbuscha*), and the chum or dog (O. *keta*). "The pink salmon first appears late in June, the runs reach a maximum about the middle of July, and remain at a comparatively high level until early August. Spawning takes place in nearly all of the streams tributary to Prince William Sound and is in active progress from late July until September. In some streams ... spawning is earlier and is complete by the middle of August.

"Chum salmon runs arc somewhat earlier than the pink runs, and they begin to enter the streams to spawn late in June. Spawning is complete by early August."

There were no family, moiety, or village rights over fishing camps and streams. This is explained by ABERCROMBIE who says that there was no need for exclusive fishing rites, since there were so many salmon in the Copper River that the natives were able to catch their whole year's supply early in the season. The fish camps at Point Whitshed and Mountain Slough have already been mentioned. These places were not claimed or used exclusively by anyone group. The natives were accustomed to stay at these camps during the salmon runs, though a number of families might remain to catch fish at the permanent villages. The fishing was done by the men, while the women cleaned and smoked the catch. [115]

Fish were speared from canoes (Galushia) and from the river bank (ABERCROMBIE).

One type of spear, described by Galushia, had two points made from a naturally forked branch, to which were lashed barbs made of fire-hardened wood. The spear was twisted to prevent the fish from wriggling free.

The other type of fish spear or harpoon is represented by a specimen purchased from Scar Stevens (P-UM 33-29-1, Plate 12,2, and Plate 13,2). This has a wooden shaft, 3.56 meters long. The diameter in the middle is about 3 cm., and the shaft tapers slightly towards both ends. It is fitted with a detachable iron head, 14 cm. long. with two barbs on the same side and a wedge-shaped tang. There is an irregular hole near the base, perhaps derived from the original use to which the piece of iron had been put. The line is attached to a round hole at the upper end of the lang, just below the barbs. The head fits into a slot at the end of the harpoon shaft, which has here been wound about with white cotton cord to prevent splitting. The harpoon line is made of the same material. For a distance of 40 cm. from the head it is made of two strands, loosely twisted together. A braid of three strands forms the next 30 cm., and the remaining portion is of three strands, neither twisted nor braided. The line is attached by a winding about the shaft, about 1 meter below the fore end, leaving about 20 cm. of slack. Below this upper winding, the line makes a single spiral turn about the shaft, 36 cm. long, and is fastened again by a similar winding. The same type of spear is described by ABERCROMBIE, who further specifies that most of the salmon supply was obtained by it.[1] Cf. also the harpoon heads described p. 110. [116]

Colonel ABERCROMBIE very generously presented the University Museum with the spear head used by Long Jim (Plate 13, 1). It was the only iron one at Alaganik in 1884. The others were made of bone or native copper, though of the same pattern. This specimen is of wrought iron, apparently shaped with a whetstone. It is 19.5 cm. long, 2.8 cm. wide, and 0.7 cm. thick. It has 4 long sharp slender barbs on the same side, and a sharp facetted point. The shaft of the head, from which the barbs are strongly detached, is very slender, and widens to a wedge-shaped tang which is drilled for the line just below the barbs. The line is of 6-strand braided sinew, 0.6 cm. wide and 2.48 meters long. It is attached to the head by a lead of rawhide, 21 cm. long. The latter is looped at both ends, and is wound throughout with sinew. One loop passes through the line hole and is twisted about the back of the head; the other loop is attached to the loop at the end of the sinew line in such a way that it can easily be cast off. The loop of the sinew braid is spliced so that no loose ends are visible. At the other end, the sinew line gradually narrows to a 3-strand braid, at the end of which are attached two sinew threads, 30 cm. long, each of double-twisted sinew. These were for attaching the line to the shaft. The shaft for a spear of this type was from 12 to 13 feet long, and the line was attached to it at the middle. If the salmon or seal got away, the spear would drag after it sideways in the water.

In the JACOBSEN collection there is a bone prong for a fish spear (B-MV, IVA 6339, Plate 13, 4). It is 19 cm. long and faintly curved. On the concave side there are five barbs and a small projection at the base, the latter evidently intended for insertion into the shaft. The butt end is split for a short distance. There is no line hole. Probably this specimen [117] belonged to a two or three pronged leister of the type in common use among the Eskimo.

According to ABERCROMBIE, the men generally fished in pairs. They had a simple scaffold, which consisted of a single log, one end resting on the river bank, the other supported over the water in the crotch of two poles, the tops of which had been lashed together. One man would stand on this, holding about 6 or 8 feet of his spear in the water, waiting until a seal or salmon came close enough to he struck. Ho would not attempt to jab the spear down into the water from the air, because the splash would frighten away the game. The hunter tried to harpoon the fish or seal near the tail, because that would most effectively cripple it, and he would endeavour to retain his hold on the spear shaft. His assistant stood ready to club the game. Generally when fishing, the assistant would have a second spear ready for his companion as soon as the latter passed hack the first harpoon with the fish dangling at the end of the line. The run of fish was often so heavy that the assistant had to work fast, cutting loose the salmon from the barbs, and replacing the head on the shaft, to be ready with the spear when his companion needed it. The slough at Alaganik would be literally packed with salmon during the run, and two men working in this way could catch enough to keep several women busy cutting up the fish. Spearing of fish is mentioned in the story of the Salmon Boy (*Tale* 4). Fish were brained with a wooden club, described by Johnny Stevens as similar to the seal club, but smaller. This is mentioned in incident 7 of the Raven cycle.

ABERCROMBIE also saw the small boys shooting at fish in the clear streams. The arrows had simply a sharpened point, hardened in the fire. Though the boys killed [118] some fish in this way, they seemed to be doing it mostly for fun.

The natives said that no nets were used for fish. In both versions of the Salmon Boy story (*Tale* 4), salmon were caught with a dipnet. It would be more correct lo say that no large

---

[1] ABERCROMBIE 1900, 397.

seines were used before they were introduced by the whites. However, the dipnet used for both herring and salmon is described by ABERCROMBIE as a round basket, made of willows tied together with wythes (Figure 14). The handle was about 6 or 8 feet (1.80 or 2.40 m.) long, running across the open top of the basket and fastened at both edges. The circular bottom was made of radiating twigs, the sides of vertically set sticks, tied to a few encircling pieces (probably by a variation of the twining technique?), The dip basket for herring was about 18 inches (45 cm.) in diameter and from 12 to 14 inches (30 to 35 cm.) deep; that for salmon was a yard in diameter and correspondingly deeper.

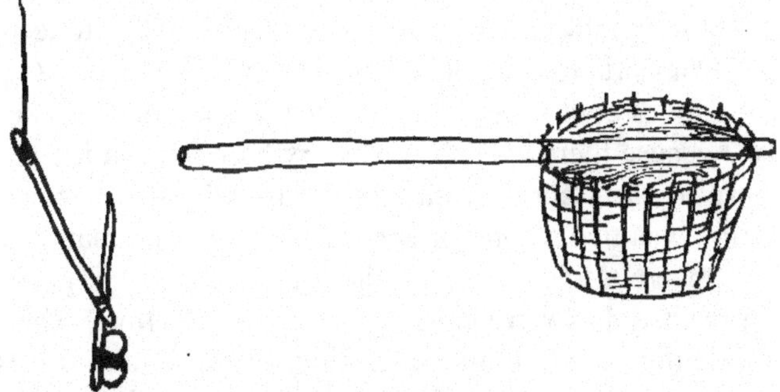

Fig. 14. Fish hook and basket dipnet, as described by ABERCROMBIE.

Herring were caught in Cordova Bay (from the canoe?), and ABERCROMBIE saw them being dried at Old Town. We quote again from Mr. THOMPSON'S letter: "Herring when mature approach shore at least once each year to [119] spawn in shallow waters. After spawning the spent herring may disappear for a time. Whether they go into deeper water or are merely widely scattered is uncertain." He mentions that in the western part of Prince William Sound herring are found early in June and remain during part of July. Late in September and in October larger herring are found there, hut he does not give any specific information for the waters around Cordova. "Thus far a well denned migration has not been traced."

Colonel ABERCROMBIE says that when catching salmon with a dipnet or basket, the men also worked in pairs. A stone corral was built on the bank of the river were there was shallow water between a rock and the shore. Since the Copper River is so muddy, salmon could be seen only in a shallow place where their fins stuck out. One man wielded the net, scooping in a downstream direction. The salmon would not turn around to escape the basket but would try to push upstream through it. The fisherman would throw the fish out on the bank by flipping the basket handle against his knee. His assistant would hook his fingers in the gills and toss the fish into the corral. They worked so fast that the passage of the salmon from the river into the enclosure seemed to be one continuous movement. When the men had a canoe load they would return to Alaganik, Where the women would unload the boat and clean the fish. This type of fishing was very strenuous. When fish were thrown into the stone corral it was not necessary to brain them. ABERCROMBIE thought that the club was used only for fish caught with a harpoon, or caught with hook and line from a canoe.

Halibut were caught by hook and line from a canoe, and might be taken in both summer and winter. *Tale* 23 mentions halibut fishing in winter. The bait was a clam [120] (compare Raven, incident 17). In incident 6, seal fat was used. The hook was made of bone or hard wood. If of bone, the parts were lashed together; if of wood, a naturally shaped branch was used. The line was made of several pieces from the small end of kelp stalks, dried, and tied (braided?) together. ABERCROMBIE described the line as made of 6(?)-strand braided fiber, dyed brown. It was dried out after use.

While the natives were not able to give a very clear description of the fish hook. ABKRCROMBIE describes in some detail that used for cod (Figure 14). This was of two pieces of bone. The shank part was about 4 inches long, circular in section, with a diameter of about ½ inch (1.2 cm.). This was tied to the middle part of the barb, a pointed piece of bone about 3 inches (7.5 cm.) long, and ½ inch (0.6 cm.) thick, somewhat flat in section. The two parts were scarfed to fit together, and the angle between them was just large enough to admit the upper jaw of the cod. To the projecting lower end of the barb was attached a lump of quartz, about an inch (2.5 cm.) long. It was grooved up cue side to fit against the bone, and was notched at the middle for the lashing. While the bait was a clam, which the natives claimed the fish could smell, the white lump of quartz also acted as a lure. The cod would often bite at it instead of the bait, and the stone would be scarred by their teeth. The stone was so light that the hook would sink slowly, swerving from side to side. The line was only 6 or 8 feet (1.8 or 2.4 m.) long, and the salt water is so clear that the natives could easily see the fish at that depth. When one took the bait, it had to be pulled in very quickly, because there was no secondary barb to hold it. The last jerk on the line sent the fish into the canoe, where it was stunned with a wooden club, about 18 or 20 inches (45 or [121] 50 cm.) long. The end of the line was tied to one of the thwarts, and one man often had a line out on each side of the canoe. Sand sharks were also caught with this rig.

Trout and whitefish in the lakes were caught with hook and line. The trout hook was described by Galushia as similar to the halibut hook, but smaller, and for these lake fish salmon eggs were used as bait. Trout and whitefish were also speared from the canoe (compare *Tale* 11). The spear is said to have been like the salmon harpoon, with a detachable iron (formerly a bone) head, barbed on one side, and fastened by a line to the shaft. If the head were rigidly attached, even for these small fish, they might squirm loose, Galushia explained. The water in the lakes is so clear that no lure was needed to attract the fish since they could be discovered from the canoe. Eyak never chopped holes in ice for winter fishing.

Eulachon were caught at night with a dipnet or a fish spear. A fire was carried in the canoe to attract them (compare Raven, incident 3). The fish spear used for eulachon was something like the two-pronged salmon spear, except that it had several barbs on each prong. These barbs were made from forked branches. The spear was scooped through the water like a fish rake. Eulachon were caught at Alaganik and Eyak from February to April.

Fish traps were also used. They were made of upright stakes, like a basket, and were of the same type as those used today by the Copper River Indians. The name for the fish trap is the same as that for a fort. These traps were set under the ice, and were without fences leading to them, though they had a funnel-shaped opening. We have no definite statement to the effect that they were used in summer for salmon, but this seems likely. [122]

The sled for bringing home fish has already been mentioned.

The Eyak did not know that salmon eggs were impregnated by the male salmon, though they knew that fish hatched from the eggs. They put salmon tails back into the water to insure the continuation of the fish supply (*Tale* 22).

When the first salmon of the run was caught, or the first lot of salmon were taken in a net. the man who made the catch would take a bath and put on clean clothes. (The others did the same?). He would cut up the fish and boil it with a little green stuff (what?). No woman was allowed to touch it before it was cooked. Every one in the village would eat a piece. If this were neglected no more salmon would come, (Johnny Stevens). Galushia knew nothing about the first salmon ceremony except that menstruating women were not allowed to touch the fish. (However, this may be only the taboo against their touching or eating fresh meat, which may have been applied to all fresh fish?).

Other sea foods utilized by the Eyak include clams, These were dug with a pointed stick at low tide (compare Raven, incident 11). Razor clams and cockles were dug and dried at the Point Whitshed fish camp in October. The natives ate little-neck (locally called "butter") clams and mussels, but did not dry them, (probably because they were too small?). Gahishia says that the Eyak did not eat sea-urchins, though in incident 10, Raven pretends to have eaten some. It seems likely that the Eyak did also. [123]

Social Culture.

Moieties and Chiefs

The Eyak are divided into two exogamous, matrilineal moieties, the Eagle and the Raven groups. Though now so reduced in numbers they still observe the moiety divisions when marrying each other or the Tlingit. Galushia did not know the origin of the moiety names. There was no claim of' descent from the moiety bird, and no taboo against killing it. Every one used to eat eagles, use eagle skins for clothing, and eagle feathers for their arrows, but no one ate the raven except in time of famine. The members of the two moieties called themselves Eagles and Ravens respectively, and considered the members of their own moiety as brothers and sisters. There was no formal subdivision of the moiety into clans or smaller groups, although as we shall see, the Wolf People and the Bark House People each formed a somewhat separate social group within their respective moieties. Both moieties were represented in each village, and Galushia denied that one moiety claimed a whole village as its own, as Chief Joe had declared. Thus, each family had a house at Alaganik and another at Eyak, and within the village a man could build wherever he chose, without moiety segregation of houses. There were no special taboos observed by members of a moiety as such.

The Wolf People and the Bark House People were [124] originally Tlingit who had emigrated after a quarrel over the inheritance of a chief's house. Galushia later modified this statement, and explained that there had been too many people living at Katalla, the nearest Tlingit village, so the Tlingit told some of their members to move out. This was before the coming of the Russians. The Wolves were adopted into the Raven moiety, and the Park House People into the Eagle moiety. The name was given to the second group because they were in such a hurry to build their potlatch house that they constructed it of bark. This tradition would seem to imply that this group, and perhaps the Wolf People also, had their own potlatch houses, but this was not supported by the list of potlatch houses nor by Galushia's express statement thai there were only two such buildings in the village, each serving the whole moiety. Actually, the name Bark House People is a clan name found among the Tlingit. A Raven clan in the Henya division was called the Tē'nedî, or "bark-house people," and a Raven clan, the Tïhît tān, "bark-house people" belonged to the Slikine division. A house group in each of these two clans actually had the name Tïhît, "bark house."[1] Thus it is clear that the name already belonged to the Tlingit before their adoption. As to the origin of the name, the Tlingit report that: "It is said that the wives of some KiksA'dî people [a Raven clan of Sanya, Stikine, and Sitka] once quarreled, and all of one side moved out into a house made of bark, from which circumstance they came to be called Bark-house people. At Wrangel the Bark-house people are credited with but one house group, but the Tē'nedî of Klawak constitute the same clan, their name being merely a variation of Tïhît tān."[2] [125]

Likewise, the name "Wolf People" is, of course, a Tlingit name, being applied both to the moiety which is called Eagle among the northern Tlingit, and to a clan within that moiety. Galushia said that the adoption by the Eyak of these two Tlingit groups took the form of a sham battle and "good time" at Alaganik, and that the Eyak moieties adopted the people they wanted.

---

[1] SWANTON 1908, 398-402.
[2] SWANTON 1908, 409.

We may be sure, however, that principles of moiety equivalence determined the choice. The most curious feature is that the Tlingit groups were apparently adopted by the wrong moieties. Thus the Wolves should have gone to the Eagles, and not the Ravens, and the Bark House People should have been adopted by the Ravens, not the Eagles. It is extremely unlikely (hat this seeming confusion was caused by forgetfulness on the part of our informants, because the information about the moiety affiliations of the two sub-groups was consistent in every way that we could check it. The confusion undoubtedly dates from the time of the adoption and is no greater than the confusion which arises when the natives attempt to equate Tsimshian and Haida and Tlingit clans.[1] The basis of this equation in these latter cases seems to have been the particular crest or crests of the clan, rather than those of the moiety or phratry. Now if we knew that the Eyak moieties had subsidiary crests, we might assume that they, rather than the main crest, were the deciding factors. Unfortunately, our native informants gave us no indication that there were such subsidiary crests. The only evidence which points in that direction, and it is admittedly most scanty, is that ABERCROMBIE describes the totem pole in Alaganik graveyard as having several animal carvings below the raven which topped it (see *Death and Burial*), and [126] the lockers in the large houses as having a variety of carvings on the doors (see Houses). The dance paddles belonging to the Raven moiety had paintings of salmon and other figures on them, while one is topped with a Raven, the other with a bear (see *The Potlatch*). The problem involved in this adoption cannot be solved without additional evidence; it might be still possible to obtain it from the Yakutat Tlingit, but it would probably be almost impossible to find a surviving Eyak who could supply it.

We do not know if this adoption was primarily a moiety or a tribal affair. In any case, the two adopted groups preserved their individual identity to some extent. Thus Chief Joe was known as a Wolf Man. A grave post of a Wolf chief was identified by Galushia in the graveyard at Alaganik. At potlatches the Wolves used to masquerade like their animal namesakes. They howled like wolves while the Eagles screamed and the Ravens croaked.

Mention ought to be made of the foreigners at Alaganik, whom ABERCROMBIE calls renegade Indians. Kai, the shaman, and Long Jim were both exiles from Taral on the Copper River. Long Jim had been sent away by Nicolai, the Taral chief, and dared not return to his own tribe. In his report, ABERCROMBIE referred to Kai as a Tlingit and said that he could speak a few words of English (see *Stories about Shamans*), but he now denies both statements. Whatever Kai's origin, he had traveled widely. He had been on the Yukon and had learned Chinook Jargon from the Hudson's Bay Company men. The Eyak accepted him, though they were more or less afraid of him. At Alaganik there was also a tall Northwest Coast Indian, probably a Tlingit, called Shorty.

At the head of each moiety was a chief. One of them [127] was the head chief of the tribe. The other chief was simply the leader of his own moiety. Galushia is not sure about the respective functions of these two men, or how a man became a chief. Below the head moiety chief was a sub-chief in each moiety. (In conversation, ABERCROMBIE explained that the chief of Alaganik was the headman of one of the two large houses; the headman of the other was a sub-chief.) The chief was supposed to be the richest man in the village, and also the strongest, though he did not have to defend his title. We imagine that Chief Joe's statement that Eyak was a Raven village and Alaganik an Eagle village means that thy head chief in these two villages belong to these respective moieties. (However, note that the totem pole in the Alaganik graveyard in 1884

---

[1] BOAS 1916, 520 ff.; NIBLACK 1890, 247f.

was topped by a raven.) Although there was a certain rivalry between moieties, Galushia said that there was none between chiefs. At the death of a chief, his brother succeeded to the position. Galushia did not know who would take the place if the chief had no brothers, though he thought it extremely unlikely that the son would be eligible since he would be a member of the opposite moiety. Even though a man might become more wealthy than the chief, he could not acquire the position during the chief's lifetime, and Galushia was uncertain if he could do so even after the chief's death. However, in *Tale* 18, we meet the statement that "he was so rich they made him head of the tribe." Though people had more respect for a wealthy than for an ordinary commoner, there was no special class of nobility, unless we mean the family of a chief, and there was no name for rich man as distinct from chief. Wealthy people and chiefs are said to have been always distributing property to the poor, in the hope of larger returns (how, if the recipient was [128] poor?) and to get luck. At first, Galushia told us that there was a chief for each moiety in each village, one of whom ranked as the headman for the village, but later he admitted that he was not sure. In view of the part played by the two moiety chiefs as leaders in the potlatch, it seems certain that there must have been an Eagle and a Raven leader in each village, even though they did not formally rank as chiefs.

Chiefs and their families were distinguished by garments of prized skins and by ornaments. It is probable, however, that wealthy persons may have worn similar clothing. While war was decided upon in a general meeting, it was the tribal(?) chief who led the war party and commanded the men to go. If he were too old to take an active part, he would appoint his son as leader, and if he had no son, the leadership devolved upon the chief's brother. Galushia commented upon the peculiarity of choosing the son. The chief was the leader of the hunting party, though an expert hunter could hunt alone and was to a large extent independent of the chief's orders. The chief did little work, and though he hunted, did not help carry back the game. He did not paddle a canoe when traveling. The chiefs were never shamans,[1] though they could command the services of a shaman in lime of war or bad weather. The chief was supposed to prefer death to capture and slavery, though a commoner who had been enslaved by the enemy was not considered degraded. All the chief's family were respected, and it was customary for the families of chiefs to marry into the families of other chiefs, though always according [129] to the moiety exogamy rules. (This surely implies moiety chiefs in each village).

While chiefs and wealthy people were supposed to give to the poor, the commoners on the other hand were supposed to give the chief a part of the meat, skins, or anything else that they acquired. It was principally the chiefs who owned slaves. For the murder of a chief (or a member of his family?) a higher payment was required than for the killing of a commoner. Only at the death of a chief's son or daughter was a slave killed as part of the funeral ceremonies.

The duties of a chief at a potlatch will be described later.

Although slaves and chiefs are mentioned in the tales, there is no story in which reference is made to the moiety division, nor to the potlatch which, as we shall see, is primarily a moiety ceremony.

With the death of Chief Joe in the winter of 1930-31, the Eyak lost their last chief, and the office has not been filled. ABERCROMBIE mentioned the "headman"[2] and a "sub-chief"[1] at

---

[1] Makari, our Eskimo ~~informant~~, told us that naɣi, the chief of the Eyak, and his second chief, *tan•a*, Old Man Dude's father-in-law, were both shamans. (Their names are given as Makari pronounced them.)

[2] ABERCROMBIE 1900, 385.

Alaganik, and made the following statement: "Their nominal chiefs are invested with very little real authority. The wealthiest man usually exerts the most influence, a not surprising condition of affairs."[2] JACOBSEN'S experience at Alaganik in 1883 would also indicate that the chief was not very powerful.When the natives stole hack from JACOBSEN the ethnological specimens which he had purchased, the latter appealed to the chief, who apparently made every effort to recover the objects, but was unsuccessful.[3]

Colonel ABERCROMBIE says that at Alaganik there was [130] some one, not the chief, who acted as peacemaker. ABERCROMBIE had distributed sonic tobacco, and a quarrel started between two men, one of whom accused the other of having stolen his share. Others joined in until the two groups were ready to fight. The peacemaker, or "policeman," dashed into a house and came out with a painted paddle, which he set up between the disputants. They stopped quarreling at once. When the photographs and drawings of the two dance paddles (Plate 15) were shown ABERCROMBIE, he said that the peacemaker's paddle was of the same type. There "was nothing about the appearance of this person to distinguish him. Apparently a stick of some kind was the recognized symbol of authority, and ABERCROMBIE'S interpreter. Pete Johnson, a white man who had married an Eyak woman, used to grab a stick when trying to enforce discipline among the natives in ABERCROMBIE'S party. There was probably some supernatural as well as civic virtue in the decorated paddle, for when ABERCROMBIE went up the Copper River, Kai gave him such a paddle to take as a protection against the Taral medicine man. However, as it was generally believed by all the natives that the latter was more powerful than Kai, (was indeed responsible for Kai's paralyzed hands), the Copper River natives only laughed at the paddle, though, of course, they recognized its significance. The Taral Indians also told ABERCROMBIE that they had a peacemaker. The white men called him John. He used to wander all over the Copper River valley, collecting tribute of some kind from the natives.

The Family

All of the grown men in a house were supposed to belong to the same moiety, and the oldest among them was the [131] head of the house group. The older brother was in a position of authority over his brothers and sisters. Chief Joe, the eldest, "used to boss his two brothers" who lived with him. They had to do all the wood cutting. Galushia told us that his older brother, Gus, has "no use" for him, because Galushia refuses to "slave" for him. The brother, and especially the oldest brother, was responsible for his sister's conduct; and if she had intercourse before marriage, or ran away from her husband, the brother would kill her (compare *Tale* 28). The oldest brother was the leader of the hunting party (when a small group went out without a chief), and the younger brothers had to carry the game home for him. They were also supposed to do other work for him. There were mutual obligations between brothers; thus, if a man were sick, his brother was supposed to support him.

The mother, of course, attended to the training of her daughters. If she died, her sister assumed that responsibility. The discipline seems to have been very strict and lasted even after the daughter's or the niece's marriage. Thus, Annie, Galushia's wife, does not dare attend a dance without first asking her mother's sister for permission, even though the dance is held in the

---

[1] ABERCROMBIE 1900, 397.

[2] ABERCROMBIE 1900, 397.

[3] JACOBSEN 1884, 389.

school house with the white school teacher as chaperon.

Marriage was always contracted between members of different moieties, and this applied even to marriages with the Tlingit. There were no rules of village endogamy or exogamy. A couple who married within their own moiety would be completely ostracised; even their closest relatives would refuse to speak to them. This feeling is still so strong that we found no case where the moiety exogamy rules had been broken. The moiety ruling could not be applied to [132] marriage with people such as the Eskimo, the Copper River Atna, whites, or Japanese, who had no such organization, although the children of such foreign mothers seem to have been given a certain standing in the moiety to which they would have belonged had their mother been an Eyak. This is reflected in the names given these children (see *Names*). The man was free to choose his own wife, subject to the approval of her parents, but the girl had no freedom of choice, A forced marriage is mentioned in *Tale* 18. Girls were often engaged before puberty, even to men old enough to be their grandfathers. A girl who was being forced to marry a man she hated might hang herself.

The prospective bridegroom would begin working ("slaving") for the girl's parents, even before her puberty seclusion. The exact services performed arc uncertain, and they apparently ended at marriage, though we do not know how long this period of engagement lasted. The prospective son-in-law was supposed to give his parents-in-law a share of all the game he killed, though no other gifts were required (Mrs. Gus Nelson). In incident 23, Raven works for his prospective bride's parents. *Tale* 7 implies that the son-in-law's obligations did not end with his marriage, since the young bear is criticised because he does not share his game with his father-in-law. Galushia said that the young man did not live with his future parents-in-law, and that after marriage he took his wife home lo his own house. Mrs. Gus Nelson, however, said that the man always lived with his parents-in-law. Naturally, this question of residence is of importance in the problem of the ownership and inheritance of the house. In *Tale* 17, a story of absurdities, the woman seems to own the house and can drive her husband out.

JACOBSEN writes: "I was permitted to share in some of [133] the household and family relationships of the Indians living on the Copper River delta. Like all the Indians of the Northwest Coast, they are married, and in consequence betrothed, when they are very young. When a daughter is born in a family, she is often betrothed on the first day of her life, but is first married in the twelfth or fourteenth year. If her father dies before she is marriageable, her future husband must take to wife his future mother-in-law until the girl becomes old enough to marry."[1] JACOBSEN seems to have made these observations while waiting for a schooner at Cape Martin, and we cannot be sure, therefore, whether they should apply to the Eyak or to the Tlingit.

A man could not speak to his mother-in-law, and had to step out of the trail if he saw her approaching. He was free, however, to talk and joke with his father-in-law. Galushia did not know of any taboo between the daughter-in-law and her husband's father, although in *Tale* 8, the Porpoise Man tells his father not to speak to the woman because she is his wife. This certainly suggests such a taboo.

Polygyny was practiced, but not polyandry. A man might have two or three wives. He would not sleep with an old wife, but an old or barren wife was not divorced. The husband would take a young wife, and the old woman would live with them and do the hard work, "like a slave." There was supposed to be no preference for marrying sisters, and no preference for cross-cousin marriage. We were given however, explicit information about the levirate and

---

[1] JACOBSEN 1884, 393.

sororate. When a man's wife died, he was given his wife's sister, unless she was already married, in which case he was given his own brother's daughter (Mrs. Gus Nelson). The mother's sister became the disciplinarian of the children after their [134] mother's death, which suggests that it was customary for the maternal aunt to become their step-mothcr. When a man died, his younger (never his older) brother, or his parallel cousin, married the widow. A man was supposed to support his brother's wife while he was away, but he was not allowed to sleep with her (Mrs. Gus Nelson). Galushia thought that when a man was away on a trip, his parents, not his brother, would care for his family. A certain amount of freedom was permitted between brother-arid sister-in-law; thus, they could joke and "rough-house" together, even when the woman's husband was present, but the man had no sexual rights over his brother's wife. It was not specified whether this joking freedom was restricted to the younger brother and the older brother's wife, or whether it was common to all the husband's brothers. Annie Nelson said, however, that a younger brother could take his older brother's wife, even during the older brother's lifetime, and that this arrangement might be permanent, provided the man treated the woman decently. Otherwise the original husband would reclaim her. The woman could not belong to both men at the same time. Neither Galushia nor his wife knew of special privileges between cross-cousins.

After first insisting that a wife was never offered to a visitor or friend, Galushia said that sometimes two men might exchange wives temporarily. The women were not consulted in this arrangement. In all exchanges, or remarriages, the children accompanied their mother. Makari told us that the Eyak and Tlingit were accustomed to offer their wives to visitors, but did not extend this courtesy to the Eskimo.

Colonel ABERCROMBIE says that the natives at Alaganik [135] persistently offered their women to him and to the members of his party. He docs not know whether the women were offered as a mark of hospitality, or in the hopes of a commercial return, whether the arrangement was expected to be permanent or temporary, nor what was the marital status of the women. The women themselves were very anxious to be taken, and kept telling the white men what good workers and excellent cooks they were. Pete Johnson, ABERCROMBIE'S interpreter, had bought an Eyak woman for a sack of flour. ABERCROMBIE says that the Nuchek Eskimo did not offer their women.

We noted one curious marriage, though we have no way of telling if it was practiced in earlier days. When Minnie Stevens's mother died, her step-father took Minnie to wife that same night. This was reported to us by the whites as a case of simple rape, though Galushia and his wife spoke of it as a marriage. Later, the step-father's (younger?) brother, Scar Stevens, married Minnie. She has a son Mike Duval, by the first union and several children by the second.

Galushia knew little about divorce, and in answer to our questions told the story of the man who feigned death in order to leave his wife (*Tale* 29). He said that if a man caught his wife with another man, he would send her away, but would not do anything to the other man. Later, Galushia said that the husband might kill his unfaithful wife, though he had already told us that this punishment would be administered by the woman's brother. A wife would leave an unfaithful husband. Galushia had never heard of murder resulting from the theft of a wife. His wife told us, however, that the Eyak often used to steal each other's wives and that the men would fight over it, and Galushia finally admitted the same. Only the older [136] brother's wife might be taken without precipitating a fight. There was no possibility of elopement, we were told, because there was no place where the couple could go. There were no hermits living away from other people.

A father or uncle (paternal? maternal?) could take a husband away from one daughter, or niece, and marry him to another daughter or to her parallel cousin. We do not know whether the basis of the man's authority was his paternal or avuncular relationship to the girls in question, or whether it was some relationship to the young man, here not explained, since the young man would probably belong to the same moiety as the older man (to the opposite moiety only in case it was the girl's maternal uncle). The only example which Galushia cited does not help to clear up the matter. Thus, Scar Stevens has threatened to take Galushia away from Annie and marry him to Scar's daughter. As far as we could find out, Scar Stevens is Annie Nelson's mother's father's brother's wife's second husband's brother, standing in the somewhat obscure position of a great uncle. Scar's marriage to Minnie, his sister-in-law's daughter, may bring him into the class of Annie Nelson's paternal uncle. In any case he belongs to the opposite moiety from her and to the same moiety as Galushia. What his relationship may be to Galushia we have no knowledge. The relationship of Scar and Minnie to Annie is probably much closer than the genealogical table (Appendix I) would show. In Table 17, one of the absurdities was that the daughter of Chief Calm Weather bought a husband from her sister. However, in the end, it was the Chief who decided which daughter should get the man, and in this case there was no possible relationship between the Chief and the young man. [137]

Grown-up brothers and sisters were not allowed to be alone together, or even to speak to each other, though the brother's wife might be present. They could only communicate to each other indirectly, or through a third person. The terms of address for parallel cousins are translated into English as "brother" and "sister," but we received conflicting answers as to whether the taboo against speaking applied to parallel cousins of opposite sex. Marriage between them "was of course, prohibited.

A childless couple might adopt a child, but it was probably never the child of living parents. The adoption was not permanent, because at puberty the child would return to his own moiety. If the couple had no children of their own, the adopted child might be well enough treated, but an orphan child taken into a family where there were already children was not usually as well cared for. Thus, Annie Nelson, an orphan in her childhood, was terribly neglected.

ABERCROMBIE made the following observations: "No bargain can be closed without the most complete and ample discussion by every man and woman present. Women occupy a more important and desirable position than with most uncivilized races. Their opinion is consulted on all points of moment, and their share of work is not excessive. Marriages are contracted at an early age without much formality, and the tie is easily dissolved. Children are treated kindly, and the men do not consider it unbecoming to take charge of them at times."[1] ABERCROMBIE adds in conversation that the natives never slapped their children.

Kinship terms and a discussion of their significance will be found at the end of Appendix II. [138]

Partnerships.

Between men of the same moiety a form of partnership might be instituted. A man would go to a member of his own moiety, not necessarily a relative, and would address him by a special term. They would hunt together, use each other's tools without asking permission, share food, and help each other. They could "play like kids" with each other's wives, but would have

---

[1] ABERCROMBIE 1900, 385.

no sexual relations with them. (See, however, Galushia's statement that friends sometimes did exchange wives). The information about this type of partnership was given in explanation of *Tale* 1A.

Another form of partnership is suggested by *Tale* 2, in which Wolverine chooses Fox as his mother's brother's son, i.e. his cross-cousin. They lived and hunted together. This cannot be the moiety partnership mentioned in *Tale* 1A, since cross-cousins belong to opposite moieties. Unfortunately there is no commentary on this story. It is possible that the relationship implied is that of brothers-in-law. We ought to remark that brothers-in-law would not be living together unless the husband of the sister was living with her in her brother's house. Since all the grown men in a household were supposed to belong to the same moiety, this arrangement may have been somewhat irregular, unless the girl's brother was a young fellow, not yet married, who did not really count as a full adult. However, no female characters are mentioned in the tale.

Kai's household will be discussed under *Stories about Shamans*. There were no clubs or secret societies among the Eyak, and the shamans and witches did not form any organization. [139]

Slaves

Slaves were captives taken in war or the children of slaves. All the slaves of the Eyak are said to have been Eskimo.[1] A captive was usually killed unless his captor took a fancy to him, in which case he brought him home as a slave. A slave might be freed for a heroic deed, such as saving his master's son from drowning. Slaves did not try to escape because of the distance from their homes, the close watch placed over them, and the bar put across the door of the house at night. Free men and women never married slaves, and slaves were never adopted into the moiety. They had no part in the ceremonial life.

Slaves slept on the floor of the main room, among the dogs and children. They did the heavy work, such as chopping wood, fetching water, packing home game, building fires, etc-They did not hunt, but were sometimes taken on hunting parties as packers, and they helped to paddle the canoe on journeys. In *Tale* 17, the slave who broke his axe while chopping wood was afraid of a beating. He also carried food to load the canoe. His master sent him on a journey under the sea to bring hack the bones of his son-in-law, and when a kneecap was needed to complete the skeleton and bring it back to life, the master took the [140] slave's own kneecap, giving him in return only a cockle shell. Finally the slave was given to the son-in-law (as a kind of wedding present?). In *Tale* 19, the slave girl carries water to the village every morning. The daughter of the chief who owns the daylight (*Raven*, incident 3) had a slave who fetched water for her. Slave women did the house work and assisted their mistress at childbirth, though they were not freed for this service. Slaves were given leftover food and used garments. They were

---

[1] COXE (1803, II 328f, taken from SHELEKHOV'S digest of the account made by ISMAILOV and BOCHANOV) reports that in 1788 the Russia expedition under ISMAILOV and BOCHANOV traded with the Tlingit in Yakutat Hay. "Among other objects of barter, the natives offered two boys about twelve years old: one of them was of the Konaghi nation [Kodiak Eskimo], and before the establishment of the Russian company in the island Kuktak [Kodiak], had been taken prisoner by the Kinaizi [Tnaina Indians of Cook Inlet], and sold by them to the Tschiipatski [Chugach Eskimo], from whom he was transferred to the Ugalakmutes [Eyak] and by them to the Koliuski [Tlingit] ... The price of his purchase was four pounds and a quarter of iron, a large coral, and three strings of beads".

never given fresh skins for clothing. They were the absolute property of their master and might be killed at pleasure, though this rarely occurred. The owner never beat them unless they deserved it.

Galushia told the following story to illustrate the power of the master. The incident occurred when he was a small boy, before he went to the United States: A party of Yakutat Tlingit were on a journey. They had not killed anything for a long time and were very hungry. Finally they secured some game and cooked it. One man had a slave with him but refused to give him any food. When they were ready to leave their camping place, the slave was picking the bones. The master beat him to death because he had kept the boats waiting. Galushia and his wife both regarded the master's conduct with horror, and we understood that the other natives at the time had disapproved of the man's severity.

A man might trade his slave for something. Galushia thought a slave might be worth a bow, but was much less valuable than a canoe.

Slaves might marry other slaves, but only with their masters' consent. There was no ceremony; the woman simply went to live with the man. Galushia did not know if any compensation was made to the owner of the woman [141] for the loss of her services in case the woman belonged to a different household.

At puberty, slave girls were secluded for the usual period. Menstruating or pregnant slaves had to observe the same taboos as free women. Galushia knew nothing about the birth customs of slaves. At death, the body of the slave was taken out of the house as soon as possible. The body was never exposed, but was always cremated, and the ashes were thrown away. Galushia supposed that it was the other slaves who disposed of the corpse. When a chief's son or daughter died, a slave was killed with a spear, and the body was cremated, but on a separate pyre, and the ashes were not saved.

At the death of their owner, slaves were usually liberated and given their choice of returning home or remaining. Sometimes they preferred to stay. In that case they would join the household of the dead man's brother, and continue to work for the widow and her children (?).

JACOBSEN reports that young people belonging to the family of a murderer might become slaves of the relatives of the victim, in cases when the murderer's family were unable to make the proper blood payment. "There are many slaves among the Tlingit, but in general they have almost as free a life as their masters."[1] Again we arc not sure whether these observations apply to the Tlingit or to the Eyak.

Crime and Punishment

Galushia said that the murder of a close relative or of a house-mate was punished lightly, if at all. By this he must surely have meant that the matter was not one of public [142] concern, for 111 *Tale* 27 the children kill their father because he has murdered their older brothers and sisters. Murder of a fellow-clansman in another household called for a small payment of property to the dead person's relatives. Murder of a member of the opposite moiety necessitated a heavy payment. Galushia thought that representatives of the two moieties would confer to determine the amount of the blood payment. Relatives of the murderer would help him to accumulate the necessary wealth. If the clansmen of the murdered man thought that the payment offered was too small, they would go outside the murderer's house and insult him in song.

---

[1] JACOBSEN 1884, 393.

Intermoiety feuds sometimes followed murder. If a member of the murderer's own moiety were killed in this fighting, the relatives might kill the murderer, since he was responsible for the feud. Payment for a killing was always necessary, no matter what the provocation. And payment was for the same amount regardless of the age or sex of the victim, since all human life was accounted of equal value. For the murder of a chief (or a member of his family?), however, a greater payment was required. For the killing of another's slave, no payment was made, unless possibly the killer might replace the other man's slave with one of his own.

JACOBSEN writes: "When someone is killed, a family council is held, and the nearest relative of the person killed arms himself and goes to the house of fhe person who committed the murder. He demands a compensation [*Sühnegeld*] from him, and if this is denied him, he threatens bloody revenge. Thereupon, a family council is called from both sides, and in open meeting the amount of the quittance [*Ablösungssumme*] in so and so many blankets is discussed. The discussion often becomes very [143] hot, especially if the relatives of the murdered man set too high demands to which the relatives of the evildoer cannot or will not agree. If the damages cannot he paid, it often happens that one or more young people from the family of the murderer give themselves into slavery, and atone for the crime through personal service."[1] Again the observations on which these remarks are based seem to have been made at Cape Martin, and we are therefore not certain to what extent they are applicable to the Eyak. Our native informants did not even mention debtor slavery or adoption to replace a relative who had been killed.

For an injury, even though accidentally inflicted, payment had to he made. Thus Galushia's mother had to give a dress to the mother of a little Tlingit girl who was hurt when playing with Galushia. A man who insulted another so that the latter committed suicide had to pay the relatives. He would give them a canoe or spear "to keep them from feeling sad." Apparently suicide as a result of a public insult was not uncommon. Thus, a native at Alaganik got drunk and insulted another man. This man attempted to kill the man who had insulted him, but he was dissuaded by his friends. Then he attempted to commit suicide, and cut his throat with a spear so that the blood spurted out with every breath. The shaman cured him, and the relatives of the man who had insulted him had to pay his relatives, but we do not know what the payment was.

In each of these cases, the offense which we would consider a crime was treated by the Eyak as a tort, to use our legal phraseology, responsibility being extended to cover the offender's relatives and even his whole moiety. However, there was no legal machinery for settlement, unless the [144] peacemaker mentioned by ABERCROMBIE had such a function. In spite oi' Galushia's statement that all human life was counted equal, we may be sure that the payments for each particular case were haggled over, and that the final settlement depended on the abilities of the two groups involved in driving the bargain.

Theft was unheard of in the old days. The tribal group was so small that the thief would be completely ostracised. (See under *Stories about Shamans*, however, that Kai used to discover what had become of lost or stolen articles. Theft was probably rare, but could hardly have been nonexistent.) If a man borrowed another's canoe and broke it, he was expected to replace it.

Marriage within the moiety would be punished by ostracism, as was failure to support a sick brother. The same penalty was probably inflicted on a son who neglected to support his parents, though we have no specific information on this point. Threat of ostracism probably was effective against stinginess and failure to share one's game with others. Adultery or unchastity in

---

[1] JACOBSEN 1884, 393.

an unmarried girl was punished by death inflicted by the brother. In *Tale* 28, bad weather and famine resulted from the concealment and non-burial of an illegitimate child. Probably breaches of taboo respecting pregnancy and childbirth were also involved, though these are not specifically mentioned. The mother and lover made atonement by killing themselves. We have no statement about punishment for rape or abduction.

The natives say that arguments were never settled by duels or feuds. Certainly the most common method of settling disputes when the participants were members of opposite moieties was for one man to go in front of his [145] rival's house and insult him in a derision song. The rival would answer in song. This was the method used when insufficient payment had been made to atone for a murder. Women never took part in these singing contests, but might be represented by their brothers. The peacemaker has already been mentioned.

One insult was a phallic gesture, made by thrusting the tip of the thumb between the first and second fingers of the clenched hand, accompanied by the word "n•'a•", implying "kiss this!" Another insult was: "Your mother has a rotten vagina!" Both of these were very terrible. Insults mentioned in the tales are: "Big nose, deep arm pits, long nose, stinking baby!" (Raven, incident 12); "Fat head, fat jaw!" (*Raven*, incident 5); "Big nose, big feet, big face!" (*Tale* 6A); and "Big hands, big eyes, big nose, big ears, big mouth, big head, big buttocks!" (*Tale* 6B).

It was impolite to address any one by his or her personal name, though there was no taboo against doing so.

War

The Eyak used to fight with spears, clubs, bows and arrows (*Tale* 25). The bow and arrow were apparently the same as those used for land-animal hunting, but special spears were used. War spears were longer than hunting spears and had an unbarbed head of bone or stone. The spear and arrow points were smeared with poison, made from a certain plant known only to a few persons (shamans?). The warrior carried three or four quivers full of arrows. The war club was of wood, tapering at the end. It was equipped with sharp spikes, formed by the ends of the branches, sharpened and hardened in the fire, or made of inserted pieces of bone. The men carried shields [146] made of a large goat skin, dried and stretched on a wooden rim. It had two handles or slings, one for the arm, the other for the hand. Galushia was not certain of the shape and did not know if the shield was painted. After some hesitation, he said that slings and throwing stones were not used.

The war apron has already been described. The faces of the warriors were painted black and red. The wooden war canoes, with the prow carved in the shape of an Eagle or a Raven head, have also been described, and mention has been made of the sealskin war canoe.

Most of the Eyak fights were with the Eskimo, who used to steal Eyak women when they were out berrying. Wars, as already stated, were decided upon by a general meeting. The war party was led by the chief, or if he were too old, by his son, and the chief could command the enlistment of unwilling warriors. Before their departure the warriors would sing war songs. On the evening before a battle no one was allowed to eat. (This taboo applied only to the fighters?) All battles were surprise attacks made during the night or early morning when the enemy were asleep, and were followed by a speedy retreat. The war cry was "'u•'u•u•!" No scalps or heads were taken. The bodies of the enemy were left where they fell, and the Eyak did not pursue those who ran away. Galushia knew nothing about purification or special observances for a man who had killed an enemy. It was believed that their shamans could protect the killers from enemy ghosts. There were no special honors, or coups, awarded for brave deeds, and a man could not become a chief through prowess in war.

If the war party had not lost any of its members, the warriors would sing joyful sungs when they returned. There [147] were no ceremonies of victory. Galushia did not know of the (Tlingit) custom of setting up the paddles at the places of those who had died as a method of announcing their death. If the party had lost any of its members, there was a mourning dance in the potlatch house which lasted several days and in which everyone took part. The warriors wore leathers stuck into a string tied around their heads. Everyone stood in a circle, and the dance consisted of motions of the body, not of the feet, and was accompanied by wailing. At intervals the chief would make an encouraging speech. No one could eat during the ceremony.

Galushia knew of no taboos observed by women in war time.

Wars were generally quite short and were usually not concluded by any peace ceremony, because the people did not trust each other enough to make an agreement. The last fight was with the Eskimo at Hawkins Island, where the Eyak fought until nearly all the enemy were killed. (Is this another version of the famous fight at Tauxtvιk between the Eskimo and the "Blackfish" — more properly "Killerwhale" — Stikine Tlingit?) Makari, our Eskimo informant, emphatically denied that the Eyak had ever fought with his people, so emphatically as to convince us that there had not only been such fights, but that the Eyak had been the victors. There still seems to be some ill-feeling between the two tribes, at least among the older people, for Chief Joe would not talk about fights with the Eskimo while his Eskimo wife was present, though he had previously mentioncd them in private (1930).

The training of warriors will be discussed under *Training of Boys*. Wars are mentioned in *Tale*s 25 and 26, and in incidents 11, 14, 19, and 24 of the Raven cycle. [148]

Fear of war is stressed in *Tale* 9. The fort as a place of refuge in time of war has already been discussed under *Houses*.

Historical Traditions and Relations with other Tribes

Galushia told us that the Eyak once lived east of Yakataga. The territory about Alaganik and Cordova was then Eskimo. (This statement is perhaps supported by the localizations of landmarks made by Raven near Katalla, see incident 2; though the story may have come to the Eyak from the nearest Tlingit with the localizations already fixed.) Galushia also said that the oldest Eyak village was Alaganik, while Makari said that the Eyak originally lived on Mountain Slough. Later the Eyak captured the territory about Eyak River and Eyak Lake. A fight with the Eskimo took place at glacatł, below Eyak River. An Eskimo scout was sitting in a tree, disguised as a bald eagle. The Eyak did not investigate because "they were not particularly interested in eagles." They were attacked by the Eskimo, but were successful. In this fight, one man (Eskimo?), when pursued by enemies, made his escape by climbing to the top of the high rock. It should be remembered that our Eskimo informant, Makari, vehemently denied this story in particular.

The Eskimo used to steal Eyak women when they were out picking berries and this caused wars. There is a story about an Eyak woman who was captured by Eskimo, but we did not learn the details. In historic times a woman and her daughter were murdered at Eyak Lake by the Eskimo. The bodies were found north of Cordova. The Eyak went to an Eskimo village on Hawkins Island, and induced the Russian trader to call all the Eskimo together. [149]

At first one man refused to come. Later he appeared wearing the squirrel skin coat of the dead woman. The trader whipped him.

We have already mentioned the fight on Hawkins Island between the Eyak and the Eskimo. Several white people also told us garbled versions of such a fight. It seems to be connected with, or confused with, the massacre of the Blackfish Tlingit by the Eskimo at Tauxtvɪk.

All the slaves of the Eyak were Eskimo. The Eyak say they did not trade with the Eskimo because they "had no use for them." They did not adopt Eskimo into the tribe. They are contemptuous of the Eskimo, even today, because the latter lack moiety exogamy. Though several Eyak men have recently taken Eskimo wives, Galushia is not certain if such marriage took place in former times. Johnny Stevens says the Eyak learned the sweat bath from the Eskimo in pre-Russian days. From what ABERCROMBIE reported, this acquisition may have been even more recent.

The Eyak sometimes, but not often, fought the Tlingit. The implication is that this was before the adoption of the Tlingit Wolf and Bark House People into the tribe. The Tlingit used to cut off the heads of their slain enemies to get the earrings. The Eyak used to marry Tlingit women, and these women were always (frequently?) stolen, but always from the proper moiety. The Eyak considered themselves more closely related to the Tlingit than to the Eskimo, because of the moiety organization of the former. They used to trade with the Tlingit — but only in historic times. Galushia thought, because formerly they would have had nothing worth trading. (Galushia has certainly underestimated the amount of prehistoric trading.) The Eyak would meet them, either in their own villages or at Katalla. [150]

They had to secure the permission of the (Tlingit?) chief by means of gifts before trading could begin. Trade was usually carried on in the summer. The Eyak even went as far as Yakutat in their wooden canoes, using the seven-mile portage between Copper River and another river. The Tlingit and the Eyak used to invite each other to potlatches. The Eagle House at Katalla was built by Galushia's Tlingit uncle to accomodate the visiting Eyak Eagles.

The Eyak also traded with the Atna from up the Copper River. The latter were thought to be "all right," but they seldom came down the river and never in large numbers. The Eyak were afraid to go to their country. Mrs. Gus Nelson said that the Eyak used to buy sinew thread from the Chitina Indians (lower Copper River), and that only the latter used to make depilated skins. Galushia thought this trade was carried on only in historic times. The Copper River shamans were supposed to be more powerful than Eyak shamans.

Colonel ABERCROMBIE believes that most of the trade between the interior and Nuchek was modern. Nicolai, the chief at Taral, had learned that the Russians wanted copper for the bolts of the ships that they were building. He started the copper traffic, sending the copper down with his second in command. (We are certain, however, that there was native trade in copper in pre-Russian days, though the Russian demand must have been a great stimulus). The route taken was originally via the Keystone Canyon of the Lowe River to Valdez, and then across the Sound to Nuchek. ABERCROMBIE found a deep and well-worn trail up the canyon and across to Tiekel in the Copper River valley. He also found a shell heap at the mouth of the Lowe River near Valdez, which he thinks represents [151] an Eskimo village founded because of the copper traffic. After the measles epidemic of 1868 this route was abandoned, due to superstitious fears, as ABERCROMBIE suggests, or perhaps due to a quarrel with the Eskimo at Ellamar.[1] In any case, the Atna then began to come down the Copper River to Alaganik in mooseskin boats; (they may have used this route in the old days also). ABERCROMBIE believes that Alaganik was founded

---

[1] DE LAGUNA 1934, 118.

about this time, because of the copper traffic. The two houses which he saw in 1884 were new. (However, from what the natives told us, Alaganik must be much older). The Copper River natives never went to Nuchck (see, however, Eskimo testimony to the contrary[1]) but paid a commission to the Eyak for delivering their copper to the trading post and bringing back trade goods in exchange. The interior natives also bartered ground squirrel parkas, mink, sable (marten), muskrat, and other light furs. They were comparatively wealthy and possessed tea, beads, and some china dishes at the time of ABERCROMBIE'S first visit in 1884. The Eyak had little or no trade goods, according to ABERCROMBIE, but we have already suggested that he may have underestimated the amount of imported articles among them. From what he said about the making of native copper bullets at Taral, we can assume that the Atna had guns.

There is no doubt, however, that the three tribes regarded each other with mutual distrust in 1884. The Eskimo who [152] brought ABERCROMBIE Alaganik stayed only long enough to unload the expedition's equipment. They did not stray more than thirty feet from their umiak. The Eyak, on the other hand, were afraid to venture into Eskimo territory after sea-otter (confirmed by the natives), and ABERCROMBIE could not induce them to ascend the Copper River above the glaciers. This was partly because of their justified and superstitious fears of the river and the ice, and partly because of their fear of the Copper River Indians. When the latter visited them at Alaganik, it was customary for the leader of the party to be invited to sleep in the potlatch house, while his men slept outside. By this trick of hospitality, the Eyak not only divided up the party but held the leader as a sort of hostage.

The Eyak could not understand Eskimo, the Atna dialect of Athapaskan, or Tlingit, though a few Tlingit words were similar to theirs. Galushia had heard that somewhere in the interior of Alaska, towards the Arctic Circle, there is a tribe that speaks Eyak. Some of the tales which we collected are specifically described as Copper River or Tlingit stories. Annie Nelson's father used to sing Atna and Tlingit songs.

Names

There were personal names, but no surnames indicating membership in the family or moiety, though the personal names are said to have been peculiar to each moiety. (However, see below, naming after the mother's father). There was no taboo against telling one's own name or that of another, though it was impolite to address a person by his name. If the person addressed was a relative, the relationship term was used; if a member of the same moiety as the speaker, a term meaning "fellow-clansman" was [153] employed; if a member of the opposite moiety the word of address was "a^nha^n," "hey!"

The child was named soon after birth by the mother, or by the maternal grandparents (?), after a dead relative of the mother of the same sex as the child. The new-born baby was supposed to be this deceased relative, revived by the Sun. Babies were sometimes born with marks on their bodies like those of the deceased. Johnny Stevens cited as a case in point several members of the same family who were born with their fingers grown together. "Lameness" is

---

[1] Cf. also PETROFF 1893, p. 66: "In addition to their other sources of wealth the Ugalentz people [Eyak] formerly enjoyed the position of middlemen between the Athapascan natives of the Upper Copper River and the traders on the coast. With the advent of the American pioneers among them this became impossible, and the Atnatena, or Atnas, now pay periodic visits to the seashore, doing their own trading at the numerous fur and fishing stations".

supposed to be inherited in Old Man Dude's family. However, in Dude's case the disability is not congenital; his fingers were shot away by a gun. Children were supposed to resemble the person for whom they were named. Whether the name was given because of the supposed similarity, or whether the naming itself insured the reincarnation of the particular relative responsible for the inherited traits recognized in the child was never stated, and it seems unlikely that this problem was ever raised by the Eyak.

The child was to them actual reincarnation of the namesake. There were never two living persons with the same name.

According to Annie Nelson, the order of preference in the choice of names for a boy was: brother, maternal uncle, father (!), and parallel cousin on the mother's side. (It is obvious that there must be an error here. A child could never be named after his own father; probably the mother's father must be meant, unless possibly Annie is referring to the custom of adopting one's own son in order to secure an heir. This is sometimes resorted to by the Northwest Coast tribes, but with so little real property to be inherited, and as far as we could ascertain no crests and privileges belonging to clans and subclans, the Eyak [154] could hardly have had any reason for such adoption.) An examination of the genealogical table (*Appendix* I) shows that among the women there are 3 who were named for the mother's sister, 1 for the mother's mother, and 1 for the mother's sister's daughter. In several cases these names have been given in succession to a group of sisters, the older girl dying in infancy before the next sister was born. It is impossible to get accurate information on the number of cases in which the girl was named for a dead sister. Among the men there are an indefinite number of cases in which the same name has been given to a succession of brothers. There are also 2 cases of naming after the mother's brother, and 1 after the mother's father. Thus Johnny MacInlyre was teased for being his own grandfather. In this case, the name passed from one moiety to the other. Minnie Stevens' son, Mike Duval, has a Tlingit name, derived from his mother's father's brother's wife's brother-in-law. Actually we suspect that this individual was Mike's mother's mother's brother. These rules for naming have not been applied to European names. In several cases the native name has been inherited but not the European name, but Malta Stevens has derived both her Christian and native name from her dead sister, and her brother Pete was also given both the names of his dead brother. In these cases, however, we were not told the European names (if there were any) of the relatives in the preceding generation for whom these children were named. Because of the common practice of giving the same name to a series of children in the same family, because of the high rate of infant mortality, and because of the taboo against mentioning the dead, it was almost impossible for our informants to tell us how many children had been born to certain couples. Thus, it is seen [155] that a name was not abandoned because several children that held it had died, and there was moreover no special clothing or protective amulet worn by a child whose older namesakes had died.

Several children of Eyak fathers but of foreign mothers were given Eyak names, just as if their mothers had belonged to the tribe. These children seemed to have been given a certain standing in the tribe, being considered as members of the opposite moiety from that of their father. The genealogical table gives us only two cases of such Eyak names for children born out of the tribe. Pauline, the daughter of Chief Charlie (Raven) and an Eskimo woman, has the same native name as the daughter of Pauline's mother's second husband's first wife (Eagle). The relationship might be described as that of "parallel cousins-in-law." if indeed fuller information would not show them to be actually parallel cousins. Johnny MacIntyre's son by an Eskimo woman is named for his father's step-father, Chief Joe. Chief Joe was a Raven, but it was not

Chief Joe's own name which was given to the boy, who is also technically a Raven, but Chief Joe's potlatch name, *stiwvn*. The potlatch name, as we shall see, is a name belonging to the opposite moiety from that of the man who bears it temporarily. The original *stiwvn* n in this case must have been an Eagle, since Chief Joe was a Raven, and it was incorrect for the name to have been given to a boy who is technically a Raven, Galushia could not understand how this could have happened, and it can only be explained by a breaking down of the old system. (Perhaps the name was distinguished in some way, and it was thought better to preserve it even though it passed into the wrong moiety). In the case of another child born outside the tribe, the rules of inheritance have been applied [156] to the Christian name, though we are unable to say what significance this may have, especially since the native names of the individuals were not given. Thus, Molly, Chief Joe's daughter by an Eskimo wife, has the same name as her dead half-sister, Molly, by Joe's first wife, an Eyak.

The name of a dead person who had not yet been reincarnated was never mentioned except at the potlatch. If the deceased were named by mistake, a present had to be given to the surviving relatives. It is partly because of this rule that so little information could be obtained about dead children. In the potlatch ceremonies persons were addressed by their potlatch name. This was the name of a member of the opposite moiety who had not yet been reborn in a namesake. When the namesake was born, the potlatch name was changed, Galushia did not know whether a child would be named for a dead person before that dead person had been honored in a potlatch through his potlatch namesake. Nor did we obtain explicit information as to how the potlatch name was chosen, except that it was given by relatives of the deceased. Chief Joe's potlatch name has already been mentioned. We do not know who the original stiwvn was, or what new name Chief Joe would have had if he had lived after Johnny MacIntyre's son was born. Scar Stevens' potlatch name was *cqəx*, after his mother's father. We did not learn any other potlatch names. Since potlatches are no longer given, this aspect of Eyak naming has become obsolete.

Puberty and Menstruation

At puberty the girl was secluded in a special hut for a month (Galushia), for twelve months (Johnny Stevens), in a special room of the big dwelling house for six months (Mrs. Gus Nelson). There she learned how to sew and [157] make baskets, which she could do better alone than with the family. Any old woman, her own mother or some one else, might teach her (Johnny Stevens). The adolescent girl was not supposed to drink water for a week (Galushia). This must mean that she could not drink it in an ordinary way, or that she was given soup instead. Gus Nelson said that the girl sucked water through a swan's bone, used special dishes of her own, and used a bone scratcher if she wanted to scratch her head, because her hair would fall out if she touched it with her hand. There seems to have been no taboo against washing. She had to stay inside, for if she walked about outdoors it would cause rain and bad weather. There was no special ceremony to mark the end of her seclusion. During the period immediately following her return to the household, the girl was not supposed to stay out of doors for long at a time, lest she get sore eyes. When she went out she had to keep her head covered, probably as a similar precaution. These same rules applied to slave girls.

JACOBSEN reports: "As among many primitive peoples, the beginning of a girl's maturity is celebrated with a special ceremony and a feast. On this occasion the young girl is separated from the other members of the family and is confined to a small room in her parent's house.

Here she must remain for thirty days, and during this time obtains only scanty nourishment from some female relative. When she lies down she must turn her head towards the south. At the end of the seclusion she can live in the house as before, and receives a new dress and other festive presents from her father or her nearest relative. And also when she marries, which usually occurs soon after this period, she, as well as her parents, receives presents."[1] [158]

Menstruating women had to stay in a special hut for five days and purified themselves with a cold bath before returning home (Johnny Stevens). This report of the seclusion of menstruating women was not supported by Galushia or Mrs. Gus Nelson. Thus the former said that when a hunter returned with game and suspected that one of the women in the house was menstruating, he would leave it outside and come in to whisper to his wife. She would tell the menstruating woman to leave while the man carried in the meat. This was kept covered up, because menstruating women were not supposed to see, touch, or eat fresh meat. (That the hunter whispered to his wife might indicate either that menstruation was not a polite topic of conversation. or that the woman was not supposed even to hear conversation about fresh meat. The former is probably the correct explanation.) A menstruating woman could eat only dried meat. We do not know if this rule applied to fresh fish, although it certainly did to the first salmon. The same taboos applied to slave women. A menstruating woman had to eat out -of her own dishes, though her food was cooked in the family pot. There is no specific mention of a taboo against the menstruating woman cooking for others, though we should imagine that such a taboo existed. Johnny Stevens later summarized his information to the effect that a menstruating woman had to have a separate bed or separate tent, separate food and water, or her family would become poor. In *Tale* 5 it is stated that it is bad luck for a hunter to stay in the house when a menstruating woman entered.

Women's taboos which apply to hunting will be discussed under *Magic*. [159]

Childbirth

A pregnant woman was not supposed to eat berries, because they would cause boils on the child. If she ate fresh liver or kidney the boy would be heavy and slow. (We do not know whether this taboo applied to dried kidneys; it will be remembered that liver was never dried.) Fish roc was forbidden, though we did not learn the reason. If the expectant mother ate fresh herring or whitefish, the skin of the child would fall off. She was supposed to move about for exercise, but not to wander far from the house. During the last weeks or so of pregnancy she must not cross or follow a hunter's trail.

The birth took place in the sleeping room of the house. All the men were sent outside, for if a man remained indoors the birth would be difficult. The mother was assisted by all the women and female slaves of the household. There were no special midwives. The mother wore her inner or summer dress, lay on her back(?), and used a strap about her body to force the child down, but no strap was fastened to the wall for her to pull against. To make the birth easy, the mother's hair was unbraided. There is no information about the untying of knots or of a taboo against crossing the fingers, though it was supposed to make the birth difficult if anyone sat in the house with crossed legs. We know nothing about the duration of labor. If the birth were painfully delayed, a shaman might he called, but he would not enter the house. Galushia says that he has never heard of a shaman being of any help.

---

[1] JACOBSEN 1884, 389.

The new-born child was washed and placed in a basket that had been prepared in advance. The umbilical cord was cut with a knife. The cord was dried and tied around the child's neck as an amulet. Galushia has kept his son's [160] cord in a bag hanging on the wall of the house. The child was supposed lo wear the cord until a year before he was old enough to hunt, or in the girl's case, until a year before puberty. Then the cord was buried in the ground. The afterbirth and bloody garments were burned by the mother as soon as her confinement was over. To neglect this would cause sickness to her and bad weather.

The woman was confined, lying down, for ten days. During that time the husband was not allowed to hunt. He could reenter the house immediately after the birth, but was not allowed to sleep with his wife (or with other wives?) until the end of her confinement. We have no information about the length of time before intercourse was actually resumed. At the end of the ten-day period, both father and mother took a bath in the water in which the skin of devilclub (*Fatsia horrida*) had been boiled.

There was no method of foretelling the sex of the child. No special taboos applied to the birth of twins, and no special dress or ornaments were worn by twins. Twins were apparently no luckier or unluckier than ordinary children.

There was no magic to make the child strong. The nursing mother drank fish and porcupine soup to get milk. The child was nursed for two or three years, whenever it cried, and it was also given a piece of seal fat on the end of a stick to suck (see *Tale* 24). This was its only food if the mother died. Foster mothers or wet nurses were not found for motherless babies, because it was feared that the nurse might steal the child.

Intentional abortion caused bad weather. It is not known what methods were used, and the practice was probably not common. Some women are said to have chewed a certain root to prevent conception. A woman recently bragged [161] of her ability to avoid pregnancy, but the others teased her: "You are just like a man!" On the whole, children were welcome and the position of the childless wife was far from enviable. We certainly heard of no case where a child was not loved by its parents, and Annie Nelson confided to us that when her first son was born she thought it the most wonderful thing that had ever happened.

We have no information about the size of the family in former times, nor of the relative number of births as compared to those of today, Galushia himself was one of a family of nine children. The largest number of births of which we have record is that of Gus and Mary Nelson who had fifteen children (counting miscarriages) of whom only three arc alive today. Disease, poverty, and drunken neglect are largely responsible for the high death rate among children today.

Unfortunately we know nothing about practices and taboos relative to miscarriages, though there must have been some type of regulation. Had weather was caused by the concealment and failure to bury the body of an illegitimate child (*Tale* 28). Galushia said that infanticide was never practiced, but JACOBSEN makes the following statement: "The population keep themselves free from deformed persons in a peculiar way, since deformed babies [*Missgeburten*] are openly burned immediately after birth; and the same thing happens every time to the afterbirth. These rules are rigidly obeyed, and their infraction is punished with death."[1] [162]

---

[1] JAKOBSEN 1884, 393.

Training of Boys

Children were taught by the old people in the household, according to Johnny Stevens. Galushia said that most of the boy's instruction was undertaken by the father, though he added as an afterthought that it was the maternal uncle who made the boy plunge in cold water every morning, while it was the father who taught him how to hunt. Apparently the vigorous part of a boy's education began at puberty. Then he was supposed to get up early in the morning (it was very bad for a man to lie in bed after the girls had risen. *Tale* 5) and take a bath in cold water. He must avoid menstruating women. Before the age of ten he was not affected by the taboo against eating or drinking from the same vessel as a menstruating woman. Boys never went into the woods to hunt alone or to seek visions because of the danger from wild animals and the Eskimo. The vision-quest of the shamanistic novice was an exception, and seems to have begun at an early age.

Sometimes a young man was specially trained as a warrior. He would lake a cold bath every morning, even when there was ice on the wafer, in order to become strong and brave. He was afterwards whipped on the upper part of the body with alder branches (with spruce boughs, according to Johnny Stevens). He was trained to carry heavy loads, and would try to pull dead branches from trees. Boys were also taught to run as fast as the animals (Johnny Stevens). A boy in training was not allowed to drink tea. If a man had been killed by the Eskimo, his relatives would train him to be a warrior. The training of warriors is described in *Tale* 25. We do not know how much of the rigorous discipline applied only to warriors and how much to all youths. [163]

In *Tale* 11 a boy was trained to dive. He was wrapped in a loon skin as soon as he was horn, and was fed on seal meat and loon meat, so that he would be able to hold his breath and stay under water for a long time like these animals.

Death and Burial

When a person died, the body was kept in the house for four days. (In *Tale* 28, the dwarfs kept the body of the man who had been killed by the mouse-"bear" in front of the house for eight days, but this was not the correct Eyak custom). The body was kept in the main room, at the "head of the house," leaning up against the wall of the sleeping room, the knees drawn up in the customary sitting or squalling position, the arms folded across the breast, or the hands placed on the breast. The limbs were held in position by cords, and the jaw was tied shut. The eyes were closed, otherwise the deceased might look at his next of kin and make him die. The corpse was dressed in his best clothes and was completely covered with his best blanket. The face was not painted and no mask was worn.

The Eyak do not like to touch a dead person, but it was the duty of the members of the opposite moiety to dress the dead, since his own relatives dared (?) not touch him. Dressing the corpse was undertaken by a group of four, six, or eight persons. Since they would receive the greatest number of gifts at the death potlatch, the members of the opposite moiety would hurry to the dead person's house in order to perform this service and receive the reward. The dead person was washed before being dressed, but Galushia believes this was a Russian custom. Beside (or before, according to Mrs. Gus Nelson), the body was piled all his belongings. [164]

During the four days of the wake there were always people watching beside the dead. The relatives painted their faces as a sign of mourning, and may also have done something to their hair(?). It was their duty to cook for the members of the opposite moiety who watched beside the dead, and who endeavored to prevent the relatives and the widow or widower from feeling sad. The brother of the dead man fed these guests. The visitors would joke. tell stories, sing and dance. The relatives would feel so sad that they would not care to eat. On the second day the visitors would notice this and offer them food, which they had to accept. The relatives would not work or play as long as the corpse remained in the house, but were supposed to be quiet. The men, however, would continue to take their cold baths in the morning. There were no special observances required of the widow, though she was not supposed to join her moiety in their fun. Her sister was free do so. (Probably the same applied to the widower.)

The dead were buried or burned, according to their own wishes or that of their relatives. (We did not learn whether there was any method of divination to discover the wishes of the deceased after death.) Cremation was abandoned after the Russians came. The corpse was never dried or mummified. A group of four, six, or eight persons to act as undertakers were chosen from the opposite moiety by the widow or the dead person's relatives. People hoped to be chosen because they would receive special gifts at the potlatch. Usually one group carried the body to the grave or pyre, usually the same group that had washed and dressed it, while a second group dug the grave or prepared the pyre. Galushia knew nothing about wearing gloves when handling the dead; none are worn now. Boards were [165] removed from the wall of the house so that the corpse could be carried out through a special opening. If it were removed through the door, the relatives would soon die. We do not know how the corpse was transported. The dead were interred squatting, just as they had sat in the house, placed to face the setting sun. Later Galushia said that they were buried on the back, with the arms and legs flexed, and the head to the cast. All the belongings to which the dead person had been particularly attached were placed, unbroken, in the grave with him. Nothing was left on top of the grave, because it was feared that a witch might steal them and use them to harm the relatives. Even now the Eyak have the same fear. Thus, when one of Gus Nelson's sons died, he had his father sink his motor boat. Food and water were placed on the grave, but only at the time of burial. Only witches (see below) ever went to the graveyard except at a funeral. If the corpse were cremated, the dead man's possessions were saved for burning at the death potlatch. The ashes of the dead were put into grave houses.

Of the deceased's possessions, only those of which he had been particularly fond were buried with him or burned at the potlatch. Other objects were saved as mementoes, to be exhibited at the potlatch. These keepsakes were never used, and were kept hidden from the sight of the relatives, lest the latter should feel sad. We may assume, therefore, that they were kept by members of the opposite moiety. Other belongings of the deceased were given away at the potlatch or might be traded off to members of the opposite moiety (see *The Potlatch*).

Galushia believes that the observances described above were the same regardless of the age or sex or the deceased, because all human beings were considered equal. When [166] a woman died, the members of the opposite moiety would cut off a little of her hair to save as a keepsake. After her relatives had recovered from the first violence of their grief, the hair was given to them. The co-wife of a woman who died had to return to her own people for two or three months, and her children would accompany her. An infant was never killed if the mother died.

When a chief's son or daughter died, a slave was killed by a spear thrust. The slave's body was cremated, hut on a separate pyre, and the ashes were not saved. Dogs were never killed at a funeral.

The body of a dead slave was removed from the house as soon as possible, probably through a hole in the wall. The body was always cremated, and other slaves doubtless took charge of the funeral. There may have been a place where the ashes of slaves were kept, but Galushia thinks this unlikely. They were certainly not preserved in a grave box.

The bodies of witches were always burned.

The graveyards at Alaganik and Eyak have been described already (see *Village Sites*). It will he remembered that the grave boxes were like small houses set on posts, or resting on the ground. In 1880 PETROFF reported: "The burial-places of the Ougalakhmute to-day exhibit the house-like sepultures of the Thlinget, but as yet without the totem."[1] Now either this statement was inaccurate at the time, or the practice of totemic markings was adopted within the next four years. It will be remembered that we observed a grave post at Alaganik in 1930, which was carved to represent a wolf (Plate 8,1), and it had certainly been there for many years. Furthermore when ABERCROMBIE [167] visited the same village in 1884 he was invited to a dance, "and I agreed to be at the casina when the sun reached the top of the totem pole standing in the center of the graveyard, which was located at the top of a knoll about 100 feet high and below the main village."[2]

Fig. 15. Picket fence at graveyard, as described by ABERCROMBIE.

In conversation ABERCROMBIE adds the following description of the graveyard at Alaganik. The entire plot, which was rectangular, was surrounded by a low picket fence, 2½ or 3 feet high. There was no gate, because it was easy to step over the fence. ABERCROMBIE hazards the suggestion that the fence was primarily intended to confine the ghosts. Each individual grave was also enclosed in its own fence. These fences were made of upright posts, set close together, and were pegged to two horizontal poles, one on the ground, the other near the top (Figure 15).At the south end of the graveyard towards the river was the large totem pole which seemed to belong to the whole graveyard. It was made of a cedar log, about 18 inches (45 cm.) in diameter, and 10 or 15 feet (3 or 4.5 m.) high. The front was carved with animal figures from top to bottom, though the back was plain. The top of the pole was cut to represent a raven with outspread wings. The figure was not very large, since it was no bigger than the diameter of the log, and the wings were not made of separate pieces. The raven was black; the other figures below it were stained black and rod. ABERCROMBIE could not identify them. Some of the individual graves were marked by a carved post at [168] the end of the grave house, inside the fence. These represented only an animal's head and were so crudely made that ABERCROMBIE could not recognize the animals intended. The large post was so much better carved that he supposed it to be the work of a Tlingit. Every grave had a small box-like house over it (Figure 16). These rested on the ground and were not set on posts as at Eyak (compare with the grave of the Wolf chief we saw at Alaganik). These houses were made of horizontally set planks, with a

---

[1] PETROFF 1884, 146.
[2] ABERCROMBIE 1900, 385.

gable roof, the ends of the gable being left open. Personal belongings were hung on the inside of the individual grave fences (comp are this with the statement of the natives that no grave goods were left above ground). There was no property hung on the fence surrounding the whole graveyard.

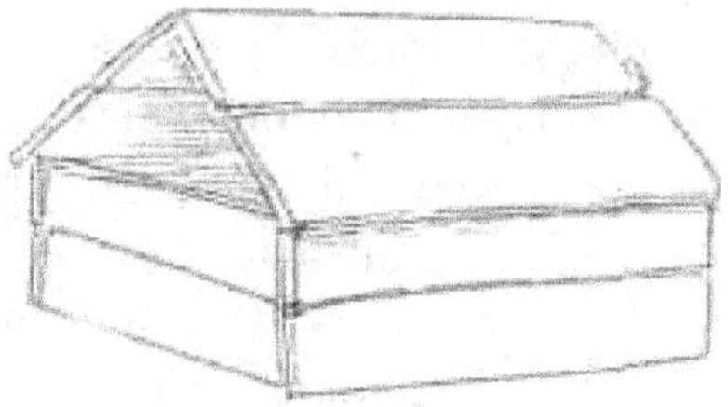

Fig. 16. Grave house, as described by ABERCROMBIE

When Old Man Dude's wife died in 1930, he buried her and built a little house over the grave (Plate 6, 2). It is made of ordinary lumber, with a gable roof, and a little window at one side. A cross is nailed to one end. Inside is a table. At the end opposite the cross is a small door, just about large enough to admit the arm. The house was freshly painted with light bluish green paint when we saw it in 1933. We were afraid to make too close an examination of it, because Old Man Dude was said to be somewhat unbalanced as a result of his wife's death (see Stories about Shamans). [169]

The Potlatch

Public ceremonies were held in the potlatch house. These seem to have been of four kinds: to dedicate a new house, to mourn those slain in battle, to commemorate a death, and to honor visitors. The last type of ceremony is mentioned by ABERCROMBIE, but not by our native informants. The term "potlatch" as used by the natives means feasting and distribution of gifts; dancing and singing were the usual accompaniments but did not in themselves constitute a potlatch. The mourning ceremony for dead warriors, already described under War, was not a potlatch because there was no feast and no distribution of gifts. The death potlatch was the most common ceremony held in the potlatch house and will therefore be described first.

Perhaps several months, or even two or three years after a death, the relatives would hold a potlatch for the dead person. The lapse of time depended on how long it took them to accumulate the necessary wealth. Such a ceremony was held only for a person who had been liked. All the members of the deceased's moiety, even those living in other villages, were invited to contribute. Such help was not obligatory, but it was expected and considered proper. The potlatch was held in summer, when people could assemble, and could be given either at Alaganik or Eyak. The potlatch house was specially decorated (how?). The guests were the members of the opposite moiety, but we do not know if all were invited. (Perhaps the number of invitations depended on the wealth of the hosts?). The guests sat in one or two rows along the walls. If there were not room to accommodate the children, they had to climb on the roof and look down through the smokehole. The festivities lasted for several days, the exact number not [170] being fixed. After the actual distribution of gifts, the guests would remain for several days and there would he dances and games. All this time the guests were fed by the hosts. For Galushia, only the feasting and distributing of gifts could properly be called the potlatch, and the events which took place on the succeeding days were of a much less solemn nature.

The potlatch ceremonies would begin in the morning, and after an interval of rest from noon until evening, would continue into the night. The ceremony was initiated by the chief(?) of the hosts who made a speech, explaining the reason for the potlatch. "So-and-so is dead," he would say. "We are giving this for him." The leader of the guests answered in a speech. The relatives of the dead man sang first. The guests would join in and continue singing while the relatives wept. Sometimes the hosts would sing the dead man's own song. This was the only occasion on which a dead person's song was sung. While singing, they would mention the name of the deceased, and weep. Even though the tears were streaming down their faces, they would continue singing. They would cry for a long time, and the guests would try to cheer them up. Then the guests in turn would attempt to sing the dead man's song, and the one who sang it best (most accurately) would receive most of the dead person's things.

A fire was burning in the middle of the potlatch house, and the chief of the deceased's moiety would put food into it for the dead person. This was done after two incomplete motions towards the fire. The chief would mention the dead man's name and ?? say "acta'" "for him." If the food was in a plate, the plate was put into the fire also, although a guest might claim the plate by asking for it. The dead man's [171] belongings, which had been saved by the relatives, would be put into the fire by the chief, one at a time. If a member of the opposite moiety wanted one of these articles, he could ask for it, naming the object and adding *sıtɬqatɬ* "I want it." The chief would take the object from the fire and hand it to him. The recipient would give the relatives something useful in exchange. From Galushia's remarks we gather that though such trading was customary, the relatives were considered greedy (if they permitted too much of it), since they and not the dead person benefitted by the exchange-The recipient of the dead man's article had to promise to take good care of it and not to misuse it. If the deceased had been particularly attached to the object, it would not be traded off but would be burned. The goods obtained in exchange were kept by the deceased's brothers, especially the oldest brother. Galushia did not think the son received anything. (Presumably if the deceased were a woman, her sisters and probably her daughters kept the traded goods.)

Food was served to the guests in order of rank. (Just what does this reference to rank imply, since we were told that there was no class of nobles?). The chief of the deceased's moiety "acted as a waiter." When the food was placed in front of the person for whom it was intended he was addressed by his potlatch name. As already explained, this was the name of a dead person belonging to the hosts' moiety who had not yet been reborn in a namesake. The recipient of the food, in accepting it, would answer: "This food is not for me, but for my dead relative, So-and-so," naming a deceased member of his own moiety who had not yet been reincarnated. Thus at a potlatch each guest was felt to be eating food for two dead persons.

Gifts of clothing and other objects were made in the [172] same way. The hosts would have a big pile of skins in front of them. Each item was taken up in turn and passed slowly down the line, while the guests sang. When the garment was placed in front of the intended recipient, he was addressed by his potlatch name and he would answer that he received the gift, not for himself, but for some dead relative. The chief of the guest clan, those who had dressed the corpse, and those who had buried or burned it received the greatest number of gifts. These presents were guns, blankets, food, furs, etc. Special gifts were also given to the man who had been able to sing the dead person's song the most accurately. After receiving these gifts, the guests danced and sang their own songs.

These ceremonies belong to the potlatch proper. We are not sure that the order indicated is correct, since the information was never given by Galushia in the form of a complete, connected narrative, but had to be pieced together from statements made at various times.

During the regular potlatch ceremonies the hosts would make a noise like their clan animal (Eagle, Raven, or Wolf — we do not know if the Bark House People had a special cry), and the guests would ask: "What do the Eagles want?" or "What does the Eagle want?" for example. The hosts would reply: "It wants to see So-and-so dance (or sing)." The person named would perform alone and would be given a special reward when the gifts were distributed.

Special costumes were worn at the potlatch. The moiety chiefs wore headdresses of skins, on which were sewn shell beads in patterns representing the moiety bird. A man from each moiety wore a mask representing the moiety bird. All the participants of both sexes had their faces painted with patterns peculiar to their moiety. The [173] men wore headbands, and may have sprinkled eagle down on their hair. A relative (the nearest of kin?) wore the dead person's best clothes and robe. (We were already told that the deceased was buried in his best clothes; the garments worn at the potlatch may have been an ordinary suit, or the corpse may have been dressed in ordinary clothes with the best robe laid over it only for the period of the wake.)

On the days following the potlatch proper, the people came in animal masquerade and acted and danced like animals. There was a prize for the man who best imitated the animal he was dressed to represent. Thus the Wolf People dressed and acted like wolves (sometimes or always?). Other animals represented were "dogs, ducks, or any kind of animal." Comic costumes were also worn, and the dances were made as funny as possible. Sometimes all the members of one moiety would go outside and file in again, making funny faces to make the others laugh. (Was this a competition, each side trying to force the others to laugh, while they themselves kept straight faces?) A prize was given for the best dance.

At or near the end of the ceremonies a bolt of calico would be thrown to the guests and they would light to secure pieces of it. When the guests left they made speeches of thanks and of regret at parting, but there were no set farewell ceremonies. The guests would take home with them baskets or sacks filled with food left over from the feasting.

When a potlatch house was built, a feast was given for a house-warming. At the last ceremony of this kind Copper River Indians and Tlingit were invited. The entire moiety that owned the house had to prepare for the occasion (that is, members from other villages were called upon to help?). As at the death potlatch, potlatch names were used when [174] addressing the guests. The guests danced first, then the hosts danced, then the guests again, and so on. Some of the dances were funny. Unfortunately, we have no specific information about these dances, and while we were told that the songs used for dances at the house-warming were different from those used at the death potlatch, we do not know in what way they differed. It seems probable, however, that comic dances and animal masquerades were more featured at the house-warming, while the death potlatch was a much more solemn occasion.

Drums were used to accompany the dances in the potlatch house. They were of the tambourine type, with a wooden rim, usually a strip about 6 inches wide, hut often made simply of a bent branch. The head was of depilated seal skin and measured about 18 inches in diameter. There was a single cross-bar across the back for a handle. There were no square drums, and a shaman's drum was never used at a potlatch. In his written account of the dances seen at Alaganik (quoted in the next section), ABERCROMBIE mentions a tambourine drum. He now suggests that he may have been mistaken, and that he recalls a drum made of a hollow(?) cedar log, about 8 or 10 feet long, on which four men pounded with a stick in each hand. Probably both types of drum were used. In JACOBSEN'S account of shamanistic performances, quoted below, several men in the audience beat with a pair of sticks on a wooden plank, while an older man beat "the big drum."

Rattles were made of a semicircular slab of wood, with a hole cut out for the hand near the straight edge. Around the curved edge were attached pieces of agate. The Eyak did not use rattles of deer hoofs, or dance mittens ornamented with rattling puffin beaks like the Eskimo of Bering [175] Strait. However, the actors or dancers in the performances witnessed by ABERCROMBIE wore bracelets of tanned skin to which were attached claws and whelk shells. The latter had small pebbles or other rattling objects inside. The dancers also wore anklets, but he cannot remember if they rattled.

The whistle used at potlatches was a hollow stick, blown across one end. There were no flutes or whistles of any other type used at potlatches. For slow dances, wooden wands or paddles were carried. These were painted black and red and had feathers tied along their whole length. Dancers often carried two eagle or swan feathers in each hand, or a whole eagle tail. The feathers were fastened together, and were often colored or striped. In his written report, ABERCROMBIE states that the shaman held a wand in his hand, and that the dancers carried feathers and other objects. The wand was actually carried by the shaman's assistant, ABERCROMBIE explains, because Kai's hands were paralyzed. It was a stick of wood, about 2 feet long, to which eider down was attached. It seems to have been used to give the actors their cues.

A complete description of the dances seen by ABERCROMBIE will be given in the next section. It is impossible for us to say to what extent the dress and ornamentation of the various performers and the form of the elaborate show itself were common to festivities held on other occasions. It will be remembered that these dances were held in honor of ABERCROMBIE, for the sole purpose, apparently, of conciliating him. Similar dances and plays may, of course, have been held during the celebrations following a death potlatch or at the dedication of a potlatch house.

Two dance paddles were purchased from Scar Stevens. [176]

They were said to have belonged to his wife's father, who must have been an Eagle. This ownership, however, is inconsistant with the explanation Scar gave of the paddles. He said that the specimen surmounted with the raven's head (Plate 15, 1) was carried into the potlatch house by the leader of the Ravens to announce the coming of his fellow-clansmen. The second paddle with the bear's(?) head (Plate 15, 3) was carried in after it to show that the Ravens were glad to come to the potlatch. We may assume that the paddles were originally the property of some Raven man. Perhaps after his death they were retained by Minnie Steven's father as a keepsake. It will be remembered that keepsakes were preserved by members of the opposite moiety from that of the deceased. We have already mentioned that ABERCROMBIE said these paddles were just like that carried by the peacemaker as his badge of office (see *Moieties and Chiefs*). It is quite possible that they had two functions. In the potlatch they may have been intended to express the peaceful and friendly feelings of one moiety towards the other; in the hands of the peacemaker they may have served to remind the quarreling moieties of their mutual obligations. Which was the primary function it would be impossible to determine without further information.

The paddle with the bear's head (P-UPM, 33-29-3) is 158 cm, long. The handle is roughly circular in section, about 3.3 cm. in diameter. It is 54 cm. long, and the lower 10 cm. of its length has been slightly narrowed for a grip. The blade is 104 cm. long, 8.3 cm. wide, and a little over 1 cm. thick. The tip is carved to represent an animal's head, 12.5 cm. long, 7 cm. wide, and 3 cm. thick. The neck is 4 cm. wide. A broken hacksaw blade is nailed to one side of the paddle. [177]

There are traces of white paint on the surface of the paddle handle and blade. This paint was evidently applied after the various figures had been painted for it does not quite reach the edges of the designs. The edges of the blade are red, and a curved black line on each side separates the blade from the handle. On the blade appear the following symbols. For convenience, those on the side of the hacksaw blade are numbered Al, A 2 and A3; those on the opposite side are BI, B2, B3, B4,and B5, from the handle to the head.

Al: At the base of the blade, below the hacksaw, are two dome-shaped figures, opposite each other, their bases at the edge of the blade. They are outlined in black, and are diagonally cross-hatched in red. Do these represent beaver lodges?

A2: Above the blade is a jumping salmon (or perhaps a killerwhale?) outlined in black, with black tail and fins. The mouth and the representation of the backbone and spines (?) are red.

A3: Above this again is a curious figure, suggestive of an insect. Both the bug and the salmon are facing the upper end of the paddle and are both right-side up when the paddle is held horizontally with the tip to the right. The body of the bug is outlined in black; the six legs. three near the front and three near the rear, are also black. A black line runs longitudinally down the middle of the body. In the space above this line are five round dots, alternately black and red from the head towards the tail. The head is detached from the body. A faint line of white paint, more distinct than that on the surrounding surface, seems to connect the head and the body. The head and the outline of the long and pointed eye are black. The outline of the pupil is red. The spaces above and below the eye are white. [178]
Unlike the paddle with Raven's head, the designs on this paddle are not the same on both sides. The figures on the side opposite the saw have their bases towards the same edge as those on the other side, and arc in consequence right-side up, when the paddle is held horizontally with the tip to the left.

B 1: At the base of the blade is a dome-shaped figure, similar to the pair on the opposite side, but somewhat larger.

B2: Above this are two diagonal lines, the lower black, the upper red. Between them is a trace of another line, too indistinct for the color to be ascertained.

B3: Above these lines is a face, human or anthropomorphic, with large detached cars. The face is round, outlined in black, with short, spikey black hairs. The curved eyebrows, and the oval outline of the eyes are black. The open mouth, in which is represented the tongue (?), the nose, and the two wrinkles at the corners of the mouth which give it a smiling expression, are red. The ears are outlined in black and have a red patch inside them. This face may represent the Sun(?).

B4: Above this again is a bug, almost like that on the opposite side. The legs, however, as well as the line down the center of the body, are red. There are curved red hairs on the hack, and curved red lines run from the middle line to the belly. No trace of white paint can be seen on the head.

B5: Above the bug, are a pair of curving black lines, opposite each other, their ends at the edges of the blade. These lines have slanting red spurs on each side, arranged in pairs. If the smiling face represents the Sun, do these figures represent the Alders of the myth? (Cf. p. 294 ff.).

As already stated, the tip of the paddle is carved to [179] represent an animal's head, probably a bear. Both sides are painted almost exactly alike. The bear on the side with the saw is 32 cm. long, including the head and the painted body on the blade; the bear on the other side is only 26.5 cm. long. Both faces and the edges of the head between them have a background of white paint. The rounded ears are outlined in black; the inside of the ears is slightly cut out and is painted red. The nostrils are outlined in blacks, with red centers. The eyes are also outlined in black but are not of the same shape on both faces. Those on the side with the saw (A), are oval, with downward curving points. On the other side (B), they are circular. Below each of the eyes on the A side, is an arching red line. These lines curve up in the middle towards the eyes, and extend all the way across the head. They are not found on the B side of the head. Do they represent face painting?

On the edges of the head, the mouth is outlined in red. Transverse bars of black, now very indistinct, represent the teeth. A curved black line at the corner of the mouth suggests the lips wrinkled back in a snarl. A pair of short curved lines on each side of the head suggest the eyes or the ears of the two faces as they would be seen in profile.

The body of the two animals is painted on the blades in solid red. Where the paddle is narrowed to represent the neck there is no paint. On each side, is a white strip down the middle of the back, crossed at intervals by red lines, which suggests the backbone. Between these crossing lines, are white areas. The two halves of the bear's body on the side with the saw are outlined in black, but there is no black outline on the other side. The tails, on each side, arc outlined in red. On the saw side, there are three black spots at the base of the tail and three spots on the tail. [180]

The general appearance of the other paddle (C-NM, H 2966) is very similar to the first, though the details are different. In the present stale it is 106 cm. long, but may originally have been slightly longer, the tip being broken off. There is a handle, 66 cm. long, roughly circular in section and about 4 cm. in diameter with a somewhat narrower grip. The blade is 80 cm. long. 6.7 cm. wide and 3 cm.thick, surmounted with a raven's head, 20 by 7.5 cm. Like the proceeding specimen this paddle has been covered with a thin, now partly worn-off coating of white paint. About 52 cm. above the tip of the handle there is a narrow, red ring. A curved red line separates the handle from the blade. On the latter there are the following symbols, which contrary to the pictures on the other paddle are identical (only slightly varying in size) on both sides:

At the base of the blade there appears a dome-shaped "beaver-lodge" (?) design with black outline and red cross' hatching similar to the two figures on the other paddle. Above the "lodge" there are two killerwhales or jumping salmon facing each other. They are also identical in outline and color with the corresponding Figure on the other paddle. On the uppermost part of the blade there is a design, probably intended to represent the frontal view of an animal's face in typical, although somewhat coarse Northwest Coast style: a broad mouth with pointed teeth, a snubbed nose, eyes, and above each eye two curved lines which may be taken to represent the ears. As in the other figures the outlines are black, whereas teeth, outlines of pupils, and nostrils are red.

The raven's head surmounting the blade is separated from the latter by means of a curved line. The beak is solid black with a red mouth, the eye is black with a pupil [181] outlined in red, and at the root of the beak as well as below the eye there are three curved, red lines. The black color of the beak is continued along the edge forming the crown of the head and the upper part of the blade.

These paddles clearly indicate contact with the whites, and were probably made after the arrival of the Americans. Not only is all the paint regular commercial house paint with an oil base, but the arrangement of the designs on the bear paddle shows that the hacksaw blade was an integral part of the decoration. We do not know what was the significance of the saw, unless it may have been used as a rattle. It was fastened by a nail through the lower hole only. A bent nail under which it slides freely is attached at what was originally a little above the middle of the saw. The upper end of the saw was not nailed.

Accounts of Potlatches

When Galushia was eight years old he attended a death potlatch given by the Yakutat Tlingit on Kayak Island. It was of the same type as that given by the Eyak. The pot-latch was given to all the Eagle people.

"We all started together from Alaganik, and Old Town [Cordova], and Eyak. It took us three days to get to Katalla. We stayed there a week. Then they sent a one-mast sloop to take us all over to that island. We stayed on the island a couple of days before they gave the potlatch. The first day there was a big feed. The second day they gave us the blankets and calico. The potlatch began early in the morning and lasted till late at night. The house was so crowded that we kids were outside, looking in through the windows. All the Yakutat people were there, but no other Tlingits and no Aleuts [Chugach Eskimo]. They gave the potlatch [182] for the people who have died. The dead party gets the benefit."

The hosts talked, telling why they were giving a potlatch. "This man that's dead, it's for him." The leader of the guests answered: "This I eat is not for me, it's for .... ," naming the deceased. (This indicates that feeding the guests conies first. Note that no potlatch names are used. Is this an error on Galushia's part, or were potlatch names not used between the two chiefs?) Then the relatives sang the dead man's song, the one he used when alive, and wept while they sang. The' crying was genuine, not just a ceremony, and there were real tears. Now the guests tried to cheer up their hosts. One at a time they sang the dead man's song and the one who sang it best received more gifts than the others.

Next the gifts were distributed. Those who had buried the corpse got the most — "guns, blankets, grub." Chiefs, too, got more than other people. After receiving these presents, the guests got up and sang their own songs and danced. (Apparently it was at this stage of the ceremonies that the hosts could ask individual guests to perform.)

After the potlatch was over (Galushia evidently means on the days following that on which the distribution of gifts had been made), the people sang and danced, each side in turn. They dressed up in animal costumes, wearing masks, and imitated the different kinds of animals. There were dancing contests, but Galushia does not remember if prizes were given.

"The hosts have to feed the whole gang until they leave. We were there a week. They sent us back on the same boat that brought us out." The food that the guests had not been able to eat they took home- in sacks and baskets. Their hosts had given away everything they owned. [183]

When Galushia was a child, the Eyak at Alaganik gave a potlatch to which the Tlingit from Kayak Island and Chilkat were invited. The Tlingit fired shots before landing, and waited in the river, singing for some time. After they landed they sang again. They did not have to sing much that first day because they were tired. They were painted and dressed in Chilkat blankets. On the second day, the hosts gave them a feast of fish and meat. Galushia did not say what was the occasion for this potlatch; it may have been the house-warming, already mentioned, though he does not here mention the Copper River Atna who were invited to that celebration.

Because he was such a small child at these two potlatches, Galushia's information is not as specific as we should have wished. When he came to describe what actually took place, he fell back upon generalized terms, and could only tell us what was supposed to have happened at any potlatch. We have tried to reproduce these accounts as nearly as possible in his own words.

Colonel ABERCROMBIE published two accounts of the dance or dances which he saw at Alaganik in 1884. In conversation he gives a very much more detailed description of the two ceremonies. When his original accounts were read to him he was at a loss to explain the discrcpencies. Some of these may have been due to loss of memory, not surprising after the passage of fifty years; others, he explains, might be errors resulting from the editing and shortening of his original manuscript, which, as we explained in the Introduction, was published without being submitted to him even for proof corrections. We give first his oral account of these ceremonies, then the printed versions with his comments and corrections. [184]

The whole village was apparently very much excited by the arrival of ABERCROMBIE and his party. Kai, the shaman, appeared with painted face to welcome them, having been warned of their coming by the Eskimo. The Eyak were much interested and impressed by the surveying instruments, especially the mercury horizon. ABERCROMBIE made a distribution of gifts. These objects, including the tobacco over which the quarrel arose, were spread out on the beach and Pete Johnson, the interpreter, passed them out. In return for the gifts the natives invited the white men to a dance at one of the two big houses. They were, in fact, invited to all the dances which were held every afternoon in the same house during the week of their stay, but they attended only the two "formal" functions.

The potlatch house was already crowded when ABERCROMBIE and his party entered. They and the other distinguished guests (Atna visitors from Taral) were {seated} just inside the door, at the front of the house, facing the open space reserved for the performers. The latter faced these guests, turning their backs on the larger audience who filled the back half of the house. Between the actors and the main audience were the medicine man, Kai, and his assistant who acted as prompter. Behind them were the four male drummers, flanked on both sides by a chorus of women (Figure 17). Two old women who sat, one on each end of the line, were the leaders of the chorus. One of these leaders was the woman who lived with Kai and seems to have been "a kind of priestess." While not on the stage, the actors or dancers crouched in the two undecorated lockers at the front of the house. Kai's assistant carried a feather wand in his hand, and when instructed by the shaman would point to the side of the house from which the performers [185] were to come. Kai would have done the prompting himself, ABERCROMBIE believes, if his hands had not been paralyzed.

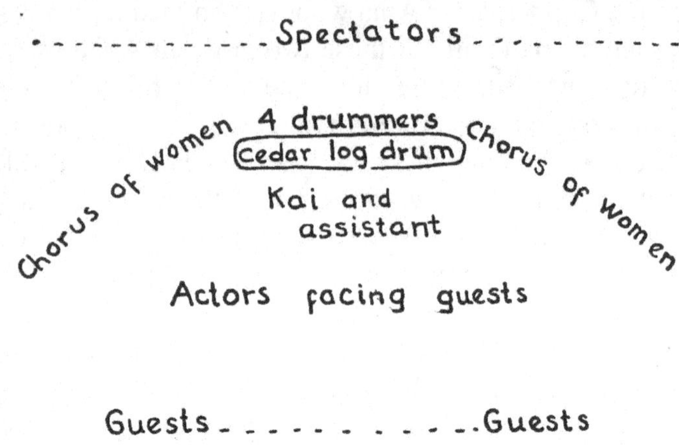

Fig. 17. Diagram of potlatch house during dances, as described by ABER-
CROMBIE. This is not the sketch referred to in his published report.

Both dances were dramas. The story was told in incidents by Kai, and then the dancers
would emerge from the lockers and act out what he had just narrated. Sometimes they carried on
a dialogue, sometimes acted or danced to the accompaniment of the singing and drumming. The
two old women who led the chorus would also talk back and forth to each other, making jokes.
The two halves of the chorus sometimes sang antiphonally, sometimes in unison. At the climax
of the Sun play the entire chorus was singing, the drummers pounding on their log, and the
whole audience joined in the singing and yelling. The chorus seems to have [186] been specially
trained, and ABERCROMBIE believes that the whole performance had been rehearsed for days.

The actors were all men, dressed in wooden masks and appropriate costumes. In the Sun
play, the part of the Sun Chief's sister was taken by a man dressed in women's clothing. The
Sea-Otter had a whole sea-otter skin on his back, the Ptarmigan and the other birds were dressed
in appropriate birdskin jackets, with wings attached to their arms and tails to their backs. The
Grouse would flap his elbows and sound as if he were drumming. The Whale had a big tail
which he brought down on the floor with a thump when he pretended to dive. The Fur Seal was
dressed in the proper furs. In the second play, an historical drama about the Russian expedition
(under SEREBRANIKOV in 1847-48?) up the Copper River, the actors were also masked — the
masks representing grotesque human faces — and the "Russians" wore fur hats. Simple
properties were used. The sister of the Sun Chief carried a small wooden box in which the Sun
was supposed to be kept, though there was nothing in it to represent the sun itself. The
"Russians" carried a whip, but no actual sled was used.

At both performances the women of the chorus had their faces painted black and red. Kai
was the only male performer with painted face, the others all wore masks. The pattern on Kai's
face has already been described (Figure 4). He impersonated the Raven in both plays. He was
dressed in a hip-length jacket of tanned skin to which raven skins had been sewn, and he had
wings on his arms and a bird's tail behind which flapped when he danced. He wore a crown or
headband with raven wing feathers, and a large wooden raven's beak was fastened to the top of
his head (perhaps to the crown) and projected over his face. His [187] assistant was dressed in a
jacket of white duck breasts. He was masked (ABERCROMBIE does not remember what character

he represented), and raven tail feathers were stuck into the edges of his mask and wooden crown. He carried a wooden wand, about 2 feet long, with eider down fastened to it. The masks and crowns of the other actors were ornamented with eagle tail or wing feathers. The masks were painted black and red, and were tied on by a cord around the head, hut were without: additional support. The actors wore rattling bracelets and some kind of anklet. They danced humped over and did excellent imitations of the animals or characters they were supposed to represent.

Some of the members of the audience had painted faces, and some of the wealthy women wore dentalium shells in their braids. In the audience were a few Copper River Indians from Taral with their slaves.

Pete Johnson acted as interpreter for ABERCROMBIE, but sometimes the dialogue was so fast that he could not understand it. In the first dance the following story was acted:

There was a Chief who kept the Sun, Moon, and Stars in a box. He took them out only when he wanted to go hunting. He always had plenty of meat but the other people had to hunt in the dark and were hungry. With the Chief lived his Sister and his Son. One day the Boy was playing on the shore when the Fur Seal came into the bay. They talked, and the Seal told the Boy he had been way down south where there was no snow and where the sun shone all the time. The Boy thought this was all a lie. Then came the Sea-Otter, who said that the Seal's story was true. He admitted that he had never been south himself, but his friend, the Whale, had been there and could verify the [188] story. So he fetched the Whale. The Whale swam all about and made big waves in the bay. This pleased the Boy. He told the animals that his Father kept the Sun in a box. The animals swam out in the bay and decided together that they "would have to get the Sun for themselves. The Seal was the leader in the plot which they invented. The animals then came back and told the Boy that they did not believe what he said, and that he must he a liar. Meanwhile, other animals had gathered until there were so many they could not all get in the bay. The Sea-Otter asked the Boy to bring the box with the Sun so they could see if he were telling the truth. The animals kept urging him to give them a peek at the Sun. They then began to show off for the Boy. The Sea-Otter showed how quickly he could dive, the Salmon how quickly he could turn. Much flattered by their attention, the Boy went to ask his Aunt for the Sun box. She would not give it to him, because her brother, the Chief, had told her never to let it out of her hands, but she consented to bring it down to the beach herself. Then the Whale took the Boy on his hack for a ride around the bay. The Boy and Aunt had never seen a whale close up before. The Seal and Sea-Otter could not carry the Boy themselves, but they swam beside the Whale to catch him if he fell off. The Aunt with the Sun box in her arms kept coming closer and closer to the water to watch. The other animals kept reassuring her that the Boy was safe. She climbed on a rock at the edge of the water to see better. Finally the Whale came back and the Boy landed on the rock. Then the Whale sounded, and he slapped the water so hard with his tail that a big wave washed the Boy and his Aunt off the rock. The box fell on a stone, broke open, and the Sun, Moon, and Stars flew up into the sky. After that, light was available [189] to everyone. The Aunt and the Boy were so horrified at the loss of these treasures that they fell down in fits.

(The Aunt put a small stone on the floor, against which she broke the box. There was actually nothing in it, but when the box broke, actors and audience shouted and followed with their eyes the pretended path of the Sun up into the sky. The Aunt and Boy were dragged off to one side of the house as if they were unconscious, then they got up and walked off the stage. ABERCROMBIE says that the natives worked up to the climax with great skill.)

The second dance told the story of the Eyaks' relations with the Russians. The purpose was to show that the Indians had always been friendly to the whites and that the trouble which occurred was due to Russian brutality. The story, or rather the historical incident, is as follows:

A Russian expedition went up the Copper River. They took Eyak Indians along to work for them. The leaders were not pure-blooded Russians, but were either Siberians of half-breeds. (This fits SEREBRANIKOV'S expedition.) They sat on the sled and drove their Indian slaves with whips. They were looking for copper and went up the Chitina River to Scoli Pass. Finally they refused to give the Indians anything to eat, so the Eyak turned on them and killed them. Then the Atna at Taral in turn enslaved the Eyak. Kai, as Raven, told the story. After the dance he came to ABERCROMBIE and explained what a fine man he (Kai) was, and how nice all the Eyak were, and suggested that ABERCROMBIE give them some sugar and tea, that is, pay for the dance, which ABERCROMBIE did.

After both performances food was served. It had been cooked outside and was carried into the house on wooden platters. ABERCROMBIE thought that it was Kai who gave the [190] feast. He and his party were invited to participate, but they did not care for the food. During the dance, there was no fire in the house, and the entire floor, including the fireplace, was filled with spectators.

We now quote ABERCROMBIE'S published accounts and give his corrections. According to this record,[1] he had exhibited the accuracy of his carbine, and had shown the natives his watch, chronometer, and field glasses.[2] "The effect was electrifying. The medicine man, who spoke Chinook, then asked me to come over to a dance, which is about the same thing as smoking a pipe of peace with the Indians of the plains. The invitation was accepted and I agreed to be at the casina when the sun reached the top of the totem pole standing in the center of the graveyard, which was located at the top of a knoll about 100 feet high and below the main village.

"As the sun neared its position we noticed an unusual stirring of the natives and a number of small canoes passing along the sloughs leading to the casina, containing women, children, and old men. Taking our bidarra [umiak] Dr. ROBINSON, myself, and interpreter, with side arms only (they being held in greater fear and more incomprehensible to the natives than a rifle, as they fire so often without reloading), we followed the narrow and tortuous channel of the slough and landed in front of the casina, which is constructed and used as follows (see Figure B): [The text figures were never published, and were apparently destroyed with the original manuscript.]

"The casina is a native hotel used for visiting and passing friendly tribes. All entertainments are given in the casina. [191] The shaman met us at the landing and escorted us to the door of the casina, announced our presence, when an old man ushered us to seats of honor in the back and center (AA), fronting the entrance.[3] The seats were covered with a piece of white drilling.[4] Our left (B B) was reserved for the performers and singers: the remainder of the house was filled with the native audience. The old native that conducted us to our seats was master of ceremonies, having a young man for doorkeeper.

"At the striking of an Indian drum on the outside, the same as used by the plains Indians, seven squaws entered, with faces painted red and black and hair and persons ornamented with swan's-down, and took station facing the dancers with backs to the audience, their left flank

---

[1] ABERCROMBIE 1900, 385.

[2] It was chiefly the mercury horizon that impressed them.

[3] Compare the description of the arrangement given above with Figure 17.

[4] There was no cloth at Alaganik.

resting on ours.[1] On the right Hank sat the drummer. At a given signal from the master of ceremonies[2] the women ~~squaws~~ {!!} began a low chant, time being kept by the young Indian with the drum, when through the door,[3] which was opened sufficiently to admit him, a young man representing the 'totem' of his family, followed by a second, third, fourth, the shaman, sixth, seventh, eighth, and ninth, their respective positions being determined by the headman and medicine man. The actors having entered, all chanting, and taken their positions, the shaman in the center with the wand in his right hand,[4] a signal to the orchestra was given and the [192] music ceased. The actors turned their backs on the audience and rested for five or six minutes. At the command of the shaman a chant was offered. The music was established, but the words were improvised by the central actor to suit the occasion. This was continued in a similar manner by other actors."

ABERCROMBIE'S second account[5] is much briefer than this, and though there are some inconsistencies in detail, it would appear that the same occasion is described.

"A proposed journey, the arrival of strangers, the return from a successful hunt, any extraordinary occasion has to be celebrated by a dance. One at Alaganik, to which an invitation was extended by the Shaman, and which seemingly was gotten up in honor of our arrival, was attended by the entire population, men, women, and children. A sort of tambour, sounding not unlike the ordinary brass drum,[6] supplied the music. When the audience had seated itself and the chorus had taken its place, leaving a portion of the floor free for the dancers, the door was suddenly thrown open and in sprang a grotesquely arrayed native with painted face,[7] who went through a variety of contortions strongly suggestive of the convulsions of nervous disorders. Before taking his place in the arena reserved for the performers, four [seven in the above account] females who took minor parts assumed their places quietly, and all began a monotonous chant, accompanying it by motions of their bodies. This concluded, each male dancer, holding in his hands feathers, or objects, the significance of which does [193] not appear, came to the front in turn, danced energetically, sang and recited, the chorus following. The ceremony was kept up several hours and was repeated in a modified form upon subsequent occasions. In some parts of the west their dances are to assist the incantations of the Shaman. But this did not seem to be the purpose at Alaganik, and to inquiries as to its object the only answer was that it was merely a dance, and had no other meaning."

Ownership and Inheritance

Hunting and fishing grounds, camp sites or house sites were open and free to all members of the tribe, regardless of moiety, family, or village affiliations. The Eyak seem to have had a clear feeling of the limits of their tribal territory, and knew they were in danger from the Eskimo

----

[1] This was the chorus.

[2] Kai's assistant, who acted as prompter.

[3] The actors came out of the locker doors, not the main house door.

[4] The shaman and his assistant have been confused in this account. It was the assistant, not Kai, who held the wand and gave the actors their cues, though Kai told him what to do.

[5] ABERCROMBIE 1900, 398.

[6] ABERCROMBIE thinks he was mistaken about the type of drum, and that It was not a akin drum hut a log. Probably both kinds were used.

[7] That was Kai. He entered from a locker.

when they trespassed on Eskimo land.

Although everyone helped to build the war canoes, these were carved with moiety emblems. Galushia said that the war canoes were the property of the whole tribe. (Should he have said that they were the property of the moiety represented?) The sealskin war canoe seems to have belonged to one individual.

The fort was undoubtedly the common property of the village. The potlatch house belonged to the moiety that built it.

Of personal property, such as clothes, weapons, tools, household utensils, dogs, and slaves, very little was inherited after the death of the owner. Almost all the dead person's things were destroyed at his death or at the death potlatch. Only a few things were saved as mementoes, or were traded to members of the opposite moiety. Nothing to which the [194] deceased had been particularly attached could be passed on in this way. The articles given in exchange for the dead man's property went to the brothers of the deceased, especially the oldest brother. The son received nothing. We have no specific information about the maternal nephew. Presumably in the case of a woman, her sisters and daughters would receive the exchange goods, but again we lack specific information. In any case the number of goods obtained in this way could not have been very significant. In 1930, Galushia made the statement that no one could keep anything belonging to a dead person, unless the deceased had given his consent. Otherwise the ghost might do harm. This most certainly refers to the goods redeemed by the members of the opposite moiety at the potlatch. In many cases the owner must have died without making any such bequests. In that case the surrender of property to guests at the potlatch must have been at the discretion of the relatives. If they traded off too much they were considered greedy.

At the death of their owner slaves were usually liberated, but instead of going home they sometimes preferred to remain with the deceased's brother(?) or with the widow(?), which would usually amount to the same thing, or with some other surviving relative(?). In any case, there were no regular rules about the inheritance of slaves, and we have no statement about the slaves owned by a woman. Perhaps it was only a man who owned slaves.

Dogs were probably the only form of personal property which was regularly inherited, since dogs were never killed. It is possible that ownership of dogs by a woman is modern (the woman in question was Galushia's mother, from whom the dogs passed to her daughter), since dogs, being kept exclusively for hunting, would naturally belong to a man. [195]

The ownership of dogs by a woman might result when there was no male relative in the family to inherit them. Unfortunately Galushia could tell us nothing about this except that when his mother died his sister took the dogs (perhaps because her brothers were too young to use them?).

The ownership of the house presents a very difficult problem. Galushia said first that the community house was owned by the family; later that only one man owned a house, though several might help him to build it. Again, he said that a group of brothers might build a house together; presumably they would own it in common, though the authority of the older brother might mean that the formal ownership of the house was vested in him. Mrs. Gus Nelson said that the house was owned by one man and was inherited by his son, but her statements are not always to be trusted. Galushia said further that the man brought his wife home to his own house. Any children born in a community house, therefore, would belong to the moiety of the mothers, not to that of the fathers. If the sons, as they married, continued to live at home, we should find the ownership of the house passing from the men of one moiety to that of the other. This seems unreasonable, since we know that no other form of property was inherited by the son, but this may nevertheless be true and an indication that the moiety organization is a recent institution, not completely incorporated into the culture of the Eyak.

On the other hand, Mrs. Gus Nelson insisted that the man and his wife Jived with her parents after marriage. Under such an arrangement, all the married men in one house would belong to one moiety, and we might infer that ownership would pass from father-in-law to son-in-law. The son-in-law in some cases was probably the maternal [196] nephew of his wife's father. The only fact which would seem to support Mrs. Gus Nelson's statement about matrilocal residence is that the father could take one daughter from her husband in exchange for another daughter. This would suggest that the young couple lived in the same place (house? village?) where the father's authority could be exerted. There is, however, some evidence, not clearly stated, that the girl's uncle also had this authority. If it were the paternal uncle the inference remains the same, but if it were her maternal uncle, it suggests perhaps cross-cousin marriage with residence in the house of the husband's father.

Galushia, however, maintained that residence was never with the wife's family. Other statements in support of his contention are: (1) At the death of a wife, the co-wife must return to her own family for a certain period. (2) The husband's father (or brother) would take care of the son's wife if the latter was away. (3) A man did not necessarily take all his wives from the same family.

Other social usages, such as individual marriages of a group of brothers to a group of sisters, and the position of authority of the older brother (and to a lesser extent of the older sister), and the authority of the maternal uncle and aunt support only the statement that a group of brothers and their families lived together. Nor does the taboo between son-in-law and mother-in-law, and the taboo (?) between father-in-law and daughter-in-law indicate in which house the married pair lived.

If we examine the tales we receive little help. In *Tale* 16 the Sun takes his human wife home to the sky. In *Tale* 6, both versions, the Bear takes the woman home to his den. In *Tale* 8 the Porpoise Prince had his human wife live under the sea in the house of the Porpoise Chief. In all of [197] these stories, however, the point of the plot requires this type of residence, so we cannot rely on them for much guidance. On the other hand, the stories also furnish us with evidence of residence with the wife's family. In both *Tales* 17 and 29, the husband deserts his wife in order to live with another wife in the latter's village or home. In *Tale* 7, the Bear, and later the two human brothers, live with their Bear father-in-law. Raven, in incident 23, lives at first with his wife's parents, then moves away with his wife to another place.

In the tales, however, we have no definite mention of community houses, though we imagine that they are implied En the following: *Tale* 25, the People who were Preparing for War; *Tale* 17, the Dwarf People; *Tale* 8, the Woman who hid the Porpoise Head in her Sleeping Room; *Tale* 6B, the Woman and her Seven Brothers; *Tale* 20, the Woman and her Nine Brothers; *Tale* 10, the Seal People; Raven, incident 15, the Whale People; incident 3, the Sky Chief who owned the daylight.

Hitherto, we have not considered the small house occupied by a single family. We unfortunately lack specific information about the early form of this house. The small houses built by the Eyak today are shacks on the American pattern (Plate 4, 3, 4), and doubtless are inherited from father to .son. However, according to the views of the American author the original small house may have been a very old element, older perhaps than the community house, and the rules for its inheritance may have been different.[1] In several tales we find specific mention of small households: *Tale* 27, a man, wife, and their children; *Tale* 24, a man and wife, [198] their daughter, their slave woman and her son; *Tale* 17, a man and wife; *Tale* 20, a Tree Man and Woman; *Tale* 18, the Sun, his human wife, and their children; *Tale* 0, the Bear, his human wife and their children. In none of these stories is mention made of the inheritance of property in any form. [199]

---

[1] The small house may have been brought by the Eyak from their original home in the interior (?). [F. DE L.]

Intellectual Culture.

Magic

Before going hunting, no one announced that he expected to kill game, otherwise he would get nothing. It was bad luck to take a sled along before the game had been secured. A man could not hunt until his wife was recovered from the confinement of childbirth, or until the dead body of a housemate had been taken from the house. If a woman touched a man's hunting weapons they had to be left outdoors for a certain period (how long?) to be purified. The evil effects might also be removed by rubbing them with devilclub (*Fatsia horrida*). No pollution resulted from the touch of a little girl. A woman was not supposed to step over a man's legs or his hunting weapons. To prevent such an accident, bows and arrow's were always kept hung up on the wall and the harpoon was kept under the overturned canoe. A woman in the last stage of pregnancy was not supposed to cross or follow a hunter's trail.

While her husband was out hunting, the wife was not allowed to leave the village or "monkey around with other men." She was not supposed to make a noise, to make new clothes, to wash or comb her hair, or gather wood. She might fetch water, cook, mend old garments, and do other work in the house. Goat hunting was the most dangerous, and so these taboos were most conscientiously observed when the man was hunting goats. [200]

When an animal was killed, the hunter cut the eyes so that it might not see who had killed it, and thus know whom to avoid {its} future reincarnation. The head of the animal was skinned and cut off and hidden under a stump, a pile of stones, or in some dry place. This rule did not apply to seals. The Eyak used to eat the brains and throw the skull away. The heads of birds did not have to be cached either. Salmon tails (*Tale* 22) and the blood and entrails of salmon (*Tale* 4) were thrown back into the river. Animal bones were not burned, lest the dead animals suffer. There was no taboo against giving them to dogs. If the taboo against sewing land and sea animal skins in one garment were broken, the hunter would lose his luck.

Galushia believed that certain people were supposed to know how to keep the animals from smelling them, but Johnny Stevens denied this belief.

In explaining *Tale* 14A, Galushia said that the hunter must rise before the crow (raven?) caws, or he will get no game. Conversely, the animal that sleeps after the crow caws in the morning will be killed by the hunter. That is why the Giant Mouse (or Mole) was killed by the crows' cawing while he was still asleep, and that was why people could escape from the Giant Devilfish (*Tale* 13B) by making a noise like a crow. Raven (incident 21) killed the first bear by throwing his spear and cawing, thus enabling men to kill bears, (We may assume that it is the raven, not the smaller crow, that is meant in these remarks).

When a bear had been killed and skinned, the pelt was lowered three times to touch the carcase before it was taken away. The people never spoke to the bear except to tease it. There was no apology made to an animal for having killed it. [201]

It is bad luck to kill small birds. To do so would spoil a person's luck in hunting and would bring other misfortune. This was explained to us by little Johnny Saski, whom we overheard rebuking another child for throwing a stone at a little bird.

When a boy made his first kill, he was not allowed to eat any of the meat. He gave the game to a relative, and it was divided up and given away. His father also made gifts of other things to members of the opposite moiety (to the boy's moiety? or to that of the father?). This observance applied to the boy's first kill of all species of animal bird, and fish.

Galushia knew nothing about special ceremonies for first fruits or the first kill of the season. The information about the first salmon ceremony obtained from Johnny Stevens has already been given in the section on *Fishing*.

If a man had been hunting for five days without any luck, he would bathe in the river. Then he would burn the spines off a devilclub and would rub the bark all over his body. Next day he would be sure to kill something. Even though his dogs barked, they would not frighten away the game. A man might also put devilclubs in his bed, but we are not sure if this was done only to cure sickness or whether it was efficacious to secure good luck in hunting also (Johnny Stevens).

In *Tale* 5, the hunter has had bad luck because (1) he lay in bed after the girls got up, (2) he ate when women were combing their hair and so became full of combings, (3) he remained in the house when menstruating women entered. Part of his purification was to take a bath in (fevuclub water and to rub devilclubs over his body.

Our information on love magic was acquired from Ma [202] Tiedemann, our Eskimo interpreter, who said she had learned it from Old Man Dude, the shaman.

When a man wishes to win the affections of a girl, he secures a piece of her clothing or hair. This is tied up with the male flower and the female flower of a certain plant that grows in lakes. The bundle is placed in a stream or lake. When it rots, the girl will be "crazy" for the man.

A woman can protect herself from love charms by passing a hoop of devilclubs over her body, drawing it from her head down to her feet. From the warnings given to Ma by Old Man Dude, we infer that love charms are still used.

The following story was told by Ma: When Ma was a little girl, Steve Vlassof's sister, Tunia (or Evdokia) lived at Nuchek. The brother of Dude's last wife, *ənaci*, who is also Annie Nelson's paternal uncle, came from Eyak in a canoe. He told the Eskimo chief, Peter Chimowitski (Makari's brother and Ma's uncle) that he wanted an Eskimo wife. The chief asked whom he wanted and he said: "Evdokia." The chief went to her parents — her father was the second chief — but the girl said she did not like the man because he was an Indian. The chief told *ənaci* to go ask her himself. He went every day for a week and talked to her, but she said: "No, I'm still going to school, and I don't want to get married now." "All right." he said. "You won't be as pretty as you are now." She had a little pimple beside her nose. Soon it spread and her whole face began to rot. The chief went to Eyak and got *ənaci*, and scared him into coming back to Nuchek. He looked at the girl and said: "Oh, you'll be all right now." He left, and right away her face began to heal up. But it looks bad even now. [203]

JACOBSEN writes: "The shamans also prepare amulets for a good price; they make especially love draughts and love amulets out of a certain kind of root, and they always find a grateful and credulous public, especially among the young people."[1]

When her husband was out chopping wood, the wife was supposed to obey the same taboos as those observed when he was hunting. If she were not quiet, or if she left the house needlessly, the axe would break.

We heard of no special women's taboos applying to war.

Although sexual abstinence was not specifically mentioned as a regular practice to secure success in important undertakings, this is implied in *Tale* 6B. In this story the brothers do not

---

[1] JACOBSEN 1884, 393.

sleep with their wives (how long?) because they want to find their lost sister. Sexual abstinence must be practiced by the shaman during the period of probation (see *Shamans*) and before attempting a cure. We must also note the prohibition against intercourse between the widower and the surviving wife for two or three months after the death of a co-wife. We do not know how soon after the death of a husband a widow might remarry.

Fasting also has magic and religious efficacy. Thus, warriors used to fast overnight before a fight, and all the people fasted during the mourning ceremonies when a warrior had been killed. During the three-months probation period the would-be shaman must not eat much, and must also fast occasionally for two or three days at a time. The shaman fasts overnight before attempting a cure. The taboos against eating certain foods have already been mentioned, but these belong to a different category from the complete fast. The taboo against eating berries which the [204] expectant mother observes is explained by the fear of causing boils on the child's body — an obvious example of sympathetic magic. The fond taboos prohibiting menstruating or pregnant women from eating or touching fresh meat may be designed to prevent the animals' souls from being offended by contact with pollution. The general fast, on the other hand, can be considered as a means of provoking the pity of the supernatural forces, or like sexual abstinence, it may be a method of keeping the body pure and receptive to supernatural powers. The fasting during the dances commemorating the slain warrior may be, like the fasting of the relatives after a, death, the traditional expression of sorrow, and without magical significance. Even here, however, sorrow and fear of danger from the ghost may both be operative.

The devilclub plays an important role in magic. This is certainly the least useful and most unpleasant plant in the region from a practical point of view but on account of its purgative and emetic powers its magic efficiency may have been "obvious" to the native mind. Bathing in water in which devilclubs had been boiled was practiced by both the father and mother after her confinement. Bathing in devilclub water and rubbing the body with the plant break the bad luck of the hunter, and rubbing hunting weapons with devilclubs removes the pollution caused by a woman's touch. During his novitiate, the would-be shaman drinks an infusion of devilclub which acts as a purgative and emetic. Devilclubs placed in the corners of the house and behind the pillow of the patient will cure disease, and a piece tied around a child's neck will ward away sickness (see Shamans). Old Man Dude told Ma Tiedman that when she went among Indians she should make a hoop of [205] devilclubs, soak it in fresh water for a few minutes, then pull it over her body down to her feet. This would protect her from love charms and shamans' spells. In *Tale* 5, as already mentioned, the hunter takes a devilclub bath to regain his luck. In *Tale* 17, the man takes a devilclub bath when searching for the daughter of Chief Calm Weather. In *Tale* 7. one of the young men is brought back to life when his Bear father-in-law and his brother make eight rings of devilclub and some other unidentified plant and "cover" his body with them, (that is, pass his body through them?). In all these instances, the devilclub acts as a purifying agent.

While bathing in cold water was practiced as part of the physical training of young men, it also seems lo possess a purifying virtue apart from any hygienic value. Thus, women bathed at the end of their monthly periods, and the would-be shaman bathed morning and night for three months before the vision quest. It is interesting to note that the sweat bath was never mentioned in the tales or by our informants as a means for purification.

Other features of hunting magic not included in this analysis will be discussed in the section on Religion, and in the same section will also be found various observances concerning weather.

While we were not told that certain numbers were lucky or had ceremonial significance, yet the following instances suggest that 4, 5, and 8 had some such virtue, perhaps the same sort which we attribute to 3 and 7. On the other hand, there is no indication that the Eyak regarded any number as unlucky, as we do 13.

The skin was removed from a dead bear after three incomplete motions, that is, on the fourth time. The dead body was kept in the house for four days, and buried on [206] the fifth. The clamshell dish was set under the corners of the house for four successive days; on the morning of the fifth day the witch's face could be seen in it.

Menstruating women were secluded for five days. After five days hunting without luck, the hunter took a bath and rubbed his body with devilclubs. Chitina Joe repeated each motion in his shamanistic treatments five times (see Stories about Shamans).

The dead dwarf in *Tale* 18 came back to life on the eighth day. The would-be shaman went on an eight-day vision quest. Eight rings of devilclubs and some other plant -were used to restore the young man to life in *Tale* 7. The Copper River shaman died and came back to life eight times (see Stories about Shamans). In *Tale* 26, the Sun and his wife have eight boys and a girl.

The group of undertakers consisted of four, six, or eight persons.

On the other hand, the following instances do not fit this suggested scheme: The childbed confinement lasted ten days. The shaman's probation or p reparation period lasted three months. Dude's wife fell ill three days after the curse, and died three days later still (see Stories about Shamans). In *Tale* 6B, the seventh and youngest brother finds his sister. In *Tale* 20, there are nine boys and a girl.

Transvestites and Witches

Among the Eyak there were men who lived like women, who did women's work and did not hunt. They did not marry other men and had no supernatural powers. They were despised and had to live on left-over scraps. The name for such a man means "no good." (Does *Tale* 25, "Good-for Nothing," refer to a man suspected of being a transvestite?). [207]

The Eyak distinguish between shamans ("doctors") and witches. Both men and women might become witches. People generally knew who were witches, though the latter tried to keep their powers secret. Witches could fly through the air in their own form, and were sometimes seen doing so, and they could also turn themselves into any kind of bird or animal. A witch gained his power by skinning a dog and putting the hide over his head. He would go to the graveyard and dig up corpses and handle the ashes. He would make a whistle out of a human arm or leg bone. Sounding this whistle, by blowing across the end of the hollow bone, was what gave the witch power to change his shape. While learning to be a witch, the novice would stay at the graveyard all night (for several nights in succession?). He would be in a crazy condition and go around in a trance. Witches never ate corpses and never killed people in order to obtain their bodies. They did not make use of the newly dead but handled only skeletons.

The witches used their power only for evil. If they could get a person's nail parings, or some of his belongings, by preference clothing, they would rub it with a woman's menstrual blood (if the witch were a woman, with her own), or with a putrefied animal carcass. As the object or garment rotted, the person would sicken and die. The witch kept the dog skin which he had worn while acquiring power and could make a man sick or unlucky by touching him surreptitiously with it. Witches did not make poison from corpses. Galushia knew nothing about the evil eye, nor of harming a person through an image made in his shape.

A shaman could force a witch in animal form to enter the house, where he would kill it. [208]

Shamans

Galushia was not able to tell us much about shamans, so that all of the information embodied in this section was obtained from Johnny Stevens, unless otherwise stated. Johnny is a shaman himself, and although he never spoke about his power to us, most of what he told us seems to be autobiographical in character.

Both men and women might become shamans, and the procedure was the same for both sexes, Galushia thought. He had never heard of a candidate who failed to obtain power. He believed that shamanistic power was inherited in some way, because the sons and daughters of a medicine man would also become shamans after his death. Johnny Stevens admitted that he had obtained his own power from a great uncle, but would say nothing more.

When a man was to become a shaman, or "doctor," the first manifestation of his spirit helper would be in a dream. This would be when he was about twelve or fourteen years old. He might hear a voice far away. He would think that someone was trying to kill him. "It came easier." said Johnny Stevens, "if your blood was clean and your life pure." The spirit would give the youth three months in which to "live right." During this period the novice had to be careful of his diet. He was not to eat much and should especially avoid sharing the food of a menstruating woman. He would bathe morning and evening in cold running water. Occasionally he would build a fire of devilclubs and boil alder bark over it. This infusion was drunk as a purge and emetic. (We are practically certain that the two bushes have been confused in this statement, and that the devilclub infusion was drunk.) We would occasionally fast for two or three days. {He} was supposed to "keep away from women." [209]

At the end of this preparatory period, the novice went into the woods alone for eight days. He was stark naked, and remained quietly in one place, without a fire and without food. This would be in summer. While fasting, something would come to him and ask him who he was. It was a spirit that came. Sometimes it was invisible, sometimes in animal or bird form. (According to Galushia, the first animal seen by the novice gives him his power. The shaman would make a doll out of the skin of this animal — or of another animal of the same species? — and stuff it with grass. Some of the shaman's dolls were in human form. Were these made by shamans whose helper had appeared in human form?). Sometimes the novice would hear somebody whistling. He would go to sleep and the spirit might come and talk to him. It might say: "You don't look well to me. You have done something wrong." Then it would make him well and would give him a song which he would remember when he woke. The song might be forgotten later, but would always be recalled when the shaman felt like singing. It meant that his spirit was returning to him. Every shaman had a song.

While the taboos of the probationary period seem, by Johnny Stevens' own statement, to be still observed (see next section), we do not think that shamans still make the vision quest as described above. Since the culture and the people are practically gone it is doubtful if there will ever be any new shamans.

A shaman may have fifty or more helping spirits. These are obtained from the earth, trees, water, winds, etc. They can carry the doctor all around the world in a few minutes. His helpers do not stay with him all the time, but come to him when needed. They can talk English, Tlingit or any [210] other language. When they are with him, the shaman can speak and understand any language. These helpers may be male or female. Johnny Stevens had never heard of sexual intercourse between a shaman and his spirits of opposite sex. He calls his spirits "my brother," "my helper," "my father," or "my uncle."

The shaman makes wooden dolls or figures of men, birds, and animals into which he puts his helpers or his own power or "mind." Johnny Stevens has seen a shaman who had dolls representing a man, a halibut, a seal, and a killerwhale. A doll bought in the store might be used. When the shaman is not using his doll, and his "mind" or his spirit helper is not in it, the image is just an "ordinary" (profane) object. During the seance the dolls will move according to their nature — walk, fly, etc. — but they cannot change their shape. Thus the image of a bird cannot turn into a fish, and vice versa. These dolls can be sent more than a thousand miles away. The dolls may he painted, but Johnny Stevens does not know what kind of paint is used.

Galushia said that he had never heard that shamans gave ventriloquist performances with their dolls, but he knew that they were supposed to be able to kill men and animals with them at a distance. These dolls could be seen and handled by women without ill effects. Once a shaman lost his doll in his bedding. His aunt found it and threw it on the floor. He rebuked her, saying: "That's my power." But the power was not impaired in any way.

In order to keep his power strong, a shaman must get others to repeat his song after him. This does not have to be done every day, but may be at irregular intervals. When his assistants repeat his song while the shaman is attending a sick person, it makes his power stronger. [211]

Galushia said that some doctors had pieces of bone (instead of dolls?), and like dolls these could be used to kill persons at a distance.

At a seance, according to Johnny Stevens, the helper would come "like somebody pushing you. You felt you wanted to sing. You would go out and get six or seven men to make a noise. You feel light as a feather; you can see things with your eyes closed. If you see a person all black it means that he will die." After falling into a trance the shaman can foretell the future.

The shaman never had to work. When he was traveling in a canoe, someone would paddle in the bow and another in the stern, but the shaman would lie in the middle with his head covered. He might tell the others that they would see something. Then a bird would appear, and by his power the shaman would make it drop dead. He would tell the paddlers to say something and the bird would fall.

During seances the shaman beats on a wooden plank with a club or drumstick (cf. ABERCROMBIE'S description of drums p. 185). These might be painted. Galushia thought that the dance paddles may have been used by shamans also.

In ordinary life the shaman wore no special dress, though the style in which he wore his hair was distinctive. When curing the sick the doctor seems to have worn a special costume though we were unable to get any specific information about it. Galushia thought that the shamans used to wear a mask of some kind, but not an animal disguise. Information on this subject has already been given under *Personal Adornment and Clothing*. The shaman put mi his special costume when fighting other shamans.

A doctor would be willing to admit his profession. Johnny Stevens, however, denied at first that he had any [212] special powers and finally would tell us only a little about them. Shamans did not form a secret society. They were always trying to fight and kill each other in order to acquire their rivals' powers. When a shaman's helper had been stolen he felt sick. Galushia did not believe that there were special shaman's words or magic formulae.

Shamans claimed that they could come back to life after death, but Galushia doubts this ability. The Copper River doctors were supposed to be especially powerful. Galushia also doubts that shamans claimed to be able to see the ghosts of the dead.

Doctors — and we should add witches — were blamed for all bad luck. They were generally killed because they were held responsible for someone's sickness, and their bodies were always cremated. When a doctor dies and his "mind" leaves his body, it travels with such force that it will blow up a mountain, "like dynamite," if it strikes one.

When a shaman is called in to treat a sick person, he is always paid in advance. The shaman never works for nothing and he can ask for anything he wants. Before attempting a cure the shaman will stay away from women and fast overnight. The sweat bath is not used by the shaman as part of this preparation, but he will not allow others to use his bathhouse. The treatment consists of singing several songs, one after the other. These songs are repeated by the shaman's assistants and this repetition makes his power stronger (Galushia). While working, the shaman would throw handfuls of down into the air all around him. (This seems to have gone out of fashion now), Sickness was formerly attributed to witchcraft, and still is, though we do not know to what extent. Sickness may be caused by the theft of the soul or by the injection of some [213] foreign substance into the body. The shaman can restore the soul by means of his song. He can also suck out the substance that is causing the illness. He will spit it out on something and exhibit it to the people. Afterwards the source of the disease is thrown away or burned up. Johnny Stevens has never seen this done and does not know if a sucking tube would be used. A shaman can also wash away the sickness by pouring water on the afflicted part. The shaman may give the patient a string to hold. He himself will hold the other end and remove the illness by rubbing the string in the direction away from the patient. We do not know how many of these methods are still commonly employed. Some of the stories about shamans (see next section) illustrate the laying on of hands. If one of the shaman's helpers fails him, he will try another.

Other items referring to the cure of sickness will be found at the end of this section.

Besides curing the sick, the shaman has power to foretell the future when he is in a trance. Then he can see things, even though his eyes are closed. As already mentioned he can prophesy a man's death if the person appears to him black. Or the shaman may move his outstretched hand back and forth; if the hand feels numb while pointing at some one, it means that person will die. Old Man Dude told us (see next section) that if his face twitches on the left side it means bad luck; if it twitches on the right side it means good luck. In order to discover whether a sick person would die, the people (shamans?) would take certain flowers, chew them, and put them under running water. These flowers were known only to certain people. If the flowers sink the patient will die. Shamans can also make people sleep by hypnotism, according to Johnny Stevens. [214]

In *Tale* 21, the shaman was the only one who could see the Invisible Being.

The shaman also has power over animals and can bring game. He has special songs for hunting, good weather, and for victory in war, as well as for curing the sick. He cannot pass on his power or his songs to another person (except when dying?). After a battle had begun, the shaman could tell how it would end, but his forecasts would not prevent the warriors from continuing the light (Galushia). The shaman could make a smoke through which the enemy could not see, or a mountain or body of water which they could not cross. These were made out of fog (Johnny Stevens). Compare these obstacles with the fog made by the Sun to help his children in their war with the Alders (*Tale* 16).

Shamans did not cut or mutilate themselves. They did not give exhibitions of ventriloquism or juggling (see, however, JACOBSEN'S account, given below). They could handle red hot stones or walk in fire without being burned, and they could walk over the surface of the water carrying heavy stones in their arms (Galushia and Johnny). These feats were not performed at special times, but were part of the regular cures(?) (Galushia). The shaman can break a glass and put it together again. He can be tied up tight and yet free himself. The shaman may get two men to stretch his belt while he lies and swings on it. From the brief descriptions of our informants, it was impossible to understand what this performance was, though it seemed to be more than a tight-rope feat. Although possibly referring to the Tlingit, the observations being made at Cape Martin, JACOBSEN'S report explains it fully. He writes:

"The medicine men make their charms [*machen ihre* [215] *Zaubermittel*} or perform the consecration of their amulets in the following manner: The shaman clothes himself first of all in his festival dress, which consists of a kind of apron, hung with bird beaks or the hoofs of wild mountain goats. He paints his face, covers his head with a kind of hat, or, according to the medicine that he wants to make, with a mask, and takes his rattle in his hand. A big fire is lit in the middle of the room, around which he performs his dance in the presence of the inhabitants who gather from all directions. The medicine man usually impresses his audience by showing them that the heat of the fire cannot harm him. For this purpose he repeatedly takes glowing coals in his hand, exhibits them all around, and throws them through a hole in the roof, without burning his fingers. The men sit around the fire along the walls of the house. Each holds a stick in his hand with which he beats out the rhythm on a wooden plank. An older man takes charge of beating the big drum. All take part in the song, and the women raise their voices as loud as possible. It is the peculiar custom that, when singing, the women hold an object of some sort in front of the mouth, as if to prevent the entrance of an evil spirit [Dämon] into it.

"The shaman does all sorts of little tricks to astonish the public. One of the favorite stunts is the following: Two men station themselves on each side of the fire and hold a rope of bast or leather immediately over the fire. The medicine man lies down, or rather hangs, on this rope, and is swung to and fro by the four bearers so that the fire is constantly under him. Often the rope catches fire and is then removed together with the man. In another trick the shaman eats a long bone before the eyes of the observers, and to their astonishment soon after pulls it out again intact [216] from his throat. The magician often makes an iron knife red hot and not only holds it in his hand but licks the blade without apparently hurling himself at all. The art of ventriloquism is employed by many shamans with a certain virtuosity. On these occasions, a sudden pause is made in the middle of the song, and the shaman bends low towards the earth, upon which a demon [Dämon], who seems to be deep under the ground, answers him.

"Since the time for the dances and similar performances did not occur during the days of my stay [late fall, at Cape Martin], I obtained part of this information through inquiries; for much of what I write here I have especially to thank the skipper of the sloop *Three Brothers*, Captain ANDERSEN, who formerly passed a whole year in this region.

"As soon as one song is ended and a new one is to be begun, the medicine man puts on another costume, or mask, or headdress, and sprinkles eagle down on his head, etc. The shaman cures sickness by removing the sickness from the patient simply in the form of a handful of bird down or a living mouse, which he eats before the eyes of the observers, so that the sickness will not be able to attack another person. The patient plays a passive role in this; he must hold himself completely quiet and with as little participation [*theilnahmlos*] as a lifeless corpse, and is laid either behind a curtain or before the eyes of the observers, according to which the shaman believes necessary. Then the shaman approaches him, while the singers and drummers observe the most profound silence and listen breathless to the prophetic speech of the magician. Each time that he says a few words the entire assembly sings as refrain '*A—hi A—hi*'

"The shaman is held by the natives in the greatest [217] esteem ... The costume, masks, and paraphernalia [*Gegenstände*] of a shaman are not kept in a house, but in the woods. [Galushia told us of finding a shaman's drum in the cave near Alaganik when he was a boy.] The natives are familiar with these things but do not dare to touch them. When a shaman succeeds in curing a sickness he receives a good fee in blankets for it. The shamans also prepare amulets for a good price; they make especially love draughts and love amulets out of a certain kind of root, and they always find a grateful and credulous public, especially among the young people. There is a shaman in every village."[1]

As already stated, sickness was attributed to witchcraft. Sometimes the sick person would dream of the person who was causing his illness. In *Tale* 18, the wife dreams of the man who murdered her husband. When the identity of the witch was not revealed by a dream, another method was employed. The relatives of the patient would take a clamshell dish and for four successive days set it under the four corners of the house in turn, so that rain water from the caves would drip into it. On the fourth night, the shell full of water was placed behind the patient's head without his knowledge. On the morning of the fifth day all his fellow-clansmen were called to look in the water. In it they would see the face of the witch who was responsible for the man's illness. Sometimes the patient might summon the witch and accuse him. The witch might or might not acknowledge his guilt. Sometimes the witch could be forced to pay an indemnity.

If a frog hopped into the house where there was a sick person it was regarded as a visitor to the patient. The people [218] would tie a bit of clothing (the patient's?) to the frog and put it back in the water. Then the patient would recover. It is not clear if the clothing was intended as a gift to the frog, or whether the frog served as a scapegoat to carry away the sickness.

When people were sick in spring and were coughing, they put devilclubs in the corners of the house and behind the pillow. They tied a piece around the children's necks to keep the sickness away. We do not know if this is still practised.

Sores or boils were opened with bone lancets. Sore eyes were washed with the juice obtained by boiling the leaves of a plant like the currant. This is the only information obtained about actual treatments, except what ABERCROMBIE reported, and that is given in the next section.

Stories about Shamans

Johnny Stevens:

Galushia explained how Johnny Stevens acquired his powers as a shaman: There was an Indian doctor at Chitina (probably Chitina Joe). His dog died, but the shaman would not bury it

---

[1] JACOBSEN 1884, 392-393.

and left it lying around for two days. Johnny Stevens buried the dog. That night he heard it crying behind the house. He became a shaman and acquired his power from the dog.

It is the common belief among the Eskimo that when Chitina Joe died he willed his power to Johnny Stevens in the shape of a beer glass, a feather, and a Y-shaped alder twig. He had used these in his cures and Johnny now uses them.

Once when they were hunting together near Shepherd Point, Johnny Stevens told (lalushia's cousin (name unknown) that they had come for nothing, because the cousin would soon die. He did (Galushia). [219]

Johnny Stevens says of himself that while he was living near Chitina his cabin burned down and all his belongings were destroyed except $5 in silver and paper money. He wondered why this had happened. He went to a Copper River shaman (Chitina Joe?), who told him to take baths and to stay away from his wife for twelve or thirteen days. He was not to think of any evil and must he better than he used to be. Johnny talked it over with his wife and they decided to try it. At the end of the time the shaman came to see him. "I see you have done everything I told you to do. It is as good as if you had been clean for three months." Since that lime Johnny has had better luck.

Is this actually the explanation of how Johnny acquired his shamanistic powers? All he told us directly was that he had received them from his great uncle, without specifying who that uncle was (Chitina Joe?), or whether the uncle was alive or dead at the time. This story may indicate that the customary three-months probation period was not required of Johnny.

Johnny Stevens has practiced among the Eskimo. LARRY NONINI, at that time superintendent of the native school at Chenega, told us that Johnny had attempted to cure an Eskimo girl who was suffering from epilepsy. For a week she seemed to be benefitted, but then had another attack which resulted in her being sent away to an asylum. Johnny had boasted of a cure, and his failure lowered his prestige among the Eskimo to a great extent.

Old Man Dude:

Old Man Dude is a famous shaman, feared by both Eyak and Eskimo. People arc very rarcful not to offend him. His great rival was the Atna shaman, Chitina Joe. [220]

Galushia tells the following story about Dude: Galushia was out trapping with Chitina Joe. They quarreled over the use of Galushia's belongings, and the latter sent Joe away. Joe told Galushia's brother, Gus, that Galushia would die that summer. Gus went to Old Man Dude, Chitina Joe's rival. Dude told him not to worry, because Joe would die before Galushia, And so it happened. The natives all believe that Dude killed Joe with his power. (See also information obtained from Ma Tiedmann).

Dude hated Chilina Joe because the latter used to tell people that Dude was a bad shaman and was killing people. Dude announced: "I'm going to get that fellow." Later Chitina Joe fell sick. He said: "I see the face of that fellow from Simpson Bay," (meaning Dude). Just before he died he said: "Old Man Dudo is killing me. He got me through the water. If he had tried to get at me overland, I could have stopped him. But he fooled me." Later Dude boasted to Ma Tiedmann: "I told you I fix him." Mrs. GEORGE MACDONALD, formerly teacher at the native school in Cordova, said that just before Joe died, the natives, both Eskimo and Eyak, claimed they could see the spirits of Dude and Joe fighting in the sky, like two flashes of light.

The following stories about Old Man Dude were told by Ma Tiedmann, who used to be his neighbor when she lived at Alice Cove in Simpson Bay.

Dude's wife, *waⁿtıcnvq*, was a strong woman and a good hunter. She wasn't sick a week when she died. Dude had accused her of relationship with Scar Stevens, who had been visiting Simpson Bay a few months before. He told her: "I'll fix you so that no man can use you again." So in three days she started to rot from her rectum to her navel. She was ashamed to tell her husband or to show [221] Ma where she was suffering. She died in three days. When Ma washed her she was rotted so that one could look into her guts. Dude saw her when Ma was washing her. "That's my fault," he admitted. He was sorry then. He buried her near his house and built a little house over the grave, with a window and a table inside. (The house was freshly painted with bluish green when we saw it in 1933, three years after her death (Plate 6, 2)). Dude will never stay away from her grave for long. Once he found a fox building a den under the grave house. He dug it out and chopped it into pieces. "No fox is going to make a home in my wife's grave!" He drinks a lot since his wife died. He is always grateful to Ma for the assistance she gave in burying his wife. He calls her "daughter," and lets her tease him about his shamanistic powers, and he has taught her how to protect herself from the magic of wicked shamans.

When Old Man Dude and Paul Eliah Chimowitski (Eskimo) were living near each other in Port Gravina, Paul used to kill lots of mountain goats while Dude got only a few. Finally Dude got jealous and wouldn't let Paul kill any more, but got them all himself. Dude told Ma this. Even now when Paul has poor hunting he blames Dude for his bad luck.

In the summer of 1933, Dude thought something was going to happen to his son Billy — that he was going to drown, perhaps. But it happened to Billy's fishing partner instead. He went on a drunken party and was robbed and pushed over a cliff by some Filipinos. Ma told this story as an illustration of Dude's clairvoyance.

When the left side of Old Man Dude's face twitches, it means bad luck – he is going to cry. When the right side twitches it means good luck. When we visited him in [222] Simpson Bay, he told Ma that all the day before (August 31, 1933) and that night the left side of his face had twitched. He couldn't sleep all night. He {knew} some native in Old Town (Cordova) was dying. That was why he and Billy had had no luck the day before. They saw several bears and each fired several shots but missed with all of them. He would not tell Ma who was dying, or even whether he knew himself who it was. We later discovered that a native woman had died in Valdez about that time. "Sure that old man was right," said Ma.

On our way back on the same trip we stopped again at Dude's house and obtained a few folk tales and natives words from him. The next morning he asked Ma if NORMAN REYNOLDS were a shaman, but warned her not to let us know that he had asked the question. We did not find out why he had this idea. It may have been REYNOLDS' rather quiet manner — a personal characteristic of both REYNOLDS and WALLACE DE LAGUNA which pleases the natives — combined with REYNOLDS' knowledge of Eyak customs and his linguistic talents.

Mrs. GEORGE MACDONALD told the following stories about Dude:

Mike Britskaloff (the oldest son of Black Stepan, an Eskimo at Chenega) brought his baby to Mrs. MACDONALD for medical treatment. The child was badly burned. He told her that he had had nothing but bad luck since he quarreled with Old Man Dude a few months before. He had loaned Dude a fishing net, and when Dude failed to return it, he had gone to Dude's house in the latter's absence and had taken it back. Soon afterwards one of his children had fallen off his boat and was nearly drowned. Later another child had been injured falling down stairs, and now his [223] baby was badly burned. "I wish I had let the old man keep the net," he said. "It wasn't worth all the trouble it caused me.

I hope he thinks he is even with me now and will let me alone."

A native woman in Cordova was dying of cancer. Willy Dude, the Old Man's older son, came to see her and told her that his father was trying to "get her," and that he had wanted him, Willy, to help. He said that he wouldn't do it, but came instead to warn her. She hung crucifixes on her bed and took other precautions, hut died soon after, convinced that Dude had killed her. Mrs. MACDONALD is not certain whether Willy was sincere in wanting to warn the woman, or whether he had come to help his father by terrifying her.

Chitina Joe Nicolai:

Since Chitina Joe has played such an important part in the lives of the Eyak, it seems worthwhile to present the information about him and about other Copper River shamans.

Chitina Joe had a power that was too strong for him to control. "He sung awful heavy." He would fail on the floor and get all his helpers together. He could plunge a knife into his heart and drive out the evil that was there. The knife made no marks. Johnny Stevens, who told us this, did not know if Eyak shamans could do the same.

Most of the information about Chitina Joe was obtained from Ma Tiedmann.

Chitina Joe was a great big fellow. Everybody liked him. He cured lots of people, but he was "kind of goofy." One day he was kalsomining the kitchen, while Ma and some other women were in the parlor. The woman of the house [224] made some tea and said: "Joe, you want some tea?" "No," he said. "And close that door. I can't do anything with you girls around." Ma said: "We're not bothering you. You're in the other room." But they closed the door just to please him. In a few minutes he said: "Lock that door. I can't work." He was always funny when women were around.

Ma's brother, Nick Chimowitski, was sick. He had some kind of pain or cold. His mother-in-law wanted to call in Chitina Joe. Nick finally agreed and Joe was sent for. He came in and said: "Nobody laugh now!" Silvester (one of the younger Chimowitskis, exact relationship unknown, claims to have succeeded to the chieftainship after the death of Chief Peter, Makari's older brother) and some other young fellows were sitting around, nearly bursting with suppressed laughter. Joe had a basin of water brought and had a hot fire made in the stove. He walked around the patient four or five times with the beer glass full of water. Then he set the beer glass on the floor and placed his forked alder stick beside it. He placed his hands on Nick's head, then wiped them together. He blew on them clasped together over the fire. He stroked Nick's back from his head down to the end of his spine, then repeated the motions of blowing on his hands over the fire. Then he stroked Nick's sides from his head down to his ribs, and repeated the motions over the fire. Then he danced five times around the beer glass with the eagle feather in his hand, while he sang. Then he took a sip out of the beer glass and made Nick drink some. This was repeated five times. Nick recovered completely next day and gave Joe $5. Joe never asked payment in advance.

Mary Chimowitski, Paul Eliah's sister and Willy Totcmoff's wife, was sick at Tatitlik. They brought her to Cordova [225] and took her to the two white physicians. Neither did her any good. Nick's mother-in-law suggested Chitina Joe. Mary was afraid at first, but finally consented to send for him. Joe knew why he was wanted, though no one had told him. He said he was not yet very strong, like the old Chitina doctors. He had Mary sit in a chair and put the beer glass full of water and his forked alder twig on the floor. Then he danced around the chair five times and sang, calling for his spirit. "You got some stuff in your ear," he said. He put his hands in the fire and blew on them, then placed them on her ear, five times. Then he gave her a drink of water (from the beer glass?) and said: "Not ripe yet. May be in two or three days it will break and come out." Two days later the car broke and she recovered. There was no pain or swelling. The white doctors hadn't known what was the matter with her.

Ma's aunt, Mrs. Nelson, who is married to a white man and lives at the site of old Eyak, met Chitina Joe in town. Later she dreamed that he was coming across Eyak River towards her, carrying something wrapped in canvas on his back. She grabbed her prayer book and holy water, and threw some of the holy water into the river. The canvas dropped with a splash and Joe ran away- A few days later she learned that Joe was sick. He insisted that he had not intended to hurt any one. Ma explains that he had been paying Mrs. Nelson unwelcome attentions.

Other Copper River Shamans

Some Copper River doctors could put a small stone on the ground and make it so heavy that no one could lift it.

A Copper River shaman died and came to life again. After four years he died and again came back to life. This [226] happened eight times. Before he died (which time?) he said: "Anytime you hear my song in the air, watch my body. I will come back to life." Two years later his power came down like a feather. They heard his song. The feather lit on his body, which was then the size of a grouse. In eight days it grew to ordinary size.

A shaman could make his son or daughter come back to life, but the child would really be dead. A Copper River doctor had a daughter ten years old. She got sick and died. He stayed by the body for two days and two nights, singing. He put his wooden doll with his power inside her. She fell asleep as if she were really dead. She was wrapped up to be buried. However, she recovered and lived to grow up. She carried the doll inside her for four of five years, when it was born as a child. She is dumb now because she is really dead.

It was felt that Copper River shamans were more powerful than Eyak shamans.

ABERCROMBIE has written a little about shamans: "In the supernatural powers of the shaman considerable faith exists, but not amounting to implicit trust. The degree of belief might be sufficient to cause delay and a demand for increased pay when disaster was predicted, but not enough to deter them from joining an expedition if the reward was sufficiently great. A previous interview with the prophet would save some annoyance in this respect. Although [not?] an Eyak himself, the shaman often with them is a half-paralyzed Thlinket, who speaks a few words of Chinook and English. His influence has been somewhat lessened by his misfortune, which is ascribed to the superior power of his rival at Yakutat."[1] [227]

In conversation, Colonel ABERCROMBIE adds further information about Kai, part of which contradicts this published statement. Kai was about 30 years old in 1884. ABERCROMBIE thinks he was not a Tlingit, but that he had originally come from the interior though he had never seen his rival at Taral. It was the latter who was supposed to have paralyzed Kai's hands. However, Kai had been on the Yukon and had learned to speak Chinook jargon from the Hudson's Bay Company men. He could speak no English. Kai lived in a little hut in the bushes, between the graveyard and the other houses at Alaganik. With him lived an old woman, not his wife, who

---

[1] ABERCROMBIE 1900, 397.

acted as his housekeeper and nurse. She was one of the leaders of the chorus at the dances and seems to have had some skill in medicine. His assistant, who acted as prompter at the dances, lived with them. None of them had to hunt or fish because the natives kept them supplied with food.

Kai and the Eyak were very much afraid of the medicine man at Taral. He was supposed to have been responsible for the failure of the Russian expeditions up the Copper River. Both the Eyak and the Atna believed that the river was controlled by a spirit subject to the Taral shaman. If a canoe ventured into white water, the spirit would pull it under. ABERCROMBIE was cautioned about this demon after one of his canoes had nearly capsized. The river water is so cold that gasses do not form in the stomach of a drowned man so that the corpse never floats. This accounts, ABERCROMBIE; suggests, for the belief that the demon is supposed to make off with drowned men. The Eskimo at Valdez had a similar belief about the Valdez Glacier river. When they heard glacial boulders knocking together in the river, they thought it was the spirit. Similarly, when the Eyak at Alaganik heard ice blocks falling from the glaciers [228] into the Copper River, they thought it was due to the Taral shaman and his familiar demon in the river. They would clap their hands to their mouths and look around anxiously. ABERCROMBIE says that this was the typical Indian gesture of surprise and fear, but it may have been intended primarily to keep out evil spirits. (Compare with the quotation from JACOBSEN in the preceding section.) The Taral medicine man was also responsible for the periods of low water and floods on the Copper River. He made the spring freshets to prevent the Eyak from coming up the river. Kai cautioned ABERCROMBIE against him, and, as already stated, gave him a carved paddle for protection. The Copper River Indians only laughed at it, for they knew that their shaman was stronger than Kai. All the Eyak believed that the Taral shaman would kill ABERCHOMBIE, and Pete Johnson half believed it, too.

Kai wore a little bag around his neck in which he kept sharks' teeth, claws, animal bones, and the like. ABERCROMBIE used to see him take these out of the bag and shuffle them about on a piece of skin or on the ground. While manipulating them he would mumble something, and from time to time glance up at the sky. He was apparently making medicine for someone. It was believed that Kai could look through the eyes painted on the doors of the houses and the lockers, and on the boxes and paddles, and see what had become of lost or stolen things.

The old woman who lived with Kai practiced medicine. ABERCROMBIE saw her doctoring the cuts of children with some kind of poultice made from fresh roots which she crushed together between two stones. The paste seemed to sting, for the children would suck in their breath with the pain, though they were too Spartan to cry. ABERCROMBIE had cut his leg on a rusty nail and the old woman offered [229] to help him. On top of the poultice or mash, she made a bandage of certain green leaves, tied about with wythes. These fell off in two days, leaving the cut covered with a scab like that produced by "Newskin." The wound itself was healed within a week. Dr. ROBINSON, the surgeon of the expedition, was much impressed with the medicine and wanted to obtain some of the plants for his own use. The old woman, however, refused to reveal what they were. Dr. ROBINSON was of the opinion that the mash made from the roots acted as a disinfectant. Pete Johnson told ABERCROMBIE that the old woman used to cook medicine for internal use.

JACOBSEN relates the following story; "Captain ANDERSEN told me that during his former stay [at Cape Martin] he was waiting for the arrival of a schooner. A shaman offered to find out by means of his magic whether the schooner would come or not. For this purpose a public gathering was appointed, and the magician first did his usual tricks. On this occasion, as he was being swung to and fro over the fire, the rope suddenly burned up and the medicine man fell into the blazing fire. With lightning speed he jumped up and out of the fire, but this hasty flight of the man who had hitherto been believed unburnable produced such a comic impression that many of those present burst out with a loud laugh. Aroused by this to the uttermost, the shaman turned his entire wrath against the unlucky schooner, and cried out that she would encounter a misfortune. That same year the ship ran by accident onto a rock near Kodiak Island, outside the Harbor of St. Paul, and the esteem of the shaman who prophesied 'this disaster' rose thereby to such an extent that even today he is honored as one of the most important medicine men of the region."[1] [230]

Religion

All animate and inanimate things have souls or spirit "owners." Each animal, Galushia explained, is supposed to have a soul that is "in charge of it, the way people are in charge of dogs." He was unable to tell us anything about the substance or appearance of these spiritual "owners." According to Johnny Stevens, trees, rocks, plants, the sea, etc, have "men or women behind them." These souls are shaped like human beings, but he thought that animals' souls looked like the animals themselves. In the tales, however, animals appear in human form in their own country or under certain conditions. To judge by analogy with the same and similar tales among the Eskimo, these characters are animals' souls or owners, and they are in human form. The soul of the animal seems to be located in the head, since the eyes of the dead animal could see the hunter, and the preservation of the head (at least of land animals) was necessary to insure the reincarnation of the animal soul. The hunter would cut the dead animal's eyes to prevent it from seeing him and recognizing him again, and would skin the head (simply in order to have the complete pelt?) before caching or burying it. Galushia said that all the souls of water animals have homes under the water, and yet no part of the seal had to be put back into the water. The Eyak did not practice the Eskimo custom of pouring fresh water on the dead seal's nose to give it a drink. The Eyak did not put animal bones in the fire, for this would cause pain to the animal's soul. We learned nothing specific about the souls of fish, except that we may assume them to be located in the tail, the blood, or the entrails, since these parts had to be thrown hack into the water to insure the return of the salmon the following season. (Note that [231] in *Tale* 4B, the Salmon Boy finally dies when his genital organs are cut.) Galushia knew nothing about Eyak notions of the cause of life and had never heard it discussed.

Galushia could tell us nothing about the size, shape, material, appearance, or location of the human soul. He did not think the soul was supposed to be able to leave the body during sleep and have dream experiences. He said the Eyak did not usually believe in dreams. A new-born baby had the soul of a dead relative, revived by the Sun, but Galushia did not know how the soul was supposed to have entered the child's body. He believed that a part of the dead person's soul may have remained separate from the part that was reincarnated. He had never heard this discussed, but thought that it must be so. Now this suggests that the Eyak may have had a vague notion of two souls, perhaps something like that of the Eskimo, who believe that each animate being has both a spirit owner, in human shape, and a life principle. When a person dies, the ghosts of all those who have died and are not yet reborn walk around the house. Ghosts are invisible, harmless, and make no noise. The popping of logs in a fire is the dead person

---

[1] JACOBSEN 1884, 392.

speaking. When this occurred, the people would put food into the fire for him. They would never spit in the fire, for the spittal would boil into a dead person's house. This was all that Galushia could tell us about the soul. He knew nothing about a spirit land, nor of any punishment for the wicked after death.

Johnny Stevens was able to supply more specific information. He also believed in reincarnation and cited as proof physical peculiarities of the dead relative which reappeared in the child. He supposed that it was the person's "mind" which is reborn. He does not know how the "mind" looks, [232] but thinks it must resemble the man, since that is how it appears in dreams. You can see animals and objects in dreams, and this shows that all things have a "mind" or soul. He does not know where the "mind" stays when it is in the body, but supposes it is in the breath. When a man sleeps his "mind" leaves him and travels around in the air, to return before daybreak. "The mind is just like the wind." If someone is wakened while his "mind" is still far away, he will be crazy. This is the explanation of (all?) insanity. In a dream your "mind" may meet someone, who asks what you are doing. You say: "I want to get help." Perhaps he will help your "mind" to return to your body. But perhaps he is bad and has more power than you; then you will feel sick for a few days after you wake.

A shaman can make a man sick by removing his "mind." Another shaman can restore it by singing and using his helpers. When a doctor is in a trance his body stays in the same place but his "mind" can travel anywhere.

In answer to our questions about the life after death, Galushia said that there was a man who died and was dead for four days. When he came back to life he told about going to heaven. He had gone up a stairway. Heaven was a pretty place with lots of colored flowers. After this, the Eyak no longer worshiped the Sun. This is obviously a recent story. It would he interesting to know just what form the new cult took, but we did not obtain further details. Johnny Stevens said also that the spirits of the dead go to heaven.

In the old days the Sun was worshiped. Galushia's mother used to go out of the house at sunrise and sunset and say prayers and make "funny motions" to the Sun, but she did not teach Galushia to do this. The old people [233] used to make offerings of some kind to the Sun. Johnny Stevens was perhaps referring to this belief when he said:

"Something up above is looking after us all the time." Kai may have been appealing to the Sun or to this power in the sky when he kept looking up while making medicine with his bag of amulets.

When asked about the nature of the moon and the stars, Galushia could only refer us to the Raven myths. People used to think the earth was flat and not very big. One could travel to the edge. There was a hole at the edge where the tide rushed in and out. Raven once went too close and fell in. Galushia knew nothing about the winds.

The northern lights appear when someone has just been killed or is about to die. The red streak in the lights is the person's blood, and the waving is the dripping of the blood. If the lights seem to approach the house, someone in it will die. People were afraid to look at the lights for fear they would he killed.

Thunder was supposed to be caused by a big bird like a raven. A man once found one of its feathers. It was so big that he could not lift even one end. Lightning is caused when the bird winks. The Thunderbird makes earthquakes when it moves. Sometimes it steals people. As long as the Thunderbird is over the ocean there will be bad weather. When thunder is heard in the fall, the bird is going in (home?) for the winter. There is usually good weather during the last of October through November and that is considered the best time to hunt. The Eyak never saw the lightning strike, and when they found a tree that had been split open they thought it was the work of another creature.

At eclipses of the sun and moon everyone was frightened, but Galushia did not know why. They probably hid in [234] the house. He knew of no solstice ceremonies, and no ceremonies of making a new fire.

We have already mentioned the belief that the Copper River was controlled by a malevolent spirit that stole people who ventured into the rapids, and that this spirit was the familiar of the Taral shaman (ABERCROMBIE).

The creature that was supposed to split open trees has sharp claws and walks like a man. It carries its young on its back, and the baby cries all the time. If a man hears the crying, he must take off all his clothes, run, and try to touch the animal. This brings him good luck.

Sometimes a man would find a young animal in the heart of a tree, wrapped in transparent skin. To bring it home insures good luck. Some people found other charms for good luck. It was believed that there was a human being in the woods who gave good luck to hunters that rose early in the morning. (Is this an echo of the Eskimo belief in *nunam cua* {Sedna}, the woman who controls the land animals?) We have already mentioned in the section on Magic rising before the raven caws as bringing the hunter luck.

Bad weather was believed to be caused by intentional abortion, and by the murder and concealment of an illegitimate child (see *Tale* 28). Bad weather is caused when children play with boats or sleds or snowshoes in winter. To spin a buzz in winter brings the north wind. If a young girl walks about during the period of her puberty isolation it would bring rain. Rain is also caused by touching freshwater clams.

Good weather can be brought back by several methods. A pregnant woman would stand in the smoke of burning branches. Scraps of skin cut from clothing would be burned [235] with spruce and hemlock boughs, while the people sing "Good weather!" An egg shell with fire in it would be set afloat. A dead bullhead or chubb would be fastened to a tree with pitch. A dead bird, the beak propped open with a stick, would be set under the eaves of the house so the rain could drip into its mouth. When the sun comes out after rain, one can keep the good weather by lighting a fire.

It was believed that if a man fed a starving animal or bird he would be rewarded by good luck in hunting and in other things (Compare *Tale* 23). The generosity of the chiefs and wealthy persons towards the poor was rewarded by good luck. It is wrong to laugh at the animals. If you laugh at Porcupine, the north wind will blow. (This was given in explanation of Raven, incident 18). If you laugh at Raven, it will be bad weather. Once Scar Stevens and Gus Nelson were playing mouth harps. Some ravens were hopping around, as if dancing, and the men laughed at them. Next day it snowed, and the people made Scar and Gus burn their mouth harps and stand in the smoke.

Ravens also announced events. When a raven flies overhead calling "*qayaq*," he is calling "us." This means that people are coming after him, over the ice or in a boat. When he calls "*qələq*", it means rain. In the Tlingit war story, *Tale* 26, disaster was foretold because a raven began to cat the extra clothing of the war party (indicating that they would have no further need of clothes?).

Formerly the Eyak would never kill the first fly or mosquito to appear in the spring. To do so would cause the death of a young boy. The mosquitoes would take him back to their home in place of the mosquito that had been killed.

In addition to the mythical animals already mentioned, the Eyak believed there were large animals living in the [236] woods that resembled gorillas. They were hairy, and had no tails. Chitina Joe once saw such a creature sitting on the bank, eating fish. He fainted. Not even shamans were strong enough to fight them. Such an animal appears in *Tale* 23. There were also giant animals like the Mouse or Mole (*Tale* 14), the Devilfish (*Tale* 15B) the Bear (*Tale* 15A) and the Beaver (*Tale* 15A). These monsters lived underground or under the water. They were all bad and ate people. Apparently, if you knew the animal's song, it would not harm you (*Tale* 14A). There were also Wolf Men, a cannibal tribe living in the interior, who made bark canoes (*Tale* 19). These people were perhaps the upper Copper River Atna, who live at Copper Center and who were believed by both Eskimo and Eyak to be cannibals, or they may have been some mythical tribe beyond them. The Tree People (*Tale* 20) were giants who lived on the upper Copper River and who sometimes came down to capture Eyak hunters to eat. They were about half as tall as a large tree, lived in brush houses, and made a magic snare that closed automatically around their victims. They may also be an interior Athapaskan tribe, translated into legend. In explaining *Tale* 18, Galushia said that there were supposed to be as many dwarfs living about the lake on Strawberry Point, Hinchinbrook Island, as there were tribes of Indians. The Owl who takes away bad, crying children and the Checkers People who take away children who play with checkers out of season appear in *Tales* 31 and 32.

Land-otters, as already observed, occupy a peculiar position in the animal world, since they are believed to be transformed men who have drowned. This notion is shared by the Eskimo and Tlingit, and is still held, at least by the older people. Besides *Tale*s 12A and B, Galushia gave [237] us other items of information. The old people used to be afraid of hurting the land-otters for fear of being killed by them. Besides, if one killed a land-otter one might kill a relative who had drowned. Once a man went out in a boat on Eyak Lake, near one of the small islands. He rocked his canoe until it was half full of water and called for help. In no time somebody came after him. It looked like a real man but it was actually a land-otter. The man killed it. He did this on purpose to show the people that land-otters do come after drowning persons. When Galushia was a little boy his brother made him a little skiff. His mother used to tell him not to go out far. "You're going to tip over," she would warn him, "and the land-otters will get you!" Once Galushia heard someone crying outside the house. He hunted but could not find anyone. The others told him it was the voice of a relative who had drowned and been turned into a land-otter. Land-otters cry when they see people, and the natives sometimes hear them crying in the woods. Some persons claim to have seen beings that were half land-otter and half human. This was before they had completely turned into animals.

Wolves and walruses were also supposed to be transformed human beings and were never hunted. If a man were attacked by wolves, he could escape injury by telling them not to hurt him. Loons were not hunted because a boy had once turned into one, but we do not know if all loons were transformed human beings. Certainly the transformation of Salmon Boy into a fish has not prevented the Eyak from catching salmon.

Finds of fossil bones of extinct animals were explained by the belief they belonged to big animals that formerly lived in the ground. [238]

Games

Children used to play with skins of little animals, such as a young beaver or seal, or a bird, stuffed with moss. The Eyak did not like dolls in human form, though we were unable to learn the reason for this. ABERCROMBIE, however, saw skin dolls in human shape at Alaganik.

Children had a popgun made out of a wooden tube through which a plunger was pushed to propel a wooden ball. Boys also had blowguns made of the wing bone of an eagle or swan, from which they shot small darts. Boys threw darts by means of a whip sling. The wooden handle was about a foot long; the string was a foot and a half long and ended in a knot which fitted into a notch cut in the middle of the dart. The dart was feathered with two, not three, split feathers, tied on longitudinally. Children also had a throwing stick for pebbles. It was made of a stick, split halfway down, with a lashing about the bottom of the split. Unlike the Eskimo toy, the upper end of the cleft was left open. We have already mentioned that ABERCROMBIE saw boys shooting at fish with bows and plain wooden arrows. Galushia played hide-and-seek as a child. One team would hide while the other team hunted until all were found. The Eyak children did not play blind-man's-buff, marbles, ball games, or skipping rope.

Children were not allowed to play with boats in winter because they would cause bad weather. To play with toy sleds or snowshoes would bring cold. Good weather could be secured by burning the toys. They also played with wooden tops and buzzes, but to spin the buzz in winter would call the north wind. The buzz was a flat piece of wood, spun on cords passing through two holes and twisted together. [239]

Both adults and children made string figures (cat's cradle). This was a game played in winter, for if played in summer it would bring rain. There were no taboos about the age and sex of those who played.

The other games described by Galushia were for adults.

He does not think the Eyak used to swim for fun before the coming of the whites, though a few individuals may have known how. The salt water is certainly too cold for anything more than a plunge, but in summer Eyak Lake is warm enough to permit bathing and swimming, and is much enjoyed by whites and natives.

The Stick Game was played by two teams, each consisting of from six to fourteen men. Any type of property might be wagered, but each player bet only with the man who sat opposite him. Every player on one team had two cylindrical sticks, small enough to be concealed in the hand. One stick in the set was marked with a bit of thong tied about the middle. The men holding these sticks would shuffle them about for a short time, their hands hidden behind their backs. Then all would hold their hands out before them, the palms closed, and one man from the opposing team would try to guess which hand held the marked stick. (Apparently at the end of the guessing the sticks were passed to the opposite team.) Small sticks, used as counters, were placed on the ground between the two teams. The number used depended on how long they wanted to play. If the guesser had correctly designated the hand in which the marked stick was hidden, the player holding it had to drop out. If the guesser failed, his opponents took one counter from the pile in the middle. After all the members of one team had been forced to drop out, their opponents took all the counters. A team had to win all the [240] counters from their opponents and from the pile in the middle to win the game.

The Partner Game was played by two pairs of partners. A small shaving was placed on a seal skin in the middle of the room. Two men sat facing each other at opposite ends of the room, the partners being divided. In turn they tossed wooden disks, two to four inches in diameter, at the shaving. The man beside the tosser watched him to prevent cheating. Points were counted according to the relative nearness of the disks thrown to the shaving. This was a gambling game.

Shinny was played on the beach. The teams were evenly matched but might contain any number of players. The two moieties might play against each other in Shinny, but rarely did in the Stick and Partner Games. The shinny sticks were naturally curved pieces of wood. The ball, a roughly rounded wooden block, was buried in the sand, and two men, a player from each team, dug it up with their sticks. The teams then tried to drive the ball across their opponents' goal line. The field was about two or three hundred yards long. There were no rules, but it was considered wrong to hit an opponent intentionally. According to Makari, the- Eskimo and Eyak used to play Shinny together.

Shooting matches with bow and arrow were also used for gambling. The target was a bundle of grass, with a stick yet up to mark the spot from which the shots had to be made. Boys had matches among themselves. A shooting match is mentioned in *Tale* 9. Makari said that the Eyak used to compete with the Eskimo in shooting contests, but that the Eyak were "bum shots."

Foot races, both sprints and distance runs. Were held [241] on the beaches, and bets were placed on the contestants. Shinny, shooting matches, and foot races were held on the beaches only during the sea-otter hunting season, i.e. in July. Tossing in a seal skin was also a favorite sport then, though we have no information as to whether it was also played at other times. Sometimes if a dog scented a porcupine in the woods, the men would race to it; the first to arrive would kill the porcupine and keep it.

The Eyak used to hold canoe races for any size canoe, including those used for war. The moieties often used to race against each other, but did not often bet on the races.

In former days the Eyak built special racing canoes, and Galushia thinks they used to bet on races in which these were used.

There were several forms of wrestling. One was for two men to grab each other and try to throw each other to the ground. Or they would lock their middle fingers together, and each struggle to straighten out the fingers of his opponent. Another form was for two men to sit on the ground with their feet braced together and try to pull each other over forward with their arms.

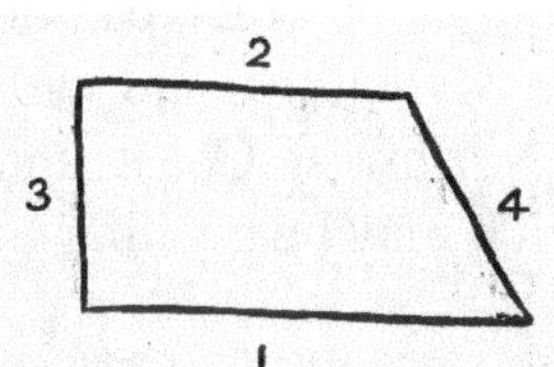

Fig. 18. Die for gambling, as sketched by Galushia Nelson.

The Eyak also used to gamble with dice. The die was a flat piece of bone, about two or three inches (5 or 7.5 cm.) long, and trapezoidal in outline (Figure 18). It was tossed into the air, and the score depended on which edge it landed and remained balanced. The longest edge counted 1, the opposite edge, which was next in length, 2, the edge at right angles to these 3, and the oblique edge 4. There was no score if it fell on either of the flat sides. [242]

The Eyak did not practice gymnastics on a stretched thong like the Eskimo.

Checkers was said to be a woman's game. In *Tale* 32, however, it is played by a young man. Galushia supposed checkers to have been an aboriginal game, and was much surprised when we told him that it had probably been introduced by the whites. As early as in 1791 SARYCHEV observed that the Aleut of Unalaska were very proficient at cards and checkers, which they had evidently learned from the Russian hunters.[1] It is possible that the latter game spread east to the Eyak before the Russians came among them to any great extent, and so appeared to the natives to be an aboriginal game. The Eyak thought it meant bad luck to play checkers at any time except during the one month when it was proper. We did not learn what month this was, nor what are the rules for the game.

---

[1] SARYTSCHEW 1805-06, I 78.

Part II
Eyak Folklore[‡]

Introduction

The [245] following tales have been written down as nearly as possible in the language of our informants. Most of the stories were told us by Galushia, prompted by his wife, from whom he had originally learned them. A few he wrote out for us. The stories which Annie told were rendered in Eyak and were translated by her husband. She told us that she had learned them from old Chief Joe. A few stories were obtained from Johnny Stevens and from Old Man Dude. The latter was hard to understand, not only because he had a poor command of English, but because he stuttered when he spoke it. He unfortunately refused to tell the stories in Eskimo, which he spoke with a good deal of fluency, although Matrona Tiedemann offered to act as interpreter for him. Dude informed us that all the myths were supposed to be sung. After giving us his version in English of the Raven Cycle, he sang the same in Eyak. Unfortunately we were not able to record cither the text or the music, Galushia told us also that all stories were supposed to be recited word-perfect, but he did not remember which ones were sung. He specified that *Tale* 6A, "Living with the Black Bear," was not sung. Furthermore, all the stories had titles, a number of these were secured in text. Where the correct title is known it is indicated by quotation marks.

Some of the stories are said to be of foreign origin. Thus, [246] *Tale* 1, "Porcupine and Beaver in Partnership," is supposed to be a Copper River story, while the war story. *Tale* 26, is Tlingit, and refers to TIingit villages. Actually there is very little in this collection which can be credited to Eyak originality. Almost every tale is found in BOAS' *Tsimshian Mythology,* and with few exceptions the plot elements have a wide distribution along the Northwest Coast and adjacent areas. Without material in text a study of the stylistic features which may be peculiar to the Eyak versions would not be very fruitful.

We have little information about songs. We have mentioned the songs used in potlatches, the songs of the shamans, and the derision songs. Apparently every person (men only?) had his own song, but when these were sung we did not learn.

The Raven Cycle

Altogether twenty incidents of the Raven Cycle were obtained, and four more were mentioned.

Ten incidents were told by Galushia, eight by Johnny Stevens, and an equal number by Old Man Dude. One of Galushia's incidents was also told by Stevens, one by Dude, and one by both. Of Dude's stories, Galushia told one, Stevens told two, and one was told by both Galushia and Stevens. Of Stevens' incidents, Galushia told one. Dude told two, and one was told by both Galushia and Dude.

‡ In addition to these by Old Man Dude, Johnny Stevens, Galushia Nelson and Anna Nelson Harry, Eyak stories were later told by Lena Nacktan, George Johnson, Sue Abraham, and Herman Kitka Sr, then published in English by John F.C Johnson 1988.

The incidents are designated as follows:

1. "Where Old Raven Made the Earth" (GN).
2. Raven Makes the Rivers and other Geographical Features (GN).
3. "Ugly Raby Crow" (Theft of Daylight) (GN and JS). [247]
4. Raven and Echo (D and JS).
5. Raven and the Grass Blanket (D).
6. Raven Steals the Fisherman's Bait (D).
7. "Where Old Raven was Walking in Back of the Waves"
        (Raven and the King Salmon) (GN, JS, and D).
8. (How Raven became Black) (mentioned by JS as conclusion to incident 7).
9. Raven Robs his Partners (D).
10. Raven and the Owner of the Tides (D and JS) (Told by GN as part of incident 11).
11. "Old Raven and Magpie" (D and GN).
12. "Where Old Raven Went Visiting the Eagle" (GN).
13. "Where Old Raven Went into a Whale" (GN).
14. "Where Old Raven Pitched the Seals' Eyes Together" (GN).
15. (Raven and the Blackfish) (Mentioned by JS).
16. "'I am Light.'" (Raven Kills his Partner) (GN).
17. Raven Pretends to Use his own Body for Bait (GN).
18. Raven and Porcupine (GN).
19. (Raven Raises an Army in the Sky) (mentioned by GN).
20. (Raven Journeys to the End of the Earth) (mentioned by GN).
21. Raven Teaches the People (JS).
22. Raven and the People with the Magic Canoe (JS).
23. Raven Marries (JS).
24. Raven Turns War Parties into Rocks (JS).

The incidents told by Old Man Dude and by Johnny Stevens are given below in the order in which they were told. Those told by Galushia Nelson were not obtained in any definite order. [248]

The Raven Cycle, Told by Old Man Dude

Old Man Dude learned the following incidents from his father. He recognized that they form only part of the complete cycle.

Incident 4: Raven and Echo

Crow first eats mussels. [It was] low tide. He was opening them. He was eating them — $h^w up$ [inhale]. Hear someone making same noise behind him. He throws the shells back over his shoulder.

When he was through he took a walk. Walk to someone's smokehouse. [It was] big. No one there. [There was a] fire there, lots of meat getting smoked. He sit down looking around. No one there. Soon pot came to the fire. Water in it. Smoked meat dropped in it. He cut, he go in the pot. [It was cut, it fell into the pot.] It got cooked. When [it was] cooked. Crow put it in

115

the plate. Crow eat it. [There was] seal's fat hanging up in the corner. Crow saw [it] when he came in. Crow go outside. He takes that fat and chewed it. Two men started to pull his hair from both sides. Crow said, "Wait a minute. I give him to you. Eat, too! Eat, too!" Crow hung up the fat and went outside.

Incident 5: Raven and the Grass Blanket

(The following is somewhat confused.)

Crow went for several days. He had a blanket. [He found a blanket on the ground.] He threw away his old blanket. He had a grass blanket [now], but it rotted, so he had no more blanket. He went to the beach. He was calling the westerly wind. "Hey Westerly Wind, give me back my blanket!" [He got his own blanket back again.] He used his own blanket. [249]

Incident 6: Raven Steals the Fisherman's Bait

He see a fisherman. He said, "What bait you got?" "Seal fat, I got for bait," he [the fisherman] hollered. Crow he picked up the water on a stick and walked under it. [He began to eat the man's bait.] He chew yet. The man feel it. He hooked Crow on the nose. Too much cheat people, that Crow. Man in the canoe want to haul him up. No. Crow held to the bottom of the canoe so he couldn't get hauled up. Pretty soon he broke the Crow's nose.

Crow fixed his nose with gum before he went to the fisherman's house. He went inside the house. "Nobody found something around here?" he asked.

"Fisherman, he found something," they said. "He hook him."

"Let me see." He look at him. "What nose is this? I don't see this kind of a live nose." [Before they could stop him?] Crow put him on his nose. He fly.

Incident 7: Raven and the King Salmon

He walk again. He see a king salmon close to shallow water. He tell that salmon: "Come ashore, that man talking bad." The salmon came to shore. Crow says, "Wait a minute." He wanted a small stick to club the salmon he couldn't find it. Salmon went in water again. Next time he killed the salmon when he came ashore.

Incident 9: Raven Robs His Partners

Crow had two partners, a bluejay and some other kind of bird. He made a fire in the beach and made a hole. He put the salmon in the hole and put fire on top to bake it. Crow told his partner: "Go look for dry wood. It don't look cooked yet." Crow dug it up when his partner went away. He ate the whole thing. Crow put the fire back on the hole. Partner came back and found him and sat down alongside the fire. They asked, "Fish baked yet?"

"No!" Crow, he walked again. [250]

Incident 10: Raven and the Owner of the Tides

Crow walked a long ways. He saw a sea-egg [sea urchin] in the water. He jump in the water. Can't get it. He got it finally.

At that time it was high ride all the time. Old girl kept the ride up. He came to [her] house. He said, "Jesus Christ, I'm cold! I get too many sea-eggs."

The old lady said, "Where you get it?"

"Where I get it? Nothing doing!" He put the sea-eggs on her bottom and rubbed it.

Old lady, she cried like hell. "Leave me alone! Leave me alone! Tide's going out," she said. He go outside. Look at tide. It was going out already. He leave her there. Don't touch her no more.

Incident 11: Raven and Magpie

He walk out and find everything: seal, halibut, codfish, all stranded. He kicked an old stick on the bottom. "Hey, get up! Help me!" Stick get up. He help.

Crow made a house over there. He got a partner yet. [The transformed stick? Or Magpie, as in GNs version?). He smoked all the stuff he found, in the house. He slept many days beside the fire. Soon, "hu hu" he dream. Soon he get up. Said to partner, "Look out, war coming. You go to war," he tell his partner.

Partner went outside. He fought him [the war]. Crow [stayed] inside. Partner come inside and look at the Crow. Crow had already cleaned up all the food in the house. Crow cheated his partner again.

[His partner put Crow in a box and tied it up.] He don't say nothing. He packed it up the mountain. Crow told his partner, "Fine day, but half the mountain got fog yet. You'll get lonesome. You going to cry." [251]

He [the partner] throw the box with Crow inside it down the mountain. Going to kill the Crow. Crow, he die. Partner stay in the house, how many days. He got lonesome. Crow was dead and his meat was already spoiled. Partner still waiting [?] for him. Partner found him and poked the Crow right on the ear. Soon Crow scratched his head. Crow said. "What's the matter? I am sleeping now."

[Old Man Dude did not remember the rest.]

The Raven Cycle, Told by Johnny Stevens

Incident 3: Raven Steals the Sun

In early days everything was dark: there were no stars, no moon, and no sun. Raven saw that a rich family had the sun, moon, and the stars hanging in a box from the ceiling.

A girl and a man went after water. Raven made himself into a feather,[1] and dropped into the water. The girl drank the water, and Raven turned into a baby inside her. The child was born a short time later after, and no one knew how it happened. The child kept looking at the box. (He was able to fly five or six days after birth.) He kept crying for the box, and at last his grandfather gave it to him. Then he flew with them [the sun, moon, and stars] through the smokehole.

---

[1] Note that the Eyak word for 'feathers' is the same as for 'leaf'. See Appendix II.

People were fishing in a dark place, getting lots of fish. Raven had come to them before and had wanted fish, but could not see. He stopped at the fishing place and opened the box. Sun, moon, and stars flew into the sky. Then people could not sleep, it was light all the time. Then Raven turned into a man with leaves (feathers) for clothes, but he still had the Raven's beak. [252]

Then he went to the first house. The people all went to sleep but they had left a watchman on duty. He saw a faint light appearing in the east but he didn't know what it was. It grew lighter and lighter. He called the people and they all came out and looked with wonder. No one knew what had happened except the grandfather who had let the sun go. The people went in to eat and the Raven kept looking at his mother, so everyone suspected he was the strange baby who had been born to her, but they were not quite sure.

Incident 10: Raven and the Owner of the Tides

Raven asked about the seawater – "Why didn't it go down?" No one could answer. He went away, walking and flying along the beach until he came to a house from which smoke was rising. He entered in the shape of a man. He spoke. The woman who lived there turned around but Raven was invisible. She groped around for the speaker.

She said, "Oh, why are my eyes so sore?"

Raven said, "Help me, and I'll help you. You make the tide go down so I can get some clams to eat. I'll make your eyes well."

The woman who kept the tides said she would do her best to get the water low enough and finally she succeeded. Raven said that would be low water and that it would come every day. The old lady's eyes grew better and she got younger.

Incident 7: Raven and the King Salmon

Raven went along the beach to a place where there was lots of fish. He was a smart fellow, that Raven. He saw a king salmon who was trying to get something that was up on the beach, but the tide was out and he couldn't reach it. He kept jumping, but each time he fell short and would [253] slide back into the water. Every time he jumped an Eagle would pounce on him, but his scales were slippery and the eagle's claws would slip off. Raven turned into a bird and went over to watch him. He cawed to attract the Eagle's attention and then said, "I'll make a big swell so that you can catch the salmon, if you give me that."

The Eagle agreed. The first wave threw the salmon up on the beach but he managed to slide back. Then Raven caused a mightly wave that threw the salmon way up the timber line. Eagle picked it up and the two birds cooked it. Two hungry men came along and asked for food but the greedy birds refused them. They went away. Before the birds could start to eat, a big landslide swept down and buried the fish, so they got none of it.

Incident 8: How Raven Became Black

They separated. Eagle going west, while Raven came east. Ravens {were} white then, but I don't know how they became black. They made the same noise as now.

Incident 4: Raven and Echo

Raven ran into a storm and had no place to go. He walked along the beach and every time he came to a headland he would fly around it. As he walked, he picked up mussel shells and ate them, and threw the shells into the wood. Every time he threw a shell he would say something and someone would mock him. It was the Echo. Raven grew angry and said, "If you are a man, then let me see your house." The Echo only repeated. Raven thought it could be no man for it was unable to answer.

Incident 21: Raven Teaches the People

Raven kept going around a point until he saw smoke coming up between the trees. He went over and there was a family who had plenty to eat. [254]

"Where do you come from”" they asked.

"I come from all over," he replied.

They gave him raw meat but Raven didn't like it.   "Where I come from," he said, "we cook our meat."

They had never heard of that, so Raven showed them how to boil meat with hot rocks and how to roast it on spits from the fire. The people were grateful and gave Raven a place to sleep in their house. Quantities of fat were hanging from the rafters. After everyone was asleep, Raven turned into a bird, seized the fat, and flew with it out the smokehole. He returned before morning and after changing back into a man, went to sleep again. The people were angry when they saw that all their fat was gone, and they knew that Raven must have taken it, but there were no marks through the doorway to show where he had gone out. They ordered Raven out. He said that he was innocent but left.

He traveled until he came to another house. He took some sea eggs in with him and said, "Have you ever seen anything like this?" The people never had. He also showed them game and fish, and they had never seen them either, for they had no weapons and knew nothing of hunting. Raven showed the man how to make bows and arrows with bone points. Then they went and shot a duck. Since that time men have hunted.

Next he took man up a mountain after bear. By and by a large bear began to chase them. Raven threw his spear and cawed. The bear dropped dead. Since that time men have hunted.

They packed the carcass back to the house and Raven showed them how to skin it and cut it up with a stone knife. [255]

"What can we use the hide for?" they asked. "You can either dry the meat side and make baskets or you can make moccasins." Before that time people had slept on grass − they had no blankets.

"How can we sew the skin?" they wondered. Raven pulled sinews from the bear's back, dried them, and showed the women how to roll them for thread. He also showed them how to cut up and smoke the meat.

The Raven went up on the mountain and killed a goat. He dragged it home. He showed the people what to do with the fat. He took bark and made a pail. The bark is taken from the trees in spring. There is one piece for the side and another for the bottom. It is sewed together with young peeled spruce roots. Holes are drilled for the lashing. Raven put the goat fat in the pail and made grease of it. It got hard, harder than butter. He did that much.

Then he went up the creek and got some fish. The people did not know how to roast meat by the fire, they knew only how to cook on hot stones. Raven then showed how to make a spit of three sticks and roast the fish.

Incident 22: Raven and the People with the Magic Canoe

After a while Raven left these people and went to another camp. He found a place where there were many people. He came among them. They wanted to know where he had come from. This was a different tribe from the one he had left, and they spoke a different language. They wanted Raven to guide them to the people that he had just left. Raven told them that they lived far away. One of the rich men had a skin canoe. The people got into it and Raven showed them the way. All they had to do was to put a pile of fish on each side of the canoe in the bow, and it would go of [256] itself without anyone paddling. When they came to the other people, they wanted to be friends and live together. They had to find out if there was enough for them all to eat. They decided to live together.

Incident 23: Raven Marries

Raven went away again. When he got a little distance from the people, he turned into a bird again. When he was with them he was like a man, all but for his beak, he could not disguise that. Then his clothes were made of different kinds of leaves [feathers]. Raven went away. He came to where there was a family living alone. They had a daughter. Raven wanted to marry her, so he "done everything". He stayed with them a long time [working for the parents?]. He married the daughter. The people liked him because he was so industrious and did not sleep late in the morning. Raven went into the woods and collected many small birds and animals. These were the people under him, he told the girl's parents. He would have lots of help in time of war.

After he married the daughter, the parents did not seem to like him. So he left the parents, taking his wife with him. He had prepared a house with lots of food ready for her. His father and mother-in-law came to visit him. He told them that he would live in that place, but that when they got old they could come to him and he would make them young again. He had a comb that would color their white hair again and make them young. That was what happened.

Incident 24: Raven Turns War Parties into Rocks

Finally his helper came and said: "There is war and trouble coming because we are too rich." He saw something coming and turned it into a rock. Soon something, another attacking war party, came again. Raven's helpers warned him [257] uand he turned them into rocks. Raven made several islands out of war parties. He lived there many years. He is said to be still living there.

The white people tried to catch him with drink. They got a drug in tea to try to make him fall asleep. Raven, however, made their boat stop and so escaped. [JS does not know what happened to the white people in the boat].

Raven never sits still. The only time he is in the house is at night. He has no children. His parents-in-law came to visit him and he makes them young.

Incident 25: Raven and the Killerwhales

Another part of the story tells how Raven came among the killerwhales. They did not like him. They live in the water in rock houses and live on meat and fish. Inside their house they look like people. Raven had to get away from them.

Raven Cycle told by Galushia Nelson

The following incidents were not told as a connected narrative as were those recited by Old Man Dude and Johnny Stevens. Each was given as a complete tale in itself, introduced by a title. The order in which we have arranged them is therefore more or less arbitrary, though we have tried to follow a logical sequence as far as possible.

Incident 1: Where Old Raven Made the Earth

$$t'c\acute{\imath}l\grave{a}cia \quad qi\partial^n\underline{x} \quad \mathrm{\upsilon}^n \quad sat\ell it\ell$$
Raven-old where earth he made

The Raven was sent down from above. He came down to the ocean. He kept flying around in a circle. Top of the tree stick out from the water and he sat down on it. All [258] the things drifted around close by. He stick it to the tree and said, "Turn into the earth!" for each stick of drift wood. The earth gets bigger and bigger each day.

After it got big, the Raven hop around the earth. "I wish a mountain would come up, too!" After his wish come, he was wishing for more mountains. "I wish there would be a beach, too!" Raven wished for mussels on the beach and all the things in the water.

After he got his wish, he flew around the whole earth. When he came down. Raven said, "Am I going to live on this earth alone?" A seagull came around. "You come to eat up everything, eh?" Then after the seagull came, all the other birds came. When each bird came, he turned them into different kinds of birds. They were all like seagulls at first. He pointed at them, "You turn into this!" He told the ducks and geese, "If there are going to be human beings, they are going to eat you."

After he made the different birds, he walked back and forth along the beach and started to cry. "I am alone in this big world. Am I going to live here alone?" Later, he was still crying for a human being, he saw a human being coming. He told the man, "You live with me here. Where you come from?" The man wouldn't answer. They made a place where they lived. After they lived there for a while, old Raven fly to some other place and the man left for some place, too.

Incident 2: Raven Makes the Rivers and Other Geographical Features

Two islands near Katalla were made by the Raven dropping rocks.

The Raven was flying around and spitting. Where he spat, that made a lake. He drew his finger through the spit [259] to form the rivers. Where he rested and stayed overnight, the spit turned into the ocean.

On the other side of Katalla is a big cave, called Raven's House, (*t'cílàcia ya' yat*). Raven was going to move away from that place. Raven threw his wooden bucket overboard because he didn't have room for it. It is a rock with a deep hole in it. The Natives get sea-eggs there at low tide. The rock is called "Where Raven Threw His Box".

> *t'cílàcia   qi'tc'   t'sa•tł uxa' sətsaxtł*
> Raven-old where box   his   threw

Right close by is another rock where Raven dragged his fish rack. There are deep scratches in the rock. This is called, "Where Raven Dragged Along His Rack"

> *t'cílàcia   qi'ᴅax wɛc uxa' tsa'səlxahti*
> Raven-old along rack his   dragged
>   where

Besides stealing daylight, and the sun, moon, and stars, Raven also stole water, and put the islands in the ocean.

Incident 3: Ugly Baby Crow Theft of Daylight

> *t'cílà   səqέ'tsəcìyέ*
> Raven baby-ugly

Once Raven was walking at night. There was no daylight then. He came to people who were fishing for eulachon. He tried to bum them for some but the fisherman wouldn't give him any.

"I'm going to make it daylight on you, if you won't give me any fish."
The fisherman said, "How could you make it Daylight?"
He left the fisherman and went on his way.
He found a chief living in one place who had everything − [260] stars, moon, and daylight. He had two slaves, one for himself, and one for his daughter. The slave of his daughter was to pack water for her. Raven came and after he saw the Moon, Daylight and Stars, he turn himself into a spruce needle and dropped himself into where they got water. When the slave came to get water he dipped water up with the spruce needle. When the chiefs daughter drank water, she drank water with the spruce needle. The chief's daughter became pregnant.

When the boy was born he grew up awful fast. In a few days he crawled all around. He wanted this and he wanted that. His grandfather think a great deal of him. When his grandfather pick him up he use to say to him, "Looks like a Raven. He got an eye like a Raven."

When the boy wants anything, he points to it and cries. He wants the Stars first. When he got it he went outside, held it up and blew it away, and it went into the sky. Next he got the Moon, after he got through playing with the Stars. Then he did the same thing with the sun. The last was the daylight. It was like phosphorescence. He had an awful time getting Daylight. When he got it he cried "qa" and flew out of the smokehole.

He went back to look for the fishermen. He tried to bum some fish again, and he told them the same thing again if they don't give him some fish he was going to make it Daylight. "How could you?" At first he made it Daylight a little bit. Then when the men saw the light they said they would give him all the fish if he would make it Daylight. So he got all the fish. [Galushia explained: The Eyaks used to fish for eulachon at night with a torch and dipnet.)

Incident 7: Where Old Raven Was Walking in Back of the Waves Raven & King Salmon [261]

t'cílàcia   qi'   tá^n ᴅlinàx qətłá•tłl
Raven old where waves behind walking
(i.e. where the Raven went beach-combing)

[This story was written down in English by Galushia]

Once a Raven was living as a beach-comber. He goes out on beach for anything that comes on beach to eat. At one time he could not find anything, so next he start with a song which he sing while he was going along the beach. "I am going by the waves. I am going by the waves."

t'a^n   *ᴅlinaqt* *ɢauxła•tł*
(*t'a^n*   *t'łinaqt* *qəxła•tł*)
waves behind   I-am-going

And the big king salmon got curiosity and came to beach but won't come close enough for Raven to kill it, so he start tease it and calling names, such as, "You big fat fish, you are so fat you could not come closer." But the fish won't come in closer until Raven call it "Fat head and fat jaw." When the king salmon got mad, it rush in so fast it got dry land, where Raven kill it and had a feast.

Incidents 10 & 11: Old Raven and Magpie Raven and the Owner of the Tides

t'cílàcia   ᴅa*x* *qɛt'sɢəguxaq'*
Raven-old and Magpie

Once Raven and an old lady were living by the beach. Raven said, "I wish we had someone to give us good luck."
Old lady said, "What is it then?"
Raven said, "I don't know what to do to make the tide low."
Old Lady said, "You wait till tomorrow morning. There will be low tide." [262]
Raven said, "How will that be?"
Old Lady said, "You will see."
Raven said, "If you made this ocean, that will happen all right." Raven didn't really believe her.
Raven had another companion in another place. That was Magpie. He went back to Magpie and told him to get up *early in* the morning. Next morning Magpie got up early and went outside without waking the Raven. Everything was dry, the tide was so low. Magpie went beach-combing. Magpie found all kinds offish and clams high and dry. He packed them all up on dry land. He found even seals.
Raven happened to wake up and he missed the Magpie. The Magpie had packed up all kind of things above the high tide line. Tide was coming in already. Raven went clam digging too. He didn't know there was so many things high and dry. So Raven started to dig butter clams, but he got only two butter clams. When he got these, he happened to look up − saw Magpie dragging a seal up above the tide line. So he went to Magpie and he helped Magpie to drag the seal up above the water line.
Magpie told Raven, "I think we got enough seals now. We get some more halibut and fish."

123

They only made one trip after the fish. But when they went for the second trip, the tide was coming in so fast they didn't have time to get another load. So Raven didn't have anything but two butter clams for himself. At high ride the Magpie started to clean his game. Raven got some driftwood, although he had never done that before. Magpie always had to do the work. When Magpie finished, he started to make grease out of the seal. Raven left and let Magpie do all the work.

When Raven left he went to the other birds, like Robin [263] and other small birds and told them to make war on this Magpie. Raven told the other birds to attack on a certain day. Then he came back to Magpie. Magpie was all through with his work.

Magpie asked Raven, "Where were you when we had so much work to do?"

Raven said, "I was looking for dry wood."

Magpie got mad and said, "You are not going to get any of these things that I have pulled up."

But Raven didn't mind what Magpie said. He said, "Nephew [*sıt'ı*^{*n*} "sister's son"], if you're tired, lay down and rest." The Raven never called him that before.

So Magpie lay down. When Magpie slept. Raven started to cook some of the fish. Raven was taking down some of the fish that was hanging up and he knocked the whole thing down on Magpie.

Magpie woke up. "What are you doing?"

Raven said, "Bluejays stealing your dried fish! I'm chasing them away."

So Magpie told Raven, "Let's bring all the rest of the things in."

So Raven said, "Let's hurry then."

When they were about through, Raven said, "Hurry up! Someone is making war on us." Raven told Magpie, "When they attack us, you go outside and I stay inside."

So Magpie was defending from outside, and Raven stayed inside. Raven was helping himself to all the food inside. He was eating it up. When Magpie was getting the worst of it, he went Inside to get Raven to help him. Raven was halfway in the big square box, drinking seal oil. Magpie pushed Raven in and pushed the top on it and tied the top down. The other birds left as soon as Magpie went in. [264]

When they were gone. Magpie told the Raven he was going to pack him up on the mountain. "I'm going to pack you up on the mountain and throw you down." So Magpie started to pack him. It was heavy. Raven began to sing. "You'll feel sorry when you see the fog halfway down the mountain. You'll think of me."

itagalέ   iyá qàk'at it'à   á•nàq' q'ətəq'ən• ì
you'll feel you sorry mountain on fog
inàⁿ•<u>x</u>   liıxàqàtłt'aɒà•<u>x</u>
on-the-side   hanging-halfway-down

But Magpie threw him down anyway. Magpie went home. Some time afterwards the clouds happened to be halfway down the mountain when Magpie got up, so he thought of what Raven said. He started to look for Raven and began to cry. When he found the box, the Raven was lying there − just the bones left.

Raven lifted his head up. "Didn't I tell you, you were going to be sorry?"

Incident 12: Where the Raven Went Visiting the Eagle

t'cílàcia   qi'   GútcGàlàq DA' <u>x</u>a'Di   Dasatł

Raven-old where Eagle   to another-place he-went

[This story was written down in English by Galushia]

Once Raven went to visit a Eagle which had a baby. When she got to Eagle 's home the Raven wanted to take Eagle baby in her arms to pat the baby, but the Eagle won't let here, as she said to her that: "You'll hurt her." but the Raven said she won't hurt her. Eagle said: "You might cave his ribs in." The Raven said she did not, so the Eagle let the Raven have the Eagle baby, and the old Raven [started?] [265] to sing for the baby, calling such as "Big nose, deep arm pits, long toes, stinking baby, " singing this song and dance the baby in his hands. while Raven was dancing the baby, he start press Eagle baby's sides in , and when he did, he throw baby to mother Eagle and said: "Here is your old baby" and went home."

Incident13: Where Crow {Raven} Went into a Whale

[This story was written down in English by Galushia]

Once Raven was out in the ocean, hunting fish. He saw a whale which he went after. Every time whale came up. Raven would be over it, waiting for a chance to go in through the blow hole of the whale, which he finally did. When he got inside the whale, he made a fire and start to roast all fat inside whale. After he roast all the fat, he cut off the heart and roast it too, so the whale died and float to beach where some of the beachcombers were and found it.

When they came to the dead whale, they heard someone singing inside, which was, "I wish someone would cut it open right over me!" And one of them happen to cut it open over him and old Raven flew out and said, "qa• qa•" and away he went.

Incident14: Where Old Raven Pitched the Seals Eyes Together

[This story was written down in English by Galushia]

Once a Crow or Raven had [an army] of warriors of light animals and birds. When they were on [their way] to war, they stopped on a seal bar where there was lots of seals. As they landed, these animals and birds jump out and act as [if] they were light as a feather and [the] seals want to know how they could be so light and they want to be as light as Crow's or Raven's warriors.

So Raven told the seals he took all [the] birds' and animals' intestines out [266] as they want to be light. The Raven asked the seals if they want him to remove their intestines, but the seals want to know how it was done and Raven told the seals that he had to stick their eyes together with pitch.

So seals want their stomachs and intestines removed. And old Raven was glad and started to pitch the seals eyes together, but he did not have enough pitch for the last seal. But the Raven started to remove their stomachs Just the same, until he came to the last one without pitch in its eyes. It Jumped up and ran away. The Raven and his warriors, which was animals and small birds, had a feast on the rest [of] the seals.

Incident 16: I Am Light Raven Kills His Partner

125

Raven and his partner [some fat animal], went for a walk. They came to a deep ravine. Raven put a piece of dry wild celery across the ravine and covered it with moss so it looked like a big log. He hopped out on it sideways. He sang, "I am light. I wish the others were as light as I am." He called to his partner, "Come on. See? It's all right!" His partner was scared but he finally came out when the Raven kept calling to him. When he got halfway out, the celery broke and he fell to the bottom and was killed. Raven went down and cooked and ate him. He had another big feast.

When he got back, the people asked, "Where's your partner?"

"Oh, he fell in the river."

Incident 16: Raven Pretends to Use His Body as Bait

Raven was living with the other birds. They went out fishing with lines for halibut. Raven used a red sweet-tasting clam for bait and caught lots of fish. He had his bait under his seat and wouldn't let the others see it. The others couldn't get a single bite. [267]

They asked Raven, "What are you fishing with?"

"I cut a piece of muscle from my leg where the blood veins run and make it red."

The others tried it and bled to death. Raven ate them up.

When he got home, the people asked, "Where is your partner?"

"Oh, he's still fishing."

The next day someone else went with him and the same thing happened. Whenever he lost his bait and put new bait on his hook, he would hold a clam down by his leg and pretend to cut his leg, hollering with pain.

Incident 18: Raven and Porcupine

The title is a verse of the Porcupine's song.

Raven fooled around the Porcupine and Porcupine hit him with his tail. Raven got quills. To get even with Porcupine he took some of his feathers and tied it into a tree [i.e., to simulate a tree]. Porcupine was going to an island on the feather log. When he got on the island. Raven took his feathers away, and the Porcupine couldn't get off. The Porcupine was singing because he couldn't get away. Finally it got cold, the water started to freeze, and at last the ice was thick enough for Porcupine to cross to mainland. [Galushia explains: if you laugh at Porcupine it will bring cold weather and the north wind will blow.]

Incident 19: Raven Raises an Army in the Sky

Raven went to the sky. He raised an army there and lowered them on a rope. They thought the trees below were men with spears pointing up and were afraid to come down.

Incident 20: Raven Journeys to the End of the Earth

Raven once went to the edge of the world. There is a [268] hole there where the tide rushes in and out. Raven got too close and fell in.

[unfortunately Galushia did not know the details of these last episodes.]

Other Myths and Legends

In addition to the Raven cycle, some thirty-two myths and folk tales were collected, by far the greater number being told by Galushia. He was generally prompted by his wife or translated for her. Seven of the stories were also collected in a second version; six of these were told by Old Man Dude, and one by Johnny Stevens. The tales are:

1A. "Porcupine and Beaver in Partnership" (GN).
1B. Porcupine and Beaver (JS, supposed to be a Copper River story).
2. "Where Wolverine and Fox were Cousins" (GN),
3. "Wolverine Man" (GN).
4A. "Taken by the Fish People (GN).
4B. Salmon Boy (D).
5. "Turned into a Ground Hog" (GN),
6A. "Living with the Black Bear" (GN).
6B. The Woman who Married a Bear (D).
7. "Brown Bear People" (GN).
8. "Porpoise People" (Written by GN).
9. "Blackfish People" (GN).
10. "He Came Back to Shore Together with the Seal People" (GN).
11. "Boy Turning into a Loon" (GN).
12A. "Where a Man Killed Lots of Land-Otters" (GN).
12B. The Man and the Land-Otters (D).
13. The Porcupines' Dance (D). [269]
14A. "The Giant Mouse" (GN).
14B. The Giant Mole (D).
15A. Giant Animals (GN).
15B. The Giant Devilfish (D).
16. "Alder People and Sun People" (GN).
17. "Calm Weather's Daughter" (GN).
18. "Around-the-Lake People" (GN).
19. "Wolf People" (GN).
20. "Tree People" (GN).
21. "One-eyed Frog" (GN).
22. The Man and the Salmon Tail (GN).
23. The Man who Fed a Starving Animal (GN).
24. The Girl and the Dog (GN).
25. "Good-for-Nothing" (Written by GN).
26. A Tlingit War Story (GN).
27. The Man who Killed his Children (GN).
28. The Illegitimate Child (GN).
29. The Man who Left his Wife (GN).
30. The Little Girl who Played with Dolls (Written by GN).
31. "Taking away by Owl" (Written by GN).
32. "Taking away by Checkers People" (Written by GN).

Tale 1A: "Porcupine and Beaver in Partnership" (GN).

Porcupine and Beaver were partners (sɪlàx̱ä[n]•nà).[1] Porcupine was like Beaver and lived in the water but he had quills even then. Once when he was traveling on the ice, Porcupine fell through the ice and couldn't get out. Beaver chewed a hole through the ice and came up under Porcupine and packed him back on the ice. They went ashore and built a fire. Porcupine started to dry himself. Beaver sat [270] down beside Porcupine, who didn't hear him come and he touched Porcupine and kind of scratched him. Porcupine hit him with his tail and got him full of quills. Beaver got mad and beat him up. Porcupine got mad then and left and went on dry land to live by himself. Beaver went back to his place. They lived apart for a while.

Later they met again and were good friends. They were getting water supplies – cutting brush – when Porcupine hit Beaver again with his tail. Beaver got mad and threw all their cutting tools away.

Porcupine got mad and said, "Now all you can use for tools is your teeth."

Beaver answered, "Well, you're going to be so you use only your teeth, too. You'll live any place, under rocks and under roots. You won't make a house like I will."

Porcupine said, "I won't have a hard time like you in the water, though. The only time you ever get out in open water is when it's warm."

Beaver said, "They [the hunters] will find you quicker than they will me. Go away! Beat it!"

Porcupine went on his way.

Tale 1B: Porcupine and Beaver (JS)

Porcupine is a bad friend of Beaver. Beaver takes tree away from Porcupine. Beaver can chop tree down, but Porcupine has to climb tree to get his food. Beaver can build a house, but Porcupine has to look around for a crack in the rocks or a place under a stump. Beaver can work for himself, can trim limbs trees for winter. Porky can't. That's why they are bad friends.

This is a Copper River story. [271]

Tale 2: Where Wolverine and Fox Were Cousins (GN)

Once Wolverine chose Fox for his cousin (mother's brother's son). He got him to live and hunt around with him. Fox was very willing because Wolverine would kill anything – he was a good hunter.

They went hunting and found a cache and Wolverine got up and threw down a goat stomach.

Fox said, "Throw them all down and I'll pack them home."

But Wolverine said, "There's nothing up here, only that goat stomach." He stayed up

---

[1] See section on Social Culture for explanation of this type of partnership.

there for quite a while.

Fox said, "What arc you doing up there all this time? f there's anything up there, throw it down and we'll pack it home. Somebody will catch us."

Wolverine answered, "There's nothing here but the blood from that stomach. I'm scratching it up." Then Fox replied, "I didn't hear anything but those wild canaries in the trees."

Fox saw the people coming and told Wolverine, "Here they come!" He grabbed the goat stomach and ran away.

Wolverine yelled, "Wait for me!" Fox said, "I told you to hurry and now I won't wait." Woverine jumped down from the platform. He had eaten so much that he burst open.

Tale 3: Wolverine Man (GN)

Wolverine Man was a good hunter, hunting goats all the time. Although he killed lots of game and brought it home, he only ate after he killed something. When he chased goats and got tired he said to himself, "Hurry up. What's making you tired?" He picked up rocks and [272] put them under his shirt. When he ran on the side of a hill he moved the rocks under his shirt around to the side towards the hill.

Another time when he chased some goats, he ran so fast that he got so far he couldn't get back − couldn't get no place from there. While he was stuck there, hanging by one hand from high place, it got dark. The biggest goat came down backwards to him. He got a hold of the goat by the tail. The goat started to pull him up and then he asked, "Are you going to kill us like you used to?"

"No," said Wolverine Man.

Goat kept asking, "Are you going to kill us and leave us without using us? What do you use us for?"

"No".

Then the goat pulled him out.

But Wolverine Man did the same thing when he got out. He happened to kill the one who saved him. While he was packing the goat home he fell over a cliff and the goat and Wolverine Man smashed to pieces.

Tale 4A: Taken by the Fish People (GN)

It was winter and the people were eating dried fish. Somebody gave a boy a moldy one. He wouldn't eat it but threw it outside, kicked it and threw it in the river. He did that all winter, throwing away moldy fish.

In summer, when the fish were running, he went to spear some fish and he got lost and never came back. They looked for him around the fish creek but couldn't find him. They thought he had drowned. They couldn't find him for over a year.

Next year they were fishing with a dipnet. They got one that made a funny noise. [273]

An old man said, "Don't touch it but put him in some feathers and put him on the drying platform above the fire."

When the fish started to get warm, he sang, "I turned into a fish! I turned into a fish!"

tä'ya' Dəqəqwɪ•łät
fish   I-turned-into

When he finished, the old man said, "Take him down."

The boy had a mother and father there. When they took him down he turned into a human being again. He told his parents and the other people:

"When you people get fish and clean them don't leave the blood laying there. Throw the blood and guts in the lake or river."

All the people did what he told them. In the fall the boy told his father to make him shavings and a fish rack and spear. He told him:

"Bring these things down to the beach for me. Give me a small box of oil. We're ready to go out again." When they got to the beach, the boy put them in the water. He told his father, "We're going now. If nothing happens to me, you'll see me next year when the fish start to run again." He went in the water and left.

While he was away with the fish people, something happened that he didn't like. He got mad and wouldn't say anything.

The Fish Chief told his people, "Go take him to the Creek-Where-We-Feel-Better (*Gótəkəlɛłtsʋaⁿ*)."

When they got near the creek, the boy started to laugh again.

After that, when the fish started to run next year again, the boy got up the wrong river and a woman cut off his head. [274]

Tale 4B: Salmon Boy (Dude)

One boy had a home. They were hungry. Wanted dry salmon.

Kid said, "No, me go."

Kid went to spear fish, but silver fish took him away, spear and all. He went to the fish home outside, and stayed all winter. The fish were like people there. Next year, when the fish came, the kid came, too. The Natives used to scoop the fish in a net. Someone caught the kid in the net with the fish. He heard the little fish make a noise.

The kid's father said, "What's the matter with that fish? Take him in the house!"

He told them to wrap him up and put him in a warm place. So the boy told the people how the fish went outside to their home. When the fish went home, the kid went outside, too. The fish outside used to eat meat spits. The kid made a boat and went to another place.

Every year the kid came back as a fish. Every year they used to catch him when the fish came. All the Natives were scared of that fish that was moving. One bad woman cut the fish's head off and found beads around his neck. He was wearing his sister's necklace. How many yards the head came back to the body and it came alive again. When they cut his organs, the white stuff started to run out from his liver. This time he died. That's all.

Tale 5: Turned into a Groundhog (GN)

There was once a man out trapping with deadfalls. He was having bad luck. He got nothing at all. He couldn't catch anything. He trapped for a long time. Finally an old woman came to him. [275]

The old woman told him, "You know why you are having bad luck?"

"No."

"You lay in bed while these young ladies get up before you. You eat, too, while your women are combing their hair. You are in the house when the sick women come back in from outside. You go take a bath in devilclubs. Rub the devilclubs on yourself."

He did that. The old lady had a cane. She laid her cane on his back. He threw up nothing but women's hair.

She told him, "Tomorrow all your deadfalls will have something in them."

He went out next day. All his deadfalls held some kind of animal. He brought them home and skinned them. He had the same kind of luck every day.

The woman told him, "Later on you are going to catch a pretty white animal in your last deadfall on your trap line. Don't take it home. Take it out and let it go."

The man caught a lot of animals and then in his last deadfall he caught a white animal, a pretty animal. He took it anyway and started home. He had a big load. He put it on top of his pack. On the way home, the animal kept falling off every little while. Finally, it started to run away. He put his pack on the ground and chased this animal. When he was chasing it, just when the animal was going in its hole, he grabbed it by the end of its tail and pulled off the end of the tail.

He sat down and felt sorry. Towards evening a woman came out of the hole. He still had a piece of tail.

The woman said, "Give me my sister's hair band."

The man said, "No. You send your sister out." [276]

"No, she's not going to come out."

The man still wanted to see the woman. Finally she came out. She was a pretty woman. She wanted that hair band back again. The man wouldn't give it back, he wanted to go inside with her.

She said, "No."

The man said, "I'll give you your hair band back if you'll let me go inside with you."

"No," she said, and started inside.

The man followed her in anyway. He turned into a groundhog.

Tale 6A: Living With The Black Bear (GN)

t'síyúq'àt   *úxi•t'i*
black bear-among   living

There was woman out picking berries. She had on a ground squirrel skin shirt. This young woman was married. They were out berry-picking. She stepped on bear dung. Bear been earing berries. She got mad and called the bear all sorts of names. "Big nose, big feet, big face!" They kept picking berries after that. Towards evening all started home. On the way home the handle of her basket was breaking every little ways and spill her berries. It happened quite a few times. When the last one passed her, she told the women, "Send my husband to meet me right away."

While she was on her way her husband met her. It was a bear who pretended to be her husband. This man started off with her. It was dark already. Finally she caught on that they were going the wrong way and she started to pull the squirrel tails from her shirt, one at a time and left them tied [277] to the bushes every little way. When she used them all up, she started to break off the tops of the bushes as she passed. They got above the bushes into the grass. She could leave no more signs for her brothers to follow. Finally they came to the bear's den.

When they missed the woman, her real husband looked for her. The found the squirrel tails and followed them, but they couldn't find her. They lost the trail amongst the grass. She was gone till next spring. She lived there with the bear, just like man and wife. She got away while the bear was out eating. When she got home she used to point where the bears' dens were to her people. She could see the smoke from their holes. Brown bears and grizzly bears make a different kind of smoke from the black bears.

Some say it's a true story.

Tale 6B: (The Woman Who Married a Bear) (Dude)

Old ladies go after berries in the summer. Had bark baskets for berries. Packed them all home. Then packed them berries in a barrel. One women slipped on bear dung, going home. Lost all her berries. She got the basket and picked up all the berries again. Again she slipped. Three times she sent a girl to the home to get her husband to help her. The rest went home, but she waited for her husband. Husband came and was packing her berries.

"What's the matter with that bear around here, making dung? He's got big hands, big feet, big nose, big ears, big mouth, big head, big buttocks!" she said.

Husband said, "Look at my hands! Where's my big hands? Look at my eyes. Where's my big eyes? Look at my nose. Where's my big nose? Look at my ears? Where's my big ears? Look at my mouth. Where's my big mouth? [278] Look at my head. Where is my big head? Look at my buttocks. Where's my big buttocks?"

He was a big brown bear!

He said, "Come on! Lets get inside the mountain." He got halfway up the mountain. "You sit down here," he said. "I'm going fishing."

He stayed with her all summer and bring her fish.

Then he said, "Let's go now into the winter-time house."

That girl had seven brothers. They didn't sleep with their wives because they wanted to find out where their sister was. They looked all fall. In Christmas month last, one didn't look yet. He stayed in the house. Some day, he go up Simpson Bay alone, early in morning, looking for sister.

Bear and girl stay in hole six months.

Last brother look all over on snow, don't see nothing. Soon he see snow balls his sister had thrown down the mountain. He saw marks of someone's hand on it. He go back to the house.

Oldest brother asked, "You see anything over there?"

"I see something."

Next day all seven brothers go over there after their sister. They have a dog that finds bear hole and barked there. The bear already had two kids by the woman. She told the two young bears to go over to their father's den. Now she goes back home.

She stay in the house. Blowing snow, nobody walk. Everybody hungry.

The girl told her brothers: "Get up early in the morning. I'll tell you where to find bear's den." Early in the morning she told them, "You see that smoke?" And pointed up the mountain.

He said, "No, I don't see it." [279]

She put something on her brother's eyes so he could see the smoke from the bear's den. That's all.

[Old Man Dude specified that this story was not sung.]

Tale 7: Brown Bear People (GN)

lıxa' *wʋla'iyu*
brown bear people

There was a bear who was married. He had an old father-in-law. They were hunting around creeks after fish. When they caught fish the young bear gave his father-in-law the worst fish and kept the best fish. There were two human brothers who watched it from far off. They watched several times.

Once when the bears were going home with fish, the old bear was taking a rest. The young men came up to the old bear.

Young men asked him, "Is that the way he treat you all the time?"

"Yes, that's the way he treats me all the time."

The young bear had two faces [two heads]. The bears went fishing again, and the young men watched them. When the old bear was resting, the young men asked him the same question.

"Is that the way he treat you all the time?"

"Yes, that's the way he treats me all the time."

The young men asked, "Where is the young bear's heart?"

"Between his eyes," the old man said.

While he rested, the two brothers got good fish and gave them to the older bear. The two young men asked him what time they came to get fish. "Just evening?" [280]

Old Bear said: "Early in the morning and in the evening."

When the bears came back, the two brothers killed the young bear and skinned it and put the skin over themselves. Got a load of fish and took it home. Old bear didn't take anything home because the brothers took it all home [for him]. The bear's wife got suspicious that it wasn't her husband that came home with her father. She got mad. She talked loud.

Her father said, "Leave him alone. He done good for me".

The she-bear went in her room. She stayed in her room until her father called her out again. Then they were living there as her husbands.

After they were living with the bears over a year − in spring when the bears were coming out − the younger brother went out and was killed by two other bears.

The female bear told her other husband, "Your brother is killed by two other bears by the creek."

The man and father-in-law went to look for her brother. When they found his body they took him home. They made eight rings out of devilclubs and another plant (*tcvkck*)[1] and cover him with them, and brought him back to life.

Tale 8: Porpoise People

(Written by GM. He later corrected the title to "Blackfish People"

k'ä'xut'ł' *wʋla'iyù*

---

[1] This plant is rare. It is like skunk cabbage; the wrinkled leaves grow in radiating groups at intervals along the stalk. It has green flowers which turn black when it goes to seed. The natives use the roots for medicine.

porpoise   people

Once a woman bring a porpoise head [in] her room and make believe it was human. She had this head in a [281] box. When she goes into her room in evening to go to bed, she talks to this head as if she was talking to a human being, and others asked her who she was talking to. She always say, "To nobody." She goes out to pick berries [for] this head and put the berries in the box the head was in. And it becomes a human being in evening. At one time while she was out picking berries again, some of [the people] take a look and saw a head of a big porpoise. And they find the highest place by the ocean to throw this in the ocean. When she come home from berry-picking, she saw that the berries was still on the box and she came [out] of her room. The other people asked her why she had the head of a porpoise in her room. She did not answer but asked what they did with it.

They said they throw it in the ocean. "What is it good for?"

She wants to know where, but they [won't] tell her. But she went and look for it, and she find the place to where she could go under the ocean to look for the head.

She find the Mussel People and asked them if they saw anybody.

They said to her: "Just before you came there was a chief's son pass."

So she went and came to Clam People and asked them if they saw anybody. They also answered that the chief's son passed a little before she came. So she went on again and asked same question [of] Butter Clam People, then the Razor-back Clam People, who told chiefs son [was] next to them, not very far off.

So she went there and find him, sitting head of the house. As soon as chief's son saw the woman, he stood up [282] to her and told his father not to say anything to her as he had lived with her for a long time.

Then he said to her: I don't believe you would follow me here."

And the woman answered:"How couldn't I follow you as I brought you to my room myself." They lived there forever.

Tale 9: Blackfish People (GN)

Gʋxut'ł   *wʋlá'iyù*
blackfish   people

Once there were some people going out hunting. While they were on their way, coming around a point, the first canoe in the hunting party saw a lot of people. They had landed, had a fire – there were lots of boats. The first canoe, before others see him, back-paddled, turned back and told the others: "There's lot of men over there at the point."

The men who back-paddled thought they were coming to make war on them. They land where they start from. They chose one man to go through the woods and come up behind the party they saw to find out whether they were acting warlike. The man came back from spying on the people.

He told his people, "I don't think they come to make war on us. They have a lot of seals roasting around the fire. They are happy. They don't act like they were going to make war."

So they all went over there with their canoes.

The Blackfish People, they thought this hunting party were coming to make war on them. So they grabbed their seals, some half cooked, and some cooked, and threw them [283] in their canoes and went off. Instead of boat going as it should go, their boats went under water. They come up some distance off shore. So the hunting party talked to them.

"We were afraid of you, too, when we saw you when you came around this point."

So they came back to land when they heard that.

They landed where they had a fire and the hunting party helped them roast the seals. After they got through eating, they had a shooting match with bow and arrow. The Blackfish People didn't have bow and arrow but they used the hunting party's. They bet each other whatever they got. The Whale People had the hunting party beat.

Tale 10: He Came Back To Shore Together With The Seal People (GN)

> *Gɛłtàq wʊlá'iyù ʊt'ł   qɛi•'yaq   stìqätłì*
> seal   people   together towards returned-he
>   with   shore   (by water)

There was once a man who killed more seals than anybody else. Wherever he went he always killed a seal. One time he went out hunting, he ripped over all of a sudden for no reason. One seal came and got him when he went underwater and brought him to where the seals came from. So he lived among the seals under the water.

At one time, the Seal People's chiefs son got speared between the shoulder blades. He got away with the spear point. The Seal People asked the man if he knew anything about it.

The oldest Seal Man pushed the man from behind. "Do you know anything about it?"

The man said, "Maybe. Wait a while." [284]

The old Seal went out with the man and told him, "Don't help him until they promise to bring you back to your old home, if you know anything about it."

So when he came back inside they asked him again: "Do you know anything about it?"

The man said, "I know. If you people take me home, I'll help him."

The Seal People thought the wound was a boil.

They said, "If you help him, we'll take you home."

So he went over to the chiefs son and looked. There was a big spear sticking on his shoulder blade. He hid it and didn't show it.

The chief said to his people, "The fastest underwater swimmer, take this man home."

Before he started to swim with the man, he told him, "Put your head against me as close as you can. If I go fast with you, you'll smother [if you don't do as I say]." The Seal told him, "I'm going to come up three times. Remember that."

When they started to swim, in one place, he went the fastest he ever went.

The Seal Man told him, "They are almost up to us."

The man asked, "What is it?"

"A devilfish is chasing us."

The man told the Seal, "Slow down. Let him catch up with us."

So he slowed down and the devilfish caught up to him. The devilfish put all his tentacles around the seal's head. The man used the spear point and broke the devilfish's bag of blueish stuff and the devilfish died.

The Seal told the man, "We like this devilfish, but this devilfish kill us. We don't get saved from this devilfish." [285]

Before they started again, the Seal ate up the devilfish. Then they started on again.

The Seal said, "I am going to come up now. I hear somebody rowing. The last time I come up, if he should spear me, make a noise."

When he came up the last time, somebody speared the seal, and the man made a noise as he was told.

The man who speared the seal asked the seal when he heard the noise, "Are you a man?"

He said, "Yes. Let's hurry to shore."

The man towed the man and the seal ashore.

When they came ashore they dragged up the seal, and the man told the other: "This seal was sent with me to take me home. Don't touch it. Don't do anything to it."

Tale 11: Boy Turning into a Loon (GN)

Once there was people living in Sheep Bay. They used to spear fish in a lake near by. Sometimes when they speared a fish it would get away and they would never find the fish or the spear again. They wondered why because the lake had no outlet.

The boy was born in one family. They started to train him to hold his breath a long time – fed him seals and big loons, animals that dive a lot. They got a big loon and skinned and dried it. When the baby was born they put him in the skin and feed him meat of animals that stay long under water.

When he got grown up and when the fish ran, he went to the lake with a fishing party. He went in the water and they never saw him again. In the evening when they started home they landed near an island [Anderson Island in Sheep Bay?]. They heard something hollering out in the water. [286] He hollered every time he came up. He went back towards the lake and kept hollering. They heard him again in the lake and went back to look for him.

They found the loon. They went back home with the boy-loon. He told them there was an underground channel to the lake. Then he turned back into a loon and went back. That's why people never bother the loon.

t
Tale 12A: Where a Man Killed Lots of Land Otters (GN)

$$Dəxɔ^n \quad qi' \quad Gəłɛsétł \quad i^nsətłàt'łɪ^n$$
man   where land-otter   killed-lots-he

Once a man went hunting. His canoe tipped over with him. He saved only himself and one stone axe. He landed on the shore. He had no way of making a fire and it was cold. In the evening some of his relatives came and landed. When they came they said, "əny^n" (an expression of sympathy]. The man jumped up and got mad at them. He knew they weren't his own people. They were Land Otters disguised as people.

He said: "You people here already? You're not going to fool me." He grabbed his axe and chased them away.

Next morning at daylight he found some dry punk and made a fire-drill and started a fire. He started to build a house. His axe wasn't good enough to build a canoe and he was a long way from home. He was making a canoe at the same time. Every once in a while the Land-Otter People came disguised as his relatives.

After he built his house they came again. He had some pitch hanging up above the fire, drying. When everything was finished, some of these people came again. He called them in the

house. He pretended that he was fooled, that [287] he believed them. He was going to kill them.
When he called the Land-Otter People up, he stayed behind on the beach and bite the edge of
their canoe. It quivers. So he knew that wood wouldn't quiver. He had dug out a urine tub
before. He was saving his urine. He put it in front of them.

"Wash your hands," he told them.

The animals just dipped the tips of their fingers in and turn their heads away. Then he
knew they weren't real human beings, got their paddles and put them above the fire inside the
house. Then he put pitch on the fire. It made black smoke. The paddles got limber and turned
into dead minks. (Land-Otters use live minks for paddles. Their canoes are live skates.)

Then the man killed the Land-Otter People, and they turned back into Land-Otters. He
skinned them, and he cut their canoe up and dried it. He kept doing that till he built his canoe.

Finally his own people came. He had been gone a long time. He still didn't believe they
were his own people even when they washed their hands. He put their paddles over the fire and
put pitch in it. They cracked and popped in (he heat and started to burn. Their canoe didn't
quiver, either, when he bit it. His house was full of land-otters and mink skins. They took him
home and all his furs. He was so rich he got to be chief of the tribe.

This story is supposed to be true. That's how they found out that the Land-Otters get
people when they drown.

Tale 12: The Man and the Land Otters (Dude)

One man went hunting all the time in a canoe. He went to the beach, got out of canoe,
alone. Soon he got up. He [288] hear something. On the side of the canoe he see two brown
bear's hands. He grabbed the tree because he was afraid. When he looked back at the canoe the
bear was gone. Bear looked back and saw the man up the tree. The man had a spear. When the
bears came to the tree, he killed both. One bear watched them and went to the hole to call
another bear. Thousand bear coming. The man cleaned them all up. The watchman bear called
more bears. The man is tired now. The watchman bear got some more bears. The man saw a
big waterfall and went under it. The bear was looking for him but couldn't find him.

Two days man stayed there. Then he went to salt water. He see another canoe coming.
He had two brothers. The brothers found him.

"Come on!" they said: "We've found him."

He go to the canoe. He went home. He had a wife and two children. It was dark when
he lay down. He got up in the night. He looked at his wife. She was a Land Otter! He thought
he was home but it was a Land Otter's hole. He killed all the Land Otters with a piece of stick.
He went out.

It was too far to walk home. He went and when he saw something to eat he ate it. Some
time later he saw a canoe, it belonged to the Land Otters. The Land Otters had taken his brother
who had drown, long time ago. He had turned into a Land Otter.

The Land Otter asked him: "Do you recognize me?"

"No!"

It was his brother who had turned into a Land Otter.

"How long ago the Land Otters got me! I know what they do. The Land Otters are
people." The Land Otter said: "Let's go home. I'll take you home." [289]

The man was scared. The Land Otter took his brother on his back and took him into the
water. He didn't feel the water. He saw everything under the water. He didn't know how long,

but his brother took him home and said: "Now you go ashore."

He saw his wife. He killed his wife. He eat her. Then he went back to the Land Otters' home. He was a devil already.

Tale 13: The Porcupine Dance (Dude)

Porky in the hole. A man watching him at night. Heard someone in porky hole. He sing – he dance. Man looked in hole. Porkies was dancing in there.

One porky said, "I'm going out to get something to eat."

The man killed twenty-five porkies. He quit; he got enough. That man die next day. Taqeikɪ, that's all. Other people watch porky hole at night, but don't see porky dance.

Tale 14A: The Big Mouse (GN)

tłuⁿtiyasləu
big mouse

Big mouse living under a cliff. He come out every time someone pass in a canoe. Kill them and eat them. He killed several people like that. There was one old man taking three women to pick berries. Old man knew the mouse's song. If you knew it, he wouldn't bother you. Sing it when passing. Old man was singing.

The youngest women said, "I wish we see this mouse."

Old man said, "Don't! What you say that for?" [290]

Just a few minutes later, the water turned red under the cliff and spread out to the canoe. The old man was still singing the mouse's song. Mouse come out backwards halfway out. He put his tail out of water and dropped it on the canoe. The old man, when he dropped his tail, jumped on the mouse's tail. He hang onto the tail. The women were all killed.

Mouse went back under the cliff with the old man. He was saved. The mouse came into a big room under the cliff. The man went to the other side of the cave from the mouse. The man sang the mouse's song so the mouse didn't bother him. He got some feed for the man. The mouse only went hunting at time of no moon, when it's dark. When the mouse goes hunting – there was a root of a tree sticking down from the roof of the cave – he [the man] tried the strength of the root. Later he climbed to the roof. The mouse had a hole clear to the top of the ground where he stuck his tail out. Man climbed clear out but came down before mouse came back from hunting and sat down where he was before. When mouse comes back sometimes he brings back seal or halibut. He puts it under himself to cook them. When it gets cooked, he brings it out and give it to man. The man eats it.

At one time the mouse went out towards morning. The mouse was supposed to be home before the raven started to make noise. When the mouse left, the man climbed the roof and got out. Before he got very far, the mouse came back. The mouse was making all kinds of noise in the cave because he missed the man. He stuck his tail out of the hole and swung it around. The man got home.

At full moon the mouse sleeps sound. When old man got home he told the young man to try to snare a crow. [291] If they snare a crow in full moon time they're going back to mouse's den. "Sharpen all that you use for your old knives, and sharpen all that you use for your old axe," the old man said.

When they caught the raven they have all knives and axes sharp. They go to where mouse sticks out his tail. Mouse had his tail sticking out the hole when he's sleeping. (Tail was like a watchman.) The old man sneaked up on him with an axe. He chopped the mouse's tail twice before he cut it off. The mouse pulled the rest of his tail down.

The young man said, "Throw the crow down that hole!"

So the crow started to make all kinds of noise down there. The mouse started to go under the cliff. He got halfway out before he died. After the mouse died, the old man went down on the root and looked at the mouse. When he found the mouse was dead, he came back up and told the other man. This young man would like to see it, so they went down and looked at it. When they came out, the mouse turned into a rock. The crow came back out of the hole, too.

[The hunter must rise before the crow makes a noise in the morning, or he will not get any game. All the animals are up before the crow. If the crow gets up before an animal does, the animal will die.]

Tale 14B: The Giant Mole (Dude)

In Yakutat was big mole. Canoe were going away. Fifty man in a canoe. Saw mole in the water. Mole hit canoe with his tail. Tipped canoe over with his tail. Broke canoe. One man from canoe went into mole's hole. Mole [292] was asleep. Mole didn't close its eyes. After a whole month he go outside, as soon as mole shut his eyes.

They were looking for crows in the night time. It wasn't daylight when water was coming into the mole hole. He [the man] looked up and saw the upper entrance to the mole hole, like a hole in the mountain. The mole put his tail out of the hole. The man was in the hole. The mole stuck his tail in the water and pulled it in full of animals. All the different animals were on his tail. The mole put a big seal under his right arm. In two minutes it was already cooked. He gave it to the man. [69] Man stay there three months. When mole was sleeping his eyes were like lamps. Three times when mole was hunting the man was watching him. Three times he cooked the seal under his arm.

The mole went out. He [the man] climbed the rocks hanging into the hole and went up the mountain. Mole went far away from home. Then he went back to his home. Water was coming in the hole from below. When he slept his eyes were like lamps. The man watched the mole. When he saw his eyes closed, he went out of the hole.

Crow filled his basket full of live people (crows). When he got enough, he went up the mountain. The mole was so big his tail stuck out the hole. The man saw it. One man went on one side, the other man went on the other side. "Look out, don't miss! You chop it." Two men chopped at the same time. Cut the mole in two. Crow helped them to throw it in the hole. Crow was making a big noise inside. Crow was scared. Mole went out the hole and floated up [dead] in the water. [293]

Tale 15A: Giant Animals (GN)

A devilfish was supposed to live in the deep hole outside of North Island in Cordova Bay. It would grab canoes if they came too close at night. When it came up, water would get so slimy that the canoe could not paddle away. The water was so deep there that a fish line could not reach the bottom. The tentacles of the devilfish were always sticking out of the water. The

Natives were afraid to go on the outer side of the island, even as recently as Galushia's boyhood. Some times people might escape from the devilfish by making a noise like a crow. The devilfish was finally driven away when the boiler from a stern-wheel fishing boat was thrown in the water.

A giant bear used to live in a lake near Martin River. There is a little slough running out of the lake that was made by the bear when he left. The name of the slough indicates that it was made in this way.

A giant beaver used to live near a glacier near Mile forty-nine (on the Copper River Railway). He had a big dam. You could see the water coming over it. He left.

There was a giant bear that lived in a lake near Gravina Bay. He was supposed to be growing bigger all the time. People were afraid to go there. They might make the bear mad. He would shake and make the earth quake.

These monsters were called *ət'stłi'yatł*. They always lived in the ground or under water. They were all bad and ate people.

[Technically, the above is not a tale or a series of storeis, but it is included here because it is, so to speak, the raw material of belief from which folk tales are built. There may well have been stories about tthese monster animals that Galushia did not remember. Such a story is told by Old Man Dude.] [294]

Tale 15B: *The Giant Devilfish* (Dude)

Devilfish near natives' house. Two brothers went out hunting in a canoe. Two days they go hunting, go back next day. One place they paddled but canoe didn't go. Don't see nothing. Kept paddling but canoe didn't budge. Soon look in water. Looks brown under them. That's big devilfish. Legs thick as a dishpan. Two fellows tie knives to their wrists. He put his paddle down [to test the depth of the water?] and the devilfish came up. It was four feet deep. They jump off canoe. They cut the devilfish. One fellow was lucky and stuck the heart. Devilfish all die, and floated up. Hundred-fifty yards wide. Another big canoe went after him. Can't make it. Can't paddle across. Water is too heavy. Was too many scales on the water.

Tale 16: *Alder People and Sun People* (GN)

Once there was a war between the Alder People and some other people. The Alder People killed off all but a woman and her daughter. Afterwards the woman and her daughter stayed outside and cried all the time.

"I wish someone would come around and marry my daughter!"

She cried there for a long time until a Frog came and asked, "What about me?"

The woman asked him, "How you going to get revenge for my brothers who were killed?"

The Frog said, "Every time when I jump from under a man's feet, I think I done something great." But the woman thought that wasn't enough.

"What about me?" The next was a little bird.

The woman asked, "What could you do?" [295]

"When I scratch up the ground I think I done something great."

But the woman didn't think much of that either.

Then came a Snipe. "What about me?"

"What could you do?"

"When I jump around the edge of the river I think I done something great."
But that wasn't enough.
The Blue Jay came next.
"What could you do?"
"When I pick up all the salmon eggs around the beaches I think I done something great."
But that was not enough.
Then Magpie came.
"What about me?"
The woman asked him, "What could you do?"
"When I find something that is hidden away, I think I done something great."
But she did not think that was enough.
Then Robin came.
"What about me?"
"What could you do?"
"When I pick those red (elder?) berries, I think I done something great."
But that wasn't enough.
The Kingfisher said, "What about me?"
"What could you do?"
"When I catch those little fish I think I done something great."
But the women didn't think much of that.
Then came the Goose.
"What about me?" [296]
The women asked him, "What could you do?"
"When I fly over seven bays without rest I think I did something great."
But that was not enough.
The Fox came next.
"What about me?"
"What could you do?"
The Fox said, "When I traveled around the world in the night I think I done something great."
The Brown Bear came.
"What about me?"
"What could you do?"
"When I start to get mad and start to run after something and tear up all the earth and break everything, then I think I done something great."
The woman thought a long time before she refused the Brown Bear.
Then came the Black Bear.
"What could you do?"
"When I slap anything and make it fly away from me I think I done something great."
But the woman refused him, too.
The Wolverine asked, "What about me?"
"What could you do?"
"When I find a cache and rob it, I think I done something great."
But that wasn't enough.
The Goat came.
"What about me?"

"What could you do?"

"When I climb the steepest hill, I think I done something great." [297]

But he was refused.

At last came the Sun Man. He had a cane.

The woman asked, "What could you do?"

"When I start to make these rivers boil and heat it all the way down the mountain. I think I done something great."

The old lady said, "Show us how you make this water boil and heat up the mountains."

The Sun Man gave the woman his cane and said, "In case I start a fire and the fire comes towards you, put this cane over the top and the fire will stop."

He left them and crossed the river and the rivers boiled. It started a fire. When the fire started to reach the woman, she raised the cane over it and put the fire out. The woman thought it was great and gave her daughter to him.

The Sun Man went home with the girl up in the sky. The woman told the Sun Man before he left that her people were all killed by the Alder People and that she wanted revenge. The Sun didn't say anything, but went home.

The Sun Man had eight boys by this girl. The eight boys didn't have no sister.

Their mother said, "When are they going to be old enough to take revenge on the Alders?"

The Sun packed half a basket of water. He dipped the boys in it and threw them above the door. When they fell on the floor they were full grown.

Then the mother said: "Are they going to be without a sister all the time?"

The man took out his bow and cut off the end, where the string is tied. He dipped it in the water and threw it above the door. When it came down it was a girl. They called her *DJɪmɪtcəkí'*, "talkative." The youngest son was .....??..... He was the boss of his brothers. [298]

The Sun's wife made a basket around her husband's thumb. When it was finished they took it off and blew in it, and it became big. They tied a rope made of roots to it. He put the oldest boy in the basket and sent him down to earth. When he got too far he saw the trees sticking up. The father had told the boy to shake the rope when he wanted to come up. He did so.

The father asked, "What's the matter?"

"Someone sticking spear up under me." That was the trees.

The father said: "Maybe not a spear."

So he sent the next oldest down. All the others was sent down, one at a time, but they all had the same story about spears. Then the girl was sent down last, and she found out it wasn't spears (because she was made of wood). When she came back, they sent all the boys and the girl down at once in the basket. The father gave them all his tools, spears, bows and war clubs. He gave the oldest a branch, like a blueberry branch. If one got killed he was to hit him with the branch and he would come alive again.

When they landed it got foggy. Their father made it foggy. They started to build a fort. The other people couldn't see them but they heard them building a fort. But they couldn't see them.

The chief of the Alders heard them and said, "What's that making a noise? I don't like it. I'm suspicious."

The Alder People said, "That's only some birds making a noise."

The chief kept repeating his question. But the Alders said: "Maybe it's just the ghosts of the other people we killed off." [299]

When they got the fort finished, the clouds drifted away and were gone. The Alder People were surprised when they saw the fort and prepared to attack it. The Alders attacked the Sun People. Seven of the Sun People went outside the fort to meet them. Just the youngest and the girl were inside. When they were fighting, the Sun People killed about half the Alder People, but none of the Sun People were killed yet. The youngest wanted to holler for the father, but the others wouldn't let him. His sister begged him not to call his father. The sister went outside and talk so much that the Alders' war canoe tipped over. The youngest boy started to rush down to meet the Alders. He ran halfway down and then ran back to his brothers. He made a bluff of attacking the enemy alone. When the woman and the youngest boy started to talk, and the youngest went inside again finally, they found that about half the Sun People got killed. The youngest wanted to call for help to his father again. The sister was scared and let her brother call for help. They did not give the oldest a chance to use his branch. The brothers didn't know he hollered. The oldest used his branch afterwards and made the others come to life.

The father heard the call for help and started to make the river (ocean) boil and that killed all the warriors in the canoes and those on land were killed by the heat. Alder were all killed off, the Sun People stayed there and hunted together.

In the evening, when the sun hit a cloud and it was pretty, the youngest said:

"I wish we could kill that color animal."

The oldest always tried to stop him from saying that kind of remarks. When the youngest said that next time, [300] he found an animal colored like a cloud. He chased it and kept chasing it, and finally chased it into the sky. All the brothers went back to the sky.

That's the end.

[Afterwards, Galushia said he had made a mistake, and that the first suitors for the girl were the birds. Then came Frog, and after him the other animals. The "blisters" on the alder bark are supposed to be wounds made by the Sun People.)

Tale 17: Calm Weather's Daughter (Diäxtsi) (GN)

There was a man and his wife. She was always getting mad at her husband.

Every time she gets mad, she says, "Get out of here. Get out of the house!" She tells him, "Go marry the daughter of the Calm Weather."

Finally the man got tired and left her.

He kept going until she saw smoke from another house. When he came to the house, he hang around outside for a while. There were two women living there.

When they heard him outside, they said, "If you are a human being, come inside."

He stayed overnight.

Same evening they asked him, "What are you doing here?"

The Man told them that his wife chased him out and told him to marry the Calm Weather's daughter. Next morning before daylight they woke him up and told him to take a bath in devilclub water. He stayed around all day. The second day they told him to get up early and go. They put up a lunch for him. They told him to look for a pretty bird that will fly ahead of him, to follow bird wherever he flies. So he did. [301]

He came to a slave who was chopping wood. He watched him from a distance. Slave broke the edge off his axe. He talked to himself about it. He was sorry.

"I guess I will get a good licking for this."

The man took pity on the slave. He went up to him and asked the slave if he knew where Calm Weather's daughter lives.

Slave said, "What you want to know for?" The man told him, "If you tell me, I'll fix this axe for you again."

The slave told him he was the slave of the Calm Weather. So the man knew where they lived. The man fixed his axe.

The old slave was glad and told him: "There are two sisters living close by their father's house."

The man told the slave, "Don't tell that you saw anybody."

The slave went home with a load of wood. Although he never drop any wood before, he dropped a piece of the wood from under the bark. The slave didn't know that he had lost k. The man followed him and found the wood and took it along with him. Late in the evening – everyone was in bed – when he was ready to come in, he put the wood in front of him and slipped in behind it into the house. He happened to go into the youngest girl's room. The girl didn't say anything though she knew someone had come in her room. The oldest girl heard the man and girl playing in the room but she didn't say anything either. (The oldest girl had a room of her own.)

Next morning the man and girl stayed in her room. So the oldest girl went to her father's house. She didn't say anything, so her father asked:

"Where is your sister?" [302]

She said, "I don't know. I heard her playing all night." Girl's father sent his slave over to find out who she was playing with.

The slave came back and told his master, "She's laying down with a man."

The oldest girl ran back without saying anything. They tried to take the man away from the girl but she wouldn't let him go. The oldest girl had a dentalium shells on the hem of her skin. She bought the man from her sister with it. So they lived together. When the youngest lost some of the dentalium shells, she wanted the man back. But she couldn't get him.

The woman told her husband, "Lets row somewhere. I got a boat on the beach a little ways."

The man went to look for the canoe but he could find only a razor-backed clam shell turned upside down on the beach. The man told his wife he couldn't find any boat but saw only a razor-back shell turned over.

She said, "That's the one. That's our boat. Turn it over and kick it on the smaller end."

So he did and the shell turned into a big canoe. Then they were ready to go. The slave was taking things to the boat. The slave brought eight bundles of dried fish and four wooden boxes of seal oil. So they got in the boat and started to go.

This man told her he had a wife before. The new wife told him, "Don't say anything to your wife if it's true you had a hard time to come to our place."

They got to the man's first home. They lived there. The second wife used to send her husband out for water. When the man came back with water, the second wife would dip a leaf in the water. The first wife used to follow the man, [303] to get water, too. The woman always spoke to him but the man never answered. Finally the man took pity on the new wife.

"How will she know if I answer my first wife?"

The second wife was making a big basket. She never went outside. She kept on working at the basket. When the man came back after speaking to the first wife, the second wife dipped a leaf in the water and when she pulled it out, the leaf was slimy.

The second wife told her husband, "You better live with your first wife. I'm going home." The woman got all her things together and started home. The man followed her down to the beach. The woman never stopped. He walked right on top the water after her.

"Turn back," she said. "I'm going to look back at you if you don't turn back."

The man kept following her until they got close to the woman's home. Then she looked back at him. The man sunk then.

When the woman got home, her father asked her, "Where is your husband?"

The woman said: "Around the point. I looked back at him and he sunk."

The father said, "Why did you do that?" "I told him not to speak to his wife and he spoke to his first wife and he spoke to her. That's why."

The chief told his slave, "Hurry and look for this man!"

The slave went to look for the man. He walked right under the ocean. The first the slave found was a big Bullhead under the water.

"Let's see," (looking into the fish's mouth), "maybe you swallow this man." [304] [He didn't see anything inside the fish.]

He saw a Shark, and asked him the same question, "Let's see, maybe you swallow this man."

Then he found a Devilfish and asked him the same question. "Let's see. Maybe you swallow this man."

Then he found a Dog Fish and asked him the same question. He just looked in their mouths. The young shark or Dogfish happened to be the one that swallowed him. So the slave cut up the Dog Fish. He just find the man's bones in there. He picked up all the bones but couldn't find one of the knee caps. He went to take them home.

When the slave got home, the father put the bones together and tried to make them stand up, but the bones always fall down again. The chief tried to make them stand up several rimes, and then he found out that one of the kneecaps was missing, and sent the slave to look for it. The slave went but couldn't find it.

When the slave come home, he cut out the slave's kneecap to put on the man. He made the bones stand up and turn into a human being again. He told the oldest daughter not to stay with the man again, so the youngest one stayed with him. So the father gave slave to man. Before he gave the slave, he put a shell, called the "cockle's baby" in as a kneecap for the slave. They lived there then.

Tale 18: Around-The-Lake-People (maⁿkaᴅιꞇłiaᴅαxɔⁿiyừ) (GN)

Dwarves as big as a thumb used to hunt and fish around the country. They were found around Strawberry Point (on Hinchinbrook Island, near Boswell Bay) at the small lake there. The little women row, the little men hunt and fish. A human captured a little man who had become [305] tangled in some roots. The dwarf gave the man all his hunting outfit − spears and bow and arrows − to let him go. One spear with an agate point he hated to part with.

When he was turned loose he returned home, but his people had gone outside the breakers. He hollered for them to come back and get him. One of his relatives came through the breakers for him. They all started home in canoes and on the way they saw a mouse, which was a brown bear to them. They all landed to try to kill him.

The little man without hunting implements was killed by the bear for he had no way to defend himself. The other people killed the bear. The bear was cut up in small pieces and left there because he had killed one of their people.

They put the body of the dead in a canoe without examining it at all. His relatives took the body home. The wife ran down to meet her husband, she didn't know he was dead. The skin of his head had been pulled off. The wife and children ran down to meet him. They were happy that their man was coming home.

The wife, when she saw her husband's head, tore a piece from the bottom of her skin and bandaged his head. They took the body and placed it in front of the left front house post. They left the body outside for eight days. On the eighth day they took the body inside.

Towards noon, the body began to move. Only the wife was there. Right at noon he moved more and more until he lifted his head. He sat up and scratched his head. He asked his wife what had happened and she told him that a bear had killed him. He asked what they had done with the bear. She said they had killed it, cut it in bits and left it there. He asked who had brought his body home. [306]

He told his wife not to worry about him and left, taking two men with him. They went to Yakutatik [?]. They were gone about a year. They came back at the time when the birds start to lay eggs. When the people saw them coming they were excited. Each man was coming in a separate canoe and all three were full of brown bear skins. When they landed the people lifted them up and carried them to the house. The man was made chief of the tribe. When he finished eating, he said to his wife: "I guess I got even with those bears."

He gave his eldest daughter to a man. She knew everything — all about making baskets and keeping house, she had already promised to marry another man, but had to obey her father and left the first man. The first man asked her husband to dig clams with him. They were digging as the tide was coming in. He made the husband stay on a sand spit. He drown there and they found the body. He turned into shrimp (or sand-hopper?).

The other man went home and told several different stories about what had happened. The drowned man's wife had a dream that the man had caused her husband to be drowned by the tide and in the dream her husband told her he had become a sand-hopper. People asked the man if that was true. He said yes. But they did nothing to him. That's all. (ᴅaqaiᴅaqa'au)

These dwarfs had many different tribes around the lake, like the different tribes of Indians.)

Tale 19: Wolf People (GN)

The Wolf People had been taking people from a village. They took quite a few away. Once a young girl was playing outside. Some old people smelled something. [307]

"Oh, there's something smell like a muskrat," they said, "It's queer this muskrat smells in the fall."

They were suspicious. It was fall and muskrats smell only in the spring. While the girl was playing outside they called her but she would not come in.

A Wolf Man was back of the house in the brush. He was showing the girl different kinds of pretty birds. The girl went up to him, and he tied her up and put her among some feathers and packed her off. While he was packing her the little girl started to throw the feathers out one by one through a little hole in the bag. They went a long way. They came to a big lake. He hollered to his people. They got him with a canoe and brought him home.

The Wolf Man was a slave of the chief of the Wolf people. He put the bag with the girl in front of the chief. The chief looked in and only found a little girl in the bag.

He said, "How did you do this? What did you do this for? Didn't you take pity on this little girl?"

When he took the girl out, instead of killing her, he killed the slave who brought her home. Another slave cut up his body and they ate him.

When they cooked the slave meat, they gave some to the little girl. She pushed it away and started to cry. After she didn't eat the meat the chief sent his sister after some goat meat. All she ate was goat meat and bear meat. She lived with them there.

She started to grow. She got old enough to pack water and to get up in the morning. The Wolf People thought the girl was just like themselves because she was growing up with them. Every morning before the others got up she packed water for the whole village. She tried to get on the good side of them so they wouldn't kill her. The chief's [308] sister told her to do things for everybody so they wouldn't kill her. She gave the girl a knife and told her while she was packing water early in the morning to put holes in all the Wolf People's canoes, except one small one the girl could handle alone.

"These people go hunting early in the evening and come back in the morning," she told her.

One morning while she was packing water, the girl cut up all the boats. It was easy because the Wolf People had birchbark canoes. Then she started away in the small canoe she saved for herself. Before she got to the other side the Wolf People found out she had got away. They put their canoes in the water and Jumped in. Before they got far the boats sank. One boat with some men bailing and others paddling got clear across. It nearly caught her.nn

The girl landed and ran behind a little waterfall and hid there. A Wolf Man landed and tracked her to the falls and lost the track. He walked around and cried and sang a sad Wolf song. [Galushia and Annie Nelson had heard the words of this song but did not remember them.]

The Wolf People gave up searching after a half a day. The girl followed the feathers home to her own people.

Tale 20: Tree People (GN)

There were people living together. In one family there were nine boys and one girl. They were hunters, always talking turns hunting. At one time the oldest went out hunting and he never returned from his hunting trip. He was caught in the Tree People's snare. The Tree People eat people. The snare opens and shuts all by itself all the time. Only time it don't move is when it got something. Next to oldest one looked for him and got into the same [309] snare. It caught eight of the boys. Finally the youngest and the sister went out to look for their brothers.

When they were on their way – the boy was leading – the boy's head was almost in the snare. The girl saw it, grabbed her brother, pulled him back.

"Didn't you see the snare?"

When they saw that snare they turned back. On their way back they picked up a rotten piece of wood. They made it in shape of a human being, put some of the boy's clothes on it. And they went back and threw it in the snare. They climbed a tree where the snare was set.

When the Tree Man saw he caught another man in the snare, he laughed.

"Hehehehehe! You got one again?" He asked the snare.

He built a fire before he started to eat the dummy. He started to cut it and found it was only rotten wood. After he found that out, he cut off a piece of muscle from his own lower leg and cooked that. After he got through eating it, he went home.

The boy and his sister trailed him home. They liked the man before he got home. Then they saw smoke and wanted to sneak up to the house. The house was made of the boughs of the tree. They looked in without the woman seeing them. They saw a foot sticking out of the woman's pot. They came into her bough house and sat across from this woman. She tried to feed them with their own brother's flesh. The boy and his sister shoved it aside. The woman tried them with another dish. She offered them hair.

"Try this seaweed."

They shoved it aside. Woman got mad and threw her *wäkck* (woman's knife) at the boy. He jumped and it went [310] under the boy. He grabbed the knife and threw it back and cut the woman's head off.

[There is supposed to be a more to this story, but our narrators ~~informants~~ had forgotten it.]

Tale 21: One-Eyed Frog (GN)

Once there was an invisible being that they sent for everything. If people wanted anything they would ask him to get it, wood or anything. [He was called:

DikqaDà'áŋ• qɛ́ yəx̱Dədəɛ́
not-seen   one-sent-for-something

Another village heard about this being. There was a shaman there who claimed he could find anything. If nobody else could find a thing, he could. They asked him if he could find this unseen messenger.

He said, "Maybe I can, I'll try. I'll try early tomorrow morning."

He started out early next morning. He kept going and traveling until he came to a one-eyed Frog.

When the Frog saw him, he asked, "What are you doing here so early in the morning?"

"I am sent to find this unseen messenger. Do you know where he is?"

The frog told him, "I do not know exactly where. There's another people live next place, Geese People – two Geese Women."

"Is it very far?"

The Frog said, "It's not so far, but you can't make it tonight."

He stayed overnight and started next morning. He found the Geese Women. [311]

They asked the man, "What you doing here?"

"I'm sent to find this unseen messenger. Do you know where he lives?"

They said, "He lives around the next point. You go over right away. You come to a house and go in it and call "məlcà!" When you find Malshaa you come by here again."

He went over there. When he got in the house, he called " məlcà ". Someone answered without being seen.

məlcà said, "I'm sent for you. Could you go with me?"
məlcà asked, "Is it very far to where you are sent for me?"

"No it's not very far. It took me three days to get here."

məlcà said, "I'll fix up my things. You wait for me at those two women's. I'll get my things ready before these people get home. You better go. If they find you, they'll eat you."

He went to the Geese Women.

They said, "Did you find məlcà?"

"Yes."

"Is he going with you all right?"

"Yes."

"If you aren't going right away you better eat with us," they told him.

While he was eating, məlcà came over. He came just like any human being, he could be seen then. He told the shaman, "Let's stay overnight. It's too late to go now."

They stayed overnight and started next morning. When they were on their way, they went around the first point and found a canoe. [312]

məlcà said, "Let's take this boat. We'll get there quicker with this boat.

The Shaman said, "No, they'll see us going."

məlcà said, "No they aren't going to see us"

They went in the canoe. The boat belonged to some people there. A boy was playing outside. He came in to his parents.

"There's an old canoe over there. There is nobody in it, but the paddles are moving!"

They ran out. They didn't believe him but they ran out and saw nobody was in the boat and it was in motion. They got scared because the boat was in motion with nobody in it. The boat never acted that way before. They followed the boat along the shore and tried to find out what made it go. When they couldn't find out what made it go, they turned back.

The shaman got home with məlcà. When he got there, the people came to meet him on the beach.

"Did you find him?" they asked.

"Yes, he's right here."

They told him, "Tell him to get out of the boat and we'll bring the canoe up."

The shaman told məlcà, " məlcà, get out of the boat now. This is where they sent me for you."

He got out and they went into the house. They went to the shaman's house. The shaman's wife had everything ready − things to eat. The shaman could see məlcà but the others couldn't see him at all.

While they were eating, the shaman told məlcà: "You will live here with us all the time."

So he lived with them there in the village.

When people brought fish to dry, all the fish started to get cleaned without anybody touching them. All the wood started to pile up around the house without anybody seeing anybody pile it. The fish hung themselves up. The fires were built. məlcà was doing all the work.

məlcà died. After he died, everybody saw his body. He was nothing but a little bit of a man.

Tale 22: The Man and the Salmon Tail (GN)

A man was walking along the river bank near Eyak. He heard someone call, "Save me!" (xu•łà!)

He looked everywhere, but at first he saw no one. At last he saw a salmon tail on the ground, full of maggots. He washed the maggots off and put the tail back in the water.

They had a hard time that winter. One day he went to the river to get water. He saw two fish tails sticking up out of the ice. He pulled up the two fish by the tails. This was a reward for being kind. That is why people always put salmon tails back in the water.

[GN believed this to be the same winter of famine as that mentioned in *Tale* 28].

Tale 23: The Man Who Fed A Starving Animal (GN)

A family were halibut fishing during the winter. They were having no luck. An animal [like a gorilla, large, hairy, without a tail, that travels in the woods] came out and cried behind the camp. The man went out to ask what was the matter.

He said, "Come to my camp."

The animal came and asked for food. The man had only a little, but he gave what he could spare. The animal went away without thanking him. Next morning the people found a pile of halibut in the camp. This happened for several days, until they were able to catch fish again for themselves.

Tale 24: The Girl and the Dog (GN)

There was a man and his wife. They had a daughter who was always playing around with the dog.

Her mother told her, "Don't play around with that bitch. Leave her alone."

They were going to move to another place. When they were ready to move, she was playing with the dog. So they left her playing with it. Before they left they tied the girl's head and the bitch's head together and left them like that.

They had a female slave, too.

The slave said, "Wait a while, I forgotten my wäkck (woman's knife)." It was just an excuse to go back and cut the girl and dog apart. She told the girl, "Don't show yourself. I'm going to get a licking if they find I cut you loose."

The slave went back to the boat and they left. The girl was still crying. They went home to where they were before.

After a year, the girl's mother told the slave, "Go to our camp, and throw their bones out. Shovel them out."

So the slave went over there. The slave find the girl and the dog. They were still alive. The house was almost full of things to eat. The dog was a good hunter. When the slave went over there, they fed her and gave her all she want to eat. She sneaked a piece of fat under her shirt for her son. The slave says, "I'm going home now. I'm staying too long. They're going to get me for it."

The girl said, "If they come back with you – when they land, you run in first. We're not going to let my father and mother in."

The slave got home.

The mother asked her, "Did you shovel the bones out?"

The slave said, "Yes."

That evening when they went to bed, the slave went to bed with her son and gave the fat to her son. After the son ate up the fat, he started to cry for some more, and called for fat: "*Gəqəxté!*"

The woman asked the slave, "What's wrong with your son? He never cried like that before."

"I tried to feed him with the breast, but it slipped out of his mouth. That's why he cried."

The boy still kept crying. The woman asked the same question.

The slave got mad, and said, "That daughter of yours that you tied to your dog got a house full of meat and gave me all I could eat. I hid a piece of fat for my son. After he ate it up he wants more."

"You want to get up early in the morning. We got to go there early in the morning. Try to stop your son from crying."

So next morning they started before daylight. When they land where the girl and dog were living, the slave grab her son, jump out and run.

The girl asked the slave, "Is that my mother and father?"

The slave said, "Yes."

The girl's mother started to run up, too.

She and her father said, "My poor daughter! My poor daughter!"

The girl pulled down a piece of fat that was hanging and threw it towards her father and mother, and said: [316] "You didn't think I was your daughter when you tied me to a dog." She said to the fat, "Turn into a glacier!"

It did − between her and her mother and father. The glacier got long, and the father and mother made a bird noise, "Däk Däk." It sounded farther and farther away.

Tale 25: Good For Nothing (GN)

Once there was one man who was good-for-nothing among rest of men who were preparing for war with other tribes. While young men and old men were in water to be strong, this good-for-nothing man would be in bed which he made by fireplace with few skins of animals. When someone have a fire going, his bedding would start to steam. The others were in water from daylight until they see smoke coming out of house. They start come out of water one by one and try to pull a part of limb on old partly rotting tree to see who was strongest, and when they come back to house, each would move this good-for-nothing with their feet and making some remarks about him. They thought this man was too lazy to go out doors [to urinate?].

This man who was good-for-nothing heard about others trying to pull a limb off tree, so he started to go in water early in morning before the other men and be in bed again before the others were out of their bed. That is reason when someone start fire going, his bedding would start to steam. But others thought otherwise. At one of the early morning's try at limb, he pulled it out but put it back in so others won't know about it, and was in bed again. When the others try it, the strongest man pull it out, and was given strong man's spear for the war.

The war was not very far off. All men was making spear points and arrow points and war clubs, but still this man [317] who was good-for-nothing was still making believe he was good-for-nothing. And then when rest was ready to go, he want to go with rest of the men, but was told that they haven't any room for useless, but begged so much they did let him go as a bailer of one of the canoes. When they got where the fight was to take place, he stayed behind rest and when they start to fight he also stayed behind, too.

But when his side was losing he take the strongest man's spear and told him to stand back and watch. The first man he killed, he did not spear him, he got a hold of him with the spear and throw him so far when he came down he was killed by the fall. And then he started on rest.

When he start he said to them, "What do you think you are doing, killing my-people?"

He only spear them once to kill them. So he won the war for his people.

Tale 26: A Tlingit War Story (GN)

(This is a Tlingit war story, referring to Tlingit villages. Mrs. Scar Stevens, who is supposed to be of Tlinget descent, confirms this opinion.)

There were some people going to visit another village in canoes to have a good time. They had had a war with those other people long before. They had killed most of the people in the other village but thought they had forgotten about it by now.

They landed at a place for overnight. A raven started to eat their extra clothes in the evening.

The oldest man said, "That's a bad sign. Let's go back." But another man had a brother-in-law in the other village and he wanted to visit him. They had married two sisters. [318]

The old man said, "All right, we will," but he was kind of sore.
When they were about halfway there in their canoes, the sky above them cracked and they saw their own shadows in the crack.

The old man said, "This is a bad sign. Let's turn back." But the man who had a brother-in-law said: "I want to see my brother-in-law."

When they got there a man came to meet them where they landed. He was the brother-in-law. He had a blanket over his shoulders and a short spear under it. When his brother-in-law stepped from the canoe he just turned away from him without speaking and went back to the house.

The people went to another house. They started to dance next night. The man who had snubbed his brother-in-law wouldn't come. They sent a man after him.

The messenger came back and said, "He's having a row with his wife."

Instead of having a row with his wife he was sharpening all his war spears.

Finally he came as far as the door. He heard a song referring to his sons and daughters. He stopped then and almost changed his mind about killing those people.

Then he thought to himself: "Maybe they'll think that I got scared."

When he came in there were two fellows dancing. He pulled out his spear and pushed them aside with his spear. He didn't mean to kill them but he pushed them apart so hard that they hit the two opposite walls and broke their heads and died. [319]

He said: "Do you people think I forgot you killed my uncles?"

His name was qaᴅúwínà. He started to kill them off. Some fell down and pretended to be dead. They had done that same trick before. qaᴅúwínà said: "Do you think you can play that trick on me again?"

Even while they were down he ran his spear through them. One of them was under some others and he didn't get him. After qaᴅúwínà left, he sneaked off. The blood was halfway to a man's knees in the room.

The man that wasn't killed got a bundle of dried eulachon that was soaked in blood. On the way home he washed them off and ate them. He had nothing else.

qaᴅúwínà had saved one woman for himself but his slave killed her without qaᴅúwínà's knowledge.

Before he killed her, the slave said, "Come on out. What's the use of hiding? What's the use of trying to save your life?"
She had a daughter. She cut her daughter's head off and jumped out of the room.

qaᴅúwínà's brother-in-law had a wife at home. When the man that wasn't killed got home, she asked him if her husband was killed, too.

"Yes."

She didn't believe him. "How is it gets daylight again then?" She finally believed it. "It's all right, too," she said. "My people were killed off by these people and we aren't even with them, yet." She was from qaᴅúwínà 's village.

They started to prepare for war again. It was the next generation. When they were on their way they met another people − another tribe. They mistook them for qaᴅúwínà's tribe. After they killed about half of them they found their mistake. [320]

Tale 27: The Man Who Killed His Children (GN)

(The title of the story is the man's name.)

Once there was a man and his wife living away from the others. This man won't let his children grow up. He kills them off as soon as they were born. Finally the woman got to think of a way to raise her children by digging in the ground and hiding her children there. When her husband returns from fishing she hide her children until they were old enough. Sometimes they would come out to play when their father was out fishing, and sometimes their father would hear them make a noise as there were twelve boys by now. When their father come in, they go in the ground again. When their father heard them make noise, he would come in and the boys would hide.

Their father would say: "Who's making that noise?"

The mother said: "I throw some clam shells out. I guess that's what your heard."

The next day father heard them and asked: "Who's making the noise?"

The mother answered: "Oh there were a lot of crows on the beach making a noise. Maybe that's what you heard."

When they were old enough, the mother told that their father had killed all of their older brothers and sisters. So they killed their father.

Tale 28: The Illegitimate Child (GN)

A chief's daughter gave birth to a child, although she was unmarried. She killed the child and hid the baby [321] behind the sloping board used for a pillow. Her younger sister discovered the dead baby and told the parents. The girl admitted what she had done and named the father of the baby.

Her brother told the man to get wood. They built a pyre for the baby. The girl asked her mother to fix her hair, so that she would not be mistaken for a slave. When they were burning the child, the girl jumped on the fire. Her lover pulled her off, and climbed on the pyre himself. She got on top of him, and they both burned with the baby.

(There was a famine. There was very deep snow, so deep that they had to climb out of the house through the smoke hole. After the girl burned herself, the snow stopped. [This is supposed to be a true story.]

Tale 29: The Man Who Left His Wife (GN)

A man who wanted to leave his wife pretended to die. He told his wife to put him on the beach with his canoe and all his belongings on top of him. In a few days he disappeared. He went away to live with another women in a different village. His wife heard about it. She went to that village and killed them both.

[This is the bare skeleton of a story told also by the Prince William Sound Eskimo. The Chugach version serves to explain the formation of Middleton and why the brown bears on Montague Island are so fierce.]

Tale 29: The Little Girl Who Played With Dolls
(Written by GN)
[This is a story told to children so they won't play with toys in evening.
They are taught to go to bed early]. [322]

Once there was a village where there were lots of children. They is not allowed to play with toys or dolls. But the children were always playing with her dolls by the fireplace and she was told many times that something would come up out of the ground to get her. But she would keep on playing night after night. One night her mother told her to go to bed and not play any more but she did not do as her mother told her to do, so she let her alone. While she was playing something did come out of the ground and pulled her down into the ground and was never seen again.

Tale 31: Taking Away By Owl
(Written by GN)

Once there was a very bad boy at one of the villages who was crying for this and that. No matter what you gave him he would want something else and would cry until he gets it. One of the wise men use to tell his mother that Owl will get him if he does not stop crying for everything. But he was hard to please, and one night a Owl did come down through the smoke hole on top of the house and take him away and was never seen again.

Tale 32: Taking Away By Checkers People
(Written by GN)

Once there was a boy who likes to play checkers and who is a good checker player. As there is a season for checkers, the checkers was played for about a month. But this boy who likes to play checkers would keep on playing as long as he could get someone to play with him. There was old man who use to tell him that the Checkers [323] People would come and get him if he didn't stop playing checkers, but he would keep on playing. Finally one night while he in bed and sleeping, someone told him to get up and go with them. Theses men and women was all small people; he had to go with them, and was never seen again.

PART III:
CRITICAL ANALYSIS OF
PREVIOUS WRITERS ON THE EYAK

Who are the Eyak?

So [327] much misinformation, so many conflicting statements have been published about the smati tribe who live between the Eskimo of Prince William Sound and the Tlingit of Yakutat Bay that we might well have begun our study by asking: Who are the Eyak? Are they and have they ever been a distinct tribal group? To the second question the information embodied in Part I makes an unequivocal answer in the alternative. The first problem, however, is less easy to solve though many solutions have been proposed from time to time. The Eyak, appearing under almost unrecognizable names, have been classed as Eskimo, as Tlingit, as Athapaskan, or even as combinations of these stocks. Even the territory ascribed to them has appeared at dill'erent places on the maps of southwestern Alaska.

Before discussing in detail the written sources on the Eyak, or before summarizing the history of this people, it may be helpful to present in tabular form the various names by which they have been called, together with the territory which they are supposed to inhabit, and the linguistic stocks and tribal groups with which they have been identified. As will be seen later, a large part of the inaccuracies and discrepancies are due to the fact that the Eyak have been confused with an eastern off-shoot of the Chugach Eskimo. Some of the names appearing on our list are included simply because some writer has attempted to identify as Evak the tribe or tribes called by these names. [328]

Name	Territory
Ugalachinuten	Mainland near "Kojak" I, especially the
Ugalach-muten	swampy coast east of Kayak I., and on the banks of several unidentified rivers [Martin River?]. Hunt sea-otter off Kayak Island.
Ugalak mutes	(same as above)
(Thuglakemut-tribe of MEARES or Wallamute	
of PORTLOCK)	
Wallaamute	"considerably beyond Comptroller's Bay to the
Wallamute	Eastward" ... "a country to the E.N.E. of Port
Wallamute	Etches"[1]
(given as name of country, not inhabitants)	
Tauglekamute[2]	live in a district rich in sea-otter
Ugalachmiuti	"le golfe du Prince Guillaume jusqu' á la baie de Jakutsit" or "bai de Bering"

---

[1] PORTLOCK (1789, 237 and 254) places the "Tacklaccimute" or "Tack-la-cumute" in Controller's Bay. These are probably the Eskimo group called the t̲xałaɣmiut, or "Shallow Water People." See the discussion on page 343f.

[2] Identified by COXE (1803, II 316 note).

Ugaljachmutzi — "in der Gegend des Berges Elias, im Norden der Berings-Bay" (Yakutat Bay)

Ugaljachniutzi — "of Prince William's Sound"
(Ougalachmioutsy) — On map he ascribes to them all of Prince William Sound and Copper River delta and an inland stretch to upper part of Bering River[1]

Ugalyachmutzi — "adjacent to Bering Bay" (Yakutat Bay)

Pritchard 1836-1837, V 370f. [330]

Ugalenzen — west of Cape St. Elias (Kayak 1). They winter
(A name given by Indians of the Copper River in a little bay east of "Kadjack" and summer
and Yakutat Bay) — on east mouth of the Copper River[2]

(The bay in question is probably Controller Bay, though inaccurately described)

Ugalentzes — "dwelling in winter to the east of the island of
Ugalezi — Kodiac, and during summer at the mouth of the Copper River"

Ugalyachmutsi — "around Mount St. Elias, they are frontier
Ugalentses — tribes to the Tshugatsches" (Prince William
Ugalents — Sound Eskimo)
Ugalyachmutsi — "near Mount St. Elias"
(language is Ugalentz)
Ugalents — "parts about Mount Elias"[3]
Ugalyach-meut
Ugalents — "near Mount St. Elias"
Ugalyackh-mutsi
Ugalenschen — somewhere west of Yakutat Bay
(name for langauge)
Ugalakmutsi — "of King William's Sound"[4] [331]
Ugalents
Ugalenzen — winter in a bay on the mainland opposite "Kajak" Island, and summer on the right bsink of the Copper River at its mouth. Marks Alaghanik on the west bank of the river, but puts the mouth too far west. Map shows their territory extending from Prince William Sound

---

[1] He places the Eskimo on Kenai Peninsula, and on the coast from Copper River to Bering River.

[2] Wrangell calls Kayak Islands "Kadjack" following an orthographical error made originally by Shelekhov in 1786, according to Bancroft 1886, 229-230, note 15.

[3] The Atna or Atnas "are occupants of the mouth of the Copper River." (1857, 67. Cf. similar statements in 1845, II 292)

[4] Has confused these people with the Prince William Sound Eskimo, following the error of Humboldt and Gallatin. He places the "Atnaer" at the mouth of the Copper River.

	to Icy Bay
Ugalachmut	(quotes Wrangell and Mithradates)
Ugalenzen	
	"West of Cape St. Elias and near the island of Kadjak"
Ugalenzen	northwest of Mt. St. Elias
Ugaljachmjuten	
Oogalenskie	"from the mouth of Copper River to Icy Bay."
Oogalensie	"Near Mount Saint Elias"
Oogalamutes	
(1) Ugalnkmuts (Eskimo)	(1) "from Icy Bay nearly to the mouth of the Atna or Copper River"
(2) Ugalentsi (Tinneh)	(2) Hold winter festivals on Kayak Island, and summer at mouth of Copper River[1]
(1) Chilkhak-mut (own name) or Ugalak'mut (Eskimo)	(1) "reside on Kayak or Kaye Island in winter, and pursue the salmon fishery at the mouth of the Atna River and along the coast nearly to Icy Bay in summer"
(2.) Ah-tena (Ugalentsi)	(2) "a small part of the coast near the Copper River mouth"[2]
(1) Ugalenz	(1) "in the interior of Alaska" (obviously based on Gallatin's map)
(2) Ugalenzes	(2) "between Mount St. Elias and Copper River" [333]
Ougalakhmute	"occupied the coast as far eastward as Mount Saint Elias." "occupying the lowlands at the mouth of the Copper river and the coast eastward to Controller bay"
Ougalentze	
Walhnnute	
Lakhaiiintes	
Oughalentze	"are now confined to two villages, Alaganuk and Ikhiak" (or "Odiak")[3]
Onghalakmute	
Ougalakmute	
Ugalentz	"Copper river delta" "extending eastward to Controller bay." Mentions villages on "Ighiak lake", at "Ighiak" and "Alaganak"
(no name)	Mentions camp on "Konno" (Eyak) Lake, and

---

[1] He lists Alaganik as an Eskimo village (p. 272). He also states that the Indians of the Copper River have pushed their way to the coast between the Eskimo Ugalukmuts and "the next tribe of Indians" [Tlingit?] (p. 410).

[2] He proposes to abandon the name Ugalentsi as applied to the Ahtena Tinneh at the mouth of the Copper River (p. 21). In 1885 he no longer uses either Ugalakmut or Ugalentsi (pp. 14ff.).

[3] Ascribes to Tlingit the territory from the left bank of the Copper River through Controller Bay.

Eyak (own name)
Ugalentsi
Ugalenzen
Ugalachmuten

Lakhamit
Lakhamite
Aglegmutes

Aglegmute
Aglegmute

Agalignuite
(own name)
(1) Eeak tella
(own name)
(2) Guth-Ie-uk-quan

Ugalakmiut
Ugalakmiut
(etc.)

villages of "Iggiak," "Allaganak," Cape Martin, and "Tschilkat" east of Cape Martin territory near mouth of Copper River. Mentions Eyak and Alaganik

Quotes Wrangell, correcting "Kadjack" to "Kajak." Mentions "Altagansik" and "Tschilkat"

In 1783 "living on the coast of the mainland from Kayak Island eastward." Since 1783 they have been pushed eastward [westward?] of Kayak Island by the Kaljushes |Tlingit]"

from the Copper River

Mentions a large village on a large river on the mainland near Kayak Island [probably Alaganik] [336]

"Eyak or Odiak village"

"occupying the eastern shores of Prince William Sound"[1]

"extending west from Cape Yaktag, through Controller Bay, and including Kayak Island"

"just east of the mouth of Copper river"[2]

"the coast at the mouth of Copper r. and on Kayak id."

Stock or Language [329]
Live constantly at war with the neighboring *'Koliuschen." They are apparently distinct from the Prince William Sound Eskimo

(same as above)

.

as Ugalak mutes, apparently without warrant

One of the 5 peoples of Russian America. The

Writer and Source
Pallas, VI, part 7, 1793, 218-225. (Ismailov & hochahov from Eskimo informants in 1788, in Shelekhov's report)

Coxe 1803, II 316-320. (Translation of Pallas)
Portlock 1791, 237, 255, 260. (Eskimo informants in 1787)

Meares 1791, II 145 f. (Eskimo informants in 1788)

*Humboldt 1811, IV 347f.

---

[1] This tribe has been identified by the *Handbook* as the Ugalakmiut (vol. 2. p. 862). They are probably the people to whom EMMONS (p. 274) refers when he mentions "an older race that descended the Copper River and peopled these shores before the coming of the Tlingit." Their language was apparently different from that of the Tlingit.

[2] The StAxā'di (?) on the Copper River are an Athapaskan Raven clan of the Yakutat Tlingit (p. 413).

others are: "Koniagi" (Kodiak I.), "Kenayzi" (Cook Inlet), "Tschugatschi" (Prince William Sound), "Koliugi" (Tlingit and northwest coast)

Language has some Tlingit words, but it cannot he proved, as resanov claims, that it is related to Tlingit — *Mithradates 1815, III 211-236. (Resanov)

Their language and that of the Kenai form one family, distinct from those of the Eskimo and "Athapascas" — *Gallatin 1836, 14 and map. (Probably Humboldt) [331]

Are a branch of the "Koloschen"of "Jakutat," and their language (like that of the "Atnaer" of the Copper River) belongs to the same stock as the "Koloschen" — Wrangell 1839, 96f, and 99.

A tribe of the "northern insular" group on the Northwest Coast, like the "Koloschcs, Atnas, Kenaies," etc. — *Scouler 1841, 218 (Wrangell)

One of the many small tribes that make up the "Koluscliian family." Their vocabulary contains "ko many Alhabascan words as to indicate an intimate intercourse with the Carriers" — Scouler 1841, 282 (Wrangell)

"Kolooch in manners and conformation." Language is "Kolooch," certainly not Eskimo — *Latham, 1845a, 270 and 272 (Wrangell and Mithradates)

Language is related to the "Kenay" — *Latham 1845b, 275

Language is Athapaskan (like "Kenay" of Cook's Inlet or Atna of Copper River) — Latham 1854, II 292

Language is Athapaskan in wider use of the term, but with Eskimo and "Kolush" affinities — *Latham 1857, 67f. (Isbister, Richardson and probably also Wrangell, and Mithradates)

Language is a dialect of "Jakutat" which includes "Jakutatschen" pro per and"Ugatenschen" — *Schott in Erman 1849, VII 128. (Veniaminov),

Belong to the same stock as the Kutchin, the Kenayer" of Cook's Inlet, the "Koltsbanen" of Copper River source, and other "Kolusch" tribes down to Lynn's Canal [333] — *Richardson, 1851, 402. (Cook)

"Thitnkithen" — Holmberg 1855, I 4 and map. (Wrangell, but note correction of Kodiak to Kayak)

Language in some ways seems to be related to Tlingit. No relationship with Eskimo or Kenai — Radloff 1859,468 ff. (Shelekhov, Wrangell, Resanov, and Veniaminov)

Ludewig 1858, 194 (obviously Wrangell)

The Kenai tribe, including the Atnas and Ugalenzen, form a separate stock, comparable — Buschmann 1859, 807

to Athapaskan	
Language is one of the two dialects of the "Yahkntat Tongue" (not Tlingit)	*Elliott 1875, 30, 227f. (Veniaminov and Tikhmenev)
(1) Innuit (Eskimo)	*Dall 1870, 410 and 430 (Gibbs, Russian traders, & probably Wrangell)
(2) Tinneh (Athapaskan)	
(1) Innuit	*Dall 1877,1,21 (Eskimo informants at Port Etches)
Tinneh	
(1) Belong to the "Kenai tribe," a branch of the Athapaskan or "Tinney"	*Keane 1878, 463f. and 541
(2) "Thiinkeets" [335]	
Formerly Eskimo, but now mixed with "Thlinket," the latter element predominating	*Petroff 1884, 29, 146
"Of Innuit extraction, but now mixed with Thlinkets"	*Petroff 1882, 568, 571
Have become "incorporated with the Thlingit family	"Petroff 1893, 66, 155, 158
Now Tlingit.	Jacobsen 1884, 386ff. (own observation in 1883)
Originally may have been derived from an interior stock, quite different from Eskimo or Tlingit. Since disastrous wars, have intermarried with both groups	
Athapaskans, intermarried with "Thiinkets," "Aleuts" (Prince William Sound Eskimo), and "Midnooskies" (lower Copper River Indians)	Abercrombie 1900, 397, 384 (own observations)
Tlingit, or related to them in language and through intermixture	Krause 1885, 99 and 323ff. (Veniaminov, Wrangell, Holmberg, Radloff, Buschmann, Petroff & Jacobsen)
Not "Yullit" (upper Copper River Indians), not "Kolosh," and not Eskimo [337]	*Bancroft 1886, 191 note 32. (Nagayev's report to Zaikov 1783. Zaikov's Journal published in Tikhmenev. Original source from Eskimo)
	Bancroft 1886, p. 327. (Baranov 1792)
	*Bancroft 1886, p. 146 (Purtov & Kulikatov 1794, in report of Shelekhov Company)
A cross between the Aleuts (Prince William Sound Eskimo?) and the "Kayak", resembling the Copper River Indians, but with a distinct language.	Elliott 1900, 739
"Of Eskimo origin," but "dominated by the neighboring Tlingit.	*Emmons 1903, 231f (Tlingit ~~informants~~?)

Have "same totemic families ... as ... the Yakutat, and from generations of intercourse the
two people resemble each other in all essential
features"

"An Eskimo tribe ... so modified by contact   Swanton 1905, p. 396
with the Yakutat as to be enumerated with the
Tlingit tribes proper, though historically it has
no right to that position"

"A tribe of Alaskan Eskimo ... so far   *Handbook* 1910, II, 862
metamorphosed by contact with the Tlingit as   (all authors starred above)
to be more properly Tlingit than Eskimo

Nomenclature

The [338] names by which these various authors have called the Eyak (or people supposed to be the Eyak) fall into several groups, the derivations of which present a problem. These forms are:

(1) Eyak (ABERCROMBIE and EMMONS). This is obviously, especially in the form Eeak tella (EMMONS), derived from the name given by the natives themselves, and which in turn is derived from the name from their village, i•γiyàq. The people call themselves "men of Eyak," i•γiyàqDəlàqέiyù (singular: i•γiyàqDəlàq).

(2) Ugalach- or Ugalyach- (with German **ch**), or Ugal- with Russian, Russo-German, or Eskimo terminations. This is the most frequently used form. WRANGELLi,[1] tells us that the name is that given by the Tlingit and Copper River Indians (Atna). PETROFF,[2] however, suggests that this name is derived from the Prince William Sound word, "ughaluikhtuk," meaning "far distant," and this is the explanation adopted by the *Handbook of American Indians*. Actually, the present Eskimo name for the Eyak is uŋa•laɣmiut, "people from the northeast."[3] The Danish author of this report would base the derivation of "Ugalach-" etc., from this Eskimo name, and suggests that the **ŋ** (ng) was rendered as **g** because the Russians lack the former sound in their language. Similarly the **ɣ** has been changed to the Russian **x** or German **ch**, translated into English as **k**.[44] In fact, it is a well-established phonetic law in the Russian language that **ŋ** is transformed into **g**. We need only cite a few examples: {Russian yroJ}, corresponding to Latin *angulus* [339] English angle, {Russian ??} < (Norse) *væring*, the personal name {Russian < (Norse) Ingvar, and Cape Taigonos {Russian TattroHoe}, < (Chukchi) taiŋənot. Nevertheless, to the American author it seems curious that the **ŋ** should have been rendered as **g**, rather than by the closely related nasal, **n**. It is possible, though, that Ugalak- is derived from the Eskimo word uŋa•laɣmiut, and that this corruption was influenced by the Eyak's own name for themselves, which would explain why the first consonant (**ŋ** or I in Eskimo, **ɣ** or the continuant **g** in Eyak) should have been rendered as g. She is of the opinion that the only consonants which would naturally be rendered as **g** by a European would be the continuant **g** (**ɣ**), the unaspirated medial G, and the ordinary sonant stop

---

[1] WRANGELL 1839, 97.
[2] PETROFF 1882, 569.
[3] Field notes, 1933.
[4] BIRKET-SMITH 1934, 219, footnote.

g. We shall return to this question.

(3) Walla- with Eskimo termination (PORTLOCK). Superficially, this would seem to be another corruption of Ugala-, provided that we may assume the first consonant to be a continuant, foreign to English speech. A similar loss of the continuant γ, is, of course, found in "Eyak." Moreover, if the word which the Eskimo informants told PORTLOCK had contained ŋ the Englishman would certainly have heard, and reproduced it correctly. The corruption of **u** to **w** is easy to understand. But the Eskimo word which we heard in 1933 was unmistakably uŋa•laɣmiut. Is it possible that at an earlier date the Eskimo used a slightly different form, something like * uɣa•laɣmiut? This may have been an Eskimo corruption of the Eyak's own name for themselves; it may later have been changed by the Eskimo to a form which has a meaning in their own language. This theory would explain the word "Ughaluikhtuk" (probably *uɣa•uix̱tʊq, or something of the sort) which PETROFF gives. This hypothesis is, however, suggested only tentatively. [340]

(4) Agalig- with Eskimo termination (ELLIOTT). This is given as the Eyak's name for themselves. It is probably a corruption of the Eskimo word, similar to Ugalak-. The same remarks about the first consonant would apply in this case, since ELLIOTT, like POTLUCK, would have heard an ŋ, if there had been one in the word, while he would have changed γ to **g**, if he had attempted to render it at all.

(5) Agleg- with Eskimo termination (BANCROFT). This seems to have been the name originally given to the Eyak by the Eskimo interpreters whom the Russians brought with them from Kodiak Island. Actually, it is the Kodiak name for the Eskimo of Port Möller on the Alaska Peninsula, and it may have been applied to the Eyak by analogy, since they, like the Port Moller people, live on the mainland.

(O) Lakh- with Eskimo termination (BANCROFT). This is probably another corruption of the Eskimo word, from which the first syllable has been entirely omitted. It is useless to speculate further, since the primary source for this form (ZAIKOV) is not available to the authors.

(7) Tauglek- with Eskimo termination (MEARES). As we suggested in u note above (page 328, note 2) there is no reason to suppose that this name applies to the Eyak. It is more likely to be a name for one of the local groups of Prince William Sound Eskimo, perhaps the people of Tatitlik.

(8) Chilkhak- with Eskimo termination (DALL, 1877). DALL identifies these with the Eyak, and says that the name is that which they give to themselves. Actually it is the Eskimo name for an Eskimo tribe, as we shall see below.

(9) Guth-le-uk- with Tlingit termination (EMMONS). These people are identified by the *Handbook* as Eyak. At first this was thought to be an error, since EMMONS [341] distinguished between the Guth-le-uk-qwan and the Eeak tella, the latter certainly being Eyak. Guth-le-uk-qwan basketry, totemic social organization, and their intercourse with the Yakutat, together with the strong presumption that the former were the "older race," speaking a language distinct from that of the Yakutat Tlingit (see page 5, note 2), all support the hypothesis that the Guth-le-uk-

qwan were actually the Eyak, and that EMMONS was in error in distinguishing between them and the Eeak tella.

Territory.

There is also considerable confusion about the territory occupied by the Eyak (or by peoples assumed to be the same as those we call Eyak). A number of designations for this territory are so vague as to be useless and may be disregarded. In this class fall such expressions as "near Mount St. Elias," etc. The errors due to the misspelling of Kayak (Kajak) Island as Kodiak (Kadjak) have already been noted, as well as those due to GALLATIN'S map, which placed the Eyak in Prince William Sound. In general, the authors quoted above agree that the Eyak occupied the mainland east of Prince William Sound, including the Copper River Delta. The eastern limit of their territory is less clearly denned. Some would place it as far east as Yakutat (Bering) Bay, or Icy Bay. A number would have it include Controller Bay and place the frontier near Cape Martin. Kayak Island is again and again included in their domain.

The Eyak themselves (Part I, pages 17ff.) claimed the mainland from the west shore of Cordova Bay to Cape Martin and did not claim Kayak Island. They specified that in historic times the Tlingit occupied Kayak Island and [342] the mainland east of Cape Martin, while they themselves expanded into Eskimo territory as far as Port Gravina.

A number of authors introduce a new element of uncertainty by ascribing the mouth of the Copper River to tribes other than the Eyak (or those identified as Eyak). Thus LATHAM[1] assigns the mouth of the Copper River to the Atna. This is the name commonly given to the Athapaskans on the middle and upper Copper River. They are usually treated as one tribe, though we suspect that they more properly form at least two groups, and for this reason try to avoid the use of the inclusive term. In 1870, DALL also places the "Indians of the Copper River" somewhere on the coast.[2] In 1877, he specifies that the Ahtena Tinneh live at the mouth of the Copper River.[3] In 1885, he places al this point not only the Copper River Athapaskans, but says that a "colony" of Chilkaht-kwan Tlingit had established themselves there since 1877.[4] SWANTON claims the mouth of the Copper River for an Athapaskan Raven clan of the Tlingit.[5]

The explanation of these apparently intrusive groups is further complicated because the Eyak (or the people identified as Eyak by these writers) have been variously ascribed to the Eskimo or Tlingit stocks. We suspect that the "Athapaskans" at the mouth of the Copper River were actually the Eyak, even though they were not recognized as such. There are certainly enough similarities between the Eyak language and the various Athapaskan dialects to explain why the Eyak might not have been distinguished [343] from their neighbors farther up the river, especially since the latter are so little known. But if the "Atna" or "Athapaskans" at the mouth of the river are really the Eyak, who then are the "Ugalakmiut" of these authors? As we shall see presently, the latter were really an Eskimo group who formerly lived on Kayak Island and the shores of Controller Bay. They have been confused with the Eyak, and this is why the Eyak have so often been called Eskimo.

---

[1] LATHAM 1857,68.
[2] DALL 1870, 272.
[3] DALL 1877, I 21.
[4] DALL 1885, 14 & 19, note.
[5] SWANTON 1905, 413.

As we have mentioned several times already, the Eyak themselves did not claim Kayak Island. According to our Eskimo informants, Kayak Island and Controller Bay were occupied by an Eskimo group, called the tiłqaɣmiut, from their village, tiłqat or Chilkat, on Bering River. These people were a branch of the txałaɣamiut, or "Shallow Water People," one of the eight tribes of the Prince William Sound Eskimo. The Shallow Water People occupied the northeastern end of Hinchinbrook Island, all of Hawkins Island and Mummy Island (txała). In historic times the inducements and pressure of the Russians concentrated the Eskimo population about Nuchek at Port Etches, Hinchinbrook Island, and the aggressive Tlingit took over the outlying territory of Controller Bay. The original Eskimo inhabitants of this eastern region were either "absorbed culturally and linguistically by ... the Tlingit"[1] or, as some Prince William Sound stories suggest, they were killed and driven out by the Indians.

As we noted above, PORTLOCK writes of the "Tacklacci-mute" or "Tack-lacumute" of Controller Bay as an Eskimo tribe. The name seems to be an incorrect rendering of txałaɣamiut, the larger tribe, of which these people formed the most easterly group. It will also be remembered that on [344] the basis of information received from Eskimo informants at Port Etches, DALL gave the name, "Chilkhak-mut," to the Eskimo who inhabited, or rather who had inhabited, Kayak Island, and further adds that this was the name by which they called themselves. His only error was in confusing these Eskimo with the Eyak.

PETROFF makes a curious statement, which we may quote in this connection, though we can adduce no satisfactory explanation. It must be understood in the light of his erroneous belief that the Eyak were Eskimo. He writes:[2]

"We have every reason to believe that formerly the Innuits occupied the coast as far as the indentation commonly called Icy Bay, but constant pressure of the stronger Thlinket tribes has caused them to recede gradually to the localities occupied by them at the present day. In the vicinity of Icy bay the glaciers of the Mt. St. Elias range of Alps reach down to the coast, forming a long line of icy cliffs, a stretch of coast affording absolutely no landing place for boats or canoes. This feature has proved an insurmountable obstacle in the way of kaiak navigation, necessitating as it does a continuous sea voyage of between two and three days without making a landing. The Innuit in his kaiak could not accomplish this, but the Thlinkets in their large wooden canoes, provided with masts and sails, could easily traverse this distance, with favorable winds, without being obliged to land ...

"From a Shaman of the Chilkhaat tribe, who boasted of his pure Thlinket extraction, I learned that a tradition exists among his people that in times past their ancestors held all the territory to the westward clear to the shores of 'another big sea,' but that the Innuits came from the north, [345] as he expressed it, like 'herrings' — each in his own kaiak. The sea was covered with men, while women and children trudged along the shore. There was much fighting, and a final retreat of the Thlinkets, but they would one day recover their own."

It is conceivable that this legend refers to an ancient clash between the Eskimo of Controller Bay and the Tlingit. PETROFF is in error in supposing that the ice barrier was

---

[1] BIRKET-SMITH 1936, 27.
[2] PETROFF 1882, 569, 575.

impassable for the Eskimo. LA PÉROUSE in 1786 actually found the remains of an Eskimo umiak in Lituya Bay, southeast of this barrier, and the Indians there reported that this was only one of eight which had visited their bay.[1] There is, however, no evidence that the Eskimo ever did more than visit this locality.[2]

Evidence from Steller and other Early Explorers.

The first account of native settlements on Kayak Island is that given by STELLER, the naturalist to BERING'S voyage of discovery in 1741. STELLER reports the following finds on the west side of the island:

On the beach he saw a fireplace, beside which was "an [346] old piece of a log hollowed out in the shape of a trough, in which, a couple of hours before, the savages, for lack of pots and vessels, had cooked their meat by means of red-hot stones."[3] Scattered about were pieces of dried salmon and fresh reindeer (caribou, or perhaps rather mountain goat) bones, some very large scallop shells and some blue mussel shells. "In various shells, as on dishes, I found sweet grass completely prepared in the Kamchadal fashion, on which water seemed to have been poured in order to extract the sweetness." This GOLDER identifies as the cow parsnip, *Heracleum lanatum*.[4] Beside the fire was "a wooden apparatus, with which, for lack of steel, they are in the habit of making fire by friction, just as in Kamchatka and other places in America:" in other words, a fire drill.[5] The Under was moss, "bleached white by the sun."[6] Farther along the beach, STELLER saw "chopped-down trees ... miscut with many dull blows," proving the use of "stone or bone axes," and along a path which he followed back from the beach he noticed "many trees recently bared of hark ... [probably] for houses or sheds."[7] Finally he discovered in the woods a spot covered with cut grass." I pushed the grass aside at once and found underneath a cover consisting of rocks; and when this was also removed we came to some tree bark, which was laid on poles in an oblong rectangle three fathoms in length and two in width. All this covered a cellar two fathoms deep." (If the Russian fathom of 7 feet is meant the dimensions of the structure were 11 by 14 feet, and 14 feet in depth. The English fathom of 6 feet would make this

---

[1] LA PÉROUSE 1797, 206f.

[2] DALL (1877, I 21) believed that the RING collection from the mouth of the Stikine River proved that the Eskimo once lived as far south as this part of the present Tlingit territory. The collection does exhibit certain Eskimo-like types (DE LAGUNA 1934, 181, etc.), but these suggest only that prior to the development of the present Northwest Coast culture there was an earlier stage, related on the one hand to the archaeological cultures of the Pacific Eskimo and on the other to that of the Coast Salish. (DE LAGUNA 1934, 218); it does not at all follow that the carriers of this culture were Eskimo. We may further add that MORICE (1906-10, I 243ff) describes the Eskimo territory as continuous as far east as Kayak Island. His view may well be disregarded, since he has no personal knowledge of the region in question, and his arguments, which are chiefly based on the etymology of the tribal names, are correspondingly weak.

[3] GOLDER'S Translation (GOLDER 1925, II 44).

[4] GOLDER 1925, II 44f and note 78.

[5] GOLDER 1925, II 45, plus note 80.

[6] GOLDER 2.-i, II 45f.

[7] GOLDER 1925, II 46f and note 86.

[347] 18 by 12 feet and 12 feet deep.) In the cellar were (1) several bark vessels about 42 inches high, filled with smoked salmon, (2) some sweet grass, (3) "different kinds of plants, "whose outer skin had been removed like hemp, which I took for nettles" (this was apparently prepared for making rope or cord), (4) "the dried inner bark from the larch or spruce tree, done up in rolls and dried" for eating, (STELLER has probably mistaken the sweet hemlock hark for the bitter spruce bark), (5) bales of seaweed thongs, identified by GOLDER as kelp, *Nereocyslis priapus*, (6) and some very long, black arrows, very well made.[1]

Of these items of culture, the following are common to both the Eyak and the Prince William Sound Eskimo:

> cooking with hot stones, wooden vessels, (though we met no mention of them as cooking pots for either people), the fire drill, clam-shell dishes for the Eyak, and probably for the Eskimo, though we have no specific information from the latter, stone adzes and axes, birchbark vessels, bark used for roofs, kelp fishing lines, dried salmon, mussels and other shellfish (especially large cockles, probably STELLER'S "scallops"), wild celery and dried hemlock bark for food. The arrows are not described in sufficient detail to be identified. The Eyak used punk for tinder with their fire drills; we do not know what the Eskimo used. The Eyak made ropes of fiber, and spruce-root cords and wythes were found in an Eskimo burial cave in Prince William Sound.[2] None of these items, therefore, gives us any clue as to the inhabitants of Kayak Island.

The underground house is, however, most certainly not [348] Eyak. While our Eskimo informants denied that their ancestors built subterranean dwellings, one of the older natives, now dead, described such houses to Mr. LEE PRATT, formerly of Cordova. and PETROFF noted them in 1880.[3] Archaeological evidence of semi-subterranean structures of some kind were found by us on Hawkins and Hinchinbrook Islands.[4] One of our Eskimo informants mentioned a temporary shelter, made by digging a pit in the ground and covering it with skins. The structure found by STELLER seems to have been rather unusual, since it was entirely subterranean, with the roof at the level of the ground so that it was practically hidden. There is no evidence, except the size, that it was used as a dwelling. The type of door or entrance is, unfortunately, not described. There can be no question, however, that it was made by the Eskimo.

KHITROV, BERING'S "Fleet Master," found traces of habitation on what we have identified as Wingham Island, near Kayak Island. In his journal he states:[5]

"We came across (on the island) a [summer] hut which was made of hewn boards; the floor was also made of these boards. [The material for the hut and floor was of good wide boards.] In place of an oven there was in one corner of the hut a fireplace. Near the hut was found a wooden basket in which were shell fish, which showed that the inhabitants here used them for food. We did not see any people, but it was quite evident that they had been here shortly before our arrival. I brought from this island [from this hut], in order to show our Captain Commander, one [349] [wooden] basket, a shovel, a small stone with copper stains on it,

---

[1] GOLDER 1925, II 47ff and note 91.

[2] BIRKET-SMITH & DE LAGUNA: *The Archaeology of Prince William Sound* (in preparation).

[3] PETROFF 1884, 21.

[4] DE LAGUNA 1934, 156, and Field notes 1933.

[5] GOLDER 1925, I 99. The interpolations in brackets are taken from KHITROV'S log, 97, note 39.

[and one common round stone with a hole]."

STELLER[1] writes of this find as: "a small dwelling built of wood, the walls of which were so smooth on the inside that it seemed as if they had been planed," which seemed to suggest that the builders had iron tools. From this building KHITHOV brought "a wooden vessel, such as is made in Russia of linden hark and used as a box." It must have been a box made with a single bent plank for the side. He also brought a whetstone, "a hollow ball of hard-burned clay, about two inches in diameter, containing a pebble, making a noise when shaken, which I regarded as a toy for small children," (KHITROV'S stone with a hole in it?) "a paddle," (KHITROV'S shovel?) "and the tail of a blackish gray fox."

The wooden hut, probably built above ground, since it is not otherwise described, might have been either Eskimo or Eyak. The box with a single bent plank for a side is Eskimo, not Eyak. The whetstone with copper stains might he from either people. While neither claim to have made rattles of baked clay, the Eyak made pottery pipes, and the Eskimo told us that they formerly made beads and animal figures of baked clay. The shovel used by the Eskimo for carrying hot stones is shaped exactly like a paddle, and it was probably this implement which KHITROV found.

That there he no remaining doubt that Kayak Island was Eskimo territory we have only to quote from MARTIN SAUER, who met an old Eskimo in Prince William Sound in 1790.[2] "He said, that they frequented (on the chase in summer) an island, which he described so particularly, as convinced us [350] beyond a doubt, that it was the Kay's island [Kayak] of Captain COOK. He remembered that when he was a boy a ship had been close into the bay on the west side of the island, and had sent a boat ashore; but on its approaching land the natives all ran away. When the ship sailed, they returned to their hut, and found in their subterraneous store-room, some glass beads, leaves (tobacco), an iron kettle, and something else. This perfectly answers to STELLER'S account of the Cape Saint Elias of Bering and is undoubtedly the very spot where STELLER landed, and where the things above mentioned were left in the cellar."

SARYCHEV makes a similar report of this conversation:[3] "One of the Americans [Prince William Sound Eskimo] then actually told us, that his father had related to him something of this ship [BERING'S]; which, however, had not landed at Tsehukli [Montague Island], but at the island of Kadjak [Kayak], that lay about two days sail to the east of this place [Nuchek], and was actually resorted to in the summer by the Americans, who went in pursuit of otters. The crew of this ship went ashore, and left them some knives and beads."[4] [351]

---

[1] GOLDER 1925, II 52f., with additions contained in notes 97 and 98 on p. 52, and notes 100 and 101 on p. 53.

[2] SAUER 1802, 193f.

[3] SARYTSCHEW 1805-06, 25.

[4] The objects left in the cellar were:

(1) "16½ arshins of green material" (between 12 and 13 yards) (Log for July 21, 1741, written by Assistant Navigator, KHARLAM YUSHIN, GOLDER, 1925 I 97).
   "a piece of Chinese silk", (STELLER in GOLDER 1925, II 51).
(2) "an iron kettle" (STELLER).
(3) "2 iron knives" (KHITROV's Journal, GOLDER 1925, I 99).
(4) "2 iron pipes for smoking Chinese tobacco" (KHITROV).
   "a Chinese pipe" (STELLER)
   "pipes" (YUSHIN)
(5) "a pound of tobacco" (STELLER)

Other statements made by the natives to various early explorers corroborate the theory that the people who frequented Kayak Island were the Eskimo. ZAIKOV'S expedition of 1783, to which we have already referred, captured several Eskimo in the neighborhood of Kayak Island and Controller Bay. They "stated that Kyak was not a permanent place of residence, but was visited only in search of game by people seen by the Russians, their homes being to the westward, at a distance of 'two day's paddling,' from which statement we may conclude that they were from Nuchek or Hinchinbrook Island."[1] NAGAYEV, as already stated, discovered the mouth of the Copper River, near which he encountered a party of natives in a large baidarka or umiak, with whom he traded. They called themselves Chugaches, and said that they came from a safe harbor, which BANCROFT would identify as Port Etches on Hinchinbrook Island.[2]

The Eskimo interpreter with ISMAILOV and BOCHAROV told the Russians that "Koiac" (Kayak) Island "was not inhabited; but was occasionally frequented by the Tschugatski, and Ugalak mutes, for the purpose of hunting sea-otters."[3]

We are, therefore, justified in assuming that the people of Kayak Island were not Eyak, but Eskimo, and that they should properly be called the tłqaɣmiut.

It is these early Eskimo inhabitants or frequenters of Kayak Island and Controller Bay who were constantly confused with their Eyak neighbors, and this is why the Eyak have so consistently been classed as Eskimo. The error [352] gained a certain plausibility from the obviously Eskimo-like features of Eyak culture. The name "Ugalakmiut" may be said to exemplify this error, and since it is not, the Eyak's name for themselves, but is only a corrupted Eskimo word inconsistently applied to several confused ethnic groups, it should be abandoned.

Confusion of the Eyak with the Tlingit

The Northwest Coast stamp on Eyak social organization and material culture, the Eyak traditions themselves, and historical records show that the Eyak have been in contact with the Tlingit for a considerable period of time. This fact should be considered when offering an explanation of why the Eyak have so often been described as a branch of the Tlingit.

Eyak traditions, as we have seen above (Part I, p. 148), say that the Eyak in very early times lived farther to the east than they did in historic times. Thus, Galushia states that once the Eyak lived east of Cape Yakataga, in country that is now Tlingit, and that they had to fight the Eskimo when they spread west to the shores of Prince William Sound. That there may be some truth in this legend is suggested by the statement made by BANCROFT (on the authority of ZAIKOV'S report) that prior to 1783 the Aglegmutes (Eyak) lived on the coast cast of Kayak Island, but that after 1783 they were driven west of Kayak Island by the Tlingit.[4] This statement is, however, somewhat misleading. According to the very earliest sources of information the Eyak were already then living at the mouth of the Copper River; they did not move to this locality in historic times. In the beginning of historic times and down perhaps to the end [353] of the 18th century, the Eskimo occupied this eastern territory (or at least part of it). If the Eyak

---

"Chinese tobacco" (YUSHIN)
(6) "20 Chinese strings of beads" (KHITROV)

[1] BANCROFT 1886, 187 note 29.

[2] BANCROFT 1886, 187f, 191 note 32.

[3] COXE 1803 II, 316f.

[4] BANCROFT 1885, 191 note 32.

lived east of Kayak Island or east of Cape Yakataga it must have been in prehistoric times.

There can be no doubt, however, about the westward advance of the Tlingit. In the prehistoric period the Eyak themselves adopted a number of Tlingit into their tribe. In 1792, BARANOV'S party on Hinchinbrook Island were attacked by a war party of Tlingit, who seem to have mistaken the Russians' camp for an Eskimo settlement. There is some doubt as to whether the Eyak joined with the Tlingit in this attack.[1] In 1799 a fleet of Eskimo and Aleut baidarkas en route to Yakutat under Russian orders was caught by a storm, and the natives who escaped shipwreck were massacred by the Tlingit near Cape Suckling.[2] This incident is also recorded in a Prince William Sound Eskimo tale, and it would suggest that at that time the Tlingit were established near Kayak Island. In 1805, the Tlingit massacred almost the entire Russian settlement at Yakutat (established in 1795), and organized a war party to attack the Russian posts in Prince William Sound. Through strategy the Eskimo, however, succeeded in killing the Tlingit almost to the last man.[3] This incident is told by the Eskimo in the story of the fight at tau<u>x</u>tvɪk on Hawkins Island. DALL wrote that since 1877 the "Chilkaht-kwan Tlingit" had established a "colony" at the mouth of the Copper River.[4] PETROFF, in both the Tenth and Eleventh Census reports (1880 and 1890), comments on the increasing [354] amount of Tlingit influence among the Eyak. He believed that the Tlingit would have advanced even more rapidly if the Russians had not stopped them, and explained the swift spread of Tlingit influence in the latter part of the 19th century to the American policy of non-interference.[5] In 1903, EMMONS ascribed the shores of Controller Bay and Kayak Island to the Guth-le-uk-qwan, a people who had the same totemic organization as the Tlingit, and who had mingled so much with the Yakutat as to resemble them "in all essential features." We believe these people were those to whom he also refers as "an older race that descended the Copper River and peopled these shores before the coming of the Tlingit," and who spoke a language that differed in some way from Tlingit.[6] As already explained, we identify these people with the Eyak, in spite of EMMONS' distinct reference to the Eeak tella "Eskimo," and in spite of his erroneous assignment of Kayak Island to their territory.

This comparatively recent infiltration of the Tlingit into country which was wrongly ascribed to the Eyak, the Tlingit-like features in Eyak culture, the social relations between the two tribes, and certain similarities between the Eyak and the Tlingit languages easily explain why the Eyak have been classed by some writers as Tlingit. This error, combined with the earlier error which confused the Eyak with the Kayak Island Eskimo, resulted in the curious explanation that the Eyak were Eskimo who had become "metamorphosed Tlingit." Actually it is possible that some of the Kayak Island Eskimo may have been incorporated into the Tlingit group who took over their territory. It is [355] unlikely that this assimilation was friendly, in view of the enmity between the two peoples, but some of the Eskimo may have been taken as slaves.

In addition to the relationships between Tlingit and Eyak that we have already mentioned, Tlingit and Tsimshian traditions indicate that there may have been others.
For example, SWANTON lists among the Raven clans of the Yakutat a group called the StAxa'di,

---

[1] BANCROFT 1886, 326f.

[2] BANCROFT 1886, 386f.

[3] BANCROFT 1886, 440f., 451f.

[4] DALL 1885, 19, note.

[5] PETROFF 1882, 569f.

[6] EMMONS 1903, 231f; 274.

an Athapaskan-speaking people on the Copper River.[1] We are not sure whether these are actually the Eyak Ravens, or the Tlingit who were adopted into the Eyak Raven moiety, or whether they are a northern Tlingit group whose territory is incorrectly described.

BOAS equates one of the Tsimshian Eagle clans, the Gun-hu'°t, or "Run-aways," wilh the Tlingil Nex'ᴀ'dî, an Athapaskan group. According to Tsimshian tradition these "Run-away" Eagles formerly lived on the Copper River, but were forced to migrate after a disastrous feud with the Raven village on the opposite side of the Copper River. In the course of their migrations down the coast they acquired additional crests.[2] According to SWANTON, on the other hand, the Tlingit Nexᴀ'di belong to the Sanyan geographical division, but are peculiar because they stand outside both of the major phratries. Raven and Eagle, with either of which they may intermarry, though they possess Eagle crests and Eagle personal names and house names. He even suggests that it is from this group that the northern Tlingit obtained the Eagle names and crests. He suggests that, instead of coming from the Copper River, these people may have been originally an Athapaskan tribe who formerly [356] lived on the shores of Behm Canal.[3] If they were from the Copper River, we would have a case where a group of Eyak had been adopted, first by the Tiingit and later by the Tsimshian, in the same way that a Tiingit group was adopted by the Eyak.

History

The history of the Eyak is rather meager. Apparently the first knowledge of this tribe was obtained by the Russian expedition under POTAN ZAIKOV that explored Prince William Sound and the waters near Kayak Island in 1783. One of ZAIKOV'S men, NAGAYEV, discovered the mouth of the Copper River. The existence of this river had already been surmised by BODEGA Y QUADRA, the Spanish explorer who came to Prince William Sound in 1779.[4] On the banks of the Copper River, NAGAYEV encountered some Prince William Sound Eskimo, who "called themselves Chugatsches, and [said] that they met in war and trade five other tribes: 1st, the Koniagas, or people of Kadiak; 2d, a tribe living on a gulf of the mainland between Kadiak and the Chugatsche country, named the Kinaias; 3d, the Yullits, living on the large river discovered by NAGAYEV; 4th, a tribe living on the coast of the mainland from Kyak Island eastward, called Lakhainit; and 5th , beyond these again the Kaljush, a warlike tribe with large wooden boats. This description of the tribes and their location was doubtless correct at the time, though the 'Lakhamite' (the Aglemules) [Eyak] have since been pushed eastward [an obvious misprint for *westward*] of Kayak Island by the Kaljushes, or Thlinkeets. NAGAYEV also correctly stated that the Yullits, [357] or Copper River natives, lived only on the upper river, but traded copper and land-furs with the coast people for sealskins, dried fish and oil."[5]

When PORTLOCK was in Prince William Sound in 1787, he learned of a region to the east of the Sound, which the Eskimo called "Wallamute" (as already explained he has confused the name of the inhabitants with that of the locality), from which many sea-otter skins were obtained in trade. "I always observed," PORTLOCK wrote, "that none of those skins were marked, as is the

---

[1] SWANTON 1908, 413.

[2] BOAS 1916, 483, 386. Cf. myth on pp. 270ff.

[3] SWANTON 1908, 409.

[4] BANCROFT 1886, 219.

[5] BANCROFT 1886, 191 note 32, based on ZAIKOV'S Journal.

usual custom when they are intended for sale, but made up into cloaks, and worn by the people, to defend them from the inclemency of the weather."[1] PORTLOCK at first thought that "WaHamute" was "considerably beyond Comptroller's Bay to the Eastward,"[2] or "E.N.E. of Port Etches,"[3] but when he came to a Tlingit village in Portlock's Harbor (near Sitka?), he believed that he had found "Wallamute." This was because the inhabitants did not mark their sea-otter skins for sale, and because they had copper daggers, similar to those of the Prince William Sound Eskimo which were said to have been obtained at "Wallamute."[4] It was COXE (cf. page 328) who identified the Wallamute with the Ugalak mutes.

Whether or not PORTLOCK had really heard anything about the Eyak, the first definite record we have of the Eyak is that left by the Russian exploring party under ISMAILOV and BOCHAROV who visited Kuyak Island and the vicinity in 1788. Their Eskimo interpreter, whom they had taken from Middleton Island (a small island in the Gulf [358] of Alaska, frequented by hunting parties from Prince William Sound), "pointed out a small rivulet [in the marshy lowland between Kayak Island and Cape Suckling, probably Martin River], which is frequented by the Ugalak mute."[5] To the west of this, an exploring party discovered a large river, probably one of the mouths of the Copper River, which they ascended for 3 versts (2 miles), and "observed a hut covered with the bark of trees, and the marks of human feet; but no inhabitants. Near this river dwell the Ugalak mutes, who are at enmity with the neighboring Koliuski."[6] DALL[7] and ALLEN[8] state that ISMAILOV and BOCHAROV established a trading post at the mouth of the Copper River. ALLEN attempts to identify the site as that of Skatalis or Sakhalis, an Eyak village. There is no mention of such a post, however, in SHELEKHOV'S account of this expedition, which is published by PALLAS and COXE. It is pretty certain that there never was a trading post on the Copper River until CHARLES ROSENBERG. built his at Alaganik in the late 1880's.

When BARANOV was attacked on Hinchinbrook Island in 1792 he thought that the Eyak had joined the Tlingit war party.[9] Two years afterwards, BARANOV sent a large baidarka party under PURTOV and KI'LIKATOV of the newly organized Shelekhov Company to "the second mouth of the Copper River." Somewhere in the vicinity they discovered a "large Aglegmule village" on a river (Alaganik?). Here they traded with the inhabitants, and succeeded in obtaining hostages, including a chief, whom they took with them to [359] Yakutat.[10] The Lebedev Company, at that time the deadly rival of the Shelekhov Company, pretended to PURTOV and KULIKATOV that they had a trading post on the Copper River, but this was untrue. (This lie, which was intended to prevent the Shelekhov Company from invading the district, may be the reason why DALL and ALLEN thought that a post had actually been established on the Copper River).

Russian attempts[11] at exploration of the Copper River began with two expeditions in

---

[1] PORTLOCK 1789, 237.

[2] PORTLOCK 1789, 237.

[3] PORTLOCK 1789, 255.

[4] PORTLOCK 1789, 260.

[5] COXE 1803 II, 317f.

[6] COXE 1803, II, 320.

[7] DALL 1870, 310.

[8] ALLEN 1887, 19.

[9] BANCROFT 1886, 327, and cf. also note 26.

[10] BANCROFT 1886, 346 f.

[11] These expeditions are listed by DALL 1870, 317f., 331, 341, 343; by ALLEN 1887, 19f.; by

1796. The first expedition under SAMOILEV was massacred. The second expedition under LASTOCHKIN (or PARTICHKEN) was only partially successful.

Other attempts to explore the river were made by BOYANOV (or BAZANOV) in 1803, and by KIMOVSKI (or KLIMOOSKY) in 1819. BANCROFT stales that in 1818-1819 two expeditions up the Copper River were massacred by the Atna. Another attempt was made by GRIGORIEV in 1843 or 1844.

In 1847 a more serious expedition was led by SEREBRANIKOV. The story of this venture is probably that which was acted out for ABERCROMBIE'S benefit at Alaganik. The expedition is also referred to in the Chugach Eskimo story of the Ten Soldiers that Ran Away from "Rooshia." This party ascended the Copper River valley as far as Tazlina River and Lake. After exploring this tributary, the expedition returned to the main river, where they were massacred by the Upper Copper River Indians, near the present site of Copper Center. The records were preserved by the Indians and were eventually recovered by the Russians. An Indian [360] from Chitina told ALLEN that three Russian parties had been massacred on the Copper River: the first by the Eyak (SAMOILEV'S?), the second by the Middle Copper River Indians, or Chitina Indians (GRIGORIEV'S?), and the third by the Copper Center or Upper Copper River Indians (SEREBRANIKOV'S). This last expedition seems to have ended Russian attempts at exploration in the region.

A few years before JACOBSEN'S visit to the Eyak in 1883, one of the Indians murdered a white man. The crew of an American gunboat arrested the murderer and took him to Portland. (JACOBSEN speaks as if this had taken place at Alaganik, but while the Eyak were upset by the event, it is not certain whether the Eyak or the Tlingit were involved. We question his ascribing this to the Eyak, simply because we found no other reference to the event, even by ABERCROMBIE who came to Alaganik the next year. It seems more likely that the Tlingit in the vicinity were involved because they were always getting into trouble with the Americans.)

Exploration of the Copper River was resumed by the United States Army expeditions under Lieutenants ABERCROMBIE in 1884 and ALLEN in 1885. It was conclusively proved that the lower part of the Copper River did not offer a practicable route into the Interior, even though it was attempted by many prospectors in the Klondike Rush of 1898. ABERCROMBIE'S expedition of that year to the Upper Copper River went in from Valdez in Prince William Sound.

The Eyak were subjected to white contact first through the Russian post at Nuchek, afterwards taken over by an American trader named HOLT, who used to visit them with a schooner. CHARLES ROSENBERG, established the first and only trading post at Alaganik, just a few years before the [361] village was abandoned. A cannery was opened at what is now Cordova between 1884 and 1890, and by the end of the century the "civilizing" of the Eyak was practically complete, and they had almost ceased to exist as a separate tribal entity. [blank 362-364]

BANCROFT 1886, 321, 525, and 576.

PART IV:
ANALYSIS OF EYAK ETHNOLOGY

Material Culture

The House

The [365] ordinary Eyak wooden house belongs to the well-known gabled type which is found all over the North Pacific Coast as far south as northern California, although interrupted by the shed type of the Nootka, Coast Salish, etc. It has been discussed by many authors, most recently by WATERMAN and OLSON. The former has published a comprehensive list of distribution; a number of additional quotations are given below.[1] This type of house does not extend into the Interior beyond the sphere of coast influence. As is only natural, the Eyak house seems to be closely related [366] to the winter dwellings of their immediate neighbors, the Chugach Eskimo, nor did it dill'er much from that of the Tnaina except for the lack of a house passage and sleeping platforms for young people. A number of structural details, like the interior partitions and the fitting of wall planks into grooved frames, point towards the Tlingit. Haida, and Tsimshian. On the other hand it was a less elaborate structure than many Tlingit houses, hut it should he remembered that the house of the northernmost Tlingit tribe, the Yakutat, was simpler than that of their more southern kinsmen.[2]

The Eyak house was described by Galushia Nelson as having walls of upright planks set into a frame of logs at the bottom and the top. Vertical split logs are used in the walls of the Kutchin "moss house" and among the Oregon and Northern California tribes.[3] In the intermediate region conditions are very complicated. The shed type has horizontal wall planks, whereas the Kwakiutl and Haida as a rule place them on end; among the Tsimshian and Tlingit

---

[1] WATERMAN 1921. OLSON 1927, 25ff. Cf. SARFERT 1909, 167 ff. — Kodiak (SCHELECHOF 1793, 202. LISIASSKV 1814, 213f.). Cook Inlet (DE LAGUNA 1934, 142ff.). Tlingit (LA PÉROUSE 1797, 196. MALASPINA 1849, 284. VON KITTLITZ 1858. 1 220f. ELLIOTT 1886, 47ff.). Nootka (MEARES 1790, 138). Squawmish {Squamish} (HILL-TOUT 1900, 485f.). Puget Sound (HAEBERLIN & GUNTHER 1930, 15ff). Washington and Oregon (LEWIS 1906, 159f, 176, 178. Gibbs 1877, 214ff.) Makah (SWAN 1870, 4ff.). Nisqually (WILKES 1844, 444). Klallam (KANE 1863, 167. GUNTHER 1927, 186.) Quinault (WILLOUGHBY 1889. 267). Chinook (VANCOUVER 1798, II 77. LEWIS & CLARKE 1814, 369 et passim. FRANCHERE 1904, 328. KANE 1863, 142). Tillamook (BOAS 1923, 3f.). Yurok (MASON 1889, 208f. KROEBER 1925, 78ff.). KAROK (MASON 1889, 208f.). Wiyot, Chulula, Whilkut (KROEBER 1925, 117, 140f.). Carrier, potlatch house (MORICE 1905, 185ff). Lower Lillooet (HILL-TOUT 1905, 134. TEIT 1900-08, 213f.). Wishram (SPIER & SAPIR 1930, 204). Shasta (KROEBER 1925, 289f.). Tnaina (WRANGELL 1839, 111. PETROFF 1884, 162f. ELLIOTT 1886, 91f. Osgood 1937a, 55ff.). Ingalik (WRANGELL 1839, 118). Atna (ALLEN 1889, 261). Koyukon, "log houses" (PETROFF 1884, 161.), Kutchin (OSGOOD 1936, 49, 52).

[2] NIBLACK 1890, 305.

[3] Cf. works cited in footnote ([1]) page 365.

the prevailing arrangement is again horizontal.[1] PETROFF states that the Tnaina house had horizontal logs grooved on the under side so that they might fit down upon the timber next below. This grooving, however, may well be due to Russian influence. From OSGOOD'S description it appears, however, that while horizontal logs were actually employed by the Tnaina of Kachemak Bay, both the Kenai and Upper Inlet divisions built their houses of upright logs. Also hybrid forms occur; the Chilkat for instance [367] place the wall planks horizontally at the rear and at the sides, but vertically in the front end,[2] and from archeological evidence the American author has reconstructed the Tnaina house in a similar way. AUREL KRAUSE has published a sketch of another Chilkat house having horizontal planks at the rear and vertical at the sides.[3] Probably the use of upright planks is the older: technically it is simpler, because shorter planks are required, and in the peripheral parts of the area only this arrangement is known. Insertion of the planks in bottom and top logs has a far more limited distribution than the use of vertical timber as a whole, being, as it seems, confined to the northernmost and most civilized peoples of the Northwest Coast.

The crude dovetailing seen by Colonel ABERCROMBIE occurs in the secondary rooms of the Tnaina houses and among the Tlingit, but may also here be of Russian origin, as suggested by ABERCROMBIE; in the case of the Eyak. In fact the dovetailing technique does not seem to fit very well with the use of corner posts which are essential to aboriginal North Pacific house building.

The Eyak house had a median ridge pole passing through the middle of the smokehole and two parallel beams forming the lower edges of the hole. These traits correspond with the roof construction on the southern parts of the Northwest Coast, whereas the Tnaina and Chugach on the one side, and the Tlingit. Haida, Tsimshian, and Kwakiuti on the other have an equal number, the middle part of the roof being more or less Hat.

A regular _smokehole_ in the roof is found both among the Chugach and Tnaina, as well as among the Tlingit, [368] Haida, and Tsimshian, whereas the Kwakiuti and Nootka art' content to push some of the roof planks aside. The _movable screen_ protrcting the smokehole has a counterpart among the Chugach, Tlingit. Haida, Tsimshian, and possibly other tribes.[4] The screen of the Tnaina house was immovable, built of planks set on three sides of the smoke-hole. Poles used as drying racks are common everywhere in the Northwest Coast houses.

Benches or platforms are found in the plank houses on both sides of Bering Sea, and so are also _separate sleeping rooms_, although they differ according to the material of the house. In the walrus-hide tent of the Chukchi and Asiatic Eskimo, and in the tent of the Reindeer Koryak it is y skin compartment, the well-known {Cyrilic полог }.[5] In the wooden house it is built of planks. As such it occurs among the Aleut and Pacific Eskimo,[6] the Tlingit, Kwakiuti and

---

[1] Cf. besides works cited above also JENNESS 1932, 94; DIXON 1933, 317.

[2] SHOTRIDGE cited by WATERMAN 1921, 53.

[3] KRAUSE 1885, 125.

[4] Information regarding Tsimshian screen supplied by Nass River Indian to the American author.

[5] Asiatic Eskimo (NELSON 1899, 258f.). Chuckchi (LUTKE 1835, II 269. WRANGELL 1839, 1 288. HOOPER 1853, 45. NORDENSKIÖLD 1881, II 24f., 95f. MAYDELL 1893. 185f. BOGORAZ 1904-09, 170 ff., 176, 180. SVENDRUP 1926, 193). Koryak (LANSDORFF 1812, 275. KENNAN 1871, 120. JOCHELSON 1908, 450f.).

[6] COOK & KING 1785, II 511. LISIANSKV 1814, 214. MERCK 1937, 129. PETROFF 1884, 141.

possibly other Northwest Coast tribes,[1] as well as the neighboring Athapaskans, i.e. the Tnaina and Atna.[2] There is also a reference from as far south as the Seechelt, a Coast Salish tribe of British Columbia,[3] but as the room here seems to be used exclusively for the puberty seclusion of young girls it is open to doubt whether it has any relation [369] to the true sleeping chamber farther north. The true sleeping rooms should not, of course, be confused with partitions of matting, etc., dividing off the sleeping quarters of each family.

The Eyak use a wooden _headrest_. Possibly a similar device was known to the Kodiak Eskimo, though the data are far from clear.[4] The wooden pillows of northern California[5] are geographically so far away that a connection is hardly feasible. It should be added, however, that according to verbal information from Dr. MELVILLE JACOBS a wooden pillow covered with skin was used in the men's house of the Coos, and a pole was used as a communal pillow among the Alsea.

We were told that the _steam bath_ was taken over from the Chugach. The early history of this type of bath in northwestern North America is rather obscure. The steam bath is, of course, widespread in North America, and there is even an isolated occurrence in South America in the north-western corner of Argentina. The typical sweat hath of the North Pacific Coast, California, and the Pueblo area is, however, a dry heat bath,[6] as is also the case among the Aleut and Eskimo of Bering Strait.[7] The steam bath is here only reported as aboriginal from Puget Sound and, in a very aberrant form, from the Kwakiutl,[8] whereas there is positive [370] evidence that it was introduced among the Aleut and Atna by the Russians.[9] This of course cannot apply to the two former cases, and the question is whether they are survivals from an early period, the dry heat bath being a later invention. If this is true (but we cannot be sure, for the steam bath at Puget Sound may also have been introduced by the Salish from the Interior since it is generally found on the Plateaus), then the steam bath of the Chugach and Eyak may be in the same position. On the other hand we dare not exclude the possibility that it is of Russian origin, just as it is among the Aleut and Atna. The type of wooden bathroom rather favors the latter view. It not only occurs among the Chugach and Eyak, but also among the Kodiak and Kuskokwim(?) Eskimo, Atna, Tnaina, and Tlingit, that is, it is found precisely in that region where Russian influence was strongest.[10] Its appearance is, moreover, quite Russian, even to such a detail as the dovetailing of

---

HOLMBERG, 1855, 96f. DE LAGUNA 1934, 144 f.

[1] WHYMPER 1868, 78. KRAUSE 1885, 127. BOAS 1897, 369.

[2] WRANGELL 1839, 111. PETROFF 1884, 163, ELLIOT 1886, 92. OSGOOD 1937a, 57ff. ALLEN 1889, 261.

[3] HILL-TOUT 1904a, 29.

[4] LISIANSKY 1814, 213.

[5] Yurok (KROEBER 1925, 92). Hupa (MASON 1889, 209. GODDAD 1903, 17).

[6] KRICKENBERG, 1934, 1f.

[7] ERMA 1870-71, III, 165). JACOBSON 1884, 160. NELSON 1899, 287f. Cf. DE LAGUNA 1935, 162. There is, however, an early reference to the steam bath among ther Kodiak Eskimo in MERCK 1937, 129.

[8] HAEBERLIN & GUNTHER 1930. 41f. BOAS 1921, 702ff. It is true that PETITOT (1876, xxx) describes the Mackenzie Eskimo as "grants amateurs de bains a vapeur " but PETITOT is often very inaccurate, and his statement should be taken with proper reservations.

[9] JOCHELSON 1925, 73. ALLEN 1889, 261.

[10] SCHELECHOF 1793a, 202f. WRANGELL 1839, 111. HOLMBERG 1856, 377f. ALLEN 1889, 261.

the logs in the Tnaina bathroom, which contrasts with the plank construction of the main room. We must still consider, however, whether the Eyak knew the dry heat bath before they adopted the steam bath and the wooden bathroom or bath house. This is possible, though we cannot answer the question definitely.

Before leaving the house we may yet call to mind that, according to tradition, the adopted members of the Eagle clan, when erecting their potlatch house, were in such a hurry that they covered it with bark instead of building a plank house. The Eyak also used bark for smokehouses. The Tnaina, Kutchin, Tahltan, and Tlingit erect [371] bark-covered houses in their summer camps, and far south, at the outskirts of the plank house area, they are regularly employed by the Shasta and Whiikut.[1] We would not infer, however, that the use of bark is a culture trait of historical importance, as it may just as well be a makeshift material.

We cannot here give the exact distribution of the *ladder* made of a notched log. It is, however, widely known on both sides of Bering Sea, both in connection with the semi-subterranean earth lodge and the plank house. A few examples will suffice.[2] Of course it is also known elsewhere in both hemispheres.

To sum up the evidence regarding the Eyak dwelling, we may characterize it as follows: It belongs to the Northwest Coast type of rectangular wooden house, and in some important details (insertion of wall planks in a bottom, and top log, smoke screen) it shows close affinity to the Tlingit house. The true smokehole, sleeping room, bench, and notched ladder occur on both sides of Bering Sea, the latter being a very widespread element. Among the neigh boring peoples vertical wall planks occur among the Chugach, Tnaina, Kutchin, and Tlingit and are probably an older feature than horizontal planks. Finally, dovetailing and the bathroom (perhaps also the steam bath) are ascribed to Russian influence, at least indirectly.

In addition to the dwelling house the Eyak had special buildings for smoking fish, for potlatches, and for defence. [372] Light *summer houses* are probably common everywhere in the fishing camps within the area of plank houses as far south at least as Puget Sound. These are frequently made of bark, as we have already mentioned, but they may also be erected of logs.[3] Among the Alaskan Eskimo the wooden summer house does not go as far north as the plank house for winter use, being replaced by the skin tent at Kotzebue Sound.[4] At their fishing places the Chugach had a smokehouse probably similar to that of the Eyak.

A special *potlatch* or *festival house* is found in many places in the boreal parts of North America, but its history is far from clear. Among the Alaskan Eskimo we have the well known *qazge* or "*kashim*" where the ceremonial masked dances take place, and which is also used as a

---

OSGOOD 1937a, 59ff. KRAUSE 1885, 128.

[1] OSGOOD 1937a, 62. Osgood 1936, 51, 55. EMMONS 1911, 37f. BANCROFT 1875, 102. KROEBER 1925, 141, 289f.

[2] Aleut (MERCK 1937, 118). Kodiak (SARYTSCHEW 1805-06, II 157). Bering Strait Eskimo (NELSON 1899, 244, 253). Tlingit (KRAUSE 1885, 126). Kwakiutl (VANCOUVER 1798, II 274). Yurok (KROEBER 1925, 79). Carrier (MACKENZIE 1801, 318). Thompson (TEIT 1900, 194). Flathead (TEIT 1930, 333). Koryak (JOCHELSON 1908, 457). Kamchadal (STELLER 1774, 214).

[3] Tnaina (OSGOOD 1937a, 55, 59, 62). Kutchin (OSGOOD 1936, 51, 55). Tlingit (MALASPINA 1849, 284. KRAUSE 1885, 134). Puget Sound (HAEBERLIN & Gunther 1930, 18f. Carrier (MACKENZIE 1801, 328).

[4] NELSON 1899, 242, cf. 247ff.

lounging, sleeping and sweating place by the male inhabitants of the village. It is, in fact, a typical "men's house", similar to the Californian dance house, the kiva of the Southwest, and corresponding structures in many other parts of the world.[1] The Central Eskimo tribes employ the word *qagje* for the great snow domes erected at their dance gatherings during the winter, but they do not diner from the ordinary dwelling huts except for their size and lack of sleeping platforms; permanent festival houses are not [373] known.[2] In Greenland the word *qagsse* only occurs in vague traditions, and although extensive excavations have been made all over the coasts, no ruin has been found which can with any certainty be identified as a *qagsse*.[3] THALBITZER has proposed to link the Eskimo word with an Ainu word and even with a Japanese sft'ni, but, as it seems, on very slight foundation.[4] On the other hand there may be some reason for associating the Eskimo dance house with the Thule culture; it seems to fit better into the pattern of the comparatively stable, whaling and sea-mammal hunting population of this stage than into that of the roving Central tribes, and the supposition of a Thule (i.e. Alaskan) origin also agrees with the fact that only vague reminiscences have reached far-off Greenland.

Among the Northwest Coast Indians special potlatch houses occur, although they do not seem to have been very common in recent times. They are mentioned from the Tlingit, KwaldutI (in which case, however, it may be an ordinary house adapted to the purpose), Bcllabella, Twana, Klallam, and Chimakum in the Puget Sound region.[5] In the interior a rectangular potlalch house is known from the Carrier.[6] According to the field notes of the American author [374] the lower Tena adopted the Eskimo "kashim" with all its features. The Tnaina of Kachemak Bay and Kenai Peninsula also had special dance houses, but they do not occur within the other bands of the tribe.[7] Very often, however, the Northwest Coast ceremonies take place in an ordinary dwelling, because this is made possible by the size of the house. It might In- templing to ascribe the disappearance of a regular dance house to the development of large, communal dwellings which made a special ceremonial room more or less superfluous. If this be so, is the dance house

---

[1] Eskimo in general cf. THALBITZER 1925, 236f. Kodiak (SCHELECHOF 1793a, 202, MERCK 1937, 142, DAWYOOW 1816, 182. HOLMBERG 1856, 378. ELLIOTT 1886, 109). Bering Strait Eskimo (BEECHEY 1831, I 367. WRANGELL 1839, 128f. SAGOSKIN 1848, 538. JACOBSEN 1884, 159, 260. ELLIOTT 1886, 385. Nelson 1899, 245f., 249f, 285ff). Point Barrow (RAY 1885, 41, MURDOCK 1892, 79f.). Colville Eskimo (STEFANSSON 1914, 189). Mackenzie Eskimo (PETITOT 1876, xxx. STEFANSSON 1914, 136, 170). It was probably also known to the prehistoric Eskimo of Cook Inlet (DE LAGUNA 1934, 162).

[2] Copper Eskimo (JENNESS 1922, 69ff. KNUD RASMUSSEN 1932, 129). Netsilik Eskimo (KLUTSCHAK 1881, 151. AMUNDSEN 1907, 256, 260f.) Caribou Eskimo (GILDER s.a. 43. BIRKET-SMITH 1929, I 269). Iglulik Eskimo (MATHIASSEN 1928,131. KNUD RASMUSSEN 1929, 227f.). Baffin Island (BOAS 1888, 600 ff. BILBY 1923, 217f, 243). Labrador (PACKARD 1891, 254f. HAWKES 1916, 59,178).

[3] THALBITZER 1920, 240ff. BIRKET-SMITH 1924, 144. Cf. also the reports on recent archaeological investigations in Greenland by MATHIASSEN, HELGE LARSON, GLOB and others.

[4] THALBITZER 1925, 252ff.

[5] EHMAN 1870-71, II 315, 3l7f. BOAS 1897, 435f. BOAS 1924, 332. EELLS 1889, 623. GUNTHER 1927, 187. HAEBERLIN & GUNTHER 1930, 17f. LEWIS 1906, 160.

[6] MORICE 1905, 185f.

[7] OSGOOD 1937a, 66f.

of the Eskimo and the North Pacific Indians an old common feature of the Bering Sea region and the Northwest Coast? This hypothesis is to some degree supported by the fad that houses with exactly the same combination of functions as among the Eskimo — ceremonies, sweat baths, sleeping and lounging place of the male population — are found in California, i.e. at the other extremity of the Northwest Coast area.[1] his gives the impression that the dance house is an old cultural feature which survived in the marginal regions, whereas it has all but disappeared in the center. For special reasons again it has lost much of its importance among the Eskimo outside Alaska.

The _fort_ is another specialized house type of the Eyak, but it was not remembered whether it was roofed or just a simple stockade. ROLAND B. DIXON recently surveyed the accounts of 18th-century authors referring to forts on the Northwest Coast and arrived at the following conclusions:

"Prior to 1800 four kinds of defensive or semi-defensive sites or structures were seen and described on the north-west coast: (1) single houses built on platforms projecting from [375] sleep hillsides, with short defensive wing-fences; (2) villages occupying the flattish summits of almost isolated, very steep-sided rocky islets, some of the houses being built on platforms which overhung slopes; (3) villages on the summits of steep-sided islets -with one or more lines of defensive palisades; and (4) defensive 'towers' not further described."[2] The last reference is to Caamaño who calls the fortifications "_torreones de madera fabricados sobre peñas escarpadas_,"[3] but as the Spanish expedition also observed guns and small cannon in the same place as the "towers," the latter may be an example of early European influence, which is known to have appeared very soon after the first contact with the whites. It seems quite certain, as is also the opinion of DIXON, that the fort erected by the Tlingit after the destruction of BARANOV'S post at Sitka, 1801,was built according to Russian patterns. On the other hand we may not be so sure that fortifications were really as rare as DIXON thinks. In legends and ethnological literature of later times they are mentioned so often that it would be natural to suppose that they formed an integral part of aboriginal Northwest Coast culture.[4] These fortifications are generally described as stockades. On the Asiatic side of Bering Sea similar structures were common in Koryak and Kamchadal villages;[5] in fact their defensive character was so pronounced that these villages acquired the name of ocTporn by the cossacks, "who considered it [376] a greater honor to conquer a fort than an ordinary open place."[6] In war times the Ainu took refuge in fortifications consisting of

---

[1] KROEBER 1925, 810ff. & passim.

[2] DIXON 1933, 326.

[3] CAAMAÑO 1849, 355.

[4] Tlingit (LANGSDORFF 1812, 110. NIBLACK 1890, 303 f. KRAUSE 1885, 131). Haida (NIBLACK 1890, 303f.). Tsimshian (BOAS 1916, 410). Puget Sound (HAEBERLIN & GUNTHER 1930, 15. GIBBS 1877, 192). Makah (SWAN 1870, 51). Klallam (GUNTHER 1927, 184). Tillamook (BOAS 1923, 5). For North American palisades in general cf. SARFERT 1909, 195ff and WISSLER 1922, 117.

[5] JOCHELSON 1908, 563f. STELLER 1774, 200, 218.

[6] STELLER 1774, 200.

an open place surrounded by earth walls, but no palisades are mentioned.[1]

Turning now to the roofed forts or log cabins we find their distribution limited to the inland Plateaus.[2] The only reference to palisades is from the Lillooet.[3] This distribution is so pronounced that it can hardly be accidental, but it is difficult to explain. The general aspect of culture is roughly speaking, more old-fashioned on the highlands than on the Pacific Coast, and as far as this goes the log cabin might well be considered an old culture clement. But this does not agree with the character of the structure, which is strikingly different from the semi-underground winter house, simple tent, and lean-to of the Plateau tribes. It will be noted that all the descriptions in question date from very recent times. So perhaps it is not very far from the mark if we assume that the log cabin is nothing but an adoption of European ideas, whether these were first derived from the Russian forts on the coast or the Hudson's Bay Company's posts in the Interior. Log houses, which did not act as fortifications, were mentioned by PETROFF from the Koyukon[4] and are now common in many places in Alaska and Canada. If a roofed fort was really known to the Eyak it may, therefore, be a recent acquisition, and the simple stockade the aboriginal type of fortification. [377]

As temporary dwellings during hunting trips and for the seclusion of menstruating girls, a brush shelter or lean-to, a dome-shaped hut, and a conical bark tent seem to have been in use, but at present it is impossible to decide whether all belong to the aboriginal culture of the Eyak, or if one or two of these types were recent intrusions. Both the simple lean-to and the ridge tent are very widely diffused in North America and northern Eurasia and are apparently very old forms of dwellings. They have previously been discussed by the Danish writer,[5] as have also the _dome-shaped hut_[6] and the _conical tent_.[7] It will appear from the lists of distribution compiled in the work mentioned and the additions given here that both the lean-to and the conical tent are found

---

[1] TORII 1919, 228f.

[2] Carrier (MORICE 1905, 195f.). Thompson (TEIT 1900, 266f.). Shuswap (TEIT 1900-08b 539). Coeur d'Alene (TEIT 1930, 117f.). Middle Columbia Salish (Teit 1928, 123).

[3] TEIT 1900-08a, 235f.

[4] PETROFF 1884, 161.

[5] BIRKET-SMITH 1929, II 21f. cf. 235f. table A 3. As far as the non-Eskimo regions are concerned the survey is far from complete and a few references are added here: Tnaina (OSGOOD 1937a, 64). Atna (ALLEN 1889, 261). Kntchin (MASON 1924, 28. OSGOOD 1936, 54). Sekani (JENNESS 1937, 34). Koyukon? (WHYMPER 1868, 203). Satudene (OSGOOD 1933, 47). Chipewyan (BIRKET-SMITH 1930, 46). Chilcotin (FARRAND 1899, 647). Shuswap (BOAS 1891, 635). Nez Percé (SPINDEN 1908, 195f.). Nespelem and Sanpoil (RAY 1933, 32). Klallam (GUNTHER 1927, 190). For the ridge tent in general cf. SARFERT 1909, 161f.

[6] BIRKET-SMITH 1929, II 43ff., 133ff., cf. tables A 1 and 3, 295ff. table B 1. To the latter add: Kutchin (OSGOOD 1936, 49, 53, 55f.). Coeur d'Alene and Flathead (TEIT 1930, 62, 333). Klamath (SPIER 1930, 55, 202). Surprise Valley Paiute (KELLY 1932, 104).

[7] BIRKET-SMITH 1929, II 33ff., 235f. table A 3, 297ff. table B 2 with the following additions: Tnaina (OSGOOD 1937a, 65). Kutchin, rare (OSGOOD 1936, 51, 54). Sekani (JENNESS 1937, 33). Satudene (OSGOOD 1933, 47f.). Coeur d'Alene, Okanagan, Flathead (TEIT 1930, 58, 227f., 332). Middle Columbia Salish (TEIT 1928, 114). Nespelem and Sanpoil (RAY 1932, 34). Ute (LOWIE 1924, 219). Surprise Valley Paiute, recent (KELLY 1932, 104). Yukagir (JOCHELSON 1926, 344f.).

among the neighboring Athapaskans and the Indians of the Northwest Coast. Their occurrence among the Eyak is therefore hardly surprising. The dome-shaped hut does not seem to be mentioned from any tribe nearer [378] than the Tahltan, and on the coast we do not meet it till Puget Sound; in both cases it is used as a sweat house. Of course its existence among the Eyak cannot be dismissed off-hand, but if it has not actually been overlooked, e.g. among the Atna, it is difficult to believe that Galushia wasright in considering it a late intrusion.

There is some uncertainty as to whether the _cache_ was a simple platform or a store house raised on poles. The former type is known from the Tnaina and Kutchin,[1] Sekani,[2] Beaver,[3] and probably other Athapaskans of the Mackenzie area, together with some Plateau tribes.[4] Otherwise the storehouse seems to he more common in this region. It is sufficient here to mention the Tlingit,[5] the Tena,[6] the Eskimo of Bering Strait and their Asiatic relatives,[7] the Koryak, Yukagir, Gilyak and Ainu.[8] The Danish author has seen similar structures among the Atna at Copper River. It is not improbable that both types may have been in use among the Eyak.

Real "_totem poles_" can hardly be said to occur among the Eyak, even though a few carved grave posts have been seen, and a post with a carving of the moiety bird was erected in front of the potlatch house. Crests being unknown, the families had no means of displaying their rank and [379] importance in sculpture. Although BARBEAU to some degree overshoots the mark when he ascribes the whole development of the totem pole to the last two thirds of the 19th century (for one thing because grave monuments are mentioned from the Tlingit before 1800,[9] and secondly because the memorial carvings of the Carrier, Tahltan, and Alaskan Eskimo arc certainly connected with them in one wav or other, and the custom could not have spread so far in that time), he nevertheless presents sufficient evidence to show that carving received its final stimulus when European steel tools were introduced.[10] Among the northern Tlingit the elaborate modern totem poles did not get a footing till very recently.[11] Under these circumstance the carved posts of the Eyak potlatch house must be considered a pure house decoration with no other heraldic meaning than that of indicating the moiety which owned the building. The grave posts were more like true totem poles, for the latter were raised primarily in commemoration of

---

[1] OSGOOD 1937a, 65. OSGOOD 1936, 51, 55. The Kutchin sometimes construct a small hemispherical shelter on the platform.

[2] JENNESS 1937, 35.

[3] GODDARD 1916, 212.

[4] Shuswap (Teit 1900-08b, 495. BOAS 1891, 635). Lower Lillooet (TEIT 1900-08a, 215). Thompson (TEIT 1900, 199).

[5] KRAUSE 1885, 133.

[6] Field notes of American author.

[7] SAGOSKIN 1848, 538. SEEMANN 1853, 59. PETROFF 1884, 128. ELLIOTT 1886, 381. NELSON 1899, 244, 256, 259.

[8] JOCHELSON 1908, 466f. JOCHELSON 1926, 344. VON SCHRENCK 1881-95, 358. VON SIEBOLD 1881, 19. HICHCOCK 1891, 454, TORII 1919, 240.

[9] MALASPINA 1849, 289.

[10] BARBEAU 1930, 505ff.

[11] EMMONS quoted by BARBEAU 1930, 510. Cf. KRAUSE 1885, 131: "In den Tlingit-Dörfern sind dies Wäppenpfiile nicht so zahlrech, wie bei ihren sudlichen Nachbarn, den Haidas und Tschimssians."

the dead, but also in this case the Eyak carvings differed from the typical specimens by not representing the crests of the deceased.

Transportation

The Northwest Coast *dugout* is widely distributed over large areas, comprising both the actual coast from Cook Inlet to northern California and large parts of the inland Plateaus. It was not very common in the Interior, however, and here its manufacture was largely stimulated by the [380] introduction of iron tools.[1] It has been subject to investigation by several authors, and recently OLSON has published a very comprehensive list of distribution.[2] In northeastern Asia the dugout is generally known among the Palaeo-Asiatic tribes.[3] As already mentioned, the Eyak canoe is very similar in shape to the Chugach specimens found by our expedition in Palutat cave, and it belongs to the same general type as that of the Tlingit, Haida, Tsimshian, and KwakiutI, though very inferior in size to many vessels of these tribes. Besides the ordinary traveling canoe, the Eyak built a smaller craft with a projecting keel at the how; this hunting canoe is also found among the Yakutat[4] and is probably a local development ou this part of the coast.

The *kayaks*, occasionally used for sea-otter hunting were evidently traded from the Chugach, or at least made according to Chugach patterns. It is not certain whether this was also the case with the large, *open skin boats* similar to the Eskimo umiak. The Danish author has previously given an account of skin boats among the North American Indians.[5] The conclusion was that even though Eskimo [381] umiaks were often traded to neighboring tribes as far as the Yakutat, among whom they were observed at the close of the 19th century bolh by MALASPINA and LA PÉROUSE, there was nevertheless sporadic evidence of skin boats from several tribes where Eskimo influence is out of the question. In these cases they seem to be survivals from an earlier cultural stage in the circumpolar region. As no particulars arc known about the construction of the Eyak skin boat, a definite answer concerning its origin cannot be given.

The pointed *crutch paddle* of the Eyak is similar to the single-bladed paddle of the Alaskan Eskimo, though there are small differences in proportion.[6] It is also not very unlike the

---

[1] Cf. FARRAND 1899, 647. TEIT 1900-08a, 228f. TEIT 1900-08b, 531. TEIT 1930, 248.

[2] FRIEDERICI 1907, 50ff. WATERMAN & COFFN 1920. OLSON 1927, 18 cf. map. A few additions may be given here: Clugash (Field notes). Tnaina (OSGOOD 1937a, 70). Crow River Kutchin, rare (OSGOOD 1936, 64). Sekani (JENNESS 1937, 43). Twana and Chimakum (EELLS 1889, 641). Okanagan (TEIT 1930, 248). Middle Columbia Salish (TEIT 1928, 120). Nespelem and Sanpoil (TEIT 1930, 248. RAY 1932, 118ff.).

[3] Chuckchi (BOGORAS 1904, 131). Koryak (JOCHELSON 1908, 541). Yukagir (JOCHELSON 1926, 375). Kamchadal (JOCHELSON 1908, 540f. KRACHENINNIKOW 1770, I 47ff.). Ainu (MOSTANDON 1937, 131f.). Cf. also OLSON 1927.

[4] GRINNEL 1902, 162f.

[5] BIRKET-SMITH 1929, II 172ff., 339f, table B 36. The following references should be added: Tlingit, Eskimo umiaks (LA PÉROUSE 1797, 208). Tnaina (OSGOOD 1937a, 68, 70). Kutchin OSGOOD 1936, 57, 62. MASON 1924, 40). Satudene, from the Mountain Indians (OSGOOD 1933, 52). Golden Lake Atgonkin and Penobscot (Letter from Professor FRANK G. SPECK).

[6] On Eskimo single paddles see BIRKET-SMITH 1929, II 79, 262 table A 51. Add to this list: Pacific Eskimo (MERCK 1937, 129. VOLKOV & RuDENKO 1910, 35). Bering Strait Eskimo

crutch paddles of the Northwest Coast[1] and in the Plateau area.[2]

In his well-known work on the navigation of the American Indians, FRIEDERICI concludes that the use of _sails_ can be proved among the Maya and Inca (or rather the Yunca of the Peruvian coast).[3] He does not consider the Eskimo, but there can be no doubt that they knew the sail before contact with the wliiles. It was observed as early as the latter part of the 10th century by FHOBISHER, the first navigator to Oavis Strait from whom we have any report since the [382] Norsemen.[4] From that time right to our own day there is an abundance of references to Eskimo sails; only (he important are cited here.[5] Their distribution coincides with that of the open skin boat, and like the latter, the sail probably belongs to the Thule culture. As the origin of the Thule complex should be looked for in Alaska, it is more than likely that the Eskimo sail is derived directly from that of northeastern Asia.[6] On the Northwest Coast the sail has been observed by several authors, but BOAS considers it of post-European origin.[7] It is, indeed, a striking fact that while the early seafarers in these waters often describe the large canoes which roused their profound admiration, none of them ever mentions the sail. Under these circumstances it is difficult to decide whether the Eyak sail is of Eskimo or European origin, but the close contact between the Eyak and the Eskimo at least suggests that the Eyak adopted the idea from their western neighbors, as was presumably also the case with the Tnaina.[8] [383]

As to the wooden _canoe stool_ sometimes used by the Eyak, only little can be said. An early writer on the Nootka says that "sometimes they make use of a kind of small stool, which is a great relief to them."[9] An appliance of this kind cannot, of course, be employed except in a dugout, both skin boats and bark canoes being too fragile, but at present we do not know whether it occurred elsewhere on the Northwest Coast, or whether there is any relation between the Eyak

---

(NORDENSKIÖD 1881, II 242). Chukchi (NORDENSKIÖD) 1881, II 98).

[1] Tlingit (NIBLACK 1890, 296). Kwakiutl (BOAS 1904, 445). Nootka (MEARES 1790, 264). Makah (SWAN 1870, 21 fig. 7, 37 fig. 19, 38). Chinook (FRANCHÈRE l904, 328).

[2] Carrier, etc. (MORICE 1905, 114f). Thompson (TEIT 1900, 256). Wishram (SPIER & SAPIR 1930, 187).

[3] FRIEDERICI 1907, 73ff.

[4] FROBISHER 1867, 284.

[5] Chugach (Field notes). Kodiak (HOLMBERG 1856, 380). Bering Strait Eskimo (NELSON 1899, 217, 221). Point Barrow (RAY 1885, 39. MURDOCH 1892, 338). Mackenzie Eskimo (PETITOT 1887, 189). Baffin Island (HAKLUYT 1600, III 38. FRANKLIN 1823, 19. PARRY 1824, 22. LYON 1824, 35. BOAS 1888, 529). Labrador (TURNER 1894, 236. HAWKES 1916, 70). West Greenland (HANS EGEDE 1925, 362. CRANZ 1770, 198. BIRKET-SMITH 1924, 258f.).

[6] Cf. BIRKET-SMITH 1936, 195. — Chuckchi (BOGORAS 1904, 129). Koryak (JOCHELSON 1908, 537f.). Gilyak (VON SCHRENCK 1881-95, 504f.), The Ainu have Japanese sails (VON SIEBOLD 1881, 22). Whereas JENNESS (1937a, 22) derives the Alaska Eskimo sail from Asia, he ascribes the Greenland sail to contact with the Norsemen. This view does not tally very well, however, with thie occurrence of sails in Baffin Island and Labrador where such contact has never been demonstrated.

[7] BOAS 1890, 817. — Tlingit (KRAUSE 1885, 174. NIBLACK 1890, 296). Kwakiutl (BOAS 1921, 97ff.). Makah (SWAN 1870, 38. WATERMAN 1920, 23ff.). Twana, Klallam, Chimakum (EELLS 1889, 642). Tsetsaut (BOAS 1895, 565).

[8] OSGOOD 1937, 69f.

[9] MEARES 1790, 263.

and Nootka types.

    If the built-up *sled* of Kutchin type was at all known to the Eyak — which is very uncertain — it must have been introduced recently. The same applies to dog traction[1] and probably also to the Yukon type of built-up sled. The built-up sleds of Alaska seem to be of North Asiatic origin.[2] The crude "sled" made of a forked branch, the only type that was certainly aboriginal among the Eyak, is evidently an extremely old culture element, just like the "sled" consisting of a skin drawn over the snow, which is used in sequestered regions of North America and northern Eurasia.[3] Bough sleds have a similar sporadic distribution. We find them for temporary use among the Yellowknife.[4] The Thompson have "toboggans made of fir-branches for sliding down snow-covered hillsides;"[5] pine branches were sometimes used by the Nespelem and Sanpoil for the same purpose,[6] and the Klamath make a bundle of willows for [384] hauling burdens over the ice.[7] Bough sleds also occur in several places in Europe.[8]

    The netted *snowshoe* is characteristic of all parts of North America north of New York in the east and northern California in the west.[9] It has recently been the subject of an excellent monograph by D.S DAVIDSON, who has been able to classify a number of types and trace the distribution of single traits.[10] The characteristic features of the Eyak showshoe are: two-piece frame with round, spliced and turned-up toe; pointed heel; two or three cross-bars; rectangular weave leaving both toe and heel compartments free; thongs attached to the frame by wrapping or reeving through perforations in the frame; and presence of a toe hole. This is a remarkable trait complex, and no exact parallels are found among other tribes.[11] The Tlingit and Tahltan, for instance, have completely netted snowshoes and as a rule use hexagonal weave attached to a selvage thong; the latter as a rule also distinguish between rights and lefts. The Tnaina snowshoe was very much like that of the Kutchin and Tahllan. There can be no doubt that several of the distinctive elements of the Eyak type are highly specialized, e.g. the spliced and turned-up toe, reeving, use of the toe hole, and more than two cross-bars. On the other hand the incomplete and rectangular netting, and the wrapping method of attaching it to the frame are probably old fcalurrs compared with the hexagonal weave and the selvage thong.[12] It is worth noticing that the advanced [385] elements of the Eyak type, notably the spliced and up-turned toe and the reeving, arc distinctly Athapaskan inventions, whereas the hexagonal weave and the selvage thong, for which the Algonkians may be responsible, are lacking. The only plausible conclusion is that the Eyak snowshoe was probably of complex origin. The underlying type was comparatively simple, but in the course of time it absorbed certain improvements of Athapaskan

---

[1] The Danish author has previously shown that at the time of the European colonisation dog traction was not used outside the Eskimo and Plains areas (BIRKET-SMITH 1929, II 169).

[2] BIRKET-SMITH 1929, II 166.

[3] BIRKET-SMITH 1929, II 163, 366 table B 32. Add: Nespelem and Sanpoil (RAY 1932, 121).

[4] PIKE 1892, 67.

[5] TEIT 1900, 257. 281.

[6] RAY 1932. 121.

[7] SPIER 1930, 171.

[8] BERG 1935, 33.

[9] MASON 1896, 383.

[10] DAVIDSON 1937. Cf. also ISEIDEL 1898, 155ff.

[11] Our information about the Chugach snowshoe is too fragmentary for allowing comparisons.

[12] DAVIDSON 1937, 35.

origin, whereas other, slill later features, such as the distinction between rights and lefts, an increased number of cross-bars, and the specifically Algonkian inventions, never reached the Eyak.

Examples of the occurrence of wooden snowshoes in North America have previously been given.[1] They all come from the Central Eskimo and eastern Algonkians or Iroquois, but the opinion was expressed that they were related to the fundamental forms of the Eurasian ski. DAVIDSON has added a number of references to the original list[2] and shares the view of their Old World origin. This hypothesis is strongly supported by the fael that wooden showshoes are now known from the Eyak and, according to our field notes, also from the Chugach.

When packing loads the Eyak use a *tump-line* across the chest. It is difficult to arrive at a clear understanding of the carrying methods in North America, because information on this topic is often remarkably meagre. The Danish author has previously compiled the available material.[3] It [386] will be noted that the chest (and forehead) method appears among several tribes close to the Eyak, such as the Tlingit, Tahltan. etc.

No study has been made of the distribution of smoke signals. It may be mentioned, however, that they are reported from the Tnaina and Kutchin.[4]

Clothing

The Eyak *shirt* or frock has the characteristic two-skin cut which is derived from the poncho and is typical of large parts of northern and western North America: the Eskimo region and the Boreal Woodlands, the northern Plateau and Plains areas, etc.[5] It is an old and widespread form of clothing which HATT has proved to belong to the pre-snowshoe or ice-hunting stage of the circumpolar region.

Shirts were also made of the skins of birds and small animals like ermines and groundsquirrels. As stated before the pattern was probably the same as that used by the Pacific and Kuskokwim Eskimo.[6] Similar shirts are mentioned from the Tnaina[7] and Atna (where they were noted by Colonel ABERCROMBIE, cf. p. 66). They probably represent a common type on both sides of the North Pacific. It is true that we are ignorant of the cut of the ancient Kamchadal shirls made of ground squirrel skins,[8] but on the other hand the characteristic horizontal strips are [387] easily recognized on the birdskin coats of the Kurilian Ainu.[9]

---

[1] BIRKET-SMITH 1929, II 36f.

[2] DAVIDSON 1937, 138ff.

[3] BIRKET-SMITH 1929, II 76, 170 f., cf. 260 table A 48 and 337f. table B 34. The following additions should be made: Chest method, Kutchin (MASON 1924, 38. OSGOOD 1936, 60, 64). Chest and forehead method. COEUR D'ALENE, Okanagan (TEIT 1930, 108. 249). Do., Nespelem and Sanpoil (RAY 1932, 122). Do., Wishram (SPIER & SAPIR 1930, 180, 191). The Tnaina employ a chest yoke like the Chugach and the Eskimo of Bering Strait (OSGOOD 1937a, 72).

[4] OSGOOD, 1937a, 116. OSGOOD 1936, 103.

[5] HATT 1914, 56ff, 82ff. cf. 227. BIRKET-SMITH 1929, II 79ff., 177ff.

[6] HATT 1914, 102ff.

[7] OSGOOD 1937a, 48.

[8] STELLER 1774, 307.

[9] TORII 1919, pl. XII cf. l60.

Gutskin coats are characteristic of the peripheral parts of the Eskimo area, but lacking among the Central tribes.[1] This distribution is the well-known criterion of the Thule culture elements. HATT has pointed out that the gutskin strips may be joined either vertically or horizontally, but the latter pattern, which is the one known to the Eyak, is limited to the western Eskimo, especially the more southern tribes. It does not seem improbable that this pattern is related to the arrangement of the material in the above-mentioned shirts of small animals' skins. The gutskin shirt must be considered principally an Eskimo garment. Outside the Eskimo region it occurs only among neighboring tribes: i.e. the Tena, Tnaina, Chukchi, and in former days Koryak.[2]

Some shirts, at least, were provided with *hoods*. In the Boreal Woodlands, shirts with attached hoods are post-European.[3] In southwestern Alaska the hoodless frocks meet [388] with the characteristic hooded coats of the Eskimo. Among the Pacific group and the Aleut bolh types as well as hybrid forms occur, though the hoodless frock was probably the most common. Originally the Eskimo coat also lacked a hood, although the attachment of a hood to the garment is an old and aboriginal feature among them.[4] The Tnaina also wore frocks with hoods attached.[5] As hooded frocks are mentioned from Prince William Sound as early as the latter part of the 18th Century,[6] there is no reason to doubt their pre-European origin among the Eyak, probably as a loan from the Chugach.

Several kinds of *headdress* are known from northern North America. The calotte-shaped cap with a crown and sides, often provided with ear-flaps, is evidently an Asiatic type which, in fairly late times, made its way across Bering Strait to the Eskimo and the Indians of the northern Plateaus;[7] we do not know it, however, from the Eyak. The fur cap made of two pieces sewn together with a median seam is, on .the other hand, an Eyak type and is also found among the Eskimo as far east as the Thule District, but not in the rest of Greenland. This circumstance, together with the fact that it cannot be traced in the ordinary Eskimo frock hood, goes to show

---

[1] HATT 1914, 119ff. — Aleut (ERLÄUTERUNGER 1781, 310. COOK & KING 1785, 509. TOLSTYKH 1933, 10. LANGSDORFF 1812, 35f. LOWE 1842, 485.). Chugach (COOK & KING 1785, 368). Kodiak (SCHELECHOF 1793a, 199. DAWYDOW 1816, 170. HOLMBERG 1856, 366f., 379). Asiatic Eskimo (MURDOCH 1892, 122. NELSON 1899, 37. BOGORAS 1904-09, 247). Bering Strait Eskimo (BEECHEY 1831, I 340. SEEMAN 1853, 53. NELSON 1899. 36f.) Point Barrow (SIMPSON 1843, 156. MURDOCH 1892, 111, 122). Mackenzie Eskimo? (RICHADSON 1851, I 358). Baffin Island (DRAGE 1748-49, I 26f., Lyon 1824. 19. BILBY 1923, 112). Labrador Eskimo (HAWKES 1916, 40f. 137. TURNER 1894, 220ff. Polar Eskimo, used formerly (Field notes of Danish author, oral information by middle-aged native, 1921). West Greenland (HANS EGEDE 1925, 370. CRANZ 1770, 183. BIRKET-SMITH 1924, 186f.). Fredrrik VI Coast (GRAAH 1832, 120). Angmagssalik (HOLM 1914, 19f. THALBITZER 1914, 575).
[2] Chukchi (HOOPER 1853, 53f. BOGORAS 1904-09, 247, 251). Koryak (JOCHELSON 1908, 599). Tnaina (OSGOOD 1937a, 50). Tena (Field notes of Amercan author).
[3] BIRKET-SMITH 1929, II 180.
[4] HATT 1914, 104, 185. BIRKET-SMITH 1929, II 81f.
[5] OSGOOD 1937a, 48f. — It is open to doubt if the hooded garments of the Kutchin (OSGOOD 1986 {1968}, 39) should be regarded as aboriginal.
[6] COOK & KING, 1785, 368.
[7] BIRKET-SMITH 1929, II 85f.

that it has also come to these tribes from the west.[1] Unfortunately we are not able to state the distribution of this type in North America outside the Eskimo area, as museum material is very scarce and the references to hoods in the available literature few and [389] without details concerning the cut.[2] It is not improbable that this kind of headgear is also of Asiatic origin, for hoods oi' the same general appearance are common among the Palseo-Asiatic tribes; as in North America, however, the cut is only known in a few cases.[3]

The true _collar-hood_ sewn together under the chin is a very interesting type to which KRICKEBERG has called attention in a recent work. He describes specimens from the Bering Sea, Polar, and Angmagssalik Eskimo and from the primitive Uru at Lake Titicaca in the Bolivian highlands.[4] It is also known to the Asiatic Eskimo and the Chukchi,[5] and was worn during the menstruation period by Tlingit and Haida girls.[6] Probably it is the same headdress which OSGOOD describes from the Crow River Kutchin us "like an aviator helmet extended into a cape generally bordered with fringes."[7] What seems to be a collar-hood was described to the American author by the Tena of the Yukon River. More doubtful are the caps of the Sekani women "shaped like bonnets, fitting around the neck."[8] KRICKEBERG cites a number of examples in Europe and southwestern Asia from antiquity right up to our own days. It also occurs among the Samoyed and Lapps.[9] This sporadic distribution, mostly [390] at the outskirts of the circumpolar region, justifies the belief also expressed by KRICKEBERG that the collar-hood is an old and nearly obsolete type.

In the circumpolar region there are, as shown by HATT, two different types of _trousers_: legging breeches derived from a pair of leggings combined with a triangular apron; and breechcloth breeches, the origin of which is presumably a breechcloth sown together at the sides.[10] The former type, which is the older, is in North America limited to the Eskimo and certain Athapaskan tribes. Very little is known regarding the American distribution of the latter type, except that it occurs among the Thompson and probably a number of other tribes on the northern Plateaus and at Puget Sound; perhaps the Tlingit should also be included.[11] The description of the Eyak trousers seems to indicate that they belong to the same type. This might be corroborated if we only knew the cut of the Tnaina garment, but unfortunately there is so far no information available.[12]

---

[1] BIRKET-SMITH 1929, II 86.

[2] The Tnaina caps were clearly different from those of the Eskimo, one piece forming the top and another one the side (OSGOOD 1937a, 48f).

[3] Chukchi (BOGORAS 1904-09, 242). Koryak (JOCHELSON 1908, 596f.). Kamchadal (KRACHENINNIKOW 1770, 57). Gilyak (VON SCHRENCK 1881-95, 393f., 397). Ainu (C-NM, A 845).

[4] KRICKENBERG 1934a, 288f. Cf. also KROEBER 1900, 296. THALBITZER 1914, 588.

[5] Eskimo drawings in C-NM. BOGORAS 1904-09, 243 fig. 175.

[6] NIBLACK 1890, 370.

[7] OSGOOD 1936, 43.

[8] JENNESS 1937, 30.

[9] C-NM, K 3: 24. VON DÜBEN (1873), 161f.

[10] HATT 1914, 140 ff.

[11] Cf. BIRKET-SMITH 1929, II 182. Add to examples given there; Chehalis (HILL-TOUT 1904b, 333).

[12] Cf. OSGOOD 1937 ii. 47.

The loose hanging, rectangular *apron* worn during the wars, and perhaps generally, by the Eyak men, should not be confused with the well-known, triangular genital covering. The latter is apparently an old circumpolar type preserved as a fork gusset in the cut of some Eskimo trousers and as an independent garment in a few isolated cases.[1] The man's [391] apron, on the other hand, has its main distribution in North America on the Northwest Coast[2] and the Plateaus,[3] and also occurred among the Pacific Eskimo.[4] We find it again in the dress of the Amur tribes and the Ainu,[5] and a survival of it is probably seen in the peculiar divided breast cloth of the Lamut. It does not seem unreasonable to regard it as a circum-Pacific type. If Colonel ABERCROMBIE'S memory is accurate, we can only interpret the breechcloth among the Eyak as recent. At any rate, its occurrence here is remarkably isolated. Although there is a single reference to the breech-cloth from the Tsimshian,[6] it was never worn by other Northwest Coast tribes, or by the Eskimo, or by the Athapaskans of the Yukon area. Among certain Plateau tribes it was not adopted until modern times.[7]

Although differing in details, the Eyak *boot* was clearly made according to the Eskimo model. This pattern of footwear is an old, circumpolar type which is limited in North America to the Eskimo and to the Pueblo Indians of the [392] Southwest, and which reappears in western Siberia among the Ostyak and Vogul.[8]

In the circumpolar region there are two styles of *mittens*, one with the thumb sewn on separately, and another on which the underside of the thumb is cut out of the same piece as the distal part of the palm.[9] Nothing is known of the cut of the Eyak mitten, so further discussion is useless. The fingered *glove* is common among most Eskimo and also among sonic Plateau

---

[1] HATT 1914, 134ff. BIRKET-SMITH 1929, II 87f. To the examples cited there add: Labrador Eskimo (SILVY 1904, 50) and Eskimo of the Thule and Inugsuk stages (MATHIASSEN 1927, I 187. MATHIASSEN 1930, 247). From Kodiak MERCK mentions "eine Schambedeckung aus einem Jewreschkenfell [skin of *Ochotona collaris*] oder Secotterschwanz" (MERCK 1937, 127).

[2] Tlingit (GODDARD 1924, 162 fig. "Una faja," MALASPINA 1849, 287. Erroneously decribed as {Russian }, i.e. ceremonial blanket, by VOLKOV & RUDENKO 1910, 44 cf. pl. VIIIa.). Tlingit and Haida (KRICKEBERG 1925, pl. 54f. figs. 3-6). Tsimshian (BOAS 1916, 53). Klallam (GUNTHER 1927, 230). Yurok and other tribes of northern California (KROEBER 1925, 76).

[3] Carrier, for ceremoniiil use (MORICE 1905, 179f.). Chilcotin (JENNESS 1932, 362). Lillooet (TEIT 1900-08a, 218f.). Thompson (TEIT 1900, 208). Coeur d'Alene, Okanagan, Flathead (TEIT 1930, 70, 233, 335. Middle Columbia Salish (TEIT 1928, 116). Surprise Valley Paiiitc (KELLY 1932, 108).

[4] Chugach (Field notes). Kodiak (SCHELECHOF 1793a, 199. LISIANSKY 1814, 104). The natives of Cook Inlet had "a small piece of fur tied round the waist" (DIXON 1789, 239).

[5] Gilyak (VON SCHHENCK 1881-95, 394). Ainu (VON SIEBOLD 1881, 14. HITCHCOCK 1891, 495. BATCHELOR 1901, 149. MONTANDON 1937, 86).

[6] BOAS 1916, 52.

[7] JENNESS 1932, 70 footnote 3.

[8] HATT 1914, 179ff. HATT 1916, 201ff. BIRKET-SMITH 1929, II 88ff., 184.

[9] BIRKET-SMITH 1929, II 87 cf. 265 table A 55, 181f. cf. 342f. table B 40. Additions: Tnaina (OSGOOD 1937a, 48f.). Coeur d'Alene, Okanagan (TEIT 1930, 73, 235). Middle Columbia Salish (TEIT 1928, 116). Klamathi (SPIER 1930, 210).

tribes, but seems everywhere to be of European origin.[1]

The _robe_ worn both by men and women has a very wide distribution in North America.[2] It is not common among the Eskimo,[3] but with this exception it occurs among most tribes in the northwestern part of the continent.[4] Even [393] on the Northwest Coast skin robes were worn as ceremonial dress. On the other hand the woven blankets sometimes used by the Eyak were clearly imported from the Tlingit; the Eyak did not know the art of weaving themselves. As early a traveller as COOK saw woollen blankets of undoubtedly Northwest Coast manufacture still further west among the Chugach.[5]

The frock was sometimes, if not always, decorated with _skin fringes_ along the sleeve seams and other seams. Among the Eskimo, fringes are used only by the Central tribes.[6] They are most often employed by the Iglulik, Netsilik, and Caribou groups, are less common in Labrador, southern Baffin Island, Coronation Gulf, and the Mackenzie delta, and are entirely lacking in Greenland and Alaska. The Pacific Eskimo and the Aleut often decorate the horizontal seams of their cormorant or gutskin frocks with isolated strips of skin or, at a later period, with bits of red cloth, but these decorations cannot be considered true fringes.[7] On the other hand skin fringes are too well known [394] from the dress of the North American Indians to need much

---

[1] BIRKET-SMITH 1929, II 31f:

[2] BIRKET-SMITH 1929, II 185.

[3] BIRKET-SMITH 1929, II 267 table A 59.

[4] Tlingit (LANGSDORFF 1812, 97. KOTZEBUE 1830, 27. MALASPINA 1849, 286f. CAAMAÑO 1849, 351. VON KITTLITZ 1858, I 222. WHYMPER 1868,78. ERMAN 1870-71, II 384. KRAUSE 1885, 146). Haida (MACKENZIE 1892, 47. BANCROFT 1875, 159). Tsimshian (EMMONS 1925, 40f.). Kwakiutl (BOAS 1909, 451). Nootka (COOK & KING 1785, 304). Makah (SWAN 1870, 15f. (GIBBS 1877, 176). Seechelt (HILL-TOUT 1904a, 28). Chehalis (HILL-TOUT 1904b, 333). Squawmish (HILL-TOUT 1900, 487). Puget Sound (HAEBERLIN & GUNTHER 1930, 37). Klallam (KANE 1863, 159. GUNTHER 1927, 230). Songish (BOAS 1891, 566). Chinook (LEWIS & CLARKE 1814, 437f., 522. BANCROFT 1875, 229. FRANCHERE 1904, 325). Tillamook (HENRY & THOMPSON 1897, 858). Hupa (MASON 1889, 210. GODDARD 1903, 18). Tahltan (EMMONS 1911, 43f). Tsetsaut (BOAS 1895, 560). Carrier (MACKENZIE 1801, 248. HARMON 1903, 243f. MORICE 1905, 164. MORICE 1890, 116). Shuswap (TEIT 1900-08b, 504), Lillooet (TEIT 1900-08a, 217f. HILL-TOUT 1905, 135). Thompson (TEIT 1900, 218f). Coeur d'Alene, Okanagan (TEIT 1930, 65f., 230 f.). Nez Percé (LEWIS & CLARKE 1814, 557. WYETH 1905, 75. SPINDEN 1908, 218). Middle Columbia Salish (TEIT 1928, 116). Spokan (WILKES 1844, 475). Pishquitpah (LEWIS & CLARKE 1814, 627). Wallawalla (LEWIS & CLARKE 1814, 532). Washington (LEWIS 1906, 187ff.). Wishram (SPIER & SAPIR 1930, 205f.). Takelma (SAPIR 1907, 263). Shoshoni (TOWNSEND 1905, 254. LOWIE 1909, 179). Ute (LOWIE 1924, 216). Paviotso (LOWIE 1924, 217). Painte (LOWIE 1924, 210). STEWARD 1933, 274. KELLY 1932, 107). Tnaina (OSGOOD 1937a, 49ff.). Sekani (MACKENZIE 1801, 205). Satudene (OSGOOD 1933, 45). Chipewyan (FRANKLIN 1823, 156). Eastern Athapaskans in general (RICHARDSON 1851, II 10).

[5] COOK & KING 1785, 363.

[6] BIRKET-SMITH 1929, II 85.

[7] Traces of fringes occur on the hem of the skin garment or robe worn by one of the Eskimo mummies found by the Expedition in Palutat cave. Like the fringes on the Eyak frocks they are probably due to influence from the Interior or the Northwest Coast.

documentation. It suffices to mention their occurrence among a few tribes in the Yukon,[1] Plateau,[2] and Northwest Coast areas.[3] This leaves hardly any doubt that the fringes of the Eyak clothing are either of inland or Northwest Coast origin.

HATT has emphasized the resemblance between hair embroidery and *porcupine quillwork*, though the latter has a far wider distribution in North America and is entirely lacking in Eurasia where the material is not at hand. The same is, of course, true of the Eskimo area. On the Northwest Coast it is at least very rare, although it occurs among the Tlingit, Tsimshian, etc.[4] On the other hand it is extremely common both in the Mackenzie region[55] and on the Plateaus.[6] [395]

Here may he inserted a few words on the *use of dentalium*, although it was not limited to dress decoration but was employed for body ornaments as well. The ordinary shells belong to the species *Dentalium indianorum*, the habitat of which is the coast waters from latitude 49° north to Sitka, comprising also the coasts of Vancouver and Queen Charlotte Islands, but they were traded all the way to Cape Mendocino, Calif, in the south and the Arctic coast in the north.[7] We found them in the Eskimo shell-heaps in Prince William Sound, and James Cook saw them among the Chugach.[8] They occur in the sites of Cook Inlet[9] and were used by the inhabitants of Kodiak and the Aleutian Islands.[10] We also find them as far east among ihe Eskimo us the Mackenzie delta,[11] and even in the Interior they are in great demand both in the Yukon[12] and Plateau areas.[13] They have also been brought to light by archaeological excavations in several

---

[1] Tnaina (OSGOOD 1937a, 52). Kutchin (MACKENZIE 1801, 48. FRANKLIN 1828, 28. PETITOT 1876, 41. OSGOOD 1930, 40). Sekani (MACKENZIE 1801, 205).

[2] Thompson (TEIT 1900, 231). Coeur d'Alene, Okanagan, Flathead (TEIT 1930, 65, 231, 335). Nespelem and Sanpoil (RAY 1932, 48).

[3] Tlingit, Haidan and Tsimshian (NIBLACK 1890, pl. XXI. KRICKEBERG 1925, pl 54ff.). Nootka (COOK & KING 1785, 304). Puget Sound (HAEBEBLIN & GUNTHER 1930, 39).

[4] Tlingit (KRAUSE 1885, 198). Tsimshian (BOAS 1916, 52). Nootka (COOK & KING, 1785, 308).

[5] Tnaina (OSGOOD 1937a, 52, 119. ELLIOTT 1886, 89. PETROFF 1884, 162). Atna (ALLEN 1889, 262. PETROFF 1884, 164). Tanana (PETROFF 1854, 161). Kutchin (RICHARDSON, 1851, I 380. SCHMITTER 1910, 4f. MASON 1924, 48. OSGOOD 1936, 40, 44f.). Sekani (JENNESS 1932, 380). Nahane (JENNESS 1932, 398), Dogrib, Slave (MACKENZIE 1801, 36). Slave, Beaver? (GODDARD 1916, 221). Satudene (OSGOOD 1933, 44, 64). Chipewyan (KING 1836, I 153. BIRKET-SMITH 1930, 56, 64. INGSTAD 1931. 189).

[6] Tahltan (EMMONS 1911, 48). Tsetsaut (BOAS 1895, 561). Carrier (MORICE 1905, 163). Lillooet (TEIT 1900-08a, 220). Thompson (TEIT 1900, 222). Coeur d'Alene, Okanagan, Flathead (TEIT 1930, 46f, 77f, 221, 326). Nez Percé (SPINDEN 1908, 216), Middle Columbia Salish (TEIT 1928, 117). Washington and Oregon, rare (GIBBS 1877, 214). Nespelem and Sanpoil (RAY 1932, 511). Takelma (SAPIR 1907. 264). Klamath (SPIER 1930, 211). Ute (LOWIE 1924, 228). Surprise Valley Paiute (KELLY 1932, 107).

[7] STEARNS 1889, 315, 320.

[8] COOK & KING 1785, 369.

[9] DE LAGUNA 1934, 113.

[10] LANGSDORFF 1812, 38. ERMAN 1870-71, III 208. PETROFF 1884, 138.

[11] STEFANSSON 1914, 164.

[12] Tnaimi (OSGOOD 1937a, 54). Tanana, Koyukon (WHYMPER 1868, 182f., 223). Tena (Field Notes of American author). Kutchin (OSGOOD 1936, 40f.). Sekani (JENNESS 1932, 380).

[13] Tahltan (EMMONS 1911, 45f). Carrier (MORICE 1905, 166f.). Chilcotin (BOAS 1891, 637).

places in British Columbia and Washington.[1] [396]

Personal Adornment

The well, known feature of _decorating the hair with loose eagle or swans down_ has a typical northwestern distribution in North America and is often of a more or less solemn character. Among the Eskimo this custom does not seem to exceed the limits of the Pacific group.[2] In the Yukon area it is, however, a widespread custom,[3] and is known to some extent also on the Northern Plateaus,[4] but the principal center is beyond any doubt on the Northwest Coast.[5] It is truly remarkable that the use of bird down is found here in an elaborate and highly developed cultural setting, for in reality it is a primitive trait which to our knowledge is not found anywhere else in North America nor in Siberia, whereas it reappears sporadically among several South American tribes, although in a somewhat modified form, as the feathers are here, as in Australia, pasted to the naked body.[6]

The _head band_ is known practically all over the northern and western parts of North America, including the Eskimo territory.[7] The custom of sticking feathers in the [397] band has obviously reached the Eskimo from their Indian neighbors and is limited to the western groups, although it is not very typical of the Northwest Coast. It seems to be one of the not very numerous links between the Eyak and the Interior. The wooden crowns of the Eyak were observed by Colonel ABERCROMBIE to be of the same type as those worn by the Atna. Very similar crowns were worn by the Chilcotin, Carrier, and Sekani.[8]

Nose ornaments and piercing the septum have a wide distribution in North America.

Shuswap (BOAS 1891, 637. TEIT 1900-08b, 509f.). Lillooet (TEIT 1900-08a, 220). Thompson (TEIT 1900, 206, 222ff.). Okanagan (BOAS 1891, 637). Washington and Oregon (GIBBS 1877, 213). Coeur d'Alene (TEIT 1930, 81f.). Nez PERCÉ (SPINDEN 1908, 220). Middle Columbia Salish (TEIT 1928, 117). Nespelem and Sanpoil (RAY 1932, 50). Cayuse (TOWNSEND 1905, 350). Wishram (SPIER & SAPIR 1930, 208). Takelma (SAPIR 1907, 264). Klamath (SAPIR 1930, 43). Shasta (KROEBER 1925. 292).

[1] SMITH 1899, 134. SMITH 1903, 141. SMITH 1900, 427. SMITH 1910, 90f.

[2] COOK & KING 1785, 354. DAWYDOW 1816, 183.

[3] Tnaina (OSGOOD 1937a, 53). Ingalik (WHANGELL 1839, 118). Tanana (WHYMPER 1868, 211). PETROFF 1884, 161). Kutchin (RICHARDSON 1851, I 381. JONES 1867, 320. SCHMITTER 1910, 4. OSGOOD 1930, 42, 45). Slave (OSGOOD 1933, 46).

[4] Tahltan (EMMMONS 1911, 46). Carrier (HARMON 1903, 262. KANE 1863, 185).

[5] Tlingit (NIBLACK 1890, 258. KRAUSE 1885, 234. LA PÉROUSE 1797, 199. KOTZEBUE 1830, 32. LANGSDORFF 1812, 98. PORTLOCK 1789, 290. PETROFF 1884, 170). Haida (BANCROFT 1875, 159). Tsimshian (BOAS 1895, 577). Kwakiutl (JACOBSEN 1884, 55. BOAS 1921, 720). Bella Coola (BOAS 1892, 421). Nootka (JEWITT 1896, 118, MEARES 1790, 112, 254). Klallam (EELLS 1889, 665. GUNTHER 1927, 232). Quinault (WILLOUGHBY 1889, 268). Cowichin (BOAS 1894, 460).

[6] METRAUX 1928, 128f.

[7] BIRKET-SMITH 1929, II 93 cf. table A 61, 185. The examples given there may easily be multiplied.

[8] MORICE 1890, 177 fig. 165.

Below we give some citations referring to the Eskimo[1] and to the tribes of the Northwest Coast,[2] the Mackenzie area,[3] and the Plateaus.[4] [398]

Nose ornaments do not extend farther north among the Eskimo than the mouth of the Yukon, the center of distribution for the Eskimo being here the Aleut and Pacific groups. In the south the distribution of the nose pin is continued far outside the Northwest Coast area (Porno, Achomawi, Maidu, Yokuts, and Mohave), and there is reason to believe that al one time it also comprised Mexico. It is true that the nose pin has not, to our knowledge, been found within the Archaic horizon there, but at the time of the conquest it was worn by the primitive Huaxteca of northern Vera Cruz, and its ancient character is further emphasized by the fact that it was sign of divine and royal dignity among the Nahua. Obviously it is a rather ancient element in western North America outside the Eskimo area. Roughly speaking, it is foreign to the North Asiatic peoples. Still a nose ring is worn by a few of the Amur Tungus (Gold, Samagir, and southern Oroche), and VON SCHRENK is probably right in considering this a survival of an old custom.[5]

Not much is known of the Eyak *ear ornaments* except that dentalium shells were used on special occasions by the chiefs and their families. In all probability this means that they had a number of shells hanging separately or in a cluster from the helix of the ear, a well-known type of ornament in these regions. Among the Eskimo such pendants are found on both sides of Bering Strait, as well as [399] in the Pacific group,[6] and they are common both on the Northwest

---

[1] Aleut (COXE 1780, 105. ERLÄUTERUNGER 1781, 309. MERCK 1937, 116. LANGSDORFF 1812, 37. WEYER 1930, 265). Chugach (COOK & KING 1785, 369). Kodiak (COXE 1780, 116. SCHELECHOF 1793a, 198f. LISIANSKY 1814, 195. DAWYDOW 1810, 183, 189. MERCK 1937, 127). Cook Inlet Eskimo (DE LAGUNA 1934, 112, 207). Bering Strait Eskimo (SAGOSKIN 1848, 531. ELLIOTT 1886, 411. WRANGELL 1839, 135).

[2] Tlingit (LA PÉROUSE 1797, 199. PORTLOCK 1780, 288. MALASPINA 1849, 287. CAAMAÑO 1849, 352. KOTZEBUE 1830, 28. KRAUSE 1885, 137f. NIBLACK 1890, 257, 261). Haida, shamans (SWANTON 1905, 40. BANCROFT 1875, 159). Tsimshian (BOAS 1916, 53). Kwakiutl (BOAS 1909, 454. BOAS 1921, 778). Bella Coola (cf. BOAS 1892, 419). Nootka (COOK & KING 1785, 271. MEARES 1790, 253. WHYMPER 1868, 53. JEWITT 1896, 114, 118f.). Makah (VANCOUVER 1798, I 218. SWAN 1870, 17. GIBBS 1877, 176). Nisqualli, Snuqalmi (HAEBERLIN & EGUNTHER 1930, 40). Klallam (WILKES 1844, 320). Quinault (WILLOUGHBY 1889, 268). Washington (LEWIS 1900, 168). Chinook (BANCTOFT 1875, 229. LEWIS & CLARKE 1814, 511). Yurok, after death only (KROEBER 1925, 77). Hupa (MASON 1889, 214).

[3] Tnaina (OSGOOD 1937a, 54). Atna (ALLEN 1889, 262). Tanana (WHYMPER 1868, fis. p. 210/11). Koyukon (WHYMER 1869. 183). Kutchin (FRANKLIN 1828, 28. HOOPER 1853, 270. JONES 1867, 320. RICHARDSON 1851, I 381. SIMPSON 1843, 190. KIRBY 1865, 418. OSGOOD 1936, 41f., 45). Sekani, pierced nose, but no ornaments mentioned (MACKENZIE 1801, 204). Dogrib) or Slave (MACKENZIE 1801, 36).

[4] Tahltan (EMMONS 1911, 45). Tsesaut (BOAS 1895. 561). Carrier (HARMON 1903, 245. MORICE 1890, 115. MORICE 1905, 166ff). Chilcutin (FARRAND 1899, 647), Shuswap (BOAS 1891, 636. TEIT 1900-08b, 510). Lillooet (TEIT 1900-08a, 220), Thompson (TEIT 1900, 222). Coeur d'Alene, Okanagan, Kalispel, Spokan (TEIT 1930, 82, 236, 340). Nez Percé (LEWIS & CLARKE 1814, 557), Middle Columbia Salish (TEIT 1928, 117). Takelma (SAPIR 1907, 264). Klamath (SPIER 1930, 214). Shasta (DIXON 1907, 413).

[5] VON SCHRENCK 1881-95, 417.

[6] BIRKET-SMITH 1929, II 39, 93 cf. 268 table A 62. Add: Aleut (COXE 1780, 247. SAIKOF 1782,

Coast[12] and the Northern Plateaus.[2] They also occur in the Yukon area.[3]

Too little is also known of the Eyak *necklaces* to make a lengthy discussion worth while. It will suffice to note a few examples from the neighboring areas, i.e. the Eskimo,[4] the Northwest Coast,[5] the Mackenzie region,[6] and the Northern Plateaus,[7] in order to show the [400] general distribution of necklaces without entering upon details of type.

The use of *body paint* is scarcely an original element of Eskimo culture, even though it is found among the western tribes; in the central and eastern groups it is entirely lacking.[8] On the other hand there are very few Indian tribes in northwestern North America who do not paint their faces and bodies, as will appear from the citations below.[9] [401]

---

285). Chugach (COOK & KING 1785, 369). Kodiak (SCHELECHOF 1793a, 198f. DAWYDOW 1816, 170. MEECK 1937, 128).

[1] Tlingit (PORTLOCK 1789, 288. KRAUSE 1885, 139. MALASPINA 1848, 287). Tsimshian (BOAS 1916, 53). Kwakiutl, "perforation of the ear does not seem to have been as prominent as among the northern tribes" (BOAS 1909, 457). Nootka (MEARES 1790, 253). Makah (SWAN 1870, 17, 47). Snuqualmi (HAEBERLIN & GUNTHER 1930, 40). Klallam, Twana, Chimiakum (EELLS 1889, 631. Chinook (BANCROFT 1875, 229). Hupa (GODDARD 1903, 19).

[2] Tahltan (EMMONS 1911, 45). Tsetsaut (BOAS 1895, 561). Carrier (MORICE 1890, 115. MORICE 1905, 166f.). Chilcotin (FARRAND 1899, 647). Shuswap (TEIT 1900-08b, 509. BOAS 1891, 636). Lillooet (TEIT 1900-08a, 220). Thompson (TEIT 1900, 222). Coeur d'Alene, Okanagan, Flathead (TEIT 1930, 82, 236, 339f.). Nez Pe-rce (SPINDEN 1908, 220). Kutenai (CHAMBERLAIN 1893, 570f.). Middle Columbia Salish (TEIT 1928, 117). Nespelem and Sanpoil (RAY 1932, 51). Wishram (SPIER & SAPIR 1930, 208). Takelma (SAPIR 1907, 264). Klamath (SPIER 1930, 214f.). Shasta (DIXON 1907, 413).

[3] Tnaina (OSGOOD 1937a, 54). Atna (ALLEN 1889, 262). Kutchin (RICHARDSON 1851, I 381). Sekani (MACKENZIE 1801, 205).

[4] Aleut (TOLSTYKH 1933, 10). Chugach (Field notes). Asiatic Eskimo (BOGORAS 1904, 256). Bering Strait (BEECHEY 1830, I 360). Point Barrow (MURDOCH 1892, 148). Mackenzie Eskimo (PETITOT 1887, 52). Angmagssalik (HOLM 1914, 33. THALBITZER 1914, 601f.).

[5] Tlingit (KRAUSE 1885, 147). Haida (NIBLACK 1890, 261). Nootka (JEWITT 1896, 115). Puget Sound (HAEBERLIN & GUNTER 1930, 41). Twana, Chimakum, Klallam (EELLS 1889, 631). Chinook (LEWIS & CLARKE 1814, 439). Hupa (MASON 1889, 212).

[6] Tnaina (OSGOOD 1937a, 54). Sekani (MACKENZIE 1801, 205. JENNESS 1937, 32). Slave, Dogrib (MACKENZIE 1801, 36).

[7] Tahltan (EMMONS 1911, 45). Carrier (HARMON 1903, 246. MORICE 1905, 170). Shuswap (TEIT 1900-08b, 509). Thompson (TEIT 1900, 223), Coeur d'Alene.,Okanagan, Flathead (TEIT 1930, 81, 236, 340). Nez Percé (SPINDEN 1928, 219). Kutenai (CHAMBERLAIN 1893, 571). Middle Culumbia Salish (TEIT 1928, 117). Nespelem and Sanpoil (RAY 1932, 50). Klamath (SPIER 1920, 215). Shasta (DIXON 1907, 413).

[8] Aleut (COXE 1780, 50, 257. JOCHELSON 1925, 96). Chugach (COOK & KING 1785, 170). Kodiak (SCHELECHOF 1793a, 201. DAWYDOW 1816, 183. MERCK 1937, 128. HOLMBERG 1856, 363. PETROFF 1884, 139). Asiatic Eskimo (BOGORAS 1904, 365f.). Bering Strait Eskimo (NELSON 1899, 329). Point Barrow (MURDOCH 1892, 140. STEFANSSON 1914, 389f.).

[9] Tlingit (NIBLACK 1890, 259. DIXON 1799, 186. KRAUSE 1885, 149f. MALASPINA 1849, 286. CAAMAÑO 1849, 352. LA PÉROUSE 1797, 199). Northwest Coast, "from the Yukntat, throughout the region south" (NIBLACK 1890, 258). Kwakiutl (BOAS 1909, 455). Nootka

Tattooing was performed by the needle-and-thread and perhaps also by the pricking method. It is not astonishing that both methods were employed, for the same was probably the case among the Pacific Eskimo. According to previous investigations of the Danish author, pricking is the older procedure and is widely diffused in North America, whereas tattooing by needle and thread is an Asiatic trait which, presumably at a later period, made its way to the Eskimo Thule culture and to certain Indian tribes in the northwestern part of the continent.[1]

It is difficult to find close parallels to Eyak modes of *hairdressing*. The bunch on each side of the head worn by the men may, perhaps, be compared with the Kutchin fashion described as "a bunch behind with a small bundle over each temple,"[2] and somewhat similar styles were worn by the Carrier and Hupa.[3] It is likewise difficult to find parallels to the single braid of the Eyak women, though two braids have a wide distribution. In fact, we can only cite one instance of women wearing one braid, viz. the Sekani.[4] It should be remembered, however, that ABERCROMBIE described the women as wearing two braids.

If the myths are to be trusted on this point a *comb* was formerly known. It is a striking fact that while the comb is common among most Eskimo and on the Northwest [402] Coast, there is no reference to combs from the Pacific Eskimo, and our Chugach informant thought they were introduced by the Russians. The Aleut combs — apart from imitations of European forms — belonged to the so-called composite type (*Stäbchenkamm*) quite different from the Eskimo and Northwest Coast one-piece comb.[5] The composite comb is also characteristic of the Plateaus.[1]

(COOK & KING 1785, 305f. JEWITT 1891, 59, 114, 116f. Makah (SWAN 1870, 17). Cowichin (BOAS 1894, 460). Nanaimo (BOAS 1889, 323f.). Coast Salish (VANCOUVER 1799, I 252. 285). Squawmish (HILL-TOUT 1900, 487). Puget Sound (HAEBERLIN & GUNTHER 1930, 40). Twana, Chimakum, Klallam (EELLS 1889, 636). Klallam (GUNTHER 1927, 231). Songish (BOAS 1891, 569). Quinault (WILLOUGHBY 1889, 268), Chinook (VANCUVER 1799, II 77. FRANCHERE 1904, 326).Tillamook (BOAS 1923, 10). Yurok (KROEBER 1925, 56). Tahltan (EMMONS 1911, 46). Carrier (HARMON 1903, 163, 245. MORICE 1905, 183. MORICE 1890, 114. Chilcotin (FARRAND 1899, 647). Shuswap (BOAS 1891, 636. DAWSON 1892, 18. TEIT 1900-08b. 511). Lillooet (HILL-TOUT 1905, 138. TEIT 1900-08a, 221). THOMPSON 1900, 228), Coeur d'Alene, Okanagan, Flathead (TEIT 1900, 86f, 236, 340). Nez Percé (SPINDEN 1908, 221f.). Kutensi (CHAMBERLAIN 1893, 560). Middle Columbia Salish (TEIT 1928, 117). Nespelem and Sanpoil (RAY 1932, 51f.). Wishram (SPIER & SAPIR 1930, 208). Umpqua (DOUGLAS cited by Lewis 1906, 177). Takelma (SAPIR 1907, 264). Klamath (SPIER 1930, 261). Shasta (DIXON 1907, 412). Shoshoni (LOWIE 1909, 182). Paiute (LOWIE 1924, 311. KELLY 1932, 116. STEWARD 1933, 275). Tnaina OSGOOD 1937a, 53). Atna (ALLEN 1889, 262). Tanana (WHYMPER 1868, 210. PETROFF 1884, 161). Kutchin (KIRBY 1865, 418. JONES 1867, 320. HARDISTY 1867, 318. PETITOT 1876, 42. SCHMITTER 1910, 10. OSGOOD 1936, 46. 48, 87). Sekani (JENNESS 1937, 32). Slave, Satudene (OSGOOD 1933, 46). Chipewyan (HEARNE 1795, 152. BIRKET-SMITH 1930, 57).

[1] BIRKET-SMITH 1929, II 24, 94 cf. 269ff. table A 64. 185ff. 344ff., table B 43. Additions: Tnaina, needle-and-thread (OSGOOD 1937a, 53). Kutchin, pricking or needle-and-thread (OSGOOD 1936, 42, 46).

[2] SCHMITTER 1910, 4.

[3] MACKENZIE 1801, 371. GODDARD 1903, 18f.

[4] MACKENZIE 1801, 205.

[5] BIRKET-SMITH 1929, II 95 cf. 271 table A 65, 187 cf. 347 table B 44. Additions: Tnaina

No combs have been brought to light by the excavations of Eskimo sites in Cook Inlet and Prince William Sound, and the tables of the distribution of the comb cited above show that its occurrence in the Boreal Woodlands is rather uncertain. If the Eyak really knew the comb it must be a Northwest Coast element in their culture. The head scratcher used by adolescent girls will be discussed later (p.469).

Tools and Techniques

The Eyak, like so many other tribes of North America, lived in a stone-copper age. They also made extensive use of bone for tools and weapons, and it is supposed that scraps of iron soon found their way to them, for iron was observed in Prince William Sound by COOK, and was known on Kodiak and the Aleutian Islands from Japanese shipwrecks even before the advent of the Russians.[23]

Very little is known of the *stone technique* of former days. That chipping was employed at least at an early period seems fairly probable, but as no particulars are at [403] hand, for instance concerning the imporlant question whether a core or a flake industry was prevalent, there is no reason for entering into details. It is highly probable that among the Eyak, as among the neighboring Indians and Eskimo, stone pecking was more important than chipping. Pecking is not much used by the Eskimo as a whole and seems limited to the Bering Strait and Pacific groups.[3] It was also practised on the Aleutian Islands and in Kamchatka.[4] That pecking was common on the Northwest Coast[5] and the Plateaus[6] is exhibited by ethnological collections from these areas. It is also well known from archaeological investigations in these parts.[7] Thus there is no doubt that within the regions with which we are concerned the pecking industry has its center on the Northwest Coast, and with respect to this art the Eyak were a Northwest Coast tribe. The art of stone polishing has an even wider distribution, including the Eskimo as a whole, so that a few references will suffice for our purpose.[8] It is difficult to say from where the Eyak

---

(OSGOOD 1937a, 53). Kutechin (OSGOOD 1936, 42, 45). Coeur d'Alene, Okanagan (TEIT 1930, 83, 236). Middle Columbia Salish (TEIT 1928, 117).

[1] BIRKET-SMITH 1937.

[2] COOK & KING 178ff, 380. JOCHELSON 1933, 22f.

[3] NELSON 1899, 91. DE LAGUNA 1934, passim.

[4] JOCHELSON 1925, 67ff. JOCHELSON 1928, 67.

[5] Tsimshian (BOAS 1916, 52). Kwakiutl (BOAS 1909, 310f.).

[6] Thompson (TEIT 1900, 182). Shuswap (TEIT 1900-08b, 473). Coeur d'Alene (TEIT 1930, 41). Nez Percé (SPINDEN 1908, 183). Klamath, Modoc (BARRETT 1907-10, 252). Shasta (DIXON 1907, 393).

[7] Lytton. B. C. (SMITH 1899, 138). Fraser River (SMITH 1903, 154, 156). Thompson River (SMITH 1900,412). Puget Sound (SMITH 1900-08, passim). Yakima Valley (SMITH 1910, 37, 74).

[8] Aleut (JOCHELSON 1925, 67, 72f.). Chugach (Field notes). Cook Inlet Eskimo (DE LAGUNA 1934, 70ff.). Old Bering Sea culture (COLLINS 1937, passim). Bering Strait Eskimo (NELSON 1899, 91). Point Barrow (MURDOCH 1892, 167). Colville Eskimo (STEFFANSSON 1914, 393). Thule culture (MATHIASSEN 1927, I passim). West Greenland (SOLBERG 1907, 24f. BIRKET-SMITH 1924, 81. MATHIASSEN 1934, 173ff.). Northeast Greenland (THOMSEN 1917, 384ff. LARSEN 1934, passim). Northwest Coast (EMMONS 1923, 23). Kwakiutl (BOAS 1909, 311).

acquired the art. [404]

Copper was cold-hammered in great parts of boreal North America before the coming of the whites, the principal resources being the deposits of Bathurst Inlet and Coppermine River in the far north, Copper River in Alaska, and Lake Superior in the east. MATHIASSEN found pieces of copper from the Thulc period at Repulse Bay, and while it has not been observed in the ruins of this stage in Greenland, copper was probably used there also, since it has actually been encountered in sites of the somewhat later Inugsuk culture.[1] Still, the general use to which it was put among the Copper Eskimo is supposed to be rather recent.[2] The Chipewyan, Dogrib, Yellowknife, and possibly other Mackenzie Athapaskans made knives, arrowheads, icepicks, etc. of native copper.[3] The Atna not only themselves worked the metal from which their native river received its name, but also traded it to their neighbors.[4] It was used occasionally by the Peel River Kutchin, the Tena of the lower Yukon, and by the Tnaina on the upper part of Cook Inlet, and it occurs in the most recent Eskimo shell-heaps of Kachemak Bay.[5] We also found it in the upper layers of the Palugvik site in Prince William Sound, [405] and COOK saw the Chugach using it.[6] The Tlingit, among whom La PÉROUSE reports copper to have been *"assez commun,"*[7] were far from being the only Northwest Coast tribe who employed this metal. It was known even to the Chinook,[8] and seems to have been fairly widespread also on the Plateaus where it probably antedated the arrival of the whites as far inland as the Nez Percé country.[9]

Information on the Northwest Coast *adze* has been summarized by OLSON.[10] The principal types are classilied according to the shape of the handle as straight, "D", and elbow adzes. The two first mentioned are more or less southern forms which do not concern us here. the elbow adze being the only one which enters into our discussion. This type was not confined to the Northwest Coast and Plateaus alone, but occurs, with a few exceptions, over the entire Eskimo area,[11] and was probably widely diffused also in the Mackenzie area prior to the

---

Puget Sound (SMITH 1900-08, passim). Shuswap (TEIT 1900-08b, 473). Lillooet (TEIT 1900-08a, cf. 203). Thomson, rare (TEIT 1900, 182). Coeur d'Alene (TEIT 1930, 41). Lytton. BC (Smith 1899, 142ff.). Fraser River (SMITH 1903, 141). Thompson River (SMITH 1900, 182). Shasta (DIXON 1907, 391), Chukchi (BOGORAS 1904-07, 309). Koryak, "not fully acquired the art ..." (JOCHELSON 1908, 608). Kamchadal (JOCHELSON 1928, passim).

[1] MATHIASSEN 1927. II 127ff. MATHIASSEN 1930, 269. MATHIASSEN 1934, 175.

[2] JENNESS 1923.

[3] HEARNE 1795. xxiii, 175. BIRKET-SMITH 1930, 59. JENNESS 1932, 388.

[4] SAUER 1802, 195f. WRANGELL 1839, 98. ERMAN 1870-71, II 386ff. GODDARD 1924, 91.

[5] WRANGELL 1839, 118. DE LAGUNA 1934, 207. OSGOOD 1937a, 102f. OSGOOD 1936, 70.

[6] COOK & KING 1785, 358.

[7] LA PÉROUSE 1797, 152.

[8] BANCROFT 1875, 235.

[9] 4 Carrier (MORICE 1890, 138. MORICE 1905, 137f.). Chilcotin (MACKENZIE 1801, 254f.). Shuswap (BOAS 1891, 637. DAWSON 1892. 11. TEIT 1900-08b, 509). Lillooet (TEIT 1909-08a, 220). Nez Percé (SPINDEN 1908, 190). Middle Columbia Salish (TEIT 1928, 117). Lytton, B.C. SMITH 1899, 133). Fraser River (SMITH 1903, 140). Thompson River (SMITH 1900, 425f.). Yakima Valley (SMITH 1910, 89f., passim).

[10] OLSON 1917, 13ff.

[11] BIRKET-SMITH 1929, II 27f. COLLINS 1937, 333f. The statement that the adze had gone of of use at Angmagssalik has since been proven to be erroneous (MATHIASSEN 1933, 116f).

introduction of the steel axe. On the Pacific coast it goes as far south at least as the Yurok, although its main distribution lies farther north. OLSON is probably right in considering it an intrusive Asiatic type.[1] It is necessary, however, to distinguish between several [406] sub-types of elbow adzes. One has a small blade set into a head of antler; this is the typical Eskimo adze, although it also occurs on archaeological sites in the Columbia-Fraser River region. Another sub-type has a somewhat larger blade set against the shoulder of a handle that differs in size according to whether it is to be grasped by one or by both hands. Finally there is the implement with a heavy, grooved blade and a T-shaped handle, somewhat erroneously called a splitting adze. Information on this sub-type was recently summarized by the American author.[2] While it is common all over Prince William Sound and Cook Inlet, it is only found in the upper layers of the Kachemak Bay deposits and seems to be entirely lacking in the Aleutian shell-heaps. It occurs, however, among the Yukon Eskimo and the Tena. On the Northwest Coast it is limited to the comparatively small area occupied by the Tlingit, Haida, and Tsimshian.[3] The obvious conclusion is that it must be a fairly recent type, probably introduced among the Eyak by the Tlingit. On the occurrence of a somewhat similar, though double-bitted adze see below.

Besides the adze, an _axe_ was also said to be used. Very little is known of the shape of this implement, which may have been replaced by an iron tool at an early date — if, in fact, the information is at all reliable, which is by no means certain. Axes are extremely rare in the northern parts of the North American continent. From the Northwest Coast they are not mentioned at all as far as our knowledge goes, except from the Coast Salish, who described some stone celts as being hafted axe-fashion as war clubs.[4] Among [407] the Eskimo the elbow-adze is dominant, but a few specimens that may he described as axes have been found. MATHIASSEN excavated a very crude hatchet, with a handle and lashing made of baleen, and a sandstone axe-blade, at the Thule culture sites at Ponds Inlet.[5] No doubt he is right in comparing these implements with a kind of axe which occurs, though rarely, among the Polar Eskimo and is used for chopping frozen meat.[6] Similar ivory-headed axes are employed by the Eskimo of St. Lawrence Island.[7] A few axe-blades have also been mentioned from Northeast Greenland,[8] but from the descriptions we suspect that they are really adzes. Anyhow, it is a remarkable fact that nowhere else in Greenland have other axes been discovered in spite of the very extensive archaeological work which has been carried out there during later years.[9] We have no information about axes in the Mackenzie area except that HEARNE speaks of the antler hatchets of the Dogrib,[10] but this may just as well refer to the stone-pointed antler pickaxes for warfare known also from the Yukon and Plateau areas. From the Yukon double-bitted, grooved stone axes are described,[11] but it should not be overlooked that the re-hafted specimen on pl. 10

---

[1] Cf. also BIRKET-SMITH 1929, II 28f.

[2] DE LAGUNA 1934, 172. cf. OSGOOD 1937a, 103.

[3] Cf. NIBLACK 1890, pl. xxiii.

[4] EMMONS 1923, 27.

[5] MATHIASSEN 1927, I 170f., II 77.

[6] ASTRUP 1895, 105. KROEBER 1900, 285.

[7] GEIST & RAINEY 1936, 103.

[8] RICHTER 1934, 129f., 201.

[9] Cf., besides the works of MATHIASSEN, LARSEN 1934; GLOB 1935; DEGERBØL 1936.

[10] HEARNE 1785, 267.

[11] KREIGER in HKDLIČKA 1930, 147ff. Cf. OSGOOD 1936, 85.

appears as an adze, and the asymmetrical shape of this object as well as the unhafted stone blades on the same plate makes this method of hafting the more probable. It is true that ALLEN mentions axes from the Atna, but without further particulars and in [408] such a manner that we suspect he refers to an imported iron tool.[1] At any rate the Eyak axe remains rather enigmatic.

The *ulo*, or woman's knife, is far less puzzling. Its distribution comprises not only the entire Eskimo area, the Northwest Coast, and the Plateaus of British Columbia, but also great parts of the Eastern Woodlands and the Old World.[2] As a culture loan it occurs among the Crow River Kutchin.[3] It seems therefore quite natural lo lind it also among the Eyak. It was said to resemble the Eskimo type, which, of course, means that of the Chugach. The latter is similar to the ulo of Cook Inlet which again approaches the northern Eskimo pattern more than it does the woman's knives of other regions.[4]

The Eyak had both crooked carving knives and knives with blades of beaver teeth. The history of the *crooked knife* is much too intricate to enter upon here. Although in its present form it must be post-Columbian, the crooked knife has, nevertheless, an extremely wide distribution.[5] The *beaver tooth knife* has a somewhat comparable distribution. Of course the latter tool is not known to the Eskimo, except the Alaskan groups living close to the forests,[6] but it was common throughout the Boreal Woodlands[7] [409] and the northern Plateaus.[8] It is also mentioned from archaeological sites at Lytton, B.C., and Pugel Sound,[9] but not from any living Northwest Coast tribe; this may be due to the early spread of metal tools over this region. The distribution of *whetstones* is, of course, nearly universal.

The *wedge* is an old and commonly diffused element in the culture of the Eskimo as well as in western North America as a whole, although it is also found in some places in the Eastern Woodlands, the northern Plains, and in Asia.[10] It is probably a very old element in the circum-

---

[1] ALLEN 1889, 263.

[2] BIRKET-SMITH 1929, II 107f., cf. 227f. table A 75, 194ff. cf. 355 table B 50. See also MATHIASSEN 1927, II 84ff., and COLLINS 1937, 350f. Add: Tnaina (OSGOOD 1937a, 102f.). The American author found archaeological speceimens in Indian sites on the Yukon below Nulato.

[3] OSGOOD 1936, 75.

[4] Cf. DE LAGUNA 1934, 184f.

[5] BIRKET-SMITH 1929, II 105f. cf. 276 table A 73, 194 cf. 353f. table B 49. To the latter should be added: Tnaina (OSGOOD 1937a, 103).

[6] Kodiak? (LISIANSKY 1914, 207). Bering Strait Eskimo (NELSON 1899, 89f).

[7] Quotations from the Mackenzie area will suffice for our purpose: Tnaina (OSGOOD) 1937a, 103). Kutchin. "awls" (OSGOOD 1936, 70, 75). Nahane (JENNESS 1932, 398). Sekani (JENNESS 1932, 379). Hare (JENNESS 1932, 390). Dogrib (HEARNE 1795, 267). Slave (MACKENZIE 1801, 39). Satudene (OSGOOD) 1933, 58). Beaver (GODDARD) 1916, 219). Chipewyan (BIRKET-SMITH 1930, 60).

[8] Carrier (MORICE 1895, 52). Shuswap (TEIT 1900-08b, 74). Lillooet (TEIT 1900-08a, 203). Thompson (TEIT 1900, 183). Coeur d'Alene (TEIT 1930, 43).

[9] SMITH 1899, 144. SMITH 1900-08, 318.

[10] BIRKET-SMITH 1929, II 114 cf. 284f. table A 90, 200 cf. 361 table B 59. Additions to the lists: General (DE LAGUNA 1934, 199). Chugach (Field notes). Frederik VI Coast, East Greenland (MATHIASSEN 1936, 42). Tsimshian (BOAS 1916, 49). Coeur d'Alenc, Okanagan (TEIT 1930, 42, 218). Middle Columbia Salish (TEIT 1928, 112). Nespelem and Sanpoil (RAY 1932, 42f.).

polar region. The *bark-stripping wedge* made of a flat and sharp stick is an entirely dinerent tool. The closest parallel to the Eyak type seems to be that of the Chugach and Tnaina.[1] It is, of course, unknown to the Eskimo generally except the Alaskan tribes among whom bark is used to a certain extent.[2] On the Northwest Coast different types are sometimes found,[3] whereas simple knife-like forms [410] occur among the Plateau tribes.[4] The bark-stripping implement is probably connected with the general use of bark for vessels, canoes, etc. in the boreal woodlands.

Dry heating of wood for bending, without steaming or soaking it in hot water, does not seem to be a very common method, or at least it has not found its way into literature. It may be employed by the Atna for making bows, but ALLEN'S description is not very clear.[5] On the northern Plains wood is heated in hot ashes.[6] Steaming or soaking in warm water is much more generally mentioned: we know it from the Eskimo, the Northwest Coast, the Mackenzie area, etc.[7]

We may here, in connection with wood working, insert a remark on the *painting of implements*, which often appeared in Eyak culture. This is certainly not an aboriginal Eskimo feature; it is never found among the eastern tribes, but only west of the Mackenzie[8] where it has probably been introduced from the Northwest Coast. Painting also occurs, on a minor scale, among the Tnaina and Kutchin and in the Plateau area as well as on the Asiatic side of the Bering Sea.[9] The principal center seems, [411] however, to be the highly developed Northwest Coast culture. The eye-ornamont painted on the Eyak doors and paddles is highly suggestive of Northwest Coast art. The paintings on the Eyak ceremonial paddles are also of a distinct Northwest Coast character.

The *lamp* is not only universal among the Eskimo but also found among several Indian and Northeast Asiatic peoples.[10] Outside the Arctic proper its distribution is, in the main, limited

---

Wisham (SPIER & SAPIR 1930, 188). Tnaina (OSGOOD 1937a, 60, 104). Kutchin (OSGOOD 1936, 75).

[1] Chugach (Field notes). Tnaina (OSGOOD 1937a, 104).

[2] NELSON 1899, 90.

[3] Tlingit, Haida (NIBLACK 1890, pl. xx fig. 79a, fig. 179 1. Kwakiutl (BOAS 1909, 371. BOAS 1921, 120f).

[4] Carrier, Sekani (MORICE 1890, 134. MORICE 1905, 76f.). Shuswap (TEIT 1900-08b, 475, 515f.). Thompson (TEIT 1900, 233). Coeur d'Alene (TEIT 1930, 43, 92).

[5] ALLEN 1899, 263.

[6] DE SMET 1859, 48.

[7] BIRKET-SMITH 1929, II 115 cf. 285 table A 92, 200 cf. 363 table B 60. Add: Aleut (LANGSDORFF 1812, 36).

[8] JOCHELSON 1925, pl. 17. DE LAGUNA 1934, 117. LANGSDORFF 1812, 42. PETROFF 1884, 139. HOLMBERG 1856, 368. NELSON 1899, 70, 198ff. MURDOCH 1892, 87, 104, 391, STEFANSSON 1914, 201, 354. PETITOT 1887, 72.

[9] Tnaina (OSGOOD 1937a, 117). Kutchin (MASON 1924, 34). Tahltan (EMMONS 1911, 48). Shuswap (TEIT 1900-08b, 475f.). Lillooet (TEIT 1900 -08a, 204f.). Thompson (TEIT 1900, 184). Coeur d'Alene, Flathead (TEIT 1930, 43, 259). Nez Percé (SPINDEN 1908, 222). Chukchi (BOGORAS 1904-09, 220). Koryak (JOCHELSON 1908, 629). Kamchadal (KRACHENINNIKOW 1770, I 54ff.).

[10] BIRKET-SMITH 1929, II 100ff., 189ff. On p. 190, 1. 19 from bottom omit: "Among the Plains Indiens ... &c" Add: Tnaina (OSGOOD 1937a, 108). Certain clay bowls from the Ertebølle

to the outskirts of the great boreal region, and according to the opinion set forth by the Danish author we arc entitled to regard it as a very old culture element connected with the ice-hunting culture. It was, however, almost completely abandoned throughout the greater part of the region when increased mobility became necessary in the snowshoe and reindeer breeding stages.[1] The Eyak lamp was very simple in pattern, being either a roughly hollowed cobble or a clam shell filled with oil. Similar crude stone lamps are found on the Aleutian Islands and sporadically elsewhere in the Eskimo area, notably among the Caribou Eskimo. According to the field notes of the American author, the Tena sometimes used naturally hollowed stones for lamps. It is peculiar that this primitive type survived side by side, so to speak, with the elaborate [412] sculptured stone lamps of Cook Inlet and the Tlingit.[2] The clamshell lamp is another primitive form which is met with again among the Nootka and Ainn and even far away in Europe among the Coast Lapps and on the Orkneys and Aran Islands, Eulachon used as candles by threading a wick through them are common on the Northwest Coast and among the Tnaina of the upper part of Cook Inlet.[3]

It is often difficult to distinguish between oval or round stone lamps and *stone mortars*. It seems, however, that mortars were formerly used by the Eyak even apart from the post-Russian wooden specimens for snuff. The stone mortar is common on both sides of the North Pacific.[4] So far the occurrence in the Kachemak Bay Eskimo culture is, however, somewhat doubtful, and even though mortars of whale vertebrae occur in the shell-heaps of Prince William Sound they cannot by any means be called common. On the other hand the wide distribution and the rather frequent occurrence in archaeological sites on the Plateaus speak [413] against the otherwise obvious inference that it is a recently introduced type, be this as it may — only close archaeological research will be able to solve the problem — there is nothing surprising in finding the mortar as an Eyak implement.

The simple *fire-drill* is very nearly universal among the North American Indians, even

---

period of the Danish stone age have recently been interpreted as lamps by MATHIASSEN.

[1] COLLINS (1937, 341ff), arrives at the conclusion that there is no direct connection between the lamps of the Arctic Eskimo and those of the Pacific Eskimo tribes. The latter he believes to be related to the stone mortars of the Northwest Coast. His arguments, however, do not seem to be entirely convincing.

[2] KRAUSE 1885, 206. DE LAGUNA 1934, 177ff.

[3] Tlingit (NIBLACK 1890, 276). Nootka (BANCROFT 1875, 190, 214 footnote). Tnaina (OSGOOD 1937a, 108).

[4] Aleut (JOCHELSON 1925, pl. 20). Cook Inlet (DE LAGU)NA 1934, 60, 174). Northwest Coast (NIBLACK 1890, 280. Tlingit (ELLIOTT 1886, 60). Puget Sound (SMITH 1900-08, passim). Shuswap (TEIT 1900-08b, 474). Lillooet (TEIT 1900-08a, 204). Thompson (TEIT 1900, 202). Coeur d'Alene, Okanagan, Flathead (TEIT 1930, 42, 217, 326). NEZ PERCÉ (SPINDEN 1908, 187). Middle Columbia Salish (TEIT 1928, 110. Fraser River (SMITH 1903, 158f, 184f.). Thompson Rivcr (SMITH 1900, 413f.). Yakima Valley (SMITH 1910, 36ff). Wishram (SPIER & SAPIR 1930, 189). Klamath (BARRETT 1907-10, 252. SPIER 1930, 177). Shoshoni (LOWIE 1908, 174f). Bannock (LOWIE 1909, 174f.). Surprise Valley Paiute (KELLY 1932, 139). Chukchi (BOGORAS 1904-09, 203f.). Koryak (JOCHELSON 1908, 578, 580). Kamchadal (STELLER 1774, 104. JOCHELSON 1928, 54, fig. 40). The Nespelem and Sanpoil seldom, if ever, made stone mortars (RAY 1932, 40. The Ainu of the present day have wooden mortars, but specimens of stone occur in tlie stone age of Japan (MUNROE 1911, 133ff.).

though the use of pyrites cannot be considered post-Columbian as WALTER HOUGH would have it.[1] The bow and cord drills are apparently rather late in North America and have been introduced from two sources. Their occurrences in the north and west is due to Asiatic influence, whereas the eastern tribes probably have adopted these methods from the whites.[2] The *pump-drill* is decidedly non-American. It is found sporadically as a fire-making impIenieiU among Ihe Iroquois and Lenape, as a tool among the Peel River Kutchin,[3] Pomo, and Pueblo tribes, but in no case is there reason for regarding it as aboriginal.

Square wooden boxes are frequent both among the Eskimo and the Northwest Coast Indians. There is a characteristic difference, however, between those made by the two groups. The more northern Indian tribes, as a rule, make boxes with a single piece of wood for the sides, bent by steam at three corners and fastened by sewing at the fourth, while the Eskimo make boxes with sides of four separate pieces pegged together. This second type also occurs among the Tlingit and the Kwakiutl, though among the latter this method is said to be recent.[4] On the southern [414] part of the coast they seem to be more common; at Puget Sound the sides may be of one piece joined by pegging.[5] As in so many other cases, the Eskimo method is more closely related to that of the southern part of the coast than to the more northern Indian method.[6] On the southern Northwest Coast pegging is the rule wherever square boxes are found. It is true that in some modern cases European influence may he suspected, but there is no reason for ascribing the type as a whole to this source. In Greenland, for instance, it is known from a period slightly later than the Thule culture. We may, indeed, feel inclined to regard it as a Thule type, even though it has not been found in the Thule culture sites in the Central area. This would explain the similarity between Eskimo specimens and those from the southern Northwest Coast, and this hypothesis is further supported by the fact that pegged boxes are rare among the present Central Eskimo and not found among the Caribou Eskimo at all.

Apparently the Eyak did not use the folded birchbark vessels so common in the boreal woodlands from Lapp-land right to Labrador, except, perhaps, for a few specimens traded from the Interior. The Eyak *hemlock-bark pails* as described to us had a bottom piece and a separate side sewn with spruce roots. It is difficult to find exact parallels to this pattern in the immediate neighborhood of the Eyak. [415]

There is a well-known Eurasian type of snuff-box with a wooden bottom and stopper; the overlapping ends of the side are interlaced. This type has also reached the Eskimo of Bering Strait.[71] Even apart from the size, the Eyak vessels differ from these boxes in having sewn instead of interlaced sides. On the other hand the Eyak type is widely known in Siberia. We

---

[1] BIRKET-SMITH 1929, II 350ff. cf. table B 47. Add: Nespelem and Sanpoil (RAY 1932, 43).

[2] BIRKET-SMITH 1929, II 97f. The Tnaina use a strap drill (OSGOOD 1937a, 45, 107f.).

[3] OSGOOD 1936, 75.

[4] NIBLACK 1890, 319. BOAS 1909, 337.

[5] HAEBERLIN & GUNTHER 1930, 35. LEWIS 1906, 161. GUNTHER 1927, 211, 224.

[6] Chugach (Spec. in Museum für Völkerkunde, Berlin). Bering Strait Eskimo (NELSON 1899, 93ff.). Mackenzie Eskimo (C-NM, P 223). Netsilik Eskiino (155 48, University Ethnographical Museum, Oslo). Iglulik Eskimo (C-NM P 27: 369). West Greenland (BIRKET-SMITH 1924, 165. MATHIASSEN 1930, 277. MATHIASSEN, 1931, 95). East Greenland (HOLM 1914, 40. THALBITZER 1914, 559ff.). Northeast Greenland (THALBITZER 1909, 519ff., MATHIASSEN 1929, 157. LARSEN 1934, 150.

[7] NELSON 1899, 274.

cannot enter upon the details of its distribution here, but at any rate it occurs among the Ostyak, Yakut, Tungus, and Gilyak.[1] In North America the same type has recently been reported from the Sanpoil and Nespelem,[2] and it may have been known to the other Interior Salish as well, though information is absent. There are also some similar containers and boxes in the Eastern Woodlands.[3] The question is, however, whether Iherc is any direct connection between the Eyak, Siberian, Salishan and Algonkian objects. We have, perhaps, a hint as to how the Eyak type should be explained in the fact that they sometimes made similar buckets of baleen from stranded whales. The Eskimo manufacture water and blubber pails with separate bottom and a rim of baleen or thin wood; they occur right from the Siberian coast to East Greenland and go back to the Old Bering Sea, Punuk, and Thule periods.[4] This may indicate that they are an old Alaskan type, and [416] they reappear, indeed, among the Kutchin and Tnaina.[5] The Tahltan also make them, evidently on a smaller scale, with sides of caribou antler.[6] It would not be surprising if there were a direct relationship belween these vessels and the Northwest Coast square boxes with bent sides.

The extensive use of bark in the boreal woodlands both of the Old and the New World seems to be a trait closely connected with the snowshoe complex (cf. the birchbark canoe, the conical tent, etc.). The natural way of making a vessel of a pliable material like bark seems to be by folding, a fact which agrees with the wide distribution of folded bark containers in the very regions where the snow-shoe complex is prevalent. The sewn bark pails of the Siberian tribes, the Eyak, and the Salish in the west and the Algonkians in the east may under these circumstances, he "translations" of an earlier wooden type into bark. Whether these "translations" were mutually independent or not cannot be decided with the incomplete material at hand.

Twined baskets have a typical center in western North America. Among the Eskimo the twined technique does not extend farther north and east than Bering Strait, but it reappears on the Asiatic side among the Koryak, Kamchadal, and Ainu.[7] The Indians of the Northwest Coast, especially the Tlingit, are experts in this kind of basketry,[8] but its distribution spreads far beyond

---

[1] Specimens in the National Museum, Copenhagen. Cf. VON SCHRENCK 1881-95, 445.

[2] RAY 1932, 38.

[3] E.g., H 1963 (Ottawa, here there is a pegged wooden bottom and sides of elm hark) and H 3046 (Naskapi), both in the National Museum, Copenhagen.

[4] COLLINS 1937, 350. MATHIASSEN 1927, II 107. To the distribution given there may be added the Pacific Eskimo (COOK & KING 1785, 372). The Caribou Eskimo, however, do not use them except when influenced by the coast dwellers.

[5] MACKENZIE 1801, 48. OSGOOD 1936, 75. OSGOOD 1937a, 104ff.

[6] EMMONS 1911, 49.

[7] Aleut (MASON 1904, 403ff. JOCHELSON 1933, 59ff). Chugach (Field notes). Kodiak (HOLMBERG 1856, 382). Bering Strait Eskimo (NELSON 1899, 204. MASON 1904, 395f.). Koryak (JOCHELSON 1908, 631ff.) Kamechadal (MONTANDON 1937, 107). Ainu (MONTANDON 1937, 103ff.).

[8] Tlingit (MALASPIINA 1849, 288. CAAMAÑO 1849, 353. KRAUSE 1885, 208. NIBLACK 1890, 313ff. MASON 1904, 406ff). Haida (MASON 1904, 414ff). Tsimshian (MASON 1904, 417). Kwakiutl (BOAS 1921, 134ff.). Puget Sound (HAEBERLIN & GUNTHER 1930, 32f). Skokomish (MASON 1904, 436). Twana, Klallam, Chimakum (EELLS 1889, 627f.). Klallam (GUNTHER 1927, 222). Quinault (MASON 1904, 435), Chinook (MASON 1904, 437). Tillamook (MASON

the limits [417] of the Northwest Coast culture and comprises the state of California as far south as the Diegueño and other "Mission Indians", although coiling reached its highest development here and the twined specimens are rather coarse.[1] We have no information about Kutchin basketry except that it was "woven".[2] The same expression is used by OSGOOD to designate the Tnaina baskets,[3] but fortunately some old Tnaina baskets arc still preserved (two of them in the Danish National Museum of Copenhagen), all of them showing twined technique. In the Plateau area both twined and coiled baskets are common,[4] the former reaching south to the western Apache. It also occurs in the cliff dwellings of the Southwest, whereas the Basket Maker remains all belong to the coiled type. Thus we have the impression that coiling was the older basketry technique which was entirely supplanted by twining on the Northwest Coast and partially displaced in the neighboring areas. WISSLER arrives at the opposite conclusion, viz. that "coiled basketry seems [418] to be a smaller area overlying a larger one of twined basketry",[5] but except for the fact that twining in more or less coarse form occurs together with coiling in the adjacent areas (a fact we may just as well interpret as a penetration from the great Northwest Coast center) it seems difficult to find evidence for this supposition. The Eyak designs are all typical of Tlingit baskets (see p. 83ff.).

So little is known of the technique and appearance of the *grass mats* spread in the sleeping rooms that a detailed discussion seems futile. It will suffice to state that grass mats occur among the Pacific and Bering Strait Eskimo as well as the Aleut;[6] whether they are related to the willow mats of the Central Eskimo is uncertain.[7] Grass or rush mats are widely used on the Northwest Coast,[8] in the Yukon area, the Northern Plateaus, and, on the Asiatic side, among the Chukchi, Koryak, Kamchadal, and Ainu.[9] [419]

1904, 436). Yurok (KROEBER 1925, 90ff.). Hupa (MASON 1889, 220. MASON 1904, 448. GODDARD 1903, 40). Wiyot (KROEBER 1925, 117).

[1] MASON 1904, 454, 463 f., 487f.

[2] JONES 1867, 321. OSGOOD 1936, 77. A single specimen, now in the U. S. National Museum, has twisted warp.

[3] OSGOOD 1937a, 76.

[4] Lower Thompson (TEIT 1900, 188). Coeur d'Alene (TEIT 1930, 48). Nez Percé (SPINDEN 1908, 190. Nespelem and Sanpoil (RAY 1932. 36f.). Plateaus of Washington (LEWIS 1906, 187). Cayuse, Umatilla (MASON 1904, 439). Wishram (SPIER & SAPIR 1930, 192ff.). Takelma (SAPIR 1907, 260. Klamath (MASON 1904, 460. BARRNETT 1907-10, 253ff.). Shasta (MASON 1904, 462. DIXON 1907, 398ff. SPIER 1930, 177). Shoshoni (LOWIE 1909, 178). Paviotso (LOWIE 1924, 233). Paiute (LOWIE 1914, 238. KELLY 1932, 123f., STEWARD 1933, 272).

[5] WISSLER 1922, 50f.

[6] HOLMBERG 1850, 322. Field notes. NELSON 1899, 202f. ERMAN 1870-71, 111 165. ERLÄUTERUNGER 1781, 311. COXE 1780, 104.

[7] BIRKET-SMITH 1929, II 56f., cf. 237 table A 5.

[8] Tlingit (NIBLACK 1890, 312 f.). Haida (BANCROFT 1875, 160. Kwakiutl (JACOBSEN 1884, 58. BOAS 1921, 125f.). Makah (SWAN 1870, 5f., 45). Squawmish (HILL-TOUT 1900, 486). Chehalis (HILL-TOUT 1904b, 333). Puget Sound (HAEBERLIN & GUNTHER 1930, 32). Washington (LEWIS 1906, 163). Twana, Chimakum, Klallam (EELLS 1889, 626f). Klallam (WILKES 1844, 320. GUNTHER 1927, 220ff). Quinault (WILLOUGHBY 1889, 267f) Quilleute (SWAN, 1870, 45). Chinook (FRANCHERE 1904, 327. BANCROFT 1875, 237).

[9] Tnaina (OSGOOD 1937, 77). Tena (Field Notes of American author). Kutchin (OSGOOD 1936,

It has formerly been shown that the *drinking tube* is common to all Eskimo as an every-day implement. whereas in North America outside the Eskimo area it has nearly everywhere acquired a more or less ritual character.[1] It must be due to the proximity of the Eskimo that the drinking tube of the Eyak — if our informant can be trusted on this point — had the same profane use.

There was a rather large variety of shape among the wooden vessels in which food was served. Ordinary *round bowls* arc used over enormous areas in both hemispheres. Exceptions are to be found in Central California with its highly developed basketry, in the pottery regions of the Southwest, and to a certain extent on the Northwest Coast and in the Amur region in Asia where wood carving had reached such a standard that people as a rule were not satisfied with the plainest of patterns. These easily explained gaps in the otherwise continuous distribution do not contradict the supposition that the round wooden howl is a very old culture element in the circumpolar region.[2] *Square bowls*, on the other hand, are a special Northwest Coast feature, more or less restricted to the higher civilized tribes of the northern part of the area, but apparently unknown [420] in the southern parts.[3] This would indicate that the square type is rather recent in the history of these tribes. The same is true of the *boat-shaped vessels*, although their occurrence also among the Gilyak and Ainu probably means that they are older than the square ones.[4]

If it be permitted to assume that the *long wooden dishes* are the same type as the trough-shaped trays of the Eskimo and others we may consider them another example of an old and widely diffused element among the Eyak. They occur over large areas both in North America

---

67). Tsetsaut (BOAS 1895, 562). Chilcotin, introduced from Shuswap (JENNESS 1934, 362). Shuswap (BOAS 1891, 636. TEIT 1900-08b, 490), Lillooet (TEIT 1900-08a, 209). Thompson (TEIT 1900, 188ff). Coeur d'Alene, Okanagan, Flathead (TEIT 1930, 47, 218f; 327). Nez Percé (SPINDEN 1908, 194f.). Middle Columbia Salish (TEIT 1928, 112). Nespelem and Sanpoil (RAY 1932, 38f). Spokan (WILKES 1844, 475). Washington and Oregon (GIBBS 1877, 220. LEWIS 1906, 186). Thompson River (SMITH 1900, 423). Yakima Valley (SMITH 1910, 84ff. Wishram (SPIER & SAPIR 1930, 190. Takelma (SAPIR 1907, 262). Klamath (SPIER 1930, 173ff). Shoshoni (LOWIE 1909, 184). Paiute (STEWARD 1933, 270). Chukchi (BOGORAS 1904-08, 170. Koryak (JOCHELSON 1908, 460, 66). Kamchadaal (STELLER 1774, 214). Ainu (BATCHELOR 1901, 133).

[1] BIRKET-SMITH 1929, II 61 cf. 243 table A 8, 143ff. cf. 312 table B 12. The following citations should he added: Tnaina (OSGOOD 1937a, 162). Satudene (OSGOOD 1933, 283). Okanagan (TEIT 1930, 283). In all these cases employed at the puberty seclusion. Cf. also BIRKET-SMITH 1929a.

[2] BIRKET-SMITH 1929, II 58 cf. 239 table A 10. 140f. cf. 305 table B 8. Add: Coeur d'Alene, Okanagan, Flathead (TEIT 1930, 64, 230, 334). Middle Columbia Salish (TEIT 1928, 115). Wishram (SPIER & SAPIR 1930, 189f.). Tnaina (OSGOOD 1937a. 104). Ingalik (P-UM).

[3] Tlingit (NIBLACK 1890, pl. xxxviii f.). Kwakiutl (BOAS 1921, 59f.). Nootka (JEWITT 1896, 102). A rude bowl with sepatate end-pieces is described by NELSON (1899, 72). It comes from the Eskimo of Saint Lawrence Island and is stated to be "the only tray of this kind that was seen."

[4] Tlingit, Haida (KRAUSE 1885, 205. NIBLACK 1890, pl. xl fig. 209, xli fig. 216). Kwakiutl (GODDARD 1934, 43 fig.). Gilyak (VON SCHRENCK 1881-95, 446). Ainu (Specimens in the National Museum, (Copenhagen).

and North Asia, but are, as it seems, to some extent replaced by a later type, the folded bark container, in the Boreal Woodlands.[1]

There is no sharp line of demarcation between the bowls and *plates*, except that the latter are flat without distinct sides. Nevertheless it seems that, with all due reservation, it can be stated that real plates are much more rare than bowls. Round wooden plates are found among the Northwest Coast Indians, and from them have spread to the Kutchin and the Alaskan Eskimo. They are also known to the Gilyak and Ainu.[2] In other words, the distribution is nearly the same as that of the boat-shaped vessel. Square [421] wooden plates occur among the Gilyak and Ainu, and STELLER'S rather obscure description may indicate that they also occurred among the Kamchadal.[3] It is not out of the question that they are due to Chinese or Japanese influence.

Spoons of wood, bone, or horn have a distribution which in North America and — remarkably enough, also in South America — almost coincides with that of the round wooden bowl.[42] The Eyak spoons of mountain-goat horn were, from the description, similar to the ordinary Northwest Coast type, though the handle of the latter as a rule was decorated with elaborate carvings, which were lacking on the Eyak specimens. The wooden *ladle* is also widespread throughout the circumpolar region.[5] As no particulars are at hand about the Eyak type it is impossible to establish its affinity with greater accuracy. The *meat fork*, in the shape of a sharpened stick, is a common Eskimo type.[6] Of its distribution in North America outside the Eskimo area practically nothing is known, although it has recently been reported from the Tnaina,[7] in which case, [422] however, it may have been borrowed from the Eskimo. Whether the same is true of the Eyak implement, we have no means of deciding. The fact, however, that the meat-fork also occurs in the Plateau area and the Eastern Woodlands may indicate that it is a widespread type which has been overlooked in many cases.[8]

Unfortunately we know little about the *stone scraper*, but from the available evidence it

---

[1] BIRKET-SMITH 1929, II 58 cf. 239 table A 9, 139f. cf. 304 table B 7. Add: Tnaina (OSGOOD 1937a. 104). Klallam (GUNTHER 1927, 210).

[2] Haida (NIBLACK 1890, pl. xlvii fig. 266). Kutchin (OSGOOD 1936, 70, 75). Bering Strait Eskimo (C-NM, P 32: 38). Gilyak (VON SCHRENCK 1881-95, 44ff). Ainu (HITCHCOCK 1891, 456, fig. 74).

[3] VON SCHRENCK 1881-95, 446. HITCHCOCK 1891, 456 fig. 74. TORII 1919, 186. STELLER 1774, 323 ("...grosse Breter, wie einen Präsentier-teller mit einem Rand versehen").

[4] BIRKET-SMITH 1929, II 60 cf. 242 table A 16, 143 cf. 309ff. table B 11. Add: Aleut (WEYER 1930, 274). Cook Inlet (DE LAGUNA 1934, 201). Chugach (Field Notes). Frederik VI Coast (MATHIASSEN 1936, 34, 37. 42). Klallam (GUNTHER 1927, 210f.). Coeur d'Alene, Okanagan, Flathead (TEIT 1930, 64, 230, 334). Middle Columbia Salish (Teit 1928, 115). Wishram (SPIER & SAPIR 1930, 185, 189f,). Klamath (SPIER 1930, 176). Tnaina (OSGOOD 1937a, 106). Kutchin (OSGOOD 1937a, 71, 75). Satudene (OSGOOD 1930, 60).

[5] BIRKET-SMITH 1929, II 59f. cf. 241f. table A 15, 142f. cf. 308f. table B 10. Add: Chugach (Field Notes). Coeur d'Alene, Flathead (TEIT 1930, 64, 334). Wishram (SPIER & SAPIR 1930, 185. 189f). Tena (P-UM).

[6] BIRKET-SMITH 1929, II 59 cf. 240f. table A 13. Add: Asiatic Eskimo (GEIST & RAINEY 1936, 144). Frederik VI Coast (MATHIASSEN 1926, 42).

[7] OSGOOD 1933a, 703.

[8] BIRKET-SMITH 1929, II 141f. Nespelem and Sanpoil (RAY 1932, 42).

may probably he inferred that it was one-handed.[1] The most common Eskimo form has a chipped end-blade, a type which MATHIASSEN has proved to be a Thule culture element, which is also true of the polished slate or jade scraper, whereas chipped discoidal scrapers and polished sandstone scrapers with bent handles are local types.[2] The chipped end scraper goes back to the Old Bering Sea culture.[3] Considerably less information is at hand i'rom other parts of North America. Here and there stone scrapers occur,[4] but any further discussion seems useless owing to our ignorance of the Eyak type. Chipped stone scrapers also occur in Northeast Asia.[5] [423] *Scrapers of clam shell*, or rather mussel shell, are still occasionally used in Greenland, and are closely related to the cup-scrapers of wood or ivory. The latter is a Thule culture type which has survived both in Greenland and Alaska.[6] Of course it is quite possible that many of the mussel shells found in the shell-heaps on the Pacific coast were employed as scrapers, and even among tribes now living the use of an implement of such a simple character may easily be overlooked. At any rate we cannot feel sure that the mussel shell scraper of the Eyak is really an element of Eskimo origin, as a superficial consideration might otherwise indicate.

The assertion by Mrs. Gus Nelson that the Eyak never removed the hair from skins is contradicted by the information obtained from other natives and the observations of Colonel ABERCROMBIE. The method of *soaking the skins* in water is nearly universal in North America except in, certain parts of the Eskimo and Northwest Coast areas where urine is employed for this purpose.[7] Urine tanning is undoubtedly the younger of the methods and, among the Eskimo, is connected with the Thule culture.[8] Concerning the use of *gutskin* we may refer to the discussion of the gutskin coats (p. 387). The Tlingit, who did not wear this type of garment, used

---

[1] As far as our knowledge goes, all two-handed scrapers in North America were made of bone. In Siberia, however, we have two-handed scrapers with blades of stone or iron inserted into wooden handles.

[2] MATHIASSEN 1927, II 90. BIRKET-SMITH 1929, II 108f. cf. 278 table A 77. Cf. DE LAGUNA 1934, 182.

[3] COLLINS 1937, 335f.

[4] A few examples from the western regions will suffice; Haida (NIBLACK 1890, pl. xx). Tnaina (OSGOOD 1937a, 103). Kutchin (OSGOOD 1936, 70). Satudene (OSGOOD 1933, 58). Tahltan (EMMONS 1911, 58). Carrier (MORICE 1895, 49ff.). Thompson (TEIT 1900, 185). Coeur d'Alene, Okanagan (TEIT 1930, 42, 44f, 217f.). Nez Percé (SPINDEN 1908, 216). Middle Columbia Salish (TEIT 1928, 111). Wishram (SPIER & SAPIR 1930, 200). Archaeological specimens have been found at Lytton and Kamloops (SMITH 1899. figg. 63f; fig. 353), near Nanaimo (SMITH 1903, fig. 114), and in the Yakima Valley (SMITH 1910, fig. 67ff.).

[5] BOGORAS 1904-09, 217f.

[6] MATHIASSEN 1927, II 91.

[7] BIRKET-SMITH 1929, 116 cf. 286 table A 93. The following instances of treating skins with hot water outside the Eskimo area will suffice: Kwakiutl (BOAS 1909, 400). Nootka (JEWITT 1896, 106). Puget Sound (HAEBERLIN & GUNTHER 1930, 33). Klallam (GUNTHER 1927, 219). Kutchin (SCHMITTER 1910. 5). Satudene (OSGOOD 1933, 59). Chipewyan (BIRKET-SMITH 1930, 62f). Tahltan (EMMONS 1911, 81). Shuswap (BOAS 1891, 636). Thompson (TEIT 1900, 185). Coeur d'Alene, Okanagan, Flathead (TEIT 1930, 44, 218, 327). Nez Percé (SPINDEN 1908, 216). Wishram (SPIER & SAPIR 1930, 200). Nespelem and Sanpoil (RAY 1932, 94). Ute (LOWIE 1924. 227. Paiute (LOWIE 1934, 226).

[8] HATT 1916, 288. BIRKET-SMITH 1929, II 116.

gutskin for wrapping up blankets.[1] [424]

    Sealskin thongs are common to all Eskimos living on the coast. While not definitely stated, it may be inferred from the descriptions of Nelson and Murdoch that the Eskimo of Bering Strait and Point Barrow cut thongs from a flat piece of skin,[2] whereas the eastern tribes cut them from a broad skin "belt." According to our field notes, the Chugach cut sealskin thongs from a skin removed whole, or spirally from the belly skin of a sea-lion. The Eyak method is the same as the last mentioned and, it may be added, also the same as that of the Woodland Indians in cutting babiche. *Lines of kelp* are typical of the Northwest Coast, although they have also been borrowed by the Chugach and the Tnaina of Kachemak Bay.[3]

    Sinew thread is used for sewing skins among the Eskimo,[4] and *in the Mackenzie*[5] and Plateau areas.[6] t was not of great importance on the Northwest Coast where tailored clothing was unknown, but when necessary it was traded from the Interior.[7] On the Asiatic coast it is used as far south as Kamchatka and the Kurile Islands,[8] whereas the Gilyak and the Ainu make thread of strips of salmon skin and elmbark fibres respectively.[9]

    The eyeless bone needle or *awl* was the ordinary sewing implement of the Eyak. The Eskimo, with the exception [425] of the Polar group, have sewing needles with eyes, and eyed needles have also been found archaeologically on pre-Columbian sites in the Pacific regions from British Columbia to the Pueblo area.[10] Needles without eyes were the only ones known to the Polar Eskimo and the Aleut.[11] Awls have a wide distribution in North America, although it is of course a impossible to decide the purpose of archaeological specimens. The Chugach use them for punching holes in heavy skin. There is definite evidence of their use as sewing implements from the Northwest Coast,[12] the Mackenzie area,[13] and the Plateau area;[14] however, in the latter region needles with eyes also occur.[15] We also have both types from the Stone Age

---

[1] KRAUSE 1885, 201.

[2] NELSON 1899, 110. MURDOCH 1892, 301f.

[3] Field notes. GODDARD 1924, 63. NIBLACK 1890, 312. OSGOOD 1937a, 79.

[4] HATT 1914, 41f. BIRKET-SMITH 1929, II 114f.

[5] Tnaina (OSGOOD 1937a, 78). Kutchin (OSGOOD 1936, 67, 72). Satudene (OSGOOD 1933, 55). Yellowknife (PIKE 1892, 50). Chipewyan (BIRKET-SMITH 1930, 64).

[6] Tahltan (EMMONS 1911, 57). Lillooet (BOAS 1894, 458). Thompson (TEIT 1900, 187). Coeur d'Alene, Okanagan, Flathead (TEIT 1930, 46, 225, 328). Wishram (SPIER & SAPIR 1930, 189). Klamath (SPIER 1930, 173).

[7] KRAUSE 1885, 185, 198.

[8] KRACHENNINIKOW 1770, I 56. STELLER 1774, 321. TORI 1919, 166f.

[9] VON SCHRENCK 1881-95, 420. BATCHELOR 1901, 144.

[10] MATHIASSEN 1927, II 98. BIRKET-SMITH 1929, II 110 cf. 281 table A 82, 197 cf. 359f. table B 55. DE LAGUNA 1934, 198.

[11] PEARY 1910, 128. JOCHELSON 1925, pl. 24, 27f. DALL 1877, 79.

[12] Tlingit (NIBLACK 1890, 263). Klallam (GUNTHER 1927, 210).

[13] Tnaina (OSGOOD 1937a, 103). Kutchin (SCHMITTER 1912, 5. OSGOOD 1936, 70). Satusene (OSGOOD 1933, 58).

[14] Thompson (TEIT 1900, 186). Flathead (TEIT 1930, 328). Wishram (SPIER & SAPIR 1930, 188). Klamath (SPIER 1930, 173).

[15] BIRKET-SMITH 1929, II 197 cf. 359 table B 55.

of Japan,[1] and there is no doubt that the eyed needle is, on the whole, quite old — in Europe, for instance, it dates back to the Upper Palaeolithic — but only the future can show the relationship between the different types. At present it seems safe to connect the awl of the Eyak with those of the neighboring Indian tribes.

The only *stitch* about which we have any information from the Eyak is overcasting. This is a very simple technique which has a universal distribution both in North America and in North Asia as far as tailored skin clothing is found.[2] The compartment *sewing bag* of the Eyak is [426] not a true Eskimo type, although it has been introduced at Bering Strait.[3] On the other hand it seems to he quite common in Hie Horeal Woodlands, and it is also found on the northern Plateaus.[4] Similar bags are used by the Kurilian Ainu.[5] It may possibly have been diffused to a certain extent as a result of contact with the whites. There is some probability that *bags of bird's feet* were also used by the Eyak. This is a type common to the Eskimo and the Boreal Woodlands, whereas it does not seem to occur on the Northwest Coast; there is reason for considering it an old culture element.[6]

Washing in urine is typical of the peripheral Eskimo groups[7] — probably as a trait connected with the Thule culture — and the Northwest Coast Indians.[8] From these tribes the custom has spread, as it seems, to the Chukchi[9] and Lillooet[10] respectively. Washing in urine should be compared with urine tanning, which also occurs in the peripheral Eskimo regions and on the Northwest Coast. The distribution of the urine tub coincides of course, with that of the use of urine for household purposes. [427]

The *snow shovel* has formerly been discussed by the Danish author, who arrived at the conclusion that it is an old culture element belonging to the ice-hunting stage.[11]

Hunting and Fishing

A great part of the economic activities of the Eyak took place on the water, but the hunting on land was by no means neglected. Both in goat and bear hunting the *dog* was an indispensable

---

[1] MUNROE 1911, 132.

[2] HATT 1914, 43f. BIRKET-SMITH 1929, II 117 cf. 286f. table A 94, 200.

[3] NELSON 1899, 105.

[4] Carrier (MORICE 1905, 149). Thompson (TEIT 1900, 201). Nespelem and Sanpoil (RAY 1932, 44).

[5] TORII 1919, 166.

[6] BIRKET-SMITH 1929, II 58 cf. 238 table A 8, 139 cf. 304 table B 8.

[7] Aleut (COXE 1780, 150, 258). Kodiak (LISIANSKY 1814, 214). Bering Strait Eskimo (SEEMANN 1853, 62. ELLIOTT 1886, 387. JACOBSEN 1884, 160. NELSON 1899, 287). Point Barrow (MURDOCH 1892, 421. Mackenzie Eskimo (PETITOT 1887, 12). West Greenland (HANS EGEDE 1925, 369. BIRKET-SMITH 1924, 212). East Greenland (HOLM 1914, 34. GRAAH 1832, 122).

[8] Tlingit (KRAUSE 1885, 166). Kwakiutl (BOAS 1909, 456, BOAS 1921, 460. Chinook (New Light ... 1897, 819).

[9] SVERDRUP 1926, 199.

[10] TEIT 1900-08a, 221.

[11] BIRKET-SMITH 1929, II 112 cf. 283 table A 87, 199 cf. 360 table H 56. Add: Chugash (Field Notes). Tnaina (OSGOOD 1937a, 106). Kutchin (OSGOOD 1936, 71, 76). For former use among the Cook Inlet Eskimo see DE LAGUNA 1934, 200f.

help. While the dog's principal function among the Arctic Eskimo is that of a draught animal, it also plays no little role in the pursuit of bears and musk-oxen, and among the Central tribes it also scents the breathing holes of the seals in the ice.[1] The hunting dog is generally used on the Northwest Coast[2] and the Plateaus,[3] [428] in the Mackenzie area[4] and in Northeast Asia.[5] There are a few instances where it is stated that hunting dogs do not occur; e.g., this is true of the Chipewyan[6] and the Klallam.[7] It is also a remarkable fact that no traces of dog traction have been found in the Eskimo Birnirk culture sites at Point Barrow,[8] nor in the Old Bering Sea and Punuk sites on St. Lawrence Island, though dog bones were not uncommon in the St. Lawrence middens. The Old Bering Sea dogs were of a different type from the Punuk breed, or the dogs used by the modern Eskimo of that region for pulling sleds.[9] Either the ancient Eskimo used dogs for hunting only, or dog traction was so little developed that no characteristic trace buckles, etc., were used;[10] the dog traction of the Caribou Eskimo, for instance, would hardly leave any archaeological trace at all. Or dog traction, which dates from the ice-hunting culture elsewhere, may have been locally lost in Alaska in Old Bering Sea and Birnirk times, as it was, for religious reasons, in the Northern Woodlands.[11] In [429] any case. the hunting dog is an old and widespread

---

[1] Chugach (Fields Notes), Bering Strait Eskimo (NELSON 1899, 120 Point Barrow (MURDOCH 1892, 263). Copper Eskimo (STEFANSSON 1921, 420. HANBURY 1904, 150). Netsilik Eskimo (AMUNDSEN 1907, 265). KNUD RASMUSSEN 1931, 183, 157). Caribou Eskimo (BIRKET-SMITH 1929, I 112). Iglulik Eskimo (PARRY 1824, 519f. MATHIASSEN 1928, 42f, 60. Baffin Island (BOAS 1880, 475, 509. BILBY 1923. 90). Labrador (HAWKES 1916, 83. Polar Eskimo (KROEBER 1900, 270. STEENSBY 1910, 300ff). West Greenland (HANS EGEDE 1925, pl. p. 46). East Greenland (THALBITZER 1914, 403f. HOLM 1914, 52).

[2] Tlingit (KRAUSE 1885, 182. ERMAN 1870-71, II 316). Tsimshian (BOAS 1916, 400. Nootka (SPROAT cit. by GUNTHRT 1927, 215), Squawmish (HILL-TOUT 1900, 490, Twana, Chimakum (EELLS 1889, 619). Yurok (KROEBER 1925, 86). Hupa (GODDARD 1903, 21).

[3] Tahltan (EMMONS 1911, 54). Shuswap (BOAS 1891, 636. TEIT 1900-08b, 520). Lillooet (TEIT 1900-08a, 226. Thompson (TEIT 1900, 244f,). Coeur d'Alene, Okanagan, Flathead (TEIT 1930, 101, 109, 243, 344). Takelma (SAPIR 1907, 260), Klamath (SPIER 1930, 158). Shasta (DIXON 1907, 431. KROEBER 1925, 294). Shoshoni (LOWIE 1909, 185. LOWIE 1924, 216). Paiute (LOWIE 1924, 195, 216, KELLY 1932, 148, STEWARD 1933, 252).

[4] Tnaina (OSGOOD 1937a, 32f). Atna (ALLEN 1889, 264). Koyukon (PETROFF 1884, 160. Kutchin (SCHMITTER 1910, 3. OSGOOD 1936, 27,127 footnote). Nahane, Slave (JENNESS 1932, 398, 390). Satudene (OSGOOD 1933, 40).

[5] Chukchi (BOGORAS 1904-9, 114). Koryak (JOCHELSON 1908, 502ff, 513). Kamchadal (STELLER 1774, 139. DOBELL. 1830, I 100). Ainu (VON SIEBOLD 1881, 21. BATCHELOR 1901, 459).

[6] JENNESS 1932, 386, footnote 1. In corroboration it may be added that the Danish author obtained no information of hunting methods where dogs were employed among the Chipewyan at Churchill.

[7] GUNTHER 1927, 215.

[8] J.A. MASON 1930, 385.

[9] COLLINS 1937, 248f.

[10] COLLINS 1937, 338ff.

[11] BIRKET-SMITH 1939, II 169f. It is a characteristic feature of the cultural development of Northeast Asia and northwestern North America that we find two fundamentally different and, in a certain measure, antagonistic aspects of the dog: as an animal of use and, on the

culture clement in the North.

The *deadfall* of the Eyak was different from the ordinary Eskimo type built of stones; a device similar to that of the Eyak was, however, described from the Chugach, and it is also common both on the Northwest Coast,[1] in the Mackenzie area,[2] and the Plateau region.[3] It occurs also in northeastern Asia.[4] The ermine *trap with a tipping plank* has a certain resemblance to the Eskimo "tower traps" for foxes. These traps seem to be typical of the Thule culture,[5] but as far as our knowledge goes there is no record of them from other regions. The *spring-bow* is hardly of aboriginal origin. It does not occur elsewhere in North America at all, whereas it is a very typical North Asiatic device[6] that may have been introduced by the Russians in early colonial times. The *pitfall*, on the other hand, is probably an old element. We find it generally among the [430] Eskimo, and it is also widely known elsewhere.[7] The same applies to the *snare*.[8]

It has been emphasized on a previous occasion that at present it is impossible to give an exact picture of the pre-Columbian distribution of the *lance* with a fixed head in North America, i.e. because the development of horse culture on the plains almost certainly meant a considerable extension of its range. Still there can be little doubt that it is a very old type of weapon in the regions considered in this work.[9]

---

other side, as an animal connected with certain cults and mythological concepts (KOPPERS 1930, 369. cf. FLOR 1930, 65ff.).

[1] Tlingit (KRAUSE 1885, 181f.) Kwakiutl (BOAS 1809, 507ff.). Puget Sound (HAEBERLIN & GUNTHER 1930, 25).

[2] Tnaina (OSGOOD 1937a. 95ff.). Kutchin (JONES 1867, 322). Sekani (JENNESS 1937, 39). Satudene (OSGOOD 1933, 60). Beaver? (GODDARD 1916, 215). Chipewyan BIRKET-SMITH 1930, 60).

[3] Tahltan (EMMONS 1911, 75ff). Tsetsaut (BOAS 1895, 563). Carrier (HARMON 1903, 253). Thompson (TEIT 1900, 249). Coeur d'Alene, Okanagan? (TEIT 1920, 104, 246). Nez Percé (SPINDEN 1908, 214. Nespelem and Sanpoil (RAY 1932, 85). Wishram? (SPIER & SAPIR 1930, 181f.). Klamath (SPIER 1930, 159). Shoshoni (LOWIE 1924, 199). Paiute (STEWARD 1933, 254).

[4] Gilyak (von SCHRENCK 1881-95, 550.

[5] MATHIASSEN 1927, II 62f. BIRKET-SMITH 1929, II 25.

[6] Chuckchi, probably also of Russian origin (BOGORAS 1904-09, 140. Koryak? (Dobell 1830, I 186). Kamchadal (STELLER 1774, 124f). Gilyak (VON SCHRENCK 1881-95, 554ff.). Ainu (HITCHCOCK 1891, 469. BATCHEKOR 1901, 461ff). In the National Museum, Copenhagen, there is allso specimens from the following Siberian tribes: Gold, Orok, Tungus, Yakut, Ostyak, and Samoyed. (Recently reported from the Koyukon).

[7] BIRKET-SMITH 1929, II 68f. cf. 253 table A 34, 157f. cf. 326 table B 25. Add: Wishram (SPIER & SAPIR 1930, 180. Ute (LOWIE 1924, 199). Pauite (KELLY 1932, 81f). Tnaina (OSGOOD 1937a, 33). Kutchin (OSGOOD 1936, 33). The Chugach did not use the pit-fall (Field notes).

[8] BIRKET-SMITH 1929, II 69 cf. 254 table A 36, 159 cf. 327ff. table B 26. Add to the lists: Chugach (Field notes). Aleut (MERCK 1937, 119). Carrier (HARMON 1903, 253). Coeur d'Alene (TEIT 1930, 103f). Nespelem and Sanpoil (TEIT 1928, 82, 86). Molalu (SPIER 1930, 158). Shoshoni (LOWIE 1924, 199). Paiute (KELLY 1932, 88). Tnaina (OSGOOD 1937a, 33, 94, 98). Kutchin (OSGOOD 1936, 25ff., 3ff). Satudene (OSGOOD 1933, 59f).

[9] BIRKET-SMITH 1929, II 65 cf. 247f. table A 26; 152 cf. 319ff. table B 18. Add: Ch ugach (Field

The Eyak apparently had both simple and sinew-backed _bows_. The latter are typical of the Eskimo, hut have also found their way to such neighboring tribes as the Chukchi, Kutchin, Tnaina, Tlingit, and Nahane.[1] The Eyak simple bow is closely related to the Northwest Coast type with a narrow grip and flat wings, a form which is also sometimes used by the Pacific Eskimo. Both the hacked and the [431] simple types must be considered related to the Asiatic composite and the American sinew-lined bows; the characteristic distinction between grip and wings of the Northwest Coast bow is a typical feature of the composite bow.

The _primary arrow release_ we find in a few cases on the Northwest Coast,[2] whereas it is very common on the Plateaus.[3] It also occurs among some Palseo-Asiatic tribes,[4] but it should be borne in mind that information on arrow release is extremely meagre from Siberia as a whole. There can scarcely be any doubt that the primary release is a very ancient way of grasping the arrow,[5] a supposition corroborated by the extensive use in a backward culture area as that of the Plateaus. Unfortunalely we are not in the position of being able to give the detailed distribution of the _wrist guard_ used in shooting. It is, at least, found among the western Eskimo and the Chukchi; it is also characteristic of the Punuk stage, but was absent in the Old Bering Sea and Thule cultures.[6]

Arrow heads of bone with a single barb we find among the Eskimo where, as barbed heads generally, they belong [432] to the Old Bering Sea. Punuk, and Thule cultures.[7] Some of the single-barbed bone points from thy lower Fraser River region, described by HARLAN I. SMITH as

---

notes). Klallam (GUNTHERI 1927, 268). Tahltan (EMMONS 1911, 67f). Shuswap (BOAS 1891, 638). Lillooet (TEIT 1900-08a, 254). Coeur d'Alene, Okanagan, Flathead (TEIT 1930, 115, 255. 359). Middle Columbia Salish (TEIT 1928, 123). Klamath (SPIER 1930, 196). Paiute, modern (KELLY 1932, 187). Tnaina (OSGOOD 1937a, 31, 85f.) Kutchin (OSGOOD 1936, 68). Sekani (JENNESS 1937, 38). Tanana (DE L).

[1] BIRKET-SMITH 1929, II 61f. cf. 224 table A 20, 147f. cf. 314ff. table B 14. OSGOOD 1937a. 86f.

[2] Kwakiutl (BOAS 1909, 515). Bella Coola (Photo by HALAN I. SMITH, National Museum, Ottawa). According to our field notes the Chugach use a modified primary release, whereas the Mediterranean release is characteristic of other Eskimo tribes. Cf. BIRKET-SMITH 1929, II 240 table A 23.

[3] Tahltan (EMMONS 1911, 66). Tsetsaut (BOAS 1895, 563). Carrier (MORICE 1895, 58). Shuswap (TEIT 1900-08b, 520). Thompson (TEIT 1900, 241). Coeur d'Alene (TEIT 1930, 98). Nez Percé (SPINDEN 1908, 213). Kutenai (CHAMBERLAIN 1893, 564). Nespelem and Sanpoil (RAY 1932, 90). Klamath (SPIER 1930, 195). Paiute (LOWIE 1924, 245. KELLY 1932, 144. STEWARD 1933, 263). Paviotso (LOWIE 1924, 245).

[4] Koryak (JOCHELSON 1908, 560). Yukagir (JOCHEKSON 1926, 384). Ainu (HITCHCOCK 1891, 469. TORII 1919, 228. MONTANDON 1937, 94).

[5] Cf. WISSLER 1926, 30ff.

[6] BEECHEY 1931, II 309f. NELSON 1899, 161f. MURDOH 1892, 209f. BOGORAS 1904-09, 155. GEIST & RAINEY 1936, 221. COLLINS 1937, 325. The Copper Eskimo have a thumb guard (STEFANSSON 1914, 97 fig. 42).

[7] MATHIASSEN 1927, II 46ff. BIRKET-SMITH 1929, II 24, 62 cf. 245 table A 21. COLLINS 1937, 323f. Cf. also the following works of MATHIASSEN: 1930, 9. 37, 57; 1931, 81; 1933, 81: 1934, 98; 1936, 73. In Northeast Greenland as well as on the Aleutian Islands and among the Pacific Eskimo they seem to be lacking.

harpoon heads,[1] may, perhaps, be intended for arrows. It is evident that our information about this type is too fragmentary for safe conclusions. *Harpoon arrows* occur sporadically more or less all over the world, but in the regions with which we are concerned they center around the Northwest Coast.[2] It seems certain that a great number of small harpoon heads from archaeological finds belong to this kind of weapon.

Arrow feathering consisting of three radial feather vanes is common throughout the greater part of western and northern North America where it has probably replaced an earlier form consisting of two tangential feathers.[3] The three-feather type is found among the western and Central Eskimo tribes as far east as Southampton Island,[4] is known from the Mackenzie area,[5] the Northwest Coast,[6] and the [433] Plateaus.[7] It is also common, however, on the Plains and may have been introduced together with the composite bow, which is also of Asiatic origin. The cylindrical or somewhat flattened *wooden quiver* belongs to the northern coasts of both sides of the Pacific. It is used by the Pacific Eskimo and their Athapaskan neighbors,[8] some tribes of the Northwest Coast,[9] and the Gilyak and Ainu.[10]

Sea-mammal hunting is, of course, less important among the Eyak on account of their rather limited access to the sea than it is among many other tribes of the north. Nevertheless the role which the pursuit of seal and sea-otter played in their economic life is sufficient to assign them to a place among the typical sea hunters of the American Northwest Coast, the Sub-Arctic, and the more or less culturally related tribes of Northeast Asia. The open-sea hunting methods in these regions are less specialized than the ice hunting of the Arctic proper. We shall, therefore, discuss the only hunting method which has a more developed character, viz, the *drive* or surround by several hunters in common. This is the typical procedure on sea-otter and white whale hunts, but it is also used sometimes on ordinary sealing expeditions among the Pacific Eskimo and Aleut.[11] It is described from the Eskimo of Bering Strait, and occasionally, [434]

---

[1] SMITH 1903, 150 fig. 17a.

[2] Aleut (MASON 1902. 298). Chugach (Field notes). Kodiak (HOLMBERG 1856, 393f.). Bering Strait Eskimo (NELSON 1899, 157, 161. JACOBSEN 1884, 251 fig. 10). Tlingit (NIBLACK 1890. 287). Tsimshian (BOAS 1916, 50). Kwakiutl (BOAS 1906, 513). Tnaina (OSGOOD 1927a, 88, 90). Peel River Kutchin (OSGOOD 1936, 68). Thompson (TEIT 1900, 243). Koryak (JOCHELSON 1908, 559).

[3] BIRKET-SMITH 1929, II 63, 149.

[4] BIRKET-SMITH 1929, II 245f. table A 22.

[5] Tnaina (OSGOOD 1937a, 88ff.). Kutchin (OSGOOD 1936, 68, 83). Sekani (JENNESS 1937, 37). Satudene (OSGOOD 1933, 62). Chipewyan (BIRKET-SMITH 1930, 19f.).

[6] Bella Coola (MASON 1894, pl. II fig. 6). Yurok (KROEBER 1925, 90). Hupa (MASON 1889, 227).

[7] CARRIER (MORICE 1895, 56). Thompson (TEIT 1900, 240. Coeur d'Alene (TEIT 1930, 99). Nez Percé (SPINDEN 1908, 213). Sanpoil and Nespelem (RAY 1932, 89). Wishram (SPIER & SAPIR 1930, 199). Paviotso (LOWIE 1924. 245). Paiute (KELLY 1932, 144. STEWARD 1933, 200).

[8] Chugach (Field notes). Kodiak (National Museum. Copenhagen, no. I b 174). Tnaina (OSGOOD 1927a, 89).

[9] Tsimshian (BOAS 1916, 50). Kwakiutl (BOAS 1909, 514f).

[10] von SCHRENCK 1881-05, 560. von SIEBOLD 1881, 20. HITCHCOCK 1891, 469. TORII 1919, 226. MANTANDON 1937, 94f.

[11] Saikof 1782, 285. coxe 1780, 77. ERMAN 1870-01, III 173. LISIANSKY 1814, 205. HOLMBERG 1856, 392f. petroff 1884, 142f. ELLIOTT 1886, 140f.

though less frequently, it was seen among the Eskimo of Baffin Island and West Greenland.[1] Returning to the Northwest Coast and adjacent regions we find it among the Tnaina, Tlingit, Kwakiutl, and Nootka;[2] probably it was common everywhere in this area, although descriptions are lacking. In Kamchatka the drives were combined with catching the seals in nets.[3]

The *barbed harpoon head* with a tang has a very wide distribution both in North America and North Asia.[4] Among the Pacific Eskimo it is more common than the toggle harpoon, whereas on the Northwest Coast a primitive form of toggle head is most often used; still barbed heads arc far from unknown. The distribution of *harpoon floats* is much more restricted. They occur on the Northwest Coast, among the Tnaina, and among the Eskimo groups hunting sea mammals in open water, i.e. the peripheral tribes. It is not certain whether the *throwing board* was known to the Eyak. For the distribution of this evidently very old culture element the reader is referred to the discussion by the Danish author.[5]

Stalking seals on the ice, the so-called *ũtoq* method of the Eskimo, is a widespread Eskimo hunting method.[6] Quite [435] probably it also appeared occasionally on the Northwest Coast when conditions were favorable, but to our knowledge is has not been mentioned from this area. At any rate is cannot, for obvious reasons, be of any importance there. On the other hand it is found in Northeast Asia, where the climate is much more severe than on the American side of the Pacific and is therefore better suited for ice-hunting methods.[7]

Sealing clubs are not much used among the Eskimo except the Pacific tribes; in the peripheral regions, however, large fish like the halibut are often stunned or killed with a simple club. The club is also found in the Thule culture and its Greenland derivations.[8] The Indians of

---

[1] SAGOSKIN 1848, 534f. PETROFF 1884, 128. BOAS 1888, 497. CRANZ 1770, 205. DALAGER 1915, 18.

[2] OSGOOD 1937a, 38. BOAS 1909, 504. BOAS 1921, 174ff, MEARES 1790, 260.

[3] STELLER 1774, 110.

[4] BIRKET-SMITH 1929, II 68f. cf. 250f. table A 30 156 cf. 323ff. table B 22. Additions: Aleut (WEYER 1930, 265 ff.). Cook Inlet (DE LAGUNA 1934, 189ff). Tnaina (OSGOOD 1937a, 83ff.). Sekani (JENNESS 1937, 38). Coeur d'Alene (TEIT 1930,105). Kamchatka (Schnell 1930, 265ff).

[5] BIRKET-SMITH 1929, II 65f. cf. 249 table A 28, 153ff. cf, 321 table B 20. Addition: Tnaina (OSGOOD 1937a, 86).

[6] Kodiak (HOLMBERG 1856, 396?). Bering Strait Eskimo (NELSON 1899, 129). Point Barrow (MURDOCH 1892, 270. Copper Eskimo (HANBURY 1904, 151. STEFANSSON 1914, 54). Netsilik Eskimo (AMUNDSEN 1907, 276f. KNUD RASMUSSEN 1931, 160). Caribou Eskimo (BIRKET-SMITH 1929, I 129f). Iglulik Eskimo (PARRY 1829, 170, 457. RAE 1850, 170. GILDER s.a., 170. BOAS 1907, 469. MATHIASSEN 1928, 45). Baffin Island (BOAS 1888, 483ff. HALL 1864, 27). Labrador (HUTTON 1912, 245). Polar Eskimo (Ross 1819, 131. KROEBER 1900, 270. MYLIUS-ERICHEN & MOLTKE 1906. 239. STEENSBY 1919, 299). West Greenland (HANS EGEDE 1925, 358. CRANZ 1770, 207. BIRKET-SMITH 1924, 326ff.). Angmagssalik (HOLM 1914, 51. THALBITZER 1914, 399f.).

[7] Chukchi (HOOPER 1853, 122f. BOGORAS 1904-09, 119). Kamchadal (STELLER 1774, 109). Gilyak (VON SCHRENCK 1881-95, 544f).

[8] Aleut (JOCHELSON 1925, 54). Chugach (Field notes). Kodiak (ELLIOTT 1886, 143. MERCK 1937, 129). Bering Strait Eskimo (NELSON 1899, 184). Copper Eskimo (STEFANSSON 1914, 51, 85). Iglulik Eskimo (RAE 1850, 170). West Greenland (BIRKET-SMITH 1924, 366). Northeast

the Northwest Coast and the Plateaus use clubs for sealing, fishing, and hunting.[1] We also find them among the Mackenzie [436] tribes[2] and in Northeast Asia.[3] Although the fishing club may be quite old, it docs not seem to belong to the earliest culture in the circumpolar region; the center of its distribution is likely to be within the salmon areas on both sides of the North Pacific.

Bird drives in the moulting season are described from certain Eskimo tribes,[4] the Yukagir and Russian settlers in Northeast Asia,[5] and the Northern Shoshoni and Paviotso.[6] It is not at all improbable that the bird drive occurs in many places where it has not been recorded, and that it is a fairly old method, comparable to the large game drives so well known in the circumpolar region.

The *leister* or multipronged fish-spear has been discussed on a previous occasion.[7] In North America the distribution covers the Eskimo area, the Northwest coast, the Plateaus, and in the east a small region comprising the Montagnais, Micmac, and Wahanaki. In Northeast Asia it is mentioned from all Palaeo-Asiatic tribes except the Yukagir. *Dipnets* occur in the peripheral parts of the [437] Eskimo area and among the neighboring Chukchi and Koryak,[8] on the Northwest Coast,[9] and the Plateaus.[1] They are also found among the Kutchin and Tnaina.[2] The Chipewyan

---

Greenland (RYDKR 1895, 321. THALBITZER 1909, 533. RICHTER 1934, fig. 82). Thule culture (MATHIASSEN 1927, II 83).

[1] Tlingit (DIXON 1789, 174. KRAUSE 1885,180). Haida (NIBLACK 1890, 282f,, 293 pl.xxvii f.). Tsimshian (BOAS 1916, 503). Kwakiutl (BOAS 1909, 478, 506). Makah (SWAN 1870, 41f.). Puget Sound (HAEBERLIN & GUNTHER 1930, 26). Klallam, Chimakum, Twana, (EELLS 1889, 634). Hupa (GODDARD 1903, 23 f.). Tahltan (EMMONS 1911, 88). Thompson (TEIT 1900, 248). Okanagan (TEIT 1930, 240). Nespelem and Sanpoil (RAY 1932, 80. Wishram (SPIER & SAPIR 1930, 178, 170 f.). Takelma (SPIER 1907, 260). Shasta (DIXON 1907, 430f).

[2] Tnaina (OSGOOD 1937a, 37). Kuchin (OSGOOD 1936, 69, 74). Nahane (JENNESSS 1932, 397). Slave (JENNESS 1932, 390). Chipewyan (BIRKET-SMITH 1930, 27).

[3] Koryak (JOCHELSON 1908, 529). Kamchadal (STELLER 1774, 109). Gilyak (VON SCHRENCK 1881-95, 545). Ainu (BATCHELOR 1901, 520.

[4] Bering Strait Eskimo (NELSON 1899, 135). Netsilik Eskimo (KNUD RASMUSSEN 1931, 187). Iglulik Eskimo (MATHIASSEN 1928, 66). Baffin Island (BOAS 1888, 513).

[5] JOCHELSON 1920, 379. MAYDELL 1893, 376ff.

[6] LOWIE 1909, 185. LOWIE 1924, 197.

[7] BIRKET-SMITH 1929, II 66 cf. 250 table A 29, 155 cf. 122f. table B 21. Additions: Aleut, for fish? (WEYER 1930, 268). Chugash (field notes). Coeur d'Alene, Okanagan, Flathead (TEIT 1930, 105, 246, 349). Middle Columbia Salish (TEIT 1928, 118). Nespelem and Sanpoil (RAY 1932, 60. Wishram (SPIER & SAPIR 1930, 178). Klamath (SAPIR 1930, 153). Paiute (KELLY 1932, 96. Kutchin (OSGOOD 1936, 68, 73, 84). Sekani (JENNESS 1937, 38). Satudene (OSGOOD 1933, 56).

[8] Aleut (JOCHELSON 1933, 52). Kodiak (COXE 1780, 117. LISIANSKY 1814, 206). Asiatic Eskimo (NELSON 1899, 187). Bering Strait Eskimo (NELSON 1899, 186f.). Iglulilk Eskimo (MATHIASSEN 1928, 65). Baffin Island (BOAS 1907, 27). Polar Eskimo (KROEBER 1900, 270. STEENSBY 1910, 283). West Greenland (BIRKET-SMITH 1924, 366f). Chukchi (BOGORAS 1904-09, 149). Koryak (JOCHELSON 1908, 531f.).

[9] Tlingit (KRAUSE 1885, 177. NIBLACK 1890, 192, 294). Haida (BANCROFT 1875. l62f.). Tsimshisn (BOAS 1916, 400). Kwakiutl (BOAS 1909, 466ff. BOAS 1921, 163ff. Bella Coola (JENNESS 1932, 340). Puget Sound (HAEBERLIN & GUNTHER 1930, 27). Klallam (GUNTHER

employ a racket-like implement for scooping up fish on to the platform where the fisherman stands,[3] but the affinity of this device to the dipnet is very doubtful. At first sight the conditions for the distribution of the latter appear to be geographical: the dipnet belongs principally to the area of the great salmon runs, or to the regions where innumerable shoals of smaller salmonides (*Thaleichlhys pacificus, Mallotus uillosus*) approach the coasts. Yet this cannot be the whole truth, for even though the number of trout ascending the rivers of the Central Eskimo area cannot compare with the multitude of salmon on the Pacific coast, there would still be ample opportunity of using a dipnet [438] if only it was known there. The dipnet seems to be an acquisition of the American Northwest, including the Thule stage of Eskimo culture. Though differing in details the peculiar basket type of the Eyak dipnet has some resemblance to the caplin scoop of the Angmagssalik Eskimo. The *fish-trap* has a distribution similar to the dip-net, i.e., it is absent among the present-day Central Eskimo tribes (with one exception, a specimen from the Copper Eskimo in the National Museum of Copenhagen, P 30:350),whereas it is known, from the peripheral tribes and Aleut,[4] the Northwest Coast,[5] the Plateau area,[6] a few Athapaskans,[7] and Northeast Asia.[8] I It is worth mentioning that the occurrence of the true fish-trap among the Mackenzie Athapaskans is doubtful, and this is paralleled by the absence of the

---

    1927, 200). Quinault (WILLOUGHBY 1889, 271f.). Washington (LEWIS 1906, 158). Yurok (KROEBER 1925, 85). Hupa (MASON 1889, 225. GODDARD 1903, 25).

[1] Tahltan (EMMONS 1911, 86). Carrier (MORICE 1905, 75). Shuswap (BOAS 1891, 635. DAWSON 1892, 15. TEIT 1900-08b, 524f.), Thompson (TEIT 1900, 249f.). Coeur d'Alene (TEIT 1930, 107). Nez Percé 1908, 210). Middle Columbia Salish (TEIT 1928, 118). Nespelem and Sanpoil (RAY 1932, 67). Washington and Oregon (GIBBS 1877, 195. LEWIS 1906, 183). Wallawalla (LEWIS & CLARKE 1814, 532). Wishram (SPIER & SAPIR 1930, 176). Klamath (SPIER 1930, 150. BARRETT 1907-10, 249f.). Shoshoni (LOWIE 1909, 187).

[2] MASON, 1924, 27. SCHMITTER 1910, 7. OSOOOD 1936, 35, 70, 74. WRANGELL 1839, 112. OSGOOD 1937a, 100f.

[3] BIRKET-SMITH 1930, 27.

[4] Aleut (MERCK 1937, 119). Bering Strait Eskimo (JACOBSEN 1884, 188. NELSON 1899, 125, 183). West Greenland (BIRKET-SMITH 1924, 362f.).

[5] Tlingit (NIBLACK 1890, 294. KRAUSE 1885, 17(i). Tsimshian (BOAS 1916, 400). Kwakiutl (BOAS 1909, 461ff. BOAS 1921, 159ff.). Nootka (COOK & KING 1785, 281. JEWITT 1896, 148). Twana, Klallam, Chimakum (EELLS 1889, 634). Chinook (LEWIS & CLARKE 1814, 431. FRANCHERE 1904, 249). Hupa (MASON 1889, 224).

[6] Tahltan (EMMONS 1911, 86). Carrier (MORICE 1905. 84ff. MORICE 1890, 129. WILKES 1844, 481. MACKENZIE 1801, 238f, 248. HARMON 1903, 252). Chilcotin (MACKENZIE 1801, 238f). Shuswap (DAWSON 1892, 16f. TEIT 1900-08b, 527ff.). Thompson (TEIT 1900, 254). Coeur d'Alene, Okanagan, Flathead (TEIT 1930, 106, 247, 349). Kutenai (CHAMBERLAIN 1893, 565). Middle Columbia Salish (TEIT 1928, 118). Nespelem and Sanpoil (RAY 1932, 61ff). Wishram (SPIER & SAPIR 1930, 177). Klamath (SPIER 1930, 152). Shoshoni (LEWIS & CLARKE 1814, 289. LOWIE 1909, 187). Paiute (KELLY 1932, 95f. STEWARD 1933, 251.

[7] Tnaina (OSGOOD 1937a, 28, 99f.). Tena (Field notes of American author). Koyukon (WHYMER 1868, 170. Kutchin (RICHAHDSON 1851, I 390. JONES 1867, 323. OSGOOD 23f., 33). The Sekani have not till recently learnt the use of fish traps from the Carrier (JENNESS 1937, 42).

[8] Chukchi (BOGORAS 1904-09, 148ff. WHANGELL 1839, II 225). Koryak (JOCHELSON 1908, 529f.). Yukagir (JOCHELSON 1926, 373). Ainu (BATCHELOR 1901, 521).

dipnet in this area.

The description of the Eyak _halibut hook_ is too vague [439] to permit of any close comparison with other types, but it seems to have been the ordinary compound form with a curved or angular shank and a straight point. Halibut hooks fashioned according to the same principle were, however, in general use on the Northwest Coast[1] (the northern and southern types differed in details) and were also used by the peripheral Eskimo tribes.[2] The neighboring Tnaina had a similar halibut hook.[3] Owing to the characteristic distribution of this type the Danish author has ascribed it to the Thule culture and considers it, therefore, to be of later origin than the simple gorge. On the other hand the American author found it in the earliest period of the Kachemak Bay culture.[4] So far, however, we have no means of solving the important question of the relationship of the Thnie stage to the cultural development of the Pacific Eskimo, and the relative chronologies of these cultural manifestations. At present we can therefore do no more than point out the distribution of the same general type of compound fish-hook along the Northwest Coast and the Polar Sea as far east as Greenland. The _hook for catching cod_, with the shank tied to the barb at an oblique angle, is different from the codfish jigs of the eastern Eskimo, but may have resembled certain V-shaped hooks from the Alaskan Eskimo and Koryak.[5] osgood figures a similar implement for catching [440] halibut from the Tnaina,[6] and it is also common on the Northwest Coast, from where, in fact, it may have been introduced among the Eskimo.

The _digging stick_ is no true Eskimo implement, even though it is used by the Chugach for digging clams, and is also mentioned from Labrador.[7] It might be imagined that the reason was purely geographical, but this becomes doubtful when we consider that the Eskimo of Bering Strait, as well as the Aleut, Chukchi and Koryak, include a fair amount, of roots and bulbs in their diet and employ a sort of mattock for digging,[8] and similar instruments are used by the eastern Eskimo for digging turf. etc. On the other hand the digging stick is found everywhere on the Northwest Coast[9] and in the Plaleau area.[10] The characteristic handles of the type within thy

---

[1] Tlingit (DIXON 1789, 174. KRAUSE 1885, 179. NIBLACK 1890, 290f.). Haida NIBLACK 1890, 290f. MACKENZIE 1892, 56). Tsimshiiin (BOAS 1916, 50). Kwakiutl (BOAS 1909, 470ff.). Nootka (VAVCOUVER 1798, II 275). Makah (SWAN 1870. 23, 40. Klallam (EELLS 1889, 634. GUNTHER 1927, 202). Nisqually (WILKES 1844, 445). Twana, Chimakum (EELLS 1889, 634).

[2] BIRKET-SMITH 1929, II 251f. table A 31. It has now been proved that fish hooks formerly occurred at Angmagssalik, whereas they were unknown there in modern times (MATHIASSEN 1933, 83 f.).

[3] OSGOOD 1937a, 101.

[4] DE LAGUNA 1934, 196.

[5] BIRKET-SMITH 1929, II 67f. cf. 251f. table A 31.

[6] OSGOOD 1937a, 101 fig. 27.

[7] HAWKES 1916, 34.

[8] NELSON 1899, 75. JOCHELSON 1925, pl. 26 fig. 1. BOGORAS 1904-09, 198. JOCHELSON 1907. 577. STELLAR (1774, 90 says that the Kamchadal use to excavate mouse-holes "mit einem Instrument von Rennthier-Hörnern gemacht," but does not give a description of it.

[9] Tsimshian (BOAS 1916. 404). Kwakiutl (BOAS 1909, 341f. BOAS 1921, 146ff). Seechelt (HILL-TOUT 1904a, 30). Klallam (Gunther 1927, 196). Chinook (LEWIS & CLARKE 1814, 433. BANCROFT 1875, 236). Hupa (GODDARD 1903, 10).

[10] Tahltan (EMMONS 1911, 86). Carrier (MORICE 1905. 84ff. MORICE 1890, 129. WILKES 1844,

latter region often occur archaeologically.[1] In the Mackenzie area the digging stick seems to be unknown. [441]

Preparation of Food

The ordinary way of boiling meat and fish was in a spruce-root basket by means of hot stones. _Stone boiling_ has a wide distribution in North America. Of course it is not used by the Eskimo, who employ soapstone pots or, in some cases, pots of poorly baked clay. Still it was known to the Chugach and is also mentioned from the Aleut.[2] On the Northwest Coast stone boiling was in general use.[3] The same is true of the Plateau[4] and the Mackenzie areas.[5] While the Chukchi and Koryak have the same method of cooking as the Eskimo, stone boiling is traditional among the Yukagir and was formerly also used by the Kamchadal.[6] Among the Gilyak and Ainu the ancient cooking vessels have been replaced by Japanese or Chinese iron kettles [442] long ago; as, however, the aboriginal pots were almost certainly made of coarse earthenware, stone boiling is improbable here even in prehistoric times.

FRIEDERICI has suggested a connection between this method and another widely known way of preparing the food, also employed by the Eyak, viz. cooking in a pit oven. The pit oven occurs over large areas in Australia and Oceania, in South America, Africa, and even in Europe,

---

481. MACKENZIE 1801, 238f, 248. HARMON 1903, 252). Chilcotin (MACKENZIE 1801, 238f). Shuswap (DAWSON 1892, 16f. TEIT 1900-08b, 527ff.). Thompson (TEIT 1900, 254). Coeur d'Alene, Okanagan, Flathead (TEIT 1930, 106, 247, 349). Kutenai (CHAMBERLAIN 1893, 565). Middle Columbia Salish (TEIT 1928, 118). Nespelem and Sanpoil (RAY 1932, 61ff). Wishram (SPIER & SAPIR 1930, 177). Klamath (SPIER 1930, 152). Shoshoni (LEWIS & CLARKE 1814, 289. LOWIE 1909, 187). Paiute (KELLY 1932, 95f. STEWARD 1933, 251.

[1] SMITH 1900, 411. SMITH 1910, 35.

[2] STELLER in GOLDER 1925, II 44. ERMAN 1870-71, III 155.

[3] Tlingit (KRAUSE 1885, 128. DIXON 1789, 175, PORTLOCK 1789, 293 f. LA PÉROUSE 1797, 198. MALASPINA 1849, 288. NIBLACK 1890, 278). Tsimshian (BOAS 1916, 49, 405). Kwakiutl (JACOBSEN 1884, 58. BOAS 1909, 407. BOAS 1921, 442, 545 f.). Nootka (JACOBSEN 1884, 110. JEWITT 1896, 108). Makah (SWAN 1870, 25). Seechelt (cf. HILL-TOUT 1904 a, 33). Puget Sound (HAEBERLIN & GUNTHER 1930, 23). Washington (LEWIS 1906, 158). Twana, Chimaknm, Klallam (EELLS 1889, 622). Klallam (GUNTHER 1927, 209). Chinook (LEWIS & CLARKE 1814, 432. FRANCHERE 1904, 238f. BANCROFT 1875, 234). Tillamook (BOAS 1923, 3. LEWIS & CLARKE 1814, 422).

[4] Tahltan (EMMONS 1911, 62. CALLBREATH 1889, 197). Carrier (MORICE 1890, 136). Chilcotin (MACKENZIE 1801, 37. FARRAND 1899, 647). Shuswap (BOAS 1891, 637). Thompson (TEIT 1900, 235 f.). Coenr d'Alene, Okanagan, Flathead (TEIT 1930, 64, 229, 333). Plateaus (LEWIS 1906, 183). Nespclem and Sanpoil (RAY 1932, 106). Wishram (SPIER & SAPIR 1930, 185). Klamath (SPIER 1930, 162). Shasta (DIXON 1907, 426). Sokulk (LEWIS & CLARKE 1814, 353). Shoshoni (LOWIE 1909, 188). Paviotso (LOWIE 1924, 233). Paiute (KELLY 1932, 91).

[5] Tnaina (OSGOOD 1937a, 45). Kutchin (JONES 1867, 321f. MASON 1924, 43. OSGOOD 1936, 29f. 34). Nahane (JENNESS 1932, 398). Sekani (JENNESS 1937, 35). Hare (JENNESS 1932, 395). Dogrib and Slave (MACKENZIE 1801, 37). Satudene (OSGOOD 1933, 39). Chipewyan (HEARNE 1795, 316).

[6] JOCHELSON 1926, 415 f. KRACHENINNIKOW 1770, I 44.

as well as in North America. Here it is widespread also outside the regions with which we are concerned, e.g. in the Gulf area, California, and the Southwest.[1] The northern limit of the method seems to be the Aleut, Tnaina, and Kutchin,[2] but it is unknown both to the Eskimo except the Chugach, and to the tribes of the Mackenzie drainage. The center of distribution in the north is the Northwest Coast[3] and the Plateaus.[4]

Roasting on a *spit* is likewise unknown to the Eskimo in general. The Danish author has a few times seen the Caribou Eskimo roast a piece of meat, e.g. a caribou shoulder-blade, by placing it in front of the fire, but never on a spit. According to NELSON, however, the Eskimo of [443] Bering Strait often roast their food over open fires, which probably implies the use of a spit,[5] and STEFANSSON actually saw the Mackenzie Eskimo "roast their fish, stuck vertically near the fire on sticks run through their mouths."[6] The Chugach also roasted meat on a spit or on a flat stone previously heated. It does not seem improbable that roast ing on spits is an Indian method of cooking introduced among the western Eskimo. It is common on the Northwest Coast,[7] in the Plateau[8] and Mackenzie areas,[9] and in Northeast Asia it is employed by the Yukagir, Kamchadal, and Ainu, whereas the Gilyak have a taboo against roasting.[10]

The Eyak used to preserve meat and fish both by *drying* and *smoking*. It is very difficult to draw a sharp line between these methods, because often in the damp air of the Northwest Coast drying was assisted by means of a fire, and therefore smoking resulted more or less unintentionally. It is with all due reservation, therefore, that the following remarks are ventured.

---

[1] On the pit oven in general cf. HABERLANDT 1913, FRIEDERICI 1914.

[2] ERMAN 1870-71, III 153 f. SCHMITTER 1910,9. OSGOOD 1937a, 43.

[3] Tlingit (ERMAN 1870-71, III 153 f). Tsimshian (Boas 1916, 45, 405). Kwakiuti (BOAS 1909, 408). Bella Bella (JACOBSEN 1884, 24). Nootka (JEWITT 1896, 108f.). Makah (SWAN 1870, 25). Puget Sound (HAEBERLIN & GUNTHER 1930, 23). Klallam (GUNTHER 1927, 209). Washington and Oregon (LEWIS 1906, 158. GIBBS 1877, 194). Chinook (KANE 1863, 140.) Tillamook (Boas 1923, 3).

[4] Carrier, Chilcotin (MORICE 1890, 135. MORICE 1905, 116). Shuswap (BOAS 1891, 637. DAWSON 1892, 9. TEIT 1900-08b, 516). Thompson (TEIT 1900, 236). Coeur d'Alene, Okanagan (TEIT 1930, 92, 240). Nez Percé (SPINDEN 1908, 199, 201 f.). Nespelem and Sanpoil (RAY 1932, 106). Plateaus (LEWIS 1906, 183). Wishram (SPIER & SAPIR 1930, 184f.). Takelma (SAPIR 1907, 258). Klamath (SPIER 1930, 160). Shoshoni (LOWIE 1909, 188). Paiute (KELLY 1932, 91).

[5] NELSON 1899, 267.

[6] STEFANSSON 1914, 153.

[7] Tlingit (KRAUSE 1885, 155f. NIBLACK 1890, 278). Nootka (JEWITT 1896, 109). Puget Sound (HAEBERLIN & GUNTHER 1930, 21ff.). Twana, Klallam, Chimakum (EELLS 1889, 628). Klallam (GUNTHER 1927, 209). Quinault (WILLOUGHBY 1889, 269). Washington (LEWIS 1906, 158). Chinook (LEWIS & CLARKE 1814, 433). Hupa (GODDARD 1903, 23).

[8] Tahltan (EMMONS 1911, 62). Thompson (TEIT 1900, 236). Coeur d'Alene (TEIT 1930, 64, 94). Nespelem and Sanpoil (RAY 1932, 106). Takelma (SAPIR 1907, 260). Paiute (KELLY 1932, 92).

[9] Tnaina (OSGOOD 1937 a, 43 f.). Sekani (JENNESS 1937, 35). Satudene (OSGOOD 1933, 39). Chipewyan (BIRKET-SMITH 1930, 31).

[10] BOGORAS 1904, 194. JOCHELSON 1926, 416. HITCHCOOK 1891, 458. VON SCHRENCK 1881-95, 431.

Drying of meat and fish is common in all the areas under consideration here: the Eskimo,[1] [444] the Northwest Coast,[2] the Plateau,[3] and the Mackenzie area,[4] although everywhere except among the Eskimo smoking seems to occur at least just as frequently. Drying is also found in Northeast Asia.[5] Smoking is clearly intrusive among the Eskimo, and is never very frequently employed,[6] but in all other culture areas it is extremely common.[7] [445]

Clams were strung on spruce roots for drying. The _needle_ for this purpose is evidently related to the ordinary fish needle used by all the Eskimo tribes.[8] Similar implements are rarely mentioned from other tribes, who often draw the fish upon any willow or twig suited to the

---

[1] Aleut, Kodiak (LANGSDORFF 1812. 42. ERMAN 1870-71, III 152). Chugach (Field notes). Bering Strait Eskimo (NELSON 1899, 267). Point Barrow (STEFANSSON 1914, 278). MACKENZIE Eskimo (STEFANSSON 1914, 139). Copper Eskimo (RICHARDSON 1851, I 314. JENNESS 1922, 99f.). Netsilik Eskimo (KLUTSCHAK 1881, 120. KING 1836, II 10). Caribou Eskimo (BIRKET-SMITH 1929, I 144). Iglulik Eskimo (MATHIASSEN 1928, 204). Baffin Island (BOAS 1888, 577). Labrador Eskimo (HAWKES 1916, 33). West Greenland (BAFFIN 1881, 35. BIRKET-SMITH 1924, 389). East Greenland (THALBITZER 1914, 538).

[2] Tlingit (ERMAN 1870-71, III 152. ELLIOTT 1886, 55). Haida (BANCROFT 1875, 163). Kwakiutl (BOAS 1921, 227f.). Makah (SWAN 1870, 7). Klallam (GUNTHER 1927, 207f.). Hupa (MASON 1889, 225).

[3] Tahltan (EMMONS 1911, 70. Carrier, Chilcotin (MORICE 1905, 92. HARMON 1903, 171, 252). Shuswap (DAWSON 1892, 15. TEIT 1900-08b, 517). Lillooet (HILL-TOUT 1905, 135). Thompson (TEIT 1900, 234). Coeur d'Alene, Okanagan (TEIT 1930, 94, 240). Flathead (DE SMET 1859, 45). Nez Percé (SPINDEN 1908, 205). Kutenai (CHAMBERLAIN 1893, 565). Sanpoil and Nespelem (RAY 1932, 73 f.). Sokulk (LEWIS & CLARKE 1814, 352). Wishram (SPIER & SAPIR 1930, 178). Klamath (SPIER 1930, 155). Shasta (DIXON 1907, 427). Shoshoni (TOWNSEND 1905, 258). Ute (LOWIE 1924, 200). Paiute (KELLY 1932, 93. STEWARD 1933, 255).

[4] Atna (ALLEN 1889, 260). Kutchin (SCHMITTER 1910, 7. OSGOOD 1936, 29, 37). Sekani (JENNESS 1937, 35). Chipewyan (INGSTAD 1931, 194).

[5] Chugach (Field notes). Bering Strait Eskimo (JACORSEN 1884, 190). Mackenzie Eskimo (PETITOT 1876, xx. STEFANSSON 1914, 137 f.). Caribou Eskimo (BIRKET-SMITH 1929, I 144). Labrador Eskimo (TURNER 1894, 252).

[6] Chukchi (SAUER 1802, 253). Yukagir (JOCHELSON 1926, 416f.). Kamehadal (KRACHENINNIKOW 1770, 165, 69. STELLER 1774, 170. KENNAN 1871, 45, 107). Gilyak (VON SCHRENCK 1881-95, 426). Ainu (HITCHCOCK 1891, 457).

[7] Tlingit (NIBLACK 1890, 276, 279. ELLIOTT 1886, 56). Haida (BANCROFT 1875, 163). Nootka (MEARES 1790, 245. COOK & KING 1785, 280, 320). Makah (SWAN 1870, 7). Puget Sound (HAERERLIN & GUNTHER 1930, 20. Klallam (GUNTHER 1927, 207f.). Washington and Oregon (GIBBS 1877, 195). Tahltan (EMMONS 1911, 70. Carrier (MORICE 1890, 129). Lillooet (HILL-TOUT 1905, 135). Thompson (TEIT 1900, 234f.). Wishram (SPIER & SAPIR 1930, 182). Shasta (KROERER 1925, 294. DIXON 1907, 427). Surprise Valley Paiute (KELLY 1932, 93, but not Owens Valley Paiute, cf. STEWARD 1933, 255). Tnaina (OSGOOD 1937a, 42). Kutchin (MASON 1924, 43f.). Eastern Athapaskans in general (RICHARDSON 1851, II 16). Slave? (BACK 1836, 92). Chipewyun (BIRKET-SMITH 1930, 31).

[8] BIRKET-SMITH 1929, II 252 table A 33.

purpose.[1] The Songish[2] and Yukagir[3] use a needle for fish and meat. As previously emphasized by the Danish author, the occurrence of the fish needle in El Gran Chaco in South America, where so many other North American culture elements reappear, characterizes it as an old acquisition.

Fish buried in the ground to rot is a favorite dish among several tribes on both sides of Bering Sea. It is eaten by the Eskimo of this general region as far cast as the Mackenzie delta,[4] as well as by the Aleut.[5] The eastern Eskimo allow seal and walrus meat to rot, but do not treat fish in the same manner. On the northern parts of the Pacific coast the ordinary way of putting up fish for the winter is by drying, but burying in the ground is mentioned from the Tnaina and Nootka,[6] and on the Plateaus we know the same method from the Tahltan, Carrier, and Thompson Indians.[7] Among the Tena, the American author has seen salmon eggs buried to rot. It is also frequent among the Koryak and Kamchadal.[8] Farther west in Siberia the [446] Tungus, Yakut, and Samoyed often bury fish in the ground, but it is said that the perpetually frozen soil prevents it from putrefying. It is not unlikely that the method originally came from Asia across Bering Strait.

Another favorite recipe among several northern tribes consists of *berries or roots put up with the oil* extracted from seal blubber, fish, or fish roe. Dishes of this kind are common among the Eskimo except in the Central regions, where vegetable food is extremely scarce.[9] On the Northwest Coast this type of dish is found at least among the Tsimshian and Kwakiuti,[10] but no doubt also among other tribes. It also occurs among the Tnaina, Kutchin, Nespelem, and Sanpoil,[11] and m Asia among the Kamchadal and Gilyak.[12] It might be tempting to express the opinion that it belongs to the peripheral parts of the Eskimo region and to the salmon areas on both sides of the North Pacific, but on the other hand the gap in the distribution within the Eskimo area seems to be environmental in character, and this type of dish also bears a close resemblance to the mixture of berries and deer fat known from the Boreal Woodlands and the Plains. Therefore we cannot dismiss the view that the idea of mixing vegetable and fatty substances is really an old and widespread culture element, slightly adapted to local conditions. [447]

---

[1] E.g. Shuswap (TEIT 1900-08b, 532f.) and Chipewyan (BIRKET-SMITH 1930, 28).

[2] BOAS 1891, 567.

[3] JOCHELSON 1926, 417.

[4] ELLIOTT 1886, 381. NELSON 1899, 267. STEFANSSON 1914, 138.

[5] ERMAN 1870-71, III 252.

[6] OSGOOD 1937a, 42. JEWITT 1896, 151.

[7] EMMONS 1911, 85f. WIIKES 1844, 481. HARMON 1903, 280. Cf. TEIT 1900, 235.

[8] DOBELL 1830, I 120. KRACHENINNIKOW 1770, I 66.

[9] Kodiak Eskimo (MERCK 1937, 130. DAWYDOW 1816, 185). Chugach (Field notes). Bering Strait Eskimo (SI:I-:MANN 1853, 62. ELLIOTT 1886, 411. JACOBSEN 1884, 279). Mackenzie Eskimo (PETITOT 1887, 239). Iglulik Eskimo (MATHIASSEN 1928, 207). Labrador Eskimo (HAWKES 1916, 35). West Greenland (HANS EGEDE 1925, 372. CHANZ 1770, 190. East Greenland (GRAAH 1832, 124. HOLM 1914, 61. THALBITZER 1914, 504, 540 f).

[10] BOAS 1916, 406. BOAS 1921, 291.

[11] OSGOOD) 1937 a, 42f. OSGOOD 1936, 30. RAY 1932, 107. The Thompson Indians mix berries and deer fat (TEIT 1900, 236). Tena (DE L.).

[12] STELLER 1774, 94, 100. VON SCHRENCK 1881-95, 439.

Social Culture

Social Organization

There is every reason for believing that the exogamic, matrilineal *moieties* of the Eyak were introduced at a fairly recent date. This impression is sustained by the facts that neither moieties nor potlatches are mentioned in the myths. From where the importation took place seems equally clear, for there can be no doubt that the idea of moieties was borrowed from the Tlingit. This applies both to the subgroups of the Wolf and Bark House People where there is a direct tradition to this effect, as well as to the two main groups, the Ravens and the Eagles. Among the Tlingit the same moieties occur, although the Eagles are called Wolves by the southern Tlingit.[1] The moieties of the Haida are also identified with Eagle and Raven, and among the four exogamic divisions of the Tsimshian proper and the Kitksan two are called by the same names, the other two being Wolf and Bear (or Killerwhale), whereas the Nass River Tsimshian have only Raven and Wolf like the southern Tlingit.[2] BOAS has shown how this moiety system can be traced, with ever decreasing vestiges, among [448] the Bella Bella and Kwakiutl, till finally it has disappeared entirely among the Nootka and Coast Salish.[3]

Among the Athapaskan tribes in the vicinity of the Eyak we find moiety systems also among the Tahltan, Tsetsaut, and Tnaina.[4] With the first two peoples the moiety designations are identical with those of the Northwest Coast, whereas the Tnaina divisions have no names. The previous existence of "clans" is also reported from the upper Tena, but they have now entirely disappeared, and nothing is known of their original character.[5] The tripartite system of the Kutchin is probably an aberrant form of the ordinary dual organization; we agree with OLSON in his view that there is no support for BOAS' belief that the triple grouping is the older.[6] In the Plateau and Mackenzie areas a sib system reappears among the Carrier, Chilcotin, and western Nahane,[7] and it has been partly copied by the Sekani and by certain Thompson and Shuswap groups.[8] A dual organization has also been suspected among the Alaska Eskimo. NELSON speaks of "totem groups" within the Bering Sea tribes, and OLSON includes them in his survey of American sib systems.[9] KNUD RASMUSSEN has shown, however, that the so-called "totem marks"

---

[1] KRAUSE 1885, 112ff. SWANTON 1908, 398. OLSON 1933, 363.

[2] SWANTON 1905, 62. BOAS 1890, 805, 819ff. BOAS 1916, 411ff. OLSON 1933, 363. According to verbal information from Dr. VIOLA GARFIELD, Seattle, all the Tsimshian groups have four phratries.

[3] BOAS 1924, 325ff. Cf. BOAS 1892, 409ff. BOAS 1897, 328ff.

[4] EMMONS 1911, 13f. CALLBREATH 1889, 197. BOAS 1895, 565. WRANGELL 1839, 104. OSGOOD 1937a, 128ff.

[5] JETTÉ 1907, 412f.

[6] OLSON 1933, 365. Cf. HARDISTY 1867, 315. JONES 1867, 326. KIRBY 1865, 418. OSGOOD 1936, 107, 122. 128. A similar system was noted by the American author among the Tena from Tanana River to Koyukuk, inclusive.

[7] MORICE 1890, 118f., 121. MORICE 1905, 203f.

[8] JENNESS 1937, 47ff. TEIT 1900, 290. OLSON 1933, 363.

[9] NELSON 1899. 322ff. OLSON 1933, map cf. p. 398.

are nothing but ownership marks, although they gradually attain something of the [449] character of an amulet through their descent from generation to generation.[1] Even though people with the same amulet may not marry, this can scarcely be called totemism, and certainly not sib organization. Moreover we were unable to find the slightest trace of a dual system among the Chugach Eskimo, the immediate neighbors of the Eyak.

It is evident from this rapid survey that the moiety organization has its center on the Northwest Coast with which we ought, perhaps, to include the adjacent parts of the Plateaus. There is evidence that this type of social organization has been spreading towards the northwest, the east, and the south. On the other hand this should not be taken as a proof that it originated on the Northwest Coast. DAVIDSON has proved that family hunting territories existed in this area prior to the moiety system,[2] and OLSON has pointed out sufficient specific parallels between the various American unilateral institutions to warrant the supposition of their common origin.[3] Old World connections are extremely probable and may belong to the wave of circum-Pacific matrilineal elements which evidently found their way across Bering Sea at a fairly remote time.[4] This problem is too comprehensive to be discussed here in detail, but one particular should not be passed over in silence: the fact that the Northwestern moieties are, at present, most prominent among the Nadene does not permit the conclusion that they were the original bearers of the dual [450] system on North American soil. There is reason for believing that it was not aboriginal among the Tlingit (and Haida?), and that it was not borrowed by the Eyak until a very late date. Some of the Athapaskans, such as the Sekani, have acquired it so recently that it had only just become established when it was abandoned again owing to contact with the whites, and the Mackenzie tribes farther east, e.g. the Chipewyan, do not know it at all. There is not the slightest trace of exogamy among the Athapaskans of Oregon and northwestern California. In the Southwest moieties and clans occur among the Navaho, the western Apache have clans but no moieties, and the eastern Apache know neither. Altogether this goes to show that the dual organization does not belong to a single stork, Nadene or other, but must have spread to a great extent independently of linguistic classifications.

The elaborate Northwest Coast system of family crests and nobility is unknown to the Eyak, among whom the only social classes occupying particular positions were the chiefs and slaves. *Chieftainship* was hereditary, but very little actual power was connected with the office. We find hereditary chiefs also on the Northwest Coast, but their position was rather that of heads of certain noble families than of political leaders with territorial authority.[5] Conditions more like those of the Eyak we find among the Pacific Eskimo[6] and the neighboring Athapaskans.[7] From the Plateau tribes it is very often stated that chieftainship was usually, but not always, inherited.[8]

---

[1] KNUD RASMUSSUN 1925-26, II 318. There is, of course, the possibility that we have here an incipient sib system. KROEBER (1923) suggests a similar origin for the Northwest Coast crest and moiety system.

[2] DAVIDSON 1928, 28ff.

[3] OLSON 1933. – We may disregard the earlier and more superficial attempts in this direction.

[4] Cf. GAHS 1929. KOPPERS 1930.

[5] Cf. MACLEOD 1924, 253f.

[6] Chugach (Field notes). Kodiak (HOLMBERG 1856, 358).

[7] Tnaina (OSGOOD 1637a {1937a}, 131). Atna (ALLEN 1889, 26i6; hereditary?). Kutchin (OSGOOD 1936, 108, 123).

[8] Tahltan (EMMONS 1911, 22). Shuswap (BOAS 1891, 636. TEIT 1900-08b, 569, 582). Lillooet

Slavery is very [451] widespread in northwestern North America and northeastern Asia.[1] We find it generally among the Pacific and Bering Strait Eskimo,[2] Aleut,[3] and nearby Atapaskans,[4] on the Northwest Coast well into California,[5] and on the Plateaus.[6] It is also common among the Palaeo-Asiatic tribes.[7] There can be no doubt that it was an old custom on both sides of Bering Sea, and was probably more developed among the semi-sedentary fisher population than among the Eskimo [452] and inland hunters or reindeer breeders, where it seems to be quite out of place in the general culture pattern. The war-like disposition of the tribes in question has, with some right, been described as the background of slavery,[8] but it cannot be the sole explanation, for it would not be difficult to enumerate many tribes of a similar spirit who do not own slaves. While their actual economic importance was not very great,[9] the desire for accumulating wealth, which is so pronounced on the Northwest Coast, cannot be left out of consideration in this context. *Slave offerings* at the burial of a distinguished person are common both among the Pacific Eskimo and Aleut,[10] and also occur in many parts of the Northwest Coast,[1] and in the Plateau

---

(TEIT 1900-08a, 254. HILL-TOUT 1905, 130). Okanagan, Flathead (TEIT 1930, 262, 376). Kutenai {Ktunaka} (CHAMBERLAIN 1893, 556). Nespelem and Sanpoil (RAY 1932, 110). Cf. also LEWIS 1906, 180).

[1] Cf. MACLEOD 1928, 638ff, 642 ff. EJUSDEM 1929. KÖNIG, 1928-29, 737f.

[2] Chugach (Field notes). Kodiak (HOLMBERG 1856, 358f. PETROFF 1884, 138). Bering Strait Eskimo (NELSON 1899, 328).

[3] VENIAMINOV by PETROFF 1884, 152. LOWE 1842, 476, 484.

[4] Tnaina (WRANGELL 1839, 110. Slavery among the Tnaina is, however, drilled by OSGOOD 1937a, 134). Peel River Kutchin, rare (OSGOOD 1936, 109. JONES 1871, 325).

[5] Tlingit (KOTZEBUE 1830, 29f. LUTKE 1835, I 195f. BELCHER 1843, 104. VON KITTLITZ 1858, I 216. ERMAN 1870-71, II 378ff. PETROFF 1884, 1165. KRAUSE 1885, 152. 161ff. ELLIOTT 1886, 64. NIBLACK 1890, 252). Haida (KRAUSE 1884, 311). Tsimshian (BOAS 1916, 499). Kwakiutl (BOAS 1897, 338). Nootka (MEARES 1790, 255. JEWITT 1896, 130f). Makah (SWAN 1870, 10). Squawmish (Cf. HILL-TOUT 1900, 475). Puget Sound (HAEBERLIN & GUNTHER 1930, 57ff). Klallam (GUNTHER 1927, 263ff). Songish (BOAS 1891, 570. HILL-TOUT 1907, 308). Washington and Oregon (GIBBS 1877, 188f. LEWIS 1906, 154f, 180). Chinook (FRANCHERE 1904, 324. BANCROFT 1875, 240). Tillamook (BOAS 1923, 4). Alsea (FARRAND 1901, 242). Yurok (KROEBER 1925, 32f.). Hupa (Cf. GODDARD 1913,15).

[6] Tahltan (EMMONS 1911, 29f.). Carrier, Chilcotin (JENNESS 1932, 362, 365. FARRAND 1899, 646). Shuswap (TEIT 1900-08b, 570, 582). Lillooet (TEIT 1900-08 a, 236). Thompson (TEIT 1900, 290). Okanagan, Flathead (TEIT 1930, 277, 380), Nez Percé (SPINDEN 1908, 245). Kutenai (CHAMBERLAIN 1893, 556). Wishram (SPIER & SAPIR 1930, 221f.). Takelma (SAPIR 1907, 267). Klamath (SPIER 1930, 39f.). Shasta (KROEBER 1925, 296).

[7] Chukchi (HOOPER 1853, 40. WRANGELL 1839a, II 226. BOGORAS 1904-09, 659ff.). Koryak (JOCHELSON 1905-08, 766). Yukagir (JOCHELSON 1926, 133). Kamchadal (KRACHENINNIKOW 1770, I 81. STELLER 1774, 235). Gilyak (VON SCHRENCK 1881-95, 646ff.). Ainu (BATCHELOR 1901, 16).

[8] KÖNIG 1928-29, 738.

[9] Cf. MACLEOD 1928.

[10] Aleut (SAIKOF 1782, 286. LOWE 1842, 478. VENIAMINOV cited by PETHOFF 1884, 154. MERCK 1937, 124). Kodiak (SCHELECHOF 1793a, 200. LISIANSKY 1814, 200). Aleut and Pacific Eskimo in general cf. WEYER 1932, 278 and literature cited there.

region.[2] They arc not reported from the Palaeo-Asiatic tribes west of Bering Strait, although it is stated that a Chukchi had the right of killing his slaves.[3] On the other hand slave offerings occurred in ancient China and Japan. The idea of slave sacrifice seems in most cases to be the same as that underlying the giving of grave-goods.[4]

We may here include a few remarks on *transvestites*, [453] even though they scarcely constituted a separate class in Eyak society. We know little about them except that the man who dressed as a woman and did woman's work was despised. It is, indeed, a very remarkable fact that, apart from such sporadic cases of congenital homosexualism as may occur everywhere and at all periods, we find transvestites and homosexual behaviour in certain well-defined areas. One of these may have been the region around the Gulf of Mexico and the Caribbean Sea — it is hard to be sure, for the accusation of unnatural vices was, like that of idolatry, the standard excuse for the slave raids of the Spaniards — and another area certainly included the regions on both sides of Bering Sea. While unknown to the Eskimo in general we find transvestism both within the Pacific group and the Aleut.[5] It is common all over the Northwest Coast,[6] but evidently of more exceptional occurrence among the Plateau tribes,[7] whereas another center of distribution is among the Palaeo-Asiatics.[8] Quite different from real transvestism, although perhaps often confused with it, are the cases of female attire worn by shamans, at least in Siberia. Here woman's dress is so far from being a token of abnormal disposition that it must rather be characterised as the opposite. As shown by STERNBERG sexual relations are often supposed to exist between the shaman and his [454] principal spirit helper, who in such cases belongs to the female sex; during the invocation, however, the shaman is not himself, but actually possessed by the spirit, and for this reason ' it is quite natural for him to dress like a woman.[9] We may, indeed, suspect that some alleged instances of homosexualism are nothing but misunderstood occurrences of this kind.

Next to observing the rules for moiety exogamy the principal condition for marriage was the acquirement of the bride by working for her parents during a period which ay have been of some considerable length, since it might start even before the bride's puberty seclusion, *bride service* is found in the North Pacific region, where it interrupts the circumpolar distribution of

---

[1] Tlingit (KOTZEBUE 1830, 30. LUTKE 1835, I 196. VON KITTLIZ 1858, I 216. KRAUSE 1885, 163. SWANTON 1908, 437). Bella Coola (BOAS 1892, 419). Makah (SWAN 1870, 10). Cowichan (BOAS 1894, 459), Songish (BOAS 1891,575). Puget Sound (LEWIS 1906, 171. HAEBERLIN & (GUNTHER 1930, 55). Chinook (BANCROFT 1875, 240. SPIER & SAPIR 1930, 223).

[2] Tahltan (EMMONS 1911, 30). Shuswap (TEIT 1900-08b, 592). Liliooet (TEIT 1900-08a, 270. Upper Thompson (TEIT 1900, 328). Wishram (SPIER & SAPIR 1930, 271).

[3] BOGORAS 1904-09, 660.

[4] Cf. BAHNSON 1882, 191ff.

[5] COXE 1780, 262. MERCK 1937, 122, 130. LISIANSKY 1814, 199. LANGSDORFF 1812, 43. HOLMBERG 1856, 400f. ERMAN 1870-71, III 154. Field notes. There seem to have been transvestites also among the Tena (Field notes of American author).

[6] BOAS 1891, 571.

[7] Thompson (TEIT 1900, 321). Flathead (TEIT 1930, 384). Wishram (SPIER & SAPIR 1930, 220f.). Klamath (SPIER 1930, 51ff.). Ute, Paviotso, Paiute (LOWIE 1924, 282f.).

[8] Chukchi (WRANGELL 1839, II 227. SVEBDRUP 1926, 236f.). Koryak (JOCHELSON 1905-08, 52ff.). Kamchadal (STELLER 1774, 289 note, 350 note.

[9] STERNBERG 1925.

bride purchase practised by the more remote Siberian and Eskimo tribes.[1] We find bride service among the Eskimo of Kuskokwim and the lower Yukon, the Pacific group and the Aleut,[2] Tnaina,[3] Tlingit,[4] and some Plateau tribes as far south as the Great Basin and the Southwest.[5] from the Northern Plateau it has spread eastwards as far as the Slave,[6,7] and it occurs, together with partial payment for the bride, in Oregon and northwestern California.[7] In Northeast Asia it is the prevailing custom among most Palæo-Asiatics.[8] [455]

Mother-in-law avoidance is found sporadically in all parts of the uncivilized world. In northwestern North America we find it, apart from the Eyak, among the Chugach, Tlingit. Haida,[9] Tahltan, Tsetsaut, Nahane,[10] and farther south among the Coeur d'Alene, Northern Shoshoni, and Owens Valley Paiute,[11] whereas it is expressly said to be lacking among other Paiute and Shoshoni groups as well as among the Ute and Paviotso.[12] The Beaver have a father-in-law taboo.[13] Mother-in-law avoidance also occurs among the Apache and Navaho, but nowhere is it more elaborately developed, or does it include a greater number of specific traits, than in California, a fact which led WISSLER to the view that this area should be considered the center of origin for this custom in North America.[14] Even though this theory may be extreme, the taboo seems to be principally a western trait in North America, for the few occurrences on the Plains among the Assiniboin, and in the Southeast among the Choctaw, Chickasaw, and Alabama, may presumably be explained by western influence, since the affinities of the Muskhogcan stock to the western parts of the continent are well-known. In Siberia avoidance is practised by the Yukagir both between fathers and their sons' wives, and between mothers and their sons-in-law,[15] [456] and although it is not expressly slated, the Gilyak probably do the same.[16] The Yakut maintain the taboo principally between women and their fathers-in-law, and a similar taboo occurs among the Buryat and Kalmuk, whereas, among the Ostyak, conditions

---

[1] KÖNIG 1928-29, 109.

[2] LISIANSKY 1814, 198. LOWE 1842, 476. NELSON 1899, 292. Field notes.

[3] WRANGELL 1839, 105. OSGOOD 1937a, 164.

[4] SWANTON 1908, 424.

[5] Carrier and others (MORICE 1890, 122). Shoshoni, Paviotso (LOWIE 1923, 150). Paiute (LOWIE 1924, 275). Also among the Apache and Navaho.

[6] Sekani (JENNESS 1937, 53f.). Nahane (JENNESS 1932, 398). Slave (JENNESS 1932, 391).

[7] Tillamook (BOAS 1923, 8). Yurok (KROEBER 1925, 29). Hupa (GODDARD 1903, 56).

[8] Chukchi (MAYDELL 1893, 196, 519. BOGORAS 1904-119, 579). Koryak (KRACHENINNIKOW 1770, I 217. KENNAN 1871, 135. MAYDELL 1893, 519. JOCHELSON 1905-08, 739ff). Yakagir (JOCHELSON 1926, 87). Kamchadal (KRACHENINNIKOW 1770, I 166. STELLER 1774, 343. DOBELL 1830, I 82). Ainu, mutual (BATCHELOR 1901, 230). The Gilyak practise bride purchase (VON SCHRENCK 1881-95, 632ff).

[9] Field notes. SWANTON 1905, 51.

[10] EMMONS 1911, 99. BOAS 1895. 565. JENNKSS 1932, 398.

[11] TEIT 1930, 172. SEWARD 1933, 302. LOWIE 1909, 211.

[12] KELLY 1932, 166. LOWIE 1926, 285.

[13] GODDARD 1916, 221f.

[14] WISSLER 1926, 103ff. Cf. KROEBER 1925, 840f.

[15] JOCHELSON 1926, 76.

[16] STERNBERG 1913, 325.

are more like those of the Yukagir.[1] The correct interpretation of these facts is far from clear, but this is of minor importance in this connection, since it is evident that the Eyak custom is most closely connected with that of the Northwest Coast. Avoidance between brothers and sisters has apparently a much more limited distribution than the mother-in-law taboo. It does not occur among the Chugach. It is, however, reported from the Tahltan, Yukagir, and Gilyak,[2] and there are also one or two instances in California.[3] Similar conditions prevail among the Ostyak.[4] Whether there is any direct relation between these occurrences, or whether they should merely be regarded as local elaborations of the general avoidance pattern, is difficult to decide.

A more or less obligatory *levirate* is practised by a great many peoples of North America and Northeast Asia. In a great many cases it is customary, but not strictly necessary. This, for instance, applies to the Eskimo.[5] It is probable that it also existed among the Aleut.[6] It is occasionally reported from the Northwest Coast[7] and very often [457] from the Plateaus as far south as the Navaho and Apache, and from California.[8] On the Asiatic side of Bering Strait it is mentioned from the Chukchi, Koryak, Yukagir, and Kamchadal.[9] According to STERNBERG group marriage is still flourishing among the Gilyak, involving full marital rights of a man in relation to his brother's wives.[10] It is not improbable that this right is only potential, depending in part upon the absence of the individual husband,[11] but at all events the close connection with the levirate is evident. In western Siberia the levirate crops up again among the Samoyed and Ostyak. The wide distribution, especially in areas with old-fashioned cultures like those of the Eskimo and the tribes of the Plateaus and California, gives the impression that the levirate is a custom of very considerable age, and it is also worth noticing that it occurs in Siberia among both the Yukagir and Samoyed who, in spite of reindeer nomadism, have preserved a great number of old culture traits.

Temporary *wife exchange* prevails among all the Eskimo from the Pacific coast to East

---

[1] CZAPLIKA 1914, 110f., 120, 127.

[2] EMMONS 1911, 105. JOCHELSON 1926, 75. STERNBERG 1913, 325.

[3] KROEBER 1925, 841.

[4] CZAPLICKA 1914, 128.

[5] BIRKET-SMITH 1927, 102ff.

[6] Cf. JOCHELSON 1933, 72.

[7] Tlingit (PETROFF 1884, 169. NIBLACK 1890, 254f, 367). Kwakiutl (BOAS 1921, 1077). Puget Sound (HAEBERLIN & GUNTHER 1930, 52). Klallam (GUNTHER 1927, 246). Songish (BOAS 1891, 576). Tillamook (BOAS 1923, 8). Yurok (KROEBER 1925, 31).

[8] Tsetsaut (BOAS 1895, 566). Shuswap (DAWSON 1892, 13. TEIT 1900-08b, 571, 591). Lillooet (HILL-TOUT 1905, 133. TEIT 1900-08a, 255). Thompson (TEIT 1900, 292. 325). Coeur d'Alene (TEIT 1930, 161). Nespelem and Sanpoil (RAY 1932, 144). Wishram (SPIER & SAPIR 1930, 220). Takelma (SAPIR 1907, 268). Klamath (SPIER 1930, 49 f.). Shasta (KROEBER 1925, 297). Shoshoni (LOWIE 1924, 278. LOWIE 1923, 150). Paviotso (LOWIE 1923, 150. LOWIE 1924, 276). Paiute (LOWIE 1924, 275. LOWIE 1923, 150. KELLY 1932, 166. STEWARD 1933, 290).

[9] BOGORAS 1904-09, 607ff. JOCHELSON 1905-08, 478ff. JOCHELSON 1926, 75f. STELLER 1774, 347.

[10] STERNBERG 1913, 323f.

[11] MAKSIMOV cited by CZAPLIKA 1914, 100.

Greenland[1] as well [458] as among the Aleut.[2] It is also reported from the Tnaina, Kiilchin, and Chipewyan.[3] It is doubtful whether the exchange of wives among the Nootka, as mentioned by MEARES,[4] had a temporary character, but on the other hand we are informed that the Shoshoni may freely dispose of their wives, apparently involving among other things, lending them to friends.[5] As shown by CZAPLICKA the so-called "group marriage" described by BOGORAS from the Chukchi should rather be considered an exchange of wives between bond-fellows.[6] The Eskimo believe that wife exchange creates especially close ties of friendship between the husbands, but actually such exchange rather results from than creates friendship. The Koryak, who arc famous for their jealousy, never practise this custom, but it is found again among the Kamchadal.[7] It is quite probable that our information about the distribution of this custom is far from, complete. It may, perhaps, be an old circum-polar trait. One thing seems fairly certain, however, viz, that it is foreign to the peoples with a clan or moiety division except in a case like that of the Eyak where the moiety organization is recent.

It is scarcely possible to draw a hard and fast line [459] between the general exchange of wives and the so-called *hospitality prostitution*, according to which an honored guest is offered the wife or daughter of his host for the night. As in the case of the Eyak, it is often doubtful, moreover, whether the latter custom is aboriginal, or is an outcome of the degenerating influence of white man's "civilization." While it can hardly be called a regular institution among the Eskimo, a foreigner will never have difficulty in finding a woman on his arrival at a village, and the East Greenland custom of "putting out the lamps" when guests are visiting the village is well known.[8] On the other hand regular hospitality prostitution is found among the Aleut, Yukagir, and Chukchi.[9] According to KRACHENINNIKOW it is also found among the Coast Koryak,[10] although JOCHELSON denies it except for those parts of the tribe that live in close contact with the Chukchi.[11] It is difficult, however, to distrust the statement of such an early and accurate observer as KRACHENINNIKOW. It may be added that the same custom is said to occur among the Tungus,[12] and MARCO POLO mentions it from Tibet. We have also reports from the Sioux,

---

[1] Bering Strait Eskimo (NELSON 1899, 292). Point Barrow (MURDOCH 1892, 413). Mackenzie Eskimo (PETITOT 1887, 104. STEFANSSSON 1914, 164). Copper Eskimo (JENNESS 1922, 233). Netsilik Eskimo (Ross 1835, 432. KNUD RASMUSSEN 1931, 195). Caribou Eskimo (BIRKET-SMITH 1929, I 195). Iglulik Eskimo (PARRY 1824, 528. MATHIASSEN 1928, 211). Baffin Island (KUMLIEN 1879, 16. BOAS 1888, 579). Labrador Eskimo (TURNER 1894, 189. HAWKES 1916, 115). Polar Eskimo (KROEBER 1900, 301. MYLIUS-ERICHSEN & MOLTKE 1906, 405). West Greenland (HANS EGEDE 1925, 373. BIRKET-SMITH 1924, 406). Angmagssalik Eskimo (HOLM 1914, 69). Cf. also KÖNIG 1927-28, 137ff.
[2] COXE 1780, 262. LANGSDORFF 1812, 43. LOWE 1842, 474.
[3] OSGOOD 1937a, 138. OSGOOD 1936, 144, HEARNE 1795, 129.
[4] MEARES 1790, 268.
[5] LOWIE 1909, 210.
[6] BOGORAS 1904-09, 602ff. CZAPLICKA 1914, 78f. Cf. SVERDRUP 1926, 134.
[7] STELLER 1774, 347.
[8] HOLM 1914, 69.
[9] COXE 1780, 172. LOWE 1842. 474. BOGORAS 1904-09, 607, JOCHELSON 1926, 62f.
[10] KRACHENINNIKOW 1770, I 196.
[11] JOCHELSON 1905-08, 756.
[12] CZAPLICKA 1914, 107.

Iroquois, Cree, and some tribes of the Southeast (Powhatan, Creek, Natchez), and from several tribes of South America. There is probably some sort of a distribution center near the coasts of Bering Sea, but we do not know whether there is any direct connection between this center and the occurrences in Central Asia on the one hand (which may include the Tungus who are of a [460] southern origin) and those of eastern North America on the other.

Broadly speaking, wife exchange is often a result of _partnership_ or bond-fellowship. It appears from the Eyak myths that the latter might be instituted both between members of the same and of different moieties, although we have no information as to whether it was of identical character in both cases. On the other hand the fact that it is mentioned in the myths may indicate that partnership is older than moiety organization. Among the Central Eskimo it is common for a man to have a friend with whom he exchanges gifts and who is his partner in singing contests. As a rule, however, they do not live in the same village and therefore do not hunt together.[1] The Eskimo of Bering Strait have a similar, though somewhat more elaborate custom,[2] and our field notes from the Chugach also refer to partnerships. They are likewise known from the Tnaina and Kutchin,[3] but their most developed form occurs among the tribes of Northeast Asia.[4] That they are not mentioned from the Chukchi may be accidental, and on the whole we cannot ignore the possibility that a custom like this, which is neither very conspicuous in itself, nor of a very extraordinary character, may have been overlooked in many cases, e.g. among the Athapaskans. It would be rash, therefore, to draw further conclusions from this scanty material. [461]

Justice.

It is a fundamental principle in Eyak society that the _hunting grounds_ are not individual properly, but are owned by the tribe as a whole. Roughly speaking, the same altitude towards territorial rights is found among all Eskimo. Only in a few cases do individual families claim certain places for setting seal and salmon nets, a circumstance which may be taken to confirm the assumption, also supported by other evidence, that nets were originally a non-Eskimo culture trait.[5] It is an interesting fact that sonic Indian tribes make a similar distinction between communal hunting grounds and private fishing places.[6] Hunting grounds are also considered _res_

---

[1] KNUD RASMUSSEN 1929, 231. KNUD RASMUSSEN 1931, 195. BIRKET-SMITH 1929, I 160. Cf. the Copper Eskimo custom that two men become "flipper associates" and give each other the hind flippers of every seal they catch (JENNESS 1923, 87).

[2] NELSON 1899, 309. KNUD RASMUSSEN 1925-26, II 365.

[3] OSGOOD 1937a, 138. OSGOOD 1936, 114, 124, 132.

[4] Koryak (JOCHELSON 1905-08, 764). Yakagir (JOCHELSON 1926, 127). Kamchadal (KRACHENINNIKOV 1770, I 160ff. STELLER 1774, 128ff.).

[5] BIRKET-SMITH 1936, 149. NELSON 1899, 307. The so-called family hunting territories of the Mackenzie Eskimo mentioned by RICHARDSON (1851, I 267, 351f.) may belong to the same category, if his statement is not — as seems more probable — simply due to a misunderstanding. At least this is almost certainly true of the "individually owned" caribou hunting territories of the Point Barrow Eskimo mentioned by MURDOCH (1892, 267). Cf. also KÖNIG 1928-29, 623f and WEYER 1932, 173ff.

[6] Klallam (GUNTHER 1927, 205). Lillooet (TEIT 1900-08a, 256). Thompson (TEIT 1900, 293). Nez Percé (SPINDEN 1908, 245).

nullius by a number of other tribes in the Mackenzie area,[1] on the Plateaus,[2] and the southern Northwest Coast,[35] whereas family hunting territories exist on the northern part of the coast. Evidence regarding land tenure among the Tnaina is insufficient.[4] Common hunting grounds are also reported from the Kamchadal and, possibly, the [462] Yukagir.[5] It seems that freedom in exploiting the hunting possibilities within the tribal boundaries should be considered an old feature in the social organization of the circumpolar region.

Obligatory *distribution of the spoils* of the chase is also a common Eskimo and Aleut trait; in some cases it is a real dividing-up of the game according to fixed rules, in other cases, e.g. when the smaller species of seal and caribou are concerned, it assumes the character of an issue of meat presents to the inhabitants of the village.[6] Similar customs prevail among a number of Indian tribes in the Mackenzie area,[7] on the Plateaus,[8] and are also mentioned from the Klallam[9] and the tribes of Northeast Asia.[10] It is remarkable that the geographic distribution of this semi-communistic attitude towards the food supply almost coincides with the lack of individual ownership as regards hunting grounds. If the appearance of this coincidence is not simply due to lack of complete evidence, then the sharing of game with one's fellow hunters is probably also an old, circumpolar culture element. [463]

The custom of *allotting the game to the hunter who inflicts the first wound*, disregarding the person who eventually brings it down, occurs in several places among the Eskimo.[11] The

---

[1] Sekani (JENNESS 1937, 44). Satudene (OSGOOD 1933, 41). Chipewyan (BIRKET-SMITH 1930, 69).

[2] Shuswap (TEIT 1900-08b, 572). Coeur d'Alene, Okanagan (TEIT 1930, 162, 277). Kutenai (CHAMBERLAIN 1893, 558). Klamath (SPIER 1930, 149). Washington and Oregon (GIBBS 1877, 186).

[3] Puget Sound (HAEBERLIN & GUNTHER 1930, 12).

[4] OSGOOD 1937a, 141f. The Tnaina of Kenai told the American author about hunting territories. A certain sandbar was claimed by one clan. When they found a member of another clan hunting seals there, they took away his baidarka and left him to be drowned by the tide.

[5] STELLER 1774, 357. JOCHELSON 1926, 123ff.

[6] KÖNIG 1928-29, 639. WEYER 1932, 176ff. Add: Aleut (VENIAMINOV cited by WRANGELL 1839, 183). Chugach (Field notes). Copper Eskimo (KNUD RASMUSSEN 1932, 105f.). Netsilik Eskimo (KNUD RASMUSSEN 1931, 147, 173).

[7] Tnaina (OSGOOD 1937a. 32). Ingalik JETTÉ 1907, 405f. Kutchin (HARDISTY 1872, 314. SCHMITTTER 1910, 6f.). Sekani (JENNESS 1937, 44f.). Yellowknife (PIKE 1892, 50). Satudene (OSGOOD 1933, 40). Chipewyan (BIRKET-SMITH 1930, 69. INGSTAD 1931, 188).

[8] Lillooet (TEIT 1900-08a, 256). Thompson (TEIT 1900, 294f.). Coeur d'Alene, Okanagan (TEIT 1930, 162, 277). Kutenai (CHAMBERLAIN 1893, 558, 564). Wishram (SPIER & SAPIR 1930, 175). Shasta (DIXON 1917, 432). Northern Shoshoni (LOWIE 1909, 185). Paiute (STEWARD 1933, 252).

[9] GUNTHER 1927, 204f.

[10] Chukchi (BOGORAS 1904-09, 631ff.). Koryak (JOCHELSON 1905-08, 769). Yukagir (JOCHELSON 1926, 124f.).

[11] Chugach, skins of animals other than sea-otter (Field notes). Copper Eskimo (JENNESS 1922, 90). Ciribou Eskimo (BIRKET-SMITH 1929, I 262). Iglulik Eskimo (MATHIASSEN 1928, 62). West Greenland (DALAGER 1915, 19). Angmagssalik Eskimo (THALBITZER 1914, 525).

Tlingit observe a similar rule.[1] Under these circumstances there is nothing strange in finding it also among the Eyak.

The most conspicuous trait in the administration of justice among the Eyak is *payment of a compensation* according to the size of the crime committed, not only as "weregild" in the case of murder, but also for minor and even accidental injuries. Outside Alaska this is entirely foreign to the Eskimo, to whom blood revenge is, practically speaking, a sacred duty. On the other hand it is a typical Northwest Coast trait, connected with the plutocratic organization of society in this area.[2] From there it has probably spread to those neighboring tribes who follow the same custom.[3] It is also practised by the Chukchi and Koryak,[4] but not by the Kamchadal, whereas it is found again among [464] the Gilyak, where it is a important duty of the clan to assist the members in the payment.[5]

Another, more informal way of adjusting personal grievances is to sing *derision songs* about one's opponent. This method of settling quarrels is well known from the Eskimo. KONIG has called attention to the important fact that it takes the form of a regular singing contest both in Greenland and on the Aleutian Islands.[6] The Central Eskimo, on the other hand, have recourse to boxing duels. However, less formalized derision songs also occur among the latter and among the Bering Strait Eskimo,[7] and we have corresponding information from the Chugach. On the other hand the evidence upon which KONIG postulates their occurrence in Kamchatka seems rather weak, for STELLER, whom he quotes, says only that the women used to compose satirical songs.[8] Evidently the Eyak custom is closely related to that of the Alaska Eskimo.

War

The small size of the tribe within historic times probably prevented the Eyak from fighting on a large scale; but the general ill-feeling towards the Eskimo, provoked by Eskimo raids for Eyak women, may nevertheless have resulted in a slate of permanent hostility between the two peoples. As bows and arrows have been discussed on an earlier occasion (p. 430 ff.) the inquiry will, in this place, be limited to the weapons of war proper. [465]

The use of *poisoned weapons* was very widespread in the western parts of North

---

[1] NIBLACK 1890, 300.

[2] Northern group in general (NIBLACK 1890, 241). Tlingit (KRAUSE 1885, 244). Puget Sound (HAEBERLIN & GUNTHER 1930, 59). Klallam (GUNTHER 1927, 266). Washington and Oregon (GIBBS 1877, 189f.). Yurok (KROEBER 1925, 28). Hupa (GODDARD 1903, 59).

[3] Tahltan (CALLBREATH 1889, 198). Lillooet (TEIT 1900-08a, 236). Wishram (SPIER & SAPIR 1930, 214f.). Takelma (SAPIR 1907, 270). Shasta (KROEBER 1925, 296). Tnaina (OSGOOD 1937a, 139). Kuchin (RICHARDSON 1851, I 387. OSGOOD 1936, 114, 134). Bering Strait Eskimo (DALL cited by KÖNIG 1925, 299f. KÖNIG Believes, but probably erroneously, that the Eskimo have adopted the idea of compensation from the Chukchi).

[4] BOGORAS 1904-09, 669ff. JOCHELSON 1908, 772f. Cf. KÖNIG 1928-29, 87.

[5] CZAPLICKA 1914, 46ff.

[6] KÖNIG 1925, 281ff.

[7] Bering Strait Eskimo (NELSON 1899, 347). Copper Eskimo (KNUD RASMUSSEN 1932, 144ff). Netsilik Eskimo (KNUD RASMUSSEN 1931, 323ff, 509ff). Caribou Eskimo (KNUD RASMUSSEN 1931), 73ff), Iglulik Eskimo (KNUD RASMUSSEN 1929, 231f).

[8] KÖNIG 1928-29, 93. Cf. STELLER 1774, 333.

America, but in most cases rattlesnake poison was employed. This was the case among many tribes of the Plateaus and the southern Northwest Coast,[1] and many tribes in the Southwest poison their arrows in the same way.[2] Plant poison is less common, but still far from being unknown; in some cases it is used in addition to animal poison, e.g. by the Thompson, Shoshoni, and Paiute. The Aleut prepared their poison from decayed corpses, as did the Chugach, but they also knew vegetable poison.[3] The Tnaina employed shaman's ashes.[4] Plant poison was also made by the Kamchadal and Ainu.[5]

The *war club* is common in northwestern North America, but it is hard to find exact parallels to the spiked club of the Eyak. The tribes of the Interior generally use a pick-axe made of an antler on which a single branch is left; the coast tribes use the characteristic "slave-killer," and farther south the equally well-known *meri*-like whale-bone or monolithic stone club. War picks with a single, spike-shaped stone head were also common among the Tlingit, Haida, and Tsimshian.[6] Spiked clubs like those of the Eyak seem to occur, however, among the Tnaina and Interior Salish. According to OSGOOD the former made clubs "from [466] a very hard species of knotted spruce found in the mountains. They cut out their club from a section two and one-half feet long and full of knots which they cut down so that the knots project like short spikes."[7] TEIT describes some Coeur d'Alene clubs as consisting of "a spike of elk or deer antler set crosswise in the end of a short wooden handle. Some were double-ended with two spikes of equal length, while others had a shorter back spike of antler, .sometimes of flaked stone."[8] They were also known to the Thompson, and "straight wooden clubs set with from one to eight spikes of stone or antler" were in use among the Okanagan.[9] The "spike clubs" of the Middle Columbia Salish were probably similar to these.[10] The Shuswap had clubs of wood with spikes consisting of prongs of antler or stone and, in later time, spear heads, sunk into the head.[11] Slightly different again is the Kutchin club "made from the jaw bone of a moose which is studded with copper along the edge."[12] The Sekani had a similar jawbone type.[13]

The description of the Eyak *shield* is not very clear, but it seems to have been different from the ordinary round shield of the Plains. Generally speaking the shield did not play a very prominent role in the northwestern parts of the North American continent, where slat or leather armor in many cases took its place. Besides, it has as a rule passed [467] out of use many years

---

[1] Lillooet (TEIT 1900-08a, 235). Thompson (TEIT 1900, 263f.). Flathead (TEIT 1930, 344). Nez Percé (SPINDEN 1908, 227). Wishram (SPIER & SAPIR 1930, 199). Takelma (SAPIR 1907, 272f.). Klamath (SPIER 1930, 199). Shoshoni (LOWIE 1909, 185, 192). Paiute (KELLY 1932, 145). Puget Sound (HAEBERLIN & GUNTHER, 1930, 14). Chinook (New Light ... &c, 808).

[2] SPIER 1928, 258.

[3] Field notes. LOE 1842, 479. PETROFF 1884, 154.

[4] OSGOOD 1933a, 704.

[5] STELLER 1774, 235f, note. BATCHELOR 1901, 454.

[6] EMMONS 1923, 34ff.

[7] OSGOOD 1937a, 111.

[8] TEIT 1930, 115f.

[9] TEIT 1930, 256.

[10] TEIT 1928, 123.

[11] TEIT 1900-08b, 538.

[12] OSGOOD 1936, 86, 88.

[13] JENNESS 1937, 37.

ago, so that our information is rather defective". It is difficult, therefore, to make any precise comparison with the Eyak type. Wooden shields occurred among the Aleut and Pacific Eskimo,[11] in the Mackenzie area,[2] and on the northern Plateaus.[3] Here the Carrier and Lillooet made their shields of wooden splinters enclosed with twine of Indian hemp,[4] while other Plateau tribes had round or oval shields made of hide.[5] There can be no doubt that the latter often were imitations of the small, circular Plains shield introduced together with the horse, the Plains costume, etc. in fairly recent times, but in other cases they were different and probably of an older type. The round leather shield of the Chinook[6] may belong to this group, and probably the Eyak shield should be classed along with it.

On a previous occasion the Danish author has tried to show that the double-edged _dagger_ — in contradistinction to the pointed stiletto — is a western element in North America.[7] It will suffice, therefore, to refer to its occurrence [468] in the Eskimo Punuk and Thule cultures,[8] the Mackenzie area,[9] the Northwest Coast,[10] and the northern Plateaus.[11]

The Phases of Life

Naming of a child after a dead person is extremely common among a great many tribes. It is a custom found throughout the Eskimo area[12] and in several cases on the Northwest Coast.[1]

---

[1] COXE 1780, 116, 155. LOWE 1842, 479. The "wooden shields" mentioned by COLLINSON from the Copper Eskimo were probably snowshoes (BIRKET-SMITH 1929, II 36).

[2] Sekani (JENNESS 1937, 37). Slave (OSGOOD 1933, 62). Chipewyan (HEARNE 1795, 115, 149).

[3] Shuswap (TEIT 1900-08b), 538). Thompson (TEIT 1900, 265). Coeur d'Alene (TEIT 1930, 117).

[4] MORICE 1890, 140. FRASER cited by JENNESS 1932, 356 note.

[5] Thompson (TEIT 1900, 265). Coeur d'Alene, Flathead (TEIT 1930, 117, 359). Nez Percé (SPINDEN 190K. 227). Middle Columbia Salish (TEIT 1928, 123). Wishram (SPIER & SAPIR 1930, 231). Klamath (SPIER 1930, 32). Shoshoni (LEWIS & CLARKE 1814, 309f. LOWIE 1909, 193. LOWIE 1924, 242). Paiute (KELLY 1932, 187).

[6] ROSS cited by BANCROFT 1875, 235.

[7] BIRKET-SMITH 1929, II 64. Add: Cook Inlet (DE LAGUNA 1934, 101f.). Chugach (Field notes).

[8] MATHIASSEN 1927, II 52. COLLINS 1937, 333. It seems, on the other hand, to be absent in the Old Bering Sea culture.

[9] Tnaina (OSGOOD 1937a, 111), Kuchin (RICHARDSON 1851, I 382. JONES 1872, 322. OSGOOD 1936, 89). Hare (JENNESS 1932, 394). Dogrib and Slave (MACKENZIE 1801, 38). Satudene? (OSGOOD 1933, 58).

[10] Tlingit (LA PÉROUSE 1797, 207. ERMAN 1870-71, II 386f. KRAUSE 1885, 244. MALASPINA 1849, 288. CAAMAÑO 1849, 353. VON KITTLITZ 1858, I 214). Tlingit and Haida (NIBLACK 1890, 283ff). Haida (MACKENZIE 1892, 50f). Tsimshian (VANCOUVER 1798, II 392). Kwakiutl (JEWITT 1896, 137). Bella Bella? {Heiltsuk} (VANCOUVER 1798, II 339). Nootka (JEWITT 1896, 140). Puget Sound (HAEBERLIN & GUNTHER 1930, 14). Chinook (LEWIS & CLARKE 1814, 433). Washington (LEWIS 1906, 170).

[11] Tahltan (EMMONS 1911, 68). Carrier etc. (MORICE 1895, 63), Lillooet (TEIT 1900-08a, 234). Thompson (TEIT 1900, 263). Coeur d'Alene, Okanagan (TEIT 1930, 115, 255). Middle Columbia Salish (TEIT 1928, 123). Archeological Lytton, B.C. (SMITH 1899. 149). Archeological Fraser R, (SMITH 1903, 174). Archeological. Thompson R. (SMITH 1900, 423).

[12] Chugach Eskimo. (Field notes). Bering Strait Eskimo (NELSON 1899, 289, 424). Asiatic

We also meet it on the Plateaus[2] [469] and in Northeast Asia.[3] There is, however, no information from the Mackenzie area, and possibly it is foreign to the Athapaskans as a whole.

The Eyak *puberty rites* for the girls, including isolation and the use of a sucking tube and head scratcher, have a definitely western character. More or less the same trait complex is found on the Northwest Coast,[4] whence it has evidently spread to the Pacific Eskimo,[5] whereas it is entirely foreign to the rest of the Eskimo. The puberty complex is also common throughout the Plateaus, even though one trait or another may occasionally be dropped, e.g. the sucking tube among the Coeur d'Alene and the seclusion among the Klamath, who practise the Californian puberty dance instead.[6] In some cases the custom of seclusion has reached the Athapaskans of the Yukon and Mackenzie areas.[7] It may be added that both the drinking tube and [470] the head or back scratcher are widely diffused in North America even outside the regions where they are employed in the puberty rites.[8] For a Full discussion of the puberty observances the reader is

---

Eskimo (BOGORAS 1904-09, 510). Colville Eskimo (STEFANSSON 1914, 161). Mackenzie Eskimo (STEFANSSON 1914, 158, 339, 363, 376). Copper Eskimo (JENNESS 1922, 167. KNUD RASMUSSEN 1932, 42). Netsilik Eskimo (KNUD RASMUSSEN 1931, 219f.). Caribou Eskimo (KNUD RASMUSSEN 1930, 61. BIRKET-SMITH 1929, I 282). Iglulik Eskimo (KNUD RASMUSSEN 1929, 58f. MATHIASSEN 1928, 212). Baffin Island (BOAS 1888, 612). Lahrador Eskimo (HAWKES 1916, 112). Polar Eskimo (KNUD RASMUSSEN 1921-25, III 17). West Greenland (BIRKET-SMITH 1924, 413). Angmagssalik Eskimo (HOLM 1914, 62, 81. KNUD RASMUSSEN 1921-25, 1 12).

[1] Tlingit (KRAUSE 1885, 217. NIBLACK 1890, 369). Haida (SWANTON 1905, 117). Puget Sound (HAEBERLIN & GUNTHER 1930, 46). Chehalis (HILL-TOUT 1904b, 322). Squamish (HILL-TOUT 1900, 484). Klallam (EELLS 1889, 656).

[2] Thompson (TEIT 1900, 291). Wishram (SPIER & SAPIR 1930, 258). Nespelem and Sanpoil (RAY 1932, 114, 131).

[3] Chukchi (BOGORAS 1904-09, 510). Koryak (JOCHELSON 1905-08, 100), Yakagir (JOCHELSON 1926, 105). Kamchadal (KRACHENINNIKOW 1770, I 176). The Gilyak do not follow this custom, and among the Ainu there is a taboo against naming a child after a dead person (BATCHELOR 1901, 242).

[4] Tlingit (LANGSDORFF 1812, 114. ERMAN 1870-71, II 318f. PETROFF 1884, 170. KRAUSE 1885, 217f.). Haida (SWANTON 1905, 48ff). Tsimshian (BOAS 1916, 531. BOAS 1890, 836f.). Kwakiutl, Bella Coola (BOAS 1890, 838). Nootka (BOAS 1891, 592f.). Makah (SWAN 1870, 12f.). Seechelt (HILL-TOUT 1904a, 32). Chehalis (HILL-TOUT 1904b, 319). Klallam (GUNTHER 1927, 239f.).

[5] LISIANSKY 1814, 201. Field Notes.

[6] Tahltan (EMMONS 1911, 104f.). Carrier, Babine (HAMILTON 1878, 206. MORICE 1890, 162f.). Shuswap (BOAS 1891, 641f. TEIT 1900-08b, 587f.). Lillooet (HILL-TOUT 1905, 136. TEIT 1900-08a, 263ff). Thompson (TEIT 1900, 311ff). Coeur d'Alene, Okanagan (TEIT 1930, 168, 282ff). Kutenai (BOAS 1890, 841f.). Nespelem and Sanpoil (RAY 1932, 133f.). Washington and Oregon (GIBBS 1877, 212). Kalispel (WILKES 1844, 485). Wallawalla (LEWIS & CLARKE 1814, 533). Wishram (SPIER & SAPIR 1930, 262). Klamath (SPIER 1930, 69). Shasta (KROEBER 1925, 299). Paiute (KELLY 1932, 162f. STEWART 1933, 293).

[7] Tnaina (OSGOOD 1937a, 162f.). Kutchin (SCHMITTER 1910, 13. OSGOOD 1936, 141, 147). Sekani (JENNESS 1937, 56). Satudene (OSGOOD 1933, 77), Chipewyan (INGSTAD 1931, 202).

[8] Cf. BIRKET-SMITH 1929, II 243 table A 18; 271 table A 66, 143, 312f. table B 12, 187f, 348f.

referred to the remarks of LESLIE SPIER.[1]

It is another typical Northwest Coast custom to *exhibit the corpse* of the deceased some time before the burial.[2] From this center it has evidently spread to some neighboring tribes.[3] It occurred, however, also in Old Mexico and a few other places in the Western Hemisphere. Much more common is the *removal of the corpse through some kind of unusual or temporary opening*, either through the smokehole, or a window, or a hole made by taking out some wall boards, or by lifting up the tent cover, etc. This custom is found everywhere in the Eskimo area.[4] and is also common on the Northwest Coast and among some neighboring tribes.[5] Curiously [471] enough we have no information about this custom from any tribe in the Mackenzie basin, but on the other hand this may be accidental. In Northeast Asia it is mentioned from the Chukchi and Koryak,[6] and we need hardly add that it is also generally observed in many other parts of the world: China, Europe, Africa, etc. Without entering into details it is safe to say that it is probably a very old procedure, primarily intended to deceive the spirit of the dead. As far as the Eyak arc concerned, their practices are intimately connected with those of the Eskimo and the Northwest Coast Indians.

Cremation was common in many places of aboriginal North America: in the West from Prince William Sound as far south as Mexico, and in the Southeast. In the regions with which we are concerned here we find it principally on the northern Northwest Coast,[7] and among the Athapaskans of Alaska.[8] Cremation is also practised on the northern Plateaus.[9] In some cases,

---

table B 45.

[1] SPIER 1930, 314ff.

[2] Tlingit (KRAUSE 1885, 222f. ELLIOT 1886, 50. SWANTON 1908, 429f.). Tlingit and Haida (NIBLACK 1890, pl. LXVIII). Haida (SWANTON 1905, 52, 54). Tsimshian (BOAS 1890, 837. BOAS 1895, 573. BOAS 1916, 534). Nootka (JEWITT 1896, 181). Puget Sound (HAEBERLIN & GUNTHER 1930, 53).

[3] Aleut (LOWE 1842, 477). Chugach (Field Notes). Eskimo of Bristol Bay (ELLIOT 1886, 50). Tahltan (EMMONS 1911, 106). Carrier (DE SMET 1859, 201). Wishram (SPIER & SAPIR 1930, 271). Ingalik (F. DE L.).

[4] WEYER 1932, 259f. Add: Copper Eskimo (KNUD RASMUSSEN 1932, 45). Netsilik Eskimo (KNUD RASMUSSEN 1931, 263), One of our Chugach informants expressly stated that the corpse was removed through the door of the house.

[5] Tlingit (KRAUSE 1885, 225. SWANTON 1908, 430). Haida (SWANTON 1905, 52). Kwakiutl (BOAS 1896, 575. BOAS 1921, 709). Makah (SWAN 1870. 83). Puget Sound (HAEBERLN & GUNTHER 1930, 53). Klallam (GUNTHER 1927, 249). Songish (BOAS 1891, 575). Yurok (KROEBER 1925, 46). Hupa (GODDARD 1903, 70), Ingalik ((CHAPMAN 1921, 307). Tahltan (EMMONS 1911, 107). Shasta (KROEBER 1925, 300).

[6] BOGORAS 1904-09, 525. JOCHELSON 1905-08, 110ff.

[7] Tlingit (KRAUSE 1885, 224f. SWANTON 1908, 430), Haida (SWAN 1875, 9), Tsimshian (BOAS 1890, 837). Northern Kwakiutl (JENNESS 1932, 342).

[8] Tnaina (OSGOOD 1937a, 166). Kutchin (HARDISTY 1872, 319. JONES 1872, 326. KIRBY 1865, 419. OSGOOD 1936, 145, 148f, 152).

[9] Tahltan (EMMONS 1911, 107). Tsetsaut (BOAS 1895, 567). Carrier (SIMPSON 1844, 160. WILKES 1844, 481f. HARMON 1903, 161, 180f. DE SMET 1859, 201. MORICE 1890. 145). Chilcotin (FARRAND 1899, 647). Klamath (SPIER 1930, 71). From the Plateau tribes cremation has spread to the Nahane (JENNESS 1932, 399) and the Sekani (HARMON 1903, 266. JENNESS

where it is not a regular custom, it is employed when a person dies far away from his village,[1] and there is archaeological evidence of its former occurrence in the Yakima valley.[2] It is also said to have 472 existed in southwestern Oregon.[3] SPIER has given a comprehensive survey of its distribution farther south.[4] There it is found in southern California and western Arizona, and in central California, but as emphasized by SPIER, it is probable that these two areas are connected at least through southwestern Nevada. He does not find evidence for connecting this double southern area with the northern one, but the gap becomes more apparent than real, if we lake into consideration the former distribution in Oregon and Washington. There can hardly be any doubt that the cremation custom of the Southwest, reaching back to early Hohokam times, is also connected with the corresponding procedure in Mexico, where it occurred both among the primitive "Chichimecas" and the more civilized tribes. The Mexican influence, which is so strongly pronounced in the culture of the Southeast, is probably responsible for the introduction of cremation in the Gulf area and the Hope-well culture of the Ohio basin. In South America it is only found among one or two tribes in the Amazon region. So cremation seems to be mainly a western element in the New World. This agrees very well with the fact that it is also found in Northeast Asia among several tribes.[5]

Earth burial in the true sense of the word is rare among the Eskimo; it occurs within the Pacific group and on the Aleutian Islands,[6] but on the other hand we cannot [473] exclude the possibility that the stone cairn burial characteristic of the Thule culture[7] is a modification adapted to the permanently frozen soil of the Arctic. The northern tribes of the Northwest Coast used to bury shamans, whereas ordinary people were burned, and also farther south burial occurred.[8] Moreover burial is common on the Plateaus,[9] including certain parts of California, in the

---

1937, 59).

[1] Shuswap (BOAS 1891, 643). Thompson (TEIT 1900, 330). Takelma (SPIER 1907, 275). Owens Valley Pauite (STEWARD 1933, 298).

[2] SMITH 1910, 143.

[3] LEWIS 1906, 177.

[4] SPIER 1928, 293ff. On North American cremation in general cf. YARROW 1880, 49ff, YARROW 1881, 143ff, BAHNSON 1882, 175 ff, MACLEOD 1925, 127.

[5] Chukchi (BOGORAS 1904-09, 522. SVERDRUP 1926, 261). Koryak (KRACHENINNIKOW 1770, 1 222. KENNAN 1871, 147. JOCHELSON 1908, 104ff.). Gilyak (VON SCHRENCK 1881-95, 764ff.).

[6] COOK & KING 1785, II 519. SCHELECHOF 1793a, 200. MERCK 1937, 131. LISIANSKY 1814, 200. COXE 1780, 173. DALL 1877, 89. JOCHELSON 1925, 41ff. DE LAGUNA 1934, 42ff, 163f. Cf. also WEYER 1930, 262.

[7] MATHIASSEN 1927 II 130f. Cf. BIRKET-SMITH 1929, II 121, 293f., table A 111.

[8] Tsimshian (BOAS 1890, 837). Kwakiutl (BOAS 1890, 839). Cowichan (BOAS 1889, 123. BOAS 1891, 841). Nisqually (HAEBERLIN & GUNTHER 1930, 53), Songish (BOAS 1891, 575). Yurok (KROEBER 1925, 46).

[9] Shuswap (BOAS 1891, 643. TEIT 1900-08b, 592), Chilcotin (JENNEKSS 132, 363). Lillooet (HILL-TOUT 1905, 137. TEIT 1900-08a, 269). Thompson (TEIT 1900, 328). Coeur d'Alene, Okanagan, Flathead (TEIT 1930, 172, 288, 382). Nez Percé (SPINDEN 1908, 252). Kutenai (CHAMBERLAIN 1893, 560. BOAS 1890, 842). Middle Columbia Salish (TEIT 1928, 127). Nespelem and Sanpoil (RAY 1932, 150f.). Kalispel (WILKES 1844, 485). Kalapooia (WILKES 1844, 394). Southwestern Oregon (LEWIS 1906, 177). Takelma (SAPIR 1907, 275). Shasta (KROEBER 1925, 300). Shoshoni (LOWIE 1924, 282). Ute (LOWIE 1924, 279f). Paviotso

Southwest, and in Mexico as far south as the Huichol.[1] It is also practised by several tribes in the Mackenzie area,[2] and by the Ainu.[3] Without entering upon a lengthy discussion about the relative age of cremation and earth burial in northwestern North America — the distribution seems to favor the priority of the latter — it can safely be stated that there is nothing extraordinary in finding both methods among the Eyak. [474]

Grave houses have a similar, although somewhat more restricted distribution in these parts than earth burial, i.e. the Pacific coast,[4] the northern Plateaus,[5] and the Yukon region with minor extensions to the Aleut on the one hand and the Slavey on the other.[6] The *giving of grave goods* is so universal throughout the whole region in question here that detailed references are superfluous. It may be mentioned that it seems more common among the Eskimo than the Tlingit, who are said to give them only in exceptional cases.[7] Sometimes they are lacking in the Mackenzie area, because all property of the dead is destroyed at the funeral.

Feasts and Games

The principal ceremonies of the Eyak, the most important of which was the feast of the dead, had the characteristic feature of the Northwest Coast *potlatch*, viz. the distribution of gifts to the guests. This feature is strongly developed, especially on the northern parts of the roast, throughout the Pacific slope from the Tlingit in the north to Columbia [475] River in the south.[8] It

---

(LOWIE 1923, 149). Paiute (LOWIE 1924, 278f. KELLY 1932, 167. STEWARD 1933, 297). Archaeological Lytton, B.C. (SMITH 1899, 158ff). Archeological Thompson River, B.C. (SMITH 1900, 431 f.). Archaeological Yakima Valley (SMITH 1910, 138ff).

[1] SPIER 1928, 295f.

[2] Kutchin (OSGOOD 1936, 145, 148). Atna (ALLEN 1889, 266). Sekani (HARMON 1903, 161). Satudene (OSGOOD 1933, 80). Eastern Athapaskans (RICHARDSON 1853, II 21). The American author found two inhumations under a house floor on the Khotol River in the lower Yukon valley.

[3] KRACHENINNIKOW 1770, I 232. HITCHCOCK 1891, 465ff. BATCHELOR 1901, 558. TORII 1919, 217ff.

[4] Tlingit (KOTZEBUE 1830, 31. ELLIOTT 1886, 50. NIBLACK 1890, pl. LXV). Tlingit and Haida (KRAUSE 1885, 230f., 311). Haida (JACOBSEN 1884, 30f. SWANTON 1905, 52). Kwakiutl (DAWSON 1888, 78. BOAS 1890, 839. BOAS 1896, 577). Bella Coola (BOAS 1892, 419). Cowitchan (BOAS 1889, 323. 1 BOAS 1894, 458). Klallam (GUNTHER 1927, 248). Quinault (WILLOUGHBY 1889, 277). Alsea (FARRAND 1901, 241).

[5] Tahltan (DAWSON 1889, 194). Carrier (HARMON 1903, 263f.). Western Athapaskans (MORICE 1905, 20). Shuswap (DAWSON 1892, 10). Thompson (TEIT 1900, 329). Nez Perce (LEWIS & CLARKE 1814, 557). Middle Columbia Salish (TEIT 1928, 127). Tribes of Columbia River (LEWIS 1906, 171, 190). Wishram (SPIER & SAPIR 1930, 271).

[6] Tnaina (WRANGELL 1839, 107). Kutchin (SCHMITTER 1910, 14. OSGOOD 1936, 148f., 152). Aleut (SAUER 1802, pl. X fig. 4). Slave, ".. .a ground cache, or perhaps something verging more toward the true burial house" (OSGOOD 1933, 80). Tena, above earth burial (F. DE L.).

[7] KRAUSE 1885, 231.

[8] Tlingit, Haida, Tsimshian (NIBLACK 189, 365ff, 372f.) Tlingit (PETROFF 1884, 171f. KRAUSE 1885, 223f, 234ff. SWANTON 1908, 434ff). Haida (SWANTON 1905, 155ff). Tsmshian (BOAS 1916, 537ff). Kwakiutl (JACOBSEN 1884, 121. DAWSON 1888, 79ff. BOAS 1897, 341ff.). Bella

has spread to the Eskimo of Alaska where there are faint traces as far north as Point Barrow,[1] and inland to the Alhapaskans of Alaska[2] as well as to the northern Plateau tribes, among whom it is still found, though in a weak form, as among the Wishram and Coeur d'Alene.[3] It is quite clear that the Eyak must have adopted this custom from their Northwest Coast neighbors.

Under these circumstances it is not surprising that we must look to the same source for the origin of the _ceremonial paddle_ carried at potlatches. Similar objects are used on the Northwest Coast[45] and by some Eskimo and Athapaskan tribes of Alaska.[5] The same origin must, of course, be ascribed to the _dramatic dances_ of the Eyak, [476] since these form such an integral part of all Northwest Coast ceremonies, and to the feather ornaments worn on the same occasions. The distribution of _masks_ has been discussed previously.[6]

Among the musical instruments of the Eyak the _drum_ took a prominent place. It had the typical Indian and Siberian tambourine shape with a central grip, in contradistinction to the Eskimo and Chukchi type with a lateral grip. The distribution of the tambourine drum in North America and North Asia has been summarized on a former occasion.[7] Whereas the drum is extremely widespread, the use of the _sounding board_ is much more restricted, being in the main limited to both sides of the Pacific. The distribution comprises the Northwest Coast[8] and certain

---

Coola {Nuxalk} (BOAS 1892, 412). Nootka (JACOBSEN 1884, 111. JEWITT 1896, 81. BOAS 1891, 588ff). Makah (SWAN 1870, 13f). Cowichan (BOAS 1889, 324. BOAS 1894, 457), Squamish (HILL-TOUT 1900, 490). Puget Sound (HAEBERLIN & t GUNTHER 1930, 55, 59ff). Twana, Chimakum, Klallam (EELLS 1889, 657). Klallam (GUNTHER 1927, 306ff.). Quilleute (REAGAN 1925, 32. In connection with whaling). Western Washington (GIBBS 1877, 205. LEWIS 1906, 156).

[1] Chugach (Field notes). Bering Strait Eskimo (WRANGEKLL 1839, 131. JACOBSEN 1884, 260ff. ELLIOTT 1886, 393f. NELSON 1899, 363ff.). Point Barrow Eskimo (STEFANSSON 1913, 87ff).

[2] Tnaina (WRANGELL 1839, 107f. OSGOOD 1937a, 149ff). Ingalik (CHAPMAN 1907, 32ff). Tena (Field notes of American author). Kutchin (JONES 1878, 326. HARDISTY 1872, 317f. OSGOOD 1936, 121f, 125ff, 137).

[3] Tahltan (CALLBREATH 1889, 198. EMMONSS 1911, 107f.). Carrier (Cf. MORICE 1905, 185. MORICE 1890, 147ff). Chilcotin (JENNESS 1932, 363). Shuswap (DAWSON 1892, 14. TEIT 1900-08b, 583). Lillooet (TEIT 1900-08a, 257ff). Thompson (TEIT 1900, 296f). Coeur d'Alene, Okanagan (TEIT 1930, 164, 277). Wishram (SPIER & SAPIR 1930, 262).

[4] Tlingit, Haida (KRAUSE 1885, 223. 234. NIBLACK 1890, 272).

[5] Kodiak (DAWYDOW 1816, 183). Bering Strait Eskimo (NELSON 1899, 353, 359. HAWKES 1913, 7). Tnaina (OSGOOD 1933a, 716). Ingalik (CHAPMAN 1907, 19ff).

[6] BIRKET-SMITH 1929, II 118 cf. 288 table A 96, 201f. cf. 365ff. table B 62. Add to the latter: Tnaina (OSGOOD 1937a, 121). Tillamook (BOAS 1923, 12). Wishram (SPIER & SAPIR 1930, 237, 257).

[7] BIRKET-SMITH 1929, II 117 cf. 287 table A 93, 201 cf. 363 table B 61. Add: Tnaina (OSGOOD 1937a, 121). Kutchin (OSGOOD 1936, 94, 100). Sekani (JENNES 1937, 57f). Satudene (OSGOOD 1933, 67). Okanagan, Coeur d'Alene (TET 1930, 278, 164). Wishram (SPIER & SAPIR 1930, 201). Klamath, recent (SPIER 1930, 89). Paiute (KELLY 1932, 147). A central grip was used by the Aleut (TOLSTYKH 1933, 12) and the Chugash (Field notes).

[8] Tlingit (KRAUSE 1885, 242). Haida (SWANTON 1905, 40). Kwakiutl (BOAS 1897, 437). Nootka (JEWITT 1896, 80, 129f.). Nisqually (HAEBERLIN & GUNTHER 1930, 79).

neighboring tribes,[1] as well as the Gilyak and Ainu.[2] It must at present remain an open question whether the sounding board is related to the plank drum with pit resonator known from California and Guiana. On the other hand percussion plates [477] of metal or stone are well known in Eastern Asia and are probably ancestors of the gong.

The peculiar semicircular *rattle* of the Eyak has no close parallels lo our knowledge, but we may surmise a connection with the Chugach rattle made of barnacle shells[3] and a certain Northwest Coast jingle rattle consisting of numerous puffin beaks attached to two or three wooden rings with a cross-shaped grip. The latter occurs among the Tlingit and Kodiak Eskimo,[4] and in the British Museum there is a specimen with a carved, nearly straight handle to which two incomplete rings are fastened, thus approaching the semicircular shape of the Eyak type.[5] Farther south the Kwakiutl, Coast Salish, Nootka, and Makah have rattles made of a willow hoop on which perforated clam shells arc strung, and strung shell rattles also occur in southern California and the Pueblo region.[6] Hoof rattles, consisting for instance of a short stick to the ends of which the dew-claws of a deer are attached, are also common on the North-west Coast, but are even more characteristic of the Plateaus, California, and, in connection with the Dog society, of the Plains.

We have no explicit information about the Eyak *whistle*, but we may infer from the description that it was probably a true whistle or flute and not a valve instrument (i.e. trumpet or clarinet). Wind instruments are not aboriginal among the Eskimo where we meet them only among the Caribou and Pacific groups, and in both cases we may [478] suspect influence from the outside.[7] On the other hand they seem to be more common in the Boreal Woodlands[8] and the Plateaus.[9] A number of different types occur, however, on the Northwest Coast,[10] and we may, therefore, with some reason look there for the origin of the Eyak instrument. This is further confirmed by the fact that wind instruments are very scarce in Northeast Asia. KACHENINNIKOW says that the Kamchadal make whistles of angelica stalks,[11] and possibly some sort of flute was

---

[1] Bering Strait Eskimo (NELSON 1899, 352). Tnaina (OSGOOD 1937a, 121). Kutchin (OSGOOD 1936, 94, 105. HARDISTY 1872, 318). Yurok (KROEBER 1935, 96). Okanagan (TEIT 1930, 278). Wishram (SPIER & SAPIR 1930, 201, 241).

[2] VON SCHRENCK 1881-95, 706f. MONTADON 1937, 169.

[3] COOK & KING 1785, 373.

[4] NIBLACK 1890, 331. KRAUSE 1885, 203, 242. BELCHER 1843, 103 DAWYDOW 1816, 183. HOLMBERG 1856, 406.

[5] British Museum. Handbook to the Ethnographical Collections. 2nd ed. London 1925, 280 fig. 268.

[6] ROBERTS 1936, 22.

[7] BIRKET-SMITH 1929, II 39. HOLMBERG 1856, 408. DAWYDOW 1816, 185f. Field notes.

[8] Kutchin (OSGOOD 1936, 94, 104). Slave (Ottawa National Museum, VI D 47). Satudene (OSGOOD 1933, 68). Chipewyan (BIRKET-SMITH 1930, 75.)

[9] Coeur d'Alene, Okanagan (TEIT 1930, 165, 278). Kutenai (CHAMBERLAIN 1893, 561). Nespelem and Sanpoil (RAY 1932, 135). Klamath (SPIER 1930, 88ff). Shasta (DIXON 1907, 449). Takelma (SAPIR 1907, 273).

[10] Tlingit (NIBLACK 1890, 331f.). Nootka (COOK & KING 1785, 311). Yurok (KROEBER 1925, 96). Hupa (MASON 1883, 235). Cf. also ROBERTS 1935, 16ff.

[11] KRACHENINNIKOW 1770, I 157.

played by the Ainu,[1] but otherwise information is lacking from this region.

Among the playthings of the Eyak children the ordinary *popgun* occurred. It is also found sporadically elsewhere in North America and Siberia.[2] Undoubtedly it is an old culture element, as it has been found in pre-Columbian strata at Ancón on the Peruvian coast. It is possible that the small *blowgun* made of the wing bone of an eagle or swan is nothing but a local variation of the popgun. The American area of the real blowgun centers around the Caribbean Sea and the Gulf of Mexico. This weapon was used by the ancient Maya, Aztec, and "Chichimecas," and was diffused as far north as the Hopi, the tribes of the southeastern United States and was even carried by the [479] Iroquois to the Great Lakes.[3] In South America its main distribution is the northwestern regions; in the literature of the 16th century it is confined to Colombia and Peru, and the extension of this area in later times is probably caused by the rapid spread of curare poison.[4] Thus it is difficult to see any connection with the Eyak occurrence.

The peculiar *throwing stick for stones* occupies a very limited area in Alaska: we found it among the Chugach, and it is mentioned from the Crow River Kutchin.[5] It has recently been suggested that certain wooden handles for implements of unknown use often found in Greenland and, in a single specimen, at Ponds Inlet, should be considered parts of a similar device, combining the characteristics of the throwing stick and the sling.[6] In fact, the Naskapi of Labrador have a somewhat similar type.[7] The Point Barrow Eskimo use a "pebble snapper" made of a small piece of wood,[8] but it is uncertain whether it has any connection with the Eyak element. On the other hand the latter may well have had a larger distribution in earlier times and he related to the ordinary throwing board, which is widely known in both Americas.[9] The "*whip sling*" for small darts is another toy which is probably connected with the throwing board. In the region which comes into consideration here it does not seem to be known except by the [480] Chukchi.[10] It also occurs among the Iroquois, but here it may be post-Columbian. Like the stone thrower (cf. the Roman *fustibalus*), it was, in fact, known in several out-of-the-way places in Europe. It needs hardly mentioning that the ordinary throwing board was also well known there in Palaeolithic times. It is a significant fact that the darts thrown by means of the whip sling were feathered with two, not three, feathers. This method of feathering is an old trait in North America where it has been retained by the eastern Eskimo and on the southern Northwest Coast, but elsewhere has disappeared.[11]

Although references arc exceedingly few there can hardly be any doubt that "*hide-and-seek*" is a common children's game among most of the North American Indians at present. The

---

[1] MONTANDON 1937, 196.

[2] BIRKET-SMITH 1929, II 121, 205 cf. 377f. table B 71.

[3] FRIEDERICI 1911, 71.

[4] NORDENSIÖLD 1924, 59ff.

[5] OSGOOD 1936, 100.

[6] MATHIASSEN 1930, 260ff. MATHIASSEN 1934, 81, 115. LARSEN 1934, 137f, 158. The suggestion was first made by the American author of this work.

[7] C-NM, H 2317.

[8] MURDOCH 1892, 379.

[9] BIRKET-SMITH 1929, II 65f. cf. 249 table A 28, 153ff. cf. 321f. table B 20.

[10] BOGORAS 1904-09, 158. C-NM. Lb 361.

[11] BIRKET-SMITH 1929, II 63 cf. 245 f. table A 22, 149f. cf. 316 table B 15. Two flat feathers were also used on Sekani children's arrows (JENNESS 1937, 37).

Danish author has observed it both among the Caribou Eskimo and the Cree, and it is also found among a number of other Eskimo tribes[1] as well as among the Tnaina and Thompson Indians.[2] Nowadays it is impossible in many cases to determine whether a game like this is genuinely American or imported. The _top_ is very widely distributed in both hemispheres and is probably an old culture element; an account of its distribution in North America and Siberia has previously been given.[3] The same applies to the [481] buzz.[4] It is worth mentioning that this element is not reported from the Northwest Coast; as far as the Eyak are concerned it is therefore most probable that it should be considered as connected with the Eskimo occurrence. _Cat's cradle_ is another widely known and apparently old culture element in North America.[5] Strangely enough this game is not reported from North Asia outside the sphere of Eskimo culture. Some sort of _hand_ or _stick game_ seems to be found in all parts of North America except the Southeast, whereas it is not known from North Asia.[6] The _partner game_ or _quoits_ is essentially western in its distribution in North America. It occurs among the Pacific and Bering Strait Eskimo,[7] as well as among some tribes of the Northwest Coast,[8] the Mackenzie area,[9] and the southern Plateaus.[10] It is also known in the Southwest. However, it is quite possible that our information is incomplete and that the distribution is really much wider. A game like this may very well be overlooked. From Northeast Asia there is no record. [482]

The distribution of _shinny_ has formerly been summarized by CULIN, and WISSLER has plotted it on a map.[11] According to the latter it covers all of the United States and southern Canada with a small outlying area in Alaska. The map, however, is not complete, for the game also occurs on the Northwest Coast,[12] so that there is really no break in the distribution from Bering Strait to Mexican frontier.

---

[1] Chugach (Field notes). Bering Strait Eskimo (NELSON 1899, 337). Copper Eskimo" (KNUD RASMUSSEN 1932, 265). Netsilik Eskimo (KNUD RASMUSSEN 1931, 356). Iglulik Eskimo (KNUD RASMUSSEN 1929, 245).

[2] Tnaina (OSGOOD 1937a, 125). Thompson (TEIT 1900, 281).

[3] BIRKET-SMITH 1929, II 121 cf. 293 table A 110, 205f. cf. 378f. table B 72. Add: Chugach (Field notes). Tnaina (OSGOOD 1937a, 124). Kutchin (OSGOOD 1936, 95, 100). Nespelem and Sanpoil (RAY 1932, 166). Klamath (SPIER 193, 83).

[4] BIRKET-SMITH 1929, II 120 cf. 292f. table A 109, 205 cf. 377 table B 70. Add: Chugach (Field notes). Klamath (SPIER 1930, 83).

[5] BIRKET-SMITH 1929, II 120 cf. 291 table A 106, 204f. cf. 375f. table B 68. Add: Tnaina (OSGOOD 1937a, 124). Kutchin (OSGOOD 1936, 96). Coeur d'Alene, Okanagan (TEIT 1930, 135. 260). Nespelem and Sanpoil (RAY 1932, 164), Klamath (SPIER 1930, 84ff). Paiute (KELLY 1932, 177).

[6] BIRKET-SMITH 1929, II 120 cf. 290 table A 103, 203f. cf. 370ff. table B 66. Add: Chugach (Field notes). Tnaina (OSGOOD 1937a, 126). Satudene (OSGOOD 1933, 69). Sekani (JENNESS 1937, 58). Klallam (GUNTHER 1927, 274f.). Coeur d'Alene, Okanagan (TEIT 1930, 130f., 260). Nespelem and Sanpuil (RAY 1932, 155ff.). Wishram (SPIER & SAPIR 1930, 267). Klamath (SPIER 1930, 77f.). Ute, Paviotso (LOWIE 1924, 257f., 262). Paiute (STEWARD 1933, 285. KELLY 1932, 171ff.).

[7] Kodiak (LISIANSKY 1814, 210. MERCK 1937, 132. HOLMBERG 1856, 403f. PETROFF 1884, 143). Bering Strait Eskimo (NELSON 1899, 332).

[8] Haida (CULIN 1907, 725). Kwakiutl (CULIN 1907, 725).

[9] Tnaina (OSGOOD 1937a, 127). Chipewyan (HEARNE 1795, 333).

[10] Shoshoni (LOWIE 1924, 261). Paiute (STEWARD 1933, 288).

[11] CULIN 1907, 623ff. (add: Chugach, field notes). WISSLER 1926, 16.

[12] Tlingit (SWANTON 1908, 445). Haida (CULIN 1907, 6142). Tsimshian (BOAS 1895, 583).

Some sort of _sporting contest_, generally foot races but sometimes also shooting matches etc., is nearly universal among the tribes under consideration here, so we need not go into details. It is characteristic that no sort of ceremonial seems to be connected with the Eyak contests, as is often the case elsewhere. _Wrestling_ is also widely known. We find it among the Eskimo,[1] the Athapaskans of the Mackenzie area,[2] and several Plateau tribes.[3] It is also reported from the southern part of the Northwest Coast[4] and the Chukchi.[5] It is quite possible that the available [483] evidence is far from being complete. _Pulling of fingers and arms_ as trials of strength are essentially Eskimo forms of sport. Both contests are mentioned from many tribes between Greenland and the Pacific, and also from the Chukchi.[6] Finger pulling also occurs among the Tnaina and Peel River Kutchin, in both cases probably introduced by the Eskimo,[7] and isolated cases of the same are mentioned from the Sekani and Coeur d'Alene.[8] This might indicate that our information is defective, but nothing can be said with certainty. _Tossing in an outstretched hide_ is known in several places in Alaska and adjacent regions.[9] According to the field notes of the Danish author it also occurs in West Greenland, but here European influence is not excluded.

The distribution of _dice_ has formerly been discussed by CULIN and later by the Danish author. Dice arc found almost over the whole of North America, though rarely in the Boreal Woodlands, which seems to conform with the fact that in Asia they are also more common in Manchuria and Central Asia than in the North.[10] It would appear that [484] gambling with dice is an old game, but one which has been partially abandoned in the northern forest regions of both continents.

---

[1] Aleut (PETROFF 1884, 159). Chugach (Field notes). Bering Strait Eskimo (NELSON 1899, 339f.). Asiatic Eskimo (WDE WINDT 1899, 246; here erroneously called Chukchi). Point Barrow (MURDOCH 1892, 383). Copper Eskimo (JENNESS 1922, 221). Caribou Eskimo (BIRKET-SMITH 1929, I 273). Labrador Eskimo (TURNER 1894, 178). West Greenland (BIRKET-SMITH 1924, 396). Angmagssalik Eskimo (HOLM 1914, 129).

[2] Tnaina (OSGOOD 1937a, 124). Kutehin (HARDISTY 1872, 314f. RICHARDSON 1851, I 385. SCHMITTER 1910, 17. MASON 1924, 23. OSGOOD 1936, 96, 106). Satudene (OSGOOD 1933, 70). Chipewyan (BIRKET-SMITH 1930, 72).

[3] Shuswap (TEIT 1900-08b, 565). Lillooet (TEIT 1900-08a, 249). Thompson (TEIT 1900, 280). Coeur d'Alene (TEIT 1930, 134). Nespelem and Sanpoil (RAY 1932, 166). Klamath (SPIER 1930, 83). Shoshoni (LOWIE 1909, 198). Paiute (STEWART 1933, 388).

[4] Puget Sound (HAEBERLIN & GUNTHER 1930, 65). Klallam (GUNTHER 1927, 279).

[5] HOOPER 1853, 148, 197.

[6] Chugach (Field notes), Bering Strait Eskimo (NELSON 1899, 339). Copper Eskimo (KNUD RASMUSSEN 1932, 267). Netsilik Eskimo (KNUD RASMUSSEN 1931, 358). Iglulik Eskimo (MATHIASSEN 1928, 221). Baffin Island (BOAS 1888, 609). Caribou Eskimo (BIRKET-SMITH 1929, I 272). West Greenland (HANS EGEDE 1925, 382. CRANZ 1770, 230. BIRKET-SMITH 1924, 396). Frederik VI Coast (GRAAH 1832, 145). Chukchi (BOGORAS 1904-09, 267).

[7] OSGOOD 1937a, 124. OSGOOD 1936, 98.

[8] JENNESS 1937, 62. TEIT 1930, 134.

[9] Aleut (MERCK 1937, 125). Bering Strait Eskimo (NELSON 1899, 338). Asiatic Eskimo (BORGORAS 1904-09, 267). Point Barrow (KNUD RASMUSSEN 1925-26, II 309). Mackenzie Eskimo (STEFANSSON 1914, 165). Chukchi (BOGORAS 1904-09, 410f. LUTKE 1835, II 275f.), Tnaina (OSGOOD 1937a, 126). Kutchin (HARDISTY 1872, 313. OSGOOD 1936, 98,101).

[10] BIRKET-SMITH 1929, II 120 cf. 291 table A 105, 204 cf. 372ff. table B 67. Add: Klallam (GUNTHER 1927, 276). Coeur d'Alene, Okanagan (TEIT 1930, 130, 260). Nespelem and Sanpoil (RAY 1932, 159), Wishram (SPIER & SAPIR 1930, 267), Klamath (SPIER 1930, 79f.), Shoshoni, Paviotso (LOWIE 1924, 258, 262), Paiute (KELLY 1932, 174ff. STEWARD 1933, 286ff.), Sekani (JENNESS 1937, 58).

Intellectual Culture

Magic and Taboo

Very [485] scanty information is available concerning the intellectual culture of the Eyak, and our discussion of this subject must necessarily be rather limited. On the other hand certain ideas and beliefs seem to be sufficiently clear to be worth mentioning.

Fasting as a magical or religious means is a typical Northwest Coast feature[1] which is also found among some adjacent tribes,[2] whereas it is entirely foreign to the Eskimo as a whole and probably also to the Athapaskans of the Boreal Woodlands. The same applies to *sexual abstinence* before some important event.[3] *Purification* by means of the devilclub has a parallel in the Tsetsaut use of a decoction of the same plant.[4] The Carriers and others use it as [486] a purgative,[5] and the shaman novices of the Tlingit eat the root.[6] The Tsimshian may drink a decoction of the plant or put some of its bark in their baths.[7] The use of plants, mostly twigs of hemlock, cedar, or spruce for ritual purification is widespread on the Northwest Coast, whereas neither the Eskimo — with the exception of the Chugach — nor the Indians of the Woodlands employ them in a similar manner.

There is, both from the Eskimo and a few tribes on both sides of the North Pacific, some scattered data about *stabbing the animal in the eye* after it has been killed,[8] but possibly our information is defective on this point. The custom of *placing a part of the game in some special place*, notably its own element, is on the other hand widely known. We find it generally practised among the Aleut[9] and Eskimo. The East Greenlanders put the seal skulls back into the sea, while the West Greenlanders are content to keep them, taking care, however, not to throw

---

[1] Tlingit (KRAUSE 1885, 285. SWANTON 1908, 429, 437, 447). Nootka (JENNESS 1932, 346). Tillamook (BOAS 1923, 10).

[2] Tahltan (EMMONS 1911, 112). Tsetsaut (BOAS 1895, 568). Thompson (TEIT 1900, 331). Coeur d'Alene (TEIT 1930, 184). When a young man among the Chugach kills his first animal of any kind, he must fast for three days, the first time he has killed a whale he must fast and keep continent for five days. (Field notes).

[3] Tlingit (SWANTON 1908, 448), Makah (WATERMAN 1920, 40). Klallam (GUNTHER 1927, 204). Tsetsaut (BOAS 1895, 568). Nespelem and Sanpoil (RAY 1932, 78). It was also practised by the Tsimshian and Carrier from whom it spread to one of the Sekani bands (JENNESS 1937, 56 note).

[4] BOAS 1895, 568.

[5] MORICE 1905, 132.

[6] KRAUSE 1885, 285.

[7] BOAS 1916, 451.

[8] Copper Eskimo (JENNESS 1922, 113). Labrador Eskimo (HAWKES 1916, 85, 114). Nespelem and Sanpoil (RAY 1932, 91). Kamchadal (Dobell 1830, I 19). Gilyak (VON SCHRENCK 1881-95, 546). The West Greenland kayak hunter will also stab the seal in the eye, but for no magical reason, only for placing the towing gear.

[9] "Von einer uns gelieferten Robbe forderte der Jäger die Galle, etwas Blut, die Harnblase nebst den Augen zurück, um sie zusammen in ein Flüchen zu werfen" (MERCK 1937, 120).

them away as long as they are fresh.[1] In Labrador a little of the seal's heart and liver is thrown into the sea,[2] and the same is done with the seal skull at Iglulik, or if it is the first seal, all the bones.[3] Among the Netsilik Eskimo a [487] careful wife always suspends from her drying rack the lower jaws of the seals caught by her husband in the present season.[4] The Caribou Eskimo take care to cover the intestines of the caribou with stones.[5] The Point Barrow Eskimo keep the walrus skulls, and the Eskimo of Bering Strait and Prince William Sound the seal bladders.[6] The Chugach leave bear and mountain-goat skulls on the land, and if they kill a sea-otter in the water what is not wanted is sunk. They also put fish guts back into the water. On the Northwest Coast and some adjacent districts it is customary to throw the bones of the salmon, or at least those of the first one caught in the season, into the sea; we find this among the Bella Bella, Kwakiutl, Nootka, Bella Coola, Cowichan, Songish, and Lillooet.[7] The Kwakiutl proceed in a similar way with the bones of the halibut and the intestines of the porpoise.[8] The Klamath will do the same with the gall of a fish caught with difficulty,[9] and on the Plateaus the Thompson Indians, Lillooet, Shuswap, Carrier, and Chilcotin show a corresponding respect towards bear skulls and bones of deer and beaver.[10] The eastern Tahltan [488] and Kaska place bear skulls on poles or in trees,[11] and among the Yellowknife and Dogrib caribou bones are sometimes put up in trees, whereas the Koyukon throw bear skulls into the river.[12] Similar customs occur among the Algonkian woodland tribes. The Kamchadal placed bear skulls and hip-bones either under their pile-dwellings or in trees, the Gilyak put seal skulls into the sea, whereas they placed white whale skulls on a tree near the beach, and the Ainu used to keep the skulls of foxes and bears.[13] As far as the bear is concerned the custom of placing the skull or other bones in some particular place seems to be part of the widespread bear ceremonialism which HALLOWELL has shown to belong to the so-called snowshoe culture,[14] but the wide range of the custom in regions which are very little influenced by the snowshoe complex goes to show that this detail may be much older, probably connected with the skull and long bone offerings studied by GAHS.[15] These bone

---

[1] HOLM 1914, 49. RÜTTEL 1917, 65. DALAGER 1915, 56f.

[2] HAWKES 1916, 9 note.

[3] PARRY 1824, 510. BOAS 1907, 161.

[4] KNUD RASMUSSEN 1931, 166.

[5] KNUD RASMUSSEN 1930, 50.

[6] MURDOCH 1892, 434. NELSON 1899, 379ff., 437. Field notes. COLLINS (1937, 248) comments on the scarcity of seal skulls in all the old sites on St. Lawrence Island, and concludes that they were thrown into the sea. He also found, in an Old Bering Sea culture site, dried seal muzzles and the skull of a bearded seal attached to thongs for suspension and thinks this was for ceremonial practices. Walrus skulls, however, were plentiful throughout the sites, and the walrus does not seem to have been accorded any honors.

[7] GUNTHER 1928, 151. BOAS 1921, 304, 612. BOAS 1891, 569, 599, 613f. BOAS 1894, 461.

[8] BOAS 1921, 246, 447.

[9] SAPIR 1930, 148.

[10] GUNTHER 1928, 155. BOAS 1891, 644. MORICE 1895, 108. TEIT 1900, 347f.

[11] TEIT quoted by HALLOWELL 1926, 141 note 608.

[12] PIKE 1892, 56. JETTÉ 1911, 605.

[13] STELLER 1774, 117. VON SCHRENCK 1881-86, 546, 548. BATCHELOR 1901, 477. 505.

[14] HALLOWELL 1926.

[15] GAHS 1928.

offerings belong both to the ice-hunting stage in the circumpolar regions and to the European Palaeolithic. Later the respectful attitude towards the bones was incorporated both in the bear ceremonialism of the Woodlands and the salmon ceremonies of the Northwest Coast. The Eyak custom of lowering the bear skin three times may be a weak reflexion of the former ceremonies.

The *first salmon ceremony* proper has been analyzed by Dr. GUNTHER who finds that it does not exist on the Northwest Coast north of the Tsimshian (in other words is [489] lacking among the Haida and TIingit), while in a southern direction it even goes as far as the northern Maidu.[1] Within the Plateau area we find it among the Lower Lillooet, Sanpoil and Nespelem, Wishram, and Shasta;[2] it is possible that it also occurs among the Carrier, and both the Paviotso and Lemhi Shoshoni celebrate a similar feast on the arrival of the trout.[3] Dr. SPIER has kindly informed us that, according to his field notes, the Okanagan have a definite first salmon ceremony. On the other hand we have no information from a number of other Plateau tribes: Tahltan, Chilcotin, Thompson, Shuswap, Flathead, Coeur d'Alene, and the Middle Columbia Salish. While the details of the ceremonial vary considerably according to the general culture pattern of the tribe, the basic ideas, i.e. the immortality of the salmon and its willingness to be caught, are the same everywhere, another common feature being the ceremonial eating of the fish with the exclusion of "unclean" persons.[4] If these characteristics are considered the criterion, the ceremony certainly exists both among the Tnaina[5] and the Eyak. There can hardly be any doubt that in spite of the gap caused by the absence of the ceremony among the Tlingit and Haida, there must be a connection with the southern area of distribution, suggesting its former occurrence also among the two tribes just mentioned. Its general character points it out as a typical Northwest Coast trait. A comparison with the first fruit ceremonies of the Interior Salish is scarcely tenable; the latter are typical sacrifices [490] to the Suprerne Being, whereas the first salmon ceremony is a purely magical measure for the increase of the fish. The ceremonial eating of the salmon would rather recall the last phase of the Gilyak and Ainu bear festival. The bear is here considered an emissary of the supernatural world, and the slaughter of the animal is by no means a sacrifice, but only an occasion of sending back its soul to the Lord of the Mountains to express the wishes of the people. After the killing, however, there takes place a ceremonial eating of the meat in which, at least among the Ainu, everybody must participate. This seems strangely out of place here and may lie a survival from an older conception incorporated in the pattern of the feast, with which are also combined the bear ceremonialism of the circumpolar snowshoe culture and influences of Indonesian ancestor worship.[6]

Love magic is foreign to the Eskimo, but typical of the Northwest Coast.[7] The magical effect of *untying a woman s hair* at the time of birth corresponds to indentical or closely allied customs known from the Eskimo and Palaeo-Asiatic tribes.[8] They may be much more

---

[1] GUNTHER 1926, 605, 609.

[2] TEIT 1900-08a, 280. HILL-TOUT 1905, 140f. RAY 1932, 71f. SPIER & SAPIR 1930, 248ff. DIXON 1907, 430f.

[3] GUNTHER 1928, 137f.

[4] GUNTHER 1928, 139ff.

[5] OSGOOD 1937a, 148f.

[6] GAHS 1929.

[7] Tlingit (SWANTON 1908, 146). Kwakiutl (BOAS 1896, 580). Shuswap (BOAS 1891, 644).

[8] Chugach (Field notes). Caribou Eskimo (BIRKET-SMITH 1929, I 281). Iglulik Eskimo, when life is felt for the first time (KNUD RASMUSSEN 1929, 169). West Greenland (BIRKET-SMITH 1924,

widespread than we have been able to state.[1]

The belief in _witches_ is, of course, more or less universal. [491] The Tlingit associate the dead body of a dog with the power of a witch,[2] and human bones are commonly employed in witchcraft on the Northwest Coast. This resembles to some degree the witch's use of a dog skin and a flute made of a human limb bone among the Eyak. No counterpart to the custom of obtaining a view of the witch by gazing in water has been met with; it has, in fact, more of an Old World than an American aspect and may be a Russian superstition. In nearly all corners of the globe it is believed that nail parings and hair combings can be used in harming a person. This belief is found, for instance, among the Eskimo — at least the eastern tribes[3] —, on the Northwest Coast,[4] the Plateaus,[5] and among the Kutchin[6] and Ainu.[7] The Eskimo and Chukchi commonly associate the _northern lights_ with death or with the souls of the deceased, although they do not, as far as we know, believe them to be omens of death, as do the Eyak.

Turning now to the _taboos_, which Sir JAMES FRAZER aptly defines as the negative side of magic, we find, as a universal and intrinsic part of the concept, the belief that violation of the taboo is automatically followed by some kind of catastrophe. In this light we must look upon the Eyak belief that storms and bad weather — which may, indeed, prove to be disastrous to the whole community — [492] are the inevitable consequences of such misbehaviour as willful abortion, killing of infants, or moving about of a girl during her puberty seclusion.

The taboo against killing dogs is a very characteristic Athapaskan trait,[8] but it is also found among the Central Eskimo,[9] and may be compared with the aversion of the Bering Strait Eskimo against heating a dog.[10] Among the Kamchadal a woman was taboo when skinning a dog.[11] Closely related to this notion is, no doubt, the taboo against wolf hunting, which is also found among the Athapaskans.[12] It does not occur among the Eskimo, but is, on the other hand, mentioned from the Kwakiutl.[13] It is probable that this attitude towards both dog and wolf

---

    408). Angmagssalik Eskimo (RÜTTEL 1917, 126. KNUD RASMUSSEN 1921-25, 135). Yukagir, untying of clothes (CZAPLICKA 1914, 131). Gilyak, untying of knots (PIŁSUDSKI cited by MONTANDON 1937, 140).

[1] Similar customs occur in many places; Lappland, Indonesia, etc. (Cf. FRAER 1923, 238ff).

[2] KRAUSE 1885, 293.

[3] Copper Eskimo (STEFÁNSSON 1913, 295). Iglulik Eskimo (LYON 1824, 155. KNUD RASMUSSEN 1929, 182). Labrador (HAWKES 1916, 112). West Greenland? (KNUD RASMUSSEN 1921-25, III 328). Angmagssalik Eskimo? (HOLM 1914, 86).

[4] Tlingit (KRAUSE 1885, 292. SWANTON 1908, 470). Kwakiutl (BOAS 1891, 613). Nootka (JEWITT 1896, 188 note).

[5] Shuswap (BOAS 1891, 644). Thompson (TEIT 1900, 630).

[6] WHYMPER 1868, 187.

[7] VON SIEBOLD 1881, 30.

[8] Kutchin (OSGOOD 1936, 24). Satudene (OSGOOD 1933, 82f). Chipewyan (MACKENZIE 1801, cxviii. INGSTAD 1931, 199). Among the Tnaina only old women will kill a dog (OSGOOD 1937a, 174).

[9] Netsilik Eskiino (KNUD RASMUSSEN 1931, 150). Caribou Eskimo (BIRKET-SMITH 1929, I 96).

[10] NELSON 1899, 435.

[11] KRACHENINNIKOW 1770, I 106.

[12] Kutchin (OSGOOD 1936, 24). Satudene (OSGOOD 1933, 82f.). Chipewyan (HEARNE 1795, 344).

[13] BOAS 1891, 613.

should be seen in a far wider connection, i.e. the typical circum-Pacific dog mythology to which KOPPERS has called attention.[1] We have found no parallels to the taboo against the hunting of walrus and loon, but it may be mentioned that the latter is often, probably on account of its uncanny cry, regarded with a kind of superstitious awe in the boreal regions, at least of the Old World. These hunting taboos are evidently all connected with the belief that wolves, walruses, and loons were originally human beings. Taboos against killing of small birds or the first mosquito of the season may or may not be specific Eyak traits; no parallels have been found. [493]

There is a general hunting taboo to the effect that nobody is supposed to laugh at a wounded animal. The same precaution against offending the game occurs among the Chugach and Thompson Indians,[2] and the Danish author believes that he years ago heard a similar opinion expressed by the Chipewyan, though at the time he failed to make a note of it. Other taboos prevent a man from hunting when his wife is in childbed, or before a burial takes place. The latter rule recalls the general Eskimo practice of staying at the village and doing no work some days after a death has occurred, whereas the former has some similarity to the custom of the Puget Sound tribes, who do not hunt during the days of their wives' menstruation.[3] The Eyak also have a taboo against talking about the animal they intend to hunt; the Eskimo of .Bering Strait and the Nespelem and Sanpoil know the same prohibition.[4] The Tnaina of upper Cook Inlet told the American author that one was not supposed to discuss bear-hunting in advance. There is every reason to suppose that hunting taboos similar to those mentioned here are much more widespread than our fragmentary knowledge indicates.

Another typical man's taboo is the obligatory fasting before a war. Like fasting as a whole it is totally un-Eskimo, whereas it is found both among the tribes of the Northwest Coast and some of their neighbors.[5] The Nootka seem to prefer bathing and sexual abstinence to fasting.[6]

Some taboos apply only to women, either in general, [494] or during menstruation and pregnancy. They are forbidden to do certain kinds of work, chiefly those that involve much activity or noise, when their husbands are hunting or splitting wood. A similar Eskimo concept forbids all noise during a dangerous occupation like whaling. The Kwakiutl women have to keep quiet during the hunting excursions of their husbands,[7] whereas, among the Thompson Indians, they are not allowed to eat.[8] Under the same circumstances a Kamchadal woman must not sew or put her house in order.[9] When a Tlingit man was chopping wood with an adze made of the precious jade, "his wife should refrain from all frivolity."[10] A curious Eyak taboo forbids women to wear clothes made of new seal skins. There is, to our knowledge, no parallel to this rule among the Eskimo to whom one would naturally look for comparisons, and the question

---

[1] KOPPERS 1930, 358ff.

[2] Field notes. TEIT 1900. 348.

[3] HAEBERLIN & GUNTHER 1930, 49.

[4] NELSON 1899, 438. RAY 1932, 78.

[5] Tlingit (SWANTON 1908, 449). Haida (SWANTON 1905, 55). Cowichan (BOAS 1889, 324. BOAS 1894, 462). Thompson (TEIT 1900, 268).

[6] JEWITT 1896. 192f.

[7] BOAS 1921. 637ff.

[8] TEIT 1900, 327.

[9] STELLER 1774, 274.

[10] EMMONS 1923, 18.

arises whether the Eyak idea may not have come into existence because they are not quite familiar with the sea. Equally peculiar to the Eyak is the taboo against mixing skins of sea and land animals in a single garment; it may be compared, however, with the Eskimo and Kamchadal taboo against cooking meat of sea and land animals in the same pot.[1] There are several instances of a woman not being allowed to step over hunting implements; in some cases the prohibition seems to apply at all times,[2] while in other cases it is only during her menstruation.[3] [495] Closely related to this is the taboo against a pregnant woman crossing a trail, which is found among a number of Athapaskan tribes.[4]

There are many rules concerning pregnant and menstruating women: the former must not eat liver and kidneys, parallels to which occur both among the Eskimo and the Plateau tribes.[5] Menstruating women must not cook in the common pot, nor eat of the common dish — an exceedingly widespread custom.[6] Neither pregnant nor menstruating women are supposed to eat fish roe, a rule which perhaps is limited to the Eyak, whereas the prohibition against touching or eating fresh, especially raw meat is nearly universal, at least during the puberty period, on the Plateaus,[7] and in some cases also in the Eskimo area[8] and the [496] Boreal Woodlands,[9] as well as on the Northwest Coast.[10] Where fish is the staple food the custom sometimes changes to a

---

[1] Cf. WEYER 1932, 367ff. STELLER 1774, 274.

[2] Labrador Eskimo (HAWKES 1916, 134). Kwakiutl (BOAS 1921,608). Carrier etc. (Morice 1905, 107). Yellowknife (BACK 1836, 213).

[3] Cowichan (HILL-TOUT 1904b, 320). Nespelem and Sanpoil (RAY 1932, 135). Kutchin (OSGOOD 1936, 320).

[4] Dogrib (DUCHAUSSOIS 1922, 332. Cf. RUSSELL 1898, 163). Chipewyan (BIRKET-SMITH 1930, 76). These statements should only be regarded as examples, not as a complete list.

[5] Baffin Island (BOAS 1907, 143). Thompson (TEIT 1900, 327). Nespelem and Sanpoil (RAY 1932, 91). Painte (KELLY 1932, 160).

[6] Kodiak (HOLMBERG 1856, 401f.). Bering Strait Eskimo (JACOBSEN 1884, 245). Asiatic Eskimo (BOGORAS 1904-09, 491 f.). Netsilik Eskimo (KNUD BASMUSSEN 1931, 505). Caribou Eskimo (BIRKET-SMITH 1929, I 292). Iglulik Eskimo (KNUD RASMUSSEN 1929, 179). Baffin Island (BOAS 1888, 596). Nootka (BOAS 1891, 594). Puget Sound (HAEBERLIN & GUNTHER 1930, 49). Klallam (GUNTHER 1927, 241). Hupa (GODDARD 1903, 56). Shuswap (BOAS 1891, 642). Lillooet (TEIT 1900-08 a, 269). Thompson (TEIT 1900, 326). Okanagan, Flathead (TEIT 1930, 288, 382). Nez Percé (SPINDEN 1908, 198). Nespelem and Sanpoil (BAY 1932, 135). Northern Shoshoni (LOWIE 1909, 214). Kutchin (OSGOOD 1936, 141, 147). Chukchi (BOGORAS 1904-09, 491f.). All cases of seclusion may, of course, be added.

[7] Carrier (HAMILTON 1878, 206). Shuswap (BOAS 1891, 641f. Cf. TEIT 1900-08 b, 592). Lillooet (HILL-TOUT 1905, 136. Cf. TEIT 1900-08a, 269). Thompson (TEIT 1900, 317). Klamath (SPIER 1930, 69f.). Shoshoni (LOWIE 1909, 214. LOWIE 1924, 274). Ute (LOWIE 1924, 273). Paviotso (LOWIE 1924, 273).Paiute (LOWIE 1924, 272. KELLY 1932, 164. STEWARD 1933, 293).

[8] Iglulik Eskimo (KNUD BASMUSSEN 1929, 179). Baffin Island (BOAS 1888, 596).

[9] Tnaina (OSGOOD 1933a 712f.). Kutchin (SCHMITTER 1910, 13. OSGOOD 1936, 141). Satudene (OSGOOD 1933, 77).

[10] Tsimshian (BOAS 1916, 531). Bella Coola (BOAS 1892, 418). Nootka (BOAS 1891, 594). Cowichan (BOAS 1894, 461. HILL-TOUT 1904b, 323). Puget Sound (HAEBERLIN & GUNTHER 1930, 49). Songish (BOAS 1891, 574). Hupa (GODDARD 1903, 56). Yurok (GUNTHER 1928, 152).

taboo against fresh fish, but the underlying idea is probably the avoidance of the raw and bloody meat, which will have a bad effect on menstruation and childbirth. In other cases the girl's observances involve a general fast.

Among other rules pertaining to the different periods of life, we ought to mention the taboo which forbids young persons to eat certain dishes, such as marrow, kidneys, bear's feet and bear's liver. Among the Thompson Indians a girl during her puberty rites should not eat bear meat of any kind,[1] and the Chipewyan say that it will make a young man slow if he eats bear paws.[2] The Eskimo avoid as a rule eating the liver of the polar bear, but as far as the Danish author has been able to ascertain, for no magic reason, but for fear of being poisoned; under certain circumstances the liver really seems to have a dangerous effect.

A very common custom forbids a young man to eat his first game alone. As a rule he has to distribute gifts to the whole village. The Eyak rule, that he must eat none of it himself, is more rarely observed. Still we find this in some Eskimo groups,[3] and also among certain Plateau [497] tribes.[4] The Klallam apply the same observance to the first salmon caught by a young man.[5]

Of seasonal taboos the only ones noted among the Eyak concern the playing with buzzes, toy boats, sleds, or snow-shoes during the winter, and making string figures in summer. Chequers were also prohibited except during a certain month. It is well known that in North America and elsewhere certain games are supposed to belong to different seasons of the year. It is also probable that the buzz, here as elsewhere, is believed to have an effect on the wind and that this idea is the reason for the taboo, but we have found no parallels to the seasonal restriction. The Chugach play with buzzes at the end of the winter to make the sun come quicker. The prohibition against playing cat's cradle in the summer is a very common Eskimo trait.[6] On the other hand the Klamath claim that when played during the winter it will make this season longer.[7]

The custom of not mentioning the names of the dead has been noted from all parts of the world;[8] it occurs among the Chugach and is exceedingly common among the eastern Eskimo with the important exceptions of the Copper and Caribou groups,[9] among the Plateau tribes,[10]

---

[1] TEIT 1900, 317.

[2] BIRKET-SMITH 1930, 32.

[3] Aleut (SARYTSCHEW 1805, II 126). Bering Strait Eskimo (STEFÁNSSON 1914, 340). Iglulik Eskimo (BOAS 1907, 515. KNUD BASMUSSEN 1929, 179).

[4] Klamath (SPIER 1930, 168). Shasta, a whole year (DIXON 1907, 432). Paiute (KELLY 1932, 80).

[5] GUNTHER 1927, 203.

[6] From Bering Strait to Coronation Gulf (JENNESS 1924, 181). Copper Eskimo (JENNESS 1922, 184. KNUD RASMUSSEN 1932, 52). Netsilik Eskimo (KNUD RASMUSSEN 1931, 167). Iglulik Eskimo (BOAS 1907, 151. KNUD RASMUSSEN 1929, 183). The Chugach make cat's cradles in the Fall in order to "tangle up the sun" and make it recede more slowly (Field notes).

[7] SPIER 1930, 139.

[8] Cf. FRAZER 1923, 251ff.

[9] Field notes. WEYER 1932, 271. Add: M'CLINTOCK 1859, 233. DALAGER 1915, 1. RÜTTEL 1917, 49.

[10] Lillooet (HILL-TOUT 1905, 138). Upper Thompson (TEIT 1900, 332.) Nespelem and Sanpoil, one year (RAY 1932, 154), Wishram (SPIER & SAPIR 1930, 258), Klamath (SPIER 1930, 60), Washington and Oregon (GIBBS 1877, 210), Ute (LOWIE 1924, 271, LOWIE 1923, 150). Paiute

and the [498] inhabitants of the southern part 6f the Northwest Coast.[1] It is also known from the Tnaina.[2] Among the Ainu it only holds good of husband and wife.[3] There can be no doubt that this custom is an old one.

Shamans

Everywhere in arctic and northwestern North America and in Northeast Asia shamanistic powers are attributed to the aid of special *spirit helpers*.[4] In the Plateau area, [499] where the power quest forms the principal part of the young man's puberty rites, there is no sharp distinction between the familiars of the shamans and the spirits of ordinary persons, but a shaman is able to conjure up his familiars at will. The very vague idea of Gahushia Nelson that the spirit helpers were inherited in some way, supported by the fact that Johnny Stevens actually acquired his power from his great uncle, corresponds very well with the Northwest Coast custom where "there is a tendency to fixed inheritance of experiences with ancestral guardians."[5] Inheritance does not exclude the dream as another source or rather manifestation of shainanistic power, but the remarkable thing is that it is also combined with a sort of vision quest; after the dream and a preparatory period the novice goes alone into the woods in order to meet the spirit.

(STEWARD 1933, 298. KELLY 1932, 168).

[1] Nootka (BOAS 1891, 576). Makah, one year (SWAN 1870, 85). Squawmish (HILL-TOUT 1900, 484). Puget Sound (HAEBERLIN & GUNTHER 1930, 46). Klallam (GUNTHER 1927, 238, 250). Songish (BOAS 1891, 576), Yurok (KROEBER 1925, 48).

[2] WRANGELL 1839, 108.

[3] BACHELOR 1901, 252.

[4] Chugash (Field notes). Bering Strait Eskimo (NELSON 1899, 427 ff. STEFÁNSSON 1914, 321f.). Point Barrow (MURUOCH 1892, 431f). Mackenzie Eskimo (STEFÁNSSON 1914, 367f., 378). Copper Eskimo (JENNESS 1922, 191ff. KNUD RASMUSSEN 1932, 27f.). Netsilik Eskimo (KNUD RASMUSSEN 1932, 294ff). Caribou Eskimo (KNUD RASMUSSEN 1930, 51ff.). Iglulik Eskimo (PARRY 1824, 551. KNUD RASMUSSEN 1929, 111f). Baffin Island (BOAS 1888, 591ff. BOAS 1907, 489. BILBY 1923, 209, 265ff). Labrador Eskimo (TURNER 1894, 194f. HAWKES 1916, 127f.). Polar Eskimo (KROEBER 1900, 304. KNUD RASMUSSEN 1921-25, III 28ff.). West Greenland (HANS EGEDE 1925, 393. CRANZ 1770, 268. GLAHN 1771, 345. GLAHN 1921, 189). Angmagssalik Eskimo (HOLM 1914, 88f. KNUD RASMUSSEN 1921-25, I 15ff.). Tlingit (KRAUSE 1885, 286. SWANTON 1908, 463. BOAS 1890, 848). Haida (SWANTON 1905, 38). Tsimshian (BOAS 1890, 848). Kwakiutl (BOAS 1890, 848. BOAS 1896, 570). Bella Coola (BOAS 1890, 848). Nootka (Boas 1890, 848). Cowichan (BOAS 1889, 326). Puget Sound (HAEBERLIN & GUNTHER 1930, 75ff). Klallam (GUNTHER 1927, 296). Songish (BOAS 1891, 581). Tahltan (EMMONS 1911, 112), Shuswap (BOAS 1891, 645). Chilcotin (FARRAND 1899, 646). Thompson (TEIT 1900, 354). Nez Percé (SPINDEN 1908, 256f.). Takelma (SAPIR 1907, 267). Klamath (SPIER 1930, 107ff). Nespelem and Sanpoil (RAY 1932, 185). Shasta (KROEBER 1925, 302). Shoshoni (LOWIE 1909, 225). Paiute (KELLY 1932, 190. STEWARD 1933, 311), Tnaina (Cf. OSGOOD 1937a, 177ff.). Kutchin (HARDISTY 1872, 317. SCHMITTER 1910, 18). Eastern Athapaskans (ROSS 1872, 307). Satudene (OSGOOD 1933, 84). Chipewyan (HEARNE 1795, 192). Chukchi (BOGORAS 1904-09, 292). Koryak JOCHELSON 1905-08, 47ff). Yukagir (JOCHELSON 1926, 155f). Gilyak (STERNBERG 1905, 463).

[5] SPIER 1930, 247.

SPIER has shown that the voluntary quest and the involuntary dream as sources of power have different distributions in North America. Acquisition through dreams occurs only in the western section of the Southwest, in the southern Great Basin, and in California as far north as the Maidu and Wailaki, whereas the quest is found on the southern Northwest Coast, the Plateaus from the Tahltan in the north to the Apache in the south, and also on the Plains; in northern California, southern Oregon and the northern Basin both methods occur.[1] This combination [500] should, however, be explained by overlapping and does not constitute a separate type. That this is the explanation is confirmed by the occurrence among the Eyak, for the combination here differs from the one mentioned above in the important detail that the Eyak novice receives the dream summons first, and the quest takes place afterwards, while in Oregon and California the events are in the opposite order. Of the Kutchin we are told that, as among the Eyak, their shamans acquire their powers through dreams, and afterwards they retire to the forest and begin conjuring.[2] Dreaming is also the ordinary method of obtaining power among the Tnaina.[3] On the whole, however, our knowledge of Athapaskan shamanism is remarkably weak. Still it may be added that ambitious hunters and warriors among the Beaver sought supernatural helpers who appeared to them in dreams,[4] but we cannot be sure that a regular vision quest is meant, nor do we know anything of the shamans in particular. Something like a quest fasting is mentioned from the Satudene, but the shamans, at least, may get power before birth.[5] The Sekani youths obtain hunting powers by a quest, but medical abilities are ascribed to dreams.[6]

If we pass to the Eskimo we find that generally a deliberate training is considered necessary, but on the other hand strange dreams, or in fact any extraordinary experiences, may lead to the acquisition of shamanistic abilities.[7] In extreme cases a man may — as we were [501] ourselves told by a Chugach informant — be a shaman without knowing it. It seems doubtful whether the training of the Eskimo novices can be compared directly with the vision quest in its more southern form; it is, at least, both locally and individually much more varied and may be the result of a special development like so many other Eskimo traits, Among the Chukchi and Koryak the original manifestation of shamanistic power may come to persons who have undergone great misfortunes or dangerous experiences, but like the Eskimo they consider a period of mental and physical preparation necessary.[8] Here, however, another factor enters. As STERNBERG has proved,[9] among a great many Siberian peoples a peculiar feature is believed to affect the acquisition of shamanistic powers, since the shaman is supposed to have sexual intercourse with his main spirit and in fact is chosen by the latter for this very purpose. Very often the Siberian shaman tries to resist the spirits, but in vain. From these remarks it seems that the area where we find a deliberate power quest is surrounded by large regions where the acquisition of shamanistic abilities is more or less due to dreams and other involuntary experiences, the special training among the Eskimo and their neighbors being, perhaps, a

---

[1] SPIER 1930, 249ff.

[2] OSGOOD 1936, 156 cf. 158.

[3] OSGOOD 1937a, 181f.

[4] GODDARD 1916, 226.

[5] OSGOOD 1933, 83f.

[6] JENNESS 1937, 68f., 72.

[7] Cf. the compilation in WEYER 1932, 428ff.

[8] CZAPLICKA 1914, 178ff.

[9] STERNBERG 1925, 472ff.

separate development. This may corroborate the supposition which is a priori the most probable, viz. that the involuntary receiving of power is older than the quest.

The paraphernalia of the Eyak shaman are scarcely as elaborate as those of the Tnaina, for instance. The _belt_ is the most characteristic insignia of the Central Eskimo shamans, but it also belongs to the shaman outfit of the [502] Aleut, Tnaina, Wiyot and Gilyak, as well as other tribes of the Amur country;[1] it may possibly he an old feature. Special neck ornaments may be worn by Tlingit shamans,[2] but we have found nothing like the shaman's hair ornament of the Eyak.

The _spirit dolls_ take a very prominent place in the outfit of the Eyak shaman. The closest parallels to them are, no doubt, the "devil dolls" of the Tnaina[3] and certain figurines of which we obtained information of the Chugach. From the Aleut there is a report of "idols who became living and had to be killed,"[4] which at least strongly recalls the same idea. From a few other Eskimo tribes there are scanty and very confused statements of what may have been similar objects. NELSON figures a carved head representing the assisting spirit of a Bering Strait shaman,[5] but we do not know if it is typical. In order to attract the caribou, the conjurers of the Labrador Eskimo erect a pole with a magic doll representing the power of some famous hunter or shaman;[6] it seems, however, to be an image of a definite person, and its identification with the dolly of the western tribes is questionable. The same applies to certain Greenlandic shaman dolls. One of these was said to speak Dutch when its master appeared;[7] in one of the legends of how the Eskimo killed the old Norse settlers in West Greenland, mention is made of a wooden shaman's doll who was able [503] to show the hiding place of the Norse chief.[8] One or two early accounts of "idols" from West Greenland[9] are, on the other hand, probably due to some sort of misunderstanding, and the carvings from East Greenland, representing evil spirits (_tupilait_) are only modern illustrations of the conception of these beings and are not intended for actual shamanistic use. If there is any connection at all between the western and eastern Eskimo magic dolls they may possibly be a Thule culture trait, since they are entirely lacking in the central area, but the whole problem is as yet far from being solved.

The Eyak and Tnaina are not the only Indian tribes in western North America, however, having dolls representing the spirit helpers of the shaman. Similar figures are described from the Carrier and their neighbors,[10] and the Coeur d'Alene used to carve stone images of their guardian spirits[11] (it should be noted that in this tribe the sharp distinction between medicine men and ordinary people does not exist). We are also told that a Quinault shaman had several figures

---

[1] BIRKET-SMITH 1929, II 181. OSGOOD 1937a, 177.

[2] SWANTON 1908, 464.

[3] OSGOOD 1937a, 179. A similar specimen was found by the American author in Cook Inlet (DE LAGUNA 1934, 114).

[4] ERMAN 970-71, III 211.

[5] NELSON 1899, 441. The wooden figure used at the doll feast, which is also celebrated by the Ingalik, seems to be different (cf. _ibid._ 379, 494).

[6] TURNER 1894, 197f.

[7] PAUL EGEDE s.a., 78f.

[8] PINGEL 1838-39, 240.

[9] DAVIS 1880, 19. OLEARIUS 1656, 176.

[10] MORICE 1890, 158.

[11] TEIT 1930, 194f.

representing his spirit helpers.[1] The Klamath, and probably the Modoc medicine men set up a carved image of a spirit on the outside of their dwellings, and the Tillamook, Chinook, and Quinaull shamans carry sticks with carvings of guardian spirits; but in these cases the analogy may be superficial.[2] It is well known that the Gilyak and other Amur tribes have a great number of wooden spirit carvings, both in human and in animal [504] shape, and that iron images of the assisting spirits are fastened to the Siberian shaman's costumes. It may be, therefore, that the scattered occurrence of spirit images in northwestern North America is due to Old World influences. As far as the Alaskan examples go, this is strongly corroborated by the fact that the above mentioned figure found at Cook Inlet has a pointed head and that pointed heads were said to be characteristic of the Chugach spirits, for this is a typical Siberian concept. As to the spirit representations of the Plateau and Northwest Coast tribes the evidence is too weak to permit of any definite conclusions.

Beliefs

It is a fundamental concept in Eyak religion that all things, whether animate or inanimate, have *spiritual "owners."* The same idea prevails everywhere in northwestern North America.[3] We find it universally among the Eskimo,[4] and it also occurs on the Northwest Coast,[5] among the Plateau tribes,[6] and in the Mackenzie area.[7] It is also [505] common among the Palaeo-Asiatics[8] and other Siberian peoples like the Yakut. It may be originally an Asiatic belief which has passed across Bering Strait to the New World.

This conception, which is really nothing but a highly developed and specialized animatism, should not be confused with the general idea of souls peculiar to human beings and animals. Like the preceeding one we find it generally spread throughout the whole area in consideration.[9] Without entering upon any lengthy discussion about the priority of animatism or

---

[1] WILLOUGHBY 1889, 278f.

[2] SPIER 1930, 270.

[3] Cf. SCHMIDT 1934, 468.

[4] Chugach (Field notes). Bering Strait Eskimo (NELSON 1899, 394f, 437f). Copper Eskimo (Cf. KNUD RASMUSSEN 1932, 31f, 35). Netsilik Eskimo (Cf. KNUD RASMUSSEN 1931, 239ff). Iglulik Eskimo (KNUD RASMUSSEN 1929, 204). Baffin Island (BOAS 1888, 591). Labrador Eskimo (TURNER 1894, 194. HAWKES 1916, 127). West Greenland (HANS EGEDE 1925, 393. PAUL. EGEDE s.a., 110. GLAHN 1771, 347f. GLAHN 1921, 179ff). Angmagssalik Eskimo (Cf. HOLM 1914, 82ff.).

[5] Tlingit (BOAS 1890, 848. SWANTON 1908, 452). Tsimshian (Boas 1890, 848). Songish (BOAS 1891, 580).

[6] Shuswap (TEIT 1900-08b, 598). Lillooet (TEIT 1900-08a, 276). Nez Percé (SPINDEN 1908, 258). Kutenai (CHAMBERLAIN 1893, 559). Nespelem and Sanpoil (RAY 1932, 172).

[7] Tnaina (OSGOOD 1937a, 169). Kutchin (PETITOT 1876, 60. OSGOOD 1936, 154, 157). Satudene (OSGOOD 1933, 81).

[8] Chukchi (BOGORAS 1904-09, 285ff). Koryak (JOCHELSON 1905-08, 30f.). Yukagir (JOCHELSON 1926, 144ff.) Gilyak (STERNBERG 1905, 252). Ainu (BATCHELOR 1901, 546, 560).

[9] For the Eskimo cf. WEYER 1932, 289ff. Chugach (Field notes). Aleut (VENIAMINOV cited by PETROFF 1884, 158). Tlingit (SWANTON 1908, 460f.). Haida (SWANTON 1905, 34). Kwakiutl (BOAS 1921, 713ff. BOAS 1891, 610). Bella Coola {Nuxalk} (BOAS 1892, 420). Nootka

animism in general, it seems perfectly clear, however, that the specialized form of the former, connected with the idea of individual "owners," is a later intrusion upon American soil than the idea of the soul.

The belief in _reincarnation_ of the soul is likewise [506] very widespread in this region. We find it referring to the reincarnation of a special "name-soul" among the Eskimo.[1] It is also common in the woodlands of the Yukon and Mackenzie,[2] and is met with both on the Plateaus[3] and the Northwest Coast.[4] Some of the Palaeo-Asiatic tribes have similar conceptions.[5] Offerings to the souls of the dead by throwing pieces of food into the fire is both a Northwest Coast and an Athapaskan custom.[6]

We had very little success in gathering information about the different _spirit being_s of the Eyak. The thunder is associated with the thunder bird. This concept is foreign to the Eskimo who, as a rule, ascribe the thunder to the crackling of a dry skin. The Koryak also have quite different ideas. Their myths, like those of the Yuki of California, identify the thunder with the Supreme Being. The Copper Eskimo, however, believe that the thunder is caused by numerous small birds,[7] and the same belief is found [507] among the Tungus and Samoyed, while the Eskimo of Bering Strait, as well as the Asiatic Eskimo and Chukchi, have adopted the idea of a

---

(BOAS 1891, 596). Cowichan (BOAS 1894, 461. Puget Sound (HAEBERLIN & GUNTHER 1930, 81). Twana, Chimakum, Klallam (Cf. EELLS 1889, 677). Klallam (GUNTHER 1927, 295f.). Alsea (FARRAND 1901, 241). Tahltan (EMMONS 1911, 108). Carrier (HARMON 1903, 255f. MORICE 1890, 158). Shuswap (BOAS 1891, 646. TEIT 1900-08b, 611f). Lillooet (TEIT 1900-08a, 286f.). Thompson (TEIT 1900, 357ff.). Coeur d'Alene, Okanagan (TEIT 1930, 183, 292). Nez Percé (SPINDEN 1908, 253). Kutenai (CHAMBERLAIN 1893, 559). Nespelem and Sanpoil (RAY 1932, 169ff.). Wishram (SPIER & SAPIR 1930, 238). Klamath (Cf. GATSCHET 1890, xcv. SPIER 1930, 101). Shoshoni (LOWIE 1909, 226f.). Paiute (KELLY 1932, 198. STEWARD 1933, 307), Tnaina (OSGOOD 1937a, 169f.). Ingalik (Cf. CHAPMAN 1907, 14. CHAPMAN 1921, 301f). Kutchin (OSGOOD 1936, 154, 157, 161). Satudene (OSGOOD 1933, 82). Chipewyan (BIKKET-SMITH 1930, 79). Chukchi (BOGORAS 1904-09, 332f.). Koryak (JOCHELSON 1905-08, 101f.). Yukagir (JOCHELSON 1926, 157ff). Gilyak (STERNBERG 1905, 470). Ainu (BATCHELOR 1901, 548 & passim).

[1] Aleut (JOCHELSON 1933, 77f.). Netsilik Eskimo (KNUD RAKMUSSEN 1931, 220). Labrador Eskimo (WALDMANN 1910, 431), West Greenland (CRANZ 1770, 257f). Angmagssalik Eskimo (HOLM 1914, 81). Among the Chugach the new-born child is not regarded as the reincarnation of a dead person (Field notes).

[2] Tnaina (OSGOOD 1937a, 160f.). Ingalik (CHAPMAN 1921, 303). Kutchin (PETITOT 1876, 59. SCHMITTER 1910, 14. OSGOOD 1936, 140, 146). Sekani (MORICE 1890, 161). Satudene, Hare, Slave (OSGOOD 1933, 75). Chipewyan (JENNESS 1932, 387). Tena (JETTÉ, MS).

[3] Tahltan (EMMONS 1911, 108). Carrier (MORICE 1890, 161). Lillooet (TEIT 1900-08a, 287).

[4] Tlingit (KRAUSE 1885, 310). Haida (SWANTON 1905,117. MACKENZIE 1892, 59).

[5] Koryak (JOCHELSON 1905-08, 100). Yukagir (CZAPLICKA 1914, 132). Ainu (BATCHELOR 1901, 237, 479).

[6] Tlingit (SWANTON 1908, 431). Kwakiutl (DAWSON 1888, 78). Squawmish (Hill-Tout 1900, 478). Puget Sound (HAEBERLIN & GUNTHER 1930, 54). Tnaina (OSGOOD 1937a, 170). Kutchin (JONES 1872, 325, doubtful). Satudene (OSGOOD 1933, 82).

[7] KNUD RASMUSSEN 1932, 24.

single thunder bird.[1]   This belief in one thunder bird is general among the Indians in northwestern North America: on the Northwest Coast,[2] the Plateaus,[3] as well as in the Mackenzie area.[4]

An analogy to the Eyak belief in a luck-bringing creature carrying a crying child on its back is clearly found in the common Northwest Coast concept of "Property Woman" who is described as having the same characteristics.[5] The Kamchadal spoke of a certain kind of forest spirits, whose wives also carried crying babies attached to their backs, but apparently nothing was known of their luck-bringing abilities; on the contrary they were supposed to make people mad.[6]

Giants appear quite often in Eskimo folk-tales, and some of them may be cannibals. They are also mentioned from the Chukchi and Tnaina.[7] The Kutchin live in great fear of hairy and gigantic cannibals.[8] Giants are also prominent [508] in the mythology of many Plateau tribes, but with some exceptions they generally show no cannibalistic tendencies,[9] whereas such notions are characteristic of both the southwestern and eastern United States.[10] There can be no doubt that the belief in giants is an old one. The same applies to dwarfs. We meet them in Eskimo myths as well as in the folklore of the Northwest Coast[11] and the Plateaus.[12] The idea of a cannibalistic wolf people may be peculiar to the Eyak.

The belief that wolves and walrusies are reincarnations of dead people — which is probably connected with the taboo against wolf and walrus hunting — may be compared to the Kwakiutl belief that the souls of the hunters on land and sea go to the houses of the wolves and killerwhales respectively;[135] but it is admitted that this parallel may be somewhat far-fetched and close analogies are lacking. On the other hand we find the belief that land-otters are really

---

[1]   NELSON 1899, 445. BOGORAS 1904-09, 328.

[2]   Tlingit (SWAN 1874, 7). Haida (SWAN 1874, 7. SWANTON 1905, 13. MACKENZIE 1892, 58). Kwakiutl (DAWSON 1888, 86). Nootka (EELLS 1889a, 332. BOAS 1891, 596). Makah (SWAN 1870, 7ff. EELLS 1889a, 329). Cowichan (BOAS 1889, 326). Puget Sound (HAEBERLIN & GUNTHER 1930, 75). Twana, Chimakum, Klallam (EELLS 1889, 653). Quinault (WILLOUGHBY 1889, 274f.). Chinook (SWAN 1874, 7. EELLS 1889a, 329).

[3]   Shuswap (TEIT 1900-08b, 597). Lillooct (TEIT 1900-08a, 275). Thompson (TEIT 1900, 338). Okanagan (TEIT 1930, 290). Kutenai (CHAMBERLAIN 1893, 575). Nespelem and Sanpoil (RAY 1932, 212). Wishram (SPIER & SAPIR 1930, 236).

[4]   Kutchin (PETITOT 1876, 60). Chipewyan (BIRKET-SMITH 1930, 81).

[5]   Tlingit (WATERMAN 1923, 450). Haida (SWATON 1905, 29). Tsimshian (EMMONS 1925, 43).

[6]   KHACHENINNIKOW 1770, I 99. STELLER 1774, 266.

[7]   BOGORAS 1904-09, 298f. PETROFF 1884, 163f. OSGOOD 1937a, 171.

[8]   MASON 1924, 59.

[9]   Shuswap (TEIT 1900-08b. 599). Lillooet (TEIT 1900-08a, 276). Coeur d'Alene, Okanagan, Flathead (TEIT 1930, 181, 290, 383). Nez Percé (SPINDEN 1908, 269). Wishram (SPIER & SAPIR 1930, 237). Klamath (GATCHET 1890, xcix).

[10]   OLSON 1933, 891.

[11]   BOAS 1916, 455. KROEBER 1925, 67.

[12]   Shuswap (DAWSON 1892, 37. TEIT 1900-08b, 589). Thompson (TEIT 1900, 339). Coeur d'Alene, Okanagan, Flathead (TEIT 1930, 180, 290, 183). Nez Percé (SPINDEN 1908, 259). Klamath (GATSCHET 1890, xcix. SPIER 1930, 237).

[13]   BOAS 1921, 727.

drowned people very pronounced among the Tlingit, Haida, and Tsimshian.[1] Among the Tahltan the otter was taboo, and the Sekani maintain that the otter makes people insane.[2] The Chugach and Aleut are of the opinion that sea-otters used to be human beings, but changed to animal shape.[3] [509] No parallel has been found to the idea that the loon is a transformed boy.

The only approach to religious ceremonial or cult which we were able to discover among the Eyak was the _reverence shown to the sun_. A real sun worship exists among the Flathead and Coeur d'Alene, it is weak among the Okanagan, Nespelem and Sanpoil, and lacking among other Salisli of the Interior.[4] Even though there is no real sun cult, the sun is, however, regarded as a mighty spirit by most tribes in northwestern North America. This is the case on the Northwest Coast[5] and the Plateaus.[6] We are also told that the Aleut used to greet the sun in the morning.[7] whereas the scattered remarks on Eskimo sun cult occurring in old works are due to misunderstanding; they were refuted, as far as Greenland is concerned, by as early an author as GLAHN.[8] In northeastern Asia, however, we find a rather distinct sun worship among the Yukagir, and the Koryak sometimes identify the sun with the Supreme Being.[9] The sun-goddess of the Ainu is probably something entirely different,[10] related perhaps to Japanese religion. Of course the little information we were able to gather among the Eyak must not be stressed, but it is nevertheless evident [510] that ideas more or less similar to their own prevail over large parts of the surrounding regions.

The belief in _charms_ and _amulets_ is too universal to need further discussion here; it will suffice to mention one important species, viz. that made of the umbilical cord of the new-horn child. This type of amulet is not rare among the Eskimo.[11] On the Northwest Coast it is mentioned from the TIingit, who, however, do not keep it more than a week, and from the Kwakiutl, Klallam, and some tribes of the extreme northwestern corner of California.[12] It is also very common in the Plateau area[13] and is reported from the Chipewyan[1] and Ainu.[2] Belief in an

---

[1] SWANTON 1908, 456. SWANTON 1900, 26.

[2] EMMONS 1911, 75 cf. 111. JENNESS 1937, 78.

[3] ield notes. LOWE 1842, 482.

[4] SCHMIDT 1934, 434ff.

[5] Tlingit (SWANTON 1908, 452. BOAS 1890, 845). Haida (MACKENZIE 1892, 57). Kwakiutl (BOAS 1890, 847. BOAS 1891, 610). Bella Coola {Nuxalk} (BOAS 1892, 420). Nootka (BOAS 1891, 595). Cowichan (BOAS 1889, 325f. BOAS 1894, 462). Coast Salish (BOAS 1890, 847). Klallam (EELLS 1889, 673). Songish, traces (Boas 1891, 580).

[6] Tahltan (JENNESS 1932, 375). Shuswap (BOAS 1891, 645). Thompson (TEIT 1900. 344ff). Nez Percé (SPINDEN 1908, 259). Kutenai (CHAMBERLAIN 1893, 559. BOAS 1890, 848). Wishram (SPIER & SAPIR 1930, 236).

[7] VENIAMINOV cited by PETROFF 1884, 153.

[8] GLAHN 1771, 338ff.

[9] JOCHELSON 1926, 141ff. JOCHELSON 1904-08, 31, 122.

[10] VON SIEBOLD 1881, 25. BATCHELOR 1901, 63f.

[11] Chugach (Field notes). Mackenzie Eskimo (STEFÁSSON 1914, 379 f.). Copper Eskimo (KNUD RASMUSSEN 1932, 41). West Greenland (HANS EGEDE 1925, 374). The Angmagssatik Eskimo use the afterbirth (RÜTTEL 1917, 176).

[12] SWANTON 1908, 429. BOAS 1921, 655, 697ff. BOAS 1896, 574. GUNTHER 1927, 234. KROEBER 1925, 45. GODDARD 1903, 52. The Haida bury the umbilical cord (SWANTON 1905, 47).

[13] Tahltan (EMMONS 1911, 101f.). Shuswap (TEIT 1900-08b, 584). Thompson (TEIT 1900, 304f).

intimate mystical connection between an individual and his umbilical cord or afterbirth is a very old conception, now almost worldwide, and is one which has been responsible for numerous magical precautions and practices.

Mythology

Unfortunately our myth material does not permit any detailed analysis. It is exceedingly meagre and evidently highly fragmentary. Besides there is scarcely a single myth which is really well told; in many instances the story is [511] hopelessly confused, the plot more or less forgotten, and many important details obviously omitted. In these circumstances we can do nothing more than point out the general character of the mythology, adding a few particulars of certain widespread tales, based chiefly upon BOAS' profound studies of Tsimshian mythology.

It is peculiar to Northwest Coast mythology that the common incidents reflect the ordinary social life of the tribes, only exaggerated by imagination.[3] The same is true of the Eyak myths, which, for example, contain next to nothing of symbolism. As has previously been emphasized there is, however, one fundamental difference from the ordinary Northwest Coast tales, in that the Eyak myths have absolutely no allusion to moieties or to the obtaining of crests through strange adventures or intercourse with animals. This lends to Eyak mythology a peculiar (older?) social aspect.

Most prominent among all Eyak myths are certainly those belonging to the _Raven Cycle_, which occurs right from the Alaskan Eskimo and, in distorted form, from the Athapaskans on the lower Yukon, as far south as the southern Kwakiutl.[4] It is also found among the Palaeo-Asiatic tribes, and there can be no doubt that it constitutes a typical circum-Pacific trait. Another widespread animal tale is the story of "Porcupine and Beaver"; the Eyak version is rather confused, but shows affinities to similar myths of the Tlingit, Haida, Tsimshian, Tsetsaut, Shuswap, Hare, and Jicarilla Apache.[5] According to the field notes [512] of the American author, the Tnaina at Kenai have a whole Porcupine Cycle. She also got a Porcupine and Beaver story from the Yukon Indians at Nulato.

The common Northwest Coast theme of a woman who gives offence to some animal which then takes her for a wife is found in the story "Taken by a Bear"; somewhat similar tales occur among the Chugach, Tlingit, Haida, Tsimshian, Bella Coola, and Rivers Inlet Indians,[6] Among the Tsimshian this tale is a part of the adventures of _Gunaxnesemg'a'd_. In the Eyak story of "Calm Weather's Daughter" there are two incidents belonging to the same cycle, viz. the slave who breaks his master's axe which is then repaired by the hero, and the hero who follows his wife over the surface of the sea, but sinks when his wife turns and looks at him. Among the Tlingit these

---

Coeur d'Alene, Okanagan (Cf. TEIT 1930, 167, 281). Middle Columbia Salish (TEIT 1928, 126). Nespelem and Sanpoil (RAY 1932, 128). Ute, Paviotso, Pauite (LOWIE 1924, 265f., 269). Paiute (KELLY 1932, 158).

[1] MACKENZIE 1801, cxxii.

[2] VON SIEBOLD 1881, 32.

[3] BOAS 1916, 875.

[4] BOAS 1916, 584. Also middle Yukon (F. DE L.).

[5] BOAS 1916, 724ff. SWANTON 1905a, 44. SWANTON 1905b, 98. SWANTON 1909. 43ff. 220.

[6] Field notes. BOAS 1916, 836ff.

themes are not connected.[1] Both incidents are known over large areas, the slave motif occurring among the Tlingit, Haida, Tsimshian, Bella Coola, Kwakiutl, Rivers Inlet Indians, Sechelt, and Nanaimo,[2] while the Sea Walkers are found among the Tlingit, Haida. Tsimshian, Kwakiutl, Sechelt, and Tillamook.[3] The incident in Calm Weather's Daughter of the husband being unfaithful to his second wife and being found out when she examines the water he has brought, is found in the Tsimshian story of the origin of the Wolf Clan as told the American author by a Nass River informant.

In the story of the Wolf People the other well-known Northwest Coast trait of the helpful animal occurs; the chief's sister gives the stolen girl a knife and advises her to [513] pierce the birchbark canoes of the wolves, but no parallel to the myth as a whole has been found. The seals show their gratitude in "He Came Back to Shore together with the Seal People," a story also recorded from the Tlingit, Haida, Tsimshian, and Rivers Inlet tribe,[4] but here referred to the sea lions. We obtained another version' from the Chugach. The most important, from an ethnological point of view, of the stories about helpful animals is, however, "The Girl and the Dog," which appears to be related to the well known theme of the girl who married a dog.[5] It is true that the Eyak version gives a sort of faded impression. It contains, for instance, no allusion to any sexual relation between the two — in fact the dog is expressly stated to be a bitch — but on the other hand there are points of resemblance in the general character of the tale (the girl left behind by her angry father and supported by the dog), which indicate a connection with the Northwest Coast theme. The latter is again related to the more elaborate myth recorded not only from the Eskimo and a great many tribes in the northwestern regions of North America, but also, like the Raven cycle, from the Asiatic side of the North Pacific.[6]

Sometimes the persons who visit the animals are transformed into animals themselves, e.g. the typical Northwest Coast story of "Salmon Boy," which is also found among the Tlingit, Haida, Tsimshian, Bella Coola, Bella Bella, Nootka, and Chilcotin.[7] The Tlingit and Haida versions are, however, most like the Eyak. Two tales refer to the general conception that land-otters are really drowned [514] human beings, viz. "The Man and the Land-Otters" and "Where a Man Killed Lots of Land-Otters." The latter resembles myths known to the Tlingit, Haida, Tsimshian, and Kwakiutl.[8] "Turned into a Groundhog" has a rather close resemblance to a Chugach tale collected by us, but is otherwise more Indian than Eskimo in character.

Parallels to "The Alder People and Sun People" were also collected by us from the Chugach. One of our informants staled that it was of Tlingit origin; we have not found any record of it from the latter, which does not prove, of course, that our informant was wrong. On the other hand another Chugach informant said that it came from the Aleut. A more Eskimo-like character is displayed in "Good for Nothing," which shows some resemblance to certain Eskimo hero tales. On the whole, Eyak mythology gives the general impression of being far more closely connected with that of the Northwest Coast Indians than with Eskimo folklore. A few myths, as we have already pointed out, also show affinity to those of the Northeast Asiatic tribes.

---

[1] SWANTON 1909-26, 245. Cf. SWANTON 1905b, 101.

[2] BOAS 1916, 955.

[3] BOAS 1916, 950.

[4] BOAS 1916, 819, 821f. Cf. SWANTON 1905b, 101.

[5] BOAS 1916, 784.

[6] KOPPERS 1930, 160ff.

[7] BOAS 1916, 770ff.

[8] BOAS 1916, 862.

Conclusions

Constituent Complexes in Eyak Culture

Having [515] studied the elements of Eyak culture separately, we may proceed to arranging them according to certain points of view. In this way we may hope to penetrate somewhat into the darkness that obscures the origin and early history of this people. But before going any farther it is necessary to reject a number of elements of which nothing can be said with any degree of certainty, either because our information is too fragmentary, or because they actually appear to be local types, or for some other reason.

These "uncertain elements" which are precluded from further discussion comprise the following: Wooden head rest; canoe stool; mitten (cut unknown); trousers (cut unknown); particular style of hair dressing; axe; bone arrow heads with a single barb; blow gun; pebble throwing stick; whip sling; "hide-and-seek"; tossing in an outstretched skin; bond-fellowship; custom of assigning game to the first hunter to hit it; several taboos, and the custom of lowering the bear hide after skinning the animal. Some other elements we may, with more or less justification, suspect of having considerable age, but so little is known about them that it seems safer to exclude them also from the discussion, viz.: Fur cap with a median seam; scrapers of stone and mussel shell; bending of wood by [516] means of dry heat; hospitality prostitution. Of the bark house we may surmise a connection with a certain Plateau type, but as the possibility of it being only a temporary makeshift cannot be dismissed we prefer likewise to disregard this evidence.

As to the compartment bag we may suspect a late spread in connection with white influence (much in the way, for instance, that floral designs have spread to northwestern Canada and Alaska). A few elements are apparently of Russian origin, or at least were introduced with Russian colonization, viz. the dovetailed log house, the steam bath(?), the automatic bow, and perhaps the detecting of witches by gazing in water. The built-up sledge and dog driving are also so recent, if indeed present at all, that they can hardly be said to belong to the culture.

Having thus paved the way for what we consider a more reliable analysis of the culture, we may proceed to enumerate those types which all have a *very wide distribution both in North America and in Eurasia*. Probably there can be no serious doubt of their relatively great age. Under this head the following are comprised:

Dome-shaped hut; lean-to; bough sledge; carrying strap; two-skin cut of frock; collar hood; hard sole boot; skin robe; simple head band; necklace; comb; head scratcher; prick tattooing; stone polishing; ulo; crooked knife (?); steaming wood for bending; simple fire drill; lamp; drinking tube; round wooden bowl; long wooden dish; spoon; ladle; meat fork(?); dehairing of skins by soaking; sinew thread; sewing awl; overcast seam; bag made of birds' feet (occurrence not established with certainty); snow shovel; hunting dog; deadfall; pitfall; simple snare; lance; primary arrow release; barbed harpoon; throwing board; [517] bird drive; leister; needle for stringing fish; stone boiling; pit oven; roasting spit; drying of meat; putting up of vegetables with fat(?); drum; levirate; wife exchange (?); communal hunting grounds; distribution of hunting spoils; naming after dead persons; removing corpse through a special opening in the dwelling; grave goods; popgun; top; buzz; string figures; shinny; wrestling; sporting contests in general; dice; hand game; earth burial; stabbing eyes of game; placing some part of game in special place; witchcraft; hair and nail taboo; taboo against menstruating women eating from common dishes; taboo against their eating raw meat; taboo against mentioning the name of the deceased; involuntary acquisition of magic power; shamanism in general; shaman's belt; animism; belief in reincarnation; belief in dwarfs and giants; amulets, especially umbilical cord amulets. Although the information is extremely meagre we suspect that also the taboos against a woman eating entrails and a young man eating his first game belong here.

As we have already mentioned, these culture elements are probably old in the history of mankind, but of course this circumstance does not necessarily mean that they are old in the culture of the Eyak. It is not without reason that this question is raised. The general distribution of the elements characterizes them as belonging to what has been called the ice-hunting stage, i.e. the earliest culture stratum of the circumpolar region.[1] However, according to the views of the Danish author, Eskimo culture is basically a specialization of the ice-hunting stage,[2] and, as it happens, an Eskimo group, the Chugach, are the immediate neighbors [518] of the Eyak. So we might, perhaps, suspect that all, or at least some, of the apparently old traits of the Eyak culture are really only comparatively recent loans from the Eskimo. However, this can hardly be true of most of the elements, simply because they are found more or less continuously not only among the Eskimo and Eyak, but also over the adjacent areas where direct Eskimo influence is entirely out of the question. Even in the case of the lamp and the throwing board (the latter, by the way, is not quite established from the Eyak) it should be remembered that both occur among the Tlingit in forms different from and independent of the corresponding Eskimo types. All taken into consideration there are, perhaps, only one instance where the occurrence of these old elements in Eyak culture may be due to contact with the Eskimo, viz. the hard sole boot. We can scarcely avoid the conclusion that a *very great number of elements in Eyak culture connect it with the ice-hunting stage.*

Some Eyak elements have a distribution which, if it cannot always compare with that of the traits just mentioned, is nevertheless very considerable. The latter are connected with the so-called *snow shoe-stage*, i.e., the complex supposed to overlie the ice-hunting culture in the Boreal Woodlands and characterized primarily by the snow-shoe.[3] As far as the Eyak are concerned the following elements belong there: conical tent; wrist guard; porcupine quill-work (?); skin fringes (?); plank and netted snow-shoes; bark-stripping wedge; beaver tooth knife (?); smoking of meat(?); platform cache (?).[4] This is really an astonishingly [519] poor array of features, when we take into consideration that the traveling route of the snowshoe complex from Siberia to the western hemisphere cannot have been very far from the habitat of the Eyak. Nevertheless they lack a number of the most characteristic elements such as the toboggan, bark canoe, blunt-headed arrows, folded bark vessel, snowshoe netting needle, two-handed scraper, hair embroidery, bear ceremonial, scapulimancy, etc. Moreover the conical tent apparently had a very inconspicuous position in the culture, and we have no information about the use of snowshoes in hunting. It should also be borne in mind that the Eyak snowshoe proved to be a primitive type which had undergone some later innovations. The inference must be that the Eyak never received the snow-shoe complex as a whole, but only scattered elements which did not modify their culture to any marked degree. In this they resemble the tribes of the Northwest Coast.

---

[1] Cf. BIRKET-SMITH 1929, II 212ff.

[2] Cf. also HATT 1916 and HATT 1934.

[3] Cf. BIRKET-SMITH 1929, 212ff. HATT 1916. HATT 1934.

[4] Skin fringes occur among the present Central Eskimo tribes. The wrist guard is characteristic of the Punuk and modern Western Eskimo cultures (Cf. COLLINS 1937, 325).

A considerable number of traits have a decidedly *circum-Pacific distribution*. Within this category we include the following: Rectangular plank house; separate sleeping room; notched ladder; stockade; raised cache-house; shirt made of horizontal strips of small animals' fur; apron; nose ornaments (?); stone pecking; stone mortar; twined basketry; boat-shaped container; round plate; wooden quiver; hunting of sea mammals in open water; weregild(?); vegetable arrow poison; digging stick (?); slavery; transvestism; bride service; cremation; shaman's dolls; attitude towards dogs; sounding board; Raven myths; tale of the Girl and the Dog. To these we may, perhaps, add: the dugout, fish buried in the ground to rot, and the mother-in-law taboo, although they are less restricted to the Asiatic shores of the Pacific than are the other traits mentioned above. [520]

It is, of course, easy to explain why the Eyak have been deeply influenced by a circum-Pacific culture drift. There can hardly be any doubt that the general direction of this drift has been from Asia, more particularly perhaps from the Lower Amur region, towards North America. In particular instances, however, it may be exceedingly difficult to decide whether an element originated on the Asiatic or the American side of the ocean, for we must not forget that the favorable geographical conditions of the American Northwest Coast give it every opportunity of developing into a cultural center, at least of secondary rank compared with the Asiatic side.

Eyak culture shares a number of elements with the northwestern parts of the American continent. More or less regularly they occur *in the Eskimo Thule culture and on the Northwest Coast*, including in some cases also the Plateaus. Some of them are obviously of Asiatic origin. although they cannot be included in any of the before mentioned groups, viz. cord and bow drill; concept of spiritual "owners"; needle-and-thread tattooing; arrow feathering consisting of three split feathers; vessels made of bent strips of wood or bark; dip net; fish trap; and fish club(?); it may be added that the cord and bow drill and the "owner" concept are probably older than the Thule culture. Of others the source is less certain: Rectangular nailed boxes; washing with urine; sea mammal drive; harpoon float; halibut hook; dagger; festival house. They may be of Old World origin, although it cannot be proved at the present time. As far as North America is concerned, they seem to belong originally to the Northwest Coast rather than to the Thule culture. Their center was indisputably the North Pacific fjord region with its genial climate and ample [521] food supply, and the influence of this region on later Alaskan Eskimo culture is well' known.

Some Eyak elements are characteristic of the *Thule culture only*, and do not occur either on the Northwest Coast or on the Plateaus: Sail (evidently primarily Asiatic); gutskin coat; truck hood; sealskin thongs; box trap with a tipping plank (?); backed bow; hunting of seals basking on the ice; derision songs. The taboo against making string figures in the summer, and the notion that the northern lights are connected with death also have an Eskimo character, although their relation to the Thule stage is uncertain. Of course the limitation of sealing on the ice is purely environmental, and there is no fundamental difference between hunting seals basking on the ice floe and on the rocks or flats.

The following elements do not occur among the Eskimo except in a few cases where borrowing from the Northwest Coast is evident, whereas they are characteristic of the *Northwest Coast and Plateau areas*: Crutch paddle; loose downs used for ceremonial purposes; feather headdress; ear ornament of separate strings of beads; body paint; use of native copper; puberty rites; grave house; quoits; thunderbird concept; reverence towards the sun; feeding the fire. Some others are now lacking on the coast, but as in these cases the primitive character of the element is unquestionable, this apparent gap in their distribution may be due to their abandonment on the coast in favor of more advanced types. For the sake of comparison the latter are added in parenthesis: Bark house (plank dwelling); spiked war club (slave killer or *meri* type); shield (armour); hereditary political chiefs (hereditary chiefs of high ceremonial rank but little or no political power); power quest (hereditary spirit helpers). [522]

Finally there are a number of elements which the Eyak must have derived *directly from the Northwest Coast*, in many cases, no doubt, from the Tlingit in rather recent times. Excluding, of course, such imported articles as the woven blanket and the like, they comprise the following items: Certain details in the construction of the house (cf. p. 371); dentalium ornaments; adze with T-handle; painting of artefacts; use of eulachon for illumination; rectangular wooden bowls; simple bow; V-shaped cod hook; art elements, including both carving and painted designs; matrilineal moieties; exhibition of corpse; potlatch; ceremonial paddle; jingle rattle; flute; fast and sexual abstinence as part of magical and religious rites; purification by means of vegetable substance; love philters; inheritance of spiritual helpers; the concepts of Property Woman and of land-otters being drowned persons.

As Just mentioned, the Eyak seem to owe all these features to their contact with the Tlingit; but when we enter into particulars we will perceive that some of them are originally Old World traits which have become more or less modified on the Northwest Coast. This holds true of the wooden house as a whole, only some details having been added. It also applies to the T-adze which is related both to the Eskimo elbow adze and the adze with a D-shaped handle from the southern Northwest Coast, all of them probably being derived from Old World adzes. The elegant curves of the simple bow, with its narrow grip and flattened wings, must be derived from the composite bow of Asia. And from Asia have probably come also the fundamentals of the social system, as far as moieties and matrilineal descent are concerned. [523]

The Building of Eyak Culture

The proceeding analysis clearly shows that Eyak culture is an extremely complicated thing which has received impulses and elements from all sides. Of course this might be expected from their geographical situation on the borders of three or four of the principal culture areas of North America and close to the main cultural gate between the two hemispheres.

The basic structure of Eyak culture seems fairly clear. More than 80 Eyak elements, i.e. nearly 45 per centage of the 183 culture traits studied here, are classed within the ice-hunting culture, and even though some are included with a certain doubt, the amount is too great to be accidental, The elements in question belong to all phases of human life, comprising dwellings, means of conveyance, dress, house utensils and tools, techniques, hunting methods and weapons, social life, sports and pastimes, magic and religion, etc. — covering in fact the whole compass of human activities. There can be no doubt that a people, with nothing but this equipment, could live in a frugal and risky, but still endurable way in these regions. This is highly suggestive, for it surely must mean that the ice-hunting stratum as a whole underlies Eyak culture, as is also the case with other specialized cultures within the arctic and boreal parts of both continents.

It is entirely different when we turn to the snowshoe stratum. It is true that this complex has been less studied than the proceeding one, and we are not as fully aware of its constituent elements. For all we know they may be much fewer in number than those of the basic ice-hunting stratum. Nevertheless, even considering the small amount of well defined snowshoe elements, exceedingly few (i.e. 10, [524] of which several are doubtful) have found their way to the Eyak, and on the whole they are of strikingly casual character. As emphasized before the only explanation we can offer is that the snowshoe complex was never adopted as a whole.

 This view entails, however, some important conclusions. It is a well known fact that the snowshoe complex is of Asiatic origin. On American soil the Athapaskans have been considered the bearers of this complex.[1] DAVIDSON even goes a step further concerning the framed snowshoe, since he supposes that it was introduced into North America with the Athapaskan invasion, whereas the Algonkians are made responsible for the spread of the plank snowshoe.[2] There are, however, serious obstacles to the latter part of his hypothesis, for the basic culture of the southern Atlantic and trans-Appalachian Algonkians seems to be decidedly "pre-snowshoe" and, indeed, characteristic of the ice-hunting stage, although modified by the more genial environment and by the intrusion of agriculture from the south.[3] This does not tally with the supposition that the wooden snowshoe formed a part of the original Algonkian culture, but agrees very well with the view that it spread to the northern groups at a period later than the first great exodus of Algonkian tribes from their primeval habitat, but still before the arrival of the primitive netted "bearpaw" type. If we turn to the first part of DAVIDSON'S hypothesis we find an apparently small, hut in reality very important difference from the view that makes the Athapaskans responsible for the spread of the snowshoe in North America. When DAVIDSON identifies the introduction of the [525] netted snowshoe of bearpaw type with the Alhapaskan invasion, he can hardly mean anything but their migration into Norlh America across Bering Strait. Let it first of all be emphasized that even if DAVIDSON is right as far as the Athapaskans go, his hypothesis cannot apply to the Nadene stock as a whole; the snowshoe complex, and even the snowshoe itself, has never got a firm footing among the non-Athapaskan Nadene groups, i.e. the Eyak, Tlingit, and Haida. If, therefore, the netted snowshoe was carried across from Siberia by the Athapaskans, the other Nadene groups must have immigrated into North America at a still earlier period. In this way the problem tapers down to the question, whether the differentiation of the Nadene stock took place in the New World or not; this it is the linguists' task to answer, but a priori it does not seem probable that the verdict should he in favor of a pre-immigration schism.

 Furthermore we find that snowshoes are not reported from a single Pacific or southern Athapaskan group, although they occur among neighboring tribes, as for instance, the Klamath, Modoc, Yurok, Ute, Paiute, and Tigua, and have frequently been found in din"- dwellings and prehistoric pueblos.[4] It would be strange, indeed, if snowshoes had gone entirely out of use among the very tribes who brought them, whereas they were retained by the tribes who had adopted them. Moreover, there seems to be archaeological evidence that the snowshoe reached the Southwest ahead of the Navaho and Apache. And if we take a fairly well known tribe like the Chipewyan as representatives of the northern division, an analysis of their culture will show an astonishing large number of ice-hunting elements besides those belonging to the snowshoe complex, viz. no less than [526] 54 per centage of the elements constituting their material culture, which can hardly be explained otherwise than by assuming that they are survivals of an earlier ice-hunting stage.[5] Under these circumstances our present knowledge cannot be said to support the view that the snowshoe complex formed the original culture of the Athapaskans and was

---

[1] BIRKET-SMITH 1918, 219. BIRKET-SMITH 1930a 27ff.

[2] DAVIDSON 1937, 153f.

[3] BIRKET-SMITH 1918, 212ff.

[4] DAVIDSON 1937, 6f., fig. 2.

[5] BIRKET-SMITH 1930, 103f.

carried by them across Bering Strait. The Nadene stock seems to have entered the New World on the ice-hunting stage, and not till a later period did the northern Athapaskans receive the snowshoe which was essential to their successful advance in the Mackenzie region.

The work of the JESUP North Pacific Expedition conclusively demonstrated the close connection between the Paleo-Asiatic tribes and the Northwest Coast Indians. In recent years GAHS has pointed out a number of cultural parallels between the Palaeo-Asiatics and Aleut on one side and Indonesia on the other: matrilinear organization, female shamans, ancestor cult connected with head-hunting in the south and bear festivals in the north, etc. According to his view the Ainu, Gilyak, and Kamchadal, together with the Indonesian tribes, represent the so-called secondary matri-lineal culture stratum of the Vienna school (*freimutter-rechtliche Kreis or melanesische Bogenkultur*), whereas, on the American side, the Northwest Coast tribes belong to the earlier, primary matrilincal stratum (*exogam-mulier-rechtliche Kreis or Zweiklassenkiiltur*), while the Koryak and Aleut occupy an intermediate position characterized by the beginning decay of the primary stratum as a result of influence of the secondary culture.[1] The theory of a connection between the Ainu and the Indonesian tribes [527] has also been advanced by STERNBERG,[2] while KOPPERS has proved that the Tungus show affinities to the Miao-tze.[3] The latter has also called attention to the distinct matrilineal stamp of the pre-Chinese culture,[4] and through a study of the dog mythology he has been able to strengthen the theory of the relationship between the pro-Chinese culture and the matrilineal culture of the American Northwest Coast.[5] The American author of the present work has proved that many elements are common to the prehistoric Eskimo culture of Cook Inlet and the Asiatic coast as far south as Japan.[6] The evidence of a circum-Pacific culture stream has gained in strength by the analysis of Eyak culture; 27 of its elements seem to belong here.

As mentioned before, the greater part at least of the 22 elements which the Eyak owe to their contact with the Tlingit (the Tlingit details of the house having been classed together as one element) must also be included among the circum-Pacific traits, as in most cases they are elaborations of Old World forms which have drifted back to the north. The matrilineal moiety system presents the most difficult problem. The ties between the matrilineal cultures of East Asia and the American Northwest Coast are so numerous and unquestionable that it is difficult to believe that the identity of the social structures could be accidental. On the other hand, it seems fairly clear that the Eyak, who like the Aleut occupy an intermediate geographical position, have not adopted the system till a rather late date; there are many features of evident pre-moiety origin, and no [528] allusion to moieties is apparent in the myths. One explanation would be that the Eyak had not always been intermediary, but had immigrated to their present habitat after the circum-Pacific culture wave had brought the moiety system to the Tlingit. But then, how shall we explain their abundant share of other circum-Pacific elements? Another explanation is the one offered by GAHS regarding the Koryak and Aleut, viz. a secondary disintegration of the dual organization due to contact with the more advanced matrilinear cultures of Eastern Asia. So far this hypothesis is nothing but a guess, and it would be more than rash to assume it for the Eyak

---

[1] GAHS 1929, 87f.
[2] STERNBERG 1929.
[3] KOPPERS 1930a.
[4] KOPPERS 1930b.
[5] KOPPERS 1930.
[6] DE LAGUNA 1934, 216f.

also. The cultural development of the northern circum-Pacific regions is far too complicated to be disposed of in a few lines, and extensive field work must still be done, before we can hope to untangle the threads.

The origin of the remaining elements of Eyak culture can be classified roughly as follows:

(1) Asiatic, without belonging to any of the well defined complexes mentioned above (9 elements);

(2) Eskimo Thule culture and Northwest Coast, chiefly found in the southern parts of the latter area (7 elements);

(3) Eskimo Thule culture (10 elements);

(4) Northwest Coast and Plateau, or in a few cases only the latter, probably because they have disappeared on the coast (17 elements).

It is true that hardly any of these groups constitutes a real complex. Most or all give the impression of a rather casual infiltration due to long cultural contact. That such contact has been of rather long duration appears from the fact that at least the elements common to both the Thule and Northwest Coast cultures must necessarily be of [529] considerable age, for one thing because most of them are limited to the southern part of the Northwest Coast and have disappeared in the northern part. A similar interpretation should be made of the Plateau traits; their presence in Eyak culture should not be ascribed to any particular intimate connection with the Interior, since these are old traits which probably occurred also in the coast area in former times. The great age of the post-Birnirk Alaskan Thule culture has been fully substantiated by COLLINS' investigations at Wales, where it seems to have been contemporary with the Punuk culture stage.[1]

A complete reconstruction of the development of Eyak culture should also include the chronological sequence of the component culture layers. So far very little can be said on this question. It seems evident that the ice-hunting stratum is the oldest, as it is certainly also in many respects the most important. The chronological relations between the circum-Pacific and Thule cultures are less clear. It is striking that none of the here-mentioned circum-Pacific traits has been carried along the Arctic coast with the eastward spread of the Thule culture, but on the other hand this does not necessarily mean that the circum-Pacific drift reached Alaska after the eastward migration of the Thule Eskimo, for it may have followed a southern route (over the Aleutian Islands?) which did not bring it into contact with the Thule culture farther north. This is an important problem, the solution of which must wait till more information is at hand.

The cultural position of the Eyak ought, however, to be fairly clear by now. We have found the following components: [530]

I., *The basic ice-hunting culture*, which they share with the rest of the circumpolar area.

II., The bulk of the later elements they have *in common with the American Northwest Coast*, viz.

---

[1] COLLINS 1937, 371f, 379.

(1) The circum-Pacific traits.

(2) Some traits common to the Thule and Northwest Coast cultures, but probably derived either from Asia or the Northwest Coast.

(3) Some other traits which so far are known only from the Northwest Coast or the Plateaus; it is important to note, however, that we do not have here a single cultural drift. Some of these elements must have come to the Eyak in the form of a reflux in recent times, owing to increasing contact with the Tlingit. For the most part they are rather insignificant details, although some, particularly the moiety system, are of deep-going character.

III., *Other influences*, of much less importance, comprising:

(1) Snowshoe traits, which have been absorbed only to a very limited extent.

(2) A few North Asiatic features which cannot be referred to any particular complex.

(3) A few elements of the Thule culture.

So the Eyak culture must be characterized principally as a Northwest Coast culture with a somewhat old-fashioned stamp, modified to a certain degree by recent Tlingit influence, contact with their Eskimo neighbors, and their proximity to the Asiatic continent. *This rather strongly supports the supposition that the Eyak have occupied their coastal habitat for a very long period* — indeed there is no evidence of immigration from any other region at all. It is generally believed that the Tlingit have [531] moved north in modern times, and certain peculiarities of their northernmost division, the Yakutat, have been explained by assuming that they have spread over a foreign substratum.[1] There is nothing to indicate that this should be Eskimo as has been supposed.[2] On the other hand it is not improbable that the Eyak once possessed a larger territory. Everything indicates, indeed, that they are a tribe in decline. Were the Eyak then the original owners of what is now the habitat of the northern Tlingit? This question is bound up with numerous other problems involving the early history of the American Northwest Coast, one of the most important areas of the western hemisphere from an ethnological point of view, and cannot be answered for the present.

To some extent our analysis has also thrown a light on the development of Northwest Coast culture as a whole. Both theoretical considerations and archaeological evidence go to show that the North Pacific coast has been inhabited for a very long period, so that when JENNESS is inclined to regard the Indians of this area as comparatively late immigrants from the Asiatic side[3] he must probably be thinking of the present day aspect of racial and cultural conditions, and not of the first appearance of Man in these parts. If, leaving the race problems out of consideration, we turn to an analysis of Northwest Coast culture, we find, on the other

---

[1] Cf. SWANTON, 1908, 407ff.

[2] MACLEOD 1924, 256f. Cf. also footnote (2) on p. 345.

[3] JENNESS 1937a, 29f.

hand, many elements of a primitive character and apparently also of a considerable age. KROEBER has emphasized the isolated position of Northwest Coast culture among the culture areas of North America; he is of opinion [532] that it only shares the most basic elements with the rest of the continent, whereas its characteristics arc cither imported from the Old World or are local developments.[1] We have found that the ice-hunting stage (which probably represents more than one culture wave) forms the foundation of Northwest Coast culture, and this stage is certainly already far removed from that of the earliest immigrants to the western hemisphere. If, however, we accept this change of KROEBER'S view, it has only been corroborated by our investigation.

This will also in a certain measure explain the cultural position of the Northern Plateaus. KROEBER believes that the old basic culture of the coast was nearly identical with the historic plateau culture,[2] but as pointed out formerly this view meets the difficulty that the latter appears essentially as a blending of ice-hunting and snowshoe elements with some later coast admixture.[3] This obstacle is removed if we consider the ice-hunting stage as underlying the culture of the coast. Hut while the introduction of snowshoe elements formed a link between the plateaus and the rest of the continent, the coast region was only very superficially affected by the snowshoe complex.

Probably we are entitled to look for the explanation of this fact in the topography of the country. Suppose the snowshoe complex crossed Tiering Strait, it would wander south along the coast until it hit the Yukon valley, entering either from the mouth, or across the numerous easy passes from Norton Sound. Being hunters, the bearers would naturally head for the Interior, up the valley which is rich [533] in game. Once they had left the coast by that route, they would find it very hard to get back. The easiest way back is down the Sushitna River from the headwaters of some of the Tanana tributaries, and so into Cook Inlet. Perhaps the Tnaina actually spread this way, since they are closely related to the Tena of the Yukon and Tanana. But the mountainous country near the mouth of the Inlet would be a barrier to a people who relied on snowshoes rather than on boats for travel, so they could not have spread much below the mouth of Kachemak Bay. As for the pass over the Chugach Mountains into Valdiz, that is very difficult, and again the Prince William Sound country is not much good for snowshoe travel. The Copper River valley is an even worse route to the coast, and would have been still more difficult in early days when the Childs and Miles Glaciers apparently met in mid-stream. Therefore the snow-shoe people must have kept to the valleys and plateaus north of the Chugach and St. Elias Mountains and east of the Canadian Coast Range. On the coast the development took an entirely different path, building up in time a remarkably isolated culture, the history of which we are just beginning to discern.

---

[1] KROEBER 1993, 7 ff. Cf. also KRAUSE 1926, 80.
[2] KROEBER 1923, 16.
[3] BIRKET-SMITH 1930a, 16.

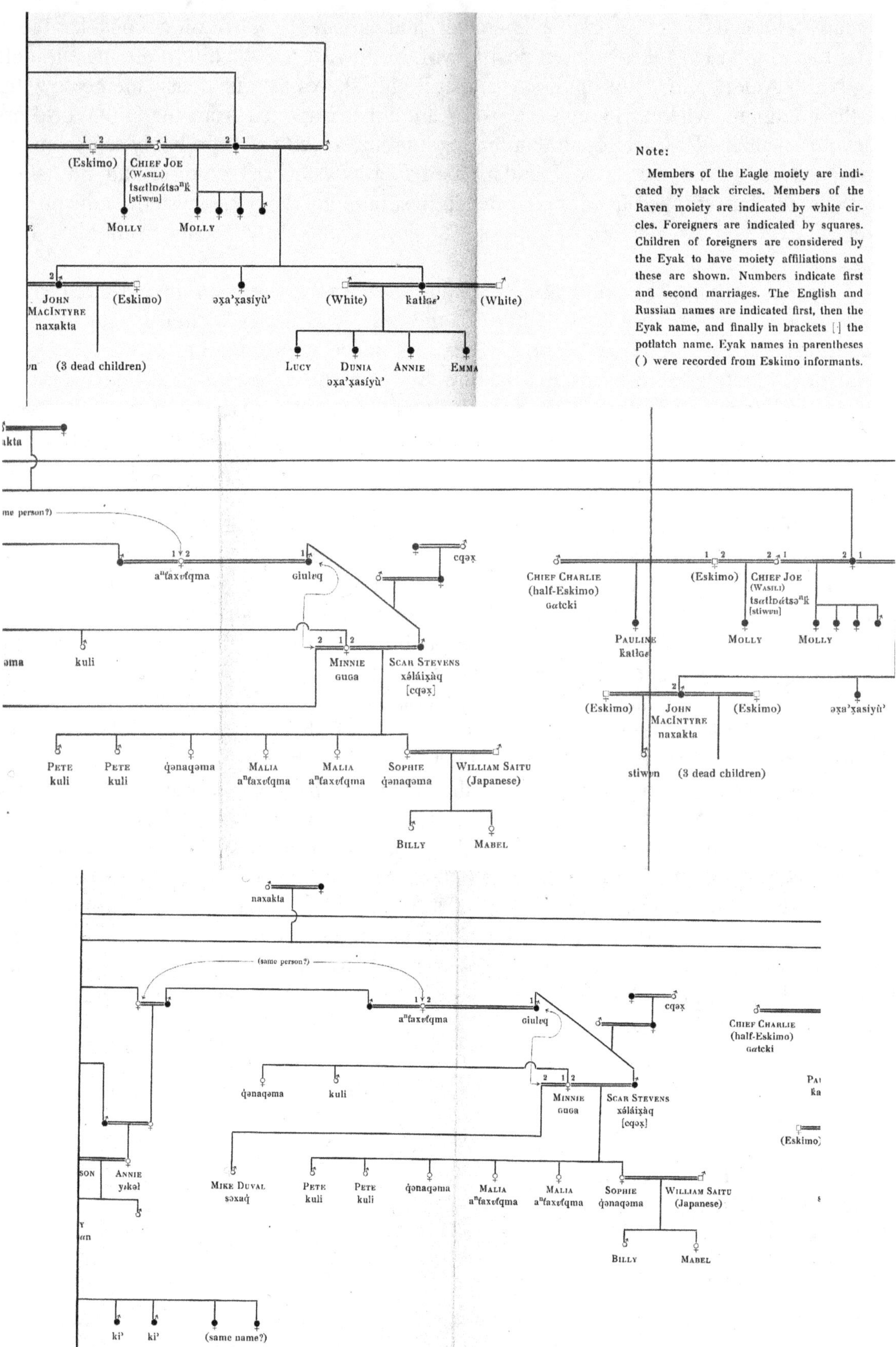

Note:

Members of the Eagle moiety are indicated by black circles. Members of the Raven moiety are indicated by white circles. Foreigners are indicated by squares. Children of foreigners are considered by the Eyak to have moiety affiliations and these are shown. Numbers indicate first and second marriages. The English and Russian names are indicated first, then the Eyak name, and finally in brackets [ ] the potlatch name. Eyak names in parentheses ( ) were recorded from Eskimo informants.

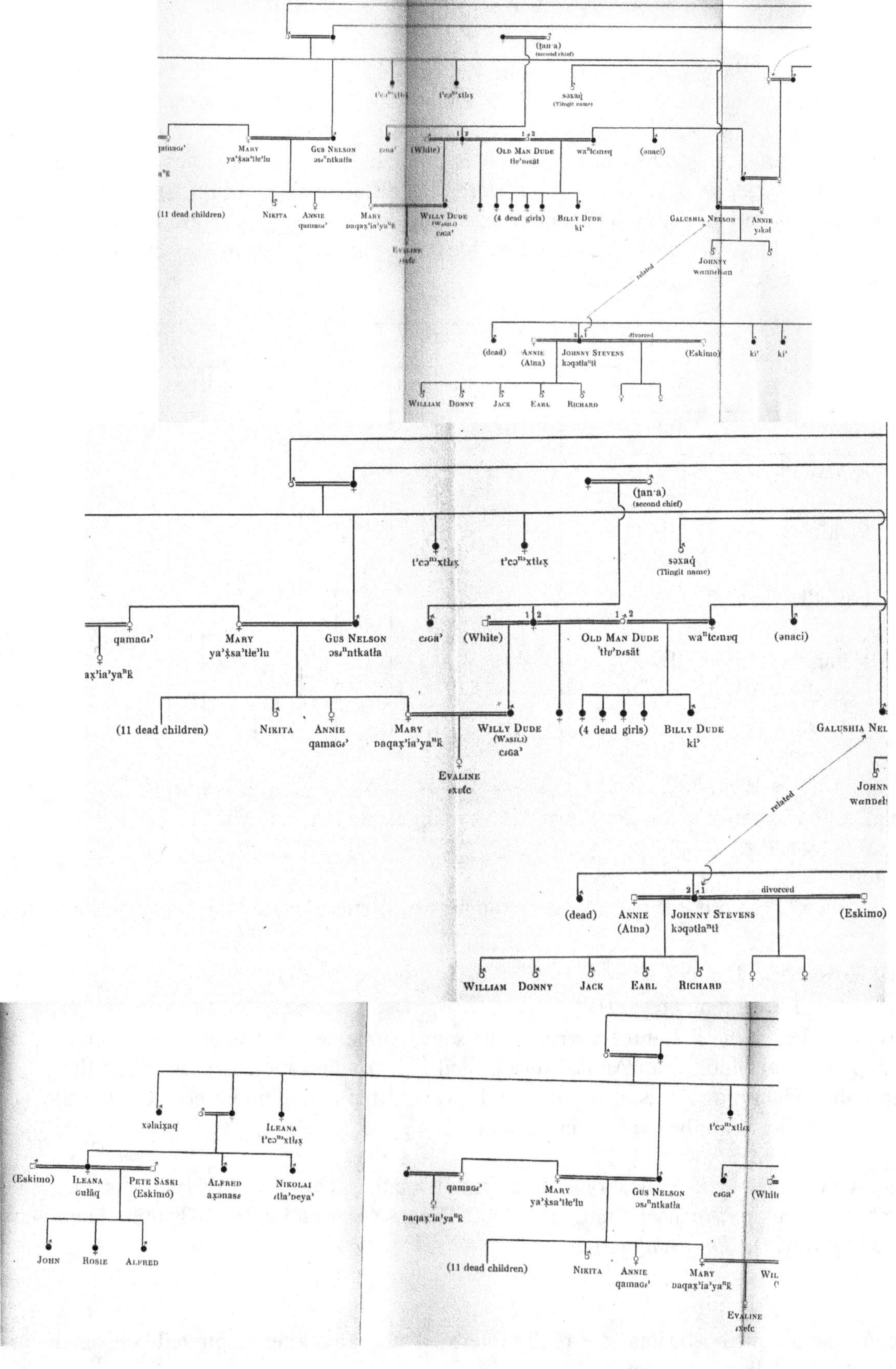
(ʈanˑa)
(second chief)
t'cɔᵐxtlɛx
t'cɔᵐxtlɛx
səxaq̇
(Tlingit name)
qamaGɪ'
MARY
ya'x̣sa'tłɛ'lu
GUS NELSON
ɔsɪᵉntkatła
cɪGa'
(White)
OLD MAN DUDE
'tłɪ'Dɛsät
waⁿtcɪnʋq
(ənaci)
ax̣'ia'yaⁿʀ
(11 dead children)
NIKITA
ANNIE
qamaGɪ'
MARY
Dɑqax̣'ia'yaⁿʀ
WILLY DUDE
(WASɪLɪ)
cɪGa'
(4 dead girls)
BILLY DUDE
ki'
GALUSHIA NELSON
ANNIE
yɪkal
EVALINE
ɪxʋɪc
JOHNNY
wɑnɒɛʰan
related
(dead)
ANNIE
(Atna)
JOHNNY STEVENS
kɔq̇ɔtlaⁿtł
divorced
(Eskimo)
ki'
ki'
WILLIAM
DONNY
JACK
EARL
RICHARD
xəlaix̣aq
ILEANA
t'cɔᵐxtłɛx
(Eskimo)
ILEANA
ɢʋłầq
PETE SASKI
(Eskimo)
ALFRED
ax̣ənasɛ
NIKOLAI
ɪtła'ɒeya'
JOHN
ROSIE
ALFRED
qamaGɪ'
MARY
ya'x̣sa'tłɛ'lu
GUS NELSON
ɔsɪᵉntkatła
cɪGa'
(White)
Dɑqax̣'ia'yaⁿʀ
(11 dead children)
NIKITA
ANNIE
qamaGɪ'
MARY
Dɑqax̣'ia'yaⁿʀ
WIL
EVALINE
ɪxʋɪc

Eyak vocabulary[‡]

The following vocabulary was obtained from Galushia Nelson, with the exception of words preceded by a **D**, which were obtained from Old Man Dude. The sometimes striking variations between the words given by these two men suggest dialectic differences. In many cases we have recorded several variations m the same word given by Galushia. This is either because the two recorders did not agree, *or* because the same word was differently heard at [536] different limes. There was unfortunately not sufficient time to check up on all these variations, and so all forms recorded are listed here. In the few cases where we can be fairly sure which is the correct from, the variants are marked with parentheses.

	Stops			Spirants			Affricatives			Nasals
	sonorant[1]	surd	glottal	snrt	surd	glt	snrt	surd	glt	
Bilabials	ʙ(?)									m
Alveolars	D	t'	't		s' c'		Dj	ts'	t's	n n^y
Patalals	G	k'	'k	γ	x ẋ (?)					ŋ(?)
Labialized Palatals				γ^w	x^w ẋ^w					
Velars	G̲	q'	'q		x̲					
Labialized Velars		q^w								
Laterals				l	ł		Dl	tł	t'ł	

Glottalization was very slight.
Breathing: h (The anterior x was not heard with a y-tinge, and may have been a harsh h).
Semi-Vowels: y and w
Glottal Stop: '
Vowels: a ä ɛ e (?) i ɪ ɔ u ʋ *a* ə (only two examples of o and w were heard. These may have been ɔ?)
Nasalized Vowels: a^n ä^n ɛ^n e^n (?) i^n ɪ^n ɔ^n u^n ʋ^n *a*^{n} ə^n (o^n should be ɔ^n?)
Diphthongs: ai *ɛi aɛ* au iɪ ɔu uʋ oɪ (?)

> (It is possible that the first three are really the same phoneme. aɛ was obtained from the kinship terms obtained from Annie Nelson, and her pronunciation is more difficult to follow than Galushia's. It is also possible, however, that hers is more correct. On the whole, we believe *ɛi* to be the correct symbol).

[‡] https://www.uaf.edu/anla/collections/search/resultDetail.xml?id=EY961K1970b is the 3000 page Eyak dictionary by Michael Krauss in 1970. The *dAXunhyuu* Learner's Talking Dictionary of 2014 is http://eyakpeople.com/dictionary.

---

[1] The consonants called "sonants" are really intermediate. Hereafter, aspirated consonants are written without diacritical marks.

(Differences in pitch are weak, and for that reason have not been heard in cases where they ought to occur.)

High Pitch: ´'

Low Pitch: `

Lengthened Vowel: •

It is possible that in addition to the consonants recorded we should have heard the labialized palatals: G^{w}', $k^{'w}$, and k^{w}; the labialized velars: $\underline{G}^{w}$, q^{w}, and $\underline{x}^{w}$ the unaspirated s and c; the affricative: DZ; and the velar: ṇ. [537]

The several examples of $\underline{x}$ and $\underline{x}^{w}$ may be x *or* h and h^{w}. ẋ ẋ̲ ẋ^{w}

The vowels ə and *a* seem to be hopelessly confused in our notes. They may be variants of one phoneme.

Natural Phenomena:

earth *or* land: ɔ^{n}• *or*'a^{n}

mainland: ta•qt

island: qa•t (D k'a:t')

shore: yəqt (in *Tale 10:*   qέi   yə'q   stıqätłi)
                                      towards shore   he-came-back

rock: (D t'sa•) (should be tsa• ?)

gravel: tsà•làxà•tł

mud (or gray): t'sɔ' *or* t'sɑ'

mountain: ıt'ł (D ıt'ł) *(In Raven 11:* it'ł á nàq' = mt. on)

glacier (cf. Tlingit): t'ła' (D t'ła')

river: 'a^{n} (D a^{n}•)

stream: (D cî)

brook: li'Galέiyà' *or* li'Galέiyà

lake: (D ma•)

lagoon *or* bay: (D x•t'łát'łaqà'à)

salt water (also table salt *or* light blue): Dı•a' (D (Dίyà')

sea.: (Dı•ya'ya't (Is this literally "salt water's house?" If so should it not end with –yat ?)

low tide: (D x̲ɔtsíx̲axtł) (Should these all be medial x's ?)

waves: ta^{n} *or* (t'a^{n} cf. *Raven* 7)

water: Gíyà (D ki'ya)

sky: ya•qt *or* (ya•kt)

sun: qátıkətł (In *Tale 16:*   qətɛqetł wʋla'iyu)
                                       Sun   people

moon: qàx̲á' *or* qàx̲á

star: la'x̲tsł *or* l la'x̲tsł [538]

northern lights: yát'qàDàq'à *or* yát'qàDàq'à

wind: k'úyı' *or* k'u•i

rain: q'ʋlέ' *or* qʋlέ

"rain" announced by Raven: qələq

fog: qətəq'ən•ì

snow: xut'ł *or* (x̲ʋt'ł)

falling snow: Dəxút'ł

wet snow on the ground: làx̱át'łéts *or* làxát'łéts
ice: t'ɪts *or* (t'ɪtc)
hail: làx̱át'ɪts *or* làxát'ɪts
summer: x̱ə'
winter: x̱alakł
fall: Gə•tłx̱álákł
spring: Gətłx̱ɔl
fire: Dəqá•q *or* stłɪq'atł (D qóät)
smoke (or, blue): tła^{n}t (D tła^{n}t)

Land Animals:

brown bear: lɪxa' *or* lɪxa
black bear: t'síyù' *or* t'sɪyù (D tsiyu^n)
caribou *or* moose: x̱ɛiyä•ni *or* x̱ɛiyá•ni
mountain goat: tła•q'ɛiya' *or* tła'x̱ɛiyə
wolverine: kʊnä'əs: *or* kʊná'əs (with strong final aspiration)
wolf: Go•tcí
fox: ná^{n}qət'sä *or* náqət'sä
ground hog: Détłəx^{w}ä•'k *or* Dətłəx^{w}ä•'k
porcupine: x̱áGəDɪnáyà' *or* x̱ákátiyà (D xakatiya) "skin is sharp"
groundsquirrel: tsətłk
dog: xəwa• *or* xəwà•
lynx: qátci• [539]
mouse: tłu^{n}tiyas
beaver: qəx̱à•c•k *or* qəxàckə *or* Gəxàckə
land-otter (or "to slide"): qətłəsət'ł *or* (In Text 8: Gəłésɛt'ł)

Sea Mammals:

seal: Gɛłtàq (or Gätłtà•q *or* Gɛłtàk)
fur seal: á•Dà•q (This is an Eskimo word, used for the Greenland seal in Greenland, and the fur seal in Prince William Sound. Chugach: aataq)
sea-lion: k'ʊmà *or* k'umàq Chugach: kammaq
blackfish whale: qa•n•q' *or* qá^n•nɪq' (Also called by the name for walrus *or* other whales)
whale *or* walrus: Goxu•t'ł (In *Tale 9*: Goxu•t'ł   wʊla'iyù)
                                 blackfish people
porpoise: qä'xútł (In *Tale 8*: kä'xútł   wʊla'iyù)
                                porpoise people
sea-otter: sa's

Birds:

raven: t'cilà
eagle: GutcGàlàq (cf. Wolf)
duck: qänù *or* qa•nù

eider duck: ɛ́lвà
goose: náx̱àq *or* náx̱əq
swan: Gɔx̱t'ł
sea-gull: àt'łáⁿnıq *or* ət'łáⁿnıq
kittiwake (gull): GəDiq
sea-parrot (puffin): Diⁿ•tıⁿ *or* Diⁿ•tıⁿ
cormorant (shag): àwáiyàq *or* àwáiyəq
loon: k'ɔq'
magpie: qɛsGəx̱aq'
humming bird (or gas boat): (D ıłätsɔⁿ
a flying bird: ıxat'a'ya• [540]

Fish:

fish (In *Tale* 4: "he turned into a fish" tä'ya')
king salmon: tɛ́i'yá'lɛ• *or* tɛ́i'yá'tłɛ• (should be: tä'yá'tłɛ• ?) (literally "big fish")
red *or* sockeye salmon: t'ca't'c
red salmon when it turns red in fresh water: qí•ŋaⁿtàq *or* qí•ŋatàq (Eskimo word?)
hump-back salmon: kack' *or* kask'
silver salmon: àDàtɛ́riyà'
dog salmon: ti•t'ł
bullhead: tca•k'
shark ("rough"): t'citcx̱
young shark (dogfish?): tcı'ntxk
trout: Dəqlà' *or* Dəqlà
rainbow trout: lí'là' *or* lí'là
whitefish: sa'qəDəqàkck *or* sa'qətəqàkck
skate: t'ciⁿtq *or* t'cıⁿtq
eulachon (candlefish): sa•k

Shell-Fish etc:

beach food (i.e. shell-fish, seaweed, etc.): lu•tc '
devilfish: tsálex̱qà
cockle: sahᵂxaq *or* sax̱x̱a'
small clam like a cockle: ("cockle's baby") sax̱ɔya'c
clam: DJiDá•Dəq
snail *or* whelk: t'ci•c
sand flea: Gətłɔtəq' *or* GətłəDəq
frog: tcíàtłq

Trees and Plants:

forest: lı•s• (in *Tale* 20: Tree Man: lí•stáDáx̱ɔⁿ)
spruce: à'Dɛ́lı•s [541]

hemlock: t'ɬɛ́iyu' *or* t'ɬɛ́iy (Is this the plural?)
alders: t'sɪn (in *Tale* 16: alder people: t'sɪn wʊla'iyu)
plant used for medicine that looks like skunk cabbage: tcʊkck
grass (or green): t'ɬɪ<u>x</u>
devilclub: t'ɬɪct' *or* k'ɬɪct'
skunk cabbage: tsɔⁿ•t *or* tsɔⁿ•t'
plant with three black petals (Kamchatka lily?): DJɪla<u>x</u>q
root of Kamchatka lily: tcʊlaq
artichoke-like plant: tcac
leaves (or feathers): t'a'tɬ *or* t'atɬ
bark: qatɬ *or* qa'tɬ
sap: sa'
kelp: Dʊ'
black seaweed: sa•qsk
seaweed with balls that pop (Fucus?): Gɔwàt's

Parts of the Body:

head (only of creatures with a neck): <u>G</u>ʊlàqà, someone's head: Da<u>x</u>ɔɔⁿ laqa (Root is: laqa)
head (of fish, shrimps, etc): täya'caw
hair: lä•ɬ
ear: Gɔtcä'<u>x</u> *or* Gɔtcä'x (Root is: tcä'x?)
eye: Gʊlà•<u>x</u> *or* (Gʊlà•x) (Root is: tcä<u>x</u>)
nose: Gʊnì•k'(Root is: nì•k' ?)
mouth: Gʊsà't (Root is: sa't)
teeth: Gəx̀ɔⁿtɬíyä' *or* Gax̀ɔⁿtɬíyá (Root is: xɔⁿtɬíyä?)
tongue: kúlà•t *or* (kuia-f) (Root is: la•t ?)
breath: Gətu'ʊq (Root is: tu'ʊq ?)
neck: Gʊtsi' *or* (Gʊt'sɪ') (Root is: tsi' ?)
arm: k'ʊt'cɪli' *or* k'ʊt'cɪli (Root is: t'cɪli *or* tcɪli ?)
hand: k'úyàqà•tc (Root is: yaqa•tc ?) [542]
finger: qaiɛ, fingers: kɪyɪtɬtsə'qsktɬ
first finger: k'ɔiyétcà•tɬ *or* qɔyátcà•'tɬ
second finger: yá'ákɑDá•lìyà *or* yá'ákəDá•lìyà
fourth finger: k'ʊyɪtɬtsɪⁿ"ktɬ *or* k'ʊyɪtɬtsɪⁿ"ktɬ
thumb: k'ʊyɪ'tcà•ɬts
fingernail: qäyɪtɬ<u>x</u>a'tstɬ *or* qäiyɪtɬ<u>x</u>a'tstɬ
leg (whole, *or* thigh only?): Gɔtɬaⁿ *or* Gɔtɬaⁿ (Root is: tɬaⁿ ?)
lower leg: k'ʊx̀^wí'ts *or* Gɔx^wits (Root is: x̀^wits *or* x^wits ?)
foot: Gʊ'q'a'c *or* Gɔ'q'a'c (Root is: q'a'c)
big toe: : Gʊ'q'ɛíyɪkʊⁿtc *or* Gɔ'q'ɛíyákʊⁿtc (Root is: q'ɛíyíkʊⁿtc *or* q'ɛíyákʊⁿtc)
toes: Gʊ'q'ɛíyɪtɬtsàq'sktɬ *or* Gɔ'q'ɛíyɪtɬtsàq'sktɬ
chest: Gʊcä•k' (Root is: cä•k' ?)
belly: Gʊkʊmà' (Root is: kʊma' ?)

umbilical cord: t'sa•
penis: Gətcɑq' (Root is: tcɑq' ?)
vagina: x̲u•1
urine: (or yellow) (applies only to dog urine?) tsā•t

Persons:

human being (or ordinary person): Dəx̲ɔⁿ *or* (Dàx̲ɔⁿ)
people: Dəx̲ɔⁿiyù *or* Dəx̲ɔⁿ'iyù
man: tɬɪlà•' *or* tɬɪlà•
woman: q'ātɬ *or* qātɬ
child: səqéts (should be: səqä•ts ?)
baby: səqä•tsəki *or* səq'ä•tsəki (-ki is the diminutive.)
boy (literally "man-child"): tɬɪlà•' səq'ä•tsəki
girl (literally "woman-child"): q'ätɬ səq'ä•tsəki
adolescent girl (is this the plural form?): yá'qɛiyù
grown, unmarried woman: ā't'q' *or* 'ā't'q'
married woman: ɪɬtaqálá•ɬta [543]
menstruating woman(?) (This name is also given for the menstrual hut):

        Dəx̲ɔⁿiyù Gəyatɬ

        people   keep-away

widow *or* widower: sətɬqätɬ
shaman: x̣ʷi•l
witch: ɪtɬGíʼɪtɬə *or* ɪtɬGíʼɪtɬà
slave: tɬá'à' *or* ɬá'à
noble: wakaiyɛkɛ (should be: wəkɛiyɛkɛ ?)
head chief *or* rich man: Gələx̲ɛ́•t'ɪ *or* Gʊləx̲ɛ́•t'ɪ
second chief (of same moiety as head chief): Gələx̲ɛ́•t'ɪ t'ca•t'cɪniⁿ *or* Gúləx̲ɛ́•t'ɪ t'ca•t'cɪniⁿ
second chief of opposite moiety: Gədɛiláq t'ca•t'cɪniⁿ
term of address for chief who is host at a potlatch: DəDé'làq (should be: Gədɛilàq ?)
my clan people: qɛiyə'qa•yu (should be: qɛiya'qiyu ?)
partner (a fellow-clansman): sɪlax̲äⁿ•nà
sick person: yík'á•'Dɪⁿ *or* yiká•Dɪ ?
murdered man: cɪcätɬ'ɪ
corpse: GələGà *or* GɔləGà *or* GúlɑGà *or* Gɔlákà
messenger: (In *Tale 21*: yəx̲Dəkù•tx́ɛ "one sent for something")

Tribes:

Eyak: (inhabitant of Eyak) í•ɣiyàqDəlàq
    plural: í•ɣiyàqDəlàqɛiyu
Tlingit: t'ɬá'x̲à'là'q *or* (tɬáx̲á'lá') *or* (qɬá'x̲àlàq)
    plural: t'ɬá'x̲à'là'qɛiyu *or* (qɬá'x̲àlàqɛiyu) (glacier-people)
Eskimo: Gədɛiyaq *or* (Gədɛiq') plural: Gədɛiqɛiyu

Copper River Indian: yáⁿnàq plural: yáⁿnàqɛiyu
Raven Man (singular(?) and plural): t'cʋlayu
Wolf People: Gotci•yu [544]
Bark House People: qatłiya ᴅət'a•xtəlaqɛiyu bark-house(?) under-people
Tree Man: lɪ•stáᴅáxɔoⁿ *or* lɪ•stáᴅ plural: -íyù
Around-the-Lake-People (dwarfs): maⁿkɑᴅɪtłiyaᴅəxɔⁿiyu (cf. Lake)
animal souls *or* owners: wʋla'iyu
salmon people: t'aiyà'ú•là•yù *or* t'äyà'úlàyù (should be: t'äyà' wʋla'iyu ?)
monster animal (singular *or* plural?): ət'stłi'yatł
Calm Weather's Daughter: (In *Tale* 17: ᴅiäxtsi)

Place Names:

Eyak: i•ɣiaq
Alaganik: ənàxànàq *or* (D ànàx̀ànàk)
Alaganik Slough ("Alaganik house", cf. ocean): ənaxanaqyat *or* (anaxanaqya't)
Eyak River: (D iɣiyákùtàt)
Mountain Slough: (cf. mountain): (D ít'łáti)
Fish Camp on Mountain Slough (cf. gravel): tsá•làxà•tłɔu
Camp called "Lots of Clams": tłɪxatł
Point Whitshed: ᴅɪkɛtłxalakt (Does this mean "Not outside the mountain" ?)
Eastern End of Hinchinbrook Island: tcɪGəxtà•ɔq (Eskimo name)
Village at Boswell Bay (cannery site) ("outside"): xəlá•st
Egg Islands (literally "outside the mainland"): xəlá•stəxɛtà•qt
Former village at Cordova (cf. whelk): t'cí•cqɛ́iGɔłɛ́
Spike Island: k'á'ᴅá'lù *or* k'áᴅálà
Hawkins Island ("island"): qa•t
Mummy Island: ᴅɪkɛtłxa (cf. Point Whitshed)
Simpson Bay: ɪlu•tɪk (Eskimo name)
Chilkat (A Yakutat village on Bering River): ᴅJɪtłqà' [545]
Cape Yakataga: yɛkutɛɣuwi
Copper River: át'à• (A Copper River word)

House Names:

Eagle House, Alaganik ("bed-house"): tcɪtłqài yàt
Raven House, Alaganik ("goose-house"): naxək yàt
Eagle House, Eyak ("skeleton-house"): qát'sʋli yàt
Raven House, Eyak ("raven-house"): t'cí•là yàt
Raven House, Gravina Bay ("the-one-we-burned-down-on-the-beach-house"): tá'uxtsà yàt *or* (táuxtsà yàt)

The House:

house: yat
roof: (said slowly) yá'tᴅa•kt, (said fast) yɑ'ᴅàkt (D tcatł) (should be: yat ᴅakt ?)

walls: qέiGɑ'x̱a•t *or* qέiGàx̱a•t

smokehole: tsɪtłqá'GɑDέiqt *or* tsɪtłqá'qɑDέiqt (D tłáⁿtɪ'ítqá'à) (cf. with smoke)

door: (D DàqétłùwàtγI)

window: (D aγalaq) (Eskimo word)

sleeping room: yá•l̀it

"head" *or* rear of the house: xɑləqDəqəst

front of the house: t'áiyàtłt'cà•t *or* t'áiàtłt'cà•t

potlatch house: (D ìDá'wàɛts)

Raven potlatch house: t'cílàyàt

Old Raven's house: (In *Raven 2*: t'cílàcia ya' yat)

Eagle potlalch house: GútcGàlàq yàt

totem pole: (Prefix with eagle *or* raven) -ləkəcktł *or* -ləkəktł

fort: (same name for fish wier) Gláctłcà•tł

hunter's lean-to ("outside house" *or* is it more properly "one-sided house"?): l̀it'cá•t'c yàt *or* l̀itcá•t'c yàt [546] girl's puberty shelter *or* cave: yá'qέiyu' yà' yàt (cf. adolescent girl) {small logs, planks over. planks run down to eaves, as overlap}

menstrual hut (same name for menstruating woman): Dəx̱ɔⁿyu Gayatł

platform cache: DɪsDɪtcɪtł

grave ("in-ground place-for-dead"): qέiyaⁿnu GəqəDətέ (cf. with bearpit)

pyre ("where- ? fire"): qɪ'qa'xɛtła•x̱a• stłɪq'atł

House Furnishing and Utensils:

bed (modern): tcɪł (D ctɪ•tł *or* qé'qä'ä't)

wooden pillow: t'sí'latł *or* tsí'làtł

grass mat ("on-ground- ?"): yánàⁿt Dətà' *or* yá'nàt Dɑtà' (cf. with grave and bearpit)

iron stove: (D ùyùq'é'qàq)

barrel: (D lá'màt)

small barrel: (D Golax̱x̱à't'o) several? many berries?

urine tub: ùyá•t'c yɪx̱GʊDà'átcx

box (the two words may indicate two kinds of boxes): t'sa•tł *or* łat' *or* łät

water-tight box *or* basket: tsɯ•tł

meat box ("meat's box"): Gɔtsä ya' lät

basket: t'ła'aq

berry basket: la'mat'wat Dətła'aq *or* la'matDətła'aq (should the tł be glottalized?)

cooking basket: uiyáx̱qəDəq'ətq' *or* uiyáxq'əDaq'ətq'

bailing basket for canoe: t'sa•qł *or* tsa•qł

plate *or* wooden dish: tsɪk' (D t's ɪk')

sucking tube: ùyəq'əGəlɪDɪt'sət's *or* úyəq'ʊGʊlɪDét'sùt's

spoon: cɪtł (D citł)

silver spoon ("money spoon"): (D Dana citł)

horn spoon: GúⁿDalέ cɪtł (GʊⁿnDέlέ cɪtł) [547]

wooden spoon: Dəkiⁿ cɪtł

drying rack (in the house?): tä'wà•tł *or* táwàtł

drying rack (out-doors?): wɛc

sewing bag: ɩɬtáqálá•tɬà
clamshell lamp: Dɩ'Dätɬ *or* Dɩ'Dä'tɬ

Basket Patterns:

1. "above-each-other pointed": ìtɬtáq íⁿtcàkɬ
2. "amphineura-shells": iⁿtɬɣɩck ìⁿtɬtsəli *or* iⁿtɬɣɩck ìⁿtɬt'səli'
3. "cockle's meat": sàẋ yá' qáqɛiyá' *or* sàẋ yá' q'áqɛiyá'
4. "Yakutat basket-straws" *or* "Yakutat design": yá•kDà•t íⁿDà•tɬs
5. "face painting": əDɩ•t'ɬà•kɬ
6. "one-after-the-other" like waves: x̱àtɬá stɬìatɬ
7. "heat-waves" (cf. drying rack): ɩⁿstɬɩwa•tɬ
8. (plain line): x̱àDɩstɩx̱àtɬ
9. "brown-bear-ulna": lɩxáɛ'Dà *or* lɩxáɣɩDà'
10. "together-each-other" (cf. "together with" in *Text 10*): ɩɬDá itɬìyatɬ
11. "raven bone": t'cìlétsəlɩ' (should be: t'cìla tsəlɩ ?)

Tools:

adze: xʊt'á•
axe: ləqəDəqà•tɬ
fire drill ("string-drill"): Gəx̱étɬ tətɬ *or* Gɔx̱ätɬ tətɬ
drill: tətɬ
drill-hearth *or* board: tsətɬ
woman's knife (ulo): wäkck
man's knife: tsatɬ
crooked knife: ʊxqəDəxəs
awl (is this the same word for drill ?): tɔtɬ *or* tətɬ
needle: tcɔ'ktɬ
lancet: ʊx̱qəDəxà•s *or* əx̱qəDəxà•c (cf. crooked knife) [548]
clam stick: saẋxa' catɬ (should be a glottal stop after the last vowel ?)
bark stick *or* peeling wedge: ca'tɬ
shovel: x̱ʊ'tɬk
snow shovel ("snow's shovel"): xʊt'ɬ yà' x̱ʊ'tɬk *or* (x̣ʷʊt'ɬiyà' xʊtɬk)
wedge: wɩɬ

Manufactured Materials:

band *or* cord: wɛ•ktɬ
thong ("cut skin"): stɬìwé•tɬ Gɔta' *or* stɬìwé•tɬ Gɔta
thread *or* sinew: k'ɔt'
straw: Da'tɬt
prepared spruce roots: qats *or* qəts
hemlock sap: sa'h

hemlock bark: t'tɛyu' (cf. bark: qa'tł)
porcupine quills: k'a'q *or* k'aq
feathers (cf. leaves): ɢʊtłt'a'tł *or* ɢʊtłt'a'tł
firewood: (D tłaq^w)
meat: ɢʊtsä' *or* ɢʊ'tsä'
boiled meat: słɩqàtkł ɢʊtsä' *or* słɩqà'tkł etc. to boil: qatk
dried meat: ᴅəsətłätł ɢʊtsä'
dried intestines: ɢənʊx̱tsä *or* ɢʊnʊqtsä
fat: ɢəqáx̱té
salmon dried with backbone hanging out: qásʊ' *or* qásʊ'
salmon dried, split up the back: qat's
dried salmon, when meat from spine is dried separately: ᴅä'ätsk
tobacco: sá'tá'ə
snuff: ɩⁿłìwàł

Weapons and Traps:

shotgun *or* rifle: (D x̣^wut'tł [549]
shell for rifle: (D ɢax̱q)
harpoon (short type used for ice-hunting): k'li' (should be: t'łi• ?) (cf. bear spear)
harpoon (used from canoe): ka'tł *or* kä'tł
spear (evidently same word as harpoon): (D ɢäktł)
harpoon head: x̣at'
bladder for harpoon: ("inflated stomach"): słx̣út'łx ɢɔtłà't'c *or* słx̣út'łx̣ ɢɔłà'tc
bear spear (cf. short harpoon): t'łiⁿ *or* t'łi
point of bear spear: t'łiⁿ sɩⁿtàiyà *or* t'łi sɩⁿtàiyà
halibut hook (cf. eulachon spear): k'a•ctł (D tcak'tł)
two-pronged fish spear: lá'ᴅá'x̱i•ya' *or* lá'ᴅá'x̱i'a
      double: la'ᴅa'x̱
      coming together: i•ya' *or* i'a
hook-like spear *or* rake for eulachon: t'cä'k'tł
club: x̱at'łk *or* (x̣atłk)
goatskin shield: tsɩlqa•t *or* tsɩlqä•t *or* (tsɩlkä•t)
bow: qʊ'tłx̱à•tł (or qɔ'tłx̣àtł)
war bow ("war-for-bow"): α'tuwɩtł wαt da qʊ'tłx̱à•tł *or* "): ə'tuwɩtł etc.
long bow for hunting in open country: ʊt'łᴅaqatłcatł (should be: ʊt'łᴅaqʊtłx̱a•tł ?)
bow string: qʊ'tłx̱àtłx̱àtł *or* qɔ'tłx̱à•x̱àtł
arrow: t'ə'ktł
arrow head: x̱ɩc
arrow feather: t'ə'ktłɩtł t'à'tł
quiver ("arrow box"): t'ə'ktłɩtł tà'
bear-pit ("in-thing-under there dig"): yàⁿnù' qɛ́i' ɢəyɛ́ilɩtł *or* yànù' — *etc.* (cf. with grave)
basket fish-trap: 'äs *or* 'as
fish weir (same name for fort): ɢláctłɩcà•tł
snare: wɛ'tł [550]

277

deadfall: Dɔx̣tł

weasel box trap: là'Dá'qá'xʊtł *or* là'Də'qə'xʊtł

Boats, Snowshoes, etc:

gas boat (same name for humming bird): (D ɬätsɔ^n)
sealskin umiak (for war): yàxəqɛ́ *or* yà^{n}xəqɛ́'
large canoe (for war): 'əx̱
small canoe (for hunting): əx̱əkí (D àx̱ákì) (should be preceded by glottal stop ?)
sail (or canvas): tɪsà• *or* təsà (D t'sɛ́sà)
mast: tɪsà•' x̱əDɛ́tłtä *or* təsa etc. (D t'səsá x̱áDɛ́tłɛ́)
paddle: kuʊsktł *or* kuʊskìl (D koɪsk)
steering paddle *or* rudder: qət'łáqɛ́iya' *or* qʊtłaqɛ́iyà
sled: x̱atł *or* xa'tł
snowshoe: t'sɔ^{n}kt *or* (tsɔ^{n}kt)
wooden snowshoe: Dəkɪ^n t'sɔ^{n}kt
pack: x̱ɛ́
pack strap: ʊx̱qʊqətɛ́x̱ɛ́ *or* ʊx̱qʊqə'tɛ́x̱ɛ́

Clothing:

shirt: qálà•q (or Gálà•q *or* Gəlà•q) (should be Gálà•q ?)
gutskin shirt: Gənʊx̱tsä' Gálà•q *or* Gənʊqtsä' etc.
hood (cap *or* hat): t'ciyàt' (or tciyàt' *or* cíàt')
cap with a peak: ʊnDɪcɪtGù•tłà t'ciyàt' *or* ʊnDɪcɪtGù•tłà etc.
trousers: Dəqətà•tł {Tlingit: tuq'ətál}
war apron (The first word is translated as "war", but cf. with the different term used in war bow):
      kúlə kʊstł
boots: si^{n}tł
blanket: qɔ'tł
mitten: tsa•q' {Tlingit: tsáx̱}
mask: áyúɣì *or* áyúɣì
head band (cf. cord): i•nà wɛ́•ktł [551]
bracelet: qa•t'ł
earrings: tcəx̱á't'łtł *or* (tcɪx̱á't'łtł)
nose ring: tłɪnɪs
good-luck charm *or* amulet: Gʊt'cátɪlisà'iyatł *or* Gʊt'cátálisà'iyàtł
dentalium shell: Gɛ́x̱à also (singular *or* plural): tcíyà
shell bead: qʊDɪłsɪlɪ kʊɣù•t *or* qʊDɪłtsɪli kɪɣù•t

Toys and Games:

doll: yalc
blowgun (cf. shotgun): Dəx̣ʊt'łk
dice (singular ?): : Gʊ'tcù

tube for popgun: t'cέiyù
plunger for popgun (cf. "wooden"): Dəskɪⁿ
stick game: *atłqα*
stick used in stick game: kɔ'Dɪ'Dɪk *or* kɔ'Dɪ'Dɪk'
shinny ("ball-hit"): yαxlαxα Dαxátłx
shinny stick: ux- (prefixed to the -word for shinny)
checkers: məkəq
partner game: qɔqɔk
shooting match ("against shooting-with-arrows"): (cf. "against" with "together-with" in *Text 10*):
    ɪtłɪxáⁿt yɪxGɔtłɪt'əktłx *or* ɪtłɪxáⁿ yɪxGɔtłɪt'əktłx
foot race: ɪtłɪxáⁿ Gɔlɪtɪqɔtł
canoe race: ɪtłɪxáⁿ " ixɪDɪqäł
cat's cradle ("tangled up"): Gutcäkt
wrestling: łútahä••'tcɛnu *or* łtłʋⁿyaⁿtck'αłαhatł
tossing in a sealskin: yá'xDáləxkì *or* yá'xDələxkì ?
story: tsa•q
song: Gɔ'tsɪn *or* (utsiⁿ') (cf. "I sing")
derision song: ("against-song-two"): łə'qà Gʋtətsɪⁿ ɪnù (should the first word be: ɪtłɪxáⁿ ?) [552]

Ceremonies and Ceremonial Objects:

potlatch: ɪⁿDákäDä'étc
potlatch at new house: yat DɛDa•xɛtc
dance: Ga'
dancing: Ga'ɪté•lέ *or* Ga'ɪtélέ
slow dance: Gɔłáⁿ•Gέ *or* kəłáⁿ•Gɪ
wand: cʋkiät
wand used for slow dances: Dαt'cà'ktł
rattle: xa'tłk
whistle ("into blowing" cf. blowgun): uyəq'έt'c Gʋx̌ùt'łk uyʋGà•tc Gʋx̌ʋt'łk (cf. mask and
    headband under *Clothing*)
wake (staying by dead body): qá'àDítłíyáłí

Non-Material Concepts:

picture *or* reflection: Gúγ^{w}ʋx̱àu *or* Gɔγ^{w}úx̱àu (Root is: γ^{w}ux̱àu ?)
ghost ("dead-person picture"): səsíⁿtłìnù γ^{w}ʋx̱àu *or* səsíⁿtłìnɔ γ^{w}úx̱àu
life *or* soul: qɔqáⁿ•tà•tł *or* qɔqωⁿ•tàtł
shaman's power: yɪDɔ *or* yɪDω
dream: stiⁿ•ts
war (cf. war apron): α'tùwɪtł *or* ətuɪtł
signal ("signal-smoke"): ʋwá•tłx̱ɔDέà'Gà łaⁿ•t
theft ("he steals"?): ìtcúⁿ
sickness: k'á'tGùtłέ *or* k'átGùtłέ ' (cf. sick) (Root is: k'at ?)
murder ("someone-he-kills"): Dàx̱ɔaⁿ cɪcätł'ɪ *or* Dəx̱ɔaⁿ cɪcätł'ɪ'

279

Numbers:

(These are used in counting. We did not attempt to get numbers used for special classes of
objects, *or* ordinals).

1. tłɪⁿkɛ
2. la•'Dɪ [553]
3. t'ú'tłkaⁿ
4. kalá'qa'qa'
5. tcɔⁿ•ɪ
6. t'siⁿ•
7. laⁿDɪtsi• *or* laⁿDɪtsiⁿ•
8. GaDɪⁿtsⁿ•
9. GʊtsDäⁿ
10. taqaq'

Colors and other Adjectives:

(The basis of classification may refer to wooden. The inserted element *-ta- or -te-* may be
related to Dəkɪⁿ• wood. On the other hand, it may refer to movable and immovable. However,
the usage is not consistent, as far as we can judge).

black: tətłDu•tc *or* Dətłtu•tck

white: x̣ʷutł *or* xʷʊt'ł

red: Glá•t'cɛ́•' *or* Glá•t'cɛ́•

green (grass): t'łx̱

gray (mud): t'sɔ *or* t'sɑ

yellow ("dog urine"): x̱əwá tsä•'t

blue (cf. salt water): Di•ya'

dark blue (smoke): tłaⁿt

brown (can be applied to an overcast sky): t'səGɔ•t *or* t'sɑGɔ•t

big (can be applied to a canoe, bird, man, dog, but not to a house *or* tree): Gu'lu• *or* (k'ulu•)
      big canoe: Gu'luʷ• x̱aki' big man: Gu'lu• yɪtłɪⁿhɪⁿ big dog: Gu'lu• x̱əwa

big (applied to house *or* tree): k'ətá'lù• *or* k'ùtálù• big tree:
      k'ətə'lù• lɪs big house: k'ətá'lu yat

giant: (suffix) -ləu giant mouse: tłúⁿtiyasləu

small (used for bird *or* pencil): ya•kʊtskɪtłɪ *or* yá•kʊtsk [554]

small (used for tree, knife, house): yáDəkʊtsk *or* yátəkʊtsk

high (use?): yà'qət'łɛ́iyá' *or* (yà'qətłi•yà)

high (used for tree): k'ʊta'au

bad *or* ugly: kəciyɛ bad baby ("baby-bad"): səqɛ'tsəciyɛ

talkative (name of Sun's daughter in *Tale 16*): DJɪmɪtcəki' *or* DJɪmɪtcəki'

old: (This may not refer to age, but may be an expression of affection *or* a similar attitude.

Cf. kinship use). (suffix) –cia

old Raven: t'cilacia

sick *or* hot: yík'à•t *or* (yíkà•t)   patient: yík'à•Dı

dead: səsıⁿtɬ (cf. murder)

double: (cf. fish spear): la'Da'x̱

wooden: Dəkì̀ⁿ• (D Dákì̀ⁿ•)

all *or* everybody: Détɬık'

unseen (cf. negative prefix for Verbs): Dık'qànà'áⁿ

unseen messenger (not-seen one sent-for-something): Dık'qànà'áⁿ qέ yəx̱Dəqtx̱έ

Miscellaneous Phrases:

to kill a member of the opposite moiety: qɔDinaq cıcätɬ'ı ("he kills" ? cf. this form with "he runs")

we are Eyaks: qìyáq í•γìyàqDəláqέiyù

they are giving a potlatch: itá'stέiyätcɬ *or* itá'stiätcɬ i

you are invited to a potlatch: ísíyätcɬ *or* ísiätcɬ "to him" (when giving food to the dead at potlatch): aⁿcta'

I want (such-and-such): — sıtɬqa•tɬ

is it you? (greeting): icu

yes (answer to greeting): aⁿ

hey! (polite mode of addressing a non-relative): aⁿhàⁿ *or* əhəⁿ'

ejaculation of sympathy: ənyaⁿ

goodby: qatu•la• (cf. with wish for good weather) [555]

thanks: aua'ta' *or* au'a'ta'

you are welcome (answer to thanks): DiDahetɬ *or* DiDakete

that's all (end of story): DàqέDàqà'àu *or* (D taqέikı)

kiss this (an insult, said with phallic gesture of thumb): na'

your mother has a rotten vagina: inyáⁿx̱á'tsi

(war cry): 'u' 'u 'u

help me: x̱úⁿtɬa• *or* x̱ú•tɬa

good weather! (called out in connection with magic rite): qətsu••lá

it's snowing (cf. with falling snow): Dəx̱ʋt'ɬ

and: Dax̱

some: (suffix) -tε

some fat (child called this when he wanted it): Gəqəx̱tέ

Prepositions:

towards (in *Text 10*): -qεi-

on (in *Text 1*: -á•nàq'

on the side of (in *Text 1*): ínàⁿx̱

together with (in *Text 10*): -ʋt'ɬ

to (in the phrase "went visiting to" in *Text 7*): -Da'

where (used in title of stories' (In *Text 3*): q'itc (in *Text 5*): qiəⁿx̱ (In *Texts 6A, 7* and *8*): qi'

along where (used with drag, walk etc.): qiDax̱

behind (used with walk) (In *Text 6A*): ᴅliinax (In *Text 6B*): ᴅliinaqt *or* t'łɨnaqt
among (In *Text 2*): -q'at
outside (cf. name for village at Boswell Bay, and name for Egg Islands): x̱əlá•st

The Possessive:

There is no modification of the noun *or* pronoun, from the ordinary subjective form. The suffix *–ya'* is placed [556] after the noun possessing and before the object possessed when that object is alienable. For inalienable objects, such as relatives *or* body parts, the suffix is omitted. Thus:

a person's head: ᴅəx̱ɔ^n laqa
puppy's father: x̱əwaki ta
dog's head: x̱əwa laqa
dog's nose: x̱əwa nɩ•k
dog's eye: xəwa la•x̱
girl's house: yá'qɛiyù yà' yàt
Old Raven's house: t'cilacia ya' yat
but Raven-potlatch house (because a potlatch house cannot be thought of without reference to its
    moiety affiliation?): t'cílà yàt (cf. also Raven-totem pole)
ghost ("dead-person's picture") also belongs to the inalienable class.

Note also the difference in the expressions for clam-stick on the one hand and meat box (box for meat) and snow shovel (shovel for snow) on the other. Arrow-feather, arrow-box, spear-point, head-band, sail-mast all belong to the "inalienable" class like clam-stick. Note, however, that the expression which we have here rendered as "shovel for snow" is literally "snow's shovel". The Eyak have a word meaning "for" (perhaps "used for") in the expression "war-for-bow."

Possessive Pronouns:

(We have written these as if they were separate words. More probably, however, they are
    prefixes).

my: (in ordinary cases, as in relationship terms): sɩ *or* si (for emphasis): x̣ʷusɩ *or* x̣ʷusi

my dog: x̣ʷusi ya' x̱əwa'

my arm: x̣ʷusi t'cɩli *or* sɩ t'cɩli

my nose: x̣ʷusi ni•k'

my head: x̣ʷusi laqa

my foot: si q'a'c [557]
your (singular): i'ɩ *or* i' *or* ɩ' (There is no special emphatic form).
your dog: i'ɩ ya' x̱əwa'   your mouth: ɩ sa't
your house: i'ɩ ya' yat   your arm: i'ɩ t'cɩli
your eye: ɩ' la•x̱   your neck: i'ɩ tsi

your eyes[1]: i"ɩ la•x̲(?)   your foot: i' q'a'c
his: *aⁿ or* αⁿ' (Note, however ux̲a for "his" in *Texts 3* and *4*)
        his dog: αⁿ' ya' x̲əwa   his mouth: αⁿ' sa't
        his house: αⁿ' ya' yat   his arm: αⁿ' tcɩli
        his mother: αⁿ' nʸa *or aⁿ* ma'

our: (you and I); qɛiyɛqa *or* qɛiyɩ'qa *or* qɛi'yɛqai
        our house: qɛi'yɛqai ya' yat   our necks: qɛiyɛqa tsi
        our dog: qɛi'yɛqa ya' x̲əwa'   our eyes: qɛiyɛq' la•x (?)
        our mother: qɛiyɩ'qa ma
        our: (he and I): αⁿDax̓u• (?)

        our eyes: αⁿDax̓u• la•x (?)
your: (plural): lax̲ɛi•lax *or* lax̲ɛilax̲ɛi
        your dog: lax̲ɛi•lax̲i ya' x̲əwa
        your house: lax̲ɛilax̲ɛi ya' yat
        your mother: lax̲ɛi•lax̲ ma (or -nʸa•)
        your eyes: lax̲i•'lax̲ la•x (?)
        your necks: lax̲ɛi•lax̲ tsi
their: αⁿ'nu• *or* αⁿ'nu
        their dog: αⁿ'nu ya' x̲əwa' their eyes: αⁿ' nu• la•x̲ (?)
        their house: αⁿ'nu ya' yat their necks: αⁿ'nu• tsi
        their mother: αⁿ'nu ma•

Verb *appears.*

(This may not be a verb at all, though it was so classified by Galushia. It may be a
        demonstrative). [558]

"red appears shirt": Gla•t'cé• kɛ'i•t'ɛ qəlaq
"black is canoe": təttɬDu•tc kɛ'i•t'ɛ' αx̲a•ki'
"sky blue is": ya•kt Di•a kɛ'i•t'ɛ'
but "green (grass) looks-like tree" (i.e. tree is green): ttɬx̲ qa'ɔ'Da'qa'Dɛ'ɛ lɩs
The form kɛ'i•t'ɛ' can only be used if the tree is moving *or* waving in the wind.
Plural: The suffix -u, -iyu, -ɛ iyu, *or* -qɛiyu
dog: x̲əwa' dogs: x̲əwa•yu
animal soul: wʊla' soul: wʊla'iyu
his: αⁿ their: αⁿnu
house: yat houses: yatɛiyu
their mother: αⁿ'nu ma• their mothers: : αⁿ'nu maqɛiyu

Texts:

---

[1] Form requested. Our informant apparently repeated "your eyes". Or is la•x̲ both singular and
        plural?

words

These are titles *or* phrases occurring in stories:

1. "You'll feel sorry when the fog is hanging half-way down the mountain."
   itàkálέ   iyà   qak'àt it'ł   á•nàq' q'ətəq'ən•ι
   you'll-feel   you sorry mountain on   fog
   ínà^{n}x   li'ιxàqàtłtà'Dà•x
   on-the-side when-it's-hanging-half-way-down (cf. sorry with sick)

2. "Living among black bears."
   t'síyú   q'àt   uxi•ti^n
   black-bears   among living

3. "Where Old Raven threw his box."
   t'cilacia   q'itc (sa'tł uxa satsaxtł
   Raven-old where box   his he-threw

4. "Where Old Raven dragged his drying rack."
   t'cílàcia   qiDax   wεc uxa' sa'sətłxatł
   Raven-old   along-where   rack his he-dragged [559]

5. "Where Old Raven made the earth."
   t'cílàcia   qiə^{n}x ɔ^n sətłιtł
   Raven-old   where earth he-made

6A. "Where Old Raven was walking behind the waves," (i.e. beach-combing)
   t'cílàcia   qi'   ta^n Dlinàx qətła•tł
   Raven-old   where waves behind was-walking

6B. "I am going behind the waves" (Raven's song).
   t'a^n t'łinaqt qəxla•tł   *or* t'a^n Dlinaqt Gauxla•tł
   waves   behind I-am-going

7. "Where Old Raven went visiting the eagle."
   t'cílàcia   qi'   GutcGàlàq   Da' xa'Di'   Dasatł
   Raven-old   where eagle   to another-place   he-went (i.e. visited)

8. "Where a man killed lots of land-otters."
   Dəxɔ^n qi'   Gəłését'h^n ì^{n}sətłàtłι^n
   man   where land-otter   killed-lots-he

9. "He turned into a ground-hog"
   Détłəx̌ä•k   sətłä'tłi'
   ground-hog   turned-into-he

10. "He returned to shore with the seal people."
   Gəłtàq wυla'iyù υt'ł   qεi•yáq   stιqätłi

284

seal   people   together-with   towards-shore returned(by water)-he

11. "I turned into a fish." (Salmon Boy's song).
ta'ya'   Dəqəq^wı•łät (should be: tä'ya' Dəqəq^wı•tłätł ?)
fish   I-turned-into

12. "Creek where we feel better" (parts not analysed).
Gótəkəlέ tsʋ'aⁿ [560]

13. "She is going after beach food."
lu•tc   qi'ya
beach-food   she-is-going-after

Verb See (cf. with "unseen"):

I see: Gəẋ^wä' *or* Gəx^wà

you see: qɛi'äc *or* qɛi'ac
he sees: a^γuqɛi'ıⁿhıⁿ *or* auqɛ'ıⁿhıⁿ
we see: qɛiyəqDa•qä'ä *or* qɛiyáq Dá•qà'à
you (pl.) see: ẋ^wu•Gəẋ^wɛlaxɛi *or* (x^wúGə'x^wέ)
they see: αⁿnu•a^γùqä'äq *or* αⁿnu•a^γùqà'à
I see you (sing.): ẋ^wui•'Gəẋ^wä *or* x^wu•ı'Gəẋ^wa
he sees you: αⁿi'qä'ä *or* αⁿi'qá'à
we see you: qaiyɛqDa•ı'qä'ä *or* qaiyáqDá•ı'qà'à
they see you: αⁿnu'ı' qä'ä *or* αⁿnuıq à'à
I see him: αⁿ'Gəẋ^wä' *or* αⁿ'Gəẋ^wέ

you see him: icαⁿqɛi'ä
he sees him: a^γuqɛi'ä'
we see him (this was the form requested): αⁿqɛi'ıⁿhıⁿ
you (pl.) see him (this was the form requested): qαláx'ıⁿhıⁿcʋ' *or* qàlaxıⁿhıⁿcʋ'
they see him (this was the form requested): αⁿnù•qέi'ıⁿhıⁿ Probaby all the G's in this verb should
    be velar G's.

Run:

I run: xatł•qɔxya•tł *or* xatł•qʋxya•tł
you run: i'xətłá•qέiyà•tł *or* i'xàtłá•qέiyà•t
he runs: i'xətłá•qέiyà•tı *or* i'xətłá•qέiyà•tı
we run: qέiyəq'Dáləqàqú•tł *or* qέiyəq'Dáləqəqú•tł
you run: ləxi•ləqəqlaxqú•tł *or* làxέilàxələxqù•tł
they run: αⁿnúləqəqu•tł
I ran: xatła si'yatł *or* xatłasiyatł [561]

285

Sing:

I sing: Gɔxtsɪⁿ(q) *or* without faint q

sing!: Gɔxtsɪⁿ(q) *or without faint* q

are you singing? (requested): k'ɔⁿtsɪⁿc *or* Gɔⁿtsɪⁿc

he sings: αⁿk'ɔⁿtsɪⁿ *or* αⁿG'ɔⁿtsɪⁿ

we sing: qɛiyáqᴅná•k'ɔtsɪⁿ *or* qɛiyáqᴅná•G'ɔtsɪⁿ

you (pl.) sing: ləxɛi•Gɔlə<u>x</u>tsɪⁿ *or* ləxɛi•Gɔlà<u>x</u>tsɪⁿ

they sing: αⁿ'nuk'ɔtsɪⁿ

I sang: k'ɔsɪtsɪⁿctł *or* Gɔsɪtsɪⁿctł

you sang: i•k'ɔsɪtsɪⁿtł *or* i•Gɔsɪtsɪⁿtł

he sang: αⁿ'k'ɔsɪtsɪⁿtł *or* αⁿ'Gɔsɪtsɪⁿtł

we sang: qɛiyəqk'ɔsɪtsɪⁿtł *or* qɛiyəqGɔsɪtsɪⁿtł

you (pl.) sang: lə<u>x</u>ɛi•k'ɔlə<u>x</u>sɪtsɪⁿtł *or* lə<u>x</u>ɛi•Gɔlə<u>x</u>sɪtsɪⁿtł

they: αⁿ'nuk'ɔsɪtsɪⁿtł *or* αⁿ'nuGɔsɪtsɪⁿtł

I will sing: k'ɔqɔ<u>x</u>tsɪⁿ *or* Gɔqɔ<u>x</u>tsɪⁿ

you will sing: : i•k'ɔqɛiyɪtsɪⁿ *or* i•Gɔqɛiyɪtsɪⁿ

he will sing: αⁿk'ɔqá•'tsɪⁿ *or* αⁿGɔqá•'tsɪⁿ

we will sing: qɛi•yíqᴅà•'k'ɔqá•tsɪⁿ *or* qɛi•yíqᴅà•'Gɔqá•tsɪⁿ

you (pl.) will sing (the informant repeated the form for second person singular. He had
   misunderstood?)

they will sing: αⁿ'nu•qa•k'ɔtsɪⁿ *or* αⁿ'nu•qa•Gɔtsɪⁿ

I don't sing: (these forms are most probably: I am not singing etc.): ᴅɪk'ɔⁿtsɪⁿ(q) *or* ᴅɪk'ɔⁿtsɪⁿq

you don't sing: ɪ'ᴅɪk'ɔⁿtsɪⁿq *or* ɪ'ᴅɪGɔⁿtsɪⁿq

he doesn't sing: αⁿ'ᴅɪk'ɔⁿtsɪⁿq *or* αⁿ'ᴅɪGɔⁿtsɪⁿq

we don't sing: qɛiyáqᴅɪk'ᴅák'ɔⁿtsɪⁿq *or* qɛiyáqᴅɪk'ᴅáGɔⁿtsɪⁿq

you (pl.) don't sing: làxi•ᴅɪk'Gɔlá<u>x</u>tsɪⁿq *or* làxɛi•ᴅɪk'Gɔⁿláxtsɪⁿq

they don't sing: αⁿ'nu•ᴅɪk'ɔtsɪⁿ

Kill:

I kill: Gɔxcä•tł *or* Gəxcä•tł (or k'ɔxcätł)

1 kill my dog: x̣ʷusi ya' xawa Gəxcä•tł [562]

you are killing a dog: <u>x</u>əwa qi•cä•tłcʋ

you (emphatic) are killing a dog: (cf. with emphatic you of *Text 1*): <u>x</u>əwa' ɪxa' qi•cä•tłcʋ

Tentative analysis of verb to sing: (Gɔ) ... tsɪ^n *or* (k'ɔ) ... tsɪ^n

Present tense	pronominal prefix	root *or* infix? Gɔ *or* k'ɔ	pronominal infix	root tsɪ^n
first person singular	–	"	X	"
second	i	"	–	"
third	α^n	"	–	"
first person plural	qɛiyaqDa	"		"
second	ləxɛi•	"	lax	"
third	α$^{n'}$nu'	"		"

It must be remembered that we did not attempt to discover if there was a dual form, *or* whether there was any distinction between we (you and I) and we (he and I). We did not attempt any analysis of verbal aspects. The infix Gɔ *or* k'ɔ may represent the aspect of the verb.

Past tense	pronominal prefix	Gɔ *or* k'ɔ	pronominal infix	past infix sɪ	root tsɪ^n	past suffix tɬ
first person singular[1]	–	"	–	"	"	"
second	i•	"	–	"	"	"
third	α$^{n'}$	"	–	"	"	"
first personal plural	qɛiyaq	"		"	"	"
second	ləxɛi	"	lax	"	"	"
third	α$^{n'}$nu	"		"	"	"

[563]

Future tense	pronominal prefix	Gɔ *or* k'ɔ	future infix qa	pronominal infix	root tsɪ^n
first person singular	–	"	qɔ	X	"
second	i•	"	qɛiyɪ	–	"
third	α$^{n'}$	"	qa•	–	"
first personal plural	qɛiyaqDa	"	qa•	–	"
second?		"	qa•		"
third	α$^{n'}$nu•	"	qa•	–	"

Negative Present tense	pronominal prefix	negative infix Dɪ(k')	Gɔ *or* k'ɔ	pronominal infix	root tsɪ^n	negative (?) suffix -q
first person singular[2]	–	"	"	"	"	"
second	i	"	"	"	"	"
third	α^n	"	"	"	"	"
first person plural	qɛiyaq	"	**Da**	**Gɔ**^{n} *or* **k'ɔ**^{n}	"	"
second	ləxɛi	"	Gɔ^n or	"	"	"
third	α$^{n'}$nu•	"	k'ɔ^n	"	"	"

---

[1] The pronominal infix *-x-* may have become elided with the initial consonant of past infix *-sɪ-*.

[2] Note that the final -Da of the pronominal prefix is here separated from the initial *qɛiyaq-* and appears as an infix preceding the infix *k'ɔ^n* or *Gɔ^n*.

287

The negative infix - ᴅɪ(k')- probably has a final k', here elided with the k' *or* ɢ of the following infix. Cf. with the negative prefix in "unseen". Note how the vowel of the infix -k'ɔ- *or* - ɢɔ- has become nasalized.

Tentative analysis of verb *to run*:　　xatła• ... yatł (singular)
　　　　　　　　　　　　　　　　　　lə ... qu•tł　(plural) . [564]

Present tense	pronominal prefix	root?	infix	pronominal infix	root?	pronominal (?) suffix
first person singular	–	x̠atła•	qɔ	x	yatł	–
second	i'ɪ	"	qɛi	–	"	–
third	– (?)	"	qɛi	–	"	ɪ *or* i
first person plural	qɛiyəqᴅa	lə	qə		qu•tł	–
second	ləx̠ɛi			lax̠		–
third	αⁿ'nu			–		–

Past tense	pronominal prefix	root?	pronominal infix	past infix	root?
first person singular	–	x̠atła•	–	si'	yatł

Tentative analysis of verb to see (ɢə) ... ä *or* (qä) ... ä

Present tense	pronominal prefix	object "you"		pronominal infix	root?
first person singular	x̣ʷu(i•)[1]	ɪ'	ɢə	xʷ	ä
(reflexive not asked)					
third	αⁿ'	"	qä'	–	"
first person plural	qɛiyaɛᴅa'	"	"		"
third	αⁿ'nu'	"	"		"

Present tense	pronominal prefix	object "him"αⁿ'		pronominal infix	root? ä
first person singular	–	"	ɢə	xʷ	"
second	ic	"	qɛi	–	"
	αⁿ'	aˠu	"	–	"

(The [565] forms for the plural seem to be hopelessly confused. Our {speaker} ~~informant~~ showed great uncertainty with verb forms).

---

[1] The final **i** of the emphatic pronominal prefix has elided here with the *-ɪ'*- following it.

A question is asked by adding the suffix -c *or* -cʋ to the verb. Cf. with "is it you?" *icu.*

Relationship Terms (used in direct address).

	man speaking	either sex speaking	woman speaking
1. father		aᴅa'	
2. mother		ama'	
3. father's older brother		ati^n	
4. father's younger brother		ati^{n}cia	
5. fathers older sister	a^{n}t		aki
6. father's younger sister	atcia		aki^{n}cia
7. mother's older brother		aqaq	
8. mother's younger brother.		aqaqcia	
9. mother's older sister		yaqέ'	
10. mother's younger sister		yaqέ'cia	
11. father's father		uca	
12. father's mother	akɩ^n (?)		kɩ^{n}ca
13. father's father's older brother		siu	
14. father's father's younger brother		siucia	
15. mother's father		wεckaca	
16. mother's mother		tcucia	
17. mother's father's older brother		qacia (or ɢɑcia)	
18. mother's father's younger brother		ciwεck	[566]
19. mother's mother's older sister	sɩtcu		aki^n (?)
20. mother's mother's younger sister	sɩtcucia		?
21. older brother	sɩxawʋ<u>x</u>		st^{n}ski
22. younger brother	siᴅaqaε		st^{n}skicia
23. older sister	siɩtki		sɩtsa'ki'
24. younger sister	siɩtkicia		sɩᴅaqaε
25. son	sɩsaqaεq		siac
26. daughter	sɩtsi		siac
27. father's older brother's son[1]		sətɩ^{n}səqaεq	
28. father's older brother's daughter		səti^{n}si	
29. father's older sister's son	sɩtɬta		?
30. father's older sister's daughter	siat		sɩtɬta
31. mother's older brother's son	siqaqcia		?

---

[1] (Forms for the children of the father's younger brother and sister were not obtained).

#			
32. mother's older brother's daughter	siat		sɪtɬta
33. mother's older sister's son	aqaqcia		yaqέ'yac
34. mother's older sister's daughter	??		yaqέ'yac
35. mother's older sister's son	??		yaqέ'caɛyac [567]
36. mother's youngest sister's daughter[1]	??		yaqέ'caɛyac
37. older brother's son	sɪx̲ʋx̲səqaɛq		??
38. younger brother's son	sɪsaqɛqcia		??
39. older brother's daughter	sɪx̲ʋx̲səqaɛq		??
40. younger brother's daughter	sitsicia		??
41. older sister's son	??		sitsaqɛiyac
42. older sister's daughter	siti^n		or siac
43. younger sister's son	??		siDaqɛiyac
44. younger sister's daughter	siti^n		*or* siac
45. son's child	siuki		sʋkɪ^{n}lakɪ^n
46. daughter's child	ciwɛckaki		sitsuki
47. wife	siat		
48. husband			sitqa
49. older brother's wife	sɪx̲ax̲at		sɪ^{n}skiat *or*
50. younger brother's wife	??		cɪtca$^{n'}$wɪ^{n}i^n
51. older sister's husband	cɪtca$^{n'}$wɪ^{n}i^n		sɪsta^{n}kiqa
52. younger sister's husband	??		??
53. wife's older sister	sitsaki		
54. wife's younger sister	siaDaqaɛ		
55, wife's older brother	siatɪ^{n}ski *or*		
56. wife's younger brother	? cɪtca$^{n'}$wɪ^{n}i^n		
57. husband's older brother			sitqax̲awax̲
58. husband's younger brother			sitaDaqaɛ [568]
59. husband's older sister			cɪtca$^{n'}$wɪ^{n}i^n *or* sitqɛtkicia
60. husband's younger sister			sitqaɛtkicia
61. husband's father			sitqa^{n}ta
62. husband's mother		(this is wife's father?)	siyɑDa^n
63. husband's father's older brother			sitqax̲uwəx̲tsi
64. husband's father's younger brother			
65. wife's sister's husband	sɪtɬta		
66. husband's brother's wife			sɪtɬta
67. co-wife			sɪtɬta
68. step-father:		(sex speaking?) sia^{n}yɪtɬ$^{n'}$i^n	

---

[1] (Forms for the children of the mother's younger brother were not obtained).

69. step-mother:		(sex speaking?) sɔt'ayɪtɬ$^{n.n}$i	
70. older step-brother:	(man speaking?) sɪtawʊxcia		
71. younger step-brother:	(man speaking?) sɪ**ɒ**aqaɛcia		

The diphthong *aɛ* is probably the same phoneme as the diphthong *ɛi*. Most of these terms were obtained from Annie Nelson, because her husband could not remember them, and her enunciation is not clear.

The suffix *-cia* means "younger," and is perhaps an affectionate diminutive. The suffix [*-ki*] may also be a diminutive, since it is used as a diminutive with other nouns.

The prefix *s-* or *c-* is probably "my." Compare with the possessive pronoun for the first person singular.

A preference for cross-cousin marriage is indicated by the fact that the man calls his wife (47) by the same term [569] as his father's older (and younger?) sister's daughter (30) and his mother's older (and younger?) brother's daughter (32). He calls his father's sister's son (29) *sɪtɬɪta* because he will marry that man's sister, and his own sister will marry that man. However, he calls his mother's brother's son (31) *siqaqcia*. Does this mean that marriage with the father's sister's daughter is preferred? Or does the use of the term (31), which might be translated as "little maternal uncle," simply emphasize the authority of the mother's brother and her son?

The woman uses the term *sɪtɬɪta* in addressing her father's sister's daughter (30) and her mother's brother's daughter (32), that is, the two women whom her brother calls "sweetheart." However, there is some inconsistency in the use of this word. The woman also uses it to her co-wife (67), her husband's brother's wife (66); and the man uses it to his wife's sister's husband (65). In these last three cases it is reciprocal and is applied to a person of the same moiety and sex as the speaker, a person whom the speaker's brother *or* sister could never marry *or* address as "sweetheart." Does this imply that the use of the word antedates the development of the moiety? Is it, in that case, a rather vague cousin-term used for a member of the same sex as the speaker?

The levirate and sororate are indicated in the use of this word towards the husband's brother's wife (66) and the wife's sister's husband (65), because the surviving brother (or sister) may inherit his (or her) spouse.

The generalized term for sibling-in-law of the speaker's sex is *cɪcta^{n}'wɪ^{n}'i^{n}* (49, 50, 51,52?, 55, 56, 59, and 60). The terms for sibling-in-law of the opposite sex, and the particularized terms for those of the same sex, are descriptive. They are [570] made up of "wife's" (or "husband's") plus that term which the wife *or* husband uses for his *or* her brothers and sisters (49 to 60).

The word for younger sibling of the same sex as the speaker is the same for both sexes speaking (22 and 24). The name for the older sibling of the same sex is different for the two sexes speaking. The woman's word for older sister (23) is related to her word for the younger sister (24), but the man's word for older brother (21) seems to be distinct from that for his younger brother. This is perhaps because the older brother is in a position of extra authority. For a woman, both brothers enjoy authority. The words for sibling of opposite sex simply add the diminutive suffix when applied to the younger. The woman's word for brother and the man's word for sister are probably related. In other words, there seems to be a grouping of siblings according to likeness *or* difference of sex (with reference to the speaker), with the exception of a man's older brother, who occupies a privileged position.

The terms for parallel cousins seem to be purely descriptive, and, as far as our information goes, are the same for both men and women speakers. The father's brother's son (27) and daughter (28) are distinguished, but the woman at least lumps together her mother's sister's children of both sexes (33, 34, and 35, 36). The man's word for his mother's sister's son (33) seems to be a diminutive form of maternal uncle (cf. especially with the mother's younger brother, 8), In speaking English, parallel cousins are called "brother" and "sister."
The maternal and paternal uncles and aunts are distinguished, but except for the terms for the paternal aunt (5 and 6) there is no difference between the terms used by [571] men *or* women speakers. However, our information may be deficient.

In the descending generation, the woman lumps together her own children and the children of her sisters, regardless of sex (25, 26, 41 to 44). Unfortunately we do not have her names for the children of her brothers.

The father distinguishes between his son and his daughter (25 and 26). His name for his older brother's son (37) is descriptive, but he calls his younger brother's son (38) "little son." His name for his older brother's daughter (39) is the same as that for her brother (37); and he calls his younger brother's daughter (40) "little daughter." It must be remembered that the Eyak practiced only the junior levirate. We lack the word for the man's sister's son, but he calls his sister's daughters (42 and 44) by a term that seems to be related to daughter (26).

The man distinguishes between his son's child (45) and his daughter's child (46). These seem to be related to the words for father's father's brother (13 and 14) on the one hand, and mother's father (15) and mother's lather's brother (17 and 18) on the other hand. The pattern for reciprocal grand-parent and grand-child terms does not seem to be clearly worked out, however.

The man's (?) word for step-brother (70 and 71) seems to be "little older brother" and "little younger In-other" depending on the relative age positions. The terms for stepfather (68) and step-mother (69) are evidently verbal nouns *or* past participles, and might be translated perhaps as: "he who has taken (?) a wife and she who has taken (?) a husband." [blank 572-3]

Bibliography

Abbreviations

A: Anthropos. Mödling b/ Wien. [573]

AA: The American Anthropologist. Washington. Lancaster. Menasha.

AAA-M: American Anthropological Association, Memoirs. Lancaster.

AAASc-P: American Association for the Advancement of Science, Proceedings. Salem, Mass.

AfA: Archiv füir Anthropologie. Braunschweig.

AGW-M: AnthropologischeGesellschaftinWien, Mitteilungen.Wien.

AnOH: Aarbøger for nordiyk Oldkyndighed og Historie. København.

AwKR: Archiv für wissenschaftliche Kunde von Russland. Berlin.

AMNH-: American Museum of Natural History. New York.

   -AP: Anthropological Papers.

   -B: Bulletins.

   -HS: Handbook Series.

   -M: Memoirs.

   -MJ: Memoirs, Jesup North Pacific Expedition.

BAASc-R: British Association for the Advancement of Science, Report, London.

BA: Baessler-Archiv. Berlin.

BAE-: Bureau of American Ethnology. Washington.

   -B: Bulletins.

   -R: (Annual) Reports.

BKRR: Beiträge zur Kenntniss des Russischen Reiches. St. Petersburg.

CGS-MAS: Canada, Geological Survey, Memoirs, Anthropological Series. Ottawa.

CI-: Canadian Institute, Toronto.

   -P: Proceedings.

   -T: Transactions.

CNM-: Canada, National Museum. Ottawa.

   -BAS: Bulletins, Anthropological Series.

   -R: Annual Report. [574]

CNAE: Contributions to North American Ethnology, Washington.

E: Ethnos, Stockholm.

GR: Geographical Review, New York.

GSS: Det grønlandske Selskabs Skrifter. København.

GT: Geografik Tidsskrift. København.

HS: Works issued by the Hakluyt Society, London.

IAE: Internationales Archiv für Ethnographie. Leiden.

JRAI: Journal of the Royal Anthropological Institute. London.

JRGS: Journal of the Royal Geographical Society. London.

MAI-: Museum of the American Indian, Heye Foundation. New York.

   -C: Contributions.

   -IN: Indian Notes.

   -INM: Indian Notes and Monographs.

MG: Meddelelser om Grønland. Kebenhavn.

MKEA-R: Museum of Far Eastern Antiquities, Bulletins. Stockholm.

NNB: Neue Nordische Beyträge. St. Petersburg & Leipsig.

PM: Peternianns Mitteilungen. Gotha.
RFThE: Report of the Fifth Thule Expedition. Copenhagen.
RSC-PT: Royal Society of Canada, Proceedings and Transactions. Montreal.
SAP-J: Societe des Americanistes de Paris, Journal. Paris.
SI-: Smithsonian Institution. Washington.
    -AR: Annual Reports.
    -CKn: Contributions to Knowledge.
    -EFW: Explorations and Field-Work.
    -MC: Miscellaneous Collections.
UA-MP: University of Alaska, Miscellaneous Collections. Washington.
UC-PAAE: University of California, Publications in American Archaeology and Ethnology. Berkeley.
UP-AP: University of Pennsylvania, Anthropological Publications. Philadelphia.
USNM-R: United States National Museum, Reports. Washington.
UW-PA: University of Washington, Publications in Anthropology. Seattle.
WB: Wiener Beiträge zur Kulturgeschichte und Linguistik. Wien.
YU-PA: Yale University, Publications in Anthropology. New Haven.
ZE: Zeitschrift für Ethnologic. Berlin.

B-MV: Berlin, Museum für Volkerkunde.
C-NM: Copenhagen, National Museum.
P-UPM: Philadelphia, University of Pennsylvania Museum. [575]

List of Works.

ABERCROMBIE, W.H: A supplementary expedition into the Copper River valley, 1884. Compilation of narratives of explorations in Alaska. Washington 1900.
— Copper River exploring expedition. Washington 1900.
ADELUNG, C. see Mithridates.
ALLEN, H.T: An expedition to the Copper, Tanana, and Koyukuk Rivers, &c. 1885. Washington 1887.
— Atnatanas; natives of Copper River, SI-AR 1886, I. 1889.
AMUNDSEN, R.: Nordvestpassagen. Kristiania 1907.
ASTRUP, E.: Blandt nordpolens naboer. Kristiania 1895.
BACK: Narrative of the arctic land expedition... 1833-35. London 1836.
BAHNSON, KR: Gravskikkc hos amerikanske Folk. AnOH 1882.
BANCROFT, H.H: The native races of the Pacific stales of North America. I. London 1875.
— History of Alaska. San Francisco 1886.
BARBEAU, M: The modern growth of the totem pole on the northwest coast. Proceedings of the 23. International Congress of Americanists 1928, New York 1930.
BARRETT, S.A: The material culture of the Klamath Lake and Modoc Indians of northwestern California and southern Oregon. UC-PAAE, V. 1907-10.
BATCHELOR. J: The Ainu and their folk-lore. London 1901.
BEECHEY, F.W: Narrative of a voyage to the Pacific and Beering's Strait... 1825-28. New ed. I-II. London 1831.
BELCHER, E: Narrative of a voyage round the world. I. London 1843.

BERG, G: Sledges and wheeled vehicles. Nordiska museets handlingar, IV. Stockholm & Copenhagen 1935.

BILBY, JW: Among unknown Eskimo. London 1923.

BIRKET-SMITH, K: A geographic study of the early history of the Algonquian Indians. IAE, XXIV. 1918.

— Ethnography of the Egedesminde District. MG, LXVI. 1924.

— Det eskimoiske slaegtskabssystein. GT, XXX. 1927.

— The Caribou Eskimos, I-II. RFThE, V. 1929.

— Drinking tube and tobacco pipe in North America. Ethnologische Studien. Leipzig 1929a.

— Contributions to Chipewyan ethnology. RFThE, VI. 1930.

— Folk wanderings and culture drifts in northern North America. SAP-J, n.s. XXII. 1930a. [576]

BIRKET-SMITH, K: Foreløbig beretning om den dansk-amerikanske ekspedition til Alaska 1933. GT, XXXVII. 1934.

— The Eskimos. London 1936.

— The composite comb in North America. E., II. 1937.

BOAS, F: The central Eskimo. BAE-R, 6. 1888.

— Notes on the Snanaimuq. AA, II, 1889.

— First general report on the Indians of British Columbia. BAASc-R, 59. 1890.

— Second general report on the Indians of British Columbia. Ibid. 60. 1891.

— Third general report on the Indians of British Columbia. Ibid. 61. 1892.

— The Indian tribes of the lower Fraser River. Ibid. 64. 1894.

— Fifth report on the Indians of British Columbia. Ibid. 65. 1895.

— Sixth report on the Indians of British Columbia. Ibid. 66. 1896.

—- The social organization and the secret societies of the Kwakiutl Indians. USNM-R 1895. 1897.

— The Eskimo of Baffin Land and Hudson Bay. AMNH-B, XV. 1907.

— The Kwakiutl of Vancouver Island. AMNH-MJ, V 2. 1909.

— Tsimshian mythology. BAE-R, 31. 1916.

— Ethnology of the Kwakiutl. BAE-R, 35, I-II. 1921.

— Notes on the Tillamook. UC-PAAE, XX. 1923.

— The social organization of the tribes of the North Pacific coast. AA, n.s. XXVI. 1924.

BOGORAS, W: The Chukchee. AMNH-MJ, VII, 1904-09.

BUSCHMANN, J.C: Systematische Worltafel des athapaskischen Sprachstamms. Abhandlnngen der Kgl. Akademie der Wissenschaften zu Berlin 1859. Berlin 1860.

CAAMAÑO, J.: Expediciən de la corbeta Aránzazu al mando del tenientede navio D....(1792). Coleccion de documentos inéditos para la historia de España, XV. Madrid 1849.

CADZOW, D.A: Old Loucheux clothing. MAI-IN, II. 1925.

CALLBREATH, JC: Notes on theTahl-tan Indians. (In DAWSON 1889).

CHAMBERLAIN, A.F: Report on the Kootenay Indians of southeastern British Columbia. BAASc-R, 62. 1893.

CHAPMAN, J.W: Notes on the Tinneh tribe of Anvik, Alaska. Congres international des améicanistes, 15. session 1906, II. Quebec 1907.

— Tinneh animism. AA, n. s. XIII. 1921.

COFFIN, G. see WATERMAN, T.T [577]

COLLINS, H.B: Archeological investigations in northern Alaska. SI-EFW, 1931. 1932.

— Archaeology of St. Lawrence Island, Alaska. SI-MC, 96. 1937.

COLLINSON, R.: Journal of H.M.S. Enterprise... 1850-5. London 1889.

COOK, J & KING, J: A voyage to the Pacific Ocean. 2. ed. II. London 1785.

COXE, W: Account of the Russian discoveries between Asia and America. Second ed. London 1780. (Fourth ed. London 1803).

CHANZ, D: Historic von Grønland. 2. Aufl. II. Barby 1770.

CULIN, S: Games of the North American Indians. BAE-R, 24. 1907.

CZAPLICKA, M.A: Aboriginal Siberia. Oxford 1914.

DALAGER, L: Grønlandske Relationer, 1752. ed. L. BOBÉ. GSS, II. 1915

DALL, W.H: Alaska and its resources. Boston 1870.

— Tribes of the extreme Northwest. CNAE, I, 1877.

— The native tribes of Alaska. AAASc-P, XXXIV. 1885.

DAVIDSON, D.S: Family hunting territories in nortwestern North America. MAI-INM, 46. 1928.

— Snowshoes. Memoirs of the American Philosophical Society, VI. Philadelphia 1937.

DAVIS, J: The voyages and works of ... ed. A. H. MARKHAM. HS. 1880.

DAWSON, G.M: Notes and observations on the Kwakiool people of the northern part of Vancouver Island and adjacent coasts. RSC-PT, V. 1888.

— Report on an exploration in the Yukon district, N. W. T., and adjacent northern portion of British Columbia. Geological and Natural History Survey of Canada. Annual Report, n.s. III. Montreal 1889.

— Notes on the Shuswap people of British Columbia. RSC-PT, IX. 1892.

DAWYDOW, (G.I): Reise der russisch-keiserlichen Flott-Officiere Chwostow und Dawydow. Berlin 1816.

DIXON, G: A voyage round the world. London 1789.

DIXON, R.B: The Shasta, AMNH-B, XVII. 1907.

— Contacts with America across the southern Pacific. (In: The American Aborigines, ed. D. JENNESS. Toronto 1933).

DOBELL, P.: Travels in Kamtchatka and Siberia. I-II. London 1830.

(DHAGE): An Account of a voyage for the discovery of a northwest passage... by the Clerk of the California. I-II. London 1748-49.

DUCHAUSSOIS: Aux glaces polaires, Indiens et Esquimaux. Paris 1922. [578]

DÜBEN, G. VON: Om Lappland och lapparne. (Stockholm 1873).

EELLS, M: The Twana, Chemakum, and Klallam Indians, of Washington Territory. SI-AR 1887, I. 1889.

— The thunder bird, AA, II. 1889a.

EGEDE, HANS: Relationer fra Grønland 1721 — 36 og Det gamle Grønlands ny Perlustration 1741. ed. L. BOBÉ:. MG, LIV. 1925.

EGEDE, PAUL: Eftlerretninger om Grønland, uddragne af en Journal 1721-88. Kiøbenhavn s.a. (1788).

ELLIOTT, C.P: Salmon fishing grounds and canneries. (1899). Compilation of narratives or explorations in Alaska. Washington 1900.

ELLIOTT, II. W.: A report upon the condition of affairs in the territory of Alaska, Washington 1875.

— An arctic province. London 1886.

EMMONS, G.T: The basketry of the Tlingit. AMNH-M, III 2.1903.

— The Tahltan Indians. UP-AP, IV. 1911.

— The whale house of the Chilkat. AMNH-AP, XIX. 1916.

— Jade in British Columbia and Alaska. MAI-INM, 35. 1923.

— The Kitikshan and their toTotem poles. Natural History, XXV. New York 1925.

ERKES, E.: Chinesisch-amerikanischeMythenparallelen. T'oung Pao, XXIV. Leiden 1926.

Erläuterungen über die tin östlichen Ocean zwischen Sibirien und America gesehehenen Entdeckungen. NNB, I. 1781.

ERMAN, A: Ethnographische Wahrnehmungen und Erfahrungen an den Küsten des Berings-Meeres. ZE, II-III, 1870-71.

FARRAND, L: The Chilcotin. BAASc-H, 68. 1899.

— Basketry designs of the Salish Indians. AMNH-MJ, I. 1900.

FLOR, F: Haustiere und Hirlenkulturen. WB, I, 1930.

F'RANCHÉRE, G: Narrative of a voyage to the northwest coast of America. Early Western Travels, ed; R. G. THWAITES, VI. Cleveland 1904.

FRANKLIN, J: Narrative of a journey to the shores of the Polar Sea 1819-22. London 1823.

— Narrative of a second expedition to the shores of the Polar Sea. London 1828.

FRIEDERICI, G: Die geographische Verbreitung des Blasrohrs in Amerika. PM, LVII. 1911.

— Der Erdofen. PM, LX. 1914.

FRORISHEH, M: The three voyages of ... 1576-78. ed. R.COLLINSON. HS. 1867. [579]

GAHS, A: Kopf-, Schädel und Langknochenopfer bei Rentiervölkern. Festschrift P.W. SCHMIDT. Mödling b/ Wien 1928.

— Kult lunariziranoga praoca kod istočnih paleosibiraca. Godišnjaka Sveučilišta 1924/25 - 1928/29. Zagreb 1929.

GALLATIN, A: A synopsis of the Indian tribes of North America. Archaeologia Americana. Transactions and Collections of the American Antiquarian Society, II. Cambridge 1836.

GATSCHET, A.S: The Klamath Indians of southwestern Oregon. CNAE, II. 1890.

GEIST, O.W & RAINEY, F.G: Archaeological excavations at Kukulik, St. Lawrence Island, Alaska. UA-MP, II. 1936.

GIBBS, G: Notes on the Tinneh or Chepewyan Indians of British and Russian America. (Reports of H.B ROSS, W.L. HARDISTY, and S. JONES). SI-AR 1867. 1872.

— Tribes of western Washington and northwestern Oregon. CNAE, I. 1877.

GILDER, W.H: Schwatka's searth. {Search} London s.a.

(GLAHN, H.C): Anmaerkninger over de tre første Bøgcr af Hr. David Crantzes Historie om Grønland. Kiøhonhavn 1771.

— Missionaer i Grønland ...'s Dagbøger 1763-64, 1766-67 og 1767-68. ed. H. Osterniann. GSS, IV. 1921.

GLOB, P.V: Eskimo settlements in Kempe Fjord and King Oscar Fjord. MG, 102. 1935.

GODDARD, P.E: Life and culture of the Hupa. UC-PAAE, I. 1903.

— The Beaver Indians AMNH-AP, X, 1916.

— Indians of the northwest coast. AMNH-HS, 10. 1924.

GOLDER, F.A (ed.): Bering's voyages, I-II. American Geographical Society, Research Series, 2. New York 1925.

GRAAH, W.A.: Undersøgelses-Reise til Østkysten af Grønland 1828-31. Kiøbenhavn 1832.

GREINER, R. see WATERMAN, T. T.

GRINNELL, G.B: The natives of the Alaska coast region. Narrative, Glaciers, Natives. Harriman Alaskan Expedition. I. New York 1902.

GUNTHER, E: An analysis of the first salmon ceremony. AA, n.s. XXVIII. 1926.

— Klallam ethnography. UW-PA, I. 1927.

— A further analysis of the first salmon ceremony. UWPA, II. 1928.

— see HAEBERLIN, H.

HABERLANDT, J.M: Die Verbreitung des Erdofens. PM, LIX. 1913. [580]

HAEBERLIN, H.& GUNTHER, E: The Indians of Puget Sound. UW-PA, IV. 1930.

HAKLUYT, R: The principal navigations, voyages, traffiques and discoveries of the English nation. III. London 1600.

HALL, C.F: Life with the Esquimaux. I-II. London 1864.

HALLOWELL, A.I: Bear ceremonialism in the northern hemisphere. AA. n.s. XXVIII. 1926.

HAMILTON, G: Customs of the New Caledonian women belonging to the Nancaushy Tine ... &c. JAI, VII. 1878.

HANBURY, D.T: Sport and travel in the northland of Canada. London 1904.

Handbook of the American Indians north of Mexico, II. ed. F.W. HODGE. BAE B, 30. 1910.

HANSÊHAK: Den grønlandske kateket ..-'s dagbog. ed.W.THALBITZER. GSS, VIII. 1933.

HARDISTY, W.L: The Loucheux Indians. SI-AR 1867. 1872.

HARMON, D.W: A journal of voyages and travels in the interior of North America. New York 1903.

HATT, G: Arktiskc Skinddragter i Eurasien og Amerika. København 1914.

— Moccasins and their relation to arctic footwear. AAA-M. III. 1916.

— North American and Eurasian culture connections. Proceedings of the Fifth Pacific Science Congress. IV. Toronto 1934.

HAWKES, E.W: The "inviting-in" feast of the Alaskan Eskimo. CGS-MAS, 45. 1913.

— The Labrador Eskimo. CGS-MAS, 91. 1916.

HEARNE, S: A journey from Prince of Wales's Fort ... to the Northern Ocean. London 1795.

HENRY, A. see New Light, &c.

HILL-TOUT, C: Notes on the Sk'qō'mic of British Columbia, BAASc-R. 1900.

— Report on the ethnology of the Sīciatl of British Columbia. JRAI, XXXIV. 1904a.

— Ethnological report on the Stseēlis and Sk'aulits tribes. JRAI, XXXIV. 1904b.

— Report on the ethnology of the Stlatlum of British Columbia. JRAI. XXXV. 1905.

— Report on the ethnology of the south-eastern tribes of Vancouver Island, British Columbia JRAI, XXXVII. 1907.

— Report on the ethnology of the Okanak•ēn of British Columbia. JRAI, XH. 1911.

HITCHCOCK, R: The Ainos of Yezo, Japan. USNM-R 1890. 1891. [581]

HODGE, R.W {FW}: see Handbook, &.c.

HOLM, G: Ethnological sketch of the Angmagsalik Eskimo. MG, XXXIX. 1914.

— & PETERSEN, 3: Legends and tales from Angniagsalik. MG, XXXIX. 1914.

HOLMBERG, H.J: Ethnographische Skizzcn übcr die Völker des russischen Amerika. Acta Societatis Scientiarum Fennicae, IV. Helsingfors 1856.

HOLTVED, E. see MATHIASSEN, T.

HOOPER, W.H: Ten months among the tents of the Tuski. London 1853.

HKDLIČKA, A: Anthropological survey in Alaska. BAE-R, 46. 1930.

HUMBOLDT, A VON: Essai politiquc sur la royaume de la Nouvelle-Espagne. II. Paris 1811.

HUTTON, S.K: Among the Eskimos of Labrador. London 1912.

INGSTAD, H.: Pelsjegerliv blandt Nord-Kanadas indianere, Oslo 1931.

JACOBI, A. see MERCK, C.H.

JACOBSEN: Capitain ...'s Reise an der Nordwestkuste Amerikas. ed. A. WOLUT. Leipzig 1884.

JAMES, E.O: Cremation and the preservation of the dead in North America. AA, n.s. XXX. 1928.

JENNESS, D: The life of the Copper Eskimos. Report of the Canadian Arctic Expedition. XII. Ottawa 1922.

— The origin of the Copper Eskimos and their copper culture. GR, XIII. 1921.

— Eskimo string figures. Report of the Canadian Arctic Expedition, XIII. Ottawa 1924.

— The Indians of Canada. CNM-RAS, 65. 1932.

— The Sekani Indians of British Columbia. NMC-BAS, 84. 1937.

— The Indian background of Canadian history. NMC-BAS, 86. 1937a.

JETTE, J: L'organisation sociale des Ten'as. Congrcs international des americanistes, XV. session, II. Quebec 1907.

JEWITT, J: The adventures of ... ed. R. BROWN. London 1896.

JOCHELSON, W: The Koryak. AMNH-M.I. VI. 1905-08.

— Archaeological investigations in the Aleutian Islands. Carnegie Institution. Publ, 367. Washington 1925.

— The Yukaghir and the Yukaghirized Tuingus. AMNH-MJ, IX.1926.

— Archaeological investigations in Kamchatka. Carnegie Institution. Publ. 388. Washington 1928.

— History, ethnology, and anthropology of the Aleut. Ibid. 432. 1933. [582]

JONES, S: The Kutchin tribes. SI-AR 1867. 1872.

KANE, P: En Kunstners Vandringer ... i Nordamerika. Overs, f. Eng. Kêbenhavn 1862.

KEANE, A.H: Ethnology and philology of America. (Appendix to H.W. BATES: Central America, in Stanford's Compendium of Geography and Travel. London 1878).

KELLY, I.T: Ethnography of the Surprise Valley Paiute. UC-PAAE, XXXI. 1932.

KENNAN, G: Tent life in Siberia. New ed. London 1871.

KING, R: Narrative of a journey to the shores of the Arctic Ocean. I-II. London 1836.

KIRBY, W.W: A journey to the Youcan, Russian American. SI-AR 1864. 1872.

KITTLITZ, F.H VON: Denkwürdigkeiten einer Reise nach dem russischen Amerika. I-II. Gotha 1858.

KLUTSCHAK, H.W: Als Eskimo unter den Eskimos. Wien, Pest, Leipzig 1881.

KÖNIG, H.: Der Rechtsbruch und sein Ausgleich bei den Eskimo. A, XX. 1920.

— Das Recht der Polarvölker. A, XXIII-XXIV. 1928-29.

KOPPERS, W: Der Hund in der Mythotogie der zirkumpazifischen Völker. WB, I. 1930.

— Tungusen und Miao. AGW-M, LX. 1930a.

— Die Frage des Mutterrechts und desTotemismus im alten China. A, XXV. 1930b.

KOTZEBUE, O VON: Neue Reise um die Welt. II. Weimar & St. Petersburg 1830.

KRACHENINNIKOW: Histoire et description du Kamchatka. Trad. du Russe. I. Amsterdam 1770.

KRAUSE, F: Über die Enstehung der nordanierikanischen Kultur-provinzen. Tagungsberichte der Deutschen Anthropologischen Gescllschaft. 45-47. Tagung. Augsburg 1926.

KRICKERERG, W: Malereien auf ledernen Zeremonialkleider der Nordwestanierikaner. Ipek. Berlin 1925.

— Der Schwitzbad der Indianer. Ciba Zeitschrift. Basel 1934.

— Beiträge zur Frage der alien kulturgeschichtlichen Beziehungen zwischen Nord- und Südamerika. ZE, LXVI. 1934a.

KROEBER, A.L: The Eskimo of Smith Sound. AMNH-B, XII, 1900.

— The tribes of the Pacific coast of North America. Proceedings of the 19. International Congress of Americanists 1915. Washington 1917. [583]

KROEBER, A.L: American culture and the northwest coast. AA, n.s. XXV. 1923.

— The history of native culture in California. UC-PAAE, XX. 1923a.

— Handbook of the Indians of California. BAE-B, 78. 1925.

KUMLIEN, L: Contributions to the natural history of arctic America. USNM, Bulletin 15. 1879.

LAGUNA, F. DE: A comparison of Eskimo and palaeolithic art. American Journal of Archaeology, XXXVI—XXXVII. 1932-33.

— The archaeology of Cook Inlet, Alaska. Philadelphia 1934.

— A preliminary sketch of the Eyak Indians, Copper River delta, Alaska. 25th Anniversary Studies. Philadelphia Anthropological Society. Philadelphia 1937.

LANGSDORFF, G.H VON: Bemerkungen auf einer Reise um die Welt. II. Frankfurt a/M 1812.

(LA PÉROUSE): Voyage de ... autour du monde. Réd. L.A. MILET-MUREAU. II. Paris 1797.

LARSEN, H: Dødemandsbugten, an Eskimo settlement on Clavering Island. MG, 102. 1934.

LATHAM, R.G: On the ethnology of Russian America. 1845a. (Reprinted in Opuscula. London, Edinburgh & Leipzig 1860).

— Miscellaneous contributions to the ethnology of North America. 1845b. (Reprinted in Opuscula. London, Edinh.& Leipzig 1860).

— The native races of the Russian Empire. (In The Ethnographical Library, ed. E. NORRIS. II. London 1854).

— On the languages of Northern, Western, and Central America. Transactions of the Philological Society 1856. London 1857.

LEWIS, A.B: Tribes of the Columbia valley and the coast of Washington and Oregon. AAA-M. I. 1906.

LEWIS & CLARKE: Travels to the source of the Missouri and across the American continent. London 1814.

LINDOW, H: Blandt Eskimoerne i Labrador. Det grønlandske Selskabs Aarsskrift. København 1924.

LISIANSKY, U: A voyage round the world 1803-06. London 1814.

LOW, AP: Report on the Dominion Government Expedition 1903-1904. Ottawa 1906.

LOWE, K: Wenjaminow über die Aleutischen Inseln und deren Bewohner. AwKR, II. 1842.

LOWIE, R.H: The northern Shoshoni. AMNH-AP, II. 1909.

— The cultural connection of Californian and Plateau Shoshonean tribes. UC-PAAE, XX. 1923.

— Notes on Shoshonean ethnography. AMNH-AP, XX. 1924. [584]

LUDEWIG, H.E: The literature of America. Aboriginal languages. With add. and corr. by W. W. TURNER. London 1858.

LUTKE, F: Voyage autour du monde. Trad. du Russe. I-II. Paris 1835.

LYON, G.F: The private journal of ... London 1824.

M'CLINTOC, W: The voyage of the »Fox« in the Arctic Sea. London 1859.

MACKENZIE, A: Voyages from Montreal ...to the-Frozen and Pacific Oceans. London 1801.

MACKENZIE, A: Descriptive notes on certain implements, weapons, etc. from Graham Island, Queen Charlotte Islands, B.C. RSC-PT, IX. 1892.

MACLEOD, W.C: Certain aspects of the social organisation of the northwest coast and of the Algonkin. Proceedings of the 21. International Congress of Americanists, I. The Hague 1924.

— Certain mortuary aspects of northwest coast culture. AA, n.s. XXVII. 1925.

— Economic aspects of indigenous American slavery. AA, n.s. XXX. 1926.

— The origin of servile labor groups. AA, n.s. XXXI. 1929.

MALASPINA: Viaje de ... Colección de documentos inéditos para la historia de Espana. XV. 1849.

MASON, J.A: Excavation of Eskimo Thule culture sites at Point Barrow, Alaska. Proceedings of the 23. International Congress of Americanists. New York 1930.

MASON, M.H: The arctic forests. London 1924.

MASON, O.T: The Ray collection from Hupa reservation. SI-AR 1886, I. 1889.

— Primitive travel and transportation, USNM-R 1894. 1896.

— Aboriginal American harpoons. SI-AR 1900. 1902.

— Aboriginal American basketry. USNM-R 1902. 1904.

MATHIASSEN, T: Archaeology of the Central Eskimos, II. RFThE, IV. 1927.

— Material culture of the Iglulik Eskimos. RFThE, VI. 1928.

— The archaeological collection of the Cambridge East Greenland Expedition 1926. MG, LXXIV. 1929.

— Inugsuk, a mediaeval Eskimo settlement in Upernivik District. MG. LXXVII. 1930.

— Archaeological collections from the western Eskimos. RFThK, X. 1930a.

— Ancient settlements in the Kangâmiut area. MG, 91. 1931. [585]

MATHIASSEN, T: Prehistory of the Angmagssalik Eskimos. MG, 92. 1933.

— Contributions to the archaeology of Disko Bay. MG, 93. 1934.

— Eskimo finds from the Kangerdlugssuaq region. MG, 104. 1934a.

— The former Eskimo settlements on Frederik VI's Coast. MG, 109. 1936.

— & HOLTVED,E: The Eskimo archaeology of Julianehaab District. MG, 118. 1936.

MAYDELL, G: Reisen und Forschungen im jakutskischen Gebiet Ostsibiriens, I. BKRR, 4. Folge I. 1893.

MEARES, J: Voyages ... from China to the north west coast of America. London 1790.

MERCK, C.H: Ethnographische Beobachtungen über die Völker des Beringsmeeres 1789-91. ed. A. JACOBI. BA, XX. 1937.

MÉTRAUX, A: La civilisation matérielle des tribus Tupi-Guarani. Paris 1928.

Mithridates oder allgemeine Sprachenkunde. ed. C. ADELUNG. III. Berlin 1815.

MOLTKE, H. see MYLIUS-ERICHSEN, L.

MONTANDON, G: La civilsation aïnou et les cultures arctiques. Paris 1937.

MORICE, A.G: The western Denes, their manners and customs. CI-P, 3. ser. VII. 1890.

— Notes archaeological, industrial and sociological on the western Dénés. CI-T, IV. 1895.

— The great Déné race. A. I-V. 1906-10.

MUIR, J: The cruise of the Corwin (1881). Boston & New York 1917.

MUNROE, N.G: Prehistoric Japan. Yokohama 1911.

MURDOCH, J: Ethnological results of the Point Barrow expedition. BAE-R, 9. 1892.

MYLIUS-ERICHSEN, L & MOLTKE, H: Grønland. København & Kristiania 1906.

NELSON, E.W: The Eskimo about Bering Strait. BAE-R, 18 I, 1899.

New Light on the early history of the Greater Northwest. The manuscript journals of A. HENRY and D. THOMPSON. Ed. E. COUES. II. New York 1897.

NIBLACK, A.P: The coast Indians of southern Alaska and northern British Columbia. USNM-R 1888 1890.

NORDENSKIOLD, E: Comparative ethnographical studies. III. Göteborg 1924.

OLEARIUS, A: Vermehrte Newe Beschreibung der Muscowitischen und Persianischen Reise. Schleswig 1656. [586]

OLSON, R.L: Adze, canoe, and house types of the northwest coast. UW-PA, II. 1927.

— Clan and moiety in native America. UC-PAAE. XXXIII. 1933.

ORCHARD, W.C: Beads and beadwork of the American Indians. MAI-C. XI. 1929.

OSGOOD, C: The ethnography of the Great Bear Lake Indians. CNM-R 1931. 1933.

— Tanaina culture. AA, n.s. XXXV. 1933a.

—Contributions to the ethnography of the Kutchin, YU-PA. 14. 1936.

— The ethnography of the Tanaina. YU-PA, 14. 1937a.

PACKARD, A.S: The Labrador coast. New York 1891.

PALLAS, P.S (ed.): Neue Nordische Beyträge. St. Petersburg & Leipzig 1781-96.

PARRY, W.E: Journal of a second voyage for the discovery of a north-west passage, 1821-23. London 1824.

PETERSEN, J. see HOLM, G.

PETITOT, E: Vocabulaire francais-esquimau. Dialecte des Tchiglit. Paris 1876.

— Monographic des Dené-Dindjié. Paris 1876a.

— Les grands Esquimaux. Paris 1887.

— Quinze ans sous le cercle polaire. Paris 1889.

PETROFF, I: The Limit of the Innuit tribes on the Alaska coast. The American Naturalist. XVI. Philadelphia 1882.

— Report on the population, industries, and resources of Alaska. 10th Census of the United States. VIII. Washington 1884.

— Report on the population and resources of Alaska, llth Census of the United States. Washington 1893. (Published under the signature of R.P. Porter, who directed the work, but the sections quoted were evidently written by Petroff).

PIKE, W: The Barren Grounds of northern Canada. London 1892.

PINGEL, C: Antiquariske Efterretninger fra Grønland. Annaler for nordisk Oldkyndighed 1838-39. Kjøbenhavn. (1839).

PORTER, R.P. see PETROFF, I.

PORTLOCK, N; A voyage round the world. London 1789.

PRICHARD, J.C: Researches into the physical history of mankind. 3. ed. London 1836-37.

RADLOFF, L: Uebcr die Sprache der Ugalachmut. Bulletin de la classe historico-philologique de l'Académie Impériale des Sciences. XV. St. Petersbourg & Leipzig 1858. (Same in: Mélanges russes. III. St. Pétersbourg 1859). [587]

RAE, J: Narrative of an expedition to the shores of the Arctic Sea, 1846-47. London 1850.

RASMUSSEN, KNUD: Myter og Sagn fra Grønland. I-III. Kjøbenhavn 1921-25.

— Fra Grønland til Stillehavet. I-II. København. 1925-26.

— Intellectual culture of the Iglulik Eskimos. RFThK, VII. 1929.

— Observations on the intellectual culture of the Caribou Eskimos. RFThE, VII. 1930.

— The Netsilik Eskimos, social life and spiritual culture. RFThE, VIII. 1931.

— Intellectual culture of the Copper Eskimos. RFThE, IX. 1932.

RAINEY, F.G. see GEIST, O.W.

(RAY, P.H): Report of the international polar expedition to Point Barrow, Alaska. House of Representatives, 48th Congress. Ex. Doc. 44. Washington 1885.

RAY, V.F: The Sanpoil and Nespelem. UW-PA, V. 1932.

REAGAN, A.B: Whaling of the Oiympia Peninsula Indians of Washington. Natural History, XNV. 1925.

RICHAHDSON, J: Arctic searching expedition. I-II. London 1851.

RICHTER, S: A contribution to the archeology of North-East Greenland. Oslo etnografiske museums skrifter, V. Oslo 1934.

ROBERTS, H.H: Musical areas in aboriginal North America. YU-PA, 12. 1936.

ROSS, J: A voyage of discovery ... for the purpose of exploring Baffin's Bay, etc, London 1819.

— Narrative of a second voyage in search of a north-west passage, 1829—33. London 1835.

RUD B.R: The eastern Tinneh. SI-AR 1867. 1872.

RUDENKO, S.I. see VOLKOV, F.K.

RUSSELL, F: Explorations in the far north. Iowa 1898.

RYDER, C: Om den tidligere eskimoiske Bebyggelse af Scoresby Sund. MG, XVII. 1895.

RÜTTEL, F.C.P: Ti Aar blandt Østgrenlands Hedninger. København 1917.

(SAGOSKIN, L:) Ueber die Reise und Entdeckungen des Lieutenant ... im Russischen Amerika. AwKR, VI-VII. 1848-49.

(SAIKOF:) Auszug aus dein Reisebericht des Russischen Steuermanns ... NNB, III. 1782.

SAPIR, E: Notes on the Takelma Indians of southwestern Oregon. AA. n. s. IX. 1907.

— see SPIER, L. [588]

SAHFERT, E: Haus und Dorf bei den Eingeborenen Nordamerikas. AfA, n. F. VII. 1909.

SARYTSCHEW, G: Achtjährige Reise im nordöstlichen Sibirien. I-II. Leipzig 1805-06.

SAUER, M: An account of a geographical and astronomical expedition to the northern parts of Russia. London 1802.

SCHELECHOF: Reise von Ochotsk nach Amerika 1783-87. NNB, VI. 1793a.

— Fortsetzung der Reise von Ochotsk nach Amerika 1788-89. Ibid. 1793b.

SCHNELL, I: Prehistoric finds from the island world of the far east. Museum of Far Eastern Antiquities, Bull. 4, Stockholm 1932.

SCHMIDT, W: Der Ursprung der Gottesidee. V. Münster i/W. 1934.

SCHMITTER, F: Upper Yukon native customs and folk-lore. SI-MC, LVI. 1910.

SCHOTT, W: Ueber die Sprachen des Russischen Amerika nach Wenjaminow. AwKR, VII. 1849.

SCHRENCK, I. VON: Reisen und Forschungen im Amur-Lande. III. St, Petersburg 1881-95.

SCOULER, J: Observations on the indigenous tribes of the northwest coast of America. JRGS, XI. 1841.

— On the Indian tribes inhabiting the north-west coast of America. Journal of the Ethnological Society of London, I. London. 1848.

SEEMANN, B: Narrative of a voyage of H. M. S. Herald 1845-51. II. London 1853.

SEIDEL, H: Der Schneeschuh und seine geographische Verbreitung. Globus, LXXIII. Braunschweig 1898.

SIEBOLD, H. von: Ethnologische Studien über die Aino auf der Insel Yesso. ZE 1881, Supplement. 1881.

(SILVY, A?): Relation par lettres de l'Amerique septentrionalte 1709-10. ed. P.C. DE ROCHEMONTEIX. Paris 1904.

SIMPSON, T: Narrative of the discoveries on the north coast of America 1836-39. London 1842.

SMET, DE: Voyages aux Montagnes Rocheuses. 4e éd. Lille 1859.

SMITH, H.I: Archaeology of Lytton, British Columbia. AMNH-MJ. I. 1899.

— Archeology of the Thompson River region, British Columbia, Ibid. 1900.

— Archaeology of the Gulf of Georgia and Puget Sound. Ibid. II. 1900-08. [589]

SMITH, H.I: Shell-heaps of the lower Fraser River. British Columbia. Ibid. 1903.

— The archaeology of the Yakima valley. AMNH-AP, VI. 1910.

SOLBERG, O: B eiträge zur Vorgeschichte der Osteskimo, Viden-skabs-Selskabets Skrifter. II. Hist.-Filos. Klasse, No. 2. Cristiania 1907.

SPIER, L: Havasupai ethnography. AMNH-AP. XXIX. 1928.

— Klamath ethnography. UC-PAAE, XXX. 1930.

— & SAPIR, E: Wishram ethnography. L'W-PA, III. 1930.

SPINDEN, H.J: The Nez Percé Indians. MAAA, II. 1908.

STEARNS, R.E.C: Ethno-conchology, a study of primitive money. USNM-R 1887. 1889.

STEENSBY, H.P: Contributions to the ethnology and anthropogeography of the Polar Eskimos. MG, XXXIV. 1910.

STEFÁNSSON, V: My life with the Eskimo. London & New York 1913.

— The Stefansson-Anderson Arctic Expedition: Preliminary ethnological report. AMNH-AP, XIV. 1914.

— The friendly arctic. New York 1921.

STELLER, G.E: Beschreibung von dem Lande Kamtschatka. Frankfurt & Leipzig 1774.

STERNBERG, L: Die Religion der Giljaken. Archiv fur Religions-wissenschaft, VIII. Leipzig 1905.

— The Turano-Ganowáian system and the natives of north-cast Asia. Proceedings of the International Congress of Americanists, 18th session. London 1913.

— Divine election in primitive religion. Congres international des amcricanistes. XXI. session, Göteborg. 1925.

— The Ainu problem. A, XXIV. 1929.

STEWARD, J.H: Ethnography of the Owens Valley Paiute. UC-PAAE, XXXIII. 1933.

SVERDRUP, H.U: Tre aar i isen med "Maud". Oslo 1926.

SWAN, J.G: The Indians of Cape Flattery. SI-CKn, XVI. 1870.

— The Haidah Indians of Queen Charlotte's Islands, British Columbia. SI-CKn, XXI. 1874.

SWANTON, J.R: Contributions to the ethnology of the Haida. AMNH-MJ, V. 1905.

— Haida texts and myths. BAE-B, 29. 1905a.

— Types of Haida and Tlingit myths. AA, n.s. VII. 1905b.

— Social condition, beliefs, and linguistic relationship of the Tlingit Indians. BAE-R, 26. 1908.

— Tlingit myths and texts. BAE-R, 39. 1909.   [590]

TEIT, J: The Thompson Indians of British Columbia. AMNH-MJ, II. 1900.

— The Lillooet Indians. AMNII-MJ, II. 1900-08a.

— The Shuswap. AMNH-MJ, 11. 1900-08b.

— The Middle Columbia Salish. UW-PA, II. 1928.

— The Salishan tribes of the western plateaus, BAE-R, 45. 1930.

THALBITZER, W: Ethnological description of the Amdrup collection from East Greenland. MG, XXVIII. 1909.

— Ethnographical collections from East Greenland. MG, XXXIX. 1914.

— Language and folklore. The Ammassalik Eskimo, II. MG, XL. 1923.

— Cultic games and festivals in Greenland. Congres international des americanistes, XXI. session. Goteborg 1925.

THOMSEN T.H: Implements and artefacts of the North-East Greenlanders. MG, M.IV. 1917.

THOMPSON, D. see New Light etc.

TOLSTYKH, A: Description of the islands discovered in the open sea ... etc. (in: JOCHELSON 1933).

TORII, H: Études archéologiques et ethnologiques: Les Aïnoii des Iies Kouriles. Tokyo Imperial University. Journal of the College of Science, XLII. Tokyo 1919.

TOWNSEND, J.K: Narrative of a journey across the Rocky Mountains to the Columbia River. Early Western Travels, ed. R.G. THWAITES, XXI, Cleveland 1905.

TURNER, L.M: Ethnology of the Ungava District. BAE-B, 11. 1894.

TYRRELL, J.W: Across the sub-arctics of Canada. London s.a.

VANCOUVER, G: A voyage of discovery to the North Pacific Ocean 1790-95. I-III, London 1798.

ВолкОВ'ъ, Ѳ.К. Этнографическія ... 1910.

WALDMANN, S: Les Esquimaux du nord du Labrador. Bulletin de la sociéténeuchateloise de geographic, XX. Neuchatel 1910.

WATERMAN, T.T: Some conundrums in northwest coast art. AA, n.s. XXV. 1921.

— & COFFIN, G: Types of canoes on Puget Sound MAI-INM. 1920.

— & GREINER, R: Indian houses of Puget Sound. MAI-INM. 1921.

WEITFISH, G: Prehistoric North American basketry techniques and modern distribution. AA, n.s. XXXII. 1930. [591]

WEYER, E.M: Archaeological material from the village site at Hot Springs, Port Möller, Alaska. AMNH-AP. XXXI. 1930.

— The Eskimo, their environment and folkways. New Haven 1932.

WHYMPRR, F: Travel and adventure in the territory of Alaska, London 1868.

WILKES, C: Narrative of the United States exploring expedition. IV. Philadelphia 1844.

WISSLER, C: Archaeology of the Polar Eskimo. AMNH-AP, XXII. 1918.

— The American Indian. 2. ed. New York 1922.

— The relation of nature to man in aboriginal America. New York 1926.

WOLDT, A. see JACOBSEN.

WRANGELL, (K) VON: Statistische und ethnographische Nachrichten über die Russischen Besitzungen an der Nordwestkuste von Amerika. BKRR, I. 1839.

— Reise des kaiserlich-russischen Flotten-Lieutenants ... längs der Nordküste von Sibirien und auf dem Eismeere 1820-24. I-II. Berlin 1839a.

WYETH, J.B: Oregon; or a short history of a long journey. Early Western Travels, ed. R.G. THWAITES. XXI. Cleveland 1905.

YARHOW, H.C: Introduction to the study of mortuary customs among the North American Indians. Ed. Bureau of Ethnology. Washington 1880.

— A further contribution to the study of the mortuary customs of the North American Indians. BAE-R, 1. 1881.

ZAGOSKIN see SAGOSKIN.

ZAIKOV see SAIKOF.

Errata.

corrected herein

Page	line	
- 19,		4 f. b: 286, read 386.
- 23,	-	13 f. t: Yukutut, read Yaktag.
- 24,	-	2 f. b: 297, read 397.
- 39,	-	2 f. t: natives, read native.
- 47,	-	2 f. t: on, read one.
- 52,	-	9 f. b: the, read this.
- 63,	-	4 f. t: pairings, read parings.
- 63,	-	9 f. t: spittal, read spittle.
- 82,	In Figure 8, numbers 10 and 11 should be transposed.	
- 84,	line	19 f. t: Emmons 6, read Emmons 3.
- 98,	-	17 f. t: bear, read beer.
- 104,	-	4 f. b: Plate 12, 4-8. read Plate 12, 4-7.
- 111,	-	6 f. t: The arrangement, read This arrangement.
- 111,	-	9 f. b: be, read the.
- 115,	-	8 f. t: 30-99-1, read 33-29-1.
- 119,	-	12 f. t: back of the river were, read bank of the river where.
- 151,	-	7 f. b: Petroff 1890, read Petroff 1893.
- 163,	-	5 f. b: for, read to.
- 184,	-	16 f. b: separated, read seated.
- 199,	-	13 f. t: present, read prevent.
- 200,	-	3 f. t: it is, read in its.
- 202,	-	1 f. t.: etc.: Tiedman, read Tiedemann.
- 208,	-	2 f. b.: We, read He.
- 222,	-	3 f. t.: know, read knew.
- 253,	-	17 f. t.: where, read were. etc.;
- 257,	-	5 f. b., etc: t'cilacia, read t'cilacia.

Indieveret til Trykkeriet den 8. April 1938.
Færdig fra Trykkeriet den 30. Juli 1938.

[592 end + Plates 1-18 = 31 images]

1. Galushia Nelson. (1933).

2. Johnny Stevens. (1933).

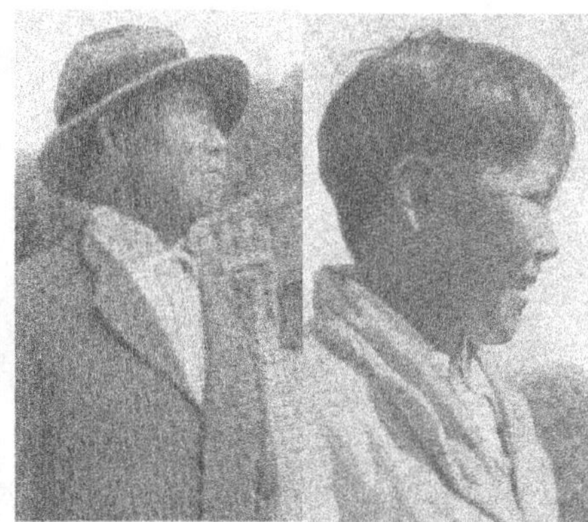

1. Old Chief Joe. (1930).   2. Johnny Nelson. (1933).

Plate 1

Plate 2

1. Galushia Nelson's family and members of the Expedition. (1933).

2. Eyak children. (1933).
From the left: unknown white child, Johnny Nelson,
John and Rosie Saski.

Plate 3

1. Eyak Lake and Copper River flats from
Mount Eyak above Cordova. (1930).

2. Eyak River with the rock of Glacatl at the left.
(Photo by Roark, Cordova).

Plate 4

1. Site of Old Eyak. (1930).

2. Alaganik Trading Post. (1930).

Plate 5

307

1. Grave near Old Eyak. (1930).

2. Grave of Old Man Dude's wife, Simpson Bay. (1933).

Plate 6

1. Old Man Dude's place, Simpson Bay. (1933).

2. Galushia Nelson's house, Old Town, Cordova. (1933).

Plate 7

1. Grave post of Wolf Chief, Alaganik. (1930).

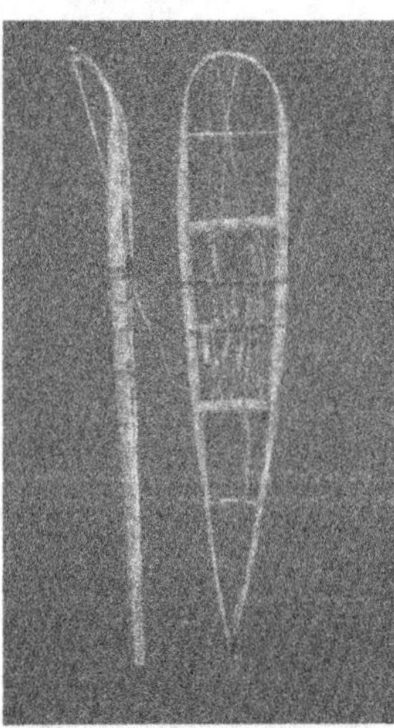

2. Gus Nelson's snowshoes. (1933).

Plate 8

1. Gus Nelson's canoe, partly finished. (1933).
2. Old Man Dude's canoe, abandoned. (1933).

Plate 9

1. Canoe on Copper River flats. (ABERCROMBIE: Photographic Album 1884).
2. Canoes and umiak at Child's Glacier. (ABERCROMBIE: Photographic Album 1884).

Plate 10

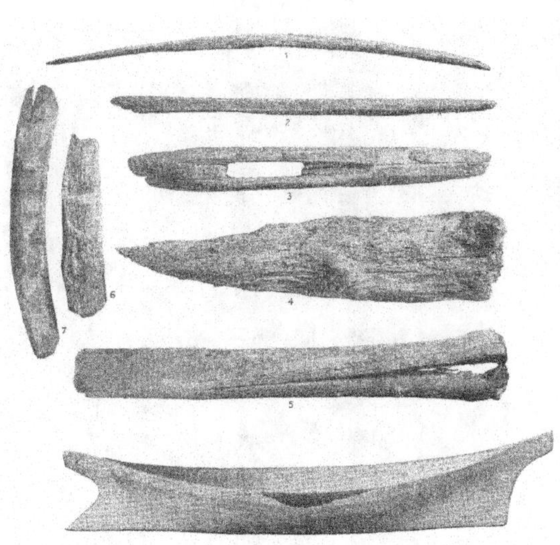

1—7. Archaeological specimens from Alaganik. 1—2. Wooden spits for fish.
3. Fragment of trap. 4—6. Wooden wedges. 7. Prow handle for canoe.
8. Model of Eyak canoe, made in 1884 for ABERCROMBIE.
(University Museum, Philadelphia).

Plate 11

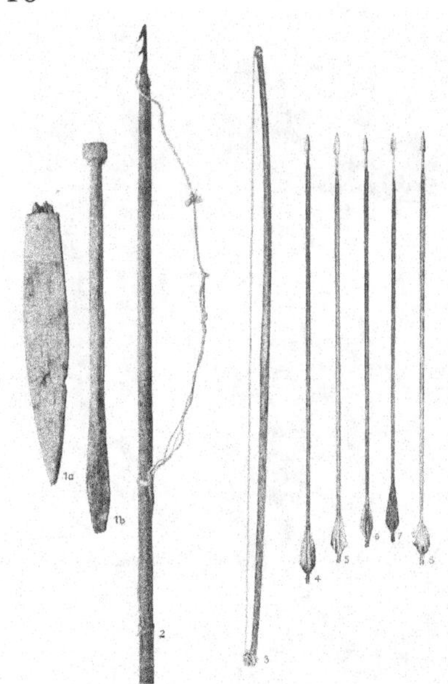

1—2. Old Man Dude's canoe paddle and Sear Steven's fish spear.
(University Museum, Philadelphia).
3—8. Bow and arrows. (Museum für Völkerkunde, Berlin).

Plate 12

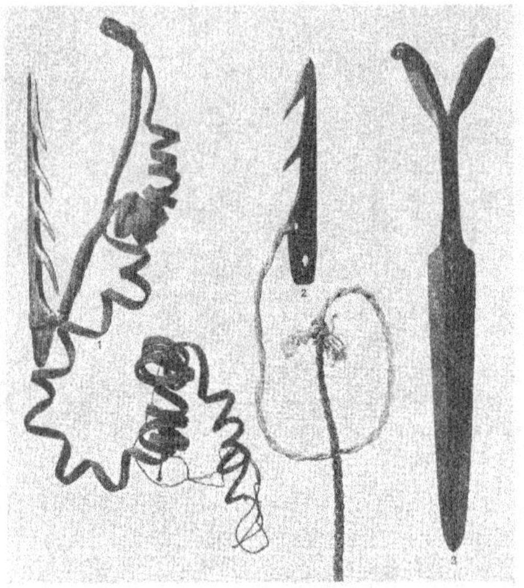

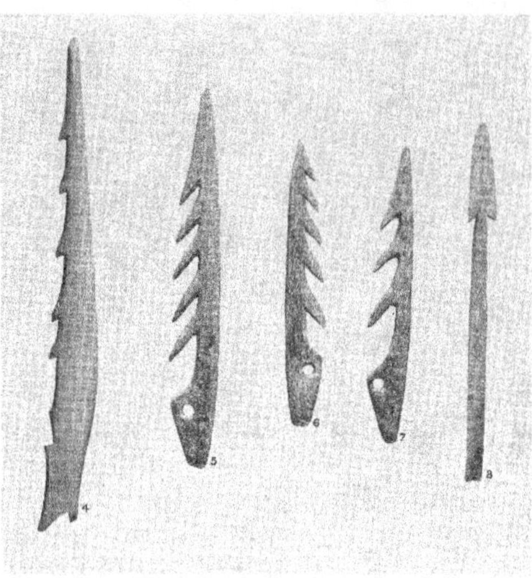

1. Iron harpoon head, collected by ABERCROMBIE 1884. 2. Iron harpoon head, detail of plate 12,2. 3. Copper dagger from Taral, collected by ABERCROMBIE 1884. (University Museum, Philadelphia).

4. Bone prong for fish spear. 5—7. Harpoon heads. 8. Arrow head. (Museum für Völkerkunde, Berlin).

Plate 13

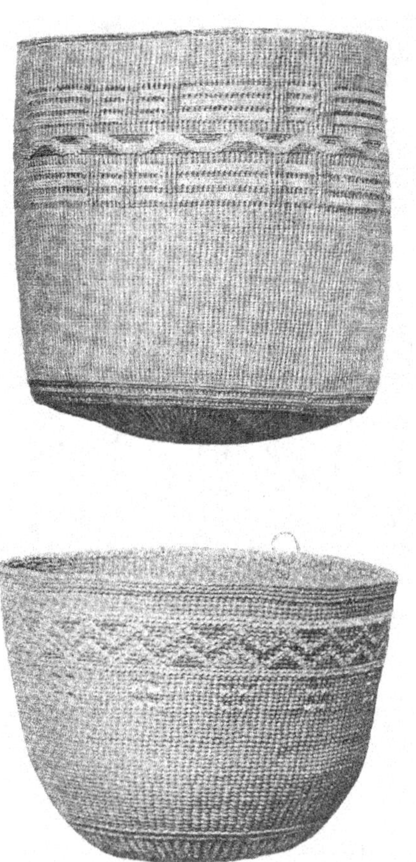

1—2. Twined baskets. (Museum für Völkerkunde, Berlin).

Plate 14

Ceremonial paddles.
1—2. Raven paddle. (National Museum, Copenhagen).
3—4. Bear (?) paddle. (University Museum, Philadelphia).

Plate 15

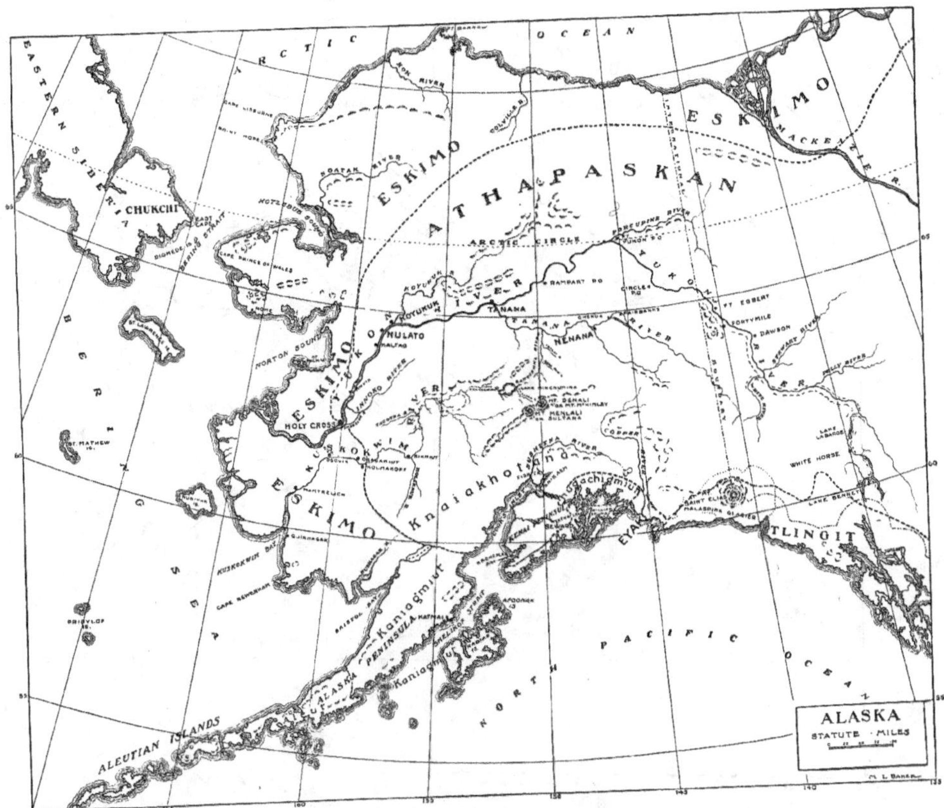

Map of Alaska, showing geographical position of Eyak territory.

Plate 16

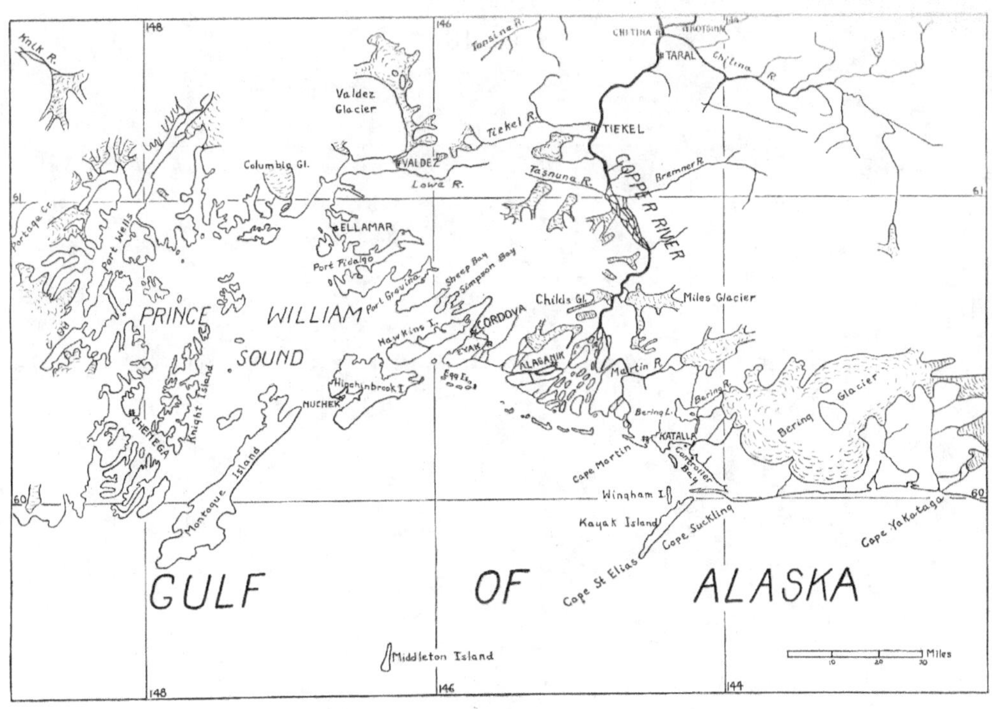

Map of territory known to the Eyak.

Plate 17

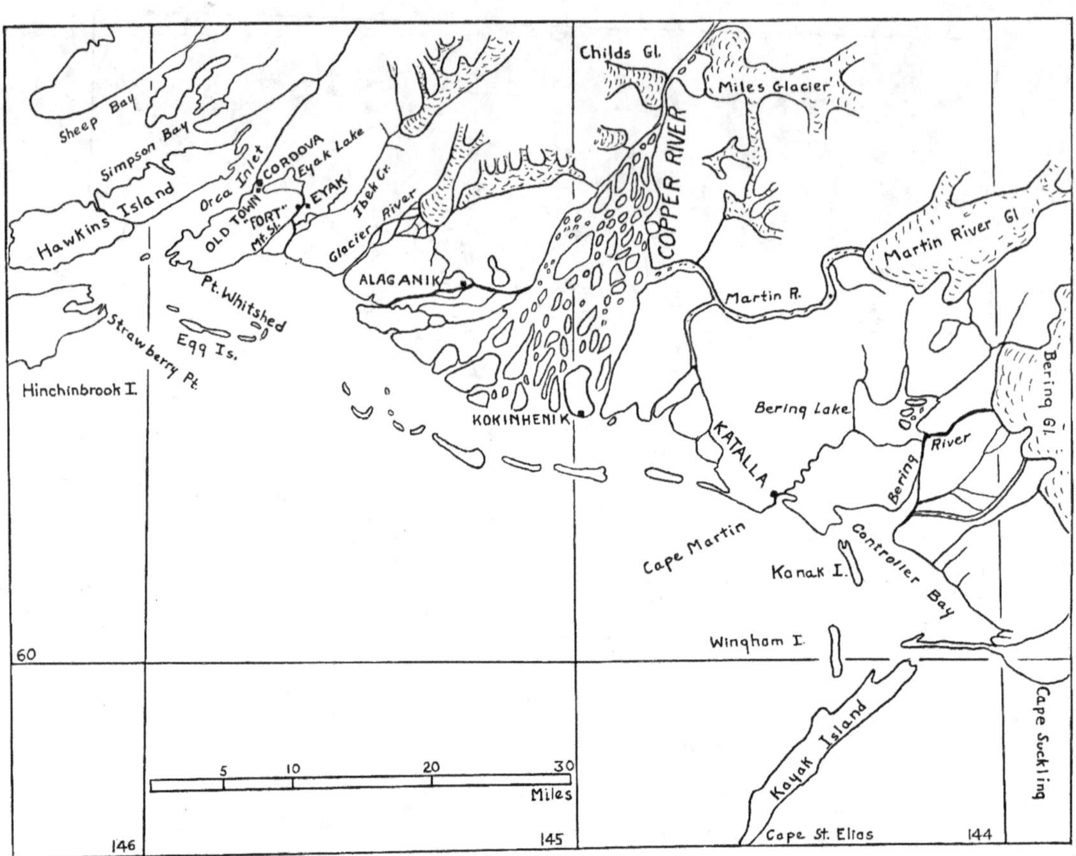

Map of territory inhabited by the Eyak.

Plate 18

Det Kgl. Danske Videnskabernes Selskab.

THE EYAK INDIANS OF THE COPPER RIVER DELTA, ALASKA

BY

KAJ BIRKET-SMITH AND FREDERICA DE LAGUNA

KØBENHAVN

LEVIN & MUNKSGAARD

EJNAR MUNKSGAARD

1938

#f = cites in next 5 pages
#0f = cites in next 10 pages

www.ingramcontent.com/pod-product-compliance
Lightning Source LLC
Chambersburg PA
CBHW081302250726
48662CB00008B/2353